Networks 2000

INTERNET, INFORMATION SUPERHIGHWAY, MULTIMEDIA NETWORKS AND BEYOND

Networks 2000

Internet, Information Superhighway, Multimedia Networks and Beyond

Edited by Melanie McMullen

mf Miller Freeman Books

LAN Networking Library
San Francisco

Miller Freeman Inc., 600 Harrison Street, San Francisco, California 94107

Publishers of *LAN Magazine*, The Network Solutions Magazine

A member of the United Newspapers Group

Cover Design: David Hamamoto

Cover Illustration: David Teich

Illustrations: Rick Eberly

ISBN 0-87930-335-2

Library of Congress Card Number 94-78802

Printed in U.S.A.

94   95   96   97   5   4   3   2   1

Contents

Introduction

The networks of the future will barely resemble the LANs and WANs of today. What is now considered top of the line in speed and throughput will be obsolete in only a few short years. More powerful microprocessors, such as Pentium, Alpha, and the PowerPC, will lead the way to high-performance desktop computers and servers. Network applications will change, too. Multimedia, for instance, will replace the basic text-based e-mail message as the preferred means of corporate communications.

On the wide area front, the Internet will continue to evolve into a powerful information resource that links millions of users worldwide and allows them access to vast storehouses of data. And the much ballyhooed information superhighway will finally emerge, giving every household a chance to be connected to a public network via a small box connected to the television set.

But what type of network technology will be able to bear this ever-expanding bandwidth burden? In the next few years, Fast Ethernet, fibre channel, and Asynchronous Transfer Mode (ATM) will usher in a new level of gigabit networking for homes and corporations. Routers and bridges will be replaced by high-speed switches, and enterprise superhubs will connect thousands of users. The network operating system will merge with the most vital component of computing, the operating system, allowing computers to quickly and easily be connected without running extra layers of software. Management and security for these powerful networks will no longer be an option but rather a necessity, handled in part by management software that will be embedded in every component on the network.

To allow you to prepare for what lies ahead, the editors of *LAN Magazine* decided to assemble this book on the future of networking. It contains the best articles on emerging technology collected in one easy-to-use reference. While the future of computing and technology will likely change courses many times over, having an idea of what potentially lies ahead should help you chart the best course.

Melanie McMullen

Editor-in-chief, *LAN Magazine*

Section 1
The Information Superhighway
and the Internet

In the last few years, everyone from the daily newspaper business reporter to Vice President Al Gore has been involved in talking about and promoting the information superhighway. This proposed wide area network, which theoretically will link individuals and companies from coast-to-coast, will facilitate a plethora of applications, including electronic commerce, video-on-demand, telecommuting, and education, to name a few.

But what exactly is the information superhighway? And who will be providing the links and applications? Those questions remain unresolved, and the answers vary depending on who you ask. Several stories in this section, "Super I-Way," "The Extra Mile," and "The Electronic Superhighway," look at how this network will–and already is–coming to fruition. Other stories look at potential problems, such as security, found in building such an extensive wide area public network.

For those who can't wait for the superhighway to surface, a very reliable wide area network–the Internet–already exists and provides links between users and databases located all over the world. "Internet Integration" and "Network of Networks" reveal some practical tips on how to hook up and find your way around the wide expanses of this sophisticated WAN.

Cruising Along The Super I-Way

CYBER-PIONEERS LOOK TO THE INFORMATION SUPERHIGHWAY TO CARRY EDUCATION, HEALTH CARE, AND COMMERCE APPLICATIONS. HERE'S A LOOK AT SIX PROJECTS.

BY PATRICIA SCHNAIDT

Drive on superhighways across the United States, and you hurtle past Jack-in-the-Boxes, Sunocos, and vast brown expanses. In your haste to arrive at your destination, the details of the scenery–the green tunnels of corn, the amusing road signs, and the litter on the roadside–are blurred. Take the local routes, and you'll get a better grasp on your environs. You're moving slowly enough to notice the finer points.

The same is true for the information superhighway. In the industry's eagerness to jump on this bit bandwagon, the uses, trials, and tolls have become obscured. So slow down, and let's see what the information superhighway is now and what it will deliver.

IF YOU BUILD IT, HE WILL COME

The superhighway won't exist. Just one superhighway won't be built. The information superhighway will be polymorphic, and a variety of institutions will build superhighways to suit their needs. Different access roads will exist, and the individual superhighways will have electronic cloverleafs connecting them. The superhighways will carry the businesses of education, health care, scientific research, commerce, government, and public services. The superhighways will use a variety of technology, from cutting edge to mundane.

This article looks at six projects of the superhighway ilk. The state of North Carolina is building an ATM network for education, health care, public services, and commerce. The National Information Infrastructure Testbed (NIIT, Washington, D.C.) is running the Earth Data System, a distributed environmental application, over Asynchronous Transfer Mode (ATM) and frame relay. Smart Valley

(Palo Alto, CA) is involved in telecommuting and electronic commerce in the San Francisco Bay Area. Pacific Bell's (San Francisco) Calren is sponsoring education, health care, and ATM-based projects in California. Digital Equipment, Times Mirror Cable (Irvine, CA), and Arizona State University are working on electronic commerce over a cable TV and Ethernet network. Microelectronics and Computer Technology Corp. (MCC, Austin, TX) is building its EINet software to enable electronic commerce.

The common denominator in these superhighways is collaboration among the organizations that are building the networks as well as among the people who will use them. Whether students and teachers, patients and doctors, scientists and researchers, or engineers and salespeople, the goal is to share information and work together more closely than networks allow today.

Networking is limited to the organizations that can afford to build their own private networks. Rarely does a company have one system that connects its customers and suppliers. It's simply too costly. For schools, hospitals, and businesses that don't find utility in building their own networks, these superhighways will provide a less-costly public infrastructure.

To some extent, the superhighways will also solve the bandwidth crunch, especially over the wide area. People quickly become dependent on e-mail for communication but find that the existing networks don't support remote sharing of more complicated information, such as CAD or image files.

Some barriers to the superhighway are technological, but most are economic and social. Sure, the physical networks have to be constructed, and they will be–using the gamut of technologies. Superhighways will be built using cable TV coax, fiber, and twisted pair. They will use ATM, frame relay, ISDN, and dial-up lines. Software developers will write applications that can be used in a distributed network. Security kinks will be straightened. Over time, the networks will be built and improved.

The biggest challenges will be the people themselves–getting groups of people to cooperate, finding funding for public-service and educational applications, ensuring access to people who can't afford to pay without heavily taxing those who can pay, delivering quality content where the superhighway delivers public services, and providing access devices that people can use easily.

Building pilot projects and then expanding their scope and scale is the only way to iron out the difficulties. Here's a status report on six projects.

NORTH CAROLINA HIGHWAY

Residents of North Carolina are no longer stuck in technological pine tar as the North Carolina Information Highway went into operation in 1994. North Carolina will use its ATM network for education, medical, governmental, and public safety applications.

"North Carolina is trying to improve educational equity and the ability to access medical care," says Andy James, public information officer for the Office of the State Controller (Raleigh, NC). "We are also working on a criminal information network that will be useful throughout the state of North Carolina, both to officers on patrol and to officers of the court, such as prosecutors and judges.

"By doing those things, we will help economic development. Perhaps businesses will want to be located in new areas. We're hoping that we'll not only save money but also generate an additional tax base to pay for other programs or to keep the tax rate stable," continues James.

BellSouth (Atlanta), GTE (Irving, TX), Carolina Telephone (Wake Forest, NC), and more than 20 other telephone companies are deploying an ATM network throughout the state. The first customer is the state of North Carolina. In 1994, 106 sites have access to the ATM network. The state plans to have 3,500 users on-line by the end of 1995, not including private businesses.

The inaugural applications on the North Carolina Information Highway include Vision Carolina and Vistanet. Vision Carolina is a distance-learning network that offers

sign language, Spanish, Japanese, health, science, and humanities courses. Vistanet provides remote access to CAT scans to develop 3D images and radiology dose calculations for cancer treatments. Both pilots have been operating over fiber, but ATM will enable them to operate in real time and exchange data more quickly.

BellSouth, which does business as Southern Bell in North Carolina, is installing ATM switches in Raleigh, Wilmington, Greensboro, Charlotte, and Asheville. GTE is installing ATM switches in Research Triangle Park and Durham. Carolina Telephone, a subsidiary of Sprint, is installing ATM switches in Fayetteville and Greenville.

"We're the lead companies because we have the size, the technical capabilities, and the financial capabilities," says Clifton Metcalfe, manager of public information for BellSouth. "As the state selects sites, then the local telcos become involved. The local telco's responsibility is to provide local facilities in those networks for those sites to be fully compatible with the network," says Metcalfe.

The fiber network uses ATM over Synchronous Optical Network (SONET). Initially, the backbone network will run at 155Mbps, with some sites running at 2.44Gbps. Within a year, the network will be capable of running at 622Mbps as needed.

The customers are responsible for purchasing the equipment needed in their sites as well as for paying the local access charges. Initially, the state will pay the line charges for the first year. For example, a school that wants to implement a distance-learning application will have to buy the students' computers, video cameras, video codecs, and multiplexers and will have to reconfigure the classrooms.

"Some of these places that are state agencies will be shifting some state money. They are also going to the community looking for donations. We will be paying the line charges. If the site can't come up with the money for the classroom, we don't have the money right now to fund everything. It's a partnership. We have our end to uphold. They have their end to uphold," says James.

Other applications can be funded in a traditional business way. For instance, private hospitals can bill doctors for their use of a telemedicine application.

James says North Carolina chose its initial sites on a first-come, first-served basis. "We want to work with everybody. The first users are the people who showed the most interest, were able to get the money, and were able to com-

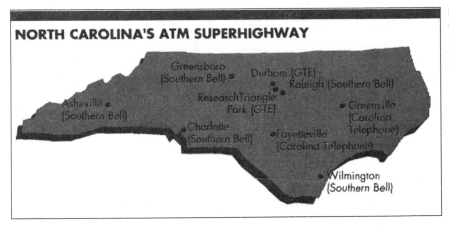

Figure 1: North Carolina will use its statewide Asynchronous Transfer Mode (ATM) network for education, medical, governmental, and public safety applications.

mit. It may not have been the ones who were the most anxious, but maybe they had more in their capital budgets," says James. "We want everybody we can get on the highway. We want all the private business we can get, since that will lead to growth, increase the tax base, and bring jobs into the state."

By the end of 1995, the carriers expect to file for a tariff and open the network for wider public access. Right now, however, they're working on building and testing their ATM networks.

Metcalfe says BellSouth has mostly completed installing the Fujitsu (Raleigh, NC) Fetex-150 ATM switches. "The Fujitsu switches are the first of their kind. We've learned about their switch as they learned about it.

"When we said this is cutting edge, it is. There are many challenges to putting together a SONET network when there's not another one like it. Plus you have to get the companies to work together. We are literally building something from scratch that no one has ever built before.

"Working together is a challenge," Metcalfe continues. "To say something is a partnership is a cliché, but it's true here. It's not just the private sector working with the government, it's all of the private companies working together."

THE NIIT

The National Information Infrastructure Testbed (NIIT) is titrating a solution of researchers, data, and distance to determine the right mixture for a nationwide, high-speed network. Its initial experiment is the Earth Data System (EDS), which assesses the impact on the environment from deforestation and ocean pollution. The NIIT plans future tests of health care, education, and entertainment applications.

The NIIT focuses on implementing real-life, practical solutions to wide-area application development and management, infrastructure scalability, security, and reliability. "Our approach is more pragmatic. ATM is starting to roll out, and frame relay is here. We are testing what people can use to start rolling out the superhighway," says Chris Caldwell, marketing program manager at Hewlett-Packard (Palo Alto, CA).

The NIIT is an industry coalition of corporations, universities, and government agencies. Its makeup includes natural competitors, such as Sprint and AT&T as well as Hewlett-Packard, Digital, and Sun, who put aside their differences to discover the real issues of moving to a high-speed distributed network model.

By cooperating in this manner, "we're effectively leapfrogging a generation of development," says Jim Payne, director of marketing and communications at Sprint (Reston, VA). "This compatibility among divergent companies is so unusual that it's almost unprecedented. It usually only happens in a war-time environment. But you never lose your mindfulness of where your competitors stand," adds Payne.

"People say the superhighway means more bandwidth, but the issues are much more important than that," says Caldwell. "The growth of the economy is in the small business arena. We've all seen the decrease in employment in large businesses. The continuing prosperity of the United-States is in small businesses. We need an infrastructure to enable applications that we can't imagine."

One of those applications is EDS, which lets researchers in different locations work with satellite images of land and oceans, weather statistics, coastline and river data, salinity levels, and fishing yields stored in a variety of public and private databases across the world. In the past, researchers had to travel, exchange tapes, or access applications by remote terminal protocols to share the same data or collaborate with other scientists. But with EDS, which is a Unix-based, distributed, multimedia application, scientists can speedily access massive data sets and easily collaborate with other researchers in real time.

EDS links nine sites across the United States using ATM at DS-3 and frame relay at DS-1, depending on the volume of data to be shared over the WAN. Locally, scientists use HP 9000 and Digital Alpha AXP workstations connected to Fiber Distributed Data Interface (FDDI) networks. Scientists are also connected to the Internet. The application itself implements OSF's Distributed Computing Environment (DCE) and uses Ellery Systems' (Boulder, CO) Open Systems for integrating the existing databases into the application (see Figure 2).

Three data sites provide high-performance computing services such as analysis and modeling as well as access to 800GB of image and text data. Six service nodes provide additional high-performance computing services, project and network management services, data conversion, and application development services. The data sites are the Institute for the Study of the Earth, Oceans, and Space of the University of New Hampshire, the University of California at Santa Barbara, and the College of Oceanic and Atmospheric Sciences at Oregon State University. The service sites are Smithsonian Astrophysical Observatory, Sandia National Laboratories in California and New Mexico, University of California at Berkeley, Ellery Systems, and Sprint.

The first phase of EDS was announced in September, 1993, and demonstrated in November, 1993. In the second phase, the EDS working group may examine advancing ATM to the desktop, adding data sets, other distributed services, and video and audio to make the application truly multimedia.

Another NIIT working group plans the health care application. They have established their goals and are developing the application and network requirements. They plan to demonstrate the telemedicine application this summer. A third working group is examining an education application. Entertainment is also a possibility, although the NIIT board has not approved it yet.

SMART VALLEY

While the NIIT is focused on the national aspects of the superhighway, Smart Valley is bringing it home–if your home is in the San Francisco Bay Area. Smart Valley has been operating since March 1993, and Harry Saal has been president and CEO since September. Smart Valley is focusing on medical, education, government, and nonprofit sectors. It also contends that a communications infrastructure would help keep businesses in the Bay Area and create more jobs.

"We are a trade association for an industry that's being formed–the information infrastructure or the superhighway industry. This industry will be as well-defined over the next couple of years as the semiconductor or PC industries are today. It will have its own software companies, its own hardware companies, and its own distribution channel," Saal continues.

Smart Valley is a superhighway advocate, although it does not promote a particular interest group or technology. "I like to think of ourselves as venture capitalists without a fund. We will help create dozens of projects. We have to select the best hundred out of thousands. Except by trying and doing pilots, how can you know which ones will be successful?" asks Saal.

Smart Valley's goal is to convene at least 12 regional collaborations in its first year. It is also working with Calren, the California Research and Education Network. It currently has two projects coursing over its synapses: Telecommuting and CommerceNet.

Smart Valley launched its Telecommuting pilot project and published the *Smart Valley Telecommuting Guide* in February. "We decided to focus on telecommuting in its own right. There is a confluence of service, productivity, economic, and environmental benefits," says Eric Benhamou, a director of Smart Valley and president and CEO of 3Com (Santa Clara, CA). "Telecommuting doesn't depend on massive technology investments."

The telecommuting pilot's goal is to involve a dozen Bay Area companies from different industries in telecommuting programs. "We'll put the *Telecommuting Guide* to the test," says Benhamou. Participants in the beta test include 3Com, Hewlett-Packard, PacBell, Silicon Graphics,

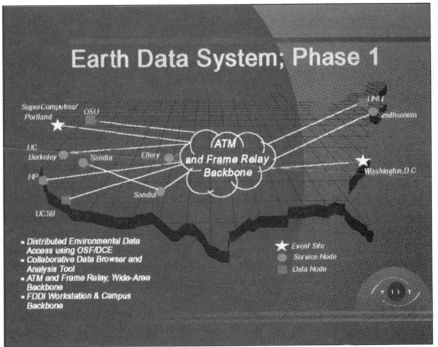

Figure 2: The National Information Infrastructure Testbed's initial experiment is the Earth Data System (EDS), which allows researchers in nine sites to interact with data and to collaborate with other researchers to assess the impact on the environment from deforestation and ocean pollution.

Stanford University, and Gray Cary Ware and Freidenrich. 3Com has 50 telecommuters whose professions range from buyers to technical publications writers to software developers. Hewlett-Packard has 300 technical support, technical documentation, and product development personnel in its telecommuting pilot. Silicon Graphics (Mountain View, CA) has 26 telecommuting engineers. Gray Cary Ware (Palo Alto, CA) has 30 employees toiling over legal documents from home.

"We expect a steep learning curve. After about six months, we'll publicize our findings," says Benhamou. In the third phase, Smart Valley will spread telecommuting more broadly in Silicon Valley. Aid for new telecommuters will come in the shape of an electronic bulletin board as well as a buddy system in which old-hand telecommuting companies adopt neophytes.

Telecommuting has broad appeal, and the benefits are easily understood. "It's not an esoteric application for people at NASA," says Benhamou. But it's not for everyone. Establishing set goals for communication, objectives, and checkpoints is mandatory. "Some people need constant communication; they'll never be happy telecommuters," Benhamou continues.

CommerceNet's goal is to examine how the Internet can and will change how business is conducted. Applications will include on-line catalogs, product data exchange, and engineering collaboration. Key technologies are Integrated Services Digital Network (ISDN) and multimedia software.

"CommerceNet is working on fully distributed catalogs that are maintained in real time. You can use World Wide Web, browse the catalogs, click on a manufacturer's name, and get their information or a surrogate who maintains their information," says Saal. "You won't have obsolete catalogs anymore. With catalogs so current, you can tie them to inventory control and forecast."

Also involved in CommerceNet is Enterprise Integration Technologies (Palo Alto, CA), which specializes in electronic commerce, and the state of California's Trade and Commerce Agency.

PACIFIC BELL CALREN

Pacific Bell announced its superhighway project in the spring of 1993, and it is still in the proposal and solicitation phase for Calren. It is offering a total of $25 million over two years to experiment with superhighway-like applications.

Calren issued two technology Requests for Proposal (RFPs) for ATM-based applications, one for the San Francisco Bay Area and one for Los Angeles. It also issued three community of interest RFPs for education, health care, and community, government, or commercial services. The community of interest applications can use frame relay, Switched Multimegabit Data Service (SMDS), single-line ISDN (SDS-IS), ISDN bundled with Centrex (Centrex IS), or Switched 56 service. The call for ATM RFPs closed in January, and the community of interest applications closed by March.

"We are looking for applications that benefit a large end-user group. It also has to be collaborative. The collaborators bring the piece parts, such as the hardware, software, and manpower. Calren funds the network service component," says Laura Sanford, Calren's communication manager. "The councils who do the evaluation toward merit are external to PacBell. They are from the community of interest and technology. For example, the education council looks at the overall impact [of the RFP] on the education community at large and looks at what it means in relation to other strategic initiatives."

DIGITAL AND TIMES MIRROR

While the state of North Carolina and NIIT are dabbling in the arts of ATM, Digital Equipment, Times Mirror Cable, and Arizona State University are dallying with some very ordinary technologies: cable TV and Ethernet. Digital is deploying Ethernet service in Times Mirror Cable's Phoenix service area, and together they are working with manufacturing companies to understand how to conduct electronic commerce. Times Mirror Cable, through its subsidiary Dimension Cable Services, is providing the cable infrastructure. Arizona State University is helping the manufacturing companies examine how they conduct business prior to the network, determine how they will conduct their business with the network, and define the usefulness of the network.

"We've tried to work with some major manufacturing companies and their suppliers to begin to look at what utility these companies can gain by being connected across a metropolitan area network," says Dave Rosi, Digital's director of video and interactive services (Acton, MA).

In this project, reality is stressed. "In a lot of these trials, people are doing nice-to-have tests," says Rosi. "If pro-

vided with the right tools, businesses will look to this type of network, embrace it, and pay for it. We have to get beyond showing things running over a public infrastructure. We're trying to assess how you make a business. The participants in this network are not just playing with devices."

Currently, Digital's Ethernet service is available in four Times Mirror Cable headends, covering about 48 miles. Digital plans to expand Ethernet service to cover 12 headends and a greater distance. Times Mirror Cable's Phoenix service area is one of the largest physical service areas. In late winter, of 1994 three companies were on-line: McDonnell Douglas Helicopter Systems, as the prime contractor, and Modern Industries and Tempe Precision Aircraft as the suppliers. Others followed shortly, so they met their project goal of having 12 to 15 companies connected by spring of '94.

Ethernet over cable TV was tried in the mid-1980s and was pretty unsuccessful. Why try again? Proponents say the technologies have improved. The throughput of the Ethernet-to-cable TV bridges is higher. The bridges are able to transmit and receive on different frequencies at will, making them easier to deploy. Also, the cable TV networks are more sophisticated. "The cable companies have begun to realize that they've been installing gigantic computer topologies that are very efficient. They've been putting in big fiber rings and putting in fiber to the neighborhood, which is more reliable and efficient," says Mike Huffaker, Digital's manager of technology (Tempe, AZ).

Cable TV networks use a tree topology, with a headend at the root. The headend receives transmissions from the inbound channels and sends them onto the proper outbound channels over coax cable. Headends are typically connected by fiber. By placing Digital's ChannelWorks Ethernet-to-broadband cable TV bridge at the users' sites, the Ethernet users may transmit and receive Ethernet packets over the cable TV network's forward and receive channels (see Figure 3). Only the transmission medium is different; applications think they're sending and receiving ordinary TCP/IP over Ethernet.

For this configuration to be successful, the cable TV network must have sufficient channels in the return path. Because cable TV networks are traditionally used to broadcast and very little data is received from the remote sites, most of the system's bandwidth is reserved for sending data. Many of the subsplit systems have three channels

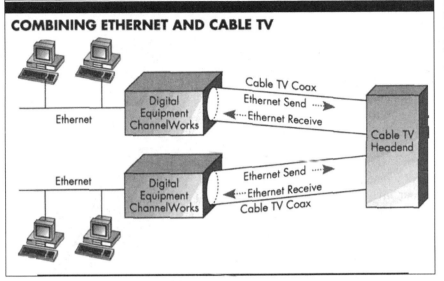

COMBINING ETHERNET AND CABLE TV

Figure 3: Digital Equipment is deploying Ethernet services over Times Mirror Cable's Arizona cable TV service area to experiment with electronic commerce. The ChannelWorks bridges reformat Ethernet traffic for transmission over the cable TV coax network.

in the return path, which usually are not used. Each channel can serve as a transmit or receive path for a LAN.

In cyber-commerce, Digital expects CAD, videoconferencing, shared whiteboards, and multimedia mail to be key applications. "The killer application is CAD. The major part of time consumption and lead time is driving across town to go to meetings. Now they can interactively use these images, interactively mark up drawings, and make changes," says Huffaker.

Videoconferencing is also an important application. "They take their handycam on the workshop floor, and later play the movie at a conference, and it's not just talking heads. They can say, 'Here's what my problem is, let me show you the machine, and listen to the noises in the machine.' It isn't the old concept of videoconferencing," says Huffaker. If this project parlays into production for Digital, the company may provide services such as data warehousing, where it or third-party companies provide on-line catalogs and storage facilities for a fee.

Digital expects electronic commerce to benefit companies both large and small. Large companies can bring their suppliers on-line, allowing them to bid on jobs, execute purchase orders, revise product specifications, and communicate. "The big companies have moved away from the attitude of working with the smaller companies. Those companies are getting leaner and are saying, 'If you want to do

business with us, you'll use the same thing we use,' " says Rosi. "It's putting the investment requirement on the little guy who can't afford it." With electronic connections, small companies can react nimbly and efficiently, for example, sending an electronic CAD file over the network instead of driving across town to deliver a hard copy of a drawing.

"This whole project is as much an experience in the technology as it is policy and socioeconomics," says Huffaker. Perhaps the more difficult aspects are the security, billing, and regulatory issues.

"The regulatory agencies haven't seen this type of network before. It's cutting across a lot of lines," says Rosi.

Rosi offers some down-to-earth hints on securing such a network. "First, take a real look at normal network security such as passwords. The other piece is to get people to think about their security. You want a drawing secured over a computer network, but how do you do it normally? Do you drive it over? We're not going to provide greater security than what you normally have unless you absolutely need it. The main thing is getting people to think about the real world," he says. The Digital network will have C2 and Kerberos security.

MCC EINET

Electronic commerce will be big business, and MCC's software is providing the network services foundation for

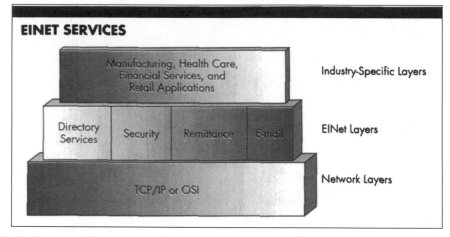

Figure 4: MCC's EINet is software intended to enable electronic commerce, including for communication, on-line product catalogs, and digital purchase orders.

EINET SERVICES

Manufacturing, Health Care, Financial Services, and Retail Applications — Industry-Specific Layers

Directory Services | Security | Remittance | E-mail — EINet Layers

TCP/IP or OSI — Network Layers

three projects of the federal Technology Reinvestment Program, which emphasizes technology investments for commercial and military applications. MCC's Enterprise Integration Network (EINet) software will be used in the Technology Network Program (TecNet), Manufacturers' EnterCorp, and Texas-One as these networks are designed and built.

TecNet will provide a prototype communications system linking the National Institute of Standards and Technology's Manufacturing Technology Centers (MTCs) and Manufacturing Outreach Centers (MOCs) and their small- and medium-size business clients to help small firms affected by defense conversion.

Manufacturers in Missouri, Kansas, and Colorado will be able to use the Manufacturers' EnterCorp network to pinpoint its clients' needs and to match them to network resources best able to fill them.

Texans can get experience with electronic commerce via Texas-One, which will be created by the Texas Department of Commerce. One application will be Borderbase, a database of demographic, socioeconomic, market, and customs data to support commerce between the United States and Mexico. Also on-line will be the Technology Assessment Center of the Texas Department of Information Resources, which provides information about hardware and software products..

EINet will also take the software lead in the Agile Manufacturing Information Infrastructure (AMII), which is under contract from the Advanced Research Projects Agency. The AMII is a venue for deploying prototyping, design ver-

ification, and process planning tools to help U.S. manufacturers be more competitive internationally.

So what is this EINet that's being used in so many government projects? Defense conversion notwithstanding, EINet could be useful for any group of companies that wants to buy and sell goods electronically.

"We're making enhancements to Enterprise Integration Network so it can be useful for the information infrastructure and specifically for manufacturing, automation, and design activities. We're trying to support anyone who wants to put manufacturing catalogs or electronic information for purposes of enabling manufacturing commerce to take place," says Brian Kushner, vice president and executive director of MCC's Information Systems Division. "We are trying to open up the world of computer-based electronic commerce. What the Ford Model T was for automobiles–low cost, lots of content, and reduced barriers of entry–we are trying to do for WAN commerce."

EINet delivers directory, security, remittance, and e-mail services that run over TCP/IP or OSI transports. It also has industry-specific modules for manufacturing, health care, financial services, and retail. It runs on Sun, Ultrix, AIX, Windows, and the Mac (see Figure 4). Connectivity is provided via the Internet, and MCC is examining other transports.

EINet's directory service, called Galaxy, takes an X.500 structure and combines World Wide Web and WAIS functions to help users move through the vast amounts of public and private information on the Internet. EINet currently uses Kerberos, and MCC is examining other types of encryption.

Remittance services are essential for electronic purchasing and payment. EINet will eventually allow for monetary transaction by electronic checks, credit cards, and letter of credits. "You have signatures on purchase orders, but on electronic forms, you don't. You need a handshake to make sure it's acceptable," says Kushner. "We are in the process of defining a pilot with a financial institution to figure out how you do it."

EINet is initially oriented toward manufacturing, but the same software can support any type of information you want to have on-line, according to Kushner. The structure that was used for a manufacturing-parts database can be applied to consulting and business planning services.

READ THE SIGNS

The superhighway will come to exist in some form, and with luck and work, it will be more than a vehicle to deliver movies on demand. If these six projects are any indication, the areas of education, health care, government, and commerce will reap the fruits of superhighway hoopla.

But as these projects and others move forward, keep in mind Saal's comments: "Most projects aren't prepared to handle success. They're prepared to handle it if 1 percent to 10 percent of the users log on. Look at the problems America Online has been having. Most projects have limits on pervasive use."

I-Way or My Way

SIGNIFICANT SECURITY, TECHNICAL, IMPLEMENTATION, AND ECONOMIC ISSUES MUST BE RESOLVED BEFORE THE INFORMATION SUPERHIGHWAY CAN TAKE TO CYBERSPACE.

BY PETER STEPHENSON

To say that Vice President Al Gore's beloved information superhighway is in trouble wouldn't be entirely accurate, since enough of it doesn't exist for it actually to be in trouble. Television and magazine advertisements notwithstanding, the National Information Infrastructure (NII) has such a long way to go to become reality that judging its health would be ludicrous. Signposts along the various on-ramps should serve as health warnings as the NII is built; however, today's NII is a collection of small sections of interstate highway connected by rural roads.

The National Computer Security Association (NCSA, Mechanicsburg, PA) held a day-long public session on the NII at ComNet (Washington, D.C.) in January, 1994. Several issues of concern to future NII travelers emerged, of which security loomed largest. "Who will be the traffic cops on the NII?" "How will I keep my information private?" "Is this NII just another Internet where hackers, thieves, network surfers, and all sorts of undesirables are after my data?" "How can I protect my system if it is connected to the NII?" Questions, questions, questions. Unfortunately, very few real answers.

Perhaps the lack of answers reflects an emerging infrastructure where no universal vision for its future exists. Or perhaps it reflects one where there's too much vision from too many people and with too little coordination. Whatever the reason, the NII has a very long way to go, and if the NCSA meeting was any indication, a lot of toes are getting stubbed on the first tentative steps.

JUST LIKE THE SUPERCOLLIDER?

Let's look at the NII from a variety of angles. What is it? What is it supposed to be? What are the technical, se-

curity, implementation, and economic issues? What could it mean to business users? What should the government's part be in implementing the NII?

Exploring the NII is like wandering the tunnels of the Superconducting Supercollider. As you wander the rough-cut corridors with bare light bulbs hanging from the ceiling, and huge tunnel-cutting machines lying idle like giant dirt-eating behemoths, you get a sense of the project's immensity.

Will these tunnels, frozen in time since the project's cancellation, and their ghost machines, waiting for operators, presage the fate of the NII? Is the NII, like the Superconducting Supercollider, too much, too expensive, and not necessary? Fortunately or not, that is doubtful. After the toe stubbing, politicking, dream spinning, and corporate greed run their course, the cybertunnels of the information superhighway will hum with life, moving information around the globe as never before. But there is lot of traveling to do on an information Route 66 before that happens.

WHAT IS THE NII?

Some people say the NII is little more than a super Internet. Others say that it's little more than hype. The NII is the proverbial gleam in its parent's eye, and a gleam whose time has come. The Internet is outmoded by about 15 years. Its capacity is based on an addressing scheme so far out of date that it is marginal even for large enterprises. The NII is also an idea for which today's technology can provide acceptable support.

The need is there, the technology is there, so what's missing? What keeps the NII from being today's answer to communications problems? First, a system like the NII needs a supporting infrastructure. Second, it needs universal buy-in with regard to contentious issues such as security.

The NII is intended to be a universally accessible, logical, and physical infrastructure for moving data of any kind throughout the United States and eventually the world. The key word is infrastructure. Infrastructure is what's lacking.

What makes an infrastructure? In the case of a "new generation" Internet, the infrastructure is a combination of physical and logical assets. The physical assets are the copper wire, fiber optics, microwave channels, routers, and other things that allow data to move between points on the network. The logical assets are the standards, controls, logical interfaces between physical network segments, and all those things that allow the physical assets to function together efficiently and securely. The physical assets are the subject of significant media and advertising hype. The logical assets are at best nonexistent and at worst significant barriers to effective implementation.

The notion that all it takes to create an information superhighway is a gigantic reel of fiber optic cable has been popularized by telephony and cable TV vendors. There can't be a single networking professional in the United States who believes that simplistic representation. The notion doesn't stop with the vendors. The Clinton administration, especially Al Gore, perpetuates the myth by making endless naive rah-rah speeches in favor of the information superhighway.

Simple political rhetoric won't suffice. The public is responding to the hype, and unless something useful is delivered, the results could be disappointing at best. What does it really take to connect the world? It sounds simple: some cable, some telephone switching equipment, and some end-user equipment. The United States can provide that technology with little difficulty. But the soft issues need to be addressed before a real information superhighway can grow.

A HEALTHY SKEPTICISM

U.S. technology can be used to build the physical infrastructure for an information superhighway. Many local and regional examples of infrastructure and intelligent use of the potential resources exist. High-speed wide-area

rings are in pilot use in Washington, D.C. In the San Francisco Bay Area, Smart Valley (Palo Alto, CA) is showing us how a universally accessed communication infrastructure can benefit society. But there is a long way to go to information gratification.

The two big concerns discussed at the NCSA meeting were security and universal access. Security is the more contentious. Security concerns boil down to privacy for both business and private users. Universal access concerns are a bit more nebulous.

Most participants in the NCSA meeting were enthusiastic about the concept of the NII and its logical extension, the International Information Infrastructure (III). None of the people I interviewed believe that the industry is within even a few years of a successful implementation. The bottom line? Where the NII is concerned, healthy skepticism should be the order of the day.

Input has come from potential providers of NII services. Much more input is needed from potential NII users. Until the buyers talk to the sellers, it's unlikely that a successful NII will emerge. Likewise, the NII users will range from megacorporations to individual households. Implementing an infrastructure that can serve equally that entire spectrum of use is a monumental task. Potentially successful vendors must understand their markets thoroughly. What is good for General Motors may not be best for Joe's Computer Integrations, and neither implementation may be the best for Joe at home.

BUILDING AN INFRASTRUCTURE

The Internet is not the NII. That statement, obvious to many, says a lot. For example, could changing the usage rules on the Internet allow it to migrate to an NII? Capacity and bandwidth issues will prevent that. Rules have been changed in recent years to allow commercial use; however, Internet mavens say it will be a year or two before the Internet runs out of addresses. The reason is that the rules have changed, allowing many more users than the system was originally intended to support.

Another example is the Internet's makeup. Portions don't have acceptable bandwidth for many of today's routine graphical applications, let alone for the high bandwidth demands that will be made by tomorrow's multimedia, multichannel services. The Internet segments were intended originally to support government data communications. Over time they have been stretched to their maximum. The Internet serves an entirely different purpose from the NII.

Another difference between the emerging NII and the Internet is that the Internet is perceived as the domain of government and academia. Many commercial companies are on the Internet, but a large percentage are technology-based. The NII, on the other hand, is a creature of the private sector, primarily the telephone companies and cable TV companies. It is a system where cable TV can, where the law allows, compete head-on with the phone companies for the public's communications dollars. Those dollars will be spent on telephone, television, and a variety of innovative communications services.

Because the cable TV infrastructure exists in most parts of the country, it will likely form a significant part of the NII physical backbone. Also, the infrastructure is very wideband and allows a lot of leeway on the types of services it carries. Finally, the cable TV industry currently carries those services right into the user's home.

The telephone infrastructure in many parts of the country seriously needs to be upgraded. In most cases, even when wideband capability exists, it stops far short of the user's home. It will take some time for the telcos to bring broadband services all the way to the user. Thus, from the home user perspective at least, the cable companies have a leg up.

The NII hype has focused almost exclusively on the private user. Despite the talk of 500 channels of television, most people seem to believe that 500 channels won't significantly improve the quality of TV. Where I live in Michigan, I have a choice of 88 channels and still have trouble finding something worth watching. Actually, a lot of those channels will provide features other than TV shows. Interactive capabilities and the capability to incorporate telephone and data communications will open new opportunities. The television will become the single most important appliance in the home.

What about business? If and when the NII becomes the III, the potential for a worldwide communications grid will become reality. A lot of barriers at the infrastructure level must be overcome. Different countries use different communications standards. Communications access laws vary widely from country to country. Most important to many

potential users, the ability to protect private information as it travels on such a grid is spotty at best.

How will a worldwide infrastructure come about? Like almost all networks, it will evolve. Various public and private organizations, tired of waiting for a real program, will build their own networks. Private and public carriers will offer on-ramps in the form of subnets. The Internet itself is likely to become an on-ramp to a future NII. The problem with this approach is that unlike the Internet, the NII will suffer from a lack of standards. The NII will need to support a multitude of protocols, and it will become a modern-day Tower of Babel. For specific users on a specific subnet, this approach poses no real problem, but the issue of universal access will not have been addressed.

KEEPING WHAT'S YOURS YOURS

Of all the issues surrounding the NII, information protection is the biggest both in scope and complexity. Information protection on the NII touches almost every aspect of its use, whether public or private, business or personal.

In researching this article I came across some of the most outrageous allegations imaginable. I also heard many legitimate concerns and received a lot of sugar-coated explanations. The one thing that came across loud and clear was that the NII is going to happen, sooner or later, bigger or smaller, and the number one barrier to its successful implementation as a worldwide business communications grid is security.

Information protection on an NII or an III covers a lot of territory. It includes the ability of an organization to protect its information intended for internal use. That definition includes data traveling on the network as well as data kept internally that could be accessed from the network. It also includes a need to protect communications between organizations.

DISPENSING WITH DES

One of the major bones of contention among companies that build data communications security products is the inability to sell those products outside the United States. Because of organizations such as the Software Publishers Association (SPA) and the NCSA, this issue has become more emotional and better understood. Both organizations are trying to place encryption export in the government spotlight, but their efforts have netted little gain.

The issue is even more confusing when you consider that Data Encryption Standard (DES) is available in the public domain. It can be compromised using current technology and has succumbed to stronger encryption schemes, some to be controlled by the government. DES-based products are available around the world from 40 non-U.S. manufacturers, according to a survey conducted by the SPA. Those 40 foreign manufacturers, some in Russia and other current and former sensitive areas, produced 123 DES-based products. But the United States can neither export nor use DES internationally. What does this issue have to do with the NII?

U.S. companies doing business internationally are forced to purchase data protection from foreign sources. One foreign source is the former KGB, which sells a DES competitor called GOST. Presumably, those companies will be communicating over the NII or III. How do they protect their sensitive information? Much to the chagrin of American developers of data encryption products, they go to the international competition.

How much revenue do those American companies lose as a result of the current encryption export policy? The National Security Agency (NSA) has stated that it can't identify much more than a few million dollars. SPA and NCSA studies indicate that the loss is actually much greater. One major U.S. company alone lost $80 million in sales in a recent 12-month period because file and data encryption in its integrated system was not exportable. This example was reported by Stephen Walker, president of Trusted Information Systems (Glenwood, MD), in testimony before the U.S. House Subcommittee on Economic Policy, Trade, and Environment, a subcommittee of the House Committee on Foreign Affairs.

The encryption export issue has been addressed by a bill before the House of Representatives introduced by Rep. Maria Cantwell (D-Washington). The bill is intended to liberalize restrictions on the export of data encryption, especially when it's part of a larger system. U.S. companies doing business on the NII would welcome this bill's passing, since it would provide a much-welcomed measure of data privacy when the NII is open to the world.

If there has been a lesson learned from the Internet, it might well be that once you open the floodgates of world-wide network access, you also open the floodgates of unauthorized intrusion. There seems to be no way to protect the information superhighway itself, so we must protect ourselves when we travel on it. The Clinton Administration recently upheld the ban on exporting data encryption so, it would seem, the Cantwell bill is more needed than ever.

SPIES AMONG US

One of the worst potential uses for the NII is keeping track of Mr. and Ms. Common Citizen. A few years ago there was an outcry of rage when Prodigy users found that Prodigy could and did capture private information off users' hard drives. From an attorney in the Pacific Northwest to a writer in New England, reports came into Prodigy forums of finding Prodigy-created files containing private information.

Prodigy began by denying that the files existed and expelling the "troublemakers" from the system. Then Prodigy admitted to the files' existence but claimed that Prodigy engineers had no access to them. Finally, they had to admit that the Prodigy computers could and did collect the information at will. The answer to irate users was that it didn't matter because Prodigy had no interest in the information anyway.

The issue to civil libertarians had little to do with whether Prodigy cared about personal information. The outrage was over the fact that Prodigy could, if it wanted, invade the privacy of its users. Issues of personal privacy have become a cause célèbre for all manner of individuals and organizations ranging from paranoid kooks to serious guardians of personal and corporate privacy such as the Electronic Frontier Foundation. The Prodigy story could be repeated when and if the government mandates use of Clipper technology as a replacement for DES according to Sharon Webb, chair of the Legislative Affairs Committee for the NCSA, and the fallout would be orders of magnitude worse than any paranoia that may have resulted from the Prodigy fiasco.

The idea behind Clipper is that it would be the only authorized encryption technology in the United States. The technology is quite strong, but it has one flaw. The system is designed so that a universal key–call it a "back door"–can unlock (or decrypt) any Clipper-encrypted data. The custodianship of the key to the back door rests with the government.

All of the encrypted American information flowing on the NII would be open and transparent to the government. The NSA's response, like Prodigy's, is that it has no interest in the general run of information being encrypted by Clipper. They are simply holding the key just in case. In case of what, we're not told.

The early response to the Clipper approach was predictably negative. After a suitable cooling-off period, Clipper is back in the news. However, the original issue of privacy has been clouded by new accompanying technologies and a new name for the project–Tessera. In essence, the facts are still the same, and recently the Clinton administration mandated use of Clipper for federal agencies.

The bottom line is that Clipper/Tessera allows government and law enforcement agencies to eavesdrop on any data transmission, including digital voice and video, encrypted with the technology. Some say this is *1984*, 10 years late.

Initiatives such as Clipper have some interesting implications for the electronic superhighway. The NCSA has information suggesting that Tele-Communications Inc. (TCI, Denver), one of the country's largest cable television operators, is working with the NSA to include Clipper technology in next-generation cable TV boxes. TCI has declined to comment.

The NII will have an immediate impact on the balance of power between cable TV and telephone providers. Since cable companies have a large investment in high-speed cable plants to serve their customers with ever-increasing numbers of channels, the next logical step (regulations permitting) is consolidation of TV, data, and telephone services over your new 500-channel cable TV system.

This emerging competition and the uncertainty of how the rules will eventually come down from industry regulators has made for some very strange alliances between former competitors and between government and industry. In many regards, business and the consumer will be the big benefactors. In some regards, alliances such as the rumored one between NSA and TCI and technology such as Clipper/Tessera could negatively impact both business and personal users of the NII.

Competition will help keep services affordable; research emerging from NII-type projects is bearing fruit.

However, if government spy agencies become involved in the already unlikely relationships, the potential exists for these officals to keep tabs on the activities of every American citizen with a cable TV box.

ENCRYPTION GYMNASTICS

The encryption export problems don't end with DES. Even though DES and its stronger competitor RSA Data Security (Redwood City, CA), can't be exported, Tessera, the Hercules of all encryption schemes, will be exported according to reports. On the surface this announcement sounds like great news for companies wanting to keep their business private as they travel through international cyberspace.

But wait a minute: What foreign power or corporation will buy an information-protection product that exposes its information to the U.S. government? Under those conditions, U.S. companies would likely be no better off than they were in pre-Clipper days.

The issue of personal and business privacy will continue to cloud the NII's horizons for some time. The answers to the "traffic cop" questions posed at the NCSA meeting at ComNet still seem to be without suitable answers. So far, the choice for the international business community at least seems to be expose private information to government snooping or take your chances in the clear.

The choice for the consumer may be privacy or 500 channels rich with options and a device that tracks every purchase, television program, phone call, and data connection made through the cable box. Clearly, we have a long way to go to reconcile technology and its benefits with the attendant costs.

SO, HOW ARE WE DOING?

With all the issues impeding the implementation of the NII, has any progress been made? It depends who you ask. *Washington Technology*, the Capitol's watchdog publication on technology issues, recently graded the Clinton NII initiative an "A" for hype and a "C" for content. Many industry watchers would lower the "C" to barely passing.

Potential start-up costs for personal use of the NII have been estimated at as much as $1,500 per household, which is probably more than most individuals are willing to pay for what could be glorified TV. With corporate giants such as MCI, Sprint, and AT&T hyping the new age information infrastructure, smaller companies seem to be concerned with affordability of access as well. Although some business users question if they would be able to afford connection services, others figure that the NII offerings, like the long distance wars in the telephone marketplace, will eventually settle down to reasonable mass-market pricing.

The bottom line is that the NII is a lot more form than substance and is likely to stay that way for the foreseeable future. In addition to the privacy and infrastructure issues, there is the dilemma of who is going to pay for all of the cable, satellite, and microwave systems needed to make it all happen. A Department of Defense employee, who declined to be identified, says, "The NII is nothing more than the telephone companies trying to get Uncle Sam to pay for installing big trunks."

If he's right, that strategy may not work. In 1992, Pennsylvania tried unsuccessfully to get taxpayers to pay for a statewide network of fiber optic communications lines. In times of tight budgets, the "what's in it for me" approach to paying more taxes is pretty strong.

The government could decide that it's in our national security interests to build an NII much like it did when the Internet was built. The Defense Information Systems Agency (DISA) is chartered with providing an open network for the military, and by all reports, DISA has made fairly good technical progress. Even though there's little consensus on what the government's role in the NII should be, the lessons of the Internet are not encouraging when it comes to government control.

One of the most interesting potential alliances affecting the development of the NII's infrastructure has fallen apart. Thanks largely to recent FCC rulings on tariffs, Bell Atlantic and TCI have called off their planned merger. The merger would have likely resulted in the most competitive commercial telecommunications infrastructure in the country and arguably could have sped along the development of the NII. With the merger off, the issues affecting infrastructure become even more precarious.

Worse than the practical aspects of the Bell Atlantic-TCI cold feet could be the psychological impact. Potential investors, already overhyped on the NII, may begin to discount NII participation as a viable investment. Bell Atlantic and TCI stocks went up slightly after the announcement, perhaps signaling that the investment community believes that cable TV and telephones don't belong together. It is ironic that the potential merger reportedly dissolved as a result of action by the very government that seeks to make its mark in the communications technology of the 21st century.

Whither the NII? At the end of the day, it's hard to say. One thing is certain: The isolated experiments, product development, and assorted on-ramps that have been spawned by the initiative are likely to be the most positive results in the near term. High-speed, high-bandwidth networking is coming of age. Whether it delivers 500 channels of cable TV or full-motion video to the desktop PCs of U.S. business is of little importance. As we enter the age of the enterprise, the developments that have been borne of the NII will have significant impact, even if the NII itself doesn't.

The Extra Mile

AS THE NATION GRAPPLES WITH THE QUESTION OF WHO WILL PAY TO PAVE THE INFORMATION SUPERHIGHWAY, POWER COMPANIES LAY CLAIM TO THE ANSWER.

BY TED BUNKER

In 1993, Bill Gates took the spotlight in a Times Square theater to describe his vision of office machines remotely controlled by telephone.

Telephones equipped with screen displays running Windows would be used to program copiers, printers, computers, and other office machines under a scheme Gates dubbed Microsoft At Work. Shortly afterward, Microsoft began collaborating with cable television giant Tele-Communications (Englewood, CO) and Pacific Gas & Electric (San Francisco) to develop a similar system for home use.

Bill Gates needs PG&E to ride the information highway?

Far-sighted, state-of-the-art vision is what you might expect from Gates, the whiz kid who turned DOS into a gold mine and made himself a billionaire. Years before he began the collaboration with PG&E, at a gathering in Boston, Gates talked about his plans to put a supercomputer-sized video server in the basement of his new home, programmed with thousands of art works and movies that could be displayed on demand on flat-panel, high-definition television screens scattered around his home. A grand scheme if ever there was one.

In PG&E, Gates may have spied what many others have overlooked in the race to construct what Vice President Al Gore believes will be an economic and communal linchpin for 21st century Americans: Power companies offer an economically straightforward rationale for building the "last mile" of optical fiber linking homes with a national, interactive broadband network.

After all, power company wires link virtually every home and business in America to what's called "the grid," the network of power lines and substations that supplies electricity throughout the country. Utilities' need for a hardwire connection will not go away anytime soon. And their interest in conserving scarce energy resources can readily justify the investment in an end-to-end fiber optic network that would have the capacity to carry 500-channel television, two-way data communications, video telephony, and more.

Sound like a pipe dream? It may be closer to reality than most imagine.

POWER TO THE PEOPLE

Entergy, a New Orleans-based utility holding company with operations in four Southern states, has already built a pilot system that allows automated and remote management of home appliances such as air conditioners and water heaters, using technology designed by First Pacific Networks (Sunnyvale, CA). Entergy says the network has enough remaining capacity to carry more than 100 channels of television and multiple telephone lines, and this system uses coaxial cable to cover the last mile from a neighborhood distribution hub.

Called PowerView, the First Pacific system is designed to let customers respond to price signals to moderate their power consumption during periods of peak demand. The technique, referred to as demand-side management, has been used for years by large consumers of electricity, corporations for example, to reduce costs and by power companies to defer construction of new generating plants.

Sexy? Not at all. Attractive? Depends who looks.

Utilities studying these applications say they can justify the cost of constructing the networks solely on the basis of the conservation they provide. And industry officials point out there's relatively little additional cost involved in substituting fiber optic lines for coaxial cable when the network infrastructure is being built.

In just the last few years, dramatic cost reductions of microelectronic data processing power and the development of interactive on-line software have combined to enable residential consumers to take advantage of the same demand-management principles used by big corporations to cut their energy bills. Essentially, it introduces a form of market-rate pricing to signal customers as to when to conserve consumption. Estimates on savings run as high as a 33-percent reduction in energy use for each home.

PILOTING THE WAY

Jack King, president of the Entergy unit that set up the pilot project in Little Rock, AR, pegged the cost of residential wiring and other hardware at $900 a home. That's easily low enough to justify the expense, when the energy savings could allow Entergy to defer until sometime in the next century the construction of new generating plants.

Power stations are expensive to build and operate. King says a new, 840 megawatt nuclear power plant, for instance, would likely cost $4 billion to build.

What's more, the excess bandwidth created by building a system with the data-transfer capacity required for two-way price and response signaling gives operators a source of new revenue from leasing that capacity to cable systems, telephone companies, or others. And some utilities have already laid fiber optic trunk lines to connect power grid control centers with local distribution nodes. Much of that idle trunk capacity, called "dark fiber" by utility managers, goes unused or is leased already to telephone companies.

In a nutshell, power companies appear to have an answer for a central problem that has confronted would-be toll-takers on the digital highway of Gore's dreams: If they build it, who will pay?

By some estimates, wiring every home, school, library, and hospital in the nation could cost up to $400 billion. That's a lot of freight, even for the likes of AT&T and its offspring, the regional Bells. Even with interactive video games, tele-shopping, and movies on demand, it won't be easy generating the cash flow to pay down debts incurred by that kind of investment. And people used to passive

television watching might not play along, especially if the costs are too steep.

But someone has to pay for the superhighway, or it won't be built. Like the television cable and telephone lines that came before, government policymakers want the electronic umbilicals to the nascent smorgasbord of video, voice, and data services to be built and operated by private interests, not public. Private interests won't build it if there isn't an economic incentive.

So sooner or later, we'll all be paying to use the electronic equivalent of driveways that connect our homes to a communal broadband network. Some–including Gore–say the superhighway will be vital to our economic health and general well-being in the 21st century. Accepting that assertion as a truism, all that remains to be seen is who we'll pay–and how much–for access to this lifeline of knowledge and commerce.

Most often when discussions of the developing national network infrastructure turn to who will build it, the answer appears to be taken somewhat for granted: Either a telephone or a cable TV company will do it, and there may not be much difference between the two in terms of services offered. Both types of companies have the technical skills required and plenty of experience raising the mountains of cash thought necessary to finance the construction.

CONTENT, NOT CARRIAGE

But when all is said and done, both come up short in offering something more than just access to the network. Content, not carriage, is by most accounts where the big money lies on the digital byways stretching into America's living rooms. Last winter's bidding war for content-producer Paramount made clear just how much phone and cable companies realize they need something customers value beyond simple access.

While cable operators and to a lesser extent phone companies look for a bit of Hollywood glitz or New York showbiz to fill that need, power companies offer a predictable, straightforward solution: conservation and the savings on electric bills that result. Couch potatoes with no interest in interactive video games or home shopping may be delighted. They can pay for it by doing nothing at all.

Utility executives at Entergy, The Southern Company (Atlanta), and several others think First Pacific Network's

PowerView could make the economics of building the information highway's "last mile" compelling.

PowerView is, says Earl Thelen, vice president and general manager for utilities at First Pacific Networks, "a technology that is economically rational.

"It costs less money for a utility to shave the peak of a critical demand period than to meet the power required during the demand period," Thelen explains.

So why haven't power companies played a bigger role? Gore has paid lip service to the idea that utilities should be allowed to get in the game. But he hasn't included them in his councils on how to map out, build, and operate the information superhighway. On Capitol Hill, lawmakers have also made paeans to the notion of power companies playing a role, but subject to current restrictions.

TOUGH ACT TO FOLLOW

Therein lies the rub. Utility holding companies with interstate operations, among the largest and most capable of building and running these systems, serving some 20 percent of the nation, face a tough legal hurdle in the form of the Public Utilities Holding Company Act, a law that dates to the Depression era. In general, PUHCA bars the holding companies it regulates from investing substantial sums into any non-power generation and distribution facilities. And state and local regulators often take their cues from federal law.

If companies such as Entergy and Southern want to build demand-management networks that can then be used for video and telecommunications purposes, they must apply for a PUHCA waiver from the Securities and Exchange Commission (SEC) to finance it. So far, most utility spending on these technologies has been carefully drawn from the earnings that would be distributed to shareholders, thus avoiding the immediate need for SEC waivers.

None of the bills pending before Congress as the winter drew to a close would modify PUHCA restrictions or any state or local laws that block utility participation in communications endeavors. Power company executives say they want to provide network infrastructure, but few want to be treated like telephone or cable companies.

"We think they [utility companies] ought to be able to play a role," Gore says, describing the Clinton administration's position as members of Congress were working over legislation to lower barriers to competition among phone and cable companies. But, he adds, "changing current energy laws is not part of our current legislation. That's something for Congress to work out in the future.

"We're not planning to offer an amendment to the Public Utilities Holding Company Act. But we do believe they have a role to play, subject to existing legal restrictions," Gore says.

Changing PUHCA might not be in the cards any time soon. When Rep. Rick Boucher, D-VA, suggested he would offer an amendment to a bill he co-sponsored with Rep. Ed Markey, D-MA, and Rep. Jack Fields, R-TX, at the start of congressional hearings on telecommunications reforms, he was met with resounding silence in the Telecommunications and Finance Subcommittee chambers.

Boucher says letting electric companies compete for a piece of the action would "promote competition, encourage more private investment, strengthen our national information infrastructure, and ensure lower prices and greater flexibility for consumers." Boucher adds that allowing power companies to get into the game would spur greater competition for the broadest consumer strata, residential users. "The last mile of the information superhighway will be put in place much more quickly," Boucher says.

But barely a week later, Boucher appeared to back away from his proposal. Joining Markey, chairman of the Telecommunications and Finance Subcommittee, and Rep. Philip R. Sharp, (D-IN), chairman of the Energy and Power Subcommittee, Boucher asked SEC Chairman Arthur Levitt whether releasing holding companies from PUHCA restraints risks opening "enormous loopholes in the scheme of prudential regulation established under PUHCA to combat the myriad of abuses to both investors and consumers that were uncovered by this committee during its extensive investigations after the 1929 stock market crash."

LEARN FROM THE PAST

The trio went on to warn that "a repeal of these restrictions might easily result in a repetition of abuses similar to those that originally led to enactment of PUHCA legislation in the first place–such as self-dealing transactions with affiliates, cross-subsidization of non-utility businesses at the expense of captive utility rate payers, the concentration of economic power in business entities that are not susceptible to state regulation, and the creation of highly leveraged and complex corporate structures controlling diversified activities that may involve increased risk."

What's going on here? Greg Simon, an aide to Gore, points out the importance of recognizing "the difference between what's practical and what's congressional." He adds that the issue may be addressed later in the legislative process, which Gore has predicted will result in a telecommunications law overhaul sometime this year. For jurisdictional reasons, Simon says, any suggestion of changing the energy laws was kept to a minimum, to prevent legislation from being held hostage by committee politics.

Interestingly, PUHCA was written by John Dingell Sr., the father of Rep. John Dingell, D-MI. The younger Dingell is chairman of the powerful House Energy and Commerce Committee and a major force behind efforts to recast the nation's telecommunications laws, along with Rep. Jack Brooks, D-TX, chairman of the House Judiciary Committee. The subcommittees chaired by both Markey and Sharp are under Dingell. As Simon notes, PUHCA "is not easily surmounted."

Obviously, legal restrictions haven't frozen power companies out of the game. Most operate their own communications networks already, linking their power-generating stations and substations with central control rooms. Industry estimates say utilities have strung more than 8,000 miles of fiber optic cable.

"They don't want to be totally dependent on the public switched networks," says Jeffrey Sheldon, general counsel at the Utilities Telecommunications Council in Washington. "The public telephone network is highly reliant on the power grid; there's a limit to how long they can operate without power."

With the emergence of legislative efforts, spurred by Gore, Sheldon says utilities have become sensitive to how changes in the law might affect them.

"Some things utilities are doing may be made so difficult they would be halted voluntarily," rather than lead to a forced opening of the network to outsiders, Sheldon says. He added that power companies don't want to find their networks treated like telephone or cable systems, unless they operate them that way in competition with phone and cable companies.

But some technologists, such as Lotus Development founder Mitch Kapor, now the head of the Electronic Frontier Foundation, say they doubt power companies have the technological sophistication to ride the cutting edge of wide-area networking technology. But that may not be giving the utilities credit they deserve.

"Until recently there's been a misunderstanding or a lack of understanding of what utilities companies' capabilities are," Sheldon adds, noting that an intensive education effort directed at lawmakers began late last year. Utilities, Sheldon says, "are installing advanced communication systems, and they have a lot of experience with advanced communications systems."

WAIT AND SEE

Some power companies with network infrastructure partially in place are holding back doing much more until Washington finishes its efforts to rewrite the laws affecting communications industries.

"We want to see how all of that ultimately plays out before we really fine-tune business initiatives," says Mike Mahoney, a spokesman for Tampa Electric. But he adds that Tampa, like many other utilities, sees customer-directed load-management programs as an important part of their future. And that will justify the construction of the information superhighway infrastructure by power companies.

"We think down the road the most compelling place for it to come is through the fiber optic cable built by the electric company," Mahoney says. "Electric utilities are really the most logical ones to build this fiber optic network, to provide voice, video, and data.

"We need it now," Mahoney adds. "We'll need full-fiber bandwidth in the future."

On the other hand, Mahoney says utilities see a future in which wireless telephones become ubiquitous, through either cellular or personal communications systems. And coaxial-based cable television systems are largely based on one-way, unswitched technology that does not have the capacity to handle the load created by 500-channel systems, two-way video telephones, and data communications between home control computers and power-management systems.

"So why not avoid multiple standalone systems? Electric companies will always need [hardwire connections] and will be the ones that will have to tie directly to the customers home," Mahoney says. "We're talking about an information highway or network built by the power company that everyone can ride on.

"The last mile link–that's where we're saying it . . . ought to be done by the electric company, because only the electric company has a legitimate reason and an ongoing need to supply that link to the customer."

THE UTILITIES' ANSWER TO 'WHO WILL PAY?'
More Power to You

Power companies trying to develop interactive, demand-side management systems to conserve energy are pursuing a variety of approaches to provide the electronic driveways linking American homes to a national broadband, interactive network.

Several of the nation's largest utilities are experimenting with a system called PowerView, from First Pacific Networks (Sunnyvale, CA). Entergy (New Orleans) is farthest along in installing a PowerView system, having wired up 50 homes in Little Rock, AR. Others eyeing the technology include The Southern Company (Atlanta), Central and Southwest (Dallas), and Portland Gas & Electric (Portland, OR).

Earl Thelen, vice president and general manager for utility systems at First Pacific Networks, describes PowerView as four integrated systems, using 386-based processors at each home and a RISC-based computer as a front end for the mainframe host in the control center.

In between are fiber optic trunk lines linked to coaxial cable, with dedicated switches. Inside the home is a network connecting appliances using standard electrical wiring.

A simple display screen gives the homeowner the ability to directly control appliances or to create and store simple programs that instruct them when to turn on or off. Thelen says the homeowner can program start and stop signals that respond to either the time of day, to price information supplied by the power company across the network, or to a combination of the two. The home processor is mounted outside the house, in a weather-hardened case, to provide access to utility service personnel.

PowerView software developed by First Pacific Networks runs the distribution network. Over that network, price signals are relayed to appliance controllers from the power company once every two seconds, while responses take 10 seconds to return, even for a network with 1,000 homes attached, Thelen says. Dozens of networks can be driven from the same front-end processor.

Homes attached to the network can also be monitored remotely by the power company and the homeowner. The power company can read the meter over the system, for instance, or detect an outage. The homeowner can remotely command appliances to turn on or off (see figure).

Entergy uses the network to signal higher electricity prices at peak load periods, such as a mid-summer afternoon. For instance, a customer who wants to save on his electric bill can program his dedicated 386 processor to adjust the air conditioner thermostat to 80 or 85 degrees from 70 degrees when rates double during the afternoon. The process allows utilities to let their prices reflect more realistically the market demand for the power–high during peak periods, low during slack times, such as the middle of the night.

SIGNIFICANT SAVINGS

Jack King, the Entergy executive in charge of the PowerView project, says an initial test with five homes conducted last year indicated an energy savings of up to 30 percent per home could be achieved. Looking at that savings rate, King says Entergy figures it could spend $400 million to deploy a PowerView system to 430,000 homes and generate enough savings to offset the need for expensive new power-generating plants. He says the company plans to spend $10 million this year building PowerView systems in several more locations.

Standard twisted-pair telephone lines simply aren't fast enough for PowerView to work, King says. It needs the speed of coaxial cable to the home from a neighborhood distribution hub or end-to-end fiber optic lines to achieve the very high-speed polling at the heart of the system. But PowerView only needs 3 percent of the carrying capacity of the network at any given time, leaving a lot of network capacity for interactive video, telephone, and cable service, among other things.

"This is a technology that enables data communications and voice communications, and it will accommodate video communications via a single broadband infrastructure," Thelen says. "It will enable television and telephone service."

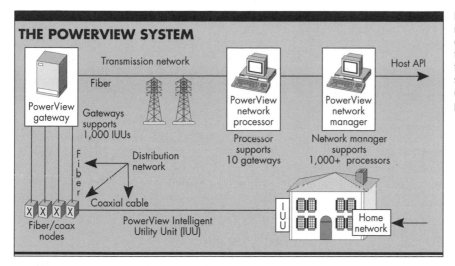

THE POWERVIEW SYSTEM

Transmission network

Fiber

PowerView gateway

Gateways supports 1,000 IUUs

Distribution network

Coaxial cable

X X X X
Fiber/coax nodes

PowerView Intelligent Utility Unit (IUU)

PowerView network processor

Processor supports 10 gateways

PowerView network manager

Network manager supports 1,000+ processors

Host API

IUU

Home network

Figure 1: The PowerView system helps reduce costs and conserve electricity by enabling homeowners to remotely control appliances, turning them on or off to curb costs at peak times of usage. The software runs the distribution network, over which the power company relays price signals to appliance controllers.

It also uses standard protocols at the home processor and standard APIs at the "head-end," or gateway that links the home network to a fiber trunk line, Thelen says. Other service providers can theoretically hook into the PowerView network, to supply video or data feeds, for instance.

A SMALL TOWN SUCCESS

In tiny Glasgow, KY, a municipally owned electric company has used similar technology not only to facilitate a demand-management system but also to supply cable television and a computer bulletin board for its customers. Billy Ray, the chief executive of the Glasgow Electric Plant Board, says the next step is to introduce an alternative local telephone service for Glasgow residents.

Glasgow began building its municipal network in the late 1980s, using $1.5 million raised with tax-free bonds. The non-profit utility, with an annual operating budget of

$14 million, figured it would save $150,000 a year once the system was in place.

The cable system, which serves about half the town in competition with a locally franchised operation owned by Scripps Howard, cost another $1.3 million to install. It costs about $400,000 a year to run and is entirely paid for out of the cable fees it generates.

Ray says the cable project, by offering 45 channels at $13.50 a month, forced the local franchise to lower its rates and double its channel capacity. Now he wants to work the same magic on the local telephone company.

Glasgow is using $10,000 in annual "excess electric revenue collections" plus $50,000 worth of equipment donated by First Pacific Networks to construct the telephone system. Ray says the city needs another $400,000 worth of equipment to finish the job.

The Electronic Superhighway

WILL THE SUPERHIGHWAY BE MARRED WITH POTHOLES, OR WILL IT BRING A WEALTH OF RESOURCES?

BY PATRICIA SCHNAIDT

The New Jersey Garden State Parkway has so many toll booths that you might as well just throw handfuls of money out the window as you drive–or so goes the old joke. Contrast that image with the freeways in California. They have more lanes and, believe it or not, fewer potholes. And most amazingly, they don't charge you for the privilege of using them.

Vice President Al Gore says the United States should have an electronic superhighway to distribute the wealth of electronic information sequestered in libraries, universities, and people's minds. The goal of the electronic superhighway is to provide an interactive network able to deliver voice, video, and data to every home and business in the United States.

If the electronic superhighway metaphor is apt, will it be marred by potholes, with drivers slowing down every couple of miles to pay toll charges? Or will the highway be easy and inexpensive to use, a true public utility?

The term "electronic superhighway" and its other moniker, the "National Information Infrastructure" (NII), are somewhat misleading in that the NII is not an individual effort nor is it the sole province of the U.S. government.

"We do not intend for the federal government to build the information superhighway. The physical network, including the fiber lines and high-capacity switches, will be deployed, owned, and maintained by the private sector," said Rep. Rick Boucher, D-VA, at the NII Round Table, a conference on the NII sponsored by 3Com (Santa Clara, CA) in June of 1993

WHAT IS THE NII?

The NII is not a distinct network. Rather, its infrastructure will include existing networks as well as technologies to be deployed. The NII is not another Prodigy or CompuServe. It is not a U.S. version of Minitel, France's information network. Rather, its services will be delivered across a host of information providers, from the Internet to the telecommunications networks to the cable TV networks to private metropolitan area networks. And its applications will be as varied.

"The NII is appropriately cast in fairly broad terms, to encompass everything from the underlying digital pipes–the fiber plowed in the ground–up through the top of the information food chain," says Tony Rutkowski, vice president of the Internet Society and director of technology at US Sprint (Reston, VA). "At the highest level, the NII is empowering institutions and individuals to utilize the available information tools effectively, creatively, and in an economically meaningful and a socially meaningful fashion–and maybe even personally meaningful."

The NII is rather an amorphous entity. It will not be built by the government, but the government will support it. It is not a single network; it will be supported by a variety of information providers.

The government targets several applications as having special merit for the NII. Most applications have social benefits, such as for education and healthcare; the commercial services, such as intercompany communication and entertainment, will be the domain of the commercial providers. Applications of the NII include: education, healthcare, information access, electronic commerce and telecommuting, and entertainment.

"The Clinton Administration is trying to serve as the NII cheerleader, but it recognizes that in terms of the government's shaping it, furnishing resources is a limited role," says Rutkowski. "The most they can do, beside being a pure cheerleader, is to take funds and channel them into projects that address sectors such as health, education, basic research, or the availability of national information resources, ranging from libraries to museums to government agency materials."

IT'S EDUCATIONAL

"The major thrust of the Clinton Administration is education reform. Technology can abet and aid that effort," said Madeline Kunin, deputy secretary of the Department of Education, at the NII Round Table. "We are trying to bridge the schism between technology and humanity. It could go either way: greater alienation or bridge building."

Some educational goals are straightforward. For instance, if there were a national student-loan program, it would require a centrally administered database. Networks could be used to connect parents to teachers, enabling parents who work to have easier access to teachers. "Unfortunately, the parents of the good kids come to parent-teacher conferences, not the poor or single mothers. They don't have time," said Kunin. Parents could also use such a network to check up on their children's homework assignments. With a distance-learning network, rural areas could get specialized teaching.

Ed Delany, marketing and operations manager for Digital Equipment's Cable TV Group (Marlboro, MA), offers a bottom-line reason for networking elementary and secondary schools. "The acquisition of this equipment is more viable if students from all over the community can use it instead of just one school. Computer-based instruction courseware is very expensive."

Kunin takes a realist's approach: "It's not enough to put in the technology and distance learning. There still are barriers. Maybe when the video generation takes over, we'll get over those barriers," says Kunin.

One barrier is unfamiliarity with electronic courseware. Teachers will need training to cope with this brave new world. "For teachers more advanced in years, this in-service training will be helpful," Boucher said.

IT'S GOOD FOR YOU

Another application of the NII is to improve the healthcare system. "Of every $1 spent on healthcare, 25 cents goes to administrative costs. In other countries with centralized systems, it's 9 to 10 cents," said Boucher. The healthcare initiative has several prongs, most aimed at reducing paperwork. Crucial to electronic record keeping is the reduction in the number of medical forms used–from the 1,500 possible to just one.

The NII calls for building pilot networks to link hospitals, clinics, doctors' offices, medical schools, libraries, and universities, so healthcare providers and researchers can share medical images and develop computer-based records. Databases would store, access, and transmit patients' medical records.

With collaborative software, healthcare providers can provide real-time treatment to patients in remote locations. "People who currently have to go to the hospital or nursing homes to have their vital signs monitored could have them monitored over the network," said Boucher.

Another application is medical evaluation over the network. Doctors could put CAT scans or MRIs on the network for evaluation by other physicians. "This is rarely possible today. It's hard enough to get a number of specialists together. Here you can have simultaneous evaluations. This is especially important in rural areas where access to even one specialist is rare," said Boucher.

With the appropriate databases, healthcare providers could have on-line access to medical information and literature. Other applications include software for visualizing the human anatomy and virtual reality for simulating surgical and medical procedures.

The NII also has applicability to the public. It calls for the development of consumer-oriented, interactive, multimedia materials for health promotion and the distribution of those materials at places such as schools and community health-service agencies. Such software could lay out the risks and benefits of patients' healthcare options.

The medical application points up an important issue: confidentiality. If there were a computer-based patient-records system, how would you authorize access to your file? You shouldn't preauthorize everyone who needs access, since you don't want your medical history to become public record. But what if you were in an accident and needed emergency medical treatment? These questions remain issues of debate.

GET KNOWLEDGEABLE

Information access is a key application of the NII. Imagine the Library of Congress on-line. Or computer access to the contents of the Smithsonian. Not all this information is cultural: Boucher also mentioned the possibility of making the government's store of satellite-taken geographical maps available electronically to the public.

Boucher envisions "libraries with no walls and no books." These libraries will be digital. "A student in his living room could dial up an electronic index, look at the document, and print it out on a laser printer in the living room within minutes. It will be achievable in a decade," said Boucher.

ELECTRONIC COMMERCE

The NII will be used for business-to-business communication. Heretofore, enterprise networks have been the domain of the large business, but with a national network with inexpensive access charges, even small companies could afford to act like big ones.

If nothing else, the NII effort mirrors what is happening in corporate networking: Individual networks are being interconnected into enterprise networks. The next logical step is to connect customer to supplier. This grandiose idea has been tried before—and ISO has all sorts of standards for Electronic Data Interchange (EDI) that few companies actually use. But on the NII level, it's not as structured. Perhaps the interconnection will come where it is needed, not where it is mandated.

"What's happened is the construction of an enormous amount of information infrastructure within businesses and organizations of all sizes for their internal information sharing," says Sprint's Rutkowski. "At the same time, the Internet, which is the concatenation of connectivity among internets, has grown to such size, and the value of inter-corporate information has become so significant, that everyone has been plugging and playing into the Internet. Interorganization communication is becoming as important as or more important than intracorporate communication.

"Increasingly you have people in a wide variety of professions collaborating in diverse ways in other places. The whole notion of 'the organization' becomes a blurry boundary around a set of people and information systems and enterprises," says Rutkowski.

Digital Equipment's Delany describes the electronic commerce arena as one "where small companies can truly become virtual departments or virtual workgroups of large companies. It's connectivity between the supplier and the purchaser and the people you're working with outside your company. This kind of connectivity is going to allow for a lot more productivity." Applications could include video-conferencing or shared, electronic whiteboards.

Wil Reiner, president of The Network Connection, a superserver manufacturer in Alpharetta, GA, sees video services for business and marketing information. What if a company were looking for a new parts supplier, but the purchasing department didn't know where to look, Reiner poses. "What if you had a channel to dial up? Just about anything that you can think of that could be presented visually could be presented this way," he says.

THAT'S ENTERTAINMENT

Interactive television and shopping are not directives of the NII, but these applications will probably come to fruition, largely from the efforts of the retailers and the cable television and telecommunications industries.

"Home shopping may go well beyond the Home Shopping Network," says Steven Harris, executive director of regulatory planning and policy at Pacific Bell (San Francisco). "It could be video shopping at your neighborhood store. It could be something more robust and personalized. Macy's is going to want to be able to connect to my house, so my wife can shop electronically."

Other applications for the entertainment business include being able to change the mix of a set of commercials on the fly as well as storing commercials and shows on server disks rather than on videotape.

A MATTER OF NATIONAL URGENCY

Many of the more politically minded bring up a matter of national pride and competitiveness when talking about the NII. Boucher reminded the NII Round Table audience that Japan has targeted the year 2015 for deploying fiber and broadband networks to every home and business. "The Germans are not far behind. They'll be able to offer a business competitiveness that we won't have," he said.

"The benefits of broadband technology extend beyond the wealthy. It's essential to the competitiveness of the economy. It will [engender] competitiveness and jobs. Jobs are for everybody," says Harris.

Singapore is building a fiber network that will link the island's business districts by 1995 and be in every home and school by early next decade. "A lot of the same things are going on in other parts of the world. Singapore's intelligent island has provided some ideas," says John Young. Young is chairman of the board of the Smart Valley project, a regional version of the NII for the Silicon Valley.

HOW TO GET THERE FROM HERE

The NII applications are grand, but what of the infrastructure? "Conceptually the information highway is a great idea, but implementation is where the difficulties come in," says Michael Erbschloe, vice president of Computer Economics (Carlsbad, CA).

"There are three components that are, to some extent, orthogonal and tugging at each other in slightly different directions," says Rutkowski. "In one direction, you've got a need to scale up the technology, in terms of performance. In another direction, you have to make an infrastructure or tools ubiquitously available. Third, you have to do things with the tools that are relevant and useful. To some extent, built-in tensions are always going to prevail. Whatever NII programs and scenarios get played out, they'll necessarily have to scale in each one of those directions."

Several types of plumbing could serve as the conduit, and many groups are eager to deliver the data pipes, including the telecommunications service providers, the cable TV providers, and the Internet. The dynamics are interesting.

The telephone companies' long-distance networks are all fiber and all digital, and they're upgrading them to SONET and ATM, so they'll be capable of transporting gigabits of voice, video, and data per second to anywhere in the nation.

Pacific Bell is one. "We will bring broadband capabilities to the entire service area no later than 2015. We will bring broadband capabilities to half of that service area in 10 years. By the end of that time, there will be 15 million lines," says Harris.

"We hope started rolling out ATM in 1994, in terms of a regular service offering. We're providing fiber optic-based services to customers who have large demands for service, such as downtown fiber rings," says Harris. In addition, PacBell is evaluating whether to bring fiber to the neighborhood or to the curb.

But there's still twisted pair in those lines, primarily in the last mile, which is the domain of the local exchange carriers. While the central offices have fiber lines, the local loop brings twisted pair up to the users' doors–and this cabling isn't the nice, data-grade twisted pair of which Ethernet users have become enamored. It's low-speed stuff; and coax and fiber can carry multiple channels.

"The phone companies don't have the bandwidth to the home that the cable companies have. The phone companies may have fiber to the neighborhood, but they have twisted-pair to the home," says Ed Zylka, director of marketing for Zenith's Communications Products Division (Glenview, IL).

With a national demand for MTV and similar entertainment, the cable companies have coaxed their way into many homes. Coax in the home gives the cable companies a bandwidth advantage, but their main transmission systems are still analog and use coax cable. The cable companies have recognized the limitations of coax for the long haul, and many are upgrading their cable plants to digital and fiber. For example, Tele-Communications (TCI, Denver), the largest cable provider in the United States, has pledged to spend $1.9 billion over the next four years to upgrade its cable TV system from coax to fiber.

Many cable companies, including TCI, will use compression to pack more data into the same 6MHz cable TV channel. The average 450MHz cable system carries 54 channels of analog TV programming. But with vestigial sideband compression, an outgrowth of work on high-definition television, the same cable plant can carry up to 500 channels.

"The superhighway is up to 1GHz. Even if you split that in half, for the forward and reverse channels of a cable TV system, that's 500 channels of 6MHz bandwidth," says Zenith's Zylka. Five hundred channels, and nothing on? Zylka says, "What the cable providers are talking about is not 500 channels of 'Gilligan's Island.' It's connections to the Smithsonian and the Library of Congress." Let's hope.

The cable companies also have a problem of topology. While the phone network is more or less a singular entity with a mesh topology, the cable companies' networks use a star topology, and they are not interconnected with one another. This gap has not gone unnoticed, and the cable operators have an initiative to use SONET rings to interconnect their regional headends.

Don't forget the Internet. There are 45,000 registered Internets, and more than half are registered as commercial internets. Plus, it has global access. "In terms of loads, the Internet will scale quite nicely for everything except really high-bandwidth broadcasts," says Rutkowski.

BEYOND THE EXPRESSWAY

Once the data freeways are in place, what about the access roads, and most importantly, the rules of the road? Little has been decided. Perhaps the debate shouldn't even be over the mechanics of the superhighway, but rather the issue is how individual users will gain access to resources easily and inexpensively.

Hark back to Congressman Boucher's example of a student dialing up library resources from his living room. The kid's workstation won't have an ATM card. Will the inexpensive way to get on and off the network be ISDN, Switched 56 dial-up lines, or through the Internet? No one can say unequivocally.

Cast it in pure economic terms. At the NII Round Table, Scott Bradner of Harvard University noted that secondary schools often have low-speed connections to the Internet, and it's hard for service providers to make money delivering low-speed services. Like it or not, a service provider is in business to make money.

"The connection to the school isn't the only problem. It's also support. Support isn't going to be like dialing 411 to get someone's number," said Harvard's Bradner.

On the service-provider side, you'll need multiprocessing superservers, which, for the most part, are here today. You'll also need inexpensive compression, which is on its way. "What we're talking about is 99 percent here. The servers we produce today will do it. Once the interaction between the viewing and transmission is worked out, then it's in place," says The Network Connection's Reiner.

The interface for the users and the service providers, as well as the applications, have yet to be worked out. But the Calren project may provide a role model.

THE RULES OF THE ROAD

The rules of the road perhaps will be the most difficult

issue to settle. The way it's cast, this electronic world is unlike anything else, with everyone, from schoolchildren to your grandmother, logging on.

"There's a problem of control," said Harvard's Bradner. "What types of resources does the instructor give the student direct access to? There are tremendous amounts of information–pornography, the reinterpretation of the Holocaust, the Valdez data–and you have to put them into context."

Also missing are encryption or even copy protection.

"The government and society are going to get heavily involved in the rules: privacy, politeness, and free speech," says Dan Lynch, president of Interop (Mountain View, CA). "It's a fascinating debate from a social viewpoint."

STOP AND PAY THE TOLL

Will the NII create a two-tiered society, in which the rich schools, businesses, and people will be able to access a wealth of information, while the poor–who cannot afford computers and even low-speed access lines–only get poorer and less informed?

"It comes down to two things: the expense and the marketability," says Erbschloe of Computer Economics. "That brings us into a very complex social issue: If your telephone rates went up \$2 a month to pay for the information highway but you never used it, then it's a serious social issue.

"Our schools are broke for the most part. There's a possibility that you could displace some instructional cost by having a national science class via cable TV," says Erbschloe. "But the majority of schools are not equipped for the service, and once they are, they would have to pay for the subscription. It's easy enough to run cable, but somebody has to pay for it and incorporate it into the curriculum."

But others point out that schools are bits away from logging on. "We already have twisted pair that goes to every school. It's safe to assume that every school has a telephone," says Eric Benhamou, president of 3Com. "Most schools have a nearby central office which sooner or later will be ISDN capable."

Purveyors of cable TV equipment, such as Zenith and Digital Equipment, point out that towns can usually negotiate free cable access and bandwidth for their schools and municipal offices when the cable provider wants to bring cable service to the homes. For example, the police and fire department of the Village of Schaumberg, IL, use their metropolitan cable TV network for fire-aided dispatch. The cable operator gave them the bandwidth for free.

It's a matter of paying the tolls. "People will have to make very hard tradeoffs. The benefits must be compelling," says Benhamou.

"In the end, the tariffs dominate the cost of ownership. The tariffs can only come down if you have critical mass. The Public Utilities Commission can help them [the RBOCs and local exchange carriers] lower tariffs, but you can't lower tariffs without PUC authorization," says Benhamou. "There are some interesting side effects: Even when PacBell gets to where there would be critical mass, the PUC may not want them to lower the tariff. This has to do with government regulations or the fact that a service can't be cheaper in one area than another."

TOO LITTLE, TOO LATE?

Has the sun set on the NII before it had a chance to shine? After all, the United States already has national and international networks, both public and private.

As Lynch explains, the NII is the outgrowth of work done some six years ago and championed by Vice President Al Gore. "The thought was that high-speed networking was going to be pervasive, but no one could afford it, so let's tie it to a supercomputer bill [because the supercomputer people are the only ones who can afford it]. Today, they're not the only guys. There's fiber collecting dust, and it's only because the phone companies can't figure out how to charge for the service without destroying their other tariffed businesses.

"If you take a step back, and say, 'What's going to happen?' the answer is going to be 'Nothing,' because of the natural paralytic factors that come into play when there is a lot of money involved.

"The data people have missed their chance. It will ride the back of the cable TV people. In the beginning, they're not going to be able to figure out how much to charge, because the data market is a little extra money to the bottom-line," says Interop's Lynch. "That may end up being wonderful for society."

THE GOVERNMENT'S ROLE IN THE NII
Uncle Sam Logs On

While the National Information Infrastructure (NII) has the backing of the Clinton Administration, the government's role is to facilitate, not to build, the network. It can fund the basic research and development and enact laws to encourage the existence of the NII. Rep. Rick Boucher, D-VA, has three bills before Congress that are relevant to the NII. He outlined the government's role:

• "To create a common set of standards and protocols to assure that data is stored in a compatible form and can be retrieved with a uniform set of commands by any person seeking to access the data."

H.R. 1757, or High Performance and High Speed Networking Act of 1993, is the information-superhighway bill presented to Congress in April. It would establish a common set of protocols and provide for research-and-development funding of advanced networking technologies.

• "The government should provide research and development funding for advanced networking technologies. These include high speed switches, a new generation of software capable of addressing and routing hundreds of thousands of packets of information travelling at gigabytes speeds simultaneously, and assure the development of applications."

Boucher said, "The funding will be targeted at the special early applications for education, healthcare, ones that deliver government information, and the classroom." This application is covered in the H.R. 1757 bill.

• "The government should assure that the 1,300 local telephone companies throughout the nation, which own the national network, design and manage their portions of the network so as to assure full interoperability for voice, images, and data travelling at high speed."

H.R. 1312, or the Local Exchange Infrastructure Modernization Act of 1993, provides this framework. If this act were passed, the local telephone companies could plan and manage the public-switched network under the aegis of the FCC. The bill would permit smaller telephone companies to share facilities and services with larger ones. It has a narrow antitrust exemption to allow the telephone companies to work together.

"We will encourage them [the local telephone companies] to work together in planning the changes. Today, there is no direct federal requirement for them to do it, and they won't do it because they are worried about antitrust regulations," said Boucher.

• "The government should assure that barriers inhibiting private sector investment in network deployment are removed."

H.R. 1504, or the Communications Competitiveness and Infrastructure Modernization Act of 1993, provides telephone companies with the economic incentives to modernize their infrastructure. It lifts the restriction in the 1984 Cable Act, which forbids the telephone companies from offering cable TV service in their telephone service areas. If this act were passed, it would allow telephone companies to compete directly with cable TV operators.

"We will provide financial incentives to build broadband networks nationwide," said Boucher.

SMART VALLEY: A BROKER BETWEEN PROVIDERS AND USERS

Get Smart

Naysayers proclaim that the National Information Infrastructure (NII) is too little, too late, but optimists are convinced that if you build it, and build it right, they will come. One way to find out who's right is to get started. The backers of Smart Valley have just that in mind.

"The NII is not about a physical network. It's about applications that bring real value to real people. This is where the ideas come from to solve real problems," says John Young, chairman of Smart Valley's board of directors and the retired CEO of Hewlett-Packard.

Smart Valley will not build a physical network, nor does the group provide venture capital; rather, this group of San Francisco Bay Area executives and politicians are trying to move forward the development of NII applications.

"I think of Smart Valley as the honest broker between the network-service providers, technology providers, application developers, and end users. We are facilitating and making the market work," says Young. As facilitators, Smart Valley's activities could be as diverse as working with the Public Utilities Commission to lower tariffs, helping companies write business plans, and encouraging manufacturers to donate hardware to needy users.

Young says, "The list of things we're doing is really quite preliminary. It ranges from a high-end, complex

medical-service network to something very simple, such as making a market in surplus food." Young envisions a social-service network that would act as a broker between the people who have surplus food–the bakeries, the caterers, and the restaurants–and the people who need food–the homeless shelters and the battered women's shelters.

"The market is the best prioritizer. Our job is to remove impediments and let the market work," he says.

Smart Valley is in its infancy. It was formed as a nonprofit organization in May, and Young hopes to have a president recruited by mid-August. He says Smart Valley will be in full swing after Labor Day. "Over the course of the next three years, we ought to see some accomplishment. I'd be disappointed if we didn't."

HURRYING THE CHICKEN, WARMING THE EGG

Calren Incubates

So far, the discussions of the National Information Infrastructure (NII) are largely theoretical. "There are a number of applications, but they're not going to happen by themselves. It's the old chicken and the egg problem. The problem is money," said Jack Hancock, executive vice president, product and technology support, Pacific Bell (San Francisco), at the NII Round Table.

In April of 1993, PacBell created the California Research and Education Network (Calren), a communications network connecting California universities, research labs, major hospitals, and some high-tech firms. Calren was launched in the San Francisco Bay Area in 1993 and was deployed in Los Angeles in the first quarter of 1994.

Calren will fund application development. "In many cases, the application builders [don't have the resources], even if the network is there," said Hancock. "PacBell will fund the development pro bono of applications. We will take requests for applications for a period of up to two years to encourage the development and writing of applications."

Calren's goals are in line with the NII's: applications for education and healthcare. Other applications include two-way videoconferencing with electronic whiteboards; virtual consortia where people in different locations can work together; electronic medical-records processing; remote patient monitoring and remote specialist consultations; interactive editing of feature-film footage; LAN interconnection; and database access.

Hancock said PacBell received 1,200 requests for funding from April 1993 to June 1993. "We created more interest than we initially anticipated." But funding won't come gratis. "Every user will be expected to come to the party with a balance of services. They will come with ideas for applications and also with their own participation," For example, Berkeley and Stanford will incorporate the elementary schools into their projects.

"We are funding the provision of a two-way interactive service," Hancock said. The infrastructure will be rolled out in three tiers: ISDN and Switched 56 service first, followed by SMDS and frame relay, and finally ATM and SONET.

Internet Integration

ESTABLISHING AN INTERNET LINK IS HIGH ON THE CORPORATE WISH LIST. HERE'S WHAT YOU NEED TO KNOW TO CONNECT YOUR COMPANY TO THE WORLD'S LARGEST WAN.

BY JOEL SNYDER

Only if you've been sequestered in Mongolia could you have missed all the hoopla over the Internet. The 1990s will be remembered as the decade that the Internet rose–and possibly fell–to the center of public attention. Newspapers from Tijuana to Bangor, ME, have been full of goggle-eyed reporters stumbling over the massive complexity of the Internet.

If your company has decided to join the headlong gold rush to connection nirvana, you may be feeling a little lost right now. You've got a line to the Internet; you've got a router; you've got some TCP/IP addresses. All the pieces are in place. But that's not good enough. You want your company, not just your network, to be connected to the Internet. Here's what to do after the phone installer's gone home. (If your company hasn't even connected yet, get a copy of *Connecting to the Internet*, by Susan Estrada, published by O'Reilly and Associates; it will tell you everything you need to know to get started).

LOCK THE DOORS

The first concern for anyone who has just connected to the Internet is security. Notice the word "concern." Security should not be an obsession. Before you make the final connection between your corporate network and the Internet, you need to decide the level of risk you're willing to take and contrast that with the inconvenience to both corporate and external users. At one end of the spectrum, your Internet-connected computers are completely disconnected from the corporate networks. The "air gap" style of security is sure to please paranoid security managers but will also annoy and inconvenience everyone who wishes to join the Internet community.

At the other end of the security space is a complete merging of your corporate network and the Internet. Unless you've got security tightly wrapped up on every single system on the corporate wires, this approach is equally inadvisable. Besides, there's little or no reason why every PC in your company needs to have peer-to-peer communications directly with the Internet.

A better approach to security would include multiple tools combined with a common-sense policy. Packet filters are a good start. Packet filtering is a capability in well-designed TCP/IP routers that lets you specify conditions for filtering out packets to and from the Internet. Make sure the router between your network and the Internet has them. To use packet filters effectively, you'll need to characterize Internet communications based on TCP/IP address and traffic type.

For example, if you anticipate that your only connection to the Internet will be for e-mail, then you can use packet filters to allow only Simple Mail Transport Protocol (SMTP) TCP traffic to enter and leave your network. Similarly, you may want to allow management traffic to enter your network, but only from your Internet network provider. In this case, you'd filter out all Simple Network Management Protocol (SNMP) UDP traffic except that coming from known addresses at your provider. If you plan to have a *gopher* server, you will want only incoming connects to TCP port 70 (the *gopher* port) to be allowed to that particular server.

The key to secure use of packet filters is to start with the most restrictive case and work your way out. Don't ignore a port just because there is no assigned service. You never know what future bugs will bring.

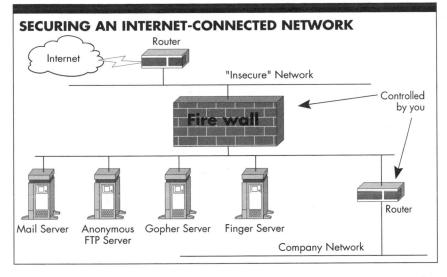

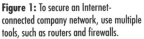

Figure 1: To secure an Internet-connected company network, use multiple tools, such as routers and firewalls.

Packet filters make your router the weak link in the entire security scheme, so protecting it from intrusion or manipulation is especially crucial. If at all possible, have your Internet provider apply filters on your incoming connection to block any and all attempts to talk directly to your router.

Some Internet service providers consider the router which connects your network to theirs part of their management domain and will either refuse to give you the configuration passwords or will insist on sharing them. In this situation, you should consider adding a second router–which only you control–to minimize risks.

A larger network or a particularly security-sensitive organization may want to build an electronic fire wall between the Internet and internal networks. Many different configurations are possible, but a typical fire wall would include a routing system with a tightly configured set of packet and address filters.

The next step beyond packet filtering, connection filtering, is a common fire wall service. In connection filtering, TCP connections are allowed only in certain directions. For example, an interactive terminal session, *telnet*, might be allowed only if it originated from within the corporate network. An attempt to enter the corporate network via a telnet session from the Internet would be denied by the fire wall.

Fire walls can be built from dedicated routers or can be part of a gateway computer which forms the bridge between the Internet and corporate networks. A gateway computer offers services to the Internet and has a limited capability to connect to the corporate network. These gateway systems, kept separate from other corporate information assets, can be used as e-mail, file transfer, and information servers for linking corporate users and public information to the Internet.

No matter how much confidence you have in the security of your Internet connection, you should still plan for a compromise in security. Take advantage of the configuration capabilities of your minicomputer networking software by activating its own port-filtering capabilities. For example, if your organization uses a small set of Class B or Class C IP network numbers, configure your minicomputers to allow only TCP connects from those network numbers. Although not as comprehensive as those offered by fire wall routers, any good minicomputer TCP/IP package will allow broad restrictions on access. Publish a set of guidelines to help minicomputer and mainframe managers add this extra ounce of prevention.

For microcomputer users, education is your primary tool. Any microcomputer with an *ftp* server is a potential opening into your corporate LAN-based data. Make sure the default TCP/IP configuration is distributed with *ftp* service disabled and passwords enabled.

TRAINING WHEELS

You can't just dump your network users into the world

of the Internet and expect them to make effective use of the resources. Your organization is paying for the connection, the hardware, and the people to support it. The company therefore has a right to expect some return on its investment. Plan from the start to have a wide variety of training services available to internal users.

Short courses of two to four hours for beginners should be a basic part of your training package. Plan for a snowball effect. What looks like little interest and small turnout will turn into overwhelming demand for training when word gets out about your new connection and the services it brings. Many training companies are now offering Internet training courses. Your network provider probably can help find good teachers nearby. If you can afford it, have a trainer familiar with your organization give several on-site classes. Internal end users will relate better to training when it is given in the context of their own responsibilities and interests.

Classroom lecture training should be supplemented with generous doses of information, both on-line and in hard-copy format. Several "how-to" books on the Internet are being distributed free of charge, including the well-written (and poorly titled) *Big Dummy's Guide to the Internet* (available for anonymous *ftp* from ftp.eff.org, in pub\Net\info\Big\ Dummy).

Commercial publishers have dumped more than two dozen intro-to-Internet books on the market in the last two years. Many are poorly written and researched or are simply formatted printouts of major on-line listings (such as the list of news groups or list of mailing lists). This particular style of "value-subtracted" publishing should be avoided. Not only are the lists out of date within minutes, but they can't be searched or effectively browsed.

Some of the best of the current crop of Internet books are listed on page 42. These books are platform-independent and assume a general interface to the Internet. PC and Macintosh users may want to browse some PC- and Mac-specific titles.

MAIL FOR EVERYONE

Most organizations have a variety of internal e-mail systems that reflect a combination of history, hierarchy, and politics. Avoid spreading the internal chaos of your e-mail systems to the Internet. Many organizations joining the Internet are using an e-mail gateway system to accept e-mail from the Internet and translate it into the appropriate internal formats. At the same time, an e-mail gateway can provide a uniform addressing scheme to simplify connections between your organization and the rest of the world.

As an example, consider the consultancy firm Opus One, which has PC, minicomputer, and mainframe e-mail systems. Rather than ask outsiders to remember and try and recreate addresses like "snydjo%venus.mis% mhs@opus1.com," which might work to actually route the e-mail, Opus One's Internet e-mail gateway allows a much simpler format: joel_snyder @opus1.com.

A well-configured gateway will both accept this aliased e-mail and properly generate aliases for outgoing mail. Thus, mail sent by "snydjo" will appear to come from "joel_snyder." This setup ensures that random and confusing addresses don't get propagated into the Internet.

The exact format of the e-mail addresses you use isn't important, as long as you enforce a consistent approach.

Gateways can have other features. By requiring that all e-mail pass through a gateway, a network manager has access to a single choke point in case of problems. A gateway can also reject or reroute e-mail that needs special handling. Some e-mail gateways include heuristics to try to deliver misaddressed e-mail by matching a partial or ambiguous address. For example, e-mail sent to "snyder @opus1.com" would be delivered if there were only one Snyder or would be returned with a list of all the Snyders if there were more than one.

SEND OUT FOR HELP

The *sendmail* package, part of most standard Unix systems, is a commonly used software package for managing an e-mail gateway. Unfortunately, it's also one of the worst choices. *sendmail* is difficult to configure, has cryptic and misleading error messages, and usually leaves few traces when a problem needs to be tracked down. Its price (free) and wide availability are the main reasons for its popularity. If *sendmail* is your only choice, make sure to get Bryan Costales' new 830-page book, *Sendmail*, (O'Reilly and Associates) which makes a valiant attempt at decoding the mysteries of *sendmail*.

Commercial vendors have played to *sendmail's* weakness by introducing a variety of enterprise e-mail gateways. Retix (Santa Monica, CA) and SoftSwitch (Wayne,

PA) are two popular, if comparatively expensive, solutions that can run on Unix platforms. SoftSwitch's roots lie in the mainframe IBM world, bringing together enterprise e-mail systems with thousands of users. Retix has approached the market from the other direction by being first with ISO standards-based networking and e-mail products, such as ITU-T X.400 e-mail. Other Unix-based vendors include The Wollongong Group (Palo Alto, CA), Isocor (Los Angeles), and Worldtalk (Los Gatos, CA).

For a combination of economy, performance, and strength under load, the OpenVMS platform from Digital Equipment is difficult to beat, particularly on the new Alpha hardware. An organization interested in a truly robust e-mail gateway should consider packages such as PMDF running on OpenVMS from Innosoft International (West Covina, CA). For a hardware and software investment of less than $15,000, you can assemble a gateway which will transfer messages between popular PC e-mail systems, along with Internet (SMTP) mail and ITU-T X.400 e-mail. Wingra Technologies (Madison, WI) offers Missive, a similar e-mail gateway product which runs on OpenVMS. And Digital has its own messaging backbone product line, called Mailbus.

ELECTRONIC 411

Hand-in-hand with e-mail services go automated directory systems. The absolute best way to discover someone's e-mail address is through what datageeks call "out-of-band a priori knowledge," or "calling them on the phone." But Internet correspondents have a curious reluctance to use this tried-and-true approach. Instead, they seek out on-line directory information. The hope, I conjecture, is to get the electronic jump on their quarry, the rough equivalent of showing up, uninvited and unannounced, at the home of a high-school sweetheart simply to see the look on his or her face.

Toward this end, a number of redundant directory-services technologies have been used by Internet-connected organizations. They include the simple *finger* and *whois* commands, with their simple syntax and limited capabilities, up through packages and experiments such as the Computing Services Office of the University of Illinois at Urbana-Champaign *ph* (phone book) protocol, Packet Switching Interface (PSI) White Pages, *whois++*, and the long-awaited ITU-T X.500-based directory databases.

Even if you have a full-featured internal electronic directory, you should probably not make that corporate database fully available on the Internet. Information that employees and other users consider reasonable to divulge to their coworkers, such as home addresses and phone numbers, may not be reasonable to publish to the entire network community.

Pick a common technology, such as the *finger* or *whois* command, and use that as a primary directory tool. Other less-common directory channels should be activated but should return only information about how to use the real directory. For example, if you chose to use *finger* as the interface from the Internet into your electronic directory, someone attempting a *whois* would get a polite message to try *finger* instead.

As X.500-based servers and, more importantly, clients become more widely deployed in the Internet, you will probably want to change to an X.500-based directory server.

A *finger* or *whois* directory server does not easily provide the capability to search based on personal attributes, something the newer directory services (such as CSO's *ph* or X.500) do with ease. Expressing a request for "the e-mail address or phone number of anyone in Accounts Payable in Chicago" through the simple *finger* protocol would be difficult.

Searches based on more common criteria, such as last or first name, are quite easy. For most organizations, though, the additional flexibility that X.500 brings does not justify the risk and difficulty of being an early adopter. Even with the relatively stupid *finger* and *whois* protocols, more specialized information can also be distributed with only a little ingenuity. For example, the California State Legislature has installed a *finger* server that, when given a California ZIP code, returns the county in which the ZIP code lies, the names, addresses, and phone numbers of the representatives who are responsible for the area, and the legislative committees to which they belong.

MAKING CONTACT

Organizations in the computer business should use their Internet connection as an opportunity to make better contact with their customers. One prime technique is through a Usenet news group dealing with your products and services. A news group can provide a forum for users of your products to discuss issues, problems, rumors, and solutions. Eavesdropping on these discussions is a valuable form of market research. Of even greater value is participation: actively responding to questions and problems, giving information about features and product changes, and keeping in touch with your most loquacious users.

Proper participation in a Usenet news group does not require huge investments of either engineering or support staff. However, your participation will be a valuable marketing edge when those customers make their repurchase decisions. Companies are finding good reputations "on the net" more and more valuable.

If a news group seems like too large a step, mailing lists are a good way to get your electronic feet wet (without a huge shock). Some corporations, such as Digital Equipment and Sun Microsystems (Mountain View, CA), have created mailing lists that are used solely to broadcast corporate information and press releases. Other companies have used mailing lists as part of a two-way communication between vendor and customer.

Mailing lists will usually require an automated list-management system. Such a system lets end users subscribe (and stop subscribing) from mailing lists without human intervention, usually by sending an e-mail message in a specific format to a specific address. High-quality, public-domain mailing list-management software is available for your e-mail gateway system, whether it runs on Unix, OpenVMS, or IBM's VM.

NAMELESS AND FACELESS

Any organization linking to the Internet should expect potential customers to come knocking at its electronic door in search of marketing information. While blatant advertising on the net is considered poor "netiquette," having a comprehensive set of information about products and services available over the wires is praiseworthy. Organizations with other information to share, such as locally developed public-domain software, databases, or random musings from the company president, will also want to establish an anonymous *ftp* area.

Anonymous *ftp* should be limited to a small number of (perhaps even as few as one) well-known computers. Internal network users must consider any bit of data on the anonymous *ftp* system as freely available, even if it isn't in common anonymous *ftp* directories. Similarly, the anony-

mous ftp computers should not have any access to organizational data stored on the network. For example, if there are network file system (NFS) disks shared between corporate computers, the anonymous *ftp* system should not have these disks mounted (or even accessible). Other disk-sharing systems, including PC network systems such as NetWare or LANtastic, should have similar restrictions to their access from the anonymous *ftp* server.

Anonymous *ftp* goes hand-in-hand with an organizational policy regarding what kinds of information can be made publicly available, how files will move from internal systems to the anonymous *ftp* system, and who will be responsible for updating the data.

Other information-based services, such as *gopher* servers, World Wide Web (WWW) servers, and Wide Area Information Service (WAIS) servers, are all admirable goals for organizations seeking to take part in the Internet's current information obesity. As long as they are well-maintained, they also help to convey a favorable impression of their sponsoring organization. On the other hand, nothing looks sloppier than a *gopher* server where most of the links jump off to electronic never-never land. Before embarking on an information publishing expedition, make sure you have management support to keep things current–or be prepared to pull them off at any time.

Some companies try to cover themselves by declaring each and every service a temporary one. This lack of commitment gets old fast; one service I use has been calling itself "experimental" since 1990.

CONTROL THE THING

When setting up these services, use some good sense about how people are going to come hunting for you. Putting your *gopher* service on a computer called Boombox is not nearly as useful as putting it on Gopher. Remember, too, that the domain name system (DNS) allows a single system to have an unlimited number of names. Even if everything is packed onto a single computer, you are better off telling people to access *gopher* on "gopher.bogus.com," *ftp* on "ftp.bogus.com," and WWW on "www.bogus.com." This setup gives you flexibility to move things around as needs and capacities change, without confusing the world at large.

The only exception to this strategy is in the area of e-mail. Although making everyone send mail to "mail.bogus.com" is perfectly acceptable, those extra five characters will simply frustrate frequent correspondents and clutter already overburdened business cards. (You were planning to have everyone's e-mail address on their business card, weren't you?)

As long as you're fiddling with your DNS servers, consider having two views of your DNS namespace, an internal one and an external one. The internal name servers would have full knowledge of your corporate TCP/IP DNS tree and would be used by internal systems as part of day-to-day TCP/IP operations. This approach is what most organizations use now. When connecting to the Internet, you may want to create a new DNS server that contains only information about the externally available systems from your corporate network. This new "external" server would be used by systems on the Internet, while the "internal" servers would continue to serve local users.

This bipartisan view of your TCP/IP network can increase network security by hiding names of systems that no one should ever connect to from the Internet. This configuration can also be used to split the load between internal and external messaging systems. For example, to the Internet, "opus1.com" might be one system used to funnel all e-mail into the corporate network. Within Opus One, "opus1.com" might be an entirely different system that has a similar function. This separation is easily accomplished with multiple DNS servers.

NOTHING IS FREE

When planning your Internet e-mail gateway, be sure to plan for the additional time needed to manage the resource and respond to random queries from the world at large. The Internet junta highly recommends that every e-mail destination have a user postmaster responsible for smooth operation and troubleshooting. The omnipresent postmaster often turns into a corporate communications officer. Every Internet postmaster has stories of random questions and demands that float in over the wires.

For example, I recently received a message from someone in India asking about a friend of his who lives in Arizona and likes to play tennis. Why was I targeted? Our corporate name server, usually known by the relatively anonymous opus1.com, had its internal name of "tennis.opus1.com" listed in an obscure database somewhere. Many novice network researchers have taken to mass-mailing surveys and announcements to every domain they can discover, usually to the attention of the poor postmaster.

Despite the interruptions that unsolicited e-mail causes, conscientious gateway managers should create a wide range of e-mail destinations to help hapless citizens in search of a contact. Good starting points, in addition to "postmaster," would include "root," "system," "operator," "hostmaster," and customer-oriented addresses such as "sales," "support," "service," "info," and, of course, "complaints." Missives don't have to necessarily flow directly from the Internet to the heart of the organization. Having someone listening should anyone knock at your electronic door is simply a good idea.

Keeping track of problems and questions should be an integral part of your postmaster's job. When outsiders make contact with an organization, they expect that their communications will be taken at least as seriously as a letter—even if you think of them as casually as a telephone call. A system to track incoming messages that ensures timely replies is a good idea. You don't want anything to fall through the cracks.

Postmasters also need to have the right attitude about handling incoming queries. Many correspondents will be confused or are beginners at the e-mail game and may need some special hand-holding. Some system managers, while technically supportive, may not have the people skills to properly represent your organization to the outside world. In the world of e-mail, where most of our normal communications cues are missing, even an innocuous message can be interpreted as hostile or insulting. If your network and system managers don't have diplomatic writing skills, you should find someone who would make a good spokesperson to read and respond to mail sent to the corporate postmaster.

FEAR NO EVIL

Linking corporate cultures to the anarchy of the Internet isn't difficult. All you need is a little discipline, a little planning, and the willingness to adapt your attitudes to the world around you. Go forth and be informative.

Network of Networks

STRETCHING ACROSS NORTH AMERICA, INTO EUROPE AND ASIA, IT PASSES 3 TERABYTES OF TRAFFIC PER MONTH; WHAT IS THE INTERNET, AND WHAT CAN IT DO FOR YOU?

BY JOEL SNYDER

A Hitchhiker's Guide to the Galaxy describes space as ". . . big. Really big. You just won't believe how vastly hugely mind-bogglingly big it is." These thoughts apply to the Internet, too. How big is the Internet? It's big enough that no one can definitively answer that question. The last time someone checked, they figured about 20 million people using a million different computers. To put it less abstractly, this figure is equivalent to the combined populations of Belgium, Benin, Bermuda, Bhutan, Bolivia, Botswana, and the British Virgin Islands–all able to communicate.

Likewise, the Internet itself defies a precise definition. It's not a single entity; instead, the Internet is a network of networks. Internet gurus disagree on exactly where the core stops and where the unfashionable backwaters begin. All agree, however, that the center is the 45Mbps TCP/IP backbone that stretches lacross North America into Europe and Asia. This backbone links the main service providers–organizations that connect your network to the Internet. Of the 7,000 networks linked directly to the backbone, about 5,000 are in the U.S. The backbone passes roughly 3 terabytes of traffic per month among Internet users.

The service providers and their customers link many other networks and protocols: Many of the 60,000 active nodes that participate in the Usenet network use the Unix UUCP protocol; Bitnet's 3,500 nodes run IBM's RSCS; Fidonet's 20,000 nodes use their own protocol; and the 50,000 nodes in SPAN use Digital Equipment's DECnet. Some links to the Internet hide the internal structure of the connecting network. When you send mail to one of CompuServe's 1,200,000 subscribers, you don't need to know which computer they're on because CompuServe takes care of routing the message for you.

The resources you can glean from the Internet are truly amazing. Once you're connected, almost all of them are free. Use this article's list of resources to convince yourself, or your boss, of the value of the Internet.

THE POSTMAN RINGS TWICE

E-mail constitutes one quarter of all Internet traffic. It is the lowest common denominator of the Internet–the one thing that links every single user. Need to get in touch with a cement supplier in St. Petersburg, FL? Want to discuss a problem with an engineer at Novell or at any major computer or software manufacturer? If you can figure out their e-mail address, you can communicate with them. Internet gateways pass e-mail from suppliers like MCIMail and CompuServe back and forth. With Telex and fax gateways, the possibilities are almost limitless.

If you're managing or using a LAN, you already know how useful e-mail within the organization can be. E-mail can help transcend barriers of time, space, and availability. To remain competitive, you have to have e-mail between organizations. A supplier who isn't available to clients via e-mail can't provide the same level of service as one who is. E-mail is no longer a curiosity; it is becoming an expectation.

Another important part of e-mail on the Internet is mailing lists. Mailing lists bring together small groups of users all over the world to discuss specific topics. There are about a thousand well-known lists. If a mailing list has at least a hundred readers, it may get turned into a Usenet news group.

ALL THE NEWS THAT'S FIT TO PRINT

One of the richest assets of the Internet is the Usenet news service. Again, people argue over names and boundaries, but what most folks call Usenet is a distributed bulletin board/ conferencing system with more than 4,000 separate conferences (called "newsgroups") on every imaginable topic, from alien visitors and alcoholism to molecular biology, cold fusion, and neural networks. Usenet originally ran exclusively over the Unix UUCP protocols and was one of the prime motivations for the UUCP network. Now, Usenet news is passed over a variety of networks using many different protocols.

The most popular of these newsgroups are read by 200,000 people a day–for example, the group named misc.jobs.offered. At the 100,000-user level are such groups as comp.windows.x, which addresses X Window, and comp.lang.c, which addresses the C programming language. Something more esoteric, such as current research directions in Japan, garners a mere 15,000 readers.

While a good portion of the Usenet is devoted to recreational and nonprofessional issues, the availability of information on computing systems and applications is unmatched. The level of discussion and quality of advice is substantially better than on local bulletin boards, and the access to technical expertise for problem solving is unmatched.

The 340 "comp" groups, aimed at computer professionals and hobbyists, cover every major and minor application package, networking technology, and topic of interest to system managers and users. If you are a PC aficionado– or an otherwise inquiring mind–who wants to find out the latest before picking up *PC Week*, or if you want to get in touch directly with users and programmers the world over, you will want to explore the 31 different groups that distribute advice for DOS and Windows users and programmers, freeware and shareware. Have a question about your Oracle database? Check the group name comp.databases.oracle. Working on a particularly knotty PostScript problem? Comp.lang.postscript. Want to know about the latest developments in massively parallel systems? Comp.parallel. Have to check a rumor about security problems in Novell? Comp.sys.novell.

A particularly interesting part of Usenet is ClariNet, which operates on a monthly subscription-cost basis, like newspapers. ClariNet brings machine-readable news of the world to your computer and can be a powerful tool.

FTP ME ABOARD, SCOTTY

Need some software? Patches and bug fixes from your applications and operating system vendors? The latest security alerts? Papers on electromagnetic engineering? Back issues of the *Biosphere* newsletter? Half of the traffic on the Internet is file transfer, people and machines busily moving information around. If Usenet is the dynamic part of the Internet, then file transfer archives are the static half. Almost everything that goes into Usenet is archived somewhere, and that's only a small percentage of what's available.

What is available? You name it–it's there. Interested in downloading the entire source code of the X Window System? It's there. Want a high quality C (or C++) compiler for every machine in your shop? Need documentation on U.S. Supreme Court decisions? How about a copy of the CIA's database on every country in the world? Or a complete set of digital maps? State Department Travel Advisories? *Roget's Thesaurus*? The list goes on and on.

You can perform file transfer via "anonymous FTP." FTP is the File Transfer Protocol, a TCP/IP utility that lets you move files from one system to another. The user name *anonymous* means you don't need to arrange your access ahead of time and you don't need a password; with it, you have access to whatever the system administrator has made available. Most anonymous FTP sites request you enter your e-mail address as the password anyway, and they can get this information even if you don't offer it, so be sure to realize that you aren't anonymous.

Like much of the Internet, no one knows how many sites are willing to let anyone log in via the "anonymous" user name and download interesting software. McGill University's Archie program tries: It indexes 1,000 sites with more than 2 million files, but that number is limited to sites that have requested to participate in the program.

THE REST OF IT

E-mail, news service, and file transfer are only the three largest services available on the Internet. Used as a wide area network, the Internet offers remote terminal access (usually called *telnet* and *rlogin*) from host to host. Telnet lets you log in to any of the time-sharing systems connected to the Internet–if you have a user name and password, of course.

The Internet is also the home to hundreds of smaller, special-purpose information services. Of course, you couldn't possibly know about all of them. Krol's *Whole Internet User's Guide and Catalog* contains several hundred resources in 120 different categories. These resources range from small databases of very local information, such as the campuswide information system at Arizona State University, to extremely sophisticated collections, such as NASA's data on nuclear decay and radiation. Many of these databases are now available using protocols based on the ANSI Z39.50 information retrieval standard, using a product called WAIS, the Wide Area Information Service, originally developed by supercomputer maker Thinking Machines (Cambridge, MA).

Almost everyone who has ever tried to find something on the Internet ends up being frustrated by the massive quantities of information and poor indexing. To help solve this problem, Internet users are working on tools for navigating through the Internet. The Internet Gopher, which originated at University of Minnesota, and the World-Wide Web (WWW), first developed at CERN, the European particle physics lab in Geneva, are two tools that build an interface on top of the Internet. Gopher is similar to a card catalog: It lets you find and retrieve resources by topic. WWW provides a trendy hypertext interface to the Internet, letting users follow links and find resources–if they're part of the "web."

Some of the resources are extremely valuable. If you're worried about security issues, the Internet is the fastest method for disseminating information about problems and fixes. The security incident reporting and management teams are all connected to the Internet, and their bulletins about problems and fixes for software and operating systems are available. Manufacturers such as Digital Equipment and Sun are also connected, and you can download the latest information and patches to their Unix operating systems from the Internet.

HOW TO CONNECT

Connecting to the Internet means finding a service provider. Providers will walk you through software and hardware installation, including phone-line installation, and will be your point of contact into the Internet. Before you find a provider, though, you have to decide what kind of service you want. For most organizations, the decision is largely a financial one, guided by the question "How much service will my current budget buy?" Naturally, the more money you have to throw at the problem, the easier the answer and the better the service.

Your choice of service provider has another important effect: It determines to which side of the Internet you get connected. Because large parts of the Internet are funded by the U.S. government, some commercial activity is regulated. As stated in the Internet policy statement, if you are connecting "in support of research or education," you can hop on pretty much anywhere. If you want to use the Internet for purely commercial purposes, you need to choose a service provider attached to the commercial side of the Internet. Your choice of service provider won't necessarily change who you can communicate with; it just ensures that commercial traffic doesn't use the federally-funded research backbone. (Any differences arising from connecting to one side of the Internet or the other are subtle ones. For example, direct TCP/IP traffic to Russia doesn't pass into the U.S. research network because it's blocked at the backbone for political reasons. U.S. educational institutions must route e-mail to Russia over a low-speed UUCP connection through Finland.)

The second half of getting connected is bringing the Internet into your organization. If you're already running TCP/IP internally, you're all set. But if you're working with a simple disk/printer operating system like NetWare or AppleShare, you'll have some work ahead of you. Most MS-DOS and Macintosh-based e-mail systems have SMTP gateways available. SMTP is the protocol used to transfer mail in the Internet; if you want to receive Internet mail in Novell's MHS, you'll have to install one of these gateways.

Bringing TCP/IP access to personal computers for network news, file transfer, remote terminal, and other services (such as Gopher, WAIS, Archie, and the WWW) means adding software.

Most medium- to large-size companies will want to have a dedicated gateway system that serves as the portal to their Internet connection. Gateway systems running either VAX/VMS or Unix are more flexible than their MS-DOS and Macintosh counterparts; they give the network manager greater control over issues such as security, mail forwarding and gateway service, access, and network management.

The gateway system doesn't necessarily have to be a large system; in fact, many organizations find that older and slower hardware is an especially cost-effective network server.

WILD SUCCESS

Getting on the Internet is relatively inexpensive. If you're on a shoestring budget, UUNet may be a good place to start. UUNet Communications was formed as an experiment by Rick Adams and Mike O'Dell in 1987 to increase the quality of service for the UUCP network. Before UUNet, several corporations and government agencies shouldered most of the burden of passing UUCP traffic around North America, a contribution they were beginning to regret as network growth exploded. UUNet was wildly successful, mostly because Adams brought the experience of running seismo, one of the major backbone UUCP sites, to UUNet with him. UUNet is now the largest provider of commercial Internet services to end users.

While UUNet provides all different types of Internet access, the low-end service they provide is one of the most popular: UUCP. The UUCP protocol family is available as freeware for every major operating system: MS-DOS, OS/2, Macintosh, Unix, VAX/VMS, and even IBM's VM. UUCP is a dial-up, store-and-forward protocol. This means that the only services you get are e-mail and network news. UUCP's primary advantage is that it's cheap: For $25 a month, you get three hours of connect time. If you use the latest modem technology, that gives you about 10MB of data a month–enough to get started with low-volume e-mail and a small set of newsgroups.

Through a provider such as UUNet (there are others), UUCP service pretty much requires a VAX/ VMS or Unix system to handle the gateway function. A workstation on a company LAN probably has more than enough horsepower to handle the low volume a UUCP connection requires.

SLIP ME ANOTHER

The next step up in organizational connection hierarchy is to almost-dedicated access. The Serial Line Internet Protocol (SLIP) and the Point-to-Point Protocol (PPP) use standard voice-grade telephone lines and off-the-shelf modems to bring a "real" Internet connection to a LAN. The difference between SLIP/PPP and UUCP is important: When the SLIP or PPP circuit is up, users on the LAN can use all of the Internet services previously described.

With SLIP and PPP, you only have to bring the circuit up when you need access. If your network provider is a long distance telephone call away, you'll probably be bringing the line up and down. On the other hand, if you live in a city without usage-based telephone service, SLIP can be even cheaper than standard communications lines. Two telephone lines (one for each end) usually cost around $50 to $75 per month; a dedicated data circuit normally starts at around $100 per month and goes up from there. Moreover, new modem technologies such as V.32*bis* with V.42*bis* mean voice-grade phone lines give higher speeds and better throughput than ordinary data lines.

SLIP and PPP are excellent transition technologies. They get you up and running quickly with minimum overhead and few ongoing costs. You don't have to deal with the phone company, and you can change network providers very quickly. The down side, however, is that SLIP and PPP are slow; the best throughput you can manage over voice-grade lines is around 15Kbps. That's great for a company with a half-dozen users, but just won't cut it if you anticipate heavy usage.

SLIP and PPP may cost more than a UUCP link, depending on your traffic volume. If you're in a major city, you probably can get a SLIP link for as little as $100 a month.

DEDICATED TO THE NET

For medium- and large-size organizations, a dedicated link provides a good answer. Most companies start out with a 56Kbps Direct Digital Service circuit; the really ambitious begin with a T-1 line–1,544Kbps. Some network providers will let you connect using a T-1 line but will limit overall throughput to 56Kbps. This setup gives good response time during peak usage but keeps the total cost down. Depending on the distance, these lines start at around $250 a month and go up from there. Add the fees your service provider charges to get your total monthly bill.

When you install a dedicated line, the service provider will want to connect to a dedicated network router. If you're already running a TCP/IP network, you may already have a TCP/IP router with an extra port that you can use for an Internet connection. If you're not currently using a router, your service provider will either lease or sell you one.

Naturally, the faster service costs more than SLIP; you can plan on spending around $10,000 a year for your connection. That may sound expensive, but it's not for the services and access you get. If you're connected to the commercial side of the Internet you can even use it as your company's wide area network.

If you can find a small group of companies in your area, you can probably share the cost of an Internet link. Most providers don't limit the number of systems you put on your end of a link. In fact, many of the smaller companies offering Internet access are doing just that–trying to leverage their investment by sharing the cost among several organizations.

CURL UP IN FRONT OF A BLAZING FIRE AND...

Read About the Internet

Here are some resources to find out more about the Internet.

The User's Directory of Computer Networks, Tracy LaQuey; Digital Press, 1990

LaQuey's 600+-page directory gives lists of systems on some of the larger networks that are part of the Internet. Primarily for network managers, the organization-to-network index in the back helps readers locate which of the connected networks links a particular organization. Call (800) 344-4825 for information.

The Matrix: Computer Networks and Conferencing Systems Worldwide, John Quarterman; Digital Press, 1990

A must-read for anyone interested in the growing world of networks and the Internet. Quarterman sought out and described networks in every country on the globe. Quarterman's obsession with networks spills over into his Matrix News, a monthly newsletter about cross-network issues. Call (512) 451-7602 for a sample issue.

Exploring the Internet, Carl Malamud; Prentice Hall, 1992

In this reference, Carl flies around the world a great deal, eats an enormous amount of ethnic food, expresses many opinions, and still manages to keep his trim figure. Entertaining and self-indulgent, I found it the perfect complement to the election returns one evening last November. Call (201) 767-5937 for a catalog.

Internetworking with TCP/IP, Volume I (2nd edition), Douglas Comer; Prentice Hall, 1991

Comer is the first and only author to provide a readable and understandable discussion of TCP/IP. If you intend to connect to the Internet using TCP/IP, you must have a copy of Comer's first book, or wallow in ignorance and confusion. For the dedicated, Volumes II and III are just as valuable, with discussions on the internals of TCP/IP software and applications. Call (201) 767-5937 for a catalog.

Internet Message, Marshall Rose; Prentice Hall, 1993

This book handles e-mail protocols and gateways in greater detail. Call (201) 767-5937 and ask for a copy of the "Prentice Hall Communications/PTR 1993" catalog.

The Internet for Dummies, John Levine and Carol Baroudi; IDG Books, 1993

The title is an insulting turnoff, but the content is good and the style is right. Not nearly as comprehensive or well-researched as some others, but it comes in the right size and style for a brief dip into the network.

Internet Passport, Jonathan Kochmer; Northwestnet, 1993

An exception in the world of poorly researched "lists of resources," Kochmer is smart enough to know where to list things and where to stand back and let the on-line listings take control. It contains the best printed resource listing currently available. Call (206) 562-3000 for information.

The Internet Guide for New Users, Daniel Dern; McGraw-Hill, 1994

A larger book that is well put together by a writer who can hold your attention. This book has special help for those new to the Unix dominated world of the Internet.

The Whole Internet User's Guide and Catalog, Ed Krol; O'Reilly and Associates, 1992

In this book for Internet explorers, Krol gives a strong explanation of the history, technology, and politics of the Internet; discusses the servers and services available; and ends with a 50-page catalog of Internet resources, from agriculture and aviation through standards, travel, weather, and zymurgy. Call (800) 998-9938 for a catalog.

TCP/IP Network Administration, Craig Hunt; O'Reilly and Associates, 1992

A complete guide for attaching a Unix system to the Internet. Call (800) 998-9938 for a catalog.

!%@.: A Directory of E-Mail Addressing and Networks, Donnalyn Frey; O'Reilly and Associates, 1992

This guide shows how to address e-mail on 130 different networks worldwide. Call (800) 998-9938 for a catalog.

Zen and the Art of the Internet Brendan Kehoe; Prentice Hall, 1993

Like Krol's book, but less expensive and a quarter the length. In this case, shorter isn't better. Call (201) 767-5937 for a catalog.

NAVIGATING THE INTERNET

Usenet Groups

Here are some of the main groupings of Usenet along with some sample topics. Remember, the complete list is more than 4,000 lines long.

comp: More than 300 groups. Covers computer science, software, and hardware and distributes freeware and shareware for every operating system.

sci: More than 50 groups. Covers science research and questions and answers about topics such as astronomy, cryptography, economics and electronics, medicine, and space.

misc: More than 30 groups on topics not easily classified, such as: buying and selling of computer systems, employment, investing and taxes, and legal issues.

soc and talk: Groups primarily addressing social issues and socializing, cultures round the world; debates and discussion fill these 100 groups.

rec: This set of about 225 groups is oriented toward hobbies and recreational activities, including antiques, science fiction, television, audio, sports, cooking, games, and music.

alt: This collection of newsgroups takes the anarchy of Usenet to its limit. There are no restrictions on alt groups, and more than 400 of them exist. Some are cutting-edge topics too new to have a home under the other categories.

biz: Twenty-five newsgroups that are carried and propagated by sites interested in the world of business products around them–in particular, computer products and services. It includes product announcements, announcements of fixes and enhancements, product reviews, and postings of demo software.

ClariNet: ClariNet is the commercial side of Usenet. Each site pays to receive Clarinet postings, which include stock quotes and reports, news from the major wire services, local news in the U.S. and Canada, and other news information.

(Source: Gene Spafford, Purdue University, IN)

WHO YA GONNA CALL?

Here's a partial list of Internet service providers who cover large parts of the U.S. You can probably get a connection from a local provider as well–call the NSF Network Service Center at (617) 873-3400 for a list of regional and international providers.

Advanced Network and Services, (800) 456-8267

JVNCnet, (800) 358-4437

UUNet/Alternet, (800) 488-6383

Merit Network, (313) 764-9430

CERFnet, (800) 876-2373

PSInet, (800) 827-7482

International Connections Manager, (703) 904-2156

SprintLink, (703) 904-2156

Section 2
Future Trends

Despite the theory that history repeats itself, predicting the future can be as much guesswork as anything else. Crystal balls won't help. Neither will five-year projections, market analysts, or highly paid computing soothsayers. When trying to envision what the state of networking will be by the year 2000, you have to look at current technology and then take a giant leap into the unknown, keeping in mind that the networks of tomorrow are directly influenced by the needs and desires of users today.

The stories in this section look at the dominant players and pieces of networking as well as the upstarts of technology. "2010: The Future of Networks" reveals a glimpse of what computing technology of the future may be like and how it will function, based on current network theories and a bit of imagination. "What's the World Coming To" takes a global view of the state of networking, and "Divining the Future" gives some insights from those in the know on which network technologies will most likely survive and thrive in the years ahead.

2010: The Future of Networks

FROM PDAS TO DIGITAL POTHOLES, HERE ARE SIX SCENARIOS OF NETWORKING IN 2010. ALMOST ANYTHING COULD HAPPEN TO HOW AND WHERE PEOPLE USE COMPUTERS.

BY THE LAN MAGAZINE EDITORS

The last frontier of exploration is not space or sea; it is the silicon and the 1s and 0s that make up computers and the information they contain and transport. From the government's national superhighway initiative to the success of cellular phones, communication and information are the powers to be harnessed and turned to our advantage.

Nothing is constant in the network universe except change. The computer industry remakes itself with every software or hardware revision. Dominant players topple to the forces of ingenious upstarts, and other up-and-comers discover they just lost their house on an idea no one would buy.

One can hardly envision the networking industry in 2010. For one, we are trapped in our prejudices of today's framework, which colors our impressions of what could occur. For another, the rate of technological change has so greatly accelerated that growth is virtually exponential.

Looking back to 1977 delivers a perspective on the vast changes. IBM and mainframes dominated, and CP/M ran on the few PCs that existed. If you look at today, storage is cheap, processing power is inexpensive and plentiful, LAN bandwidth is nearly free, and WAN bandwidth is becoming more affordable. That trend will only continue.

So what will the networking industry look like in 2010? Will it be one of complete mobility, with digital assistants handling the mundane details of our lives? Will it be a world of digital entertainment, delivered by a high-powered superhighway? Or is inertia omnipotent, and nothing will change, with the current morass of incom-patibility dragging down business users and consumers alike? Or will growth in networking be truly exponential, and we will live in a Buck Rogers-like world? And finally, how will technological advances affect society and the economic order?

Here are six scenarios of networking in 2010. In them, the LAN Magazine *editors describe the computing environs and how they came to be, what technologies and companies are key, and how the services are paid for and delivered.*

RIDING ON THE INFORMATION HIGHWAY
Tune In, Pop Around

Beavis and Butt-head and 499 other shows any time of the day you want. That's the information superhighway in 2010, at least from the entertainment perspective. Fortunately, only a fraction of the people use this national high-speed network to learn how to set fire to cats, as the two scatologically obsessed teens educate. Instead, they learn about the Great Barrier Reef or the Civil War, play interactive games, and send video greeting cards to their families.

This high-speed network, which connects most U.S. homes to most other U.S. homes, is used primarily for entertainment. The real money is made by mass-producing inexpensive, entertaining products and services. The superhighway is predominately based in the United States, but it has sent roots to other continents, particularly in North America, Western Europe, and the Pacific Rim.

With the gigabit-per-second national backbone, bandwidth is not an issue. And access is inexpensive. Basic services are $65 per month (inflation hasn't risen much since the 1990s), as long as you send less than 500MB per month at a speed of 45Mbps of less. You pay a per-Mbps charge for additional transmission, but you are not charged a premium for distance when making calls in North America.

ENTERTAINING USES

Superhighway applications include:

Movies on demand, much to channel surfers' delight and convenience. The solution to people not knowing ho to program their VCRs is that they don't have to anymore; the telecable companies–the fruition of the telephone and cable company merger mania–download whatever program people want to watch. People buy or rent movies from the infotainment providers.

Personal home videos. Instead of having friends over to the house to watch the video of Junior taking his first steps, people film their own videos using their digital cameras with built-in optical disks, then broadcast the videos to their friends and relatives. (Videophones aren't popular, because the beauty of the phone is that you can lay on the couch with peanut butter on your face and still sound as if you're wearing a charcoal-grey power suit.)

Video shopping. As a venue for shopping, video is no longer considered lower than Sears. Even Neiman-Marcus offers electronic shopping. People interact directly with the video catalogs, checking availability and pricing with the stores' databases and even trying on clothing in electronic dressing rooms (Finally, a solution to three-way mirrors).

Interactive games. The network's high-speed nature makes it practical and close to realistic to play interactive games, which are particularly popular with the MTV generation and their kids. Virtual reality has been widely recognized as not reality. One popular game, SimWorld, is the contest of dominating the global economy down to the last leveraged buyout. Tiffany Trump, the Donald's daughter, is the game master.

Education. The superhighway brings classes and research materials to people everywhere. Half the materials in the Library of Congress are on-line. Navigation software makes it easier to locate information, but even in a digital dimension, the trick is knowing where to look. But digital education and research solve the problem of your needing to have the data in hand.

Information publishing. Multimedia commingles video, still photos, sound, and text to deliver the day's news or other information. With interactive publishing, you can find as little or as much information as you want just by asking your navigation software for help.

BUSINESS ON THE SIDE

Because the network was developed to serve entertainment purposes, it is less flexible than a network designed to serve business needs. But much of corporate North America uses the superhighway, particularly for internal communications.

Leading-edge companies don't use the superhighway for internal communications, since they need the advantage of controlling their information destinies. Also, the security and privacy aren't sufficient. These companies are experimenting with ATM 2.

In 1994, networks were used to make internal communication and information exchange more efficient, but pathetically few tools existed to help individual corporations communicate. Electronic Data Interchange (EDI) was a farce. Companies wouldn't build intercompany networks, because they forced the companies to enter into a committed relationship in an era when only the short term mattered.

The superhighway is the underpinning for business-to-business communication. The network is used for document communication, worker collaboration, and videoconferencing but never as a primary means of making deals and communication. Nothing replaces face-to-face meetings, because viewing a two-dimensional image of a person is inherently untrustworthy. The virtual corporation was a pipe dream of the 1990s, since companies could not survive with disenfranchised individuals sprawled throughout the globe.

THE PLAYERS

The computer, information-delivery, and entertainment industries have blossomed since the advent of the superhighway. Everything from high-speed hardware to intuitive software is needed to run the information superhighway.

The ATM superhighway, with its ISDN on-ramps, is owned by the bit pushers, or the telecable companies. Once the Federal Communications Commission deregulated the cable TV and the local exchange carrier markets, any provider could deliver any type of information. Bits is bits, whether they're carried by a company that has 20-year-old roots in cable TV or telephone service.

Fiber is run to homes in progressive areas (the leader, Pacific Bell/CableVision, has five more years to make good on its promise of fiber to the home, but it's 78 percent there). Nearly all businesses have fiber connections to the superhighway.

The services carried by the bit pushers are owned by the infotainment industry. Sony owns Time/Warner. The powerhouse of business information is RJ Reynolds/IBM/Dow Jones (RID), which not only publishes news and user-navigation software but also has the marketing expertise to deliver it to nontechnical consumers. In retrospect, Louis Gerstner was a brilliant choice as the leader of the new IBM.

In the homes, televisions have fiber-optic connections, brawny CPUs, digital cameras, and optical disks. They also have links to the phone. People select their programming using a device of their choice. Some use the Sharp remote PDA, which uses the old Apple interface. Others prefer the drag-and-drop interface of the Microsoft/Intel selectors. Others use audiotext, the basic service offered by the tele-cable providers. All telephones have an integrated data/fax modem. The telephones and televisions share the high-speed, fiber-optic connection to the superhighway.

Consumers finally understand that the quality of service is the same regardless of which company they purchase phone and data service from, but they remain confused over the perceived differences of video-service providers.

The Gore initiative for the superhighway had limited success, because of the government's lack of clout and technical acumen needed to pull it off. The Library of Congress is nearly on-line, but the proposed citizen's medical database was about as popular as Selective Services registration.

The danger of the superhighway is that the people are so bombarded with information and accustomed to the MTV-rate of image changes that they are becoming desensitized to any substantive information. On the bright side, Barney the Dinosaur and Tabitha Soren don't appear on all 500 channels.

PRIVATE NETWORKS, PRIVATE USE
Build Your Own

The information superhighway as a vehicle to deliver business information was a failure. The cable/phone companies built an infrastructure suitable for downloading movies to homes, but the priority was not on delivering reliable, flexible service to businesses. The large corporations that ship terabytes of data per day rely on their own expertise and the skills of their seasoned systems integrators to build highly functional, private networks. These networks are used not only for internal communication but also for business-to-business communication.

Building a high-speed public backbone was a good theory, but in practice companies could not afford a level playing field when global competition is so intense. Corporations need ownership of their own networks, affording them even a megabyte of competitive advantage. Companies learned that building intercompany networks among their most favored trading partners gives them a significant edge.

With their speedy private networks, companies are free to disperse their employees to the most convenient locations. If manufacturing is best done in Mexico (as it has become since the North American Free Trade Agreement passed), then the network can accommodate those workers and their data as easily as if they were on the other side of the main corporate campus.

Most companies lease their wide-area bandwidth (usually ATM or clear-channel T-4) from the WAN service providers. The cable/phone companies pulled so much fiber in the heyday of the superhighway that more dark fiber is installed than can be used in decades.

DESKTOP DUTY

Power users have desktop computers with 128-bit operating systems. Microsoft's RNT/4 multiprocessing operating system, with its integrated file, mail, print, and fax services, dominates the desktop. AT&T/Novell NetWare is the main remote operating system, and it provides robust back-end services. Users' desktop computers have 155Mbps interfaces to the internal networks.

Directory services help users locate what services are available on their networks. For network-to-network communication or for access to public information, people typically subscribe to a directory-update service, provided by most cable/phone providers. Many corporations look to the Universal Directory Service standard to integrate the cacophony of directory standards used over the past two decades. And with the current incompatibilities in directory structures, being the first to know a piece of information and act on it provides a significant business advantage, which can translate directly into increased profits.

The biggest advance since the 1990s is application integration. People still have to commit to buying a certain operating system–RNT/4, PowerOpen/6, or any one of the seven flavors of Unix–but they can point, click, drag, drop, and speak from application to another. Gone are the days when people composed a letter in one application and used two others to deliver the information. Now they link applications and devices using their object drivers. Voice recognition works for simple commands such as "print to the LaserJet" or "fax to Mike at Mystery Science Theater 3000."

The difficulties of collaborative work have been solved, at least from a technical perspective. While it's easy enough for a group of people to work together on a document, the most difficult aspect is the people themselves. People like control over their work, and collaboration forces people to give up some autonomy.

At last, the lawyers are beginning to budge on the legality of digital signatures. Initially, the lawyers feared that they would be replaced by computers, but the legal issues of electronic copyright and privacy will keep lawyers in billable hours for many decades.

CCD BECOMES PC

Mobile Madness

To appreciate the free-floating computers of 2010, you have to first understand the shortcomings of their pre-Mobile Age ancestors. Look at what happened to the most basic device, the plebeian PC.

The personal computer of the 1990s was a boring, uninspired machine. Regardless of whether you upgraded the monitor to add a palette of screen colors, loaded a hundred zippy Windows applications onto its hard disk, or even knife-etched your name into its beige disk-drive dashboard, the personal computer was still a square, stale heap of hardware. Strapped by network wiring and trapped to the desktop by an overweight and clunky CPU–not to mention the constraints of its necessary accessories, such as the keyboard and the then-mighty mouse–the PC reached its zenith in the early 1990s and headed soon thereafter into permanent retirement.

But the humdrum technology alone did not cause the PC to peak and sink. The PC world was hit by two unrelated but detrimental trends. First, as PC development progressed, many manufacturers, instead of enhancing the droll device they had, chose the easy, non-R&D method and cloned the PC, peddling it a few bucks below everybody else. Although prices dropped, the lack of innovation in PCs meant no new buying groups were added.

Second, the PC and even the easy-to-use Macintosh and their respective operating systems never got easier to use, only increasingly complex, which further limited the existing base. Manufacturers then had to kiss goodbye any possible consumer interest. People who didn't regularly use any VCR features other than "play" would surely never understand Program Manager. These twists of fate, technology, and marketing left a mere 3 percent of the world's population in 1993 using the pitiful PC.

CUTTING LOOSE

But shortly after that, the technology track began to split, and life as we know it in 2010 officially began. Around the year 1995, while the IBMs and Compaqs were still avid Pentium pushers, the consumer-electronics companies quietly built computer products aimed at that 97 percent who were computer illiterate. These visionaries were experienced at selling sophisticated electronics with no-brainer user interfaces; in fact, a whopping 30 percent of the world's population in 1993 used such a device: the television.

As early as the 1970s, these electronics companies had beta-tested their ability to lure the common man into computers with a foray known as the Atari Age. But by the early 2000s, they had much more marketing skill and extended their appeal way beyond the 5- to 15-year-old boy lured by those amazing Mario Brothers. This time they wrested an entire unsuspecting crowd into computer addiction.

In addition to experience, Sony and Sharp, the wizards of electronics, had foresight–and cheap products. In the early 1990s, they knew that life in the yet untamed world of PDAs couldn't begin until the devices hit the magic $200 price point.

Apple Computer, on the other hand, was forced into a survival merge in the late 1990s with Radio Shack, creating Apple Shack, a place where consumers could buy, among other things, a MultiMedia Newton that came bundled with a handy Tandy Ni-Cad four-pack, a recharger, and a sheepskin cover. John Sculley, who rejoined the company as an advertising spokesperson, sold the Shack's Newt Paks on the Home Shopping Network, and every night he reconfirmed to his viewers that the first-generation device never recognized his last name as "Scurry."

GEE WHIZ

Now back to now, 2010. Via the retail channel, Sony and Sharp grossly outsell the PC desktop dinosaurs of old with their portable consumer computing devices (CCDs). More common now than Cheez Whiz was in the 1990s, CCDs are basically a set of exotic, compelling, and cheap devices that come with a wide variety of network options and in designer colors.

For these devices, the pen proves to be mightier than the keyboard. Their users don't want to download dissertations from the Internet; they just want to fax in a pizza order. These portables are small, lightweight, and energy efficient, running off a watch battery. Network protocols for local and remote access are embedded into the Personal Operating System (POS), with infrared transmission for the short trek and spread-spectrum radio for long distance access to public and private networks.

The operating systems for these CCDs, while not common among devices, are compatible with other CCD POSs and allow for information interchange. This interchange is crucial to their usefulness, since most consumers are inclined to purchase more than one CCD (remember that the average household in the 1990s had seven AM/FM radios).

After a heated IEEE standards battle, CCDs connect in peer-to-peer networks over Slow Ethernet, the victor over 10Base-TinyLAN. This transmission rate more than satisfies the needs of the machines humming along on 486 chips that Sony picked up cheap when Intel switched to RISC manufacturing. Voice annotation is also standard, as well as a variety of personalized security guards, such as a fingerprint lock, which keeps intruders from siphoning personal information from a CCD if a user accidentally leaves one at a bus stop.

JUST SAY NODE

While CCD-based consumer networks proliferate, business users have equal mobility and even more sophistication. Motorola and AT&T dominate now, due to their ability to reach out, touch, and control the deep Cs–chips and communications. Executives who can afford AT&T's $10,000 Personal Electronic Organizer Node (PEON), with its built-in fax, copier, scanner, phone, and printer, are the envy of their coworkers.

Motorola, shooting for the low-end executive, bought Microsoft and ported Windows 8.0 to its pagers, allowing users to view multiple incoming phone numbers simultaneously via pull-down menus. Motorola renamed its RAM cellular network to CRAM when it hit overflow capacity and could no longer guarantee air time.

IBM, in an attempt to give users of its 128-bit OS/2 8.1 some extended telephony features, purchased Northern Telecom. And true to the adage that history repeats itself, mobile business users hungry for information turned their backs on distributed servers and decided that upsizing to gigantic consolidated databases was the only way to maintain a manageable environment. This nondistributed two-faced commit rendered the IBM mainframe, now with its fully integrated PBX, king.

THE MORE THINGS CHANGE ...

Same Ol', Same Ol'

It has been said that the brain is the world's most efficient computer network. If we do use only 10 percent of our brains, then we must use only 5 percent of our LANs.

Some would say our network evolution is summed up in the old saw, "The more things change, the more they stay the same." Networks continue to elude management and have no clear end points. As in the past, today's network environment is full of grey areas. Remember the grumpy old man who says, "Nothing will ever change"? Evidently, he was right.

A LOOK BACK

Companies in the network industry are following the same vectors they did before the turn of the century. Connectivity, though far easier, is still not a given. Products come with built-in network capabilities. Where and how it connects is another matter. A proliferation of standards–software and hardware–has the industry bollixed. Every time a technology curve flattens, and people become at ease with the status quo, innovation from another company changes everything.

Microsoft is still the largest player in the computer industry despite government intervention that forced Microsoft to break up into Baby Bills. Novell has aligned itself with huge physical network purveyors (read that as cable and phone companies, the ones that survived the aftermath of the megamergers in the 1990s) but is a smaller force these days. CEO Ray Noorda says he will retire soon. IBM also plays a reduced role, although OS/2 is still found in many large corporations.

The larger hub vendors are prospering; separation of phone and data services still extends only to the outer wall of the building. Also prospering are private (external) cabling and radio service firms, busy installing services for use in homes and businesses. Application vendors just keep releasing new versions and running back and forth from the bank.

PLAYING A NEW GIG

Even in 2010, speed remains a problem. Remember when we thought 100MHz was fast? Users clamor for 1GHz just to process the bologna-size chunks of data coming across the airwaves or wire.

While voice-driven systems are convenient, many users complain of talking all day and getting a dry throat. Eye strain, caused by small viewers, plagues the masses. The new computing environment has its own hazards; gone are the days of the screen radiation and carpal tunnel syndrome so prevalent before the turn of the century. The real winners in 2010 are otolaryngologists and voice trainers.

Ease of use is still a lie for most users, and getting the products you want is still an exercise in deductive reasoning. For the ultimate in specialized products, you contact a manufacturer. More commonplace products are at the dealer. Even more common products are at the mall. For the ultimate in commoditized products, you turn on the TV and buy, buy, buy. Prices and profits are highest at the manufacturer and lowest on your home screen. Delivery systems aren't the greatest. Even with the post-2000 trend of localized manufacturing, you still have to wait for the truck.

THE OFFICE AFFAIR

The work environment has not changed drastically, except that fax machines are almost extinct. And people don't have as many computers, either. Just as networking cured the multi-PC desktop, so advances in manufacturing and software eliminated the need for separate desktop and portable machines. In fact, the darn things have become fashion statements, following the pedigree of beepers and car phones.

Management of these devices is a nightmare, since they're literally all over the place. While the computing units can be tracked easily, you can't get a picture of what's on each RAM array at any given time. And forget about tracking in bad weather.

One change helping managers is the automatic license metering that comes with all off-the-shelf software. Updates are still problematic, though; once initiated, they are automatic, but getting the users to initiate them is a problem.

Security is still shaky, too. All these computing units are walking around with people attached to them, and someone can easily grab an active unit and mess up the network. Even if the perpetrator isn't much of a hacker, he or she can still destroy someone else's computing space. Welcome to 2010.

TAKE THE FAST TRAIN

The Virtual Head

Dave flicks the switch to turn off his virtual-reality (VR) glasses. He pushes them up and blinks in the bright sunlight streaming through the window of the commuter train. He nudges his reading glasses back down, and they automatically switch into sunglass mode. All around him, people read newspapers, magazines, and books projected on their VR glasses. These wonder glasses take their viewing orders wirelessly from the people's wrist-mounted personal communicators.

Most of Dave's fellow commuters wear the newer, lightweight glasses that look like Ray-Bans of old, but he can't see what type of personal communicators they sport. He chortles that he is the first on the train to own the AT&T PerCom 2100. This 3-ounce personal communicator has been on the market for a week, and at $149.95, it is sure to be a hit, especially since it weighs 2 ounces less than the nearest competitor's.

Dave sits upright in his seat and watches the scenery whiz by at 100 mph. The new commuter train into the city makes his weekly personal attendance at departmental meetings at work less painful than before he telecommuted.

He mulls over the idea of moving back to the city. With so many people telecommuting, the commercial real estate market had hit bottom, until the developers converted office buildings into expensive executive condos. He decides he isn't ready to give up suburban life just yet.

OUTER SPACE

His company has dramatically reduced their office space by rotating the assigned day for each department's meeting. Dave sighs as he gets another whiff of the too-strong perfume from the woman sitting next to him. Somehow he always seems to end up sitting next to her on these trips to the city. He wishes the company could reduce these meetings to semimonthly meetings.

Dave sees from checking his PerCom that he has another 15 minutes before the train pulls into the station. He turns on his PerCom, and his reading glasses go opaque. He browses through a menu of options that include selections from *Rolling Stone, Newsweek,* and *SportsWorld's Digital Replays.* He selects *Newsweek's* "25 Years: A Look Back" from the menu and taps the speed-control button on his PerCom to boost the reading speed.

Dave remembers the boom in the 1990s when publishers realized electronic publications would be hot. Back then, each publisher had to select a single on-line service or bear the incompatibility burden of supporting many different interfaces. Or they had to ship expensive CDs to their subscribers, who always complained how dated the information was by the time the package finally arrived in the mail.

But all of that was before ConnectNet, a national, value-added information publishing network. It cost only $50 a month, plus $5.95 for books and magazines.

The success of personal communicators was critical to the success of ConnectNet, because dealing with modems, telephone lines, and a hundred different communications protocols was a big hassle.

Dave recalls those first personal communicators. Sure, they had combined the functionality of those old PDAs with cellular phones, beepers, and global-positioning systems. But at more than 2 pounds and hampered by a wire

to the viewing screen, those old hand-helds had been barely usable. No wonder they had been a big bomb.

As Dave's train pulls into the station, he realizes how nostalgic the *Newsweek* article has made him. He shakes his head to clear his thoughts and flips off his PerCom.

THE SOFT UNDERBELLY
OF THE INFORMATION AGE

Who is the Network Manager?

The computing environment and the world's social fabric is polarized into the technological haves and have-nots. In the decade before the turn of the century, economic problems in the United States led to a lack of support for public education. Many city dwellers fled to the suburbs and, finally, to outlying towns.

Since the dawn of large-scale integrated circuits, electronic and computer technology has been accelerating exponentially. The technologically best and brightest have been on a wild ride just to keep up with the pace of development. Too many others have been left in the dust.

In the 1990s, companies around the world went on a reengineering binge to pare their workforce, using technology to do more with fewer people. Competition for jobs for the unskilled and semiskilled became brutally intense as a smaller portion of the employer pool offered jobs to those without specialized skills. The computer literates in the workforce fared better than the computer illiterate, but even in this group polarization occurred–not everyone had cutting-edge computer skills. Cobol programmers suffered.

THE NETWORK MECHANIC

The development of computers ushered in the Information Age. The Industrial Revolution was characterized by automation, but the tasks that were automated were the routine, mechanical jobs that were easy for machinery designers to imitate. Automating office work was harder, partly because of the ad hoc nature of the work and also because, in addition to actions, office work involved thought, analysis, and decision-making, which are difficult to automate with mechanical technologies. The banking and insurance industries embraced the new technologies, since they had large numbers of relatively routine and therefore easy-to-automate clerical jobs.

In the Information Age, the key ingredient in companies' successes turned from capital to information. Those companies and individuals that could discern the new trends and position themselves to take advantage of them prospered mightily, far surpassing the growth rates of the old organizations that relied on capital for their growth.

Wall Street investment firms had their own form of an information arms race, as they moved rapidly to acquire and put to use the then-new engineering workstations. Hot-shot mathematicians and programmers that could spot a stock trend seconds before the rest of the market stood to make millions. Compute power, and the knowledge of how to best use it, gave people a very important edge over the competition. Information replaced capital as the key wealth-building factor. Companies that couldn't or wouldn't adopt the latest technologies soon fell by the wayside.

HAND-ME-DOWNS

Today, a large gap separates the technological haves and have-nots. The haves possess all the latest hardware and software, while the hand-me-downs, aging 486- and Pentium-based machines, are all many companies can afford.

The same trend holds true among individuals. While those who are computer illiterate could still hope to find some jobs for the semiskilled in the 1970s, the world today is quite different. Those without basic technological literacy are effectively shut out.

The polarization continues, because big-city schools lack sufficient computers to train their students well. Those people who succeed tend to come from private schools, which can better afford the extensive computer labs and top-notch instructors, or from public schools in the wealthier, outlying communities.

Even among the haves, technology has taken its toll. While students completing college may be quite computer literate, few had to go through the mathematical drills of basic multiplication and division. A whole generation has grown up with the electronic calculator and is ignorant of the process of performing very simple, routine mathematical calculation. Checkbooks go forever unbalanced.

THE CRABGRASS THEORY

Network managers play an important role as the world becomes more and more networked. Compute power is so cheap that it has spread all over the world. Likewise, memory is getting so cheap that concentrating data bases in a few geographical points makes little sense. Inexpensive, high-speed, wide-area communications are another factor leading to dispersed databases. Companies are migrating from the clean, simple hierarchy of SNA to the ad hoc, crabgrass model the Internet represents.

Advances in remote management mean larger companies can run networks with fewer network managers. Smaller companies depend on contract networking consultants who provide part-time remote management. Cheap communications mean the network manager can be in another state or another country, but having people nearby still has some advantages, especially in case of a hardware failure.

While network managers play a vital role, they aren't at the top of the pay or social scales. Those at the lowest rungs of network management play the roles of plumbers and keep the data flowing. The highly skilled network consultants don't get involved in the day-to-day chores of network management. Rather, they design the new networks or serve as linebackers for front-line network managers. To stay in the vanguard, those on the forefront need a steady diet of education, much the same as with doctors and scientists.

Future Perfect: 21 Steps

21 TRENDS IN BUSINESS AND TECHNOLOGY TO GUIDE YOU THROUGH THE ODYSSEY OF THE NETWORKS OF TODAY AND TOMORROW

BY THE LAN EDITORS

You arrive home from a hard day at work in front of the computer, you ease into your favorite chair, pick up your remote control, pop on the television, and decide what movie you would like to download from the video store. Your television (or more precisely, the computer and modem inside) calls the computer at the video store, and in seconds, you're watching "2001: A Space Odyssey." It's all been downloaded over a nationwide network.

Networks delivering entertainment services aren't as futuristic as you might initially suspect. NBC is experimenting with news you can download to your home PC. It may take a while longer for you to program your coffeemaker from the node next to your bed, but the technology exists. Ask anyone who's seen some of the demos at Interop where toasters and trains are controlled by SNMP.

Technology is a good thing, but the more pressing question is, which network technologies are useful and practical? Some technologies apply only in the laboratory, not in the office. Which are not only future perfect, but future practical?

Once a technology toy, networks are quickly becoming a strategic business asset. From silicon to software, networks are maturing rapidly, shouldering the responsibilities of a grown-up technology. And it's only the beginning. Just where are networks going?

Here are 21 trends for the 21st Century as compiled by the *LAN Magazine* editors.

1: BUSINESS EMPHASIS
Out of the Technology Chrysalis

One sign of networks' maturity is their emergence from the technology chrysalis. Able to survive without pu-

rified air and outside the tender care of a technologist, LANs have evolved. As their wings unfold and dry, a pattern of business spots appears.

Business–not technology–is rapidly becoming the driving factor behind networks' installation. The justification for a network is no longer as simple as sharing an expensive printer; the real use lies in sharing information. Corporations are realizing that their networks exist to help a business function more efficiently. That glaring realization means networks are analyzed, budgeted, charged back, and cost justified. Under that interrogation, some functions show themselves to be cost-effective and productive, while others do not. Some tasks are subcontracted to groups that can better perform them. For example, support is regularly outsourced.

The LAN administrator must adapt to this new business. MIS must regroup to meet these business requirements or find themselves extinct. MIS must work together with the business-line managers. They must work with the telecommunications managers. They must understand the business problem and evaluate technology in that light, selecting those products and strategies that are the best for the company's bottom line. Suddenly, an understanding of basic accounting practices will come in very handy for network administrators who thought they were safe from such pecuniary knowledge.

2: PROTOCOL PROLIFERATION
Mind Your Ps and Qs

TCP/IP, IPX/SPX, AFP, NetBEUI, SMB–the alphabet stew boils as if in a cauldron. Protocols are proliferating, and getting them to communicate meaningfully requires a magician's legerdemain and lion tamer's sense of timing. A lack of interoperability among products causes many network managers' cauldrons to boil over.

Faced with different systems and the users who demand access to any and all of them, the network designer's pat answer is to set corporate standards and to reduce the number of protocols on the backbone. Giving advice is easy; actually making it all work isn't.

These protocols were never designed to work in the same memory space, and, when forced, they often collide. Even simple protocol problems can present deceptively difficult challenges. Getting different vendors' TCP/IP implementations to work together is one thing, but adding IPX/ SPX into the stew is another. Compound the situation with applications, and the permutations of problems is far greater than sorting out the differences among a few vendors' Ethernet chips–and even that level of interoperability took years to achieve.

For now, stack all of the protocols together, wrap the network with bailing wire, and stick a wad of Wrigley's in the cracks. Spit twice and throw salt over your shoulder.

3: GLOBAL NETWORKS
A GAN and a GAN

LANs are not a local phenomenon, physically or geographically. As LANs become internetworks, they move beyond their initial geographic boundaries. LANs are going global.

Companies outside the U.S. are recognizing the benefits of LANs, including their low cost and high flexibility. Many network product manufacturers report that 40 percent to 60 percent of their sales are outside the U.S. With the globalization of the economy and a rise in nationalism, corporations must have a local presence if they want to be international. Suddenly, each country's variations in telephone systems, modem requirements, and electrical voltages are more than something you deal with on vacation.

Europeans' differing political climate causes them to favor different technologies. OSI, the salvation that brought no relief to the protocol proliferation in the U.S., has disciples in Europe. ISDN brings harmony to the cacophony of different countries' PTTs and makes wide area networking remotely affordable. Unix and NetWare are widely installed, and some European countries even install LAN Manager.

Networking happens beyond the Continent as well. On the Pacific Rim, the Japanese market will be the next to pop, with interest mainly in Ethernet and Unix.

4: REMOTE ACCESS
Turning Up the Dial

Words such as *maturing, burgeoning, exploding,* and *mushrooming* are commonly used to describe the remote access market. In a time when growth in most areas of the computer industry is moderate to flat, telecommuters are multiplying like rabbits, sitting in quiet hutches all over the world.

According to International Data Corp. (IDC, Framingham, MA), the installed base of laptops in 1990 was a mere 8.8 million units, but this number will hop to 22.5 million by 1995. And these workers, although physically remote, won't be isolated from their livelihoods. IDC also estimates that by 1995, 3.7 million LANs will support 59 million PCs. Here's where remote access products come in.

Name your poison: asynchronous communication servers, dial-in routers, network modems, data and voice PBXs. All of these products–regardless of maker or function–are in; expensive leased lines are out. Workers in the outer limits can phone in to their home base and, using methods such as single-node routing, participate in network functions as simply and fully as someone sitting in the main office. Data and commands, rather than the entire application, cross the phone line. Already Apple, Banyan, Microsoft, and Digital Equipment supply versions of their software that do so. This virtual node networking will complement the more traditional remote control networking.

This technology will only improve, driven by new players and strong competition. Users will be able to pick from a lineup that includes cheap modems to high-speed access servers with management capabilities. Client-server applications will boost the ease of virtual networking. And someday in the not-so-distant future, employees who actually come to the office could be virtually nonexistent.

5: WIRELESS WANDERERS
Hitting the Road

They've been called the disenfranchised, the untethered, the nomads. They may number nearly 8 million, or twice the population of Los Angeles. And if these mobile maniacs don't have sufficient connectivity to the rest of the world, expect riots.

Fortunately in the network industry, where there's a need and a niche, there's a product. Wireless connector-uppers are shooting from every direction, with vendors producing spread-spectrum desktop adapters, infrared PCMCIA cards, wireless hubs, and parallel-port adapters. These options will allow the wanderer to connect to the network using whatever device is handy, including palmtops, laptops, pen-based devices, or any of the upcoming family of personal digital assistants that should surface this year.

While wirelessness has been a staple of the retail industry for several years, the idea is just coming to fruition for office LANs. When coming from a wire-replacement angle, wireless network vendors left network managers unconvinced, and early sales of the slow, wireless, in-building products sagged.

But last year, as vendors started to push collaborative, *ad hoc* computing, a brave new world arose. Wireless networks could simply come together; managers with laptops could meet and share data in a conference room LAN, or an isolated workgroup across the street from the main office could connect to the home servers. For single mobile users, salespeople could drop by the office and use a wireless connection to download dollar figures into the central database. A roving worker on a factory floor could move from server to server without a hitch or a glitch; software for performing this feat has already been announced.

Ad hoc networks, both wired and wireless, could show up everywhere, with plans already in progress for in-flight networks on airplanes that run FDDI to the tray table. These networks would allow passengers to order drinks and meals or have a nice e-mail conversation with that cute blond in 34C.

To facilitate spontaneous LANs, more network integration will occur on mobile devices. Ethernet and Token Ring chips on the motherboard may become standard fare on laptops. And look out—you may someday have more Windows running on your home computers than you have windows in your living room.

6: BEYOND FILE SHARING
More NOS Service

While the need to share files and peripherals often pushes companies to install LANs, most network operating system vendors have emphasized these basic, workgroup-level services for too long. Fortunately, this trend has begun to change. More back-end services, most notably messaging and directory services required for enterprise networking, are being integrated into the NOS, either as add-on modules or as part of the system software. Third-party developers can build more robust applications faster based on these infrastructures.

Many years ago, Banyan pioneered integrated NOS services with its StreetTalk product for VINES, and now it has broken these services into separate offerings, giving customers more choices and flexibility in constructing their networks. Novell finally has caught on. Its NetWare Global Messaging serves as an interim step; NetWare 4.0 will have integrated messaging and directory services. For the Macintosh platform, Apple's Open Collaboration Environment, an extension to the next release of System 7, provides developers with back-end functions such as directory services.

Because application developers can leverage the NOS vendors' work through APIs, they no longer have to devote valuable time and resources to reinventing the wheel. They can concentrate their efforts on adding functionality and enhancing user interfaces. The net result is more and better applications.

Look, too, for imaging and workflow services at the NOS level. Now, if only print services really worked. . . .

7: DISTRIBUTED LAN SERVICES
Un-stuffing the Server

One trend this year reverses completely a trend from last year. Like zany college kids stuffing a multitude into a phone booth, last year vendors were helping users stuff as many NLMs into their NetWare servers as possible.

Just as the pictures of the phone booth prank resembled a Picasso painting—filled with torsos and limbs and heads, in random order—so, too, did network administrators view their servers. "Put the comm server in the file server," said some companies. "Put the fax server in there, too," said others. "Backup belongs in the server," said a few key vendors. Lots of things at the server, lots of NLMs running concurrently. (NLMs are much more well-behaved than their VAP parents, but still, when you have 100 of them . . . .)

Now users have seen the light, and they're shining it in

the direction of software and hardware vendors. A combination of products and technologies may have ushered in a new era of LANs that includes distributed services in a big way.

Most people think of the NetWorth NetWare Hub. This hub includes the NetWare Application Engine. It lets users design their own hub and lets other services exist there, too: fax server, gateway, router, and other network devices can exist at the hub.

Is the hub such an obvious place to put these things? For some, yes, because of the ability to deal with the whole network in one physical (and logical, most times) place. But even without the hub, one can see the possibilities with a product like Runtime NetWare, a version that will let you run NetWare applications, including NLMs, anywhere on the network.

Perhaps this year your file server will breathe a little sigh of relief, too.

8: PEER-TO-PEER GROWS

Peer Pressure

Peer-to-peer architectures have existed as long as networks have, but peer-to-peer is gaining a new respectability and making market gains. The peer-to-peer architecture is a requirement of distributed processing, since all nodes must be able to communicate directly with all other nodes (the definition of peer-to-peer). So as distributed systems and cooperative processing become more prevalent, peer-to-peer's fortunes will rise along with them. Even the venerated client-server architecture is a simpler form of peer-to-peer, where all clients talk to one server.

Peer-to-peer networks can be desktop or background implementations. Desktop implementation consists of an entry-level network, where all users communicate with each other and no dedicated server exists. Artisoft's LANtastic and Sitka/Tiara's 10Net are but two examples of the typically NetBIOS-based herd. A background peer-to-peer network has a "system" rather than a "user" orientation; it features communication at the layers below the desktop machine's display and local processing levels.

Desktop peer-to-peer will continue to expand in functionality and size, especially those networks based on LANtastic, which is quite scalable. Also, Microsoft's foray into the peer market with Windows for Workgroups is notable, but expect the Redmond giant's network offerings to be subject to intense scrutiny for historical and technical reasons.

Background peer-to-peer has been around since card readers were state of the art. It has attracted a variety of different aliases in its time, including VAX clusters, Datapoint's Arcnet, and APPN and LU6.2 within SAA. Background peer-to-peer applications may be more difficult to develop because of their scope, but they run the core of a company's business.

Advanced peer-to-peer operating systems–both desktop and background–will make continued market headway in the coming year, as the client-server model increasingly is seen as a restrictive way to construct networks.

9: NETWORK MANAGEMENT

The Call to Order

The Desktop Management Task Force (DMTF) has developed an API called the Desktop Management Interface (DMI), which Intel has implemented in a single 10KB terminate-and-stay-resident (TSR) utility incorporating–at last count–eight major desktop management programs in a Windows package called LANDesk. While it is true that the other major vendors are taking a cautious approach to DMI, Intel resembles E.F. Hutton: "When Intel ships, people listen."

Products built on DMI might mean an end to the nagging problem of console overlap, where every utility has its own interface and its own agent and overlaps with functions provided by other products. Console overlap occurs because each product designer functions like a visionary in isolation, creating the "ultimate" platform for everyone. Add up all the visionary solutions and you have a conglomerate "control panel" sporting a thousand lights and 200 switches, with each piece speaking its own language and begging for individual attention.

Another way to ditch such bells and whistles could be Novell's NetWare Management Services (NMS), which provide a nice set of APIs for Novell network management using the Windows interface. But get moving Novell: Craig Burton of The Burton Group (Salt Lake City) has postulated that DMI-based LANDesk might surpass NMS to become the *de facto* standard for managing the NetWare LAN. And high prices on the user and developer versions certainly aren't helping Novell's position.

Network agents represent another bright spot in the battle to make the workstation a "synchronized" part of the network, rather than the "asynchronized" unit that it is now. Agents are proliferating on the LAN, in the guise of NLMs, TSRs, and Windows programs, in ways that were nearly impossible during the DOS Age. While the presence of so many agents represents a positive step in terms of functionality, it is unfortunate that every vendor is writing its own: Agents will be proliferating in the coming year.

10: HIGHER-LEVEL CONCERNS

Climbing the OSI Ladder

As little as three years ago, vendors were trying to convince us that Ethernet was better than Token Ring, or vice versa. "Too many collisions," accused the Token folks. "Too much overhead," said the Ethernetters.

And so, who won? Apparently, both Ethernet and Token Ring won; both enjoy a healthy existence. The access method has become a moot point. Manufacturers are comfortable with the fact that there are multiple protocols on internetworks, all pointing to a trend toward moving up the OSI ladder away from physical and data-link layers (What kind of media am I using? And what protocol takes care of contention for the network?).

A lot of work has been done in the network and transport levels in the past year. The Burst Mode NLM and the large-packet IPX capability born recently exemplify such a move up the ladder. There is even a renewed move to peer-to-peer networking (session level) and a breakdown of peer-to-peer into low end (with NetBIOS) and high end (typified by APPN/ LU6.2, IBM's large-scale, peer-to-peer network protocol).

What does this trend mean? That we as users don't really care how a message is packetized (Ethernet or Token Ring): We are beginning to care more about things such as guaranteed delivery, as dictated in the transport layer (typified by the ISO's nascent TP4 protocol), and even higher-level protocols for client and server services (Novell NCP, Apple AFP, FTP, FTAM, etc.).

We can rest easy, knowing that even though the wars on the lower OSI rungs rage on, we (and vendors) can concentrate on what's really important.

11: FDDI

Bandwidth Buster?

For $1,000, you can buy an '85 Chevy pickup, a queen-sized bed, a used Mac, 77 CDs, or an FDDI-over-UTP card. An FDDI card for $1,000? Absolutely. According to manufacturers, prices are soon to sink, with cards for fiber connections coming out this year with $1,400 tags, and FDDI-over-copper cards with a sticker price of $995.

Cheaper parts are largely responsible for lower card costs. Recently, a low-cost fiber transceiver came to market that will help card vendors shave several hundred dollars off existing adapter prices (these currently range from $1,500 to $8,000). Although the maximum node-to-node distance will be reduced from two kilometers to 500 meters, the cost trade-off should offset any distance problems. Transceivers for copper, also expected to drop in price, are already cheaper than their fiber counterparts, making them a downright bargain for 100Mbps speed.

So if FDDI does indeed hit the low road in price, and network managers take advantage of the copper twist, will it connect to every desktop? Doubtful; not even good marketing could make that scenario happen. But consider two relevant points: Rewiring is a one-time cost to companies, and more than 35 vendors, including IBM, now sell FDDI products, making for an aggressive market.

User need may also drive FDDI popularity. Pressure for greater bandwidth is building to near-explosive levels. And network managers are being forced to make some technology decisions that will anticipate the dreaded killer app. Ethernet is cheap but insufficient for the megatraffic of the future. Dedicated Ethernet can solve a few bottlenecks, but it becomes a stopgap measure to the speedy stuff. Then there's ATM and 100Mbps Ethernet–Vaporware with a capital "V"; enough said. That leaves FDDI. As a backbone technology, traditional FDDI over fiber will remain a strong contender: Users will continue to use it in the high-energy areas, such as between wiring closets, between servers–including backup servers running NetWare SFT III–and from concentrator to concentrator. It's standardized, highly fault tolerant, and getting lower in price.

Any of the options running 100Mbps via copper will remain in vertical markets for a while. But if the killer app arrives in this decade, 35 vendors will come knocking.

12: HARDWARE PRICE WARS
And We'll Throw In a Desk

"GAS WAR," said the sign. Underneath, the price: "25." This really happened in the not-so-distant past. One of the great things about aging is that you can remember things like gas wars. In retrospect, people (especially the 20-something set) must think that gas station owners were out of their minds, matching artificially low prices.

Will our children think computer manufacturers had the same disease? Twenty-five years from now, will we wonder how a firm could sell a 486 for less than $1,500, or the new Pentium for $2,000?

At the rate things are going, the price wars may never stop. This fact has not escaped the manufacturers. You may remember the Apple printer commercials that gave a retail price on the screen. Next to the price was an asterisk, which referenced a statement, "But who pays retail, anyway?" The message is clear. The 1990s are the era of the hardware bargain.

Even IBM is rolling the price dice. Whereas three years ago, you felt good about getting a souped-up 386 for less than $2,500, now an IBM ValuePoint 486 with 8MB RAM, a 120MB hard drive, and OS/2 already installed, sells for less than $2,000.

But the price wars have also precipitated the exodus of resellers from hardware sales. The margins just aren't there. Most LAN VARs carry machines less for bottom-line reasons and more for customer convenience reasons. The good news is that prices continue their downward slide. The bad news is someday the hardware may only be available in computer superstores, leaving users in markets such as Bagdad, AZ, or Macedonia, IL, high and dry.

13: UNIX AND PC LANS COUPLE
Unix Multiplies

Unix, they say, isn't just for academics anymore. It's a serious operating system for serious corporate applications. This mantra is about as familiar as "The Year of the LAN." Perhaps more important is the intersection of the two. Unix systems are becoming accepting of LANs, and LANs are becoming accepting of Unix.

For LANs to run those sought-after business-line applications, the network operating system and application software must be fast, robust, and reliable. Most NOSs

lack the necessary discipline and power, but Unix can bring these characteristics to the coupling. When it comes to ease of use and low cost, PC software dominates the gene pool. Univel UnixWare offers a prime example of the offspring.

It has taken a couple of tries, but then parents always practice on the first kid.

14: ADD IMAGING LATER
The Image of Things to Come

Re-engineering is a buzzword, but don't let that stop you from doing it. And while workflow remains more fantasy than reality, imaging is coming, so prepare yourself. The key is that all three concepts go together, and you'll need to change either the technology you use, the way you work, or both to benefit from them.

Dropping hardware prices, the increased number of LAN-based applications, and imaging services integrated into network operating systems will contribute to the growth of imaging systems. But these systems are harder to implement successfully than it might appear.

One problem is that people often confuse workflow with imaging; you can do workflow without imaging (although not the other way around)–and often you should. And when it comes right down to it, you don't really want the images, you want the data they contain.

Underneath it all, imaging systems are based on storage and retrieval. You can't just look at the application; you must take into account issues such as storage capacity, retrieval times, and how the increased traffic affects your network performance. While you can set up efficient imaging systems, expect to hear about frustrated users who jump in too quickly, without carefully thinking through both the complex business and technical issues imaging systems involve. For success stories, look to vertical markets, such as banks and insurance companies, that developed mainframe-based imaging systems and are transferring this expertise to the LAN.

As far as multimedia applications go, don't hold your breath. Getting imaging applications to work will take a while. But the learning curve could be shortened if imaging experts and network gurus–as well as the two fields' resellers–teach each other.

15: INTERACTIVE APPLICATIONS
A Two-Way Street

The philosophy that brought us object-oriented programming–don't reinvent the wheel–brings us software that depends on applications provided by other vendors or that can talk to other programs.

Interactive applications can have conversations with each other that the user initiates and the application controls and monitors. Interdependent applications comprise products whose services can be extended when used in concert with another vendor's program. For example, if one vendor's fax server software is linked to another vendor's e-mail, the user gains two fully functional applications that work together as one. So, users not connected to a particular e-mail system could receive a fax of a message originally sent as e-mail.

Vendors are recognizing the value of building applications that integrate with other vendors' existing products. Such integration drastically reduces the time to bring new features to market and allows smaller vendors to stand up to the bigger companies.

For networks, interactive applications can make tangible the dream of real-time systems. Just think about how much time during a typical day your personal computer sits idle, cycling and waiting. If the network were to use those wasted processing cycles effectively without affecting the user, you could send your mainframe to the Smithsonian.

Additionally, some networks exhibit interactive workgroup features–a direct result of the LAN's evolution from a group of connected individuals to a group of individuals acting as individuals on a system that orchestrates their work. Interactive applications hold the possibility of enabling you to leapfrog over the real-time fantasies of the mainframe world–enabling workgroup solutions that may change the possibilities of a personal computer.

16: TAKING LICENSE
Software's New Network Face

Do you know what's on your desktop? What about what's running on the 100 or 1,000 nodes connected to the network? The network should be the perfect conduit for software information, but its potential has yet to be fully realized. To manage software, you need to know what you're dealing with. The buzzword here is asset management, and once mastered by software makers and end-user companies, it will be a double-edged sword in the realm of licensing.

With the Software Publishers Association breathing down the neck of corporate America, more and more companies are clamping down internally to ensure that installed software complies with licensing requirements. We'll see software vendors and consortia, such as the Desktop Management Task Force, making it easier for companies to use the network to manage the desktop through standard APIs and asset-management software. With its implementation of SNMP, Apple, for example, added a Macintosh agent that provides desktop software and hardware information to third-party management systems.

But once companies master software inventorying, they'll find both oversubscribed and underutilized licenses. With hard information, they can play hard ball when negotiating site licenses. We'll also see a buying push in more companies toward standardizing on fewer products, again for more favorable licenses as well as for easier management. Vendors also will restructure pricing to reflect more accurately the network environment. Microsoft's new "enterprise pricing" with its latest release of LAN Manager, for example, acknowledges that client and server software should be priced differently.

Two more software trends: software being sold electronically and electronic software distribution on PC networks. Resellers Software Spectrum (Garland, TX) and Softmart (Exton, PA) announced electronic shopping systems last year. Look for more offerings from resellers and also directly from companies.

Lots of companies are talking about electronic software distribution; unfortunately, it can be more complicated than sneakernet. Look at players with mainframe-based systems that are transferring their knowledge to the LAN environment. Annatek, for example, was recently acquired by Novell. Its Network Navigator technology will serve as a base for Novell to build electronic software distribution services for NetWare. Workflow software vendors often use electronic software distribution as an example of what their products can do. Be careful here. While software distribution is a process, it takes time and care to define all the steps. More specialized products (or sneakernet) could save you time and headaches in the long run.

17: SECURITY AND PRIVACY

My LAN is Not Your LAN

In a democratic embrace of information sharing, people often forget that some information was never intended to be shared. Like passwords. Like your company's salary structure (especially if you're in upper management). Like the angry e-mail about your boss you sent to friend.

Trusting users survive in an innocent state, blissfully unaware of their impending fall from grace. One bite of the apple will tear away their ignorance of security and privacy issues.

Encrypted passwords solve only a fraction of the problem. Networks are largely unsecured. Diskettes promise possible viruses. Every modem is a security risk. Add the proliferation of notebooks and their users' desire to connect to the home LAN, and suddenly security is your business, not just the spook's down the street.

What is private on a network? On many networks, the administrator has carte blanche to directories, files, and applications, as well as all the sensitive data contained within. Systems administration should not entitle you to someone else's corporate secrets.

For networks to be a serious business tool and not be the downfall of a corporation, security and privacy must be addressed, because my LAN isn't always your LAN.

18: FROM COMPONENTS TO PRODUCTS

Silicon Sandwiches

How can manufacturers of components leverage their positions into successful markets for the 1990s? For some, the solution is to step up production and to venture into new markets. Intel, for instance, caught up to market needs with its 386 chip a couple of years ago and provided the 387 for the few million folks who insisted on having "Recalculate" turned on inside their Lotus spreadsheets. Filling this need put Intel a step closer to the end user.

Intel again got a step closer to the end user (however, via the reseller channel). Such a move was pioneered, in the network interface card business, anyway, by SMC. SMC was a formidable competitor in the silicon business; it manufactured many chips used in a plethora of cards. But the company also had skills in board integration, and, eventually, became one of the premier driver houses, too.

All these factors, plus the advantage of making their own parts, made SMC a formidable board competitor as well.

Intel did the same a couple of years ago. It seemingly started with the 387 and other devices that were add-ons for the end user–a wide departure from the strategy of having the heart of computers made (and sold) by someone else. Then with the purchase of LAN Systems' software stable and board-level products, the LAN end user was deluged with Intel products.

Olicom is another player who has entered the market. Although the company always was a board-level product company, it was mainly through OEMs that Olicom developed a North American market. Now, however, the OEMs are staying, but Olicom is marketing its own card, too.

National Semi, too, was in the fray. But National has had problems with channel conflict. A case in point was Network Interface Corp. (NIC) dropping National as its chip provider because National was in effect competing with NIC. Now, NIC is using Fujitsu, who has stated it will not come out with board-level products. For its part, Intel has publicly committed to avoiding channel conflict.

19: THE ROLE OF MAINFRAMES

Big Iron Oxidizes

The mainframe continues to move down to its rightful place in the network. As a LAN person, you could consider the mainframe a big file server, or better yet, an overweight node.

One result of the network's increasing viability as a strategic decision-support platform is that fewer mainframe vendors are being asked to offer a total solution. Instead, MIS departments are asking the LAN/ WAN providers to bid competitively against the Big Iron people– and the LAN foot soldiers are winning because of lower cost, the larger number of vendors available, and a shorter time to deploy.

Intel-based file servers now pack the power of some mainframes. Multiple CPUs, redundant drives, error-correcting memory, redundant power supplies, and long mean times between failure have quickly become the standard descriptors of superservers. Although the price tag of superservers may seem high to those used to buying PCs at Akbar & Jeff's Computer Hut, the initial price of purchase and the cost of maintenance are far lower than those of mainframes.

On the application side, corporations are beginning to pit the typically younger networking project-development groups against the older mainframe development groups, each entity submitting competitive project proposals. The result: The networking people are being given the development projects because of cost, staffing (mainframe workers tend to be expensive since they've been around a while), and time to deployment.

Still, don't be lulled into thinking that the mainframe is a corpulent heart attack candidate in his last few moments; the database software companies peer into the glass house from the outside. The maturity and stability of mainframes performing level-two synchronized transactions will keep the LAN/WAN from putting this overweight node on too strict a diet in the near future. But the strategic support systems, the ones that hurt (but don't kill) the business if they go down, are moving to networks.

20: PCMCIA

A Tiny Takeover

The waiter heads for your table and cordially hands you back your dinner bill and your card. "I'm sorry, sir," he says, "but we don't accept this card." Your date looks aghast, you're horrified; you've handed the waiter your PCMCIA Ethernet adapter.

Yes, smaller than your American Express, PCMCIA cards are literally the next thing in network adapters, modems, faxes, and memory for portable computers. The PCMCIA 2.0 form factor is based on a standard ratified in September 1991 by the PC Memory Card International Association (hence the name PCMCIA). This standardization allows for interchangeability, both in cards and hardware. Users have the freedom to pop the cards in and out, making the cards the epitome of simplicity. The user plugs the PC card into the socket and connects the cable to the network. Unlike with network adapters, the computer's cover never has to be opened, nor do jumpers for interrupts need to be set. The wireless PCMCIA adapters coming to market this year go even one step further than their wired cousins, creating the ultimate in mobility by letting the user merely roam within range of the receiving desktop unit or server to access the network.

This ease of use, coupled with the surge of popularity in laptops–Forrester Research (Cambridge, MA) reported that laptop and notebook computers accounted for 40 per-

cent of all PCs sold in 1993–will translate into PCMCIA cards becoming the hottest items in networking since 10BaseT. And lots of users will be leaving home with these cards; more than 1.1 million PCMCIA Type II LAN adapters (for Ethernet and Token Ring) will ship by 1995, according to analysts at AP Research (Cupertino, CA), a market research firm for silicon products.

Currently more than a dozen computer manufacturers are shipping laptops and palmtops with the PCMCIA slot, but expect that figure to double in the next few years. It's very likely that desktop computer vendors will enter into this massive mini-market and add PCMCIA slots to their machines, too.

Apple plans to include a PCMCIA Type II slot in the Newton that will connect to an internal 32-bit high-speed bus. The initial pen-based offerings from Grid and TriGem already have PCMCIA 1.0 memory card slots, and plans are underway to migrate to 2.0 compatibility soon. In other words, buy a slew of those credit-card holders for your wallet now; because sooner than you think, your PDA will need its PCMCIAs.

21: FLASH PROM UPDATES

Wire You Copying Files?

A nagging problem for hardware/ software device manufacturers has always been upgrades. Most of the time, advances in the new product rendered the old one obsolete (which was performing well on the end user's network). Innovation time was change-the-product time.

That's no longer the case. Many manufacturers, especially of products that function at the physical layer, are offering an alternative: flash PROM. The technique consists of updating software and drivers over the wire by updating the flash PROM chip with the new information. For manufacturers, it means only coming up with the new code and distributing it. (A related trend is electronic software distribution, finally coming to the forefront.) For end users, it means no trashing of product before the amortization schedule is done. If only cars could be this way.

Who's doing flash PROM? Proteon, for one, is incorporating the concept into its routers, then into its entire internetwork/hub product line; it seems to Proteon that flash PROM updates are easier for all parties. SMC, too, already has flash PROM in one of its hubs, and will put it into other hubs, too. Intel even has it on the adapter board. Shiva has been using flash PROM for several years.

Flash PROM touches other trends, too, like network silicon on the motherboard. No need to pull the chipset off the motherboard when it's time for an update (barring any huge gains in silicon technology). The technology also gives manufacturers and end users a longer product life, and the capability, someday, of direct sales over wires. Scary? You bet. Will it happen? Probably not. But it's interesting to think about the ramifications of such a, well, handy methodology.

What's the World Coming To?

"GLOBAL ARMAMENT" MAY BE TAKING ON A NEW MEANING AS ASIA AND WESTERN EUROPE ARE CLOSE ON THE HEELS OF U.S. ENTERPRISE ADVANCEMENTS.

BY JACK POWERS

As the Information Age goes global, network managers in the United States are extending their enterprise networks across countries and across continents, juggling differences in hardware, software, telecommunications tariffs, infrastructure development, and management cultures to tie together international operations.

While the United States leads the world in local area network connections and in advanced network applications, such as client-server databases, e-mail, and groupware, users overseas–especially those in Western Europe and Asia–are catching up technologically and, in some cases, leapfrogging ahead with government technology initiatives and regional telecommunications standardization.

In general, the state of world networking stacks up as you might expect: The major countries in Western Europe, the key Pacific Rim nations, and Australia and New Zealand are the most advanced; developing nations in Africa and South America are the farthest behind; the emerging former communist bloc nations are struggling to link up to the modern world's telecommunications network; and the rest of the world is a complex mixture of high-tech, low tech, and no tech. Surprisingly, Japan is not highly networked, with a little more than one quarter of the PCs there linked to LANs vs. nearly 80 percent in the United States, according to the experts I interviewed.

WESTERN EUROPE

"France, Germany, and the United Kingdom are about a year to a year-and-a-half behind the United States," said Craig Johnson, director of product marketing for Asanté Technologies (Sunnyvale, CA), which has been selling its products abroad. Other leading hardware and software vendors interviewed for this story agree with this general timeframe.

But the Big Three European Community (EC) leaders are catching up. In 1991, the United States was five years ahead; by 1994 or 1995, the gap will be closed, the experts say.

Through the 1980s, Johnson says, most European firms were still running on twin-axial cables (IBM mainframe coaxial cable) and Systems Network Architecture; now every new European installation uses a fiber-optic backbone with twisted pair to the desktop.

Further behind are the southern European countries. Government regulation through the Post, Telephone, and Telegraph authorities (PTTs) and the inclination to hold back until EC-wide standards are in place have also inhibited network connections on the Continent. Italians, for example, are heavy users of PCs, but industry is very fragmented into regions and network connections are relatively new.

Tim Shaffstall, president of international distributor Shaffstall Marketing (Indianapolis), thinks European business culture may also inhibit LAN connectivity there. "A lot of European companies are running on centralized minicomputer-based systems, and they're reluctant to give up control by moving over to a network," he says.

The network management and transaction accounting capabilities of minis and mainframes mirror the tight control that European technical managers have over their operations. The cultural implications of distributed desktop computing clash with the more traditional top-down approaches to business organization.

User demand in this environment has not generated new LAN development. "The average user in Europe is not as familiar with networking," says Joann Rockwell, international products manager for Artisoft (Tucson, AZ). "Our challenge in Europe is to build end-user awareness of such LAN concepts as peer-to-peer and client-server computing." The company markets localized versions of its LANtastic peer-to-peer software throughout Europe and finds it has to evangelize the market before pitching product.

While LAN penetration on the Continent may be a bit slow, WAN links are booming. Europe's E-1 dedicated lines are twice the speed of U.S. T-1 circuits, and 56Kbps X.25 lines are common. Moreover, many PTTs offer Integrated Services Digital Networks (ISDN) links to the office at a time when ISDN is still hard to come by in most U.S. cities.

In synchronous fiber-optic links, Europe's Synchronous Digital Hierarchy (SDH) rivals the U.S. Synchronous Optical Network (SONET) for transmission speeds higher than 155Mbps.

The United Kingdom and France lead the Continent with sophisticated telecommunications services. "X.25 and ISDN are very hot, very big in Western Europe," says Richard Weissberg, director of international product management for Lotus Development (Cambridge, MA). He cites France Telecom's pioneering Minitel videotex system with 6 million users as an example of an "extremely large, already installed base of value-added services" that might be ported to a network environment.

Similarly, the market in the United Kingdom is a sophisticated one with heavy use of on-line databases, e-mail servers, and new groupware networks based on Lotus Notes and Folio (Provo, UT) Views.

The organizing power of Notes is especially popular in Germany, which has more Notes developers than France, the United Kingdom, Switzerland, and the Benelux countries combined. (For reference, there are more than twice as many Notes VARs in California alone.)

SCANDINAVIA

LAN penetration is very high in Denmark, Iceland, Norway, and Sweden, on a par with or ahead of the U.S. market, according to Asanté's Johnson. Norway has as many PCs as people, and the advanced telecommunications infrastructure supports sophisticated services, such as digital cellular communications and ISDN links.

EASTERN EUROPE

In networking as in most commercial areas, the countries of the former Soviet Union and the nations emerging from behind the Iron Curtain present some tough problems for Western technologists. On the one hand, 40 years of communism have left behind little usable technology infrastructure. On the other hand, when your first computer is a 66MHz 486 and your first modem runs at 9,600 baud, you can jump very far ahead. "They're not even bothering to put up old generation telephone systems," says Lotus' Weissberg. Instead, these countries are leaping ahead to standardize on digital telecommunications equipment.

Each of the countries of Eastern Europe is at a different stage of development, however. Those that began breaking away from the Soviet bloc earlier are further along the networking path. Asanté's Johnson points to Poland's international software-consulting and contract-programming businesses as examples of the budding "intellectual sweatshops" springing up in the East. Unfortunately, most high-tech computer services in Eastern Europe are for export: More developers exist there than do users–for now.

Networking entrepreneurs are translating LAN products for the marketplace–a local VAR has created a Czechoslovakian version of LANtastic for Artisoft, for example –but the installed base of all high-tech equipment remains small. Money is also a problem. Few Silicon Valley developers accept zloty or roubles, and hard currency has other priorities than Ethernet boards and e-mail packages.

For those who absolutely, positively need to network, the solution may be a do-it-yourself communications system that doesn't depend on installed communications lines. Cellular telephones get around the lack of land lines for voice communications, and some companies are using satellite technology to link data.

Ethernet and Token Ring cards for very small aperture terminals (VSAT) were recently introduced by AT&T Tridom (Marietta, GA) and Hughes Network Systems (Germantown, MD). A satellite dish on the roof of a factory in the Urals can receive data from a centralized hub at 512Kbps and transmit back at 128Kbps, not as fast as a T-1 circuit but not as slow as waiting in line to get wired up.

ASIA

For a generation, the superheated economies of Taiwan, Singapore, Hong Kong, and South Korea have focused on high technology as the key to economic success, and networking has been an important part of many government/private sector initiatives. South Korea, for example, is Artisoft's second-largest overseas market for LANtastic. Singapore was the first country to offer nationwide ISDN service in the 1980s. And worldwide telecommunications networks converge on the region's world-trade and financial markets.

As labor rates in the fastest-growing Southeast Asian nations rise, manufacturing jobs are moving to Thailand, Malaysia, Indonesia, and the Philippines, and modern networks will surely follow. It's still hard to get phone service in out-of-the-way places, but telecommunications infrastructure is high on the list of most countries' development plans, and holding actions, such as cellular telephony and VSAT links, will take up the slack in the meantime.

Like Poland, India is mainly an export market in computer-software services. Major U.S. and European corporations have long used Indian contract programmers and consultants for custom work, but the penetration of networks in the subcontinent itself is rather light.

Japan remains a fairly protectionist environment for American-style networking, and the small penetration of LAN connections there is also attributable to the language problems of Kanji computing. Both Artisoft and Lotus have released Kanji-based versions of LANtastic and Notes, although the interoperation of these systems with Roman-alphabet computers is not an easy task.

"What if you're in Tokyo working for Saab, and you're sending an electronic-mail message to Sweden?" asks Lotus' Weissberg. "We have to make sure the Kanji and Nordic character sets link properly. What if somebody has Kanji characters in his name or in his electronic address book? It's something we're trying to get real smart about real fast."

Ideographic character sets are also a part of the fastest-growing market in Asia, the People's Republic of China. Although the prospects for democracy are as bleak as ever, China is booming after more than a decade of economic reforms that saw a fourfold increase in gross national product. All that growth has severely taxed the already deficient infrastructure, however, and full integration into the worldwide telecommunications network will not occur anytime soon. With 1.2 billion people to hook up to tele-

phones and cable TV, business networking is likely to take a back seat to consumer applications in the next five years.

THE CARIBBEAN

For U.S. firms, the Caribbean has long been a source for high-tech, back-office functions such as data entry–a source of cheap English-speaking labor. As part of the North American Free Trade zone, Barbados, Jamaica, and Trinidad have special tax incentives for white-collar, data processing-type workers as opposed to most developing countries' blue-collar manufacturing jobs. Companies such as American Airlines operate private data networks through PTT-run satellite facilities, and local telcos make telecommunication links between the United States and the Carribean very economical. Regular telephone service is poor, however, and there is little indigenous network usage.

SOUTH AMERICA

In the aftermath of the South American debt crisis, several countries have undertaken economic reforms to reduce government regulations and to develop high-tech infrastructures. Brazil's import deregulation in 1992 sparked a boom in computing and networking; until the regulatory barriers fell, an AppleTalk network linking a Mac to a laser printer required a special permit from the PTT. Mexico and Venezuela, for example, are ranked tenth and eleventh in newly industrializing economies in science and technology by the World Competitiveness Report, produced by the Singapore National Technology and Science Board, a government research arm.

LANs are not part of the South American scene today. "Third-world nations don't have networks because they don't have computers," says Shaffstall. "From an American or European perspective, it's absolutely amazing how many business functions are still carried out manually [in South America]."

AFRICA

Similarly, Africa has very few computers, let alone networks. What telecommunications development there is is clustered in South Africa and in sporadic government-backed initiatives. An AT&T/Cable & Wireless satellite network, for example, links sites in Africa with the Caribbean, the United States, and the United Kingdom, but use comes mainly from American and British multinationals down-loading to their local offices.

GLOBAL NETWORKING PROSPECTS

Like the rest of high technology, the future of network-ing is a story of the haves and the have nots. Countries that invest in telecommunications and computing devel-opment will take their place on the global network; those that don't–or that cannot afford to–will be stuck in the technological backwater.

Low labor rates and cheap natural resources are no longer the keys to national development. Companies look-ing to invest in developing nations would rather invest in a place that has LAN and WAN capabilities than in one that doesn't.

Some believe the impediments to worldwide network-ing are inevitably temporary. Asanté's Johnson thinks "globalization and competitiveness issues will make the barriers to networking fall down." In Europe, he says, things have gotten a lot better in recent years. Where once a hardware vendor needed the approval of 15 separate PTTs for a network card, now "if you can meet Germany's requirements, you'll probably get everybody else [to ap-prove]."

Regional structures, such as the European Community, the North American Free Trade Area, the Association of South East Asian Nations, and the Caribbean Basin Initia-tives are drawing countries and companies closer together electronically.

Network vendors see an almost unlimited opportunity for worldwide networking growth in the years ahead. In-dustry analysts expect the U.S. LAN market to start flat-tening out by 1994 as the total number of PCs on LANs ap-proaches 100 percent. Continued growth in networking will come with growth in the rest of the world, especially the newly industrializing countries in the Pacific Rim and South America.

For software vendors, one highlight of increased LAN connections is the extra control it gives to catch unautho-rized copies. In many developing nations, software copy-right protection is applied only loosely, and, for every le-gitimate copy of a program, dozens or even hundreds of bootlegs may exist. With more users migrating to net-works and groupware applications, the ability of applica-tions software to catch unauthorized copies of a program

running on the network increases, making it harder to cheat. Says Lotus' Weissberg, "Eventually those people who now make unauthorized copies will be brought into the family of modern technology users."

A GLOBAL ENTERPRISE NETWORK

International network growth will be driven from the developed world, from U.S. and European firms trying to extend their enterprise networks to regional and local of-fices around the world. In the foreseeable future, it's likely to be the U.S. network manager–in collaboration with lo-cal staff–who creates the networking plan, promulgates enterprisewide standards, picks hardware and software, and gets the network up and running.

George Hoenig, vice president of strategic planning for Artisoft, advises managers to look at network issues on a country-by-country basis. "Different countries are at very different levels of development."

At the basic hardware- and software-driver level, local vendor support is a must: Products familiar to U.S. buyers may run with a different voltage, frequency, and operating systems in another country.

Just as in the United States, networking VARs and deal-ers operate at various levels of competence in most coun-tries, and finding the right vendor is much harder when you communicate mainly via fax. In general, the wilder and woolier a market, the greater the need for vetting the local LAN supplier.

Telco links also require some local assistance. Most mo-nopoly PTTs still need written notification before hooking modem equipment to their wires, although many users ig-nore the formal procedures and network-friendly PTTs are lax in enforcement.

For higher-volume applications, dedicated E-1 lines running at 2.048Mbps are available as point-to-point links in Europe, and T-1/E-1 bridges link U.S. and European lines directly. In general, the deregulated U.S. telecommu-nications business offers a far wider choice of communica-tions options; in most other countries, a single PTT rules.

Connecting multiple sites between the U.S. and over-seas means negotiating with different telcos that all have different tariffs and different equipment availability. In Spain, for example, clean digital lines are very hard to come by.

Several telcos offer end-to-end support for LAN managers faced with linking different networks in different nations. BT North America (NY, a former subsidiary of British Telecom), for example, sells frame-relay service between the United States and 12 countries in a turnkey package.

A LAN manager with sites in Chicago, New York, London, Paris, and Singapore, for example, would write one contract with BT North America for a complete multipoint system. The monthly price would include: a properly configured bridge/router at each site; a Channel Service Unit or Data Service Unit (CSU/DSU) to link each site to BT's point-of-presence via a digital line; and a negotiated committed information rate (CIR) based on anticipated network utilization. The price does not include the local digital-line charges between the sites and the points of presence.

At a CIR of 128Kbps, BT would install lines capable of burst transmission up to 256Kbps. The user pays only for the CIR; there is no extra usage charge. The bundled price for the equipment and the service for the five sites at 128Kbps is $51,472 per month. Outside of the obvious benefit of having a single source responsible for end-to-end service and for negotiating the local telco links, users estimate that BT's frame-relay approach saves about 20 percent off a comparable private network built country by country.

NETWORK DEVELOPMENTS

In a world that is downsizing, LAN managers don't have the staff or the time to deal with the complexities of multinational network connections. Larger firms will be able to buy turnkey services from major international telcos, but as smaller companies find themselves in the international marketplace, the levels of risk and complexity for establishing international interconnects must come down.

In Western Europe, Scandinavia, and Singapore, ISDN standards are already making digital connections as easy as sending a fax. Although a few telco-level inconsistencies still exist in ISDN implementations, by the time the signal reaches the user, the links are consistent.

In the United States, the situation is both better and worse. The deregulated telecommunications marketplace offers an embarassment of interconnect riches–T-1s, T-3s, Switched 56Kbps, frame relay, and asynchronous transmission mode (ATM), as well as somewhat standardized ISDN and all sorts of off-the-rate card deals–but the lack of a governmental hand on the networking tiller makes the formation of a unified national network more difficult.

On the system side, networking software, bridge/routers, and the security overlays that go along with them are relatively stable and mature. Enterprisewide networks begin with the first in-house interconnects, and the extension of networks around the world are really just building on that basic foundation

Divining the Future

EVEN MARKET RESEARCH CANNOT PREDICT THE FUTURE, BUT, COUPLED WITH SOLID ANALYSIS OF INDUSTRY TRENDS, IT CAN HELP YOU NAVIGATE YOUR COURSE.

BY DAVE BRAMBERT

As the network business sails strongly forward, it leaves a mighty wake. Catching no one off guard, Novell has put in another powerful year. In 1993 Banyan went public and scored a hit with ENS. Microsoft, while putting in low numbers in network-product sales, has done record business in applications software. Microsoft also reported that it hired 2,500 workers in 1993. Despite successes, some big ships list in today's squalling economy.

IBM took on water. Even as plans take shape to cut the crew by another 25,000 souls, $5 billion turns into bilge, and captain Akers is mutinied. These latest cuts, when combined with early retirements during the past few years, would fill a city roughly the size of Peoria, IL.

The stock market was not kind. IBM's hull was rocked by stock devaluation, leaving the industry wondering what's happening in the deep Blue sea. Industry watchers sometimes forget the number of hands left on the IBM deck–plenty remain, and they're bailing as fast as they can.

But IBM also made some progress. The Austin-based network-software group has had success with OS/2 2.0. The network people in Raleigh, NC, are busy dividing and conquering network products. Small groups–of 50 or fewer workers, minuscule by IBM standards–are changing the way IBM works and are getting first-time products to market in as little as six months. Although Akers is out, credit is due him who masterminded the distributed approach.

Digital Equipment Corp. (DEC) also took a pounding and weathered a change at the helm, too. But the financial community has been impressed with the velocity of DEC's comeback; it's happening faster than outsiders predicted, although it's not exactly soaring.

Activity remained high on the business side. Novell bought Unix System Laboratories (Summit, NJ) and so has a greater stake in the Unix market. Standard Microsystems (Hauppauge, NY) bought Sigma Network Systems (Reading, MA), getting into the switched-hub market. Microtest (Phoenix) an entrepreneurial firm, went public. In short, the partnering and acquisition in the industry won't stop soon.

USER TRENDS

Talk to anyone in IS or network administration, and they'll tell you the network world is changing. According to Dataquest Worldwide Services Group Director Jeff Kaplan, customer trends include:
- more technologies;
- more end users;
- more mission-critical applications;
- more networked environments;
- more support issues created by Windows; and
- more costly support demands.

Dataquest has compiled a three-year study of the Fortune 1,000 and large nonprofit organizations. Figure 1 shows the study's first conclusion: Computing power is migrating to the desktop, with PCs and workstations in 1994 basically doubling their share of the computing power from 1990. Mainframe-computing share is cut just about in half, and minis triple their workloads.

The customer LAN-budget allocation was not significantly different in 1994 than it was in 1990. LAN hardware and software acquisition will took up 42.4 percent of the budget, followed by in-house LAN support (personnel, training, etc.) at 37.7 percent. Externally provided LAN

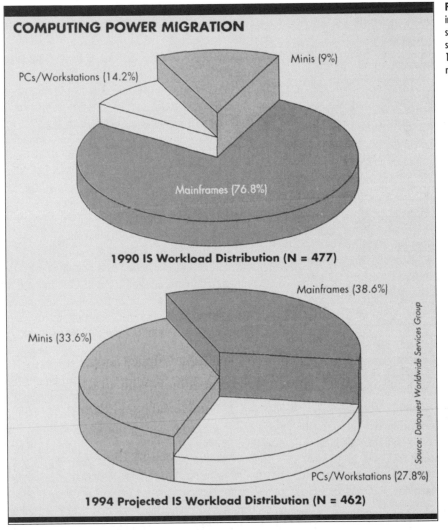

COMPUTING POWER MIGRATION

Minis (9%)

PCs/Workstations (14.2%)

Mainframes (76.8%)

1990 IS Workload Distribution (N = 477)

Mainframes (38.6%)

Minis (33.6%)

PCs/Workstations (27.8%)

Source: Dataquest Worldwide Services Group

1994 Projected IS Workload Distribution (N = 462)

Figure 1: Computing power is migrating to the desktop, with PCs and workstations in 1994 nearly doubling their share of the computing power from 1990 to 1994. Mainframe share of the market will decrease significantly.

support was at 13.7 percent, with the ubiquitous "other" at 6.2 percent.

Of the 37.7 percent of the budget swallowed by in-house support, here is a breakdown:

• end-user support, 24.7 percent;
• maintenance, 21.3 percent;
• adds, moves, and changes, 14.6 percent;
• research and planning, 14.2 percent;
• network-application development, 13.7 percent; and
• network operations and management, 11.5 percent.

Dataquest reports the following breakdown of external

services and the percentage of the external budget (13.7 of the total LAN budget) spent on each:

• maintenance and operating system support, 42.5 percent;
• end-user training, 21.4 percent;
• network-operations and management services, 21.1 percent; and
• network-application development, 14.9 percent.

Dataquest also looked at the industry from a vertical-market perspective. The study measured network professional-services (consulting, integration, and so forth) opportunities for 12 industries from 1990 to 1995.

Figure 2: The two-year growth rate for the number of LANs in companies with revenues greater than $1 billion is 61 percent. For companies with less than $1 billion, it is 82 percent. Five-year growth is 120 percent for companies greater than $1 billion; for those below $1 billion, it is 205 percent.

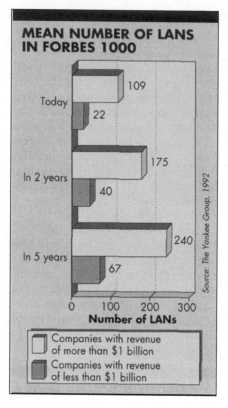

MEAN NUMBER OF LANS IN FORBES 1000

Source: The Yankee Group, 1992

Number of LANs

- Companies with revenue of more than $1 billion
- Companies with revenue of less than $1 billion

years." The report concludes that the SNMP market, which reached $14 million in 1990, will grow to $236 million in 1994.

The burgeoning corporate network is fueling the need for network management. Look at Figure 2 and Figure 3 for a taste of LAN growth over the next two years to five years. The charts are useful not just for what they say outright but for what they suggest. For instance, Figure 2 reveals that the two-year growth rate in LANs for companies with revenues greater than $1 billion is about 61 percent. For companies with less than $1 billion in revenues, that number is closer to 82 percent. Five-year growth in the number of LANs is 120 percent for companies with revenues greater than $1 billion; for those with revenues below $1 billion, the growth rate is 205 percent.

Figure 3 shows the growth in LAN internetworking. While the number of standalone LANs remains fairly static, the number of interconnected LANs in 1994 jumped to four times or five times the number for 1990. The number of multiprotocol routers sold worldwide also supports this trend. Routers will enjoy a 35 percent CAGR from 1991 to 1995.

The Yankee Group estimates that in 1992, costs per workstation were $352 for network administration; $200 for service, support, and maintenance; $152 for installation; and $92 for training. This total, the Yankee Group notes, does not include the costs associated with network downtime, another study in itself.

If the average downtime per LAN is 2 percent per year, then the Forbes 1,000 loses $1,000 to $1,500 in productivity per employee, according to The Yankee Group. The average Forbes 1,000 company loses between $4.2 million and $6.3 million per year in lost productivity.

Can network management come to the rescue? Not likely; major companies are still finding management strategies hard to implement. The greatest barriers to internetwork management, according to The Yankee Group, are, in order of frequency:
- complexity;
- lack of standards;
- lack of expertise;
- lack of commitment;
- politics;
- lack of products; and
- cost.

Telecommunications, with a growth rate of about 27 percent, will experience the highest compound annual growth rate (CAGR) of those industries. Distribution, state government, and discrete manufacturing each will grow more than 20 percent. The largest number of service opportunities belongs to discrete manufacturing, followed by state government and distribution.

ABOARD THE ENTERPRISE

Many businesses are busy building internetworks in hopes of creating an enterprise network. But, according to the Yankee Group (Boston) in its 1992 study, *Managing the Enterprise LAN*, "The vast majority of companies today are not close to implementing enterprise LANs. However, they are aggressively building internetworks."

The study notes that although no off-the-shelf solutions for internetwork management exist, tools are available. "The market for internetwork management systems," the study continues, "will be the fastest-growing segment of the network-management market during the next four

Readers are almost sure to find a familiar barrier among these. One important result in The Yankee Group's survey concerns which vendor offers the best internetwork-management capabilities. Who won? If you said Novell, you're wrong; that firm garnered 7 percent. Even IBM scored only 11 percent. DEC? No, DEC logged a respectable 15 percent. The winner? No one, with 26 percent of the vote. Vendors with sense will realize that the internetwork-management game is far from over.

In agreement with the importance of management is Market Intelligence Research Corp. (MIRC, Mountain View, CA). According to a study called *LAN/WAN Network Management Software, Service, and System Markets*, enormous growth will take place in this area. In 1991, revenues generated by network-management software, services, and systems were almost $3.2 billion. MIRC expects that figure to grow fivefold by 1998, to $15.8 billion.

MIRC says 11.5 percent of this market in 1993 was owned by network-management software. In five years, that total will be 18.5 percent (of a $15.8 billion market). Intelligent hubs will also increase network-management market percentage, from 21 percent this year to 27 percent in 1998. Network-management services will fall from 53 percent this year to 40 percent in five years.

These figures do not mean that outside services will shrink, though. *The U.S. Market for Network Outsourcing*, a study by Frost & Sullivan (New York), informs us that rapid developments in technology will fuel rapid growth in network outsourcing. The study predicts revenues to more than triple, from $2.6 billion in 1992 to $8.4 billion in 1997. About half of those revenues will go to outsourcing companies and computer suppliers; the other half will go to telecommunications-equipment makers and service suppliers.

PC LANS AHOY

On the good ship PC LAN floats hope. This sector of the market will be awash in dollars once again, and the waves of money will crest. MIRC estimated that the total PC LAN market was $9.5 billion by the end of 1993; in 1998, that number will grow to $22.4 billion. International Data Corp. (IDC, Framingham, MA) sets the network-products market size at $9.3 billion in 1994.

The number of networks will also grow, albeit on a flatter curve. The reason for the flattening is that many com-

panies already have their networks in place and are upgrading when a change is imminent. Peripheral Strategies (Santa Barbara, CA) reveals in its 1992 *PC LAN Storage Management Report* that the installed base of PC-based LANs was about 2.8 million, and by 1997, that number will grow to about 3.3 million.

Surprisingly, the survey shows that peer-to-peer LANs will increase in number as a part of the total installed base; market share of server-based LANs will drop. In 1993, server-based LANs accounted for about 1.8 million of the 2.8 million total, and 1 million networks were peer-to-peer. Server-based networks accounted for about two-thirds of the market.

These statistics all change by 1997, according to Peripheral Strategies. By then, server-based LANs will number about 1.9 million, and peer-to-peer networks will number about 1.3 million.

Before thinking that peer-to-peer is taking over the industry, take a look at the following numbers. Peripheral Strategies measured the number of PCs in peer LANs, in server LANs, and in no LAN. In 1993, slightly more than 11 percent of PCs were on peer-to-peer LANs. Almost 43 percent of all PCs were on server-based LANs, leaving 46 percent of PCs not on any LAN. Peripheral Strategies predicts that, by 1997, those numbers were about 17 percent on peer-to-peer LANs, 70 percent on server-based LANs, and 13 percent on no LAN at all.

REAL OPERATORS

Of the server-based NOS vendors, Novell is expected to retain its market share. In 1993, says Peripheral Strategies, the top five NOS vendors had the following market share:
- Novell, 66.6 percent;
- IBM, 15.1 percent;
- Microsoft, 9.6 percent;
- DEC, 5.5 percent; and
- Banyan, 2.6 percent.

In 1997, the numbers will look more like this, according to the study:
- Novell, 69.1 percent;
- IBM, 22.2 percent;
- DEC, 3.3 percent;
- Microsoft, 2.4 percent; and
- Banyan, 2.4 percent.

NetWare 4.0 will make significant gains in the Novell

Figure 3: The number of interconnected LANs in 1994 will jump to four times or five times the number in 1990.

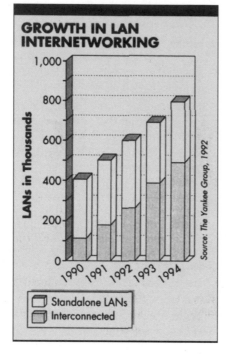

market, the survey predicts. From no market share in 1993, NetWare 4.0 will account for about 835,000 licenses by 1997 (of a total of about 1.33 million).

By 1997, 90 percent of server-based networks will consist of more than 100 nodes, with about 9 percent comprising between 10 nodes and 100 nodes. A tiny fraction of a percent of networks will consist of fewer than 10 nodes (down from about 10 percent in 1993).

Network storage capacity will rise in proportion to the number of nodes. Networks in the 5GB-capacity range will tumble in number. Networks with a capacity of greater than 100GB will experience a sharp increase, from just a few thousand in 1993 to about 95,000 in 1997.

One trend that is impossible to ignore, but hard to quantify, is that network operating systems are including more services. NOS vendors want to be the conveyor belt for e-mail, fax, and other application services. Novell should continue to make strides in hub management, server hubs, tape backup, and other services.

RING TWICE

In terms of services, electronic mail is growing at an amazing rate. The Yankee Group, in its *YankeeWatch*

white paper, says e-mail and the collaborative applications it has begun to spawn are more likely to affect individuals in the enterprise network than any other enterprise application. The firm estimates that the PC LAN messaging market will grow to $1.45 billion in 1995, up from $570 million in 1993.

In 1993, 38.9 million electronic mailboxes existed in the United States. Of those, 15.1 million (about 39 percent) are PC LAN-based. In 1995, the number of mailboxes will increase to 75.5 million, and the number of LAN-based mailboxes will rise to 38.7 million, or roughly 51 percent of all electronic mailboxes. (Mainframe, midrange, and Unix mailboxes will drop from 50.6 percent to 36.3 percent over the same period.)

A side note: Novell and Banyan have purchased a $500,000 stake each in Beyond (Cambridge, MA) whose BeyondMail uses a rules-based engine for handling mail intelligently.

THROUGH THE CHANNEL

One of the biggest questions facing network buyers is, "Where do you buy network products, anyway?" It's not that network products are unavailable. Quite the contrary, lots of products exist, and, as of this year, many more places to buy them will exist as well.

Much of the momentum that drives catalog sales for IBM, Compaq, Hewlett-Packard, DEC, et. al., can be attributed to Dell and its direct-to-end-user sales strategy. Much as K-Mart battles Wal-Mart for a few tiny points of a margin, the computer giants are trying to get those potential users who operate outside of the usual channels. Like those discount retailers, major computer makers are putting out promotional materials that are straightforward, no fuss, no muss.

Yet conflicting trends have begun. In a study done by Charles River Strategies (Boston) for IBM, small VARs (less than $2 million) grew in terms of total LAN products sold. Over a two-year span from 1990 to 1992, the small VAR increased market share, from 21 percent of network products sold to the end user to 26 percent. Large VARs actually increased in raw number but decreased in percentage from 27 percent to 24 percent of market share.

Small VARs, it seems, make the most gains in marketshare. But who buys from these small VARs? About 57 percent of the small VAR's business comes from other small businesses. Medium businesses accounted for 18 percent, large businesses for 7 percent. Interestingly, government accounted for 12 percent of small VAR LAN-product sales. Education was last at 6 percent.

The number and quality of certain channels has increased, too. The ranks of participants in Novell's Platinum program, which started with 25 resellers, has swelled to numbers in the three digits. Microsoft, too, has expanded its reseller base past the planned 600 network specialists.

IBM, even while offering a product catalog, has expanded its reseller program tremendously. What was in January 1990 a three-member channel (direct sales, advanced-product dealer, and industry remarketer with vertical value added) has become a program with 13 ways to get product to the user.

Big Blue's vision is clear, at least in the channel. The company will "expand distribution of low-end networking products, and put into place consistent certification requirements and enhanced support offerings," according to Dave Nichols, IBM PC Company's director of reseller channel management.

YIN AND YANG

What's the secret to successful implementation for users in this windy, whitecapped market? According to Mike Zak, associate at Charles River Ventures, it's a dual driving force. "User behavior can be attributed to two things: value and frustration. Each addresses a different aspect of user behavior.

"There is a lot of frustration among users," says Zak, "especially on the part of those who sign the checks and who make the purchases. I think those people have begun to wonder about value and the extent to which value is attained in a network investment."

Zak feels that this uncertainty arises from the confusing number of choices and from the dynamism of the industry itself. He also notes that almost every company still has some problems with unfinished installations, and major portions of many companies' computing plans do not work.

Not surprisingly, he feels that the best is yet to come in networking—even given the blustery business environment. "There is a contradiction," Zak states. "On the one hand, you might think mergers or buyouts imply consolidation and a reduction in new players. But we see new players popping up all the time, creating lots of opportunities for their owners and investors.

"The communications and networking sector is complicated, it's pervasive, and a lot of demands are placed in this area. The technology we apply to this problem is still in its early stages. There are many significant networking companies we have yet to hear about. The opportunity to provide new solutions is extremely good. I can only express excitement at the appearance of new players."

Zak points to hot spots for innovation. "A couple of areas remain wide open. The whole ease-of-use problem has not been dealt with. Another aspect is ease of support. Despite claims, no one has figured out how to make this technology work out of the box. We have an entire VAR and consultant channel that exists solely because of the complexity of the products. There is great opportunity here. People are sick of buying products that have engineers attached to them."

Section 3
Multimedia

The networked computer user is no longer limited to viewing flat, text-based screens full of static information. While sharing this type of information over the network was once satisfactory, users now want more. With the advent of high-speed, high-bandwidth network technology, sending a message that contains data, voice, and a video clip is now possible. With the right network infrastructure, hardware, and application software, multimedia can bring the desktop to life, opening up new methods of lively communication between users.

But what sort of performance and technology boosts do you need to have on the network to be able to tap into the excitement of multimedia? The stories in the section reveal the latest technology and network applications in the areas of imaging and multimedia. These features look at all aspects of using multimedia on the network, including the crucial and often overlooked component of information storage. And at the end of the section, "High School Goes Prime Time" and "Never Forget" offer real-life case histories of multimedia in action.

A Sharper Image

IMAGING VENDORS WORK FOR OPEN STANDARDS AND ARE
INTEGRATING IMAGING INTO DESKTOP APPLICATIONS.

BY MIKE HURWICZ

The election-day slogan in Chicago used to be, "Vote early–and often." Such trickery would be difficult if poll workers could positively establish every voter's identity.

Of course, voters have to show ID, but even teenagers know how easy it is to substitute their picture on the ID of someone whose birthday qualifies them to enter establishments where minors are not welcome. However, if the bartender had a book with the picture of every licensed driver, a lot of kids would be drinking Coca Cola instead of Coors.

Having such a book might sound far-fetched, but using the latest imaging technology, the government of Mexico is embarking on a project that might sound almost as difficult: setting up a system to check the identities of some 45 million voters expected to turn out for national elections in the summer of 1994. The government will give poll workers a book with a picture, signature, and thumbprint of every citizen registered to vote at that location. Poll workers can match all three items to identify the voter.

IMAGING FOR THE MASSES

Like most imaging applications past and present, the Mexican voter registration system targets one mission-critical task rather than a general improvement in productivity. But it typifies today's systems, not yesterday's, in that PCs are a critical component of the system: When imaging first emerged, it was out of reach for ordinary PC LAN folks with their slow PCs, small disks, and nascent networking. So imaging systems were built around Unix, mainframe, and minicomputer platforms. But now the PCs are fast enough, the disks are big enough, and the networks are in place.

As imaging comes to PCs, it should help PC users in their everyday tasks, such as general-purpose filing. So far, however, hordes of images are not invading the average user's desktop.

"The technology to deal with images on an occasional basis is getting put in place," says Bruce Silver, vice president of BIS Strategic Decisions (Norwell, MA), a market research and consulting firm. "What's lacking now is a compelling reason to buy [desktop imaging applications]."

The problem is straightforward: payback. The return on investment (ROI) for line-of-business applications essential to business operations is usually easy to quantify. For example, an insurance firm that can process claims faster can service more customers and bring in more money. However, determining the ROI on imaging as a substitute for paper filing at most offices is more difficult.

Vendors of desktop and workgroup imaging products, consequently, are struggling to find a market for their increasingly inexpensive and easy-to-use products. Nevertheless, Silver believes that desktop imaging will become a significant market force within about two years to five years.

Now, however, customers are spending most of their imaging dollars in the line-of-business arena, according to BIS. Line-of-business vendors are flourishing despite the fact that they often sell expensive products that can be installed only by VARs handy with sophisticated workflow and database programming.

At this point, most users of general desktop imaging are experimenting rather than implementing on a broad scale, says Jennifer Mitchell, principal analyst at Dataquest's (San Jose, CA) digital documents service. In early 1994, a Dataquest survey of 250 IS professionals in companies with more than 100 employees found users were focused on production systems, not desktop imaging.

In such a potentially large market, even experimental use of desktop imaging systems will continue to outsell line-of-business applications in terms of number of seats, as BIS' 1993 figures show. However, because of its cost, line-of-business imaging is still ahead in dollar earnings).

MAKING IT LOOK GOOD

While line-of-business applications bring imaging to small workgroups doing specific tasks, imaging as a substitute for everyday paper filing is applicable for nearly everyone on a LAN. So even though users on the whole aren't jumping up and down demanding desktop imaging, the thought of all those desktops makes vendors' mouths water: Vendors are working on making the technology so cheap, so attractive, and so easy-to-use that users just won't be able to resist.

In addition, vendors are incorporating imaging into network and server operating systems. It is becoming an almost-invisible component of everyday applications such as e-mail, database management, and document management.

For instance, while the voter-registration system in Mexico was custom-built, the vendor, Genesys Information Systems (Hunt Valley, MD), could just as easily have made Windows or DOS applications capable of imaging. "If a customer has an existing database and applications that satisfy the company's information management needs, we can enable a full set of imaging capabilities within that environment," says Braun Jones, president of Genesys.

Then users can access images from existing applications without any change to the applications other than the addition of thumbnail-size icons that users click on to bring up the images. In the Windows environment, Genesys uses Microsoft's Object Linking and Embedding (OLE) to enable systems for imaging. In the DOS environment, the company uses a "screen-scraping" technique for reading text in certain locations on the screen to determine which image is desired.

Through the use of these kinds of techniques, imaging as a separate product category will begin to disappear. Imaging won't remain a separate application; it's becoming part of the desktop environment, where the prevailing

attitude is, "Images should be seen but not complicate my life." With image-enabled systems, users can integrate images smoothly into other desktop functions; they don't have to think about or manage them differently just because they're images.

While highly focused, specialized imaging applications are not going away. Ron Arenson of Wang (Lowell, MA) states, "Within two to three years, there will be no discussion of an imaging market per se. Images will be subsumed in the information-processing market as an object type." This projection from a man whose title is director of image marketing.

Some vendors are already redefining themselves so they don't get pigeon-holed in the disappearing imaging niche. ViewStar (Alameda, CA), ostensibly an imaging company, defines itself this way: "ViewStar develops client-server software systems for business process automation which address mission-critical, line-of-business workflow and document management applications in large corporate environments." The company doesn't mention imaging anywhere. Yet if you look at what ViewStar does today, it usually starts with converting large quantities of paper documents into image files.

Imaging applications, such as fax distribution programs or scanning large quantities of documents, will still exist. Far more frequently, however, other applications, such as word processing, spreadsheets, e-mail, and database and document management, will have imaging features right alongside their other functions.

One of the companies interested in making imaging easier and more attractive is Watermark Software (Burlington, MA). It makes image-enabling software that not only scans, prints, and displays images but also uses Windows OLE to place a thumbnail of a document in any OLE-capable application screen. The user double-clicks on the thumbnail, the image appears, and the user can then use Watermark to type text, write freehand, highlight, draw arrows, and add voice comments and other OLE objects to the image. Watermark Discovery Edition costs $149 for a single-user version, while the Professional Edition is only $295. The Professional Edition lets users access the Watermark server and integrates with document management services. "You can get the software to display, scan, and print for $100 a seat," says BIS' Silver.

At the same time, computer-based fax vendors such as

Alcom (Mountain View, CA), RightFax (Tucson, AZ), Cheyenne Software (Roslyn Heights, NY), and Optus Software (Somerset, NJ) sell network fax capabilities for about $1,000 per server. Fax files are image files, and the increasing use of these programs may eventually highlight the need for image management.

Nifty, low-cost desktop imaging applications, however, will not be enough to make the desktop imaging market explode. That kind of growth will require powerful back-end services to manage those images.

BEHIND THE SEEN

Image files are unstructured, unlabeled bags of bits, with no header information to reveal their content or text to use for indexing purposes. While desktop imaging products such as PC fax programs can create lots of image files and programs such as Watermark Discovery Edition can edit them, the facilities for managing those files are typically based on the DOS file system. When the number of files gets into the hundreds or thousands, tracking them becomes difficult using DOS alone. In addition, magnetic disks fill up quickly with large image files.

Line-of-business imaging vendors solved these problems long ago with two back-end services: document management and mass storage. These services let users store and retrieve large quantities of images efficiently.

A document management service is typically based on a database product that indexes and retrieves images according to user-defined criteria. For instance, an insurance adjuster wants all the documents relating to the fire-damage claim filed by Joe Jones in August 1989. Previously defined indexes stored externally, not in the image file, enable users to search by date, type of document, and the person who submitted the claim.

A mass storage service is usually 99.9 percent transparent to users. For instance, such a service may automatically migrate files from magnetic to optical media after the files haven't been accessed for a certain period of time. When a user requests a file that has been migrated, the system automatically brings it back to magnetic media. The delay may be so small that users may not even notice. Or it could take half a minute to get a file from an optical jukebox. For the most part, though, users are unaware of the location of their files.

These two kinds of services make imaging practical, either for line-of-business applications or for widespread desktop deployment. Users of PC LANs, however, need to have the services running on the kinds of servers that dominate LANs, primarily NetWare, Windows, and OS/2 servers. Services running on those operating systems have been emerging for several years.

MUSCLE SERVERS

"Powerful server technology to manage documents and jukeboxes, network and communications services, as well as centralized scanner and fax capabilities, if that's desired, are critical to enabling imaging applications on a departmental level and higher," says John Robinson, Genesys' director of marketing.

For line-of-business applications, back-end services have historically run on highly scalable Unix boxes, either servers or workstations. Today, line-of-business application-development vendors may also offer PC-based servers. FileNet (Costa Mesa, CA) and ViewStar offer Unix-based servers, and ViewStar also has servers running under Windows, OS/2, and DOS.

Imaging vendors who started out targeting the desktop market, avoiding competition on the line-of-business front, have generally limited themselves to PC-based servers, on the theory that their customers didn't want the cost or the complexity of Unix. For instance, the image server for LaserFiche Windows/ NLM, from Compulink Management Center (Torrance, CA), is a NetWare server running a Compulink NLM. Imara Research's (Toronto) server is an OS/2 machine, as are the servers for Lotus Notes:Document Imaging (LN:DI) from Lotus Development (Cambridge, MA) and Genesys' Image Extender. Optika Imaging Systems (Colorado Springs, CO) uses Windows-based servers.

A PC-based server strategy has had severely limited scalability in the past. Unix-only imaging vendors argue that it still does. However, high-end PCs and superservers running OS/2, Windows NT, and NetWare 4.x are expanding the upper limits of PC scalability.

FOLLOW THE GREEN PAPER

Armed with more powerful server platforms, some PC-based vendors have gone where the money is and are expanding their business into line-of-business imaging. For instance, Compulink, LaserData (Tyngsboro, MA), and Optika are all moving that way. Genesys, which may have been the first image-enabling vendor in mid-1991 and which has had an OS/2-based image server product for several years, has also moved strongly into line-of-business programming, as evidenced by the Mexican voter-registration application.

Thus, vendors who staked their claim in PC LAN imaging find themselves competing with the line-of-business vendors. Those vendors, while secure in their market, still have to race the upstarts for the desktop market.

Other vendors are entering the act, too. For example, PC-based document management vendors such as KeyFile (Nashua, NH) have added imaging capabilities to their products. In Apri, 1994l, Watermark announced an NT-based image server, based on Microsoft SQL Server, designed to support optical media and including both document management and mass storage services. The Watermark image server is accessed using Watermark Professional Edition as the client. Together, they bring Watermark out of the nifty-front-end-but-where's-the-back-end category.

The Watermark server manages images only, but Watermark Professional Edition and the image server can work with document management systems from PC DOCS (Tallahassee, FL) or SoftSolutions Technology (Orem, UT) for users who want to manage images and other kinds of files through a single interface. The images are managed by the Watermark image server, using the Microsoft SQL Server database, but the user employs the PC DOCS search function, for instance, to find the desired images.

Vendors of all stripes see an opportunity in offering not just a complete solution for imaging but a way of handling files of all kinds, as well as related functions such as faxing. On the one hand, all this competition means a wide variety of products, from vendors with different strengths and backgrounds. Competition is forcing prices down and the number of features up. Users might be tempted to say, "Let the vendors go at each other, and may the best products win." Unfortunately for the user who would like to go with a clear winner now, there isn't one.

STANDARD BEARERS

One factor that should help customers is the development of open standards. For instance, perhaps users would be more willing to buy a low-end imaging server if they knew that later on they could access its document management service from a higher-end imaging product, without having to throw away the low-end server. Similarly, a utility such as Watermark would be much more useful if it could access the image server or mass storage service of an existing line-of-business imaging application from FileNet or ViewStar instead of from just its own Watermark server.

Today, neither of these scenarios is possible. An image server based on a SQL database, as most of them are, is open to any application that can send SQL commands. Unfortunately, most low-end imaging products can't even spell SQL. Besides, the SQL approach requires custom programming.

Meanwhile, inexpensive imaging utilities may support Windows standards such as OLE or Dynamic Data Exchange (DDE). But that support doesn't provide access to back-end internals such as image server pointers to multiple images comprising a document or to mass storage rules for migrating files to optical media. Today, such access can be accomplished only via proprietary APIs.

Because of the lack of standard APIs, multivendor cooperation is slow in coming. For instance, to operate with the Watermark image server, PC DOCS and SoftSolutions created special Windows Dynamic-Linked Libraries (DLLs) to interface with a proprietary Watermark document management API.

Simplify Development (Nashua, NH), is also developing links between its MailRoom for Windows/ShareScan and other vendors' offerings. Simplify's product is an image-document builder that serves as a central coordinator for other products, which together form an imaging system. For instance, MailRoom for Windows can use e-mail and workflow products such as Lotus' cc:Mail, Beyond's (Burlington, MA) BeyondMail, WordPerfect's (Orem, UT) WordPerfect Office, and Microsoft's MS-Mail. It supports optical character recognition (OCR) products from Caere (Los Gatos, CA), Calera Recognition Systems (Sunnyvale, CA), ExperVision (San Jose, CA), and Xerox Imaging Systems (Peabody, MA), and fax products from Delrina (San Jose, CA), Alcom, Optus, and Intel. Simplify also supports document management products from PC DOCS, SoftSolutions, and Saros (Bellevue, WA), and optical storage products from Conner (Lake Mary, FL), Novell, Cheyenne, and Palindrome (Naperville, IL).

PICKING A LINCHPIN

Vendors such as Simplify and Watermark can offer nicely integrated multivendor environments for imaging and document management. However, because some of the integration depends on proprietary APIs, certain parts don't work without the Simplify or Watermark product, making it difficult to substitute another vendor's product to meet some functions. Users become locked in.

While users may not want to make an application vendor the linchpin of their imaging system, they may be willing to make that kind of commitment to a NOS vendor. Take Novell, for example. NetWare 4.x will provide standardized document management and mass storage services under Image and Document Management Services (IDMS, formerly Image Enabled NetWare). Novell shipped a functionally complete developer's kit for IDMS in December 1993. Novell says that IDMS itself will be shipping to end users by the end of this month. End-user products should follow.

Watermark was planning to base its image server on IDMS but went with NT instead because of delays in IDMS availability in late 1993. Watermark is looking closely at IDMS now that the NT server is out the door, says Arny Epstein, Watermark's chief technical officer. Support for IDMS would give Watermark users simultaneous transparent access to images stored on Watermark NT-based image servers and images stored on IDMS servers.

IDMS requires NetWare 4.x services, such as the global directory. However, a single NetWare client can access both 3.x and 4.x servers. IDMS is thus a viable option for enabling all NetWare desktops. "Our goal is to make all 30 million NetWare clients [capable of imaging]," says Scott Wells, Novell's product line manager for NetWare application services.

That's fine for NetWare desktops. However, to have any chance of harmonizing imaging applications and services in all the computing and networking environments found in today's corporate LANs, users and vendors need open, cross-platform interfaces to back-end services. An industry consortium, the Shamrock Document Management Coalition (represented by the PR firm of Waggener Edstrom, Portland OR), is working on APIs to provide those interfaces.

On St. Patrick's day, 1993, while you and I were out spilling Guinness on our green clothes, Shamrock, a dedicated group of document management professionals, met to define APIs to support three kinds of interoperability:

• Multiple clients talking to a single back-end service. Users could buy workflow software from one vendor and imaging software from another, yet have both sets of software access the same document management back end.

• A single client talking to multiple back ends. A single client could access document management services from, for instance, IBM and Hewlett-Packard.

• Back ends talking to each other. Middleware registers and accesses various back-end services, which might be the ideal way to transfer large numbers of files from one back-end repository to another.

Shamrock APIs will address document access (how to open a session with a service and request a document), security (determining whether a user should be allowed to access the requested service, document, or portion of a document), and document content architecture (how to define compound documents that may consist of multiple images, text segments, voice annotations, and so on).

"With the turnkey applications of the past, document management and mass storage have been fairly tightly integrated with the application," says Frank Dawson, senior programmer in the Software Solutions division of IBM. "But suppose I want to integrate marketing and engineering applications. I need a common back-end system and looser coupling between the application and the back-end service. Shamrock is trying to enable that type of integration by defining API functions that back-end systems ought to provide. I hope [back-end] vendors will expose those functions through that API. I think that will go a long way toward helping us reach the goal of being able to pick the desired client and service and use them together."

IBM and Saros created the original Shamrock specification. In April 1994, a draft was released to other vendors, users, consultants, and systems integrators for review. The importance of the standard to the imaging industry is indicated by the presence on the review board of such vendors as ViewStar and Wang Laboratories (Lowell, MA).

Even vendors not part of the original thrust are enthusiastic. "Openness at the service level will be a competitive advantage," says Watermark's Epstein. Look for Watermark to get involved in industrywide standards for back-end services such as document management and mass storage.

WE KNOW WHO YOU ARE

Across the Border

The government of Mexico has embarked on an ambitious voter-registration drive and is making use of imaging technology to fulfill the goal of one citizen, one vote. During 1993, voter-registration workers have been stationed in 6,000 locations around Mexico with Polaroid (Cambridge, MA) cameras and laminating equipment. Voters are coming in, having their pictures taken, and putting their thumbprint and signature on an ID card. The voters take home the laminated card.

Besides the ID card, registration workers also produce a receipt, which they forward by courier to one of 17 imaging sites. There, the receipts are scanned and stored on a Genesys Information Systems (Hunt Valley, MD) image server, a 50MHz PS/2 Model 95 running OS/2. Windows clients, running imaging software based on Genesys' Image Extender product, connect to the Genesys server over a NetWare 3.12 network. IBM de Mexico is coordinating the project, which also includes Oracle (Redwood Shores, CA) SQL database servers running on IBM RS/6000s under AIX.

At the imaging sites, workers take three images from each receipt–a photo, thumbprint, and signature–and store them on the Genesys server. The receipt also has a bar code containing textual information, such as the voter's name and date of birth. The workers scan the bar code to have that information automatically transferred into an Oracle database. When all the receipts have been processed, the final step will be to produce the voter-registration books.

The government also created a central nationwide database to ensure that no one is registered twice. In implementing this system, the government of Mexico is not just leapfrogging its neighbors to the north and south; it is installing the first imaging-based voter-registration system of this magnitude anywhere in the world.

PRICES DOWN, NUMBER OF FEATURES UP

How Low Can You Go?

How soon will imaging come to your desktop? That depends on products and prices. Here's a quick look at some vendors' offerings.

Alacrity, based in Hackettstown, NJ, sells its single-user Office-In-A-Box for $599, including a low-resolution–300 dot-per-inch (dpi)–Ficus black-and-white scanner. The software scans, stores, retrieves, prints, and handles incoming and outgoing faxes. Alacrity also offers a workgroup solution, which costs $2,495 for a 10-user system, including software and a single controller card that serves as a fax card, printer controller, and scanner controller.

QMS (Mobile, AL), the printer company, has come out with something it calls the QMS 2001 Knowledge Machine, a combined printer-scanner-fax-copier that sells for $3,999. That price includes hardware and software.

Caere (Los Gatos, CA) makes a document and image management program, PageKeeper, that goes beyond conventional search techniques to help you find documents. It focuses on image documents, including scans and faxes, with content that can be converted to text through optical character recognition (OCR). PageKeeper isn't a new product; it's been shipping since December 1992. But it's relatively inexpensive, at $195 for the single-user product and around $300 a seat for network editions.

What it can do is pretty amazing. Other document managers may offer three kinds of searches:

• keyword indexes, in which you assign specific keywords to a document and retrieve them according to those keywords;

• full-text searches, which allow you to retrieve text documents according to any word or combination of words in the document; and

• fuzzy searches, which will find documents with close matches to the words you specify.

PageKeeper goes beyond these three offerings. Using natural language processing, PageKeeper examines text and builds a profile of the document based on sentence structure, not just the occurrence of particular words. For instance, it can tell the difference between nouns and verbs and can thus determine which words represent key subjects in the text. PageKeeper allows you to make unconstrained queries in which you specify one or more keywords. In response, you get a list of topics ranked by relevance. You can also take a document you've already found and use its profile as the basis for another search, in effect saying, "Find me more documents like this one." When it displays a document, PageKeeper can display both the original image (so you can view non-textual material) and the OCR text.

PageKeeper also includes a compression algorithm that can compress text files by as much as 50-to-1. Caere started out in OCR software, where it is still a leader, so the OCR capability in PageKeeper is first-rate. PageKeeper has also inherited some of the qualities of its forerunner, OmniPage. For instance, PageKeeper supports more than 50 different scanners, many of the drivers having been brought over from OmniPage.

Imaging: Save the Green

SEEING THE IMAGING FOREST FOR THE MONEY TREES

BY DAN CARROLL AND MIKE HURWICZ

CareAmerica Health Plans, an HMO headquartered in Chatsworth, CA, has saved more than 900,000 sheets of paper during the past two years through an imaging system that handles enrollment. It expects to save $4.4 million over the next five years through the new system.

Furthermore, retrieving an enrollment application from the CareAmerica files used to take three to five days. Today, the same task takes about 20 seconds. The difference? Document imaging.

"Now we can answer members' questions immediately," says Bob Steiger, director of health plan systems for CareAmerica. "We don't have to call back. As a result, we're providing better customer service than before. We are handling 25,000 member inquiries per month."

To handle this many requests using the previous paper filing system, CareAmerica would have had to hire five new employees, says Steiger. With the new system, the HMO has gone from 150,000 to 200,000 members without increasing customer service staff.

The key to handling the increased volume is scanning enrollment applications when they come in. After that, the applications are accessible over the document-imaging network. That system is much faster and more reliable than the previous one, in which the customer service representative had to fill out a request form and send it to the distribution department. Distribution department staff then retrieved the requested application from a file drawer, photocopied and replaced it in the file drawer, and sent the photocopy to the requester.

With a paper filing system, a document could be misfiled every time it was used. Today, once an image document is correctly filed electronically, subsequent misfiling is nearly impossible.

Also, CareAmerica has linked the document-imaging system from FileNet (Costa Mesa, CA) with its AS/400 minicomputer, where a member-eligibility database resides, and with an SQL database server that simplifies distribution of images to Windows-based desktop applications.

NECESSITY, DESIRE, CONVENIENCE

Working with images in electronic form on networks has become necessary or desirable for many businesses. In some cases, it's just a matter of convenience. For instance, taking the place of a fax machine, a fax server can take text or image files and turn them into outgoing faxes. Incoming faxes become image files, too. Similarly, a document-imaging system, which scans paper documents and stores them as files on the network, replaces a paper filing system.

Image files are created by many applications, among them paint/draw, computer aided design (CAD), photo-retouching, screen-capture, and animation programs, as well as video "frame grabbers," and digital still cameras.

You can manipulate and manage electronic images, wherever they come from, in ways that are impossible with paper. For example, you can:
• access an image instantly, without going to a file drawer;
• share a single copy of an image among multiple users, anywhere on the network, even over a WAN;
• allow many users to view and change the same image at the same time, using object linking technology;
• embed images in word processing documents or use them in computer-based presentations;

• e-mail or fax images directly from disk;

• print or plot images, achieving better speed or quality, or lower cost, than with a photocopier;

• manage images with standard databases or specialized image storage-and-retrieval systems;

• integrate images into electronic forms and workflow packages;

• use screen scrapers to automatically read portions of the screen and take appropriate action;

• edit and enhance images with paint, draw, CAD, or photo-retouching software;

• annotate images with text, sound, or video;

• use optional character recognition (OCR) to convert electronic documents to text, then use that text to index and later to retrieve them; and

• attach bar codes to images–a nearly foolproof indexing and retrieval method.

Networked imaging systems offer many advantages beyond easy access and manipulation. For instance, paper consumption and handling can be minimized, saving time, money, and the lives of innocent trees. A user can look at a fax, act on and delete it, for instance, without ever touching ink or paper.

Trips to the fax and copy machine, as well as time spent waiting in line, can be reduced or eliminated. Electronic images also take up less physical space than paper images. With compression, a filing cabinet full of documents can be stored on a single compact disk. An optical jukebox that fits in a small closet can replace more than 100 filing cabinets.

However, imaging on networks can raise potentially difficult issues. Usually, one of the first things users think of is overflowing storage devices and the network buckling under the weight of huge image files. Indeed, you have to expect slower response times when accessing a 500KB image than when loading a word processing document or a spreadsheet. On the positive side, standard network optimization techniques, such as segmentation and distributing functions to different network nodes, are effective for imaging systems.

A more difficult problem for some is the sheer number of imaging products available. This variety can make it difficult to hone in on the one that suits you best.

Standards have been yet another major stumbling block for imaging users looking for assurances that today's

investments will be in the mainstream of tomorrow's imaging solutions, that they will not be "orphaned." Happily, standards for networked imaging are emerging.

TWO ROADS DIVERGED

Basically, there are two approaches to imaging. They're often categorized as "high-end" or "low-end" solutions, a description not entirely inaccurate. More precisely, these solutions might be defined as "transaction oriented" or "ad hoc."

Each solution suits a different market. The transaction-oriented market consists of customers who want to maximize the number of transactions, such as scanning and indexing a receipt or invoice, performed in a given period of time. Such customers may need a system to handle large numbers of transactions (say, more than 5,000 or 10,000) every day. Usually, such users also need to store many millions of pages, often from one million to 10 million, sometimes upwards of 70 million.

Such customers usually buy hardware and software from a single vendor, and integration services are often part of the deal, too. These customers don't worry about a thing, except cost and perhaps the survival of the vendor, on whom they depend.

Long-time vendors in this arena include FileNet, IBM, Recognition International (the Dallas company which acquired Sunnyvale, CA-based Plexus) and ViewStar (Emeryville, CA). Total hardware, software, and integration costs usually range upwards of a quarter of a million dollars, and million-dollar installations are not unusual.

While these systems are implemented on LANs, NOSs such as NetWare or LAN Manager are not usually a central element. For instance, the image server, where images are stored, is typically a RISC box running Unix. One exception is ViewStar, based on the Sybase (Emeryville, CA) Structured Query Language (SQL) database server, which can run on OS/2, on the IBM RISC System/6000 under AIX (IBM's version of Unix), or as an NLM on Compaq 486 and higher server platforms. The NetWare server is a highly specialized environment, not just a plain vanilla NetWare server.

The ad hoc approach is geared toward intermittent, as-needed access. It usually involves fewer than 5,000 or 10,000 transactions a day, and total images on-line or near-line in the low millions at most.

Figure 1: TIFF, Group 3, Group 4, Windows, Dynamic Data Exchange (DDE), and Object Linking and Embedding (OLE) are firmly established standards in the imaging world. Image Enabled NetWare (IEN) will provide standard APIs and services for NetWare LANs. Open Database Connectivity (ODBC) is a Windows-based standard for interfacing database front ends to database servers.

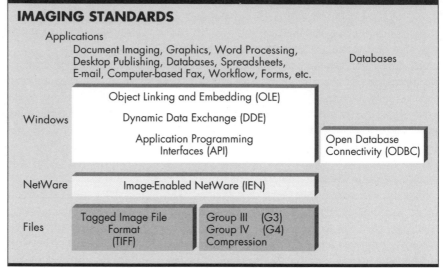

Figure 1: TIFF, Group 3, Group 4, Windows, Dynamic Data Exchange (DDE), and Object Linking and Embedding (OLE) are firmly established standards in the imaging world. Image Enabled NetWare (IEN) will provide standard APIs and services for NetWare LANs. Open Database Connectivity (ODBC) is a Windows-based standard for interfacing database front ends to database servers.

However, modular, distributed client-server architectures can help achieve much higher numbers of total images stored and transactions per day. For instance, Optika Imaging Systems (Colorado Springs, CO), with its File-Power family of Windows-based products, claims it has users who scan more than 125,000 pages per day.

Ad hoc systems are based on shrink-wrapped software and commodity image servers, such as NetWare file servers, Windows, or OS/2 machines. In most cases, you can set up a small system yourself. You may want to hire someone to set up a larger or more complex system, but such vendors probably won't provide products and services geared to the mass market. For such custom installations, you might contract with a team of VARs or consultants, including someone specializing in imaging. Or you may contract with a VAR with broad network expertise, including imaging.

Products in the ad hoc class include Alacrity System's Alacrity (Hackettstown, NJ), Compulink Management Center's (Torrance, CA) LaserFiche, Imara Research's (Toronto) Imara, KeyFile's (Nashua, NH) KeyFile, LaserData's (Tyngsboro, MA) GroupFile, Optika Imaging Systems' FilePower family, Pinnacle Micro's (Irvine, CA) Paperless 1 Imaging System, TechKnowlogy's (Salt Lake City) Imaging Software for Windows 4.0, and Westbrook Technologies' (Westbrook, CT) File Magic.

Dozens more of these vendors exist, and they keep popping up like sheets out of a fast scanner. Systems are typically priced at about $200 to $1,000 per user, with $2,000 per user at the high end.

Some vendors may be poised to bridge the ad hoc and transaction-oriented worlds. For instance, Nien-Ling Wayman, CEO of Compulink Management Center, says the company's new LaserFiche NLM product positions Compulink to compete with transaction-oriented systems in some instances. LaserData and Optika are others that seem to be headed in this direction.

INVESTMENT PROTECTION

Transaction-oriented document-imaging systems have historically been self-contained, with little concern for multivendor interoperability. Because of differences in Unix versions and hardware platforms, as well as close links between hardware and software, moving from one transaction-oriented imaging system to another generally means throwing out most of the old system and starting over.

Ad hoc systems, in contrast, run on standard platforms. You can drop one DOS-based imaging package and install another without changing hardware or operating systems, for instance. Still, multivendor interoperability has been limited historically.

Until recently, established vendors in the PC LAN arena–whether applications vendors (for example, Word-

Perfect, Lotus, and Microsoft) or NOS vendors (such as Novell, Microsoft, and Banyan)–haven't paid much attention to imaging. As for the companies that led the charge into LAN-based imaging, industry observers wondered which of these smaller companies would be around in a few years' time.

But the imaging industry is gaining support and popularity. Vendors such as Novell and Microsoft have entered the fray, and a number of standards are emerging to provide a stable infrastructure for imaging applications. Multivendor interoperability has made significant progress. You can mix and match auxiliary tools, such as faxing or image-editing tools, without changing your document-imaging software, and you can change your imaging system without giving up all your tools; the OS and hardware can remain in place no matter what else you change.

Standards driving such increased capability include (see Figure 1):

• *Tagged Image File Format (TIFF)*. Nearly everybody supports this file format now. However, TIFF is not a perfectly uniform, 100-percent interoperable standard. "Not all TIFF readers can read all TIFF files," warns Ed Feldman, senior product manager, of Alacrity Systems. "It depends how the reader is implemented. Some are very narrow [in terms of the number of implementations of TIFF they can read]; others are very broad." TIFF also allows custom tags, which can only be read by the vendor's own TIFF reader, Feldman notes.

• *Group 3 and Group 4 compression*. Support for Group 3 is widespread; support for Group 4 is growing. Problems and mismatches still crop up, however. We found that LaserFiche NLM, for instance, required imports in Group 4 formats. None of our other programs would produce such files.

• *Open Database Connectivity (ODBC)*. This Windows-based, Microsoft-sponsored standard facilitates the creation of Windows-based tools that can access multiple databases. Most imaging vendors say they will support ODBC, making it easier to get into a single image database with a number of different Windows-based tools or to use the same tools with image databases from different vendors.

• *Microsoft Windows*. Windows APIs, as well as features such as Dynamic Data Exchange (DDE) and Object Linking and Embedding (OLE), facilitate tighter integration

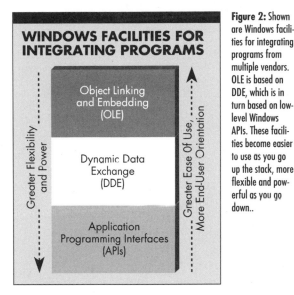

Figure 2: Shown are Windows facilities for integrating programs from multiple vendors. OLE is based on DDE, which is in turn based on low-level Windows APIs. These facilities become easier to use as you go up the stack, more flexible and powerful as you go down..

among programs from different vendors. APIs, DDE, and OLE form a three-layer cake, with greater ease of use and less flexibility as you go up (see Figure 2.)

APIs are a very flexible way to integrate programs, but they're relatively difficult to work with, and developers, not end users, must perform the integration.

DDE is a client-server technology. Only those functions that have been specifically implemented in a DDE server can be requested by DDE clients. Thus, working at the DDE level offers less flexibility than working with the Windows APIs underlying DDE. But life is also simpler at the DDE level than at the API level. Developers can use DDE through APIs, and users can access DDE capabilities through macro or script languages.

Simpler yet is OLE, which allows you to make one document or file an object inside another "container" object or file. You see the contained (linked or embedded) object displayed, and you can double click on it to bring up the application that created it. Then only the application limits what you can do. OLE is very easy to work with. Developers implement OLE as a generic means to achieve the same goal, whereas APIs and DDE usually perform a variety of tasks in addition to object manipulation. Users do the actual embedding and linking through standard procedures that require only a few more clicks.

Big-name companies are making more of a commitment to imaging, too. For example, in August, 1993, Word-

Figure 3: These are three strategies for avoiding hardware and software conflicts in imaging systems.

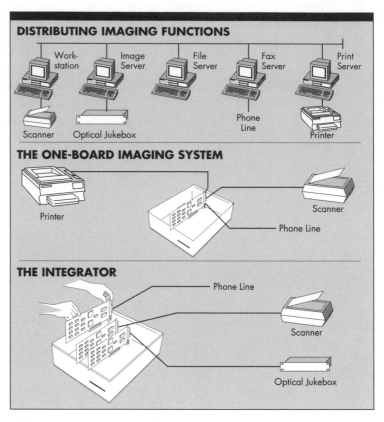

Perfect announced that WordPerfect Office will serve as a distribution vehicle for electronic images using OLE and DDE. Windows software products from four partners will take advantage of this capability:

KeyFile and PaperClip Imaging Software (Hackensack, NJ) both provide document-imaging and management software. Simplify Development's (Nashua, NH) MailRoom allows users to include document images in business communications using e-mail and computer-based fax. Watermark's (Burlington, MA) Watermark Discovery Edition enables users to incorporate images into any OLE-compliant Windows application and provides tools for viewing images and performing editing tasks such as annotation and highlighting. (Imagery Software of Bedford, MA, which was a partner, no longer sells to end users.)

Meanwhile, on the NOS side, Novell has partnered with Kodak to produce Image Enabled NetWare (IEN) for NetWare 4.0, a set of NLMs offering enhanced image-oriented

services such as storage and retrieval, indexing, and manipulation.

IEN will provide several benefits. Users will gain a richer imaging environment with more choices. They will be able to use imaging tools from various vendors with a single image database on the NetWare file server. This interoperability results from the fact that vendors use the same NetWare-based APIs to store, retrieve, and manipulate documents in the image library. IEN also defines the format of the image file, ensuring compatibility at that level.

In addition, because IEN supports multiple vendors simultaneously, users will be able to migrate more easily from one vendor to another.

With IEN providing the infrastructure, vendors can focus on higher levels of the application. Users will get more capable applications more quickly and at a lower cost. In addition, more vendors will be encouraged to enter the imaging market. And users will receive more stable platforms with ongoing support.

IEN's limitations in features, in single-server performance, and in capacity are not yet known. Some observers believe that, initially, IEN will be more suited to casual, ad hoc applications than heavy transaction-oriented ones.

Novell, however, says that IEN will be suitable for both kinds of applications. In any case, those interested in transaction-oriented processing can get around single-server performance and capacity limitations by storing images on multiple servers.

"Management of multiple databases, servers, storage resources, and security will be one of NetWare 4.0's strongest attributes," says Garron Bailey, principal consultant for imaging systems with Compulink.

Actually, even single-server capacity limits may not affect the majority of users, who need fewer than, say, 3 million documents. However, realistic limits on numbers of documents for IEN have not yet been established. (The beta version is not even available at this writing.)

NOT TO WORRY

One problem that users probably won't have to worry about is RAM requirements on the server. Some observers have fretted over the fact that, according to Novell documentation, a million files could require 144MB or RAM under NetWare 4.0, for example. Although some of today's higher-end servers and superservers, such as the Compaq SystemPro/XL, can support 144MB of RAM, the boxes and the RAM are expensive. Servers are, of course, always expanding RAM support. Today, however, we don't know of any that support more than about a gigabyte of RAM.

Still, thanks to a NetWare 4.0 facility called the Real-Time Data Migrator users need not worry too much about RAM considerations. The Real-Time Data Migrator allows for files to be stored without the RAM overhead of NetWare, according to Dave Lakness, vice president of engineering at Imagery. It avoids NetWare RAM requirements by storing the files on the file server without using the NetWare file service.

In addition, vendors can address the RAM problem. For instance, Micronet Software (Silver Spring, MD) is porting its O!V Document Management System to IEN. O!V manages images using object-oriented index struc-

tures that don't require any RAM and only 20B of disk space per object, says Harvey Fineman, president. However, disk storage is generally slower than RAM storage.

IEN performance will, of course, be highly dependent on hardware. I/O problems, for instance, can typically be solved with a good superserver and enough money. That being said, a point may come when the same performance can be attained more simply or more economically using a transaction-oriented system such as FileNet, IBM's ImagePlus, Recognition's Plexus, or ViewStar.

IEN's initial release may not include all the bells and whistles sophisticated users want. For instance, IEN does not provide *prefetching* services, which automatically move files from optical to magnetic media based on workers' upcoming requirements. Sources at Novell say implementation of many features will be left to third parties.

TAKING NOTES

Lotus Notes provides sophisticated information-management tools.

Lotus Notes 3.0, from Lotus Development (Cambridge, MA), is a sophisticated distributed information manager. It permits users to create and secure distributed databases, access them via customized forms, and link data from different databases into documents. Users can have multiple databases anywhere on the internetwork as a unified system. Notes provides extensive facilities for managing and replicating directories. It also includes a mail function.

But Lotus Notes is not for the meek–nor for the OS/2 novice. It's a complex program, with a very steep learning curve. The Notes Server runs on OS/2. Those not already familiar with OS/2 are really in for a learning experience.

And Notes is not for everyone. The software, equipment, installation, and learning time it requires are just too costly. However, for large or far-flung LANs, it's worth considering, especially if you already have OS/2 expertise. Just the ability to manage multiple databases under one platform is reason enough to consider Notes. However, for most small, geographically localized LANs, using Notes would be overkill.

DOING THE LN:DI

Lotus Notes:Document Imaging (LN:DI) is a Lotus

product licensed from Eastman Kodak. It comes with its own storage-management system, called Mass Storage (MSS). MSS resides on the Notes server and supports and manages various image media, including hard disks, removable optical drives, and jukeboxes.

MSS keeps track of document location as well as linking and embedding information. It also provides a staging area on the file server's hard drive, to provide quick access to recently used documents. MSS moves linked documents to the staging area, too, when you access a *container* document, one that contains linked or embedded documents. The MSS *migration manager* moves data from the staging area to the various storage media. User-defined rules govern when and where data moves.

Add a GammaLink fax card and Notes Fax Gateway Software from Lotus and you can send faxes. With the addition of Notes Incoming Fax Gateway software, you can also receive faxes on any LN:DI workstation.

You'll need a scanner on at least one workstation. You can then share that scanner with any other LN:DI workstation or use it as a standalone. A user must go to the shared scanner station to set up the scan, including specifying a mail recipient for scanned pages. You can first send pages to the optional OCR server, which resides on the Notes server, and then to any user.

INSTALLATION

Installing LN:DI is not a task for the average person. However, if you have already mastered OS/2 and Notes, you should be able to pull it off. It's all well explained in the 100-plus pages of the *Administrator's Guide*.

First, install named pipes, the protocol used by LN:DI to communicate between workstations and the MSS server. This task is complex enough to require 14 pages of instruction.

Next, install the MSS server software–another 12 pages. Proceed to the LN:DI incoming fax software, jukebox software (if needed), the OCR server, shared scanner, and client software. Finally, you are ready to test the connection between the client and the MSS server.

Each step is not all that difficult, but most steps will take time. Expect to spend time on the phone with support people. In addition, you will probably find it necessary to get a few update files from your NOS vendor.

USING LN:DI

LN:DI enables the user to add single or multipage image documents to Notes databases. The first step is to create an image document, either by receiving a fax, scanning, pasting from the Windows clipboard or importing TIFF or PCX (PC Paintbrush) files. Then the document must be linked or embedded, through Object Linking and Embedding (OLE), into a Notes document for storage.

Linked and embedded image documents appear in the container document as image icons. Clicking on an icon opens the associated image documents. However, Notes handles linking and embedding differently.

For linked documents, Notes stores only the link information in a database. The image document is stored outside Notes in the MSS. A linked document can be accessed by multiple users and can be modified when opened. In contrast, Notes stores the entire embedded document in a database as "read-only."

Users can add annotations, in the form of embedded objects, to image documents. You can access, edit, print, or fax an annotation by selecting the icon representing it. When printing or faxing a container document, you can print annotations as separate pages.

Annotations in LN:DI are linked text files. Contrast this setup with programs such as Watermark or WinFax Pro, which allow you to add highlighting or text that appears right on the page. While Notes annotations are fine for display on a screen, they don't work for receiving, modifying, and resending faxes.

RETRIEVING DOCUMENTS

You retrieve documents through Notes. The Notes administrator creates retrieval macros that you access through an easy-to-use graphical interface.

You can search documents using word searches (if the database has a full-text index), by form types, and with formula-based macros. For creating formula-based macros, Lotus Notes 3.0 supplies 100 different functions, including Boolean operators (for example, AND, OR, and NOT). Functions are fully described in 111 pages in the *Application Developer's Reference*.

Notes' search capabilities are competitive with those provided by other document-imaging systems and are easy to use, once the search macros have been created.

However, creating them takes administrator time and effort.

LN:DI is fully featured and performs all the functions of the best document-imaging programs. Its purchase price is attractive. In addition, Notes offers many unique features. However, labor costs for installation, administration, and training will discourage many users. We wouldn't install OS/2 and Notes just to get LN:DI. However, if you've already made a decision to use OS/2 and Notes, give LN:DI a look. Otherwise, look at the competition first.

The Paper Chase

DOCUMENT-IMAGING SYSTEMS OFFER MORE THAN THE KNOWLEDGE THAT YOU ARE HELPING TO SAVE TREES: THEY CAN MAKE SOUND BUSINESS SENSE.

BY DAN CARROLL AND MIKE HURWICZ

The idea of the paperless office has been around for a long time. And mostly, it's been just that–an idea. Every year, American offices devour 5 million to 6 million tons of paper for forms and repro-graphics such as plain-paper copying, according to the American Forest and Paper Association (New York and Washington, D.C.). Paper consumption in these areas is growing faster than the Gross Domestic Product (GDP), the AFPA says.

So, what's wrong with paper? For starters, consider the environmental impact of overharvesting trees.

In addition, the paper itself is expensive. Consider, too, the time it takes to file and retrieve it from filing cabinets, the time it takes to copy and fax it, and the storage space it requires. Paper is also prone to errors: It can easily be misfiled, lost, or destroyed. A spilled cup of coffee can render it illegible. Since several people usually can't read the same piece of paper at the same time, important documents are often copied over and over.

Many companies have addressed these problems–to some extent–through e-mail. They have eliminated many memos routed via paper mail and replaced them with e-mail messages routed across the network. Some e-mail programs support incoming and outgoing faxes and can incorporate images such as those created by scanners or by paint or draw programs.

For instance, you can scan a document, modify it, and e-mail it. Documents can be e-mailed to multiple recipients, viewed on the screen, and later deleted, all without using any paper.

However, e-mail usually lacks tools for working with images. E-mail programs seldom include functions for scanning images, for instance. Indexing of messages is usually limited, too; often, all you can do is put messages in different "folders."

E-mail presents a more basic problem: Each user manages his or her own messages, as if they were letters in a private mailbox. This private handling can be inefficient if many users need copies of the same documents. (Sometimes, behind the scenes, e-mail systems do store what appears to be multiple copies as a single copy. This method only works for users who share a single post office.) In addition, the private mailbox paradigm doesn't facilitate central administration. For example, no convenient way exists for a central administrator to deny a user access to a document once the user has received it as a message.

E-mail, because of shortcomings in a number of related areas–including image-related tools, indexing and retrieval, information sharing, and central administration–often doesn't fit all the needs of the office.

WHEN E-MAIL ISN'T ENOUGH

Databases can provide shared access to information, acting as a single filing cabinet that can be accessed by many users. Databases also offer centralized administration, flexible security, and excellent indexing. Many databases now support Binary Large Objects (BLOBs) such as scanned images and images imported from paint or draw programs. For example, in a personnel database, one of the fields in each record could be a picture of the person. You could search for the record based on the person's name, birth date, or any other information in the record. The data screen might include an icon of a face. Click on the icon to display the person's picture.

However, like e-mail programs, databases seldom integrate tools for working with images. Setting up a convenient system for accessing, faxing, and e-mailing scanned documents, for instance, would take a lot of custom programming.

Several tools exist for integrating images into Windows via Object Linking and Embedding (OLE). For example, Watermark document-image processing software from Watermark Software (Burlington, MA) enables users to embed image documents, such as faxes, invoices, and forms, into their e-mail or other Windows applications. The images, even after they've been embedded in other applications, can be stored, retrieved, and modified with Watermark's annotation tools. Watermark is inexpensive. Watermark Discovery Edition costs $149. Watermark Professional, to be available in the second half of 1993 for around $395, adds an image server which provides faster multiuser access to images and optical jukebox support.

Products such as Watermark basically allow you to click on an image icon in a Windows program to display an image. A document-imaging system, on the other hand, is a complete, integrated imaging environment. Basically a database of documents created by scanning or faxing or by software such as draw and paint programs, a networked document-imaging system consists of a server, usually with a scanner and a printer attached. The system may also include a shared fax board at the server. Documents may be stored on the imaging server or on a separate file server. Workstations may have no special hardware, but just software that allows them to access documents on the imaging server and print, send, and receive faxes–if the imaging system includes a fax function. Alternatively, workstations may also have scanners, so that users can duplicate or fax hardcopy without leaving their desks.

In addition to database-like features, such as indexing, centralized administration, and shared access to information, the document-imaging system offers integrated scanning and printing and perhaps integrated faxing, e-mail, and optical character recognition, all without custom programming.

Other Windows programs may be able to hook into document-imaging systems through Dynamic Data Exchange (DDE). For instance, Alacrity Systems' (Hackettstown, NJ) E-Quip document-imaging system offers a DDE programmer's toolkit. Using these tools, a programmer could make E-Quip into an imaging service for another program. For example, a database programmer could put menu items in the database to send and receive faxes through E-Quip.

Document-imaging systems can save paper, storage space, filing effort, and trips to the copy machine by making convenient the scanning of documents and their electronic storage and access. Even when they only automate operations that do use paper, such as printing, faxing, and copying, document-imaging systems save valuable employee time.

AT WHAT PRICE

Unfortunately, document-imaging programs can add significant costs to your operation, too. For example, magnetic information is vulnerable to different kinds of threats than is paper. A thief may be able to slip out with a 6-by-6-by-3-inch hard disk containing information that, in paper form, would fill a filing cabinet. So, you might want to consider extra security with your document-imaging system. A power spike can destroy magnetic information which, in paper form, would be safe from anything but a major fire or flood. So, you might want to consider off-site backup and/or nonmagnetic media such as optical disks.

As you convert more of your company's information into electronic form, a computer outage becomes a more serious problem. You might want to invest in fault-tolerant computer systems. Finally, working efficiently with images requires a fairly burly computer system. You may find that you need faster CPUs, larger screens, and bigger hard disks.

Then, of course, there's the cost of the document-imaging software and accompanying hardware, such as scanners. Not so long ago, you could barely touch a document-imaging system for less than $50,000. Most of the good ones were minicomputer- or mainframe-based. That's no longer true.

Now a number of popular document-imaging systems exist in the $25,000 to $50,000 range. Filenet (Costa Mesa, CA) is doing well with its WorkFlo Business System, which runs $50,000 and up per network. At the low end of the high end, Compulink Management Center (Torrance, CA) LaserFiche LAN costs between $495 and $37,495 per network.

These products, though they may have Windows and DOS versions, are likely to support Unix hosts, minicomputers, or mainframes. They may hook into heavy-duty database software, such as products from Oracle and Ingres.

Vendors sell these high-end systems based on their performance, scalability, integration with enterprise computing and communications systems, support for enterprise standards such as Structured Query Language (SQL), and a host of features, such as fast and sophisticated indexing and retrieval, document routing and workflow management, document annotation, and automatic archiving. In general, such programs require a technically sophisticated end user for successful deployment of a complex high-end document-imaging system.

AT THE LOW END

At the other end of the scale, however, is a burgeoning market in low-cost PC LAN-based document imaging. Currently nearly two dozen LAN-based document-imaging systems are available for about $10,000 or less. Some of these systems are versions of more expensive products, licensed for fewer users.

For instance, a five-user license for Advanced Technology Services (Atlanta) Optidoc 3.5 is $8,400. Icar 4.0 from Alared (Lakewood, NJ) costs $10,000 per network. Paper-Clip from PaperClip Imaging Software (Hackensack, NJ) costs $10,850 for five users, while PaperGate from ImageTech (Southfield, MI) costs $10,500 per network, and a two-user license costs $2,995. Cheaper still are programs such as SeaView from Science and Engineering Associates (Albuquerque, NM), at $6,450 for a five-user network, and

DMS Pro, from Van Der Roest Group (Santa Ana, CA), at $550 per network user.

But wait, there's less: FilePlus from Greengage Development (San Jose, CA) costs $1,995 per scan station and $295 per view station. QuickView Plus from Seabreeze Engineering Associates (Altamonte Springs, FL) costs $1,595 per network. Keyfile from the Nashua, NH company of the same name costs $2,995 for its workgroup edition and $4,995 for its OS/2 document-server Enterprise edition. VisagePro from Document Image Development (New York) costs just $1,495 per server, $295 for a retrieval station, and $795 for a scan-and-print station.

The low-cost programs typically run on PCs, under DOS or Windows or sometimes OS/2. They don't usually integrate with specific databases and may not support SQL access. Performance is geared toward the small workgroup with modest workloads.

Indexing and retrieval are likely to be simple. And such products may not offer such features as document routing, workflow management, document annotation, and automatic archiving.

What these low-end products do offer is a familiar environment, low-cost software and hardware, and– ideally– ease of use. They're designed with the budget and technical resources of the small office, workgroup, or department in mind.

The person who can set the jumpers on a network card or edit an initialization file in Windows should be able to install, configure, and manage most low-cost document-imaging systems.

Hungry for More

SATISFY YOUR USERS' CRAVINGS FOR DATA BY PROVIDING THEM WITH STORAGE THEY NEED VIA NETWORKED CD-ROMS

BY TOM HENDERSON AND TERRY HICKMAN

Our appetites for data are gargantuan, as are the capacities of CD-ROMs. You might be tempted to sate your users' desire for greater capacity by deploying CD-ROM drives in each network workstation, but that would add a linear cost per seat. Another temptation exists: to apply one of the cornerstone philosophies of networking–sharing peripherals and data access–to CD data and drives.

There are three methods of networking CD-ROMs. First, you can use network software that allows other users to access a workstation's CD-ROM drive. This method proved to be largely unusable: All the software we tried slowed the workstation–a 386/33 PC–considerably during CD-ROM drive access from other users. Perhaps a much more powerful PC would have the capacity to deliver CD-ROM data without such a hefty impact on workstation performance. Two methods remain: CD-ROMs may be networked through a network file server or through a standalone CD-ROM server. We examined both methods and their variants by evaluating products from four vendors–CBIS, Online Computer Systems, Meridian Data Systems, and Corel Systems.

A DIFFICULT DECISION

No other medium enables the transfer of up to 673MB of data between so many computers so handily. Still, deploying CD-ROMs as networked, shared devices has historically been a difficult decision for network designers and administrators to make and a difficult concept for vendors to grasp.

Microsoft's Multimedia Personal Computer (MPC) specifications require that the CD-ROM drive be connected locally to the workstation. To some vendors, sharing CD-ROM data natively across a network is a foreign concept, even an unnatural act.

Additionally, administrators' reluctance to network CD-ROMs also may have been exacerbated by the fact that CD-ROM technology was slow to take off, as well as its plain slowness. Sony's CD technology is only 11 years old–relatively young considering that most components in desktop computing have been around since the early 1970s. Additionally, as an online, random access device, the data CD is very slow when compared to hard disk technologies. The fastest CD-ROMs–those with an average access time of 230 milliseconds–are slower than all but the most sluggish of hard disks. Many CD-ROM drives are barely faster than floppy disk drives but are almost always faster than the near-line, non-random access tape drives.

All these factors lead to the conclusion that demand for CD-ROM drives will increase only with the demand for data and greater storage capacity. The large capacity of CD-ROMs initially caused the greatest excitement among database publishers, and the earliest implementers of CD-ROM technology were public librarians.

Today, the number of CD-ROM titles published is staggering. Seven new public titles appear daily. The CDs fall into six general categories: operating system/programming environments, databases, application software (especially graphical or statistical software), resource software (fonts as well as data not within database structures), reference software (books, magazines, and trade journals and publications), and games.

For some people, just the thought of having 600MB of randomly accessible, online data brings joy. For others, such as Ford Service Centers, the data replace stacks of manuals, and the information can be updated as soon as the latest CD arrives.

THE FINER POINTS

Of the four products we examined, two were freestanding CD-ROM servers–the one from Meridian Data Systems, which can also operate as a file server-based product, and the one from CBIS. Two were strictly file server-based products–the one from Corel and the one from Online.

Each product tested was easy to install. The performance, or speed of data access, appeared to be comparable among all the products, although we did not check this parameter quantitatively. If your usage is heavy, you should expect system performance degradation. Each of these products provides some form of caching and/or other performance enhancing scheme.

In short, there were no earth-shattering differences among the products; they all perform the basic job of networking CD-ROM service. But you are likely to select such products based on some of the more subtle differences in their features sets. We evaluated these products by paying close attention to the characteristics that seemed most likely to influence purchasing decisions. These characteristics include:

• platform support;
• ease of use;
• network operating system support;
• windows support;
• bundled utility functions;
• device driver type; and
• price per network user.

OTHER CONSIDERATIONS

Key to determining cost per seat is that CD-ROM software licensing agreements have a bit of catching up to do relative to their non-CD counterparts. Non-CD software typically allows you to monitor software usage, but not all CD-ROM packages provide this capability.

Most network application software has caught up to the network age: Network licenses are monitored not according to individual licensees but rather according to the number of concurrent users legally permitted under the licensing agreement. The initial network license costs some amount, and subsequent licenses cost some fraction of the initial cost–even less where the subsequent licenses don't include collaterals such as media or documentation.

But CD-ROM licenses have been slower to mature. Many disks are still distributed according to single-usage rules, and, naturally, licensing arrangements affect the cost per user. For this reason, and because piracy is now a felony, we considered the software's handling of licensing as an additional decision maker at the point of purchase.

MERIDIAN DATA SYSTEMS

The Meridian Data Systems software comes in two flavors: In one incarnation, it is a process in a Novell file server; in the other incarnation, it can be a NetBIOS-based standalone server. We loaded the software into the Beach Labs file server, a Compaq SystemPro LT running NetWare 3.11b. Connected to the server was an Online Systems' four-drive CD-ROM, SCSI-controlled subsystem.

Because Meridian's otherwise complete documentation contained no mention of what kind of hard disk controller could be used, we called technical support and discovered that the only currently supported hard disk controller was the Adaptec 15XX/17XX SCSI controller card. Luckily, we had one around. We used this hardware platform to test all NLM-based products.

Meridian's CD Net uses the popular Advanced SCSI Programming Interface (ASPI) software driver. The Meridian package requires that the CD-ROM subsystem attached to it have a Meridian ROM in its mouth during the boot-up process and only during boot up–an inconvenience for networks that restart more than once in a while. This requirement is also very inconvenient, even painful, for network administrators who work from remote locations. We expected broader SCSI adapter support. Once we determined which driver to use, the CD-ROM server came up.

Meridian software's distinguishing features start with the bundling of a DOS menuing system that comes in both character mode and Windows mode. This menuing system can help provide a script for launching the CD-ROM applications from a user-defined menu. The menu administration module guides a user through the process of defining exactly what happens when the user selects the option from the list. This feature is convenient for end users and adds a level of security to the network because it includes the capability to prevent users from escaping the menu system or rebooting the computer by typing <ESC>, <CTL>-C and <ALT>-<CTL>-<DEL> keystrokes. This feature would be useful where workstations are unattended, open to the public, and vulnerable to misuse as in libraries and self-service help desks.

The Windows software installs easily, providing a simple yet effective Windows menu system for accessing CDs in the drives.

Other software can control the doors on the drives so inquiring fingers won't purloin the CDs. The CD-ROM drive doors are locked upon insertion of a CD. To unlock the drive door and remove the CD, you must use Novell's MONITOR NLM or the Meridian utility–another inconvenience.

On the plus side, the Meridian software doesn't use the MSCDEX driver. Like the CBIS package, Meridian chose to save licensing costs by using a driver that's loadable and unloadable, rather than Microsoft's MSCDEX–a DOS device driver that cannot be unloaded. The capability to unload all relative modules from overcrowded workstation memory can be quite an attractive feature since it saves memory and helps eliminate potential conflicts. The alternative is to maintain different CONFIG.SYS files and to reboot the station after copying the correct one to the boot directory.

The documentation claims that the server software has cache and read-ahead algorithms that enhance overall throughput. Although we did not test this feature extensively, we are not convinced that caching may have much of an effect unless the CD-ROM data is read sequentially.

Similarly, the manual describes the software's load-balancing scheme as follows: "If the CD-ROM subsystem has two or more copies of the same CD, load balancing routes multiple user requests to the device that can process the read request the quickest." However, unless you have a protocol analyzer capable of debugging SCSI commands, you can't know for certain that this one is the activity taking place.

Overall, the Meridian manuals are very good at explaining each of the software commands, what they do, and what their correct syntax is–making customizing nearly foolproof.

As far as platform operability, at this writing, Meridian's software runs on NetWare and has a NetBIOS standalone server available. However, the company has announced that upcoming versions will include NetBIOS

support. And, the package has no provisions for license policing.

You pay slightly more per user with the Meridian package. In exchange, you get a high degree of customization, a convenient setup for Windows users, and a DOS device driver that can be removed from memory. This package looks like it was designed for the VAR or integrator–someone trying to pave a pretty bumpy road. Think of it as the Cadillac of the packages we tested.

COREL SYSTEMS

Although there are a few exceptions, virtually all CD-ROM drives are connected to PCs, Macintoshes, and their servers via the SCSI bus interface. Up to seven CD-ROMs can be cabled together and connected to a single SCSI controller card. But then a problem arises for DOS PCs–they run out of logical drive letters to associate with a physical drive. Most PC-based servers, therefore, use up to 24 drives, leaving drives A: and B: for floppy disk usage.

Corel's CD-ROM server software product is unique in that it is bundled with its universal SCSI device driver software, CorelSCSI. This software includes support for most types of SCSI devices, including disk and tape drives, CD-WORM drives, rewritable optical drives, scanners, printers, and optical jukeboxes. In addition, the package contains SCSI device testing and diagnostics, a tape backup program, and support for playing audio CDs.

An additional per-seat licensing fee of $5 is required for the use of Microsoft's MSCDEX.EXE. The need for MSCDEX.EXE also means that the workstation modules cannot be unloaded from memory.

Windows-based utilities enable you to manipulate the various aspects of the package's functions. The manuals are well written and provide useful information on all aspects of operation. The drive doors can be locked and unlocked via the utilities included.

The version of CorelSCSI tested runs under NetWare only. Concurrent license agreement enforcing is not automated.

The inclusion of such a wide variety of functions in an inexpensive package ($99 for a 100-user license) is attractive. If the Meridian product runs like a Cadillac, the Corel product resembles an economy car–it is an efficient and reliable package that doesn't exactly offer luxury but does provide a few niceties at a good price.

CBIS CD CONNECTION

The CBIS product is a standalone CD-ROM server system and as such requires a dedicated computer. CD Connection was installed on a CBIS CD-ROM server–essentially a 386/ 33, monochrome clone in a very large tower case that has many bays for CD-ROM drives. Our system contained three CD-ROM drives connected to one (included with the server) Advanced Storage Concepts' ASC-86 SCSI controller. We installed an SMC Ethernet NIC and NetWare IPX for network access. We tested all standalone products on this platform regardless of vendor.

The workstation was a 386DX/33 Beach clone with LSL.COM, IPXODI.COM, and NETX.COM on top of an NE2000 NIC over thin Ethernet. The software can run on six different networks: CBIS Network-OS Plus, Generic NetBIOS, Novell with NetBIOS, Novell IPX, Intel OpenNet, and Banyan VINES. The manual describes the installation procedure for each of these network types in adequate detail. You need to know the characteristics of the target network, although we changed very few of the system defaults, and everything worked just fine.

For our network, NetWare IPX, the server diskette contained DOS, the SCSI device driver, IPX.COM, and the CBIS software. The system must be able to connect and login to the network before attempting to use it as a CD-ROM server. The NIC must be installed, and the hardware and software must also be configured before you are up and running.

The CBIS product performed well. Once it was installed, we found logging in and accessing the data on the CD-ROMs to be easy and efficient. CBIS provides the server and workstation drivers, which can be unloaded from memory without rebooting.

CBIS does not provide Windows-based software, nor does it include provisions for automatically enforcing concurrent licensing agreements.

The documentation is concise and useful. A nice feature is the inclusion of technical bulletins on various hardware connectivity and software issues. Of particular importance are the bulletins providing information on integrating the product with Windows and the Macintosh. The manuals also provide an extensive description of the results of the company's testing of individual CD-ROM-based products. This application-specific information explains about the CD-ROM product and how to get it up and running on the CBIS CD-ROM server.

For the money, CBIS does not provide as much customization as the Meridian package. However, you have more flexibility in terms of the number of network platforms it works on, and the driver software is a little more robust, especially for Windows. The CBIS driver software has enhanced software resembling MSCDEX so you could run multiple concurrent animated CDs–and play three active games concurrently, for example.

ONLINE'S OPTI-NET

Online Computer Systems' Opti-Net comes in three flavors–NetBIOS, NLM, and VAP versions. We tested only the NetBIOS and NLM products. After installation, the products performed in a similar fashion. In fact, the workstation side of the system seemed to be exactly the same for both types of software.

We installed the NetBIOS version on the CBIS ROM server hardware described earlier. As with all the products, the installation required the creation of a server boot disk and workstation configuration. The installation software created batch files for both sides of the connection.

For the NLM software, we had an Online Systems' four CD-ROM SCSI subsystem attached to our file server. The NLM version of the software also guided us through the process. The NLM software generally has the familiar feel of Novell-supplied software such as SYSCON, MONITOR.NLM, and INSTALL.NLM. It provides the console operator the ability to check and modify network devices, attached users, and performance. Operation of the NLM is predictable and easy.

In general, the Online product behaved well. We encountered nothing spectacular or unusual during operation. The workstation software requires MSCDEX.EXE and allows you to unload programs for the workstation by way of a supplied utility program.

Online includes Windows support in the form of a utility for attaching to or detaching from an optical server, opening and closing databases, and querying the status of the CD-ROM databases. Using DOS CD-ROM applications from Windows requires the user to run TBMI.COM and TASKID.COM (provided) to allow the application to issue direct calls to IPX/SPX. Each time you run such an application, you must insert TASKID first, then remove it after termination. Although this process may seem like a pain, it is fairly easy to do via batch files and will be necessary for all DOS-based products. None of the other products' manuals covered this aspect of system operation.

Another bonus is that you can automate the policing of licenses by instructing the server software to limit the number of concurrent connections to individual CD-ROMs in the system.

The documentation is adequate and provides the user with all pertinent information on software installation and use. Extensive technical tips regarding known problems and system enhancement information are also included.

Online provides CD-ROM subsystems and other hardware and software products.

With network CD-ROM services, you can take many different directions to the same destination. In this evaluation, we found few actual functional differences between the packages. Sure, one CD-ROM server maker may have called its program OFRED and another maker may have called its software CFRED, but underneath, they are all FREDS. They all perform the basic job correctly. The major differences lie in where the program lives and in which frills it adds and leaves out.

Certainly, one tangible difference is in the CD-ROM server's cost per user. The cost of these products ranged from $100 per user to $6 per user. What you pay for within that range is the robustness of the software, its flexibility, and the number of platforms on which the product works.

Multimedia Mail

**NEW MULTIMEDIA MESSAGING STANDARDS AND INNOVATIONS
MEAN MORE POWER AND BETTER INTEROPERABILITY
FOR ENTERPRISE E-MAIL.**

BY NED FREED

Multimedia mail is rapidly becoming a fact of networking life. Workstation users are no longer satisfied with sending simple, plain-text messages. Now they want to send word processing files, spreadsheets, and other data files as e-mail messages. And they don't want to go through the hassle of manually encoding and decoding to reduce information to the plain ASCII text required by yesterday's mail systems.

Demand is also increasing for network applications that can support digital audio and video messages. In the best of all possible e-mail worlds, a user should be able to exchange multimedia business presentations that would be the envy of Cecil B. deMille, complete with PostScript text, video with accompanying audio, lots of fancy graphics, and spreadsheets.

If you are dealing with a single computing platform, such as PC or Macintosh, then you can always shop around for a platform-specific e-mail system sophisticated enough to meet your multimedia needs. But very few sites rely on only one computing technology and one set of network protocols. In today's world, you have to interconnect different workstations with different audio and display capabilities running different operating systems. This complexity requires a standards-based e-mail system. You need a common language to bring down this electronic tower of Babel. You need a protocol that provides a common thread, allowing you to exchange multimedia messages across disparate platforms.

YOURS AND MIME

The Multipurpose Internet Mail Extensions (MIME) standard was developed by the Internet Engineering Task Force (IETF) to address just this need. MIME was specifically created as a format for multipart/multimedia messages on the Internet, but it is rapidly gaining acceptance for use in enterprise networks. A number of vendors, including Frontier Technologies (Mequon, WI), Innosoft (West Covina, CA), and Z-Code Software (San Rafael, CA), among others, have incorporated MIME support into their commercial e-mail systems.. Users of their products can exchange multimedia messages with those on LAN and WAN infrastructures as well as across the Internet. And since MIME is an open standard, different MIME-capable e-mail packages can be installed to support different e-mail environments at any point in the network.

The advantages offered by MIME are virtually endless. Corporate users have already discovered that MIME is the perfect vehicle to ship binary files around the network. Consider, for example, that you have just finished your quarterly sales report, and you want to submit it to the vice president of sales and marketing. Rather than generating a printout with the appropriate spreadsheets and pie charts, you can format the document as a MIME message and send it electronically. The graphics files, spreadsheets, text, and even the PostScript formatting all remain intact and identifiable with a MIME-capable e-mail system.

MIME brings new muscle to e-mail, and it marks the beginning of a new age in electronic communication. Once MIME-capable e-mail systems become commonplace, other new technologies can emerge. These include active mail, which uses e-mail messages to initiate applications such as interactive electronic forms, and Electronic Data Interchange (EDI), which allows users to utilize e-mail for business transactions.

The advent of multimedia mail brings, of course, a range of new headaches as well. E-mail security becomes a bigger and more serious issue than ever before. Network administrators also have to start thinking seriously about how they want to enable multimedia mail for their users and what impact lots of large multimedia messages will have on their networks.

But before taking a look at the future possibilities and problems presented by multimedia mail, let's consider the state of the MIME standard and explore the multimedia options currently available to network administrators.

THE BIRTH OF MIME

The MIME standard has been proliferating steadily since it was first issued as a Request for Comment (RFC) by the IETF in June 1992. MIME has been approved as two draft standards by the IETF: RFC 1521 and RFC 1522. Virtually all vendors interested in e-mail are beginning to embrace these new standards.

What exactly does MIME offer to the network user? MIME provides a standardized way to define multipart/multimedia messages, so different types of formatted message data can be sent across any computer network, including the Internet, without losing structure or formatting information. For example, MIME makes it possible to send PostScript images, binary files, audio messages, and digital video across IP-based networks either as standalone messages or as individual parts of a multipart message. For example, a user can send a video message with accompanying audio and a plain text transcript.

Since MIME was designed to be an Internet standard, it has to support all sorts of message types as they pass through the transports and gateways that make up the links of the Internet. So MIME was written as an extension to RFC 822, the current Internet e-mail message format standard. RFC 822 specifies that Internet mail messages use the ASCII character set. And like all RFC 822 messages, the content of MIME messages can be limited to relatively short lines of seven-bit ASCII. Nontext data, then, has to be converted to ASCII characters of seven-bit bytes before they can be transmitted over the network. This conversion is usually done automatically.

If all types of mail messages–text, PostScript, audio, and video–are reduced to the same kind of seven-bit ASCII data, the mail system has to have a way to determine what kind of message format is being sent or received. The MIME standard uses RFC 822-style headers to describe different message types and different multimedia body parts, so the mail system can properly interpret each part of the e-mail message and assemble and present the pieces correctly.

The MIME specification defines four different header fields:

• A MIME-Version header, which labels a message as MIME-conformant. This header allows different MIME-aware mail user agents to process the message appropriately.

• A Content-Type header field, which is used to specify the data types within the message. Within the Content-Type header are various fields used to describe different message types and subtypes. There is a "text" type, a "multipart" type (for multiple parts in a single message), an "application" type (for data shared between applications, such as a spreadsheet), a "message" type (for encapsulated mail messages), an "image" type, an "audio" type, and a "video" type.

• A Content-Transfer-Encoding header field, which can be used to specify the encoding used to get the message through a given message transport, such as the Internet.

• Two optional header fields, a Content-ID and a Content-Description header, which serve to label and identify the data in the message.

MIME DELIVERS

MIME was really designed to be an information delivery mechanism. Specifically, it is a standardized way to identify different types of messages using headers to label and describe different message types and different parts of a multipart/multimedia e-mail message. Although this labeling sounds simple enough, the framework created by MIME opens up an entire realm of new possibilities for e-mail.

For example, IETF committees are currently working on specifications for multinational character sets. With such character definitions in place, e-mail correspondents will be able to exchange mail in Swedish, Korean, Japanese, Vietnamese, Russian, or other languages using much broader character repetoires than ASCII provides. And since each of these definitions is defined within the MIME framework, they are encompassed by the MIME standard and can be specified using MIME headers.

Figure 1. Unlike conventional e-mail agents, a MIME User Agent (UA) includes a parser, which identifies message components, and a dispatcher, which forwards those components to the appropriate display device.

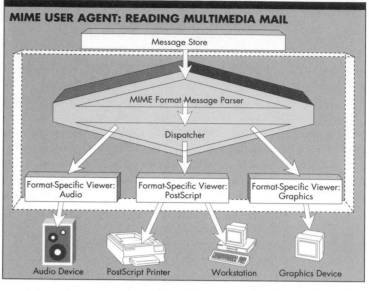

Another group is working with MIME to create a set of definitions for e-mail audio types that would be compatible with most phone messaging systems. These definitions would create a set of compressed audio types that would be ideal for applications such as voice mail, where audio fidelity is not a major issue. Once these definitions are in place, we will see e-mail systems emerge that are capable of interfacing with voice mail systems, sending and receiving e-mail as voice mail.

Remote printing is another potential application. For example, an additional image subtype based on the TIFF specification has been developed, enabling users to send e-mail messages to remote printers, including fax machines.

Another specification for vector graphics is being developed to allow users to transmit critical drawings, such as schematics and blueprints, as e-mail. Another group is working on rich text and related formats specifically for the Windows environment. And other groups are developing MIME definitions for proprietary document formats, such as WordPerfect. The possibilities seem to be nearly endless.

AN EXTENSIBLE USER AGENT

No matter what specific support definitions emerge, MIME's power is in its ability to support different types of e-mail transmissions across disparate computing platforms. Some of the MIME-capable e-mail products starting to emerge, such as Innosoft's PMDF e-Mail Interconnect 4.3 and Z-Code Software's Z-Mail 3.0, are using MIME as a canonical or intermediary format to handle message conversion. In these systems, a message can be received by a MIME e-mail system in any format, converted to a MIME message, then reconverted to any other e-mail format. For example, an incoming cc:Mail message is converted to MIME, then reconverted from MIME to DEC's Message Router format for receipt without losing data. Since MIME is capable of dealing with any kind of electronic message, MIME is an ideal intermediate format for gateways.

Some MIME-capable e-mail systems can also be configured to convert the actual contents of MIME messages. For example, the Conversion Channel in PMDF can tell the difference between spreadsheets, graphics, files, and word processing documents sent as e-mail using the MIME headers. The Conversion Channel can then call on a conversion library, such as Digital's Compound Document Architecture (CDA) Converter Library, to automatically translate messages to a different format. For example, an incoming Lotus 1-2-3 spreadsheet could be automatically translated into a Microsoft Excel spreadsheet.

The real cornerstone of any MIME-based mail system is the MIME-capable mail user agent (MIME UA). In fact, the MIME standard describes how mail user agents identify different message types, so the user's mail interface

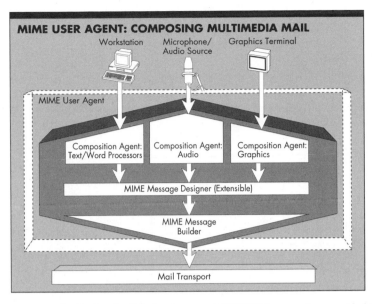

Figure 2. To create MIME messages, the Message Designer calls various composition agents to build a multimedia message.

can properly display the data for the user. A MIME UA can handle complex multipart messages, regardless of the mail transport agent, computer operating system, or network operating system. The trick, however, is finding a MIME-compatible user agent that is not only MIME-aware (able to interpret incoming MIME messages) but also MIME-capable (able to create as well as read MIME e-mail messages).

A MIME UA differs from a conventional mail user agent. Where most mail agents have a simple viewer to display text e-mail messages, the MIME UA has a MIME parser and a dispatcher (see Figure 1). To display a multipart/multimedia message, the MIME UA first passes the message through a parser, which identifies the different components of the message from the header information. The UA's dispatcher then accesses a specific viewer for each message type, specifying output as a graphic, text, PostScript, and so forth. MIME capabilities can also be added to an existing e-mail user agent, or you can install a new user agent that has MIME support built-in.

The MIME UA offers the user real advantages because it means his or her MIME-compatible e-mail package can be extended easily. For example, to support new image formats, the user can purchase new viewer software and then tell the MIME UA how and when to call it; you don't have to buy a new user agent, as would be the case with a conventional e-mail system. Furthermore, add-on viewers can

be provided by virtually any vendor. So as your needs change and expand, your multimedia e-mail support can change and expand as well.

IF YOU BUILD IT

To create MIME-compatible e-mail messages, the MIME UA uses a MIME Message Builder, which communicates with the mail transport system and a Message Designer to assemble the parts of the MIME message (see Figure 2). The Message Builder uses different composition agents called by the MIME Message Designer. The idea is that you tell the Designer what you want to build, and it, in turn, calls the various available composition agents to build a MIME e-mail message. For example, to create audio messages, the composition agent may provide an interface to a microphone, or to create graphic messages the composition agent may interface to a graphics terminal. And since the Message Designer is extensible, you can add composition agents to support almost anything–MacPaint, Microsoft Word, Lotus 1-2-3.

When shopping for a MIME e-mail system, remember that creating a user agent that can compose MIME messages is much more difficult than creating a MIME-aware user agent that can simply read MIME messages. Ultimately, if you are building really complicated, interactive messages, you will stretch the capabilities of any MIME

Figure 3. By creating a MIME-capable e-mail enclave, you can add a multimedia interface to your existing e-mail system.

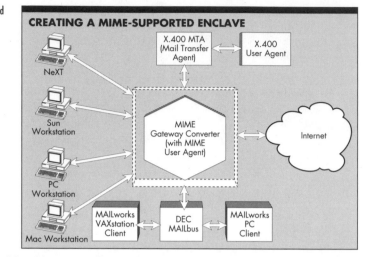

user agent. No MIME Message Design Tool will be able to write programs for you, and this kind of message is really a kind of program. However, the MIME UA model does work as a simple programming language and lets you compose simple multimedia messages, making it something akin to a fifth-generation programming language.

ADDING MIME SUPPORT

If you already have an existing proprietary, multimedia-capable, e-mail system such as NeXTMail, Microsoft Mail, cc:Mail, or QuickMail, then you can add MIME support to your system using an enclave approach (see Figure 3). The universal problem with proprietary multimedia mail packages is message format compatibility. If you are using Microsoft Mail, for example, and you need to send multimedia messages over the Internet, there is no guarantee the recipient is using the same sort of system with the same e-mail software or viewing capabilites. And even if they have the same system, the Internet mail infrastructure won't be able to support the binary structure of Microsoft Mail attachments. Without the MIME infrastructure to package the message, that message can no longer be either transportable or decipherable.

The solution is to create an e-mail enclave by installing a MIME-capable e-mail gateway between the local workstations and the WAN or Internet mail transport. The MIME gateway would be responsible for converting all e-mail messages to and from MIME. The MIME e-mail gateway can act as a repository of all knowledge about the e-

mail system. For example, if you are supporting cc:Mail users, then the gateway knows how to handle incoming MIME messages to make them compatible with cc:Mail.

The enclave design offers some real advantages. Since the gateway acts as the repository of all local e-mail knowledge, it can also be configured to act as an e-mail converter system. Converter libraries can be installed on the gateway to handle conversion of both message formatting and content. If you have a user registered with the gateway who prefers to receive text as Microsoft Word files, for example, the gateway can be programmed with that information, and incoming text messages are automatically converted from their original format, say WordPerfect, to Microsoft Word before they are forwarded to that registered user. Similarly, incoming Lotus 1-2-3 spreadsheets can be received as MIME messages by the gateway, then converted to Microsoft Excel before they are forwarded.

The enclave concept is finding its way into many computer networks as an interim solution, but it may also offer advantages for the long term. It has the advantage of looking to the past, allowing the user to leverage the software and file formats already installed on the network. It also looks to the future, allowing the user to more easily extend the e-mail infrastructure as new formats proliferate. Just as the MIME user agent is extensible to support different multimedia viewers, a MIME-capable e-mail gateway can be set up with conversion libraries to make it extensible to support multiple proprietary formats. A network no longer has to offer universal coverage of all known e-mail formats. As the world of e-mail becomes more complex, this modular approach allows the administrator to specify filters for incoming messages, so those messages can be read easily by local users.

For the enclave premise to be practical, it has to be tied to a directory of information where user preferences can be registered and stored. There are two logical models to register user preferences: You can either give everyone free choice with regard to e-mail formats, or you can provide preference templates that limit the selection to specific formats.

If you run the network at a small high-tech company with 25 employees, then per-user selectability makes sense, since each user has specific technical needs and preferences that should be addressed. If you have a company with 200,000 employees, then the preferences available for word processing software will be limited, and the cookie-cutter approach offered by templates is clearly more practical and cost-effective.

The use of preference templates allows you to limit the choice of e-mail conversion formats to reflect available computing resources. For example, if the accounting department is all PC-based and only uses WordPerfect, then you can direct them to register for e-mail services using WordPerfect templates for PC services only. So by using templates, you can limit the users' e-mail format choices to a specific set of conversion parameters.

Some software products currently available, such as MAILbus Conversion Manager from Digital Equipment, allow the system administrator to create specific e-mail templates for different groups of users. Unfortunately, such approaches are complex and difficult to use with large user populations. Most likely, user preferences will eventually be registered in the X.500 directory.

Developed as a part of OSI, X.500 was designed to handle large applications with decentralized directories that reside on servers scattered throughout the network. These directory servers periodically exchange information about their users to keep directory information current. The advantage of using X.500 services as a basis for creating e-mail registration templates is that X.500 is a network standard, which means it is platform-independent and, like MIME, extensible. MIME-capable channels can be added to X.500 directory services easily, so when a user browses the e-mail directory for an address, the user not only gets

an e-mail address for the recipient but also could receive a GIF or TIFF picture as a MIME message as well.

No matter which model you choose when creating your e-mail system, adopting MIME as the messaging format allows the system to become extensible, so it can embrace virtually any new format or mail system. MIME's modular architecture makes it relatively easy to add new e-mail channels and format conversion channels without having to migrate to an entirely new e-mail platform. And the MIME architecture paves the way for other e-mail possibilities as well.

INTERACTIVE MULTIMEDIA E-MAIL

One of the challenges with MIME is that multimedia messages become quite large, and not all users will have the computing power needed to read every part of a MIME message. What if you are a PC user who receives a MIME message consisting of plain text, spreadsheets, audio, and video parts? Unless you have the right hardware and software, you won't be able to view the audio and video segments; but the text and spreadsheet body parts may be meaningful to you. Rather than trying to break the message apart yourself, you could use a client-server e-mail approach and access only those parts of the message you want.

The Interactive Mail Access Protocol (IMAP), as specified in RFC 1176, is designed to support just this kind of client-server e-mail environment. The concept behind IMAP is that large messages should be handled by powerful server systems, and clients should have to run only lightweight e-mail agents to access those message parts they can handle. So smaller workstation systems, such as PCs, don't have to process unnecessary e-mail and large blocks of data that are meaningless to them.

Compared to the MIME user agent model, IMAP offers a more primitive method for users to filter their own MIME messages. Since IMAP lets users preview a message's structure before they receive it, and since MIME messages are clearly described by MIME headers, users can simply access the header information, then determine which parts of the message they want to receive. This option is particularly valuable for users who access e-mail from multiple locations. For example, if the IMAP server is configured to send multimedia messages to the Sun workstation in your office, but you are accessing e-mail from your laptop at home, you can manually filter the message beforehand, access the text messages you can read on the laptop, and save the multimedia portions for review on the Sun in the office.

ACTIVE MAIL

Now that MIME offers the ability to send binary files in a uniform fashion around local and wide area networks and the Internet, new possibilities, such as enabled or active mail, become available. Enabled mail implements additional processing at different stages in the e-mail process. The enabled mail model becomes clearer if you visualize it as three distinct processes: delivery time, the point at which e-mail reaches the recipient's delivery system; receipt time, the point at which e-mail crosses the threshold into the delivery system; and activation time, the point at which the recipient actually reads the message. Proprietary e-mail systems that support enabled mail have their own scripting languages to create specified computational processes that are executed when the mail message is received.

Enabled mail brings in the concept of active mail. Traditionally, e-mail, including multimedia mail, has been passive–messages are received and displayed by the recipient. With *active mail*, a message can contain a program that can be executed when the recipient reads it. Of course, the potential offered by active mail could be a godsend to some users, providing an easy way to handle bug fixes or provide remote activation of everyday computing services, such as system backup. It could also prove to be a nightmare, giving malevolent outsiders another means to attack your computer system.

MAIL FRAUD

Clearly, some specific issues have to be addressed to make active mail workable. First is the security issue. A means has to be defined to read any active mail message without doing potential harm to a user's system. For example, if you open an anonymous active mail message, you don't want to trigger a bad reaction, such as erasing your hard drive or sending vital files across the Internet.

Work is currently under way to define e-mail languages that would support safe active mail transactions. Put simply, these mail languages would remove any features that could do potential harm to a computer system and replace those functions with new primitives that allow only lim-

ited operations on public files. By replacing general-language primitives with safe primitives, the active mail environment can be rendered safe for general applications.

A number of proprietary e-mail programming languages have evolved, as well as one or two more general languages. Safe-TCL was jointly developed by Nathaniel Borenstein of Bellcore (Morristown, NJ) and Marhsall Rose of Dover Beach Consulting (Mountain View, CA) as a base language with the syntax to support many enabled mail primitives. The authors say that Safe-TCL is sufficiently secure, with safe primitives that are powerful enough to support most active mail applications. Safe-TCL also has the added advantages of being extensible and portable, so it can support a variety of functions on multiple mail platforms.

Once a universal e-mail language has been defined, MIME messages can be incorporated into active mail via a relatively simple process. Binary files for applications can be sent along with execution instructions written in active mail. As a simple example, consider an interactive birthday card delivered in something akin to Safe-TCL and MIME. When opened, the active mail language instructs the computer to activate the audio and video readers on the recipient's workstation and then automatically accesses the audio and video MIME messages enclosed to show the sender singing "Happy Birthday."

ELECTRONIC DATA INTERCHANGE

Another e-mail technology that can take advantage of MIME is EDI. EDI is actually much further along in the development process than enabled mail. Defined by both the ANSI EDIFACT and OSI X.12 standards, EDI provides a standardized way to set up electronic forms. Many companies are exploring EDI applications to support computerized purchase orders, employee review forms, insurance claim forms, and other applications where a user can effectively fill in blanks on an electronic form.

EDI itself doesn't define the actual appearance of the form but rather the meaning associated with each field in the form, such as which field is a part number and which field is a unit price. Once the information is entered, it is sent to a central location for processing. The information is usually transferred as a batch process, and it can be sent to a local EDI server, or it can be sent to a remote location as e-mail.

MIME becomes an important part of the EDI infrastructure, since with a MIME-capable e-mail gateway, EDI-formatted information can pass unscathed through the e-mail infrastructure. MIME recognizes EDI data just as it handles any other kind of specially formatted information.

GET THE MESSAGE

With all these potentialities, multimedia mail is at the forefront of a whole new way of thinking about electronic messaging. Today's MIME-compatible e-mail systems offer users a range of new applications for e-mail. And the beauty of MIME is that it is an industry standard; it's extensible and modular and can be retrofitted to most existing e-mail infrastructures. MIME is an enabling technology that can be used as a basis for a whole host of exciting new applications. Once multimedia messaging becomes commonplace, the possibilities for extensive e-mail applications seem almost infinite.

MIME-capable E-mail Systems

The following products currently support the Multipurpose Internet Mail Extensions (MIME) standard. Note that other MIME-ready e-mail systems are being developed, so this list is not comprehensive.

Frontier Technologies
10201 N. Port Washington Rd.
Mequon, WI 53092
(414) 241-4555
Super-TCP/NFS for Windows

Developed for the PC platform, specifically Microsoft Windows, Super-TCP/NFS includes a MIME-capable e-mail handler as part of its e-mail support. The same e-mail package includes support for SMTP, POP 2, and POP 3, and has distribution lists, address books, and automatic forwarding.

Hewlett-Packard
19310 Pruneridge Ave.
Cupertino, CA 95014
(800) 752-0900
MPower

MPower is a suite of collaborative multimedia tools for Unix (specifically HP-UX) developed to run on HP Series 700 workstations, Series 800 multiuser systems, and X terminals. Included is the MPower mailer that uses the Unix sendmail command and includes support for MIME.

Innosoft International
1050 East Garvey Ave. S.
West Covina, CA 91793
(800) 552-5444
PMDF e-Mail Interconnect V4.3

Developed to run on the Digital OpenVMS and OSF/1 platforms, PMDF was the first commercial e-mail distribution and routing system to incorporate MIME. Building on the MIME-capable PMDF user agent, PMDF has e-mail channels to interconnect a wide range of messaging systems, including cc:Mail, All-in-One, VMSMail, SMTP, and Novell's MHS. Support packages are also available to connect to Digital's Message Router and X.400 systems and to provide e-mail-to-fax services.

International Messaging Associates
1389 Mitchell Ave., Suite 102
South San Francisco, CA 94080
(415) 871-4045
Internet Exchange for cc:Mail

IMA's Internet Exchange for cc:Mail is a cc:Mail-to-SMTP/MIME Internet mail gateway that runs under Windows 3.1. It was specifically developed to provide a standards-based multimedia connection between cc:Mail and SMTP, giving e-mail users a means to exchange multimedia messages with the Internet.

Z-Code Software
4340 Redwood Hwy., Suite B-50
San Rafael, CA 94903
(415) 499-8649
Z-Mail 3.0

Z-Mail 3.0 is a Unix-based e-mail system that includes full MIME support. MIME messages can be passed through both SMTP and X.400 transport protocols and gateways. In its current release, Z-Mail also supports Motive 1.2 and has added features, such as directory services.

High School Goes Prime Time

IN RURAL OKLAHOMA, SCHOOLS BREAK GROUND WITH THEIR USE OF INTERACTIVE MULTIMEDIA

BY LESLIE GOFF

Television in the classroom used to mean sitting and watching a PBS-produced music or art lesson while your real teacher graded papers, but today, thanks to fiber-optic networks, TV is transforming the classroom. The ability to send large amounts of video and audio is making possible one of the biggest revolutions in modern education: distance learning.

Distance learning, like business teleconferencing, provides a two-way channel for teachers and students in separate locations to interact. Applications range from voice-only to full multimedia so teachers and students in several different locations can see and hear each other.

For the rural school systems using the technology, distance learning pushes the envelope of courses available to students and the community at large without straining staff and other resources. The importance of distance-learning technologies can be seen in the Grady County Public Schools in South Central Oklahoma, where a 50-mile fiber optic-based interactive network has enabled the five participating schools to meet the requirements of the Oklahoma Education Reform Act (see Figure 1).

The act, passed in 1991, mandates that schools widen their curriculums with more of the advanced coursework needed for acceptance into four-year colleges and universities. However, in Grady County, and rural areas like it, where the entire student body may comprise as few as 400 students, courses such as calculus draw such low enrollments that offering them is not cost-effective.

"If I have three students who want calculus, I have the option of hiring a teacher for it, which would be about $18,000 a year," explains George Tiner, assistant superintendent for the Canadian Valley Area Vo-Tech school in Chickasha, OK, "or, for about $17,000 a year, we can lease the lines for the fiber-optic network and have access to many other teachers without any additional staff costs."

But by pooling their resources, sharing staff and courses over the network– known as the Grady County Interactive Educational Television Network (IETN)–the schools are providing German I and German II, Spanish, psychology, art, calculus, and trigonometry–courses that were impossible to offer before because of small class sizes.

Tiner says, "We offered some of these classes before, such as trigonometry, but the class size would vary, and it just wasn't economically viable."

Moreover, the network provides increased flexibility for students who want to attend half-days at Canadian Valley Area Vo-Tech. Before, schedule conflicts prohibited many students from exercising this option if it meant they would miss a required academic class such as English. Now, over the network, an additional English class is available.

"We knew the network would allow us to meet the needs we had identified–the ability to broaden our course offerings, to better schedule classes, and eventually, to offer classes back to the community," Tiner says.

IETN, which encompasses the Vo-Tech school and the high schools in the towns of Alex, Amber-Pocasset, Ninnekah, and Rush Springs, is serving some 128 students in its first year and will likely expand next year to include the Grady County community at large, which will hook in through the local cable-television network. Plans are to provide one-way viewing with interactive audio over the phone, Tiner says.

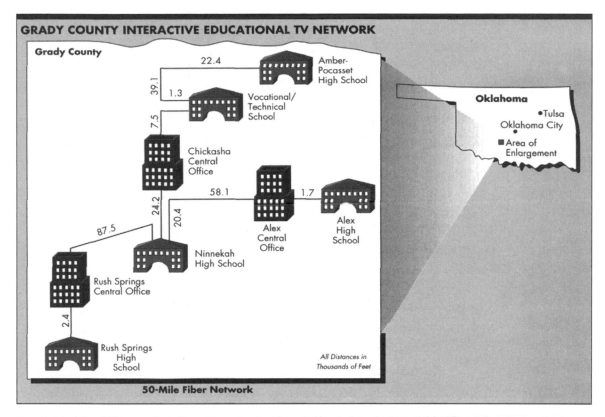

GRADY COUNTY INTERACTIVE EDUCATIONAL TV NETWORK

50-Mile Fiber Network

Figure 1. In South Central Oklahoma, a 50-mile fiber-optic interactive network has enabled five schools to widen their curriculums with more advanced coursework.

Southwestern Bell (St. Louis) built the fiber-optic network and provides turnkey services to the schools, including network design, equipment procurement, engineering, installation, training, ongoing maintenance and repair, and the transmission link.

The network is a single-mode wide-bandwidth fiber multichannel transmission system that allows video, data, voice, and fax signals to be combined on one optical wavelength, says Conti Roberts, senior design consultant for Southwestern Bell in Oklahoma City. Roberts, along with Steve Curry, the company's area representative, oversaw the Grady County project.

Each school is equipped with one send and three receive channels, so up to four classrooms can interact at once.

"A teacher couldn't logically handle more than four classrooms at once," Roberts says. "It's a de facto standard for the other distance-learning networks we've installed."

In fact, the state limits classroom sizes on distance-learning networks to 10 students at any given site and 25 students total across all sites, an adequate number, Tiner says.

"We want the teacher to feel that he or she can effectively deal with the size," he adds. "That's more important when you're introducing new teaching methods."

LIVE, IT'S CALCULUS

The analog system that carries the video and audio from the live classroom to the remote classrooms uses 7MHz of bandwidth, which is equivalent to a digital transmission of 45Kbps, Roberts says, adding, "There's no compression so it's just like live TV, which the kids were surprised to see. There's no degradation of the video signal."

Southwestern Bell subcontracted the analog transmission system, dubbed the FN6000, from American Lightwave Systems (Meriden, CT). The FN6000 architecture is comprised of plug-in modules for mix-and-match transmission capabilities that can be altered to suit individual needs. This equipment, including lightwave transmitters and receivers, video modulators and demodulators that carry the signals, audio and data modems, power supplies, and network-management hardware and software, resides in a cabinet at the back of each remote classroom, where the fiber terminates. The cabinet also houses the TV and VCR hook-ups.

The heart of the system lies in the five dedicated remote classrooms—one at each school—each of which is equipped with eight TV monitors, three cameras, five microphones and a lapel mike, speakers, a fax machine, a VCR, a camera control panel, and an Elmo EV308 Visual Presenter, a portable document stand with its own camera that serves the same function as a blackboard (see Figure 2). Ford Audio-Video Services (Oklahoma City, OK) provided all of the classroom hardware except the VCRs and fax machines, which each school purchased through its own educational-products vendors.

SAY "CHEESE"

Three of the monitors let the teacher see the students at each of the three remote classrooms. Three others enable the students to see each other in each classroom. The remaining two allow the students to view the teacher and what he or she is writing on the Elmo document stand. Two of the three cameras are focused on the teacher and the students, respectively, and the Elmo has its own camera mounted over the board on which the teacher writes.

The fax machine is used to send and receive homework, quizzes, and tests, while the VCR records presentations for students who miss class. Taped classes also enable students to review material, and they serve to record discipline problems.

Teachers can operate the VCRs in each remote classroom from a central control panel in the live classroom, a feature that helps maintain order without having an adult supervisor in each class. For instance, if a student is disruptive and fails to heed the teacher's warning, the teacher can turn on the VCR remotely and record the incident.

AIN'T MISBEHAVIN'

"They don't realize how sensitive the system is," says Lori Howell, a teacher at Alex High School, who teaches a psychology class over the network. "The first day of school, I recorded the classes and played it [the tape] back for the students so they would know they can be monitored. We don't tolerate much misbehavior. If problems continue, we recommend them to another class."

The principal at each school on the network also has a monitor, so teachers can ask them to observe discipline problems and intervene. The principal, after checking the monitor, can then go to the classroom or speak to the student over the intercom system.

While the Orwellian feel of the monitoring system is not lost on the administrators, as Tiner points out, "We were concerned about providing a classroom with a good learning environment. Part of that is controlling the environment with discipline."

A teacher also can use the control panel to operate the cameras in his or her classroom. For instance, teachers can pan the classroom, zoom in on a student who's speaking, or tilt a camera for a better angle. Next year, the schools want to add the capability to control the cameras in the remote classrooms, as well, which would further increase a teacher's ability to maintain discipline, since now students are able to inch out of camera range. The control panel also has an antifeedback feature so the sound in each classroom can be monitored with maximum efficiency.

Implementing a technology—such as an interactive distance-learning network—that so radically alters a process presents many management hurdles, including consistent class scheduling, establishing procedures for substitute teachers, mastering the technology, and meeting the costs.

INVESTING IN EDUCATION

"We were unable to find any outside funds within the timeframe that we needed them," Tiner says, "so all of it was funded by the schools and by a $40,000 grant from the State Department of Education that went back to the schools to offset expenses."

Each school paid for its own classroom, which cost $32,000 each to equip. All five schools share the cost of leasing the fiber-optic lines—two cables providing a total of 16 channels—which is $1,450 per month fixed over a 10-year period, a special rate for the education market. Roberts estimates that the typical commercial lease would be in the ballpark of $1,700 per month. At the end of the lease, the schools will renegotiate a usage fee with Southwestern Bell.

"Laying the cable incurred the biggest cost," Roberts says. "But we know schools are on a limited budget, so, basically, we developed a special price for the education market."

Compared, however, with the cost of hiring the additional staff at each school to teach the extra courses being offered this year, the network is paying for itself, Tiner says.

"It is one of the best things to come along in years for schools of our size," says Rocky Stone, superintendent of the Ninnekah Public Schools. "Without it, it would be very difficult to offer the things that we will have to offer in the next few years. It wouldn't be feasible."

Southwestern Bell was already laying fiber-optic cable for long-distance service in the area when approached by administrators to build the interactive network, Roberts says. The company then proceeded to lay a loop in every town from the central office to the school, and, to lay brand-new fiber to Alex and Rush Springs. "We're trying to lay fiber proactively in rural communities," Roberts says, "but in this case, we got a request for service."

The company already had implemented numerous similar systems across Arkansas, Texas, and Kansas, proving that necessity is the mother of invention. Rural areas are leading the rest of the country in establishing distance-learning networks, noted Gerry Segal, director of College Systems for the Bank Street College of Education in New York. Bank Street has been progressive in the research and use of multimedia technologies in education.

"It is one of the few areas where being rural is being at the forefront," Segal says. "Especially in Canada and Alaska, they've been doing it for years [using satellite dishes] because of the need to reach sparse populations and not having the resources to do it."

Canada, for instance, has a 30-year or longer history of using satellite-based distance-learning networks to deliver noninteractive audio and video to remote areas, Segal says. The advantage of laying fiber-optic networks in rural areas is the ability to transform distance learning into an interactive environment.

Tiner says he first learned about interactive distance-learning networks at a conference on technological innovations in education. Later, he saw a network in action that Southwestern Bell had set up for a Texas school district.

"I sat on it for about a year, but in the process of monthly meetings with other school superintendents, I brought it up," he says. "Then we began a joint effort of talking about what we wanted and where to find it."

Tiner knew Southwestern Bell was already laying fiber-optic cable in the area and was personally acquainted with Curry, the company's Oklahoma City representative. Curry put him in touch with educators in South Central Kansas who were already using a 141-mile fiber-optic distance-learning network to link students and teachers at Cowley County Community College with four Kansas high schools in Caldwell, Conway Springs, Oxford, and Udall.

"We spent a day there looking at the system, visiting with teachers and students," Tiner says. "It was helpful in understanding the system's actual capabilities."

COOPERATION AND COMMITMENT

Tiner and the other four school superintendents—Stone of Ninnekah; Vernon Florence, superintendent of the Alex Public Schools; W.L. Jackson, superintendent of the Amber-Pocasset schools; and Roy LeMar, superintendent of the Rush Springs district—discussed the system for about a year before contracting with Southwestern Bell. It took an additional three months to four months to lay the cable, install the equipment, coordinate school schedules, and smooth out the details.

"The key for a network like this to work is cooperation of all the schools involved to the extent that they will sit together at a table and say, 'We're determined to see this through even if we have to go outside of what we usually do,' " Tiner says. "There has to be a willingness to make a commitment to details."

For instance, class period starting and ending times have to be precisely the same at each school, down to the second, he says, so several different bells will not be ringing during the last minutes of a class on the network.

When the Grady County IETN was ready to go, Tiner and the other superintendents sent their teachers and school counselors to South Central Kansas for a personal indoctrination to distance learning. The students in the five participating schools were notified about the network and the new opportunities it would provide last August.

"It was short notice, so the numbers we have participating are excellent, all things considered," Tiner says.

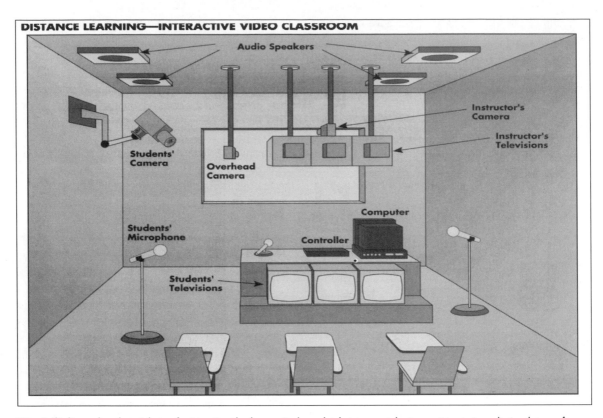

DISTANCE LEARNING—INTERACTIVE VIDEO CLASSROOM

Audio Speakers

Instructor's Camera

Instructor's Televisions

Students' Camera

Overhead Camera

Computer

Students' Microphone

Controller

Students' Televisions

Figure 2. This diagram shows the typical setup of an interactive video classroom. Teachers and students in separate locations can interact using applications that range from voice only to full multimedia.

"They all bought into the technology, the delivery system, everything."

CANDID CAMERA

Although both teachers and students were initially apprehensive about the technology–the main problem was stage fright, fear of the camera–it was just a matter of time before they were sold. Howell, the psychology teacher, says that, after a period of reluctance at the beginning, her students now "can't wait for their turn to do something on camera. It's an honor to be in a fiber-optic class."

Stone adds that students enjoy socializing with students at other schools whom they wouldn't know otherwise. For instance, Tiner says schools competing in sports events good naturedly hang spirit banners in their fiber-optic classrooms for the other schools to see, and there have been interschool dances that wouldn't have taken place otherwise.

"They didn't realize at first that they would be on TV, and they were reluctant to speak," Stone says, "but now they're excited about it and see that a fiber-optic class is like any other class."

The teachers who have been asked to work with the system have been enthusiastic, Stone adds, but some resistance remains among "veteran teachers who don't want to change things."

In general, teachers have to be better prepared when teaching a class on the network. Howell notes, "You can't wing it in front of the camera. You've got to have everything you need right in front of you, and students have to have handouts ahead of time."

The superintendents already are planning changes and improvements to the network for the next academic year, including adding more schools to the network, linking the network with a local college to offer continuing education classes for the community, tying into the local cable system to offer home-based distance learning, expanding high school course offerings, and continuing to work on the small details.

Florence, the Alex superintendent, says that among the glitches still to be worked out are what to do if one school closes because of weather conditions, if one school is having an assembly during a scheduled network-class period, or if a participating teacher is out for a day.

"The main problem is if the sending school has a conflict," he says. "We're also trying to deal with substitute teachers by getting one of the other teachers who is familiar with the system to take the class."

New classes under evaluation for transmission over the network include public speaking, creative writing, an introduction to computers, and a science class, as well as additional language and advanced-math courses.

The superintendents are talking to several local colleges about tying into the network, but Florence says, "Nothing is even close to being signed yet." If the link materializes, the schools could offer high school seniors concurrent enrollment in college classes, provide ongoing education for teachers, and extend opportunities for adult education.

Florence also says two other schools originally involved in the fiber-optic network planning talks that dropped out early on now have renewed interest in joining the IETN. There is interest in forming a second network of four or five schools, and then linking the two networks, a plan that would ease scheduling and transmission.

At the top of the list, however, are plans to incorporate additional technologies into the existing network if funding allows.

They would like to enable teachers to control the cameras in the remote classrooms for increased interaction and discipline. The superintendents are also considering whether to install a personal computer and printer at each teacher's station and a digital response pad for each student. Teachers then could give interactive quizzes and in-class assignments and would have immediate access to students' answers.

"It [installing this additional technology] would be quite expensive but it's a one-time expense, and after it's installed it [the new network] shouldn't be any more expensive than a regular PC network," Florence says. "We fax over fiber now, so the technology is in place."

Stone says a future goal is to provide a computer link over the fiber-optic network into the libraries at each school with a shared electronic card catalog on CD-ROM. Periodicals also could be shared on a networkable CD-ROM system.

"Then we'd have an interlibrary loan system with some way to transport books among the schools," he says. "There's so much technology available it's unbelievable."

KEEP TALKING

As of presstime, a meeting was scheduled to talk about new classes and long-term goals. "Talks have to take place continually for it to work," Tiner says, adding that the network itself has contributed to its own development.

"We use it for staff-development opportunities and for teachers to teleconference on common problems," he says. "We administrators can use it to meet for 30 minutes without driving 20 miles. I know it will be more and more valuable."

As for the future of distance-learning networks in general, Bank Street's Segal says advances in video-compression standards could pave the way for providing interactive multimedia over existing copper-wire phone lines. Two visual compression standards, known as JPEG and NPEG, can compress and decompress 1b of data every 18th of a second and are improving, he adds. If multimedia applications can eventually be transmitted over existing cable, both business and education will benefit without the difficulty and expense of laying fiber-optic cable.

"Fiber is a good delivery system, because you don't have to worry about the visual content," he says. "It transfers a lot of information very quickly, but it will take many years to rewire the entire country with fiber. But if you can use video- and data-compression techniques so this can work on a copper-wire phone system, then you've got a very interesting system that can be delivered anywhere, anytime."

Never Forget

NATIONAL HOLOCAUST MUSEUM BUILDS AN INTERACTIVE MULTIMEDIA LAN TO PRESERVE MEMORY.

BY SUKETU MEHTA

The U.S. Holocaust Memorial Museum in Washington, D.C., is dedicated to presenting the history of the persecution and murder of 6 million Jews, millions of Roma (gypsies), homosexuals, Jehovah's Witnesses, dissidents, Slavs, handicapped, and other victims of Nazi tyranny from 1933 to 1945.

One of the principal components of the museum is the Wexner Learning Center, where visitors can take advantage of a state-of-the-art multimedia network to conduct a self-guided tour through the history of the period.

The amount and range of data on the Holocaust available to visitors of the Learning Center is immense: An electronic form of the MacMillan Encyclopedia of the Holocaust, with articles linked to thousands of photos, interviews with Holocaust survivors, documentary footage, historical audio recordings, a day-by-day chronology spanning the 16-year era, and detailed computer-graphic maps, was created specially for this system. The Center is the product of more than three years of in-house design and production efforts, which required a staff of more than 30 historians, video producers, writers, cartographers, computer and multimedia professionals, musicologists, recording engineers, and content experts.

Says Yechiam Halevy, director of Information Services for the museum and head of the Learning Center creation effort, "We recognized early on that the Permanent Exhibition could not completely educate the public about the Holocaust. The Wexner Learning Center was created so that visitors, no matter how much or how little they might know about the Holocaust, could find the answers they're looking for in their quest for an understanding of this time in history."

VIDEO PCS

The Learning Center has 26 IBM PS/ValuePoint 486DX2 computers running at 66MHz. Twenty-four of them serve as audio/video workstations, each equipped with an Intel ActionMedia II digital video interactive (DVI) card, three sets of headphones, and a Mitsubishi 20-inch VGA monitor with an Elographics acoustic touchscreen device which is, literally, transparent to the user; it does not require an overlay to be placed on the monitor screen. Each workstation is equipped with a 200MB hard drive, primarily used for storage of local graphics and audio prompts. Another of the PCs is a printer station, and the last one serves as a console that controls the workstations, performing functions such as limiting access time. An overhead-projector system is connected to one of the workstations for larger groups of visitors.

Visitors can access on-screen articles in four ways: by choosing from a broad list of Holocaust topics; by typing in a specific term or place name; by looking through lists of the various media on the system; or by paging through a chronology of Holocaust events.

A unique "ID Card" system operates in the main museum. Upon entering the Permanent Collection, each visitor is given this card, which resembles a passport. The card has the photo, name, and an outline of the personal history of a Holocaust victim of the same gender and age as the visitor. When the visitor enters the Learning Center, she can use the card to further explore the people and places she has just learned about. A thousand personal histories are stored in the database.

RESPONSIVE TO THE TOUCH

Visitors interact with the system by touching a highlighted term in an article, which then calls up a grouping of related media terms associated with that term, such as other articles, maps, or survivor interviews. If the visitor wants to see an interview, she has full control to play or pause the interview at any time, see the next interview segment, or return to the previous article. The system keeps track of the visitor's path through the material and can help guide her back to any point in her journey. Visitors can print maps and articles of interest from the network printing station and take them home.

When evaluating servers for this network, the museum looked at several offerings, including servers from Starlight, Tricord, and NetFrame. The Starlight server was a dedicated video server, but the museum also wanted to use its server for other purposes, such as applications development. At the time, the Tricord server had a limit on the number of disk drives it would support in the configuration the museum wanted. According to Michael Blakeslee, a consultant closely involved in setting up the network, the museum found that, "at the time, NetFrame was the box that met our criteria."

The NetFrame server functions primarily as a video server and a multimedia storage device, though it's also used for applications development. It features a 486-based processor with eight I/O subprocessors that handle the SCSI subsystem and the LAN subsystem. It also has 30GB, count 'em, 30GB of mirrored storage. That's more storage than you can shake a stick at, but it's needed to store the huge files that make up the video portion of the database. The museum considered implementing RAID but found cost savings were offset by performance loss.

The NetFrame server is linked via three Token Ring segments to the Learning Center. It is also linked to the main network of the entire museum on another Token Ring and to the technical department on a fifth ring. The network uses Madge ISA bus 16Mbps Token Ring cards. "Our benchmarks at the time showed that the Madge cards had the highest throughput of all the cards we tested," says Blakeslee. Database materials can be retrieved from the server in real time at an average bandwidth of 150KBps, enough to support the needs of full-motion DVI video, along with audio and subtitles.

MULTIMEDIA ON THE NETWORK

The NOS is Novell's NetWare 3.11, which will be up-

graded to NetWare 4.0 in coming months. To deliver video over the network, the Learning Center turned to Video-Comm multimedia networking software from ProtoComm (Trevose, PA). This software provides the video streaming, or the timely delivery of video and audio data, to workstations.

The VideoComm software turns a NetWare file server into a video server. It achieves this feat by using several techniques including optimizing disk I/O, utilizing a client-server video protocol, prioritizing video screens, and preventing network overload by limiting the number of video screens per network segment. (ProtoComm recommends five screens per segment on Ethernet LANs and up to nine for Token Ring LANs, such as the one at the Holocaust Museum.)

The software runs as an NLM on the server. On the client side, there is an interface to the workstation platform. The version of the software in use at the Learning Center is called the Highpak-25, which supports up to 25 simultaneous video streams emanating from a server.

All the data—text, video, and audio—15GB's worth, currently resides on the NetFrame server. As the volume of data increases, Blakeslee would like to get another server, but currently, all the video has to reside on one server. The server has enough storage space to carry 40 hours' worth of video. Currently, some 25 hours of video has been digitized, using Intel's DVI format. This format supports 30-frames-per-second playback of digital video, comparable in image quality to ¾-inch videotape. "Our plans are to be able to support multiple types of digital video, not just DVI," says Blakeslee. "VideoComm is a temporary solution." He would especially like to support MPEG, a file format and compression algorithm that has attracted the support of many vendors including Intel.

To allow video to be played back over PC screens, the museum had to digitize its video. In doing so, video data has to be compressed. Two techniques are available for video compression. Symmetric compression is performed on a PC with a DVI card from Intel. Asymmetric compression is performed on a high-end multiprocessor system and incorporates higher-powered algorithms for compression to produce production-level video. Because the museum had a large amount of video to be digitized, it outsourced this process to NB Engineering (Crofton, MD), which used asymmetric compression to convert the video into digital form.

The software video platform in use at the workstation level is NewWorld, developed by Digital Video Arts (Dresher, PA). It is an operating system that provides a library of routines for playing audio and video, and it exercises Intel's ActionMedia II boards.

The development team used FoxPro from Microsoft as the database-development environment and wrote the code to access the database for the delivery system in codebase, a generic dBase API. A mammoth task, still not completely finished, is the text-retrieval system that plucks information the visitor wants to see from the mass of data. Currently, a full-text retrieval system isn't in use; data is just keyworded and doesn't allow for connections to be made from the data being accessed.

But an Israeli company called 2001 has donated a full-text retrieval system called XRS. This software consists of a set of programming libraries that allows the Learning Center to index all its data based on the words and the descriptions in the full text. Instead of picking from a list of keywords, the visitor will be able to search the full text based on any word that she types. The software has a thesaurus built in, which is important because the text contains 25,000 different place names. "This is very important when you're dealing with transliterated languages and the general vocabulary of Eastern Europe. With this software, variations on the spelling of, for example, Cracow [in Poland] will get you the same term," Blakeslee says.

The museum designed its own front end for each workstation. It is based on a GUI, and, because it performs only the functions needed for the museum application, it needs a workstation equipped with only 2MB of RAM. "Our use of GUI is much simpler than what's provided by Windows, so we don't need the overhead," explains Blakeslee. "We chose not to use Windows or one of the commercial GUIs because of our use of DVI. At the time we were developing the application, there wasn't a programming API for DVI."

Extended memory on the workstations, that is memory above 1MB of RAM, is used to cache video graphics and to run a protected-mode terminate-and-stay-resident (TSR) program constructed by Blakeslee. This TSR acts as a data-retrieval mechanism—it takes data (textual material and linkages between the various presentation modules) from the server, formats it, and feeds it to the workstation.

As for the network wiring, the museum purchased SynOptics Token Ring hubs, which connect to a fiber optic backbone serving all the museum departments; from the hub to the workstation, the wiring is copper. According to Blakeslee, the museum eventually plans to switch to an FDDI network with Network Peripherals FDDI cards.

Sensitive to the noble purpose of the museum, vendors donated much of the equipment in the Learning Center. IBM donated all the 486 PCs; NetFrame donated a portion of the purchase price of the server; and 2001 donated the XRS text-retrieval software.

CREATIVE CARTOGRAPHY

Among the main concerns of the Learning Center's network planners was allowing the user to "navigate" through the data. Blakeslee explains, "Making the navigational connections is very hard to do. Building the map that allows the user to navigate through the data is difficult. There aren't a lot of packages available–we home-brewed our mechanisms. It's not unlike making a movie. This is an interactive movie, and there are many pathways through the data, many ways this [information] can be presented to the user. It's a network of data."

Blakeslee would like to make it easier for users to retrieve the information. Currently, he says, "We provide a roadmap for the user. You can travel anywhere on any road that is defined. You can't make your own roads right now. Our intention is to allow you to define your own roads into the data. In the future, a user will be able to put things together in a way that is useful to her. A researcher wanting photos and films on a particular subject will be able to access those."

Blakeslee would also like to port the entire system to OS/2. "OS/2 provides a multitasking platform which has the video API built in to it." He also considered Windows. "Right now I'm not crazy about that particular multimedia API." The museum is also considering producing a foreign-language version of the application in use at the Learning Center, which should be relatively simple since it doesn't involve changing the software but mostly involves changing the textual material to another language.

In addition, Halevy has plans to broaden the scope of the Wexner Learning Center to include not only visitors to the museum but also people and institutions anywhere that are interested in using the Center's database. "We plan to create a CD Atlas using maps from the system, to be available for schools. We want to create a subset of all the media on the system to be put on a set of multimedia CDs for school and home use. And eventually, when computer data links allow, we hope to support telephone access to organizations and individuals outside the museum."

POWER USER

The network, first installed in the museum in late March of this year, is now fully functional. A prototype of the network had been running since mid-June of 1992, and at that time, the museum carried out extensive testing with focus groups to enhance the usability of the system.

On April 22, 1993, the museum was dedicated and the Wexner Center was visited by the First User himself, President Bill Clinton. The museum's visitors have been very positive about the system at the learning center, reports Blakeslee, because "most people don't even see the technology." Five thousand people a day visit the museum, and the Wexner Center is used "pretty solidly" from 10 a.m. to 5:30 p.m., according to Blakeslee. The average user sits down at the workstation for about 25 minutes, although lots of visitors use it for longer than that.

One of the museum's design criteria for the project was that the technology not get in the way of the people using it. The fact that the center's workstations don't need keyboards, just touch screens as the user interface, gives visitors an interface that is easy to grasp. "People under 40, and especially people under the age of 25, can walk in and use the system without assistance," Blakeslee says.

Section 4
High-speed Networking

Much like automobiles, computer hardware and software has to be better, more reliable, and faster with each new release. What worked a few years ago, or even a few months ago, can quickly be deemed inefficient or overburdened as users start to experiment and expand. Such is the case with network technology as well.

As mainframes are carted off to trash heaps and PC-based file sharing becomes an integral part of every business, network pathways can quickly become clogged with traffic. What begins as simple file and printer sharing on a LAN can almost overnight escalate into extensive data transfers involving databases, spreadsheets, and graphics and imaging applications, choking 10Mbps Ethernet links.

But help is on the way, coming in the form of new technology as well as updated solutions based on familiar network techniques. Asynchronous Transfer Mode (ATM) could be the high-speed panacea for the future. Or if you prefer a more common approach, maybe a faster Ethernet would be best. Although the official standards are still stalled by debate and politics in IEEE committees, 100Mbps Ethernet products are already on the market. "Plug in at 100" and "Twice as Nice" explain the details of this next generation of Ethernet. And don't overlook the internetworking bottlenecks of high-speed data transfer. Maybe a switch to switching technology is also in order; "Switch Hunt" and "Sizzling Switches" should help you decide.

ATM Takes Off

OFFERING BETTER BANDWIDTH MANAGEMENT, ATM MAY BRING ABOUT THE UNIFICATION OF COMMUNICATIONS.

BY CHARLES FELTMAN

For the one or two of you who may not have heard, Asynchronous Transfer Mode (ATM) technology is circling above your network, about ready to land. The buzz surrounding cell-relay technology has grown immensely, to the point where you might well expect to be offered a choice between an ATM cup or a Jurassic Park cup with your burger at McDonald's.

Almost every company that sells LAN or WAN equipment has announced a product or, at least, a plan for a product; a few have already shipped products. The networking and communications trade shows are full of ATM news. Some seminars even offer the promise of demystifying ATM.

The lure and excitement of ATM can be attributed, in part, to the role it will play in WANs and LANs. ATM offers the eventual promise of a grand unification of all communications, from the desktop to the WAN, at speeds of 2.488Gbps and beyond. As a local-area networking technology, ATM will help ease congestion on the backbone, reduce the proliferation of Ethernet segments, and bring unlimited bandwidth to the desktop for high-volume data applications such as imaging, voice, video, and multimedia.

THE BIG PICTURE

Although helpful for the LAN, ATM may bring about some of the biggest changes in the way people and businesses communicate across the WAN. For starters, ATM will allow the same high-bandwidth applications that can be run over LANs to be transported across the WAN, impossible using existing technology. In addition to bandwidth, ATM networks will have the ability to support data, voice, and video traffic on the same network.

Some of the wide-area applications the carriers will initially support with ATM-based services are LAN interconnection, host-channel extension, multimedia distance learning, and disaster recovery. ATM will also eventually obviate the need, at least technically, for the multiple separate networks (such as data, voice, and video-conference) most companies maintain, allowing corporations to build a single enterprise WAN carrying all their communications traffic.

In addition to supporting new applications and consolidating traffic, ATM has the potential to allow network managers to cut their telecommunications costs because of more precise bandwidth management. Just how much savings users will realize will be largely a function of ATM service pricing, which has yet to be set by any of the carriers. However, according to market-research firm Vertical Systems Group (Dedham, MA), the recurring cost of leased lines and services makes up 44 percent of the average company's telecom budget. So even a small savings in this area can be valuable.

A VESTED INTEREST

Yet amid all the hoopla surrounding this new technology, the public telecom carriers–those who would bring us wide-area ATM–have been uncharacteristically quiet, keeping to the fringes of the ATM circus. Some have announced general ATM strategies but have been reticent to share the specifics of their plans for providing and pricing public ATM services. They are keeping their cards close to the vest and playing them cautiously.

Behind the poker-player fronts, however, the telephone companies have been hard at work on ATM. The interexchange carriers (IECs) and the Regional Bell Operating Companies (RBOCs), who provide local telecommunications service in the United States through the local exchange carriers (LECs), have been working on how and when to incorporate ATM technology into their infrastructures and how to best provide ATM-based services. This implementation, it turns out, is no simple task, and considerable work still needs to be done before ATM becomes a viable wide-area public service.

In fact, even though several carriers have announced user trials for late in 1993 or early 1994 with general availability soon to follow, industry observers predict ATM services will not be in widespread use until the latter half of this decade. For starters, the types of wide-area applications that require that kind of bandwidth (45Mbps to 155Mbps and up) are currently few and far between. This lack of obvious applications, combined with the amount of work that still needs to be done on the carrier side, will likely push implementation of practical, cost-effective wide-area ATM beyond 1995.

For the carriers, providing public communications services means simultaneously solving several difficult problems, including:

• deciding what their "ATM services" will actually be;

• determining how to provide them; ensuring that T-1, frame relay, Switched Multimegabit Data Service (SMDS), and other existing service offerings will work in conjunction with ATM services;

• pricing ATM-based services to be attractive to users without simply cannibalizing existing services;

• deploying ATM and Synchronous Optical Network (SONET) technologies in their communications infrastructures to reduce costs and improve users' network capacity and manageability; and

• making sure that ATM switches from different vendors can interoperate with each other and with users' customer-premise equipment (CPE).

To complicate matters, the carriers are deciding on these issues before several of the critical interface and management protocols for ATM have been fully defined or standardized. This ambiguity leaves the carriers and their switch vendors to define their own protocols, make them work, and hope that they won't have to make too many changes when standards are finally completed.

FEEDER PIPES

"The big question is, 'Just what are the carriers' ATM services going to be?' " says Rosemary Cochran, principal analyst of Vertical Systems Group. "Will they just be 45Mbps pipes with other services as feeders, or will they offer some kind of T-1 ATM? Is it just going to be AAL5 [ATM Adaption Layer Type 5], or will they offer other Adaptation-Layer protocols to handle voice, video, and other traffic?"

Most likely, carriers' initial public ATM services will be a combination of high-bandwidth ATM pipes for customers who can use them and smaller feeder pipes running frame relay, SMDS, and T-1 services. The carriers are building high-speed ATM switching and transport backbones to carry traffic within their networks. The ATM services they plan to offer are at once independent of this effort yet closely tied to it.

The carriers recognize that in the near term, most users will want access to the WAN at something below DS-3 speeds (45Mbps), the lowest speed of the two "native" ATM interfaces defined to date (OC-3 at 155.52Mbps is the other). Few companies today have enough traffic from one application, or even aggregated traffic from multiple applications, that could justify a DS-3 connection. So in addition to DS-3, most carriers will initially offer access to their ATM transport backbones from frame relay, SMDS, or T-1 services around the "edge" of the network (see Figure 1).

The ATM Forum, a consortium of equipment manufacturers, service providers, researchers, and users, has begun to define a specification for a native ATM interface using DS-1 (1.544Mbps). T-1 services, which are ubiquitous in private networks throughout the United States, are based on DS-1 access.

The move to develop a DS-1 interface specification for ATM is being driven primarily by the carriers, who are hearing their customers express concerns that they won't be able to cost justify DS-3 access for several years. For many, it isn't a matter of buying one but rather two DS-3s for redundancy.

THE MANY OR THE FEW

The IECs are concerned that if they can't offer native ATM at a lower–and affordable–access rate, too few customers will buy the service. At the same time, many people involved with the technology say ATM doesn't make much sense at speeds below DS-3. The cost benefits of the technology come from the ability to aggregate and transmit large amounts of traffic at high speeds on a single channel.

However, as Ron Jeffries, editor of the *ATM User Newsletter* (Santa Maria, CA), points out, "In most cases, the user will only have to pay for a DS-3 pipe from his premise to the [long distance] carrier's POP [point-of-presence]. It's expensive for the distance, and he won't be using all that bandwidth, but he'll benefit from the low latency of a 45Mbps channel. Once his traffic gets to the POP, all he'll have to pay is the carrier's charge for an ATM [permanent] virtual circuit. Depending on how carriers end up tariffing their services, users will most likely be able buy virtual circuits from the IECs at speeds lower than 45Mbps."

Using DS-1 as an access for native ATM may prove to be too-little bandwidth, according to Jeffries. WAN access from small- to medium-size sites often pushes 1.544Mbps. A single router may be using 512Kbps. So users may find that even though they are a long way from filling a DS-3, they will need more than a single T-1. Managing multiple T-1 access could become a bigger nightmare for the carriers than trying to get customers to pay for DS-3s.

As a result, the IECs will lean harder on the RBOCs to lower their prices for T-3 service (which is based on DS-3). Vertical Systems Group's Cochran points out that the IECs have been exerting pressure on the LECs to cut T-1 access rates for a while, because the high rates have discouraged use of long-haul public T-1. "So far, there has not been similar pressure on T-3, but that may come with ATM," she says.

Comments from the IECs support Cochran's assertion. A planner working on ATM for one of the IECs, noting that DS-3 access is very expensive, put it this way: "The RBOCs will have to get a lot more aggressive in their DS-3 pricing for this thing to fly, and we [carriers] are going to be working with them on that issue."

ACCESS SERVICES

Other services, such as frame relay and SMDS, are better suited to provide cost-effective connectivity at speeds in the range between 64Kbps and DS-3. Accordingly, all the carriers are planning to provide access to ATM services via frame relay or SMDS. Of these two, the IECs are focusing primarily on frame relay, seeing it as the service of choice for their customers. AT&T has gone as far as to state publicly that it will provide SMDS access only if it gets enough customer demand. And for now, it will offer only frame relay.

The problem, at least in the short run, is that the standards for converting frame relay to ATM are incomplete. As with all evolving technology, standards are being developed, but interface standards are not yet available. Initially, carriers and their switch vendors will implement the functionality in a partly proprietary fashion to provide frame relay-to-ATM service. This proprietary setup means that interoperability between carriers may be limited for the first year or two.

The benefit to users, though, is that they will be able to buy a service that matches their application requirements today and migrate to ATM when the need arises. The carriers may also be offering modified (that is, lower) frame relay tariffs as part of ATM services.

CLASS OF SERVICE

One of the major benefits of ATM in the WAN is that it can accommodate different types of traffic, including data, voice, and video. The technology provides specifically for the handling of four different classes of service (see Table 1). Within the ATM protocol suite, the AAL is responsible for taking data from higher-layer protocols and packaging it into the 48-byte information payload portion of the 53-byte ATM cells in a way appropriate for the type of data being transmitted. In other words, the AAL protocol is what determines, among other things, the class of service given to the data by the ATM network.

At this point, three Adaptation-Layer types are well defined enough to be used in public ATM services: AAL1, AAL3/4, and AAL5. AAL5 offers some advantages over AAL3/4, the most important being bandwidth efficiency. AAL3/4 has 4 bytes per cell of overhead, whereas AAL5 has no per-cell overhead. In addition, since AAL5 is well-suited to handling frame relay traffic over ATM, carriers can more easily provide close links between the two services. For these and other reasons, AAL5 has gained broad acceptance among the carriers.

Any given AAL type can theoretically support all four classes of service, although some handle certain services better than others. For example, AAL5 is far less efficient for handling a video-conferencing application than AAL1. So the AAL types offered by each carrier will determine which applications their service will best support. All the carriers will initially offer AAL5 service for applications such as LAN interconnect, host-channel extension, and frame relay traffic. Most will also provide AAL1 to support voice-circuit emulation (as opposed to direct voice support) and video.

In addition, AAL5 can carry frame relay traffic over an ATM network between two frame relay end nodes. However, AAL5 does not define how to translate frame relay traffic into ATM traffic. Methods for accomplishing this translation have been proposed by WilTel and an AT&T/Stratacom/Cisco consortium, among others, but a standard specification may not exist for several more years (1996). In the meantime, each carrier will do the translation its own way.

ATM INTEROPERABILITY

Because ATM at 45Mbps is beyond the needs and means of most users today, interoperability between ATM and existing WAN services, such as frame relay, is critical to its general acceptance by the market. Good, clean interoperability will allow users to gradually evolve their networks toward ATM as requirements dictate.

Another area in which interoperability is just as important is between different vendors' products. The public ATM switches themselves need to interoperate flawlessly. Each carrier will provide its own service using one or two different vendors' products, ensuring interoperability within its own infrastructure. However, the carriers won't all choose the same switch vendor. So switch interoperability is key to a national, and eventually global, ATM service.

When a customer with sites in different parts of the United States signs up for an ATM service, its traffic will have to cross Local Access Transport Area (LATA) boundaries. The LECs will provide ATM service within the LATAs but by law are required to use the IECs to carry traffic between LATAs.

While some nationwide customers may use IECs to bypass the LECs, many will have multiple sites concentrated within a single LATA and will use the LECs' ATM, frame relay, or SMDS services in conjunction with an IEC's ATM

service. IECs will also contract with the LECs to aggregate traffic from multiple points within a single LATA.

The key manufacturers of telco capacity public ATM switches are AT&T, Siemens, Fujitsu, NEC, Northern Telecom, Alcatel, and GTE Government Systems. Most will initially ship products with DS-3 interfaces that will be upgradable to OC-3. But this upgrade path doesn't begin to ensure interoperability between their switches, which contain some fairly significant architectural differences. To date, interoperability testing has fallen primarily to the carriers and their switch vendors.

U.S. West, for example, has incorporated ATM switch-interoperability testing into an ongoing testing program. According to Will Walling, manager of broadband services, U.S. West has just completed individual trials of Fujitsu, AT&T Network Systems, and Siemens switches in a test bed using a multimedia distance-learning application between a teaching hospital and two other hospitals in Minneapolis. The next phase of trials will get to the heart of the matter, however, as the group tests the different vendors' switches together on one network.

The carriers have also been working closely with leading ATM CPE vendors to ensure interoperability. The manufacturers of ATM routers, DSU/CSUs, and local-premise switches want to make sure that users who purchase their products can connect to the public ATM network when the time comes. The carriers also require that customers have compatible equipment. Each of the carriers has (or will have) some type of certification program for manufacturers. When prospective ATM customers go to their service provider, they can get a list of certified ATM CPE manufacturers. Users planning future implementations of ATM will need to pick equipment providers whose products will interoperate with the equipment that the carrier uses to provide ATM WAN services.

MANAGEMENT MANIA

With ATM, unified management may prove to be one of the most powerful differentiators between the carriers' offerings, especially when looking at inter-LATA ATM services involving multiple IECs and one or more LECs.

"We realize that when a customer purchases ATM, frame relay, or any other inter-LATA service that involves our company and an IEC, they want it to look like one network," says Bill Bjorkman, staff director for broadband

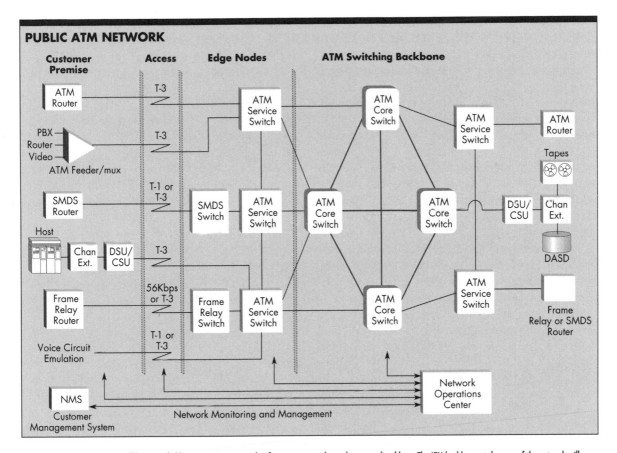

PUBLIC ATM NETWORK

Figure 1. Public ATM services will be [provided by carriers over network infrastructures similar to the one outlined here. The ATM backbone at the core of the network will consist of a large ATM switches. The edge of the network will have smaller ATM switches, some with protocol conversion. Routers, DSU/CSUs, and ATM feeder multiplexers will connect to ATM switches.

planning at Nynex (White Plains, NY). "This means providing comprehensive management across the entire network." Nynex has been working with the IECs to develop such management capabilities between networks as part of its service, according to Bjorkman.

Another aspect of management has to do with allowing users to monitor and configure their networks. Now that network managers are getting the tools they need to comprehensively manage their local campus networks, carriers that can also provide ways to manage the enterprise WAN will have a strong advantage. Simple Network Management Protocol (SNMP), which has become the de facto standard for LAN management, will be offered by some carriers as part of their ATM packages.

The carriers are acutely aware of the need for enterprise management, and most are working on some type of user system that will allow customers to manage their networks as a unified whole. Some have announced or demonstrated systems, while others are still in the design stages. None is far enough along yet to really meet customers' needs, however, and users can expect to find most early systems limited.

THE PRICING FACTOR

Pricing is a critical factor that will affect the time required for the market to adopt public ATM. The tariffs for ATM-based services will be set by the carriers, and they are putting much care, effort, and research into how to price ATM services. To date, none of them has publicly discussed its strategies for pricing ATM-based services, nor has any carrier announced any specifics.

One thorny problem the carriers face as they try to define tariffs for ATM is cannibalization of revenues from existing services. For most of them, the primary concern is T-1 private-line service. Depending on how it is priced, ATM service may offer some significant cost savings over private T-1, possibly opening up carriers to heavy revenue loss if too many users exploit it. Some of the IECs also have substantial investments in frame relay, and the RBOCs have sunk considerable resources into SMDS services, neither of which they want to see bypassed right away for ATM.

ATM services may be tariffed in one of several ways. One method is to price a set bandwidth channel, a permanent virtual circuit between two sites, and then charge for additional bandwidth used above that rate. Another is to charge for two bandwidth rates, an average rate and a peak rate, with a maximum amount of time allowed above the average rate. These models are similar to current pricing methods applied to frame relay service.

Other methods use ATM switches' ability to count cells and to implement a variety of priority levels. Some or all of a tariff could be built around actual per-cell usage with different cell-priority assignments. Some switches can also distinguish between virtual connections between two sites, potentially allowing a carrier to charge based on the number of connections established by the user and/or the amount of time a connection is used.

All these possible tariffing schemes and the many permutations that can be derived promise potential savings for some customers and increased costs for others. Most users realistically expect that ATM WAN services will be expensive initially, but they could very quickly realize moderate to significant savings. This expectation assumes that ATM will offer bandwidth on demand. Users look forward to having a great deal more control over the allocation of bandwidth for their WAN applications than they do today with private networks or even with switched public services.

PVCS AND SVCS

Initially, however, customers of ATM may be in for some disappointment in bandwidth savings. For one, out of the starting gate, the carriers will offer only permanent virtual circuit (PVC) service. The earliest that a switched virtual circuit (SVC) service will arrive is late 1995 to early 1996. SVCs would allow users much more flexibility and control over their bandwidth usage.

For example, users could bring up and tear down circuits between any two sites on an as-needed basis, much like we make telephone calls today. The assumption is that, like a phone call, users would have to pay for only the time used, which could offer many companies significant cost savings. SVCs could also be used to add bandwidth to an existing PVC temporarily, such as while a large file is being transferred.

ATM may not be a cost-effective service until it incorporates SVC capability. Nynex's Bjorkman agrees that customers could benefit from bandwidth-on-demand over the wide area. But he is quick to point out that users will still be able to realize some savings from PVCs, depending on how ATM is tariffed.

Terry Lindsey, vice president of technical development at WilTel's (Tulsa, OK) Advanced Development Group, says customers can derive some cost benefits from PVC-based ATM. ATM circuits allow the carriers to allocate and manage bandwidth over their networks more efficiently, and the savings can be passed along to users. In addition, and again depending on how ATM is tariffed, customers may be able to purchase PVCs for only the maximum bandwidth they require between sites and no more. Technically, bandwidth allocation, and therefore charges, could even be varied by times of day and days of the month.

CONGESTION AND SECURITY

ATM users are concerned with a few other issues, including how the carriers will handle network congestion. As with frame relay, when an ATM network becomes congested, cells will get discarded, depending on their priority.

The carriers have engineered their networks to accommodate peak traffic for the first year or two of use, during which they expect that specifications for congestion management will be standardized. How the carriers handle the congestion problem, the policing of bandwidth utilization, and cell priorities, will be a key factor for users interested in subscribing to a specific carrier's ATM service.

Another area of concern is security. Most commercial users haven't dealt with this issue because they run their data over private networks. As they migrate to public ATM services, however, some are beginning to take more than a passing interest in how secure their data will be.

FUTURE SHOCK

ATM is not going to be the communications user's panacea for many years to come. A great deal of work still needs to be done on all fronts, including completing critical specifications and building equipment that incorporates them; assuring interoperability between ATM switches, services, and CPE; working out the management issues between LECs and IECs and between local- and wide-area network elements; establishing tariffs that make the services cost-effective for a broad spectrum of users; and determining how best to provide services for different applications.

The initial phase, in which the carriers will be beta-testing various services, has already begun. The second phase, which will probably last 12 to 18 months, will see the carriers introducing at first limited, then successively broader, ATM services. During this time, carriers will also be working to resolve many of the open issues and simultaneously will be upgrading their network infrastructures to accommodate heavier ATM traffic. A handful of early adopters, mostly Fortune 100 companies, will implement the initial services and provide valuable feedback.

Many more companies will begin building campus ATM networks and start using new, high-bandwidth applications on LANs as a result. By the latter half of 1995 or early 1996, many of them will be ready to take advantage of public ATM wide-area services, and the third phase will begin. The applications that can make use of its bandwidth will be up and running, and cost and competitive issues will drive users to higher bandwidth WANs. If the carriers are ready by then, and if they have resolved most of the outstanding problems and gained the confidence of the early adopters, ATM may start to realize its promise of revolutionizing how companies communicate and do business.

GOING GLOBAL

ATM includes one more critical piece. The U.S. carriers today are focusing on providing coherent nationwide ATM services. The joint AT&TPKDD (Japanese PTT) trial that started in July of 1994 and will be running for the next three years is the first attempt at international ATM.

Sam Shuler, communications strategy manager for Texas Instruments (Dallas), would like to see international ATM services evolve right along with U.S. offerings. "Public ATM has to be a globally available and realistically usable service. Otherwise it won't really meet the needs of companies such as TI."

Shuler and his colleagues in other multinational companies look forward to wide-area ATM with a combination of anticipation and concern. The latter comes from years of experiencing the pain and frustration of trying to stitch together global enterprise networks out of a patchwork of mismatched equipment, technologies, and services.

Their fervent hope is that ATM will be much more similar in the United States, Europe, the Pacific Rim, and Latin America than current services, allowing them to make use of its unique features as the core of global enterprise networks.

SERVICES VS. PRICE

ATM: The Early Years

As the major carriers unveiled their first ATM services and continue to offer new ones, they will try to differentiate their services. They will all offer comprehensive, end-to-end, solution-oriented services and provide CPE (such as routers and DSU/CSUs). Most will offer some management system that gives users the ability to monitor and configure their WAN.

AT&T (Holmdel, NJ) began customer trials in the second half of 1993 and offered general availability of services in late 1994. AT&T supports data and multimedia applications, with support for voice "when it makes sense," according to Dave Nelson, product manager for AT&T's InterSpan ATM Services.

"One of our key differentiators will be interoperability between our InterSpan ATM, frame relay, and Information Access Services (IAS). A user will be able to purchase ATM for some sites, frame relay for others, and even IAS dial-up services, and link them via our ATM backbone network," Nelson says.

Sprint has turned on two switch sites in California and will be beta-testing services this summer, with general availability to follow. It hopes to be an early provider of

ATM services to the federal government and large commercial users.

One of the benefits of Sprint's (Reston, VA) services, according to Dave Crosby, director of Data Product Management, is that the company will focus on providing end-to-end services for many types of applications. Sprint is working with router, hub, and DSU/CSU vendors to offer these products.

MCI's (Washington, D.C.) Paul Weichselbaum, vice president of data marketing, says his company will be offering ATM over Synchronous Optical Network (SONET) technology. "What will users want to do with ATM initially? LAN-to-LAN, data and voice overflow, imaging and host-channel extension are some of the key applications we're gearing up to support," says Weichselbaum.

One of the differentiators Weichselbaum stressed was that MCI will offer strong application-engineering support. "It will be going from private-line networks to virtual public networks, and it will need help making the transition gracefully."

WilTel (Tulsa, OK) has been the most detailed of the IECs regarding its ATM service. In March of 1993, it announced ATM service specifically for channel extension over a wide-area network. Describing WilTel's strategy, Terry Lindsey, vice president of technical development, notes that channel networking is a well-defined application for a mature technology that raises few problems on an ATM network.

"We'll have an opportunity to really see how ATM works, while at the same time providing our customers with a clear set of benefits for channel networking, including savings over a leased-line network and a great deal more flexibility," according to Lindsey. The channel-extension service began in the second half of 1993. WilTel's next service, turnkey LAN interconnect, began during the first half of 1994.

The RBOCs have also been working on ATM services to add to their SMDS and frame relay and complement the IECs' offerings. One key issue for the RBOCs is interoperability with IEC equipment and services. The more closely RBOCs can work with the IECs to provide unified networks, the better off both sides will be.

But the RBOCs will also have to confront competition for their traditional markets from the alternate, or bypass, providers, such as MFS Datanet (San Jose, CA). Although small, these companies are less restricted by regulations than are the RBOCs, and with aggressive pricing these providers may take considerable business away from their larger competitors.

ATM: The Grand Unifier

BY DELIVERING MORE BANDWIDTH, ATM PROMISES TO SOLVE A WIDE RANGE OF NETWORK PROBLEMS, INCLUDING THAT OF INCREASED SEGMENTATION.

BY CHARLES FELTMAN

Asynchronous Transfer Mode (ATM) is the Grand Unification Theory of communications. For those of you not familiar with this holy grail pursued by physicists for the last half-century, the GUT, as it's commonly called, promises to unite the theories of particle physics (the very small, "local" interactions of matter and energy) and the theories of cosmology (the interactions of space and time on the very big scale). ATM is the GUT of the communications business, promising to unite data, voice, video, images, LANs, MANs, and WANs from desktop to desktop around the world.

Its most ardent proponents portray ATM as a technology that will solve current networking problems and usher in a brave new era of communications in which multiple users can synchronously or asynchronously share images, text, and video and voice data on their workstations, linked over a network that transcends current notions of LAN and WAN.

How much substance lies in the promises behind ATM? The potential applications of ATM technology are impressive. For many communications managers, ATM offers real hope for solving some of the formerly intractable problems of local and wide area networking technologies, including the leading problem of increased network segmentation.

The number of users is growing at an explosive rate, and so is the demand for bandwidth. To keep the network from crawling, managers are using routers or bridges to divide LANs into more segments with fewer users on each.

Unfortunately, this solution is like the proverbial medicine that cures the symptom but kills the patient. Such solutions often alleviate congestion while increasing the complexity of network management. As LANs become more complex, hubs run out of card slots, and response time and data loss go up while more links go down. But the underlying problem, which cannot be solved by increasing segments, is that of running up against the fundamental limitations of shared media networks.

Other problems with current LAN technologies also loom. The exodus from centralized to distributed, client-server computing will soon begin to swamp internetworks. At the same time, desktop computers are becoming relentlessly more powerful, and multimedia, video, and other new applications will require more bandwidth.

Over the long haul, ATM is the best way out of this morass. It is a switched networking technology with low-latency, high-bandwidth, and multiprotocol, multimedia capabilities. With ATM, users don't have to contend with a fixed amount of network bandwidth. Each connection is guaranteed the capacity it requires, no matter how many other connections exist over the network at a given time.

With its 45Mbps to 2.488Gbps capacity, ATM will also be able to support even the most powerful workstations and allow general implementation of bandwidth-hungry applications that most current LANs and WANs just can't support. And it can support different types of traffic, including data, voice, and video over the same network links.

Distributed CAD/CAM, engineering visualization and joint design, medical imaging, and wide-area supercomputer channel extension are powerful applications that, although typically used on experimental networks today, will become widespread on ATM networks. Other applications, such as multimedia, desktop video, and distance learning are still in development, waiting for the networking technology that will enable them.

As Sam Shuler, communications strategy manager for Texas Instruments (Dallas), observes, "Over the past 10 years, there has been rapid growth in computer applications and the horsepower to drive them, but our local area networking technologies haven't changed much at all in the same timeframe.

"I don't see any single 'killer application' that will drive migration to ATM," Shuler adds. "Instead, it [the migration to ATM] will come from the aggregated requirements of a variety of problems and applications."

EVOLUTIONARY IMPLEMENTATION

ATM has been touted by some as a revolution in networking. Truth is, the technology is more evolutionary, a descendant of time-division multiplexing (TDM) and Narrowband Integrated Services Digital Network (N-ISDN) wide area networks. Its implementation won't be a flash-cut from current LAN/WAN infrastructures, either, as some of the hype might suggest. Instead, ATM will gradually infiltrate all sectors of the enterprise network over the next several years.

It will probably be first implemented in campus network backbones, sometime between 1993 and 1994. Initially, ATM switches will link hubs equipped with an ATM port (see Figure 1), which can be done via an ATM card added to an existing product. This use of ATM technology is a straightforward extension of most current LAN architectures, and the specifications exist in complete enough form to allow products to be built, installed, and used.

"This is the low-hanging fruit for the equipment vendors," says Rosemary Cochran, a principal of Vertical Systems Group, a Boston consultancy. "The technical problems involved in building ATM campus backbone switches are minimal at this point. Users can buy one switch at a time, so they can add to their networks without replacing anything. And, most importantly, ATM in this form will help solve an existing problem by greatly increasing performance over the backbone."

In fact, a few vendors have already begun sampling this fruit. Within the past 10 months, Fore Systems (Pittsburgh), Network Equipment Technologies (N.E.T., Redwood City, CA), SynOptics (Santa Clara, CA), Hughes LAN Systems (Mountain View, CA), and Newbridge Networks

(Kenata, Ontario) have announced or introduced ATM campus switch products.

Jennifer Pigg, program manager for Data Communications at The Yankee Group (Boston), agrees with Cochran that ATM's first widespread use will occur at the campus backbone, but she believes that backbone products will be preceded by ATM workgroup switches and adapters used to connect pockets of high-performance workstations in engineering labs, universities, and other similar environments.

"Technical workstation groups will be the earliest production users of ATM. Most of the campus switch vendors have introduced ATM adapters for high-performance workstations, such as Sun SPARCs, that will allow them to link directly to the switches," Pigg points out. The Yankee Group expects to see this section of the market begin development seriously about mid-1994.

This architecture uses the switch as an ATM hub. And, since a switch is essentially useless without a workstation or a router connected to it, the ATM switch manufacturers have at least one ATM adapter available for Sun Microsystems' SBus. Fore Systems also has adapters available for systems from DEC, HP, NeXT, and Silicon Graphics, making it the leader in ATM workstation adapters.

Following quickly on the heels of ATM switches for the campus backbone will be a new generation of ATM switching hubs. In addition to ATM ports, these hubs will have interfaces for shared Ethernet LANs, dedicated Ethernet, bridges and routers, and Token Ring LANs (see Figure 2). The hubs will connect to other hubs, ATM campus switches, and ATM WANs via the ATM ports.

Within the switching hubs, routers will serve to link Ethernet LANs to the internal ATM switch. Four of the vendors mentioned earlier—N.E.T., SynOptics, Hughes LAN Systems, and Newbridge—plan to expand their products in this direction within the next 12 to 18 months. Fore Systems has opted for a different strategy, focusing purely on ATM networks. However, it has teamed with Cabletron (Rochester, NH) to provide ATM capability for its hub products. Initially, Cabletron will simply provide connectivity to the Fore switches, but Cabletron plans to introduce by late next year an ATM hub that fully incorporates Fore's technology.

The final phase of ATM implementation in the LAN environment will come with ATM adapters for PC-class sys-

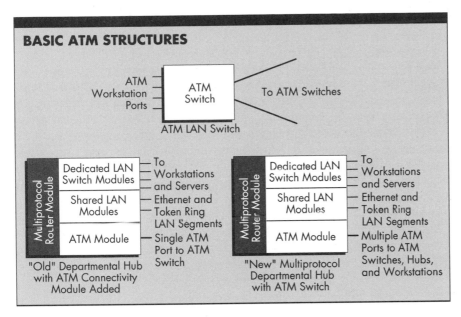

BASIC ATM STRUCTURES

ATM Workstation Ports — ATM Switch — To ATM Switches

ATM LAN Switch

Multiprotocol Router Module
- Dedicated LAN Switch Modules
- Shared LAN Modules
- ATM Module

- To Workstations and Servers
- Ethernet and Token Ring LAN Segments
- Single ATM Port to ATM Switch

"Old" Departmental Hub with ATM Connectivity Module Added

Multiprotocol Router Module
- Dedicated LAN Switch Modules
- Shared LAN Modules
- ATM Module

- To Workstations and Servers
- Ethernet and Token Ring LAN Segments
- Multiple ATM Ports to ATM Switches, Hubs, and Workstations

"New" Multiprotocol Departmental Hub with ATM Switch

Figure 1. Here are the basic functions of the ATM LAN switch, enhancements to existing hubs, and future integrated ATM departmental hub.

terns. These products will begin to appear as early as 1994 for use with PC-based servers. But servers will probably be the only PCs provisioned with ATM adapters until about 1995 or 1996, when the cost of ATM chips and adapters should come down.

But the market probably will not be ready for ATM to the desktop much before then. As Jim Capabianco, ATM product line manager at Ungermann-Bass (Santa Clara, CA), notes, studies by McQuillan Consulting (Boston) have shown that less than 5 percent of desktops today need speeds higher than 10Mbps. Fortunately, that figure means network managers can continue to meet their users' communications requirements without having to replace adapter cards for some years yet.

Users clearly aren't going to throw away their existing network gear and replace it with ATM all at once, but they do want to take advantage of some of ATM's benefits for the campus backbone. Managers at several companies evaluating or currently using ATM products all say that integrating ATM with current network equipment and applications is a key issue. The integration issue hasn't gone unnoticed by the equipment vendors, most of whom plan to deliver backbone switch and hub products that support existing Ethernet, Token Ring, and adapters.

THE RIGHT STUFF

Understanding whether ATM can integrate with and add significant value to existing LANs, as well as enable the transfer of new, high-bandwidth mixed-media, requires delving into how the technology works. Ethernet and Token Ring networks use variable-length packets to carry data over a shared medium. Every station on the LAN (or LAN segment) looks at each packet sent over the network, accepting or rejecting it based on the packet's address. Packets can be routed between LANs or LAN segments using one of several routing protocols that use some form of network address embedded in the packet.

ATM transports data in fixed-length cells. Each cell is 53 bytes, or octets, long, including a five-octet header identifying the cell's route through the network and a 48-octet payload for user data. The user data includes any headers or trailers required by higher-layer protocols.

ATM is a connection-oriented technology. Rather than broadcasting cells onto a shared wire or fiber for all nodes to receive, a specific virtual circuit is set up between two end nodes before data is transmitted. Cells identified with a particular virtual circuit are only delivered to nodes on that virtual circuit.

One or more ATM switches may relay cells along the path between the two end nodes. The switches and connections between them can be considered shared media to the extent that they switch and transport cells for many different virtual circuits. However, each end node has its own dedicated link to the switched network and does not contend for a fixed amount of bandwidth as do nodes in shared-media LANs.

This dedicated link means that data transfers by any number of end nodes can occur simultaneously on an ATM network without causing an overload. Any number of new end nodes can also be added to the network (limited by the number of physical hub or switch ports available) without danger of overloading the network.

The ATM cell header contains a virtual connection identifier consisting of a virtual path identifier (VPI) and a virtual channel identifier (VCI), which together serve to identify connections. The VPI/VCI pair associate an individual cell with a particular virtual circuit across a single link. Cells arriving at an incoming port on an ATM switch can easily be directed to the appropriate outgoing port using the VCI pair. This process takes place in hardware, and its simplicity makes ATM switches very efficient.

Network designers can scale ATM networks from moderate to very high speeds and sizes because of ATM's short, fixed-length cells, combined with predetermined virtual connections. An ATM network can accommodate any combination of speeds from 45Mbps to 2.4Gbps, and possibly higher. ATM networks are not confined to one particular medium but can be run over shielded twisted-pair (STP) and unshielded twisted-pair (UTP), coaxial, and fiber optic cable.

The concept of a virtual circuit in the ATM world derives from its heritage in time-division multiplexing networks. TDM bandwidth reservation is static. Each TDM circuit is allocated a specific position, or time slot, in a synchronous series of frames transmitted across a channel. Data from a particular circuit is placed only in its assigned time slots, and any switch in the network knows where to look in the bit stream to find data belonging to that circuit. If no data is to be sent over that circuit, the time slot remains empty, effectively wasting the bandwidth.

ATM uses the virtual circuit identifiers to tag cells as belonging to a particular virtual circuit instead of assigning them to specific time slots; thus, bandwidth is used only when data needs to be sent on an ATM network. When no data is destined for a given circuit, the bandwidth

can be used by cells from other virtual circuits (see Figure 3). However, ATM does provide ways to reserve bandwidth for a given virtual circuit over a period of time.

The basic ATM network model incorporates end nodes and intermediate nodes linked in a point-to-point topology. End nodes can be host systems, routers, DSU/CSUs, PBXs, or any other type of customer premise equipment (CPE). Intermediate nodes are ATM switches.

Two major types of network interfaces are defined within ATM: the User Network Interface (UNI) and the Network-to-Network Interface (NNI). Since ATM started out as an architecture for public WAN services, the UNI was originally intended to be the interface between ATM CPE and a public ATM switch. When the technology began to be implemented in LANs, the term UNI was broadened to cover the interface for any end-user device connected to an ATM switch, public or private. The term "public UNI," however, now describes the interface between CPE, including private ATM switches such as those used in a LAN backbone, and public switches used by WAN service providers.

The NNI, originally designed to serve as the interface between switches in the public ATM WAN, is now used to describe the interface between private ATM switches, as well. Unique NNIs exist for private switch-to-private switch connections, which are links between public ATM switches owned by local exchange carriers (LECs) and deployed within each Local Access and Transport Area (LATA) and between switches used in the interexchange carrier's (IEC's) long-haul networks. The public UNI is used between a private ATM switch and a public-carrier switch. The ATM Forum is defining the UNI between an LEC's switch and an IEC's switch, called the Broadband Inter-Carrier Interface, or B-ICI. The B-ICI will help ensure that the IECs and LECs can develop a uniform ATM service.

While several different ATM interfaces exist, they are all very similar and are designed to work together to form a unified network that can be easily scaled from local workgroup to global proportions. The primary differences between these interfaces are related to connection administration and signaling. For example, UNIs and NNIs generally differ in that the only type of signaling across a UNI is the signaling needed to set up a virtual circuit for a specific data transfer, while NNI signaling also includes exchange of information, such as routing tables. A UNI is

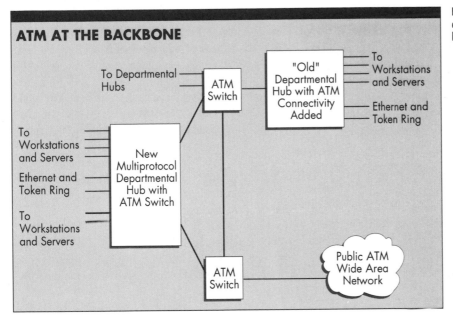

ATM AT THE BACKBONE

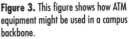

Figure 3. This figure shows how ATM equipment might be used in a campus backbone.

used between a private and a public ATM switch because public network regulations forbid exchange of anything other than connection setup information between those two types of devices.

Although not a standards body, but a consortium of manufacturers, service providers, and users, the ATM Forum has adopted prestandard "specifications" for both public and private UNIs. However, to date no commonly agreed-on NNI specification has been established for switch vendors. In the interim, most public and some private switches are using the UNI, while others have implemented proprietary NNIs.

MAKING THE CONNECTION

ATM is a connection-oriented networking technology. When an end node wants to communicate with another end node, it requests a connection to the destination node by transmitting a signaling request across the UNI to the network. The request is passed through the network to the destination. If the destination node agrees to form a connection, a virtual ciruit is set up across the ATM network. A virtual circuit mapping is defined between the UNIs and between corresponding input and output ports on all intermediate switches. This virtual circuit is identified by a unique combination of VPI and VCI values at each switch point.

The end nodes also tell the network about the characteristics of the desired circuit, such as average bandwidth, variation or burstiness, and sensitivity to delay, all of which determine the required quality of service for the circuit. The network uses this information to allocate appropriate overall bandwidth.

In other words, the network will determine, based on probabilities, the total number of virtual circuits of all types that can be handled over a given link while maintaining the required quality of service. If the network can't meet the end node's request for a circuit with a necessary quality of service, the responding node's UNI will reject the request until the bandwidth is available. *Admission control,* as this process is referred to, helps maintain the network's ability to assure quality of service for all circuits.

Once a virtual circuit is established between two end nodes, data from the end nodes are segmented and put into cells. This segmentation process can be applied to any kind of traffic, including LAN packets, digital voice, or video. If a particular end node has more than one virtual circuit assigned across the UNI, it can interleave cells for each circuit into the cell stream as it chooses, based on demand, class of service, priority, or other parameters.

The term *class of service* refers to the class, or type, of traffic for which a circuit is used. ATM is designed to carry any of four classes of traffic, A through D. If a circuit carries Class A voice traffic, which is highly sensitive to delay, it can be guaranteed the necessary bandwidth; that is, cells will be placed into the cell stream over time on a regular-enough basis to ensure the required level of quality for that class of service. The ability to guarantee a circuit a given quality of service is one of the biggest advantages of connection-oriented networks.

After cells have been transmitted across the UNI, the switches will relay them from link to link to the destination node at very high speeds, because very little processing is required. Essentially, the switches read and change the VPI/VCI values and direct the cells through the switch matrix to the appropriate output ports. The switch doesn't "care" what type of data the cells carry; it simply relays them from an input link to the appropriate output link.

THREE-LAYER MODEL

ATM networks can guarantee quality of service for different types of traffic, allow bandwidth on demand over its circuits, and provide high-speed transmission over different media using a layered stack of protocols, each of which provides services to the layers above and below it. In the simplest form, ATM protocols are defined in three layers of a reference model similar to the OSI model: the ATM Adaptation Layer (AAL), the ATM Layer, and the Physical Layer. Data and control information from higher user and control layers passes through these three layers of protocols.

The ATM protocol reference model is more complex than the OSI model in that it also incorporates user, control, and management "planes," somewhat analogous to protocol suites. However, the basic operation of ATM can be understood by looking at the functionality of the protocols in the three ATM layers.

The Physical Layer is segmented into the Transmission Convergence (TC) and Physical Medium Dependent (PMD) sublayers. This structure separates ATM transmission from the actual physical interface, allowing ATM communications to support a variety of interfaces and media.

The TC sublayer performs two key functions. One is delineating cells out of the bit stream handed off by the PMD. The second is decoupling the speed of the cell stream to the physical interface from the data that is passed on to the ATM Layer within the switch by inserting idle cells. In other words, the switch may process cells much faster internally than the transmission speed of the network medium does.

The PMD sublayer handles medium-dependent functions of the Physical Layer. ATM can use twisted-pair, coax, and fiber optic media as well as different interface speeds associated with the media. To date, three Physical-Layer specifications have been defined that are suitable for both public and private ATM network interfaces, including:

• DS-3, a standard public-carrier interface and transmission standard that runs at 45Mbps, associated with T-3 carrier service.

• OC-3, a standard Synchronous Optical Network interface and transmission standard that runs at 155Mbps over single-mode optical fiber, but can also be run over other media.

• TAXI (AMD's Transparent Asynchronous Transmitter/Receiver Interface chipset), a 100Mbps multimode fiber interface that uses the same optical fiber physical medium and line coding (4B/5B) as the FDDI physical layer. This standard was defined to allow the early deployment of low-cost private ATM networks, which can be built using the AMD (Sunnyvale, CA) TAXI chip (hence, the name).

The term *native ATM* is sometimes used to refer to direct ATM interfaces that have been specified by a recommending body. The ATM Forum is working on an OC-12 (622Mbps) specification for native ATM. Several vendor consortiums have proposed a number of alternatives for a native DS-1 (1.544Mbps, associated with T-1 carrier service) interface for connecting to public ATM networks.

CELLS AND CLASS OF SERVICE

The ATM Layer deals with cells. In an end node, it exchanges a cell stream with the Physical Layer and takes segmented data from the upper layers, assembling it into cells. Its other major end-node function is to police quality of service for each circuit. The ATM Layer will refuse a request for a virtual circuit if it determines that quality of service cannot be maintained. In some ATM implementations, the ATM Layer may also provide traffic shaping at the source node and policing of service-quality parameters in the intermediate and end nodes. (*Traffic shaping* is a process whereby an ATM client node negotiates with the

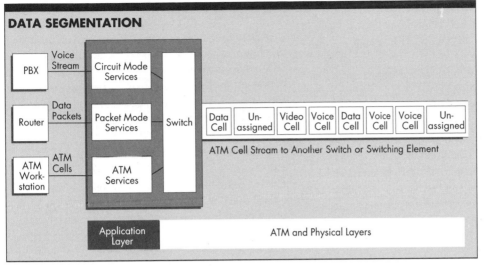

Figure 4. Here data is segmented into ATM cells.

network's connection-management service to obtain an approved burst rate and throughput for each virtual circuit.)

In ATM switches the ATM-Layer responsibilities are simpler. It assigns the proper VPI/VCI values to each cell that comes in to an input port so that the cell gets to the correct output port. Since these values have only local significance, meaning they may be changed at each switch, the ATM Layer manages this procedure. The ATM Layer also handles cell ordering (ATM cells must stay in order) and ensures that system requirements are met. At the switch's output port, it passes cells to the Physical Layer for transmission over the next link. Finally, the ATM Layer in a switch may also set congestion-control bits in cells and handles buffering of cells when there is network congestion or contention for a given port.

The ATM Adaptation Layer (AAL) provides services to the higher layers that support classes of service for transported data and is primarily responsible for its segmentation and reassembly. Four different AAL types are defined for ATM and correspond to the four classes of service. AAL1 is designed to support Class A service; AAL2, Class B service; AAL3/4, service Classes C and D; and AAL5, which will also be used to support Classes C and D.

While in theory any AAL type can support any class of service, each has distinct functional properties designed to best support a particular class of service. The ATM Adaptation Layer implements the appropriate AAL functionality for the type of data each virtual circuit will carry. One of the key benefits of ATM is its ability to support very different types of traffic over the same network, and it does so by using AAL types.

AAL1, AAL3/4, and AAL5 specifications have been sufficiently defined to allow vendors to implement them in products. However, users can expect enough variation in AALs in the first generation of ATM end-node products to make general interoperability a problem. Early on, interoperability can only be assured with vendors who have developed their own adapter hardware and software or with vendors who have partnership agreements.

AAL5 was developed as a "lightweight" AAL for variable bit rate, asynchronous traffic (Classes C and D). AAL3/4 is more complex and utilizes more bandwidth. For this and other reasons, most vendors and public carriers are initially implementing AAL5 for these classes of service.

CONSIDERING ATM

Just about all networking vendors have announced some type of ATM functionality for their products. More often that not, announcements for ATM support come in the form of a future product or enhancement. But users, market analysts, and vendors alike agree that widespread availability and use of ATM products is coming, and planners should be prepared.

As TI's Shuler notes, "One of the biggest tasks I face with ATM is figuring out how, practically speaking, to implement it. We [his company and users in general] need to understand how to manage and administer the technology as an element in our network. We have to learn how to build the engineering model for using applications over ATM. We have to figure out logistically how and where to implement ATM products in the network over time. And, maybe most importantly, we have to understand the real cost of implementation."

Key implementation issues include switch design, signaling and circuit types, connection management, LAN services, network management, and interoperability.

ATM switches are major elements in networks. Whether switches serve solely as ATM concentrators or are integral to ATM/Ethernet/Token Ring hubs, users should be aware of a few switch issues. From a design standpoint, the most significant features of a switch are the switch fabric, the location, the number, the size of cell buffers, and the mechanism(s) used to handle contention within the switch.

Much of the debate surrounding the relative merits of time division vs. space division multiplexing architectures as the basis of the switch fabric has been generated by vendors looking for ways to differentiate their products. While some distinct differences between the architectures exist, neither architecture yet offers a clear advantage over the other. Probably more important considerations are the use of cell buffers in the switch and the handling of contention for switch ports. These elements of switch design will affect the cost of building a switch (and therefore its selling price), performance, and growth capacity.

Switch cost can be compared in terms of total cost, cost per port, and cost per cell. Depending on the role an ATM switch will serve in the network, each of these parameters can be a valuable assessment tool. You should look at cost for more than one system size. For example, for a small number of ports, one vendor's cost per port may be higher than another's. But when the switch or hub is expanded, the cost per port may drop much lower than the cost of a competing system.

SIGNALING AND CIRCUITS

Signaling, the procedures for setting up and managing circuits across an ATM network, is a new concept for most LAN administrators. LAN nodes don't need signaling because they don't set up circuits; they just transmit data as necessary. But circuits and signaling are the lifeblood of people who come from the telecommunications side of the industry.

Two types of virtual circuits are used in ATM. One, a permanent virtual circuit (PVC), is always available for end nodes needing to establish a connection. The circuit itself is established by some means outside the ATM network–for example, by a network administrator–and therefore doesn't require the set-up signaling that switched virtual circuits (SVCs) need.

An SVC, on the other hand, is set up when requested by a node and is torn down when no longer needed. For ATM to be used as a private LAN technology, SVC service is a prerequisite; maintaining PVCs between every end node on an ATM LAN would make it unusable. But SVCs do require more complex signaling. The ATM Forum is currently evaluating an SVC signaling specification called Q93B. However, most vendors with products currently on the market are using some form of proprietary signaling scheme which, of course, they plan to change when the standard is finalized.

The decision of whether to use PVCs or SVCs is a much bigger issue in the public WAN arena. Since PVCs don't require the extensive signaling that SVCs do, the first public ATM services offered by the carriers will only be PVC based. While PVCs offer considerable bandwidth flexibility, many users believe that wide-area ATM will be cost justified only with the use of SVCs, which will allow true WAN bandwidth on demand.

Another important differentiator of ATM implementations is the location of the connection-management software. Basically, two options exist. One is to make the software internal to the switch, an approach that distributes the functionality throughout the network. The other is to implement the software in an external system, such as a SPARCstation, somewhere on the network. Each has its relative advantages and disadvantages.

The distributed approach requires greater intelligence be built in to each switch, making them and the whole network a little more complex and costly than they would be with centralized connection management. When the administrator upgrades software, he or she must download every switch in the network, whereas a centralized scheme requires upgrading only one system. However, distributed connection-management software allows the network to be more easily scaled from small to very large. It can also be faster, theoretically, because the resources are all local to the switch and don't have to be transferred across the network. Finally, a decentralized scheme does not have the problem of a central point of failure, inherent in a centralized scheme.

LAN PROTOCOLS OVER ATM

If ATM is going to be able to integrate with and support existing LAN technologies, the products will have to provide certain services. Three that are high on this list are support for multicasting, LAN emulation, and address mapping.

To run unmodified across an ATM network, LAN protocols, such as TCP/IP and IPX, require support for multicasting. When a TCP/IP node, for example, wants to get the media access control (MAC) address of another node, it broadcasts an Address Resolution Protocol (ARP) packet out to the network addressed to "everybody." Since ATM is connection oriented, the switch needs to have some mechanism for duplicating the ARP and sending it to all other end nodes in the network.

Multicasting is essentially free in shared-medium networks, but in switched networks it makes an additional demand on the switch hardware and/or software. The most efficient place to perform multicasting is in the switch fabric itself, where most vendors have implemented it. No standard exists for handling multicasting over ATM networks, but the ATM Forum is working on the issue and should have a specification ready sometime next year.

Initially, most end nodes will continue to talk to an Ethernet or Token Ring concentrator card in a hub. The protocol exchange between a shared-medium LAN and the ATM network will take place in the hub, typically as a function of a router or bridge card that will make use of the multicasting function. In this way, Ethernet traffic, for example, will be "bridged" over the ATM network between hubs, where it will be handed off to shared Ethernet segments or dedicated Ethernet ports.

But this arrangement doesn't solve the inability of LAN protocols such as TCP/IP, IPX, XNS, AppleTalk, DECnet, or OSI to talk directly to the ATM network. The solution to this problem is called LAN emulation. Both the ATM Forum and the Internet Engineering Task Force (IETF) have a TCP/IP LAN emulation specification. But because no emulation specification exists for the other protocols, other packets remain out of the loop, including about 60 percent of all LAN traffic that reportedly uses IPX protocols.

Part of the LAN-emulation puzzle is internetwork address mapping. In a TCP/IP network, for example, when a node wants to find the MAC address for another node so it can send data, the sending node broadcasts an ARP. When the destination node receives the ARP, it sends back information about its 48-bit MAC address, at which point the source node can begin sending packets. But no standard specification exists yet for mapping a MAC address to an ATM address.

In the absence of standards, vendors devise their own schemes so they may get products to market. Some will be better than others, but none will interoperate. Because multicasting, address mapping, and LAN emulation are critical to integrating ATM into existing networks, users will be bound to a single vendor's products until standard specifications are defined and implemented.

GETTING FROM HERE TO THERE

ATM switches will provide multicast and other services that support the requirements of LAN routers such as Open Shortest Path First (OSPF), Cisco's Interior Gateway Routing Protocol, Intermediate System to Intermediate System (IS-IS), and Routing Information Protocol (RIP). However, no direct link exists between ATM and router networks, which sit outside the ATM network and use it as a transport service. Nor does a standard exist for ATM interswitch routing. Most ATM vendors will use a derivative of the OSPF algorithm, but ATM routing will remain separate from IP routing.

This architecture is best for allowing ATM to be integrated easily into current enterprise networks, and it assures that ATM switches won't have to bear the burden of multiprotocol routing. In the short run, router networks will remain intact, and routers will continue to serve their functions of delineating and connecting network segments across both local and wide areas. As networks migrate toward ATM, the routing function will continue to exist, but routers as we know them may become obsolete.

Congestion management is another area in which the ATM Forum, let alone a standards body, has yet to establish specifications. Fortunately, because of the immense amount of bandwidth available, congestion with ATM (what little congestion may occur on campus backbones or even pure ATM LANs) can be handled easily with a simple, reactive control scheme.

Congestion management is a more important factor in wide-area ATM networks. Embedded in ATM technology are several methods for managing congestion. They include congestion notification, handled in much the same way as on frame relay networks, and traffic shaping from the end node. Also embedded in ATM are procedures for prioritizing cells and ensuring that higher-priority traffic always gets through.

MANAGING ATM

One of the most critical factors, whether integrating ATM into an existing network or building a pure ATM LAN, is network management. Again, no management standards have been specified yet, and the ATM Forum has recently taken up the challenge. Most vendors either have or have plans for some type of SNMP management by placing SNMP agents in ATM switches and adapters and developing or enhancing management platforms.

ATM management includes the ability to monitor and control SVCs and PVCs, overall network topology, and the health of each of the elements in the network. Congestion reporting will be important in ATM networks, as well. How it is reported–per port, per VCI, and/or per VPI– makes a difference for network operators. One of the important differentiators between vendors will be how well their management system integrates ATM management with monitoring and control of existing LANs.

VENDOR STRATEGIES

Who will emerge as the key players in ATM? The first three market segments to develop will be for ATM-only technical workstation networks (switches and adapters), campus backbone switches, and ATM "smart hubs." Switches for ATM backbones that link to upgraded shared-media and dedicated Ethernet hubs will have a fairly short window before a third "smart hub" (combined ATM and shared media) market emerges.

The traditional hub vendors, such as SynOptics, Cabletron, and Hughes LAN Systems, with their large installed bases and distribution networks, are probably best positioned for these markets. N.E.T. and Newbridge, both taking a run at these markets from their traditional niches as WAN switch vendors, will have a harder time because they lack the distribution channels.

At least one important player in the hub market, Ungermann-Bass (UB), has articulated a long-term ATM strategy to build switches and hubs in conjunction with Bolt, Beranek and Newman (BBN, Cambridge, MA), but in the near term the company is focusing on its Dragon-Switch product, an Ethernet switching hub that incorporates Virtual Network Architecture (VNA) functionality. VNA gives users the ability to assign virtual Ethernet segments in software, which can also be done with ATM. They are banking on users being interested in a subset of ATM benefits at a lower price for the next 12 to 18 months. UB and BBN recently announced the formation of an independent, jointly owned company called LightStream to develop a line of ATM products.

IBM also recently announced a panoramic ATM strategy that includes the eventual development of products from hubs and switches down to ATM semiconductor chips. Its initial offerings, slated for introduction in 1994, will be an intelligent ATM hub being developed in partnership with Chipcom (Southboro, MA) and adapter cards for workstations and servers.

Today's hub vendors have a vested interest in providing ATM connectivity for their users' existing shared-media networks, allowing them to transition to the new technology over time. Vendors entering the hub market for the first time with ATM offerings will also be vying for these customers. But a market for pure ATM LANs to connect high-performance workstations will also exist, and Fore Systems has staked out an early claim on it with their switch and broad array of technical workstation adapters.

The PC-adapter market will be a few years in coming. Users are too heavily invested in current technologies to open up to ATM for a while. But when the market does take off, it promises to be huge, and the traditional adapter vendors are already laying plans for attacking the market.

The router vendors, however, are in a curious position

with respect to ATM. Those router vendors who have done so well providing bandaids for the shared-media congestion problems may find that the market for routers per se will decrease significantly as the ATM market grows. Router vendors will forge alliances and partnerships for developing routing functionality in ATM switches and hubs. Some router vendors will also shift their traditional focus somewhat.

OUTSTANDING ISSUES

Everyone has his or her list of outstanding issues for ATM. Key questions for network managers and planners are: What will ATM do for me that I can't get from extensions of my existing LAN technologies, such as 100Mbps Ethernet or FDDI over copper? What changes will I have to make to implement it? What will ATM implementation really cost?

The need for ATM is not obvious to many LAN managers. Few individual applications even come close to justifying the current cost of ATM. And virtual LAN architectures, combined with faster versions of Ethernet, will help many users hold the line against network congestion and increased segmentation for a while and will likely cost less than ATM in the short term.

But these technologies are limited in their ability to scale from small to very large networks. And as TI's Shuler points out, the cumulative demand of many applications will really drive ATM. For this reason many of the world's biggest, most communications-intensive companies are already lining up behind ATM, working closely with vendors, directly and through the ATM Forum, to push the industry forward.

"Hughes Aircraft has made a conscious decision to step over the so-called transition technologies and go right to ATM as the basis for our enterprise network architecture," says Bud Huber, manager of strategic planning for Hughes. "ATM is the best foundation for extending current applications and building the future of our business."

ATM will not appear overnight, nor will it solve all of our problems. For some it will be too slow in coming and they may get frustrated. It will undoubtedly create new problems even as it solves old ones.

But at this point it is clear that ATM is coming. ATM's flexibility, speed, and ability to form the basis for a single, unified enterprise network architecture will eventually convert enough users to reach critical mass. It will solve many current problems, and, perhaps more importantly, it will enable new applications that will make companies more efficient, more effective, and more competitive.

Plug in at 100

AS 100MBPS ETHERNET VIES FOR THE TOP RUNG ON THE HIGH-SPEED LADDER, THE STANDARD MUST SCALE SLIPPERY POLITICAL AND TECHNOLOGICAL SLOPES.

BY PATRICIA SCHNAIDT

A s networks have become an integral part of corporate computing, their pathways have become clogged with users. With a single Ethernet or Token Ring unable to sate users' appetites for bandwidth, network managers have called in routers to segment networks. Routers have cleared many congestion ills, but they are no panacea. The speed of the LAN itself is the next target for improvement.

The market for high-speed LANs is vast, potentially as great as the size of the entire network market. In this high-stakes contest, the vendors are vitriolic, as they elbow each other for the right to plug in a 100Mbps , each proclaiming its technology to be the true descendant of Ethernet or the chosen path for multimedia.

THE NEED FOR SPEED

As corporations distribute their data, networks become populated with more users and more data. The applications are becoming more demanding as well. No longer home to character-based productivity applications alone, networks are running mission-critical applications and databases. With the advent of better graphics, file sizes are larger. Distributed applications such as Lotus Notes have healthy appetites for bandwidth.

Not all big-bandwidth applications are quotidian. On the horizon is multimedia, although whether multimedia will ravage the business application landscape or stay a home application remains to be seen. If your idea of mul-timedia is playing prerecorded, digitized video and send-ing multimedia e-mail on a small scale, today's networks will be able to handle it. Once you try to broadcast video to many users or want to do interactive videoconferencing, you'll need a network technology with more bandwidth

and a greater attention to latency than current networks offer.

Just which network will deliver the additional band-width and lower latency has yet to be settled. A variety of technologies are clambering for the top rung on the ladder, including Fiber Distributed Data Interface (FDDI), local Asynchronous Transfer Mode (ATM), and 100Mbps Ether-net, but none has gained a strong foothold. Sage Network Research (Newton Centre, MA) surveyed 256 network pro-fessionals on which high-speed LAN technologies they were most likely to evaluate. Sage found that 63 percent of the respondents were likely to evaluate 100Mbps Ethernet, 54 percent were likely to evaluate ATM, and 53 percent were likely to evaluate Copper Distributed Data Interface or CDDI (see Figure 1). It's a close call.

FDDI and its twisted-pair cognate CDDI have been available the longest but are still costly. Running ATM to the desktop is even more expensive and experimental than FDDI. ATM is a virtual circuit technology, which is very different from the shared-media LANs people use. 100Mbps Ethernet is still in the vendors' labs and in the standards committees, but it has gained a large mindshare.

The development of 100Mbps Ethernet has been fraught with political machinations. IEEE committee meet-ings, once among the dullest assemblies on earth, now showcase some of the network industry's biggest political maneuverings. Putting politics aside, let's look at the dif-ferent 100Mbps Ethernet technologies, their relative use-fulness, and when they will become available.

100MBPS ETHERNET

The effort to deliver 100Mbps Ethernet is split into two

main camps: IEEE 802.12 and IEEE 802.3. 802.12 is working to standardize a version of Hewlett-Packard's (HP, Roseville, CA) 100VG-AnyLAN, which uses the demand-priority media-access method; accommodates Ethernet and Token Ring frame formats; and transmits over four pairs of Category 3 UTP wire, Category 5 UTP, STP, or fiber. 100VG-AnyLAN is so named because it runs over Category 3 UTP, which is both voice grade (VG) and data grade cable, and can work with both Ethernet and Token Ring frame formats (any LAN).

The 802.3 100BaseT committee is working to standardize a 100Mbps Ethernet that uses a carrier sense, multiple access with collision detection (CSMA/CD) media-access method with either a 100BaseX or a 4T+ signaling scheme. 100BaseX is an amalgamation of CSMA/CD and the FDDI physical layer; it requires two pairs of Category 5 wire but also runs over STP and fiber. 4T+ marries CSMA/CD with a new signaling scheme; it requires four pairs of Category 3 wire.

The two standards efforts will result in completely different networks, but both will use the Ethernet frame format. Which one will be appropriate for you depends mostly on the type of wire you have installed, but also on your vendor loyalty and the urgency of your bandwidth needs.

WIRED FOR SPEED

Bear in mind the history of 10BaseT: In the early days, vendors proclaimed that you could use ordinary telephone wire to transmit data at 10Mbps. In reality, the existing telephone wire usually wasn't of sufficient quality to carry 10Mbps data, and many sites ended up pulling new data-grade UTP, now referred to as Category 3.

As networks take a tenfold increase in speed, wiring will be at the heart of the matter. Once again, perception is reality. The typical 10BaseT installation uses Category 3 UTP in the wiring runs to the desktop, 25-pair Category 3 bundles in the wiring closet, and fiber optics in the building risers and on the backbone. 10BaseT transmits over two-pair Category 3, and at least one four-pair bundle is pulled to most desktops. What those other two pairs are doing is critical, but difficult, to quantify. Are they used as a voice line or a modem line? Are they idle? No one knows for sure.

For new installations, most people pull Category 5 UTP.

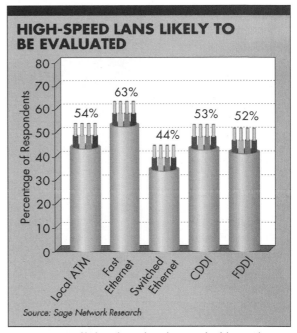

Figure 1. A variety of high-speed networks are being considered, but none has gained a strong foothold, according to Sage Network Research.

Category 5 costs a bit more than Category 3, but the Electronic Industries Association (EIA) has rated it for 100Mbps transmission, which makes it suitable for FDDI, 100Mbps Ethernet, ATM, and other high-speed LAN transmissions. The EIA has rated Category 3 for transmissions up to 10MHz. Most sites with Token Ring use STP. That's the accepted wisdom for wiring.

Let's hope conventional wisdom is right, because little statistically meaningful research on the quantity and type of wiring exists. 100Mbps Ethernet vendors mostly cite surveys that were conducted within their customer base or use very small sample sizes. It's hard to get a good cross section of what cabling is installed, yet the quantity and type of available wiring is pivotal in this race to plug in the next high-speed LAN.

JLP Associates, a Santa Jose, CA, consulting firm, surveyed 150 companies with revenues of $20 million to $88 billion, and it found that 34 percent had four pairs of UTP installed at the desktop, 13 percent had six pairs installed at the desktop, and 22 percent had eight pairs at the desktop (see Figure 2). Forty-two percent of the respondents in the JLP study run 25-pair bundles of UTP in the wiring

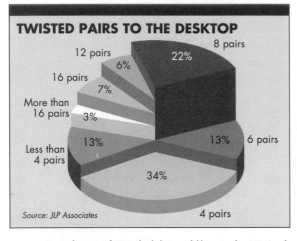

TWISTED PAIRS TO THE DESKTOP

12 pairs — 6%

8 pairs — 22%

16 pairs — 7%

More than 16 pairs — 3%

Less than 4 pairs — 13%

6 pairs — 13%

4 pairs — 34%

Source: JLP Associates

Figure 2. Having four pairs of UTP to the desktop available is critical to 802.12 and 4T+. JLP Associates' survey found that 34 percent had four pairs installed at the desktop, 13 percent had six pairs, and 22 percent had eight pairs.

closet; only 18 percent use them in the horizontal wiring subsystem. The JLP study confirmed that Category 5 is the choice for new installations. Of those surveyed, 65 percent said that their cabling standard was Category 5; 16 percent said it was Category 3, 6 percent said it was Category 4, 5 percent said it was STP, and 5 percent said it was thin coax.

"The people who specify wiring typically say 'Let's pull lots of wire and plan for growth,' " says Paul Ahrens of National Semiconductor (Santa Clara, CA). Ahrens is 100Mbps program manager and president of the Fast Ethernet Alliance, a consortium of vendors interested in the 100BaseT cause. "What ends up happening is that the facilities department pulls the wire. Facilities has a tighter budget than telecom, so facilities may or may not pull it. They definitely pull it to the wiring closet, but very few companies know what goes on from wiring closet out to the desk."

If you have a Category 3 wiring plant, you may be able to use either an 802.12 or 4T+ implementation. If you have a Category 5 plant, you may be able to use 802.12 or 100BaseX. Be forewarned that not all Category 5 wiring plants are completely Category 5. Category 5 wire has been shipping for about a year, but the Category 5 cross connects and patch panels have been available for about six months.

Wiring won't always be a Gordian knot. The impend-

ing EIA 568 specification for commercial building wiring should resolve some confusion, since it calls for installing four pairs to the desktop. Many companies are now recommending running eight pairs to the desktop.

A LOOK AT 100BASET

100BaseT is being developed under the aegis of 802.3. 100BaseT uses a CSMA/CD media-access method, an Ethernet frame format, and either the 4T+ or the 100BaseX signaling scheme. If 100BaseX is targeted for Category 5 installations, then 4T+ is slated for the existing Category 3 installations.

"10Mbps Ethernet started with thick coax, then moved to thin coax, FOIRL [fiber optic interrepeater link], 10BaseF, and UTP. There has been a history of multiple media for same LAN type. We're just starting with two media types," says Peter Tarrant, chairman of IEEE 802.3 100BaseT task force and director of product management at SynOptics (Santa Clara, CA).

The primary objectives of 100BaseT are to provide:
• An unchanged media-access control (MAC) layer (IEEE 802.3, CSMA/CD). The Ethernet MAC remains unchanged, except for the interframe gap, which is specified in time. The remaining Ethernet MAC attributes are specified in bits, which does not change if the speed is increased. In Ethernet, the interframe gap is 9.6 microseconds; in 100BaseX, it is .96 microseconds. Both are 96 bits.
• A 100Mbps data rate.
 Support of cabling systems compliant with EIA 568 and TSB 36.
• A network span of 250 meters. At 250 meters, the network diameter of a 100Mbps Ethernet network is one-tenth the size of 10Mbps Ethernet.
• 100-meter links between workstations and hubs. Ninety percent of the workstations are within 100 meters of the wiring closet.
• Implementation costs less than twice 10Mbps Ethernet's costs.
• Emissions satisfying FCC Class B and the European equivalent, EN 55022B.
• Error robustness equal to or better than that of 10Mbps Ethernet.

The two signaling types–100BaseX and 4T+–will be interoperable at the station and the hub. Interoperability at the station will be achieved via the media-independent interface (MII), which is an AUI-like interface. Interoperability at the hub will be achieved via a repeater. 100BaseT will specify a *universal repeater* which will support both physical layers. A 100BaseT network can support up to two universal repeaters 10 meters apart. 100BaseT will also specify *line-level repeaters* for each technology that will support extended distances.

When 100BaseT ships, expect to see 100Mbps adapters as well as ones that are speed switchable from 10Mbps to 100Mbps, as was done with 4/16Mbps Token Ring.

"At the price 10/100 adapters are going to be sold, we think there will be little end-user resistance to them," says Tom Slykhouse, SynOptics' group manager of connectivity.

100BASEX FOR CATEGORY 5

100BaseX adapts the full-duplex signaling mechanism of FDDI to work with the Ethernet MAC. Because it uses FDDI's Physical Medium Dependent (PMD), which is the encoder/decoder and transceiver, 100BaseX uses the same cable types as FDDI. When implementing the FDDI Twisted Pair PMD (TP-PMD), 100BaseX uses two pairs of Category 5 UTP. With the other two pairs properly terminated, they should be able to carry voice but not another high-speed LAN. TP-PMD uses stream-cipher scrambling and MLT-3 bit encoding. 100BaseX also supports the FDDI Fiber PMD, which calls for 62.5/125 micron multimode fiber. The Fiber PMD uses unscrambled, Non-Return to Zero, Invert on ones (NRZI) bit encoding.

The 100BaseX specification calls for a *convergence sublayer*, which maps the FDDI PMD's continuous signaling to the start-stop, half-duplex system expected by the Ethernet MAC (see Figure 3). Using FDDI's four binary, five binary (4B/5B) encoding, the PMD carries five-bit code groups, which are mapped to symbols.

These symbols are mapped to represent 16 data values, four control codes (for packet delimiters, which in Ethernet is done via the carrier sense and transmit signals), and the idle code. The remaining symbols are declared invalid. If the MAC transmits while the sublayer receives, a collision occurs.

David Systems (Sunnyvale, CA), Digital Equipment, Grand Junction Networks (Fremont, CA), Intel (Hillsboro, OR), National Semiconductor, Sun Microsystems (Chelmsord, MA), SynOptics, and 3Com (Santa Clara, CA) are the principal sponsors of 100BaseX.

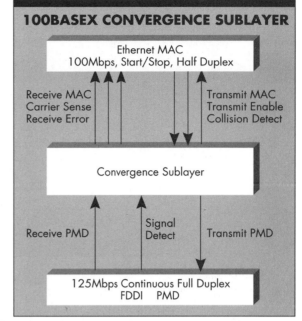

Figure 3. 100BaseX's convergence sublayer maps the FDDI physical layer's continuous signaling to the startstop, half-duplex Ethernet MAC.

4T+ FOR CATEGORY 3

The 4T+ signaling scheme enables 100BaseT to run over existing Category 3 wiring. 4T+ is a half-duplex signaling that transmits and receives over four pairs of Category 3, 4, or 5. Three pairs are used to transmit data in each direction, while the fourth pair is used as receive only for collision detection.

Like 10BaseT, 4T+ uses pairs 1 and 2 to carry data and for collision detection in one direction only. Unlike 10BaseT, 4T+ uses pairs 2 and 4 bidirectionally to carry data (see Figure 4). 4T+ does not support 25-pair Category 3 in the horizontal wiring.

In 4T+, data is encoded in an eight binary, six ternary (8B/6T) code set, which delivers a good DC balance, according to Robert Heaton, director of hardware engineering at Standard Microsystems Corp. (SMC, Irvine, CA). 8B/6T is a new bit encoding scheme, although it is technologically akin to MLT-3. Bandwidth is limited to below 30MHz. 4T+ also uses a quiet idle state, like 10BaseT but unlike 100BaseX.

4T+ will support the 100BaseT universal repeater. Ac-

Figure 4. 100BaseT's solution for transmitting over four-pair Category 3 is 4T+. In this half-duplex signaling scheme, three pairs are used to transmit data in each direction, while the fourth pair is used as receive only for collision detection.

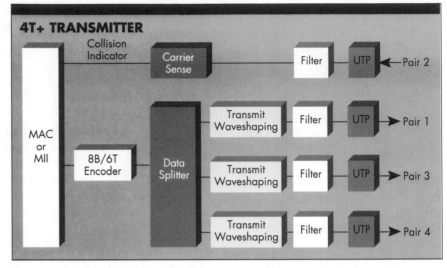

Figure 4. 100BaseT's solution for transmitting over four-pair Category 3 is 4T+. In this half-duplex signaling scheme, three pairs are used to transmit data in each direction, while the fourth pair is used as receive only for collision detection.

cording to Nariman Yousefi, SMC's manager of analog engineering and coauthor of the physical-layer portion of the 4T+ specification, the 4T+ group is also working on a line-level repeater that will potentially support three levels of repeaters. 4T+ also plans to specify a fiber repeater.

SMC, 3Com, and Intel developed the 4T+ specification.

HOW FAR WITH 100BASET?

100BaseT proponents contend that little will change for 10BaseT network designers and managers. "The bulk of the connection is the same. The only difference is how you interconnect the hubs," says 100BaseT task force Chairman Tarrant. Both 100BaseX and 4T+ support distances of 100 meters from the hub to the workstation and a distance of 10 meters from hub to hub. Vendors say that the small network diameter isn't a problem, since networks typically use routers for segmentation.

"Most people will run fiber to the basement, which then connects to a wiring device. A two kilometer flat network is not practical. People want a demarcation point," says George Prodan, 3Com's high-speed product line manager. "For the desktops, 100 meters is all you need."

100BaseT advocates contend that managing a 100BaseT network will be similar to managing a 10BaseT network. 100BaseT will use the 802.3 repeater management specification, with a modification to indicate whether the repeater is a 10Mbps or 100Mbps device. "We

may change the management indicator as to the speed, but you can use identical MIBs [management information bases]," says Slykhouse.

The Fast Ethernet Alliance will conduct interoperability testing. It will define the test suites, but third-party testing houses may perform the actual tests. Slykhouse expects the tests to be ironed out by about March.

100Mbps Ethernet is developing. No standards-compatible products exist, as the standards are still on the drawing board. "With all of the work that's been done, there will be reasonably mature drafts by second quarter. The back end of the standards process will be done in the second half. The standards will be formally done by the end of '94," says Tarrant. "The 100BaseX specification is slightly ahead, but the 4T+ group has done a lot of work over the last three months."

EXAMINING 802.12

Demand priority is being developed under the auspices of 802.12. Spearheaded by HP, but supported by IBM, Proteon (Westboro, MA), AT&T Microelectronics (Berkeley Heights, NJ), Ungermann-Bass (Santa Clara, CA), and others, 802.12 specifies a 100Mbps network that uses the demand-priority access method, an Ethernet or Token Ring frame format, and quartet signaling for encoding. The 802.12 spec will operate over four pairs of Category 3, STP, Category 5, and fiber. Networks are designed in a star topology, supporting up to three levels of cascaded repeaters and up to 100 meters between the re-peaters and the stations. A network may be up to 4,000 feet in diameter.

Demand priority is a round-robin arbitration method in which the central repeater regularly polls its connected ports–in port order–to determine which have pending transmission requests and whether those requests are normal priority or high priority (see Figure 5). High-pri-ority requests are serviced before normal-priority re-quests. Demand priority institutes different levels of pri-ority to service both data and real-time video needs.

Ports that are not transmitting issue an idle signal. When the repeater selects the next station to transmit, it clears the idle signal to that station. Once the station has sensed the silence, it begins to transmit. The repeater alerts the other stations that they may receive an incom-ing message, and the repeater decodes the incoming packet's destination address as it is received. The repeater looks in its link configuration table for the port belonging to that destination address and sends it to that port and to any promiscuous ports.

The *root repeater* controls the operation of the *priority domain*, which may include up to three levels of cascaded hubs. Essentially, interconnected repeaters act as a single large repeater. All traffic is sent to each repeater, and each polls its active ports for requests after packet transmis-sion.

To ensure fairness, no station is permitted to transmit twice in a row if other stations have requests pending at the same priority level. At the root, a high-priority request is not permitted to interrupt a normal-priority request that's already in progress; however, in a lower-level re-peater, the normal-priority request is preempted, so the high-priority request can be executed. To ensure that a re-quest doesn't starve while waiting for the CPU, normal-priority requests that have been pending longer than 250 ms are elevated to high-priority status.

802.12 uses a quartet signaling encoding scheme. Data is encoded as five binary, six binary (5B/6B) characters and transmitted across the wire in four sequential code streams. It uses NRZ encoding. Like 4T+, quartet signal-ing is a new encoding scheme.

Unlike 100BaseT, 802.12 supports 25-pair Category 3 bundles in wiring runs between the stations and the re-peaters; however, the repeaters must implement a store-

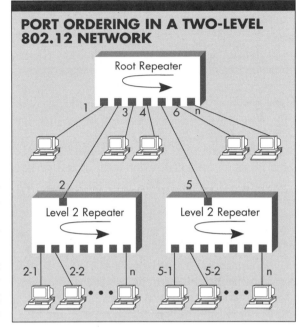

PORT ORDERING IN A TWO-LEVEL 802.12 NETWORK

Figure 5. The 802.12 root repeater polls each port in physical port order for trans-mission. In the example, the portorder is 1, 2-1, 2-2, . . . , 3, 4, 5-1, 5-2, . . . 6, . . .

and-forward operation rather than their normal cut-through switching. Because of Category 3's lower electro-magnetic characteristics, the hub cannot transmit and re-ceive simultaneously because of crosstalk. Category 5 repeaters will be able to support 25-pair cable without buffering. The repeater operates in store-and-forward mode when transmitting multicast or broadcast packets, also because of the crosstalk.

Although 802.12 supports both Ethernet and Token Ring frame formats, all hubs in a priority domain must support either Token Ring or Ethernet. However, says Brice Clark, HP's strategic planning manager for the Ro-seville, CA, Networks Division, "We're looking at an ex-tension to the standard to detect which type of packet is coming in. It's not particularly important in the first stan-dard. Hardly anybody puts Ethernet and Token Ring in the same wiring closet." Until they do, a modular hub con-taining a Token Ring-to-Ethernet bridge/router will pro-vide simultaneous support for the two packet types.

In its implementation of 802.12, HP plans to offer a product that transmits on two-pair STP, two-pair Category

5, and one strand of fiber. It accomplishes this transmission by multiplexing the four code blocks onto the higher-capacity wire.

"With STP, the bandwidth is much higher. You can double the signaling rate on those two pairs and put two code blocks onto one pair, whereas on Category 3, the code blocks will be on their own pairs," says Clark. "The two-pair Category 5 solution will look like the STP solution with different impedance matching."

Clark notes that the 802.12 signaling approach uses the same silicon for the different wire types, while 100BaseT uses different signaling schemes. "The technology for Category 5 is completely different than the technology for Category 3."

GET YOUR PRIORITIES STRAIGHT

Priorities are an important part of 802.12 and a brave new world for network managers. Something–an application, a supervisory function on the server, or the NOS itself–tells the adapter card the transmission priority. Existing applications won't know about the priority scheme, and by default they'll transmit at normal priority. Applications that carry time-sensitive payloads, such as video or voice, would ideally take advantage of the priority scheme.

"We have a lot of multimedia software developers on the early list for products. They're panting to get their hands on the technology. They can enable applications to set a high priority for the multimedia portions of their products," says Clark.

"With so much bandwidth available, the real need for multimedia is low latency and guaranteed bandwidth. We've done extensive modeling. We can have 60 full-motion video channels on a VG net. We could have several hundred videoconferencing channels," he says.

Clark says that as the 802.12 network gets larger, you would want to impose a check-out scheme on the priorities. For example, you might want to limit the number of priority slots, so you can ensure all traffic gets a fair share of the bandwidth.

The work on priorities has just begun. "We've approached 802.1 and have about 25 companies interested in developing a standard. It will take a while for the technology to roll out and for people to run into bandwidth problems," says Clark.

Also akin to the Fast Ethernet Alliance, 802.12 propo-

nents assert that a 802.12 hub will be managed similarly to a 10BaseT hub and will use Simple Network Management Protocol (SNMP).

"The MIB variables will look like Ethernet MIBs and Token Ring MIBs, although a few parameters don't make sense any more. There are no more collisions and token rotation times," says Clark.

Clark says that 802.12 has "a pretty solid draft specification" that he expects will be voted on at the IEEE Plenary meeting in March. "By mid-1994 we will have our draft standard, which people will feel fine about implementing. Dotting the i's and crossing the t's on 10BaseT took two more years," he says. As with the Fast Ethernet Alliance, Clark cites interoperability as a major goal of the standards effort.

THE UPSHOT

Do you need 100Mbps now? If you want products based on existing standards, then your only real choice is FDDI, either as a shared-media hub or as a switch. You may want to look at full-duplex transmission. If you're willing to go with prestandard 100Mbps Ethernet, Grand Junction is shipping FastNIC 10 and FastSwitch 10/100, which combines a 10Mbps Ethernet switch with 100Mbps Ethernet. If you can wait until the 100Mbps Ethernet standards are complete–optimistically by the end of 1994–you can take advantage of the lower cost, standards-based 100BaseT and 802.12 technologies.

Until the standards are complete and products are shipping, deciding which technology is "better" is an academic exercise in reading IEEE specifications. The real test is implementation, cost, and interoperability.

In the meantime, closely examine your wiring plans. If you're going to pull new cabling, by all means, pull Category 5. It only costs a bit more than Category 3, and it will be capable of transmitting 100BaseT, 802.12, FDDI, and ATM. If you have a Category 3 wiring plant and you don't want to upgrade (or can't afford it), then your choices are more limited. If you've got four pairs available to the desk, great. Otherwise, you're going to have trouble reaching 100Mbps, no matter which technology you select. If you've got STP, your cable has the bandwidth necessary to carry you into the next stage of high-speed computing.

To install any high-speed network, you'll need the appropriate high-speed wire testers and signal testers. Category 5 wiring testers are now coming to market, but a set of testing parameters that make a Category 5 plant pass or fail a test has not been formulated. Vendors of cable testers are vying to have their methods adopted as the standard.

Also look closely at the cost of implementing 100BaseT and 802.12. At twice the cost of 10BaseT, the target price for both camps is slightly less than FDDI.

HP's Clark says, "I think the $400 total cost is still too high. At comparable volumes, VG will cost no more than 10BaseT. By the end of '95 or mid-1996, the street price will be below $200 for the hub and adapter."

Switches are more expensive than repeaters; their electronics are more complicated. 100BaseT networks have a small diameter, which means you need bridges and routers. The typical network is heavily segmented for traffic purposes, so chances are you won't get rid of any of the segmentation by going to a faster technology. If anything, the segmentation will increase.

FULL-DUPLEX VS. HALF-DUPLEX TRANSMISSION
Double Your Pleasure

Whether you choose 10Mbps Ethernet or 100Mbps Ethernet, you might want to consider the technology's ability to run in full-duplex mode. Traditional Ethernet is *half duplex;* it can either transmit a packet or receive a packet, but it cannot transmit and receive simultaneously. Simultaneous transmit and receive is *full duplex.* A 10Mbps Ethernet running in full-duplex mode would be able to transmit and receive at 20Mbps. If 100Mbps Ethernet ran in full-duplex mode, it would have a rated speed of 200Mbps.

Taking advantage of full-duplex transmission requires full-duplex adapter cards connected to a switch rather than to a shared media hub. A switch can send and receive simultaneously, while a shared-media hub cannot. Because a switch uses more complicated electronics, it is also more expensive.

Pay attention to where you need the bandwidth improvement. If your applications are throughput intensive, as multimedia is, for example, you probably want to upgrade the entire workgroup.

In most cases, the server is the bottleneck, and you can improve performance by putting the servers on a faster network. Servers are required to send and receive data simultaneously, since they must respond to client requests, so full-duplex transmission might be a boon. Workstations generally don't need full-duplex transmission, because they either send or receive data but don't send and receive at the same time.

If full duplex sounds right for you, also consider the improvement in speed.

"If you're going to replace every adapter, why go from 10Mbps to 20Mbps?" asks Jack Moses, vice president of marketing at Grand Junction Networks (Fremont, CA). "The real cost isn't the price of network adapters; it is the cost of sending people out to replace the adapters. Companies are not going through that hassle for a potential increase to 20Mbps."

For 100Mbps full-duplex transmission, you should look to 100BaseT's 100BaseX implementation rather than 4T+. 100BaseX uses the FDDI Physical Medium Dependent (PMD), which is inherently full duplex, although full-duplex transmission is not currently specified. 4T+, which runs over Category 3 UTP, is half-duplex.

But not everyone is a fan of full duplex. "Full duplex is irrelevant. It's a FUD [fear-uncertainty-and-doubt] factor," says Brice Clark, strategic planning manager for Hewlett-Packard's Networks Division (Roseville, CA). "You can use full duplex, but now you're talking about very expensive switching hubs that cost $1,000 a connection. We can build fully switched VG hubs. We can also run VG higher than 100Mbps on Category 5, fiber, or STP. We can do 200Mbps on Category 5."

Twice As Nice

100MBPS ETHERNET PROMISES 10 TIMES THE SPEED AT TWICE THE PRICE OF 10BASET. BUT WHEN YOU NEED THE SPEED, WILL 100MBPS BE AVAILABLE?

BY PATRICIA SCHNAIDT

While you wait for your 386 PC to churn out the recalculation of a 1,200-cell spreadsheet under Windows, you have plenty of time to dream about the fast life: Your Pentium-powered PC running the 32-bit Windows NT, cranking through the recalculation of that enormous financial model. You dream of sending your boss that gargantuan file, along with an e-mail that includes a video clip of you saying: "We're going to make oodles of money this quarter. Look at cells A6,935 to G8,902."

If you manage to talk your money-powers-that-be into that cool new Pentium machine, you'll also have to think about the LAN pipe. If you're using an EISA, MCA PC, or RISC workstation, you might want to give your LAN a second thought. These machines may have enough power to prompt the need for high-speed networks to the desktop.

Infonetics (San Jose, CA), is finishing a study on the shipments of FDDI adapters for PCs and workstations. "It looks like the long-awaited upturn of desktop FDDI is occurring," says Michael Howard, the market research firm's president.

But high-speed LANs don't necessarily mean FDDI anymore: The IEEE 802.3 committee has formed a study group to throw its beloved Ethernet hat into the high-speed LAN ring. What that network will be, and whether you can call it Ethernet, is a hotly debated issue. Going by the monikers "Fast Ethernet," "100Mbps Ethernet," and "100BaseVG," this offspring of 802.3 is causing a stir. In short, 100Mbps Ethernet promises to deliver 100Mbps of bandwidth to the desktop computer over unshielded twisted-pair wiring. And the proposed price tag should tantalize even the most budget-constrained MIS manager–

only one-and-a-half times to two times the current price of 10BaseT.

ONE MORE FAST NETWORK

Those of you awaiting the ballyhooed explosion in FDDI to the desktop may wonder if users really need 100Mbps at their fingertips, regardless of what access method is chosen to deliver it. But the network manufacturers are insistent: We're going to need mega-bandwidth at workstations.

"The majority of our customers who have larger networks have a need for more bandwidth," says Surya Panditi, general manager of the Access/One business unit for Ungermann-Bass (Santa Clara, CA). "They're already looking at ways of creating smaller physical segments." Ungermann-Bass recently introduced DragonSwitch, an Ethernet switch that enables users to configure virtual networks.

"You've got to have high-speed networks–whether it's TCNS, FDDI, or something," avers Walt Thirion, president of Thomas-Conrad (Austin, TX), a maker of TCNS, a 100Mbps network. "We're really pushing the bandwidth of existing networks."

According to Thirion, multimedia isn't the application driving high-speed networking, "This is not far-out stuff; they are real-world corporate applications. It's the data that's killing the network. Whether it's factory-floor automation or groupware that lets users share the latest version of some document, it's all going across a network." The need for bandwidth is also predicated on the client-server architecture and downsizing. "If you take a mainframe and blow it apart, you have to compete with those speeds," says Thirion.

Brice Clark, strategic planning manager of Hewlett-Packard's (HP, Roseville, CA) networks division, says the quotidian applications of 486 PCs, graphical user interfaces, and printers attached directly to the network are driving the need for bandwidth. So is a new class of application that can "enhance human communications. The applications that customers are experimenting with are real-time multimedia and diskless workstations," says Clark.

But what has happened to FDDI, the traditional panacea of the speed-choked?

ETHERNET IS BIG BUSINESS

FDDI hasn't arrived, even with the glucose-rich infusion of copper wiring into the 100Mbps token-passing network. FDDI, in its fiber form, is used as a backbone; this summer, FDDI vendors will ship products that implement FDDI over UTP, and the official ANSI standard should follow shortly, some two years after its proposal. In the meantime, the Ethernet people have said, "Hey, we can do that–and we can do it less expensively."

HP's Clark says,"FDDI has provided a solution at a price that is prohibitive. There's very little direct-connect FDDI installed because it costs a minimum of $3,500 for the hub and card, and that doesn't factor in the cost of the fiber.

"The reason that [Grand Junction's] Fast Ethernet and our implementation, 100BaseVG, are getting so much attention is cost. It's the cost of the hardware–specifically the adapters, hubs, and cabling. It's also the cost of integration with existing networks–migrating the installed base gradually, as opposed to using different technology," he says. HP offers connections to managed 10BaseT hubs for less than $200. "That is the baseline for today. Customers don't want to spend more than one-and-a-half to two times what they pay for 10BaseT. FDDI is 10 times the cost of Ethernet," says Clark.

Both HP and Grand Junction (Union City, CA), two of the more visible players in 100Mbps Ethernet, predict that they'll be able to sell products for one-and-a-half times to two times the current cost of 10BaseT. Both to shipped prestandard products at the end of 1993.

Cost isn't the only reason users have been slow to buy FDDI. FDDI is a sophisticated network, and people who design, install, and manage FDDI networks must be quite experienced. In contrast, vast numbers of people are familiar with 10BaseT and unshielded twisted-pair.

The Ethernet manufacturing community looks at the huge installed base of Ethernet and is hoping that the current users will move to 100Mbps Ethernet, instead of migrating to some alien token-passing solution such as FDDI.

Others disagree. "There's no correlation at all," says Thirion. "Once they break out of those modes, it will all come down to perceived cost. It's the cost of the politically correct decision, the tools to troubleshoot, and everything that goes into the cost of ownership."

SO WHAT IS FAST ETHERNET?

The 802.3 Higher Speed Ethernet Study Group has established 10 objectives. Technical proposals have been made and will continue to be made until its July interim meeting; no technical proposals have been accepted. The objectives are:

• It will support a speed of 100Mbps.

• The distance from hub to hub or from hub to station is a maximum of 100 meters.

• The 802.3 frame format or packet size will be retained.

• It will support twisted-pair wiring that conforms to the Electronic Industries Association (EIA) 568 standard for commercial building and wiring.

• It will meet the same error detection requirements as 802.3.

• It will meet emissions and susceptibility for FCC Class B and the European equivalent, EN55024-3.

• It will support dual speeds of 10Mbps and 100Mbps. A hub port will detect the dual speeds as does a 4/16Mbps Token Ring hub port. The adapter cards can optionally support the dual-speed mode; they can be 10Mbps, 100Mbps, or both.

• It will include a specification for a media-independent interface such as the AUI port.

• The topology will support multiple 100Mbps hubs.

• It will use the ISO 8877 connector, which is the international flavor of the RJ-45 connector.

That is 100Mbps Ethernet. Very little else has been decided–even whether this Ethernet network will use Carrier Sense Multiple Access with Collision Detection (CSMA/CD), a trait that has been critical to an Ethernet network's identity.

The Higher Speed Ethernet Study Group has divided into two camps over access method: CSMA/CD or not. The CSMA/CD camp includes Grand Junction, SynOptics, 3Com, Cabletron, Chipcom, and others. The "not" camp includes Hewlett-Packard, Ungermann-Bass, Wellfleet, Plaintree, and RCE. Neither group concurs on wire type, signaling, or media access method (MAC).

Hewlett-Packard has made a technical proposal to the study group that uses a packet switch with the Ethernet frame format. The so-named 100BaseVG runs over Category 3 and Category 5 unshielded twisted-pair (UTP) wire. Grand Junction has made a technical proposal to combine a CSMA/CD MAC with the FDDI signaling scheme. The Grand Junction proposal, called Fast Ethernet, runs over Category 5 UTP.

THE HP PROPOSAL

HP's 100BaseVG is a fundamentally different type of network than 10BaseT, although HP says 100BaseVG will look like Ethernet to the end user. 100BaseVG is comprised of quartet signaling and demand priority.

Quartet signaling transmits using all four pairs in a twisted-pair bundle, or it uses all four pairs for receiving signals. In contrast, 10BaseT uses two pairs of wires–one pair for receiving data and one pair for transmitting. Using 100BaseVG requires twice the number of pairs that 10BaseT needs. Quartet signaling also uses a different data-encoding scheme than 10BaseT. The combination of quartet signaling and a different encoding scheme makes it possible to run 100Mbps of data over Category 3 UTP.

100BaseVG uses *demand priority* to control access to the network. Demand priority implements a packet switch in the hub, and the hub manages access to the network. A node tells the hub it wants to transmit, and it requests either a normal- or high-priority class of service. If the hub receives more than one request at a time, it services the higher-priority ones first. The hub receives the packet from the node and immediately switches it to the outbound port with that destination. The switching architecture affords low latency and minimal delay.

Still, demand priority isn't perfect. It polls the clients to see if they have a transmission, and, if enough high-priority transmissions are queued, the normal-priority transmissions would never get serviced, in a process called *starvation*. Clark says that 100BaseVG could handle 100 real-time video channels coming in from a 1Mbps codec, and starvation wouldn't be an issue. "We don't need to rush to get bandwidth allocation in place. We're a long way from needing it."

Because of demand priority, the HP approach can guarantee bandwidth to high-priority applications. "Bounded delay is a big deal for diskless workstations because you can reduce the amount of memory needed in the workstation," says Clark. You can also use 100BaseVG's bounded-delay feature to give higher priority to servers than to clients. And of course, it's useful for multimedia.

Operating systems and applications must be built to accommodate these priorities. "Priorities are something that Novell would support in its NOS. NetWare might use a higher priority for servers and a normal priority for clients," says Clark.

THE GRAND JUNCTION PROPOSAL

To create 100Mbps Ethernet, Grand Junction proposes to use the CSMA/CD access method with the FDDI Twisted Pair-Physical Medium Dependent (TP-PMD), the latter being a fancy way of saying encoder/ decoder and transceiver.

With a technology Grand calls 100BaseX, Ethernet's four functions–transmit, receive, carrier sense, and collision detection–are mapped to the FDDI PMD, which natively has receive, transmit, and signal detect. The receive and transmit functions map directly. To get a collision-detection signal from an FDDI PMD, 100BaseX performs a logical AND of the receive and transmit streams. Carrier sense is equivalent to NOT idle.

Despite the FDDI signaling, Grand says it can maintain all of the Ethernet MAC attributes, except the interframe gap. In Ethernet, the interframe gap is 9.6ms, which equals 96 bits at 10Mbps. Fast Ethernet still uses 96 bits, but at 100Mbps, the interframe gap must be specified at 96 nanoseconds. Maintaining the MAC, says Grand, ensures a quick time to market and an easy migration path for users, network managers, and product manufacturers.

The FDDI TP-PMD uses the MLT-3 encoding scheme, which enables high-speed data to run over Category 5 twisted-pair and meet FCC Class B emissions. Fast Ethernet requires Category 5 UTP, which is very high-quality UTP; however, very little Category 5 is installed.

Jack Moses, vice president of marketing at Grand Junction, admits that Grand's approach faces challenges. "It's a hard sell, because it's emotional. There's a negative visceral reaction against anything from ANSI X3T9.5," the committee that specified FDDI. The Higher Speed Ethernet Study Group, says Moses, is "interested in building something new."

A BIG MAC ATTACK

Over the past several years, network people have largely stopped debating which type of MAC is better (usually it was token passing vs. collision detection) and moved to the problem of network interoperability. But the MAC debate is back.

Why is an 802.3 committee–the IEEE group for CSMA/CD networks–considering a non-CSMA/ CD proposal? "The chair of 802.3 made a decision to bring a proposal into the group, because she determined that all 100Mbps [research] should take place in one forum," says Peter Tarrant, chairman of the Higher Speed Ethernet Study Group and an employee of SynOptics. What Tarrant carefully does not say is the chair of 802.3, Pat Thaler, is an HP employee. Infer what you wish; in the IEEE committees, everyone is supposed to represent themselves, not their employers.

"802.3 is a CSMA/CD committee, and the [Hewlett-Packard] demand-priority scheme is clearly not Ethernet or CSMA/CD as we know it," says Tarrant.

Others are more forceful in their opinions. "The chair made the unprecedented decision to hear non-CSMA/CD proposals," says Moses. "It opened up a Pandora's box. Even FDDI could now present to the 802.3 committee."

A fulcrum of 100Mbps Ethernet is the MAC. Changing the MAC would cause irreparable damage to the industry, according to some accounts. Others say as long as you preserve the frame format, little will change.

"Only the frame matters. The MAC doesn't matter one iota to the customer," says Clark. Clark says Grand Junction and the others who want a CSMA/CD solution are holding onto something that isn't important to the customer. Users sitting at their desks don't know or care how the network arbitrates access to itself. "They [Grand Junction] are valuing the internal industry of CSMA/CD more than the customers' investment. They want to hold onto CSMA/CD no matter what," says Clark.

"HP says it's just the MAC changing, so it's no big deal.

But it's a long chain of supply. If you change the MAC, it obsoletes investments made along the way," says Moses. "Each change in isolation may not be a big deal, but the accumulation is a disruption through the supply chain. It's an enormous waste, and HP trivializes it."

"There are a lot of implications and impacts on the industry if the MAC layer is changed," says Howard, the independent analyst. "If you don't change the MAC layer, you don't have to change the management software or the testing equipment, and you don't have to teach as much new technology to the industry. You only have to talk about minimal changes [such as drivers]. If that happens, then you really can talk about 'fast Ethernet.' "

WIRED FOR SPEED

Although hardly a glamorous subject, the wire is at the crux of this matter. One reason so many people installed 10BaseT was the widely held belief that it could use existing telephone wire (whether end-user companies really used existing wire is another issue). Two wire types are relevant to 100Mbps Ethernet: Category 3 and Category 5.

Most 10BaseT networks use Category 3. The EIA 568 standard rates Category 3 for speeds up to 10Mbps. Category 5 is a four-pair UTP wire that has much lower capacitance and crosstalk than Category 3. The EIA has approved it for speeds up to 100Mbps, but 155Mbps are possible.

The dilemma is installed base vs. quality. Category 3 has the largest installed base of UTP; Category 5 has existed for only two years. Category 5 is slightly more costly.

HP's proposal runs on Category 3; Grand's network needs Category 5 to succeed. The Higher Speed Ethernet Study Group says that it will use only EIA 568 wiring. Grand Junction is hoping that enough people will install Category 5 wire during the time that it takes to form a 100Mbps Ethernet standard–then wire type will no longer be an issue. "The biggest impediment is that we don't have a Category 3 solution," Moses says.

Conventional wisdom says that people won't rip out their existing UTP just so they can bring 100Mbps of bandwidth to the desktop. After all, many companies rewired their buildings a scant few years ago when they installed 10BaseT.

If you buy into the conventional wisdom, says Paul Callahan, an analyst for Forrester Research (Cambridge,

MA), then you're "probably missing something out there." According to Forrester, in 1991, 2.6 million connections were made using voice-grade UTP; in 1992, 2.4 million connections were made; and in 1993, that number decreased again, to 2.1 million connections. Contrast those figures with the upwardly mobile data-grade UTP market (Categories 3, 4, and 5): In 1991, 1.26 million connections were made; in 1992, 3.7 million connections were made; and in 1993, 5.2 million connections were made.

Callahan attributes the change to crashing prices and high turnover of existing wiring. When Underwriters Laboratories (Northbrook, IL) began testing data-grade UTP, nay-sayers projected that certification would make it more difficult for small players to enter the market. "It actually made it easier for smaller manufacturers to enter the market because they could get certified," says Callahan. "Suddenly people said, 'Category 5 cable has dropped by almost 30 percent. What am I doing putting in this stuff that won't support higher bandwidth?' With a drop like that it started to impact people's thinking about the longevity of installation."

Callahan also points to a qualitative reason for the sharp increase in data-grade UTP shipments. People turn over quite a bit of their wire. People expected that structured wiring would do away with that. But a company's management makes a change, and workers mow down modular furniture and rip out all of the wire.

He offers quantitative data to back up his impressions. In 1992, he studied the wiring habits of more than 50 companies in the Fortune 1,000. In that group, 20 percent replaced more than half of their horizontal wiring in less than three years. "It's the best laid plans of mice and men."

"How long do you support legacy wiring? You have to make a break with legacy technology at some point. Maybe this is one of those points," says Moses. "Take a look at Microsoft. They made a decision to obsolete 8088s and 8086s to get the functions of their new software [Windows]." Will customers discard their equivalent of XTs to get a perceived benefit? It depends on the cost. According to Moses, "the cost differential on Category 3 vs. Category 5 is trivial, since installation is the bulk of the cost. The difference is $20 on a link cost of $400."

Another key issue is the number of pairs a twisted pair bundle contains. Using the four-pair wire is a question of availability and skill. The HP demand-priority scheme uses all four pairs in a Category 3 bundle. 10BaseT uses only two pair. Whether HP's approach requires a radical or migratory change hinges on the availability of that extra pair in a four-pair bundle. Or even having four pair pulled to the desktop.

Independent market research statistics do not exist on the number of pairs actually in use at the desktop. HP offers anecdotal evidence only, saying that 90 percent of HP's installed base has four-pair wire to the desktop. Grand Junction conducted a survey of 100 U.S. companies with revenues greater than $250 million. It found that 45 percent have four or more pairs available for data.

For many years, Northern Telecom specified pulling six pair of wire–three for voice and three for data–to the desktop but has since changed its specification to eight pair. Type 1 cabling, part of the IBM Cabling System, is a two-pair bundle of wire. Using 25-pair bundles is also a standard of structured wiring specifications. HP's solution supports 25-pair bundles; Grand's does not.

Even when four-pair wire has been pulled to every desktop, not all pairs are available. "Some people string four pair to an office, and use two pair for phones and hook up AppleTalk or Ethernet on the other pair or two. Certainly once you string the four pair and use one pair for telephone, you only have three pair left," says Howard.

SEND IT TO COMMITTEE

Which way shall prevail?

"There's already a majority in a committee [for CSMA/CD] and we have to move forward to gain consensus," says Tarrant. "When we see companies like the hub vendors, Cabletron, SynOptics, and Chipcom, who are blood competitors, and 3Com, SMC, and Intel, who make adapter cards, and workstation companies like Sun Microsystems, all pushing CSMA/CD . . . ."

Tarrant says, "We're confident that we'll solve the transmission issues on wiring. We believe it is possible to run CSMA/CD over Category 3; you would use more pairs. With Category 5, you would use two-pair. People are gluing things together. I see no reason why the transmission scheme can't be glued together."

Both Grand Junction and Hewlett-Packard argue that their solution will ensure the shortest time to market. And with standards processes taking years to complete–10BaseT took three years to write, and it's considered one of the speedy ones–time to market is a pressing issue, especially as the standards-based FDDI-over-UTP products begin to emerge this year. In March of 1993, the Higher Speed Ethernet Study Group targeted June, 1995 as its submission date to the IEEE Standards Review Committee.

In the end, users will have their choice of switched Ethernet, 100Mbps Ethernet, and FDDI over UTP for high-speed workgroups. Switched Ethernet is appropriate when you don't want to change the adapter cards in the workstations; it will give your network a performance boost for the least money. And it's available now.

When you're willing to change adapters and hubs, you can choose from 100Mbps Ethernet and FDDI over UTP. The right solution is a matter of which one is cheaper and which one is available.

As analyst Callahan says, "If people can actually produce a 10/100 switchable 10BaseT/ 100Base-whatever adapter for a 50-percent premium over 10BaseT, then it will be a compelling situation. People will be embarrassed to not have made that choice."

Switch Hunt

SEPARATE HYPE FROM REALITY IN SWITCHES, AND YOU CAN RELIEVE NETWORK CONGESTION, SOLVE SERVER BOTTLENECK, AND AVOID BUYING ANOTHER ROUTER.

BY PATRICIA SCHNAIDT

Network congested? Get a switch. Well, they call themselves switches, but most of them aren't switches per se. Most are multiport Media Access Control (MAC) layer bridges, renamed and made more powerful than their ancestors.

Marketing goes to the core of switches. Just some of the many heated debates center around which architecture–cut-through vs. store and forward–is better, is latency really an issue, what type and how many high-speed ports are needed, and whether Network-layer routing is necessary. Most of these switches are for Ethernet, although a few are for Token Ring and Fiber Distributed Data Interface (FDDI). The Asynchronous Transfer Mode (ATM) switch debate is best left to another time and article.

Perhaps the most meaningful distinction to make among the switches is where in the network their makers intend them to reside. First, switches help with the problem of congestion. Networks carry more traffic than ever, and MIS needs some way of segmenting traffic. Bridges used to serve that function before they got a bad rap from router vendors. Since then, routers have been used for network segmentation. But routers are expensive to purchase and complex to configure. MIS departments can justify the extra effort when building a wide area network, but in a local network, a switch is simpler.

"When selling routers, we noticed that a lot of people didn't need routers for local applications," says Randy Fardal, associate vice president of marketing for Retix (Santa Monica, CA). "Unless they need to do subnetting for network addressing, it's easier to bridge."

Call them bridges or call them switches, but these devices segment local networks less expensively and with less maintenance hassle. So we're back to the bridge vs. router debate, but this time it's switch vs. router.

"Internetworking is a WAN phenomenon," says Dave Zwicker, director of marketing for Standard Microsystems Co.'s (SMC's) Enterprise Division (Hauppauge, NY). "We're using the word *intranetworking*. The goal of internetworking is to connect the premise network to off premise. The goal of intranetworking is to accelerate bandwidth, to segment networks, and to provide virtual LAN capabilities so you can segment a LAN by performance rather than dividing it by community of interest."

Second, switches can help with server bottlenecks. Networks have many clients trying to access the resources of a few servers–a setup that makes the servers the bottlenecks. Workstations can continue to use their shared LANs–Ethernet, Token Ring, or something else–and servers can have higher-speed pipes.

A SWITCH TAXONOMY

Switches can be used to connect hubs, to connect servers, or as part of a collapsed backbone.

• **Switch of hubs.** Switches can be used to segment existing Ethernet hubs, instead of using a router for segmentation or building a flat LAN (see Figure 1). Most switches are deployed this way today. Like a bridge, a switch operates at the MAC layer and can be dropped in virtually anywhere. The network topology doesn't have to change. Simply connect the LAN segments to the switch ports, and you have instant bandwidth improvement.

If your bandwidth problems are really bad, you might give each user his own private Ethernet by attaching one user per switch port. A debate rages as to how prevalent the need for private Ethernet is

The type of switches used in this solution tend to have ports all of the same type, such as all Ethernet. Also, the requirements for fault tolerance and redundancy tend to be low. As the market develops, these types of switches will become inexpensive.

• **Switch of servers.** Switches can connect servers. For MIS departments with servers physically located in the departments, servers can be attached to the high-speed ports on the switch, thereby increasing throughput (see Figure 2). Here's where you should consider switches that have higher-speed ports, whether they're FDDI, 100Mbps Ethernet, ATM, or full-duplex Ethernet.

Many MIS departments choose to centralize their servers, setting up a server farm, instead of having servers distributed throughout the department. With this setup, the old 80/20 rule of 80 percent of traffic remaining local and 20 percent being remote won't hold true–all of your users' traffic will have to traverse the network to and from their own server. By setting up servers one to a switch port, you can increase the throughput of the network. For this setup, you'll want the switches not only to have several high-speed ports but also to have high-performance and fault-tolerant capabilities. Also check whether the switch has a nonblocking architecture.

• **Collapsed backbone.** The high-end switches are capable of taking on routers in a collapsed backbone (see Figure 3). These switches have a variety of port-speed interfaces, from Ethernet to ATM, can perform Network-layer routing, have very high packet-forwarding rates, and sport fault-tolerance and redundancy features that many others lack. With this type of switch, a nonblocking architecture becomes essential. These high-end switches won't replace routers entirely, but they can certainly give them a run for their money. Companies in this market segment tend to downplay competitiveness, since, "No one wants to jab a stick in the eye of Cisco," explains Jack Moses, vice president of marketing for Grand Junction (Fremont, CA).

SWITCH ARCHITECTURE

Most, but not all, switches are really MAC-layer bridges. "Switch is a marketing term," says Tom Medrek, director of marketing for 3Com's Switching Division (North Billerica, MA), formerly Synernetics. At the heart of

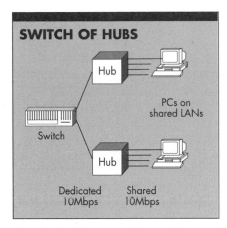

Figure 1. Switches can be used to segment existing Ethernets. Connect the LAN segments to the switch ports, and you have instant bandwidth improvement.

the which-architecture-is-better debate are the issues of latency and error checking.

Kalpana (Sunnyvale, CA), the inventor of Ethernet switches, has patented its cut-through architecture. As a packet is coming in from a port, the switch reads the packet's MAC layer destination address, then looks up the address in an internal table to determine on which outgoing port it must send the packet to reach its destination. It shunts the packet to the proper port, often before the packet is finished being received. This strategy leads to very low latency and very high packet-forwarding rates.

Most of the other switches are high-density MAC-layer bridges. They gain their speed by doing packet processing on the individual cards, rather than having a central CPU do all the work as in old-style bridges. Also, the CPUs are much more powerful, using either RISC processors or custom Application Specific Integrated Circuit (ASIC) designs.

"The design needs to be all-ASIC," says Gordon Stitt, vice president of marketing for Network Peripherals (Milpitas, CA). "RISC is expensive to do it right and costly to do it fast." Others prefer the RISC architecture. For example, the 3Com LANPlex uses a RISC processor with a packet processor on every card, and Cisco Systems' (Menlo Park, CA) Catalyst uses a central RISC processor with ASIC packet processors for the interfaces.

Kalpana says its EtherSwitches have a 40 microsecond latency, or delay, as compared to bridges' 800 microseconds latency and routers' 1,800 microsecond latency. But the time through the switch isn't the only factor in latency–latency is systemwide. Users push a button and expect a certain response time; everything that happens from

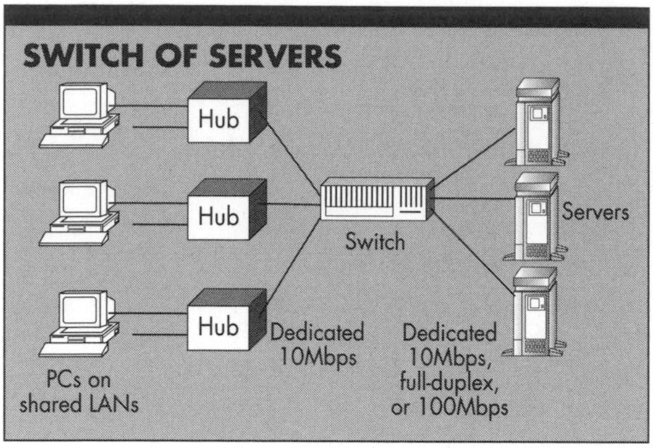

SWITCH OF SERVERS

Servers

PCs on
shared LANs

Dedicated
10Mbps

Dedicated
10Mbps,
full-duplex,
or 100Mbps

Figure 2. You can set up server farms by attaching servers to the high-speed ports on a switch and attaching shared Ethernet segments or single users to the 10Mbps ports.

that button push to the return answer can be lumped into latency. Servers, workstations, switches, and routers contribute to latency.

Medrek has seen the latency issue come to a head with VAX clusters, since they were designed to be local. Introduce any device, and hence a delay, between the VAX cluster and the terminals, and the applications tend to time out. Switches, however, provide a sufficiently low latency.

Latency is an issue with time-sensitive applications, such as full-motion video. "People say that they need low latency for a constant bit-rate transfer. But with the desktop videoconferencing, the quality is so low, what's the difference if it jitters a little bit more anyway?" asks Mike Harrison, director of Advanced Product Engineering at Cabletron (Rochester, NH). Many isochronous applications will run on ATM networks.

One way Kalpana gets low latency is by passing packets without doing any error checking or cyclic redundancy check (CRC) calculations. Consequently, fragments from Ethernet collisions are passed on as if they were valid packets, and the packets will travel to their destination node before the error is discovered. With a bridge or other device that performs error checking, the error is discovered immediately, and the packet can be retransmitted. If the switch is set up with only one user per port, this collision scenario will not occur, since no collisions will happen. If multiple users share a port, then collisions are a real issue.

Another factor contributing to system performance is

the transport protocol. Packets must acknowledge that they've arrived safely at their destination, as defined by the rules of most transport protocols. Most modern protocols, including IP and burst mode IPX, do not require each and every packet to be acknowledged, rather they allow groups of packets to be acknowledged. This so-called sliding window reduces the overhead.

Kalpana says its cut-through architecture is particularly useful because packets don't have to be acknowledged before they're passed along; however, the current versions of IPX and IP have sliding windows. In those cases, a cut-through switch delivers a performance advantage only on the very first packet sent; the remaining packets within the "window" will be acknowledged as a group. With the older implementations of IPX, then, Kalpana's EtherSwitch retains an advantage.

SPEED ANYONE?

Many of the switches include several high-speed LAN ports for attaching servers. FDDI, 100Mbps Ethernet, full-duplex Ethernet, and eventually ATM will be among the technologies used. So far, most switch vendors with high-speed ports use FDDI, since it is a proven technology, although many are looking toward the various flavors of 100Mbps Ethernet when those standards solidify.

If you are mixing LAN types, especially FDDI and Ethernet, make sure the switch you choose supports the various frame flavors that occur on your network. For instance, people refer to Ethernet generically, but Apple uses EtherTalk, NetWare 4.0 uses Ethernet 2.0, and NetWare 3.x uses 802.3 formats. "The switch must look into the packet header and perform the standards conversion," says Jayshree Ullal, director of marketing with Cisco Systems.

Which LAN technologies the switch supports is a matter of the maker's preference and customer demand; however, for all of the technologies except full-duplex, a store-and-forward architecture will be necessary. Low-speed packets can be racheted up to the high-speed technology fairly easily; however, the high-speed packets will have to be buffered before they can be transmitted onto the lower-speed LANs. In either case, the packet formats will have to be translated into the other type, usually by going through an intermediary "neutral" packet format.

Kalpana's EtherSwitch does not support buffering, and therefore it cannot support FDDI, 100Mbps Ethernet, or

ATM in its current incarnation. Blair says that store and forward in the EtherSwitch is inevitable, but it won't ruin his position on the superiority of cut-through switching. "It's a case of how efficiently you handle the light networks. If you look at comparisons between Ethernet and FDDI or Ethernet and 100Mbps Ethernet, how efficiently do they handle the Ethernet-to-Ethernet traffic? If you look at the traffic patterns, the majority of this traffic is moving across the Ethernet."

FULL DUPLEX: IS 20MBPS ENOUGH?

Kalpana proposes full-duplex Ethernet as its high-speed port for servers as well as its switch-to-switch connection. Kalpana is the biggest proponent of full-duplex, although IBM and Cabletron are also supporters. "Full-duplex Ethernet is low-hanging fruit. It's easy to do," says Blair. "It's evolutionary, not revolutionary."

"When we first started doing confidential disclosures to our customer based on what we were doing with full-duplex, it was obvious to them," says Michael Murphy, senior planner of IBM Network Systems Division (Research Triangle Park, NC). "Sometimes it was more difficult for people to understand where the benefit was in ATM and 100Mbps Ethernet." IBM resells Kalpana's EtherSwitch.

To implement full-duplex Ethernet, you need a full-duplex Ethernet NIC and a full-duplex Ethernet port on the switch. The device to gain full-duplex needs dedicated access to the Ethernet port. 10BaseT is wired for full-duplex transmission, but the protocol is half-duplex. Because the machine has a private port, a collision cannot occur–it is not a shared medium–so by disabling the collision-detection function and modifying the underlying protocols, data can be carried on that return path. The theoretical throughput can be effectively doubled from 10Mbps to 20Mbps. The different vendors' implementation of full-duplex Ethernet does not necessarily interoperate; no official standard exists.

Many of the Ethernet cards are capable of transmitting full-duplex but currently use only half-duplex. For some, the change can be made in software, which is a less-expensive venture than swapping out cards. For instance, IBM isn't charging a premium for its full-duplex Ethernet NICs.

"Over time that full-duplex capability will be there as the installed base grows. As people require greater perfor-

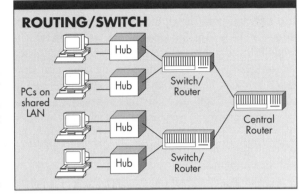

Figure 3. Switches can be used to complement routers. These switches usually have a variety of port-speed interfaces, from Ethernet to ATM, can perform Network-layer routing, have very high packet-forwarding rates, and sport fault-tolerance and redundancy features.

mance from these workstations, they have an alternative of either going to a higher-speed LAN, such as SDDI [Shielded Twisted-Pair FDDI], 100BaseT, or 100VG, or the simple alternative of reconfiguring the adapter, changing the wiring closet connection to the switch rather than to a repeater, and they have 20Mbps," says Murphy.

Many switch vendors dismiss full-duplex, saying that the difficulty of replacing adapter cards and deploying switch ports to the servers isn't worth a bandwidth improvement to only 20Mbps. That amount of effort requires a higher payback in speed, say to 100Mbps with FDDI or 100Mbps Ethernet. "Full-duplex Ethernet is a Band-Aid," says Medrek.

COLLAPSED BACKBONE

Pure switching is suitable for workgroups and to connect clients and servers. But switches can be used to connect internetworks. The switches that serve as front ends to the enterprise routers will include router functions, including performing Network-layer routing and the ability to build fire walls against broadcasts and security breaches. Most of these switches will not include the laundry list of routed protocols of enterprise-level routers, but they will handle the short list of popular ones–IPX and IP most certainly. Many players in this market see switch/routers as a migration path to ATM.

The most interesting aspect of adding Network-layer routing to a switch is to provide an effective antidote to the epidemic of adds, moves, and changes by delivering a virtual LAN function. The virtual LAN concept is most often associated with ATM, but it can be done using current network technology. A virtual LAN lets network managers set up workgroups that are not hard-wired to a physical location. Users can be added and moved without physically changing which hub they plug into, and workgroups can be set up according to people's business relationship rather than physical proximity. Users and their servers may be on different physical segments, but the performance will be as if they were local.

How's it done? Virtual LAN should be easier than older methods. For example, MAC-layer bridges have long permitted industrious administrators to configure filters that define which MAC addresses can communicate. Filter definitions are static, and the administrators find themselves in a Sisyphean struggle to keep filters current.

Virtual LAN will come about through software. The network administrator can assign workgroups by Network-layer address or by port number, rather than by MAC-address. For example, IP subnetting can be used to provide a virtual LAN. Aspects of the ATM Forum's upcoming LAN-emulation standard will also be used to build virtual LANs the ATM way.

Sizzling Switches

FOUR YEARS AFTER THEIR INTRODUCTION, ETHERNET SWITCHES ARE HOT. HOW DOES ETHERNET SWITCH TECHNOLOGY WORK, AND IS IT FIERY ENOUGH TO BURN OUT ATM?

BY CHARLES FELTMAN

Ethernet switches are suddenly hot products, and they're fast igniting a new LAN switching market. Some people see them as the logical precursors to switched Asynchronous Transfer Mode (ATM) networks. But others believe that the technology behind switched Ethernet, which has already been extended to Token Ring and Fiber Distributed Data Interface (FDDI) and will eventually include 100BaseX and 100VG-AnyLAN, will eliminate the need for widespread implementation of ATM in LANs, relegating it to a niche technology.

One of the key differences between current LAN technologies (Ethernet, Token Ring, and FDDI) and ATM is that today's LANs are based on a shared network medium over which all traffic is broadcast to every node, while ATM switches traffic between nodes along dedicated network paths. This switching approach is primarily what allows ATM to provide network bandwidth ranging in the hundreds of megabits and even gigabits per second.

So what is an Ethernet switch, and what does it do?

For a growing number of network managers who have implemented them, Ethernet switches offer a bridge over very troubled water between their heavily congested networks of today and still uncertain future technologies.

Take Kirby Hess, for example. Not long ago, Hess, senior telecommunications technician for Applied Materials, a leading worldwide supplier of semiconductor manufacturing equipment, faced a rapidly growing problem on his company's LAN.

Applied Materials' 1,500 users are housed on a 14-building campus in Santa Clara, CA. Each building was configured with a single Ethernet segment that served multiple departments or workgroups. The way the Applied

Materials network matured, every workgroup had its own server located in the same building. Segments from all 14 buildings were tied to routers in the company's computer room via a Raycom (Van Nuys, CA) FiberRing 100 backbone.

Hess's problem was rampant congestion on the Ethernet segments. Users were bringing new, bandwidth-hungry client-server applications online. In addition, the number of network users had been steadily growing. These changes were combining to fuel a bandwidth crisis.

After considering different approaches to controlling bandwidth on the segments, including adding multiport routers or bridges in each building, Hess and his staff came across a product called EtherSwitch from Kalpana (Sunnyvale, CA). As the name implies, the device "switches" Ethernet. By deploying a switch in each building Applied Materials has been able to provide every workgroup with its own private 10Mbps Ethernet segment at minimal additional cost.

The switch keeps all intergroup traffic within its segment, which means that each workgroup is isolated from traffic on other segments. At the same time, if any user needs to access any server or other device on the company's worldwide enterprise network, he or she can do so without an extended delay.

A BRIDGE BY ANY OTHER NAME

Kalpana's EtherSwitch was the first such device to hit the market. "We brought the product out in the spring of 1990 and spent the next two years trying to explain what an Ethernet switch is," notes Larry Blair, Kalpana's vice president of marketing.

What was a novel concept four years ago is fast becoming a key element in today's networks. Over the last two years, several vendors have introduced variations on the Ethernet switching theme, and at least two vendors have recently rolled out Token Ring switches. "The market for LAN switches ballooned to somewhere between $50 million and $75 million in 1993," says Fred McClimans, program director at Gartner Group (Stamford, CT).

But, as McClimans explains, this market is a difficult one to track because the boundaries between what vendors are calling "switches" and devices such as bridges and routers are somewhat fuzzy. Also, important variations–both functional and technical–separate the different products currently being marketed as Ethernet switches.

SEND REINFORCEMENTS

If one constant prevails across all Ethernet switching products, it is that they are finding their way onto more LANs every day. The main reason for their sudden popularity is that they are effective reinforcements for beleaguered networks.

The basic problem is that for a growing number of users 10Mbps shared Ethernet is reaching its limit. It can handle only so much traffic before things start to slow down for everyone. And the problem isn't just on the backbone; it's often more serious on the segments supporting workgroup applications.

The company that puts in a high-speed backbone often finds itself in the same boat as the city that builds a rapid transit system to carry people quickly between major stops, then finds that the streets leading to the transit stations are hopelessly clogged.

ATM, with its promise of gigabits per second transmission rates, is still too far out on the horizon to be of much help for most networks today. Closer at hand are other "fast LAN" technologies, such as FDDI, FDDI over copper, and the 100BaseX/100VG-AnyLAN twins separated at birth. But the network manager looking at any of these technologies for relief is confronted with a major stumbling block: They require considerable capital outlay for expensive new equipment–hub modules, desktop adapters, and, with FDDI, fiber cabling.

Companies with heavy investment in a 10Mbps Ethernet infrastructure just aren't prepared to jettison what they've got if it can be made to carry them two or three

years further. Next-generation networking technology still poses too much uncertainty.

So companies are looking for inexpensive ways to relieve congestion and boost bandwidth without trading out their existing networks. And products that "switch" existing Ethernet network traffic are proving to be the most effective solution. Ethernet isn't the only LAN technology with a large installed base that can benefit from switching. Token Ring installations can also make use of switches, and at least two vendors–Standard Microsystems Corp. (SMC, Hauppauge, NY) and Fibronics (Pembroke, MA)–have introduced Token Ring products that provide this functionality in addition to Ethernet switching.

The symptoms of congestion–low throughput, long response times, frustrated and underproductive users–can be alleviated in the short term by dividing a large network into smaller segments with fewer users on each. This function is the basic benefit that all Ethernet switches provide.

Most switches on the market offer between four and 16 ports and are configured as either a standalone box or a plug-in module for a hub. Each port supports a separate 10Mbps Ethernet segment. You can attach many nodes or just a single device to each segment. In practice, typically one or more cascaded 10BaseT concentrators is attached to each port on the switch (see Figure 1).

Each switch port filters traffic sent over its attached segment. Traffic that is destined for a node on the same segment does not cross the switch's port boundary. If a node on one segment needs to send packets to a node connected to a different segment–that is, a different switch port–those packets will be forwarded across the port boundary and through the switch fabric to the appropriate destination port. The switch ensures that multiple simultaneous 10Mbps connections can be supported between segments.

One of the primary applications for switching is network microsegmentation, the technique Hess of Applied Materials uses. Network managers can determine how many nodes each segment can support before congestion starts to become a problem and limit each segment to that number without limiting any user's access to the network.

CLIENT-SERVER RELATIONS

David Willis, information technology analyst for American National Can Co. in Chicago, was looking at a similar problem when he found Artel's (Hudson, MA) Glactica Su-

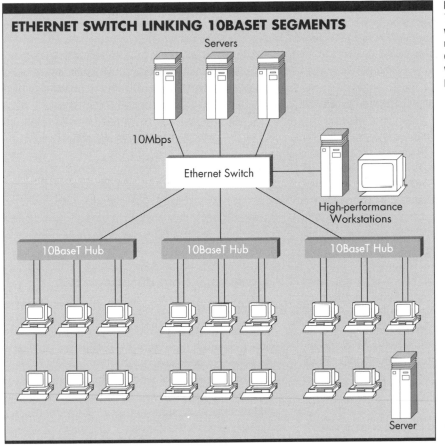

ETHERNET SWITCH LINKING 10BASET SEGMENTS

Servers

10Mbps

Ethernet Switch

High-performance Workstations

10BaseT Hub   10BaseT Hub   10BaseT Hub

Server

Figure 1: Here, an Ethernet switch links 10BaseT segments with servers and workstations on dedicated 10Mbps segments. In a multifunction hub, switch and 10BaseT concentrator modules would be linked across the hub's backplane.

perSwitch. (Note that Chipcom and Artel are negotiating a merger at this writing.)

Like Applied Materials, American National Can was undergoing rapid growth in the number of users on its network and was introducing client-server applications with high bandwidth requirements.

The American National Can network supports 750 users in the company's multistory headquarters building. Some 100 of them work on Unix-based CAD stations, while the rest use NetWare client PCs with access to four Novell servers. Willis implemented the Glactica Super-Switch, a switching hub that can hold up to four eight-port switch modules, to give each floor its own segment.

Because of the way data is used by the company's employees, each of the four Novell servers has to be available to any user on the network. To ensure enough bandwidth

to handle peak demand for access to the servers, Willis has given each server its own dedicated 10Mbps segment.

For American National Can, Ethernet switching proved to be the most cost-effective solution to the bandwidth crunch. Other alternatives, such as routing between segments or putting multiple adapter cards in each server to form different subnets, would have been much costlier and would have introduced additional, unwanted complexity to the network, according to Willis.

Microsoft (Redmond, WA) uses 3Com's (Santa Clara, CA) Switching Modules in LinkBuilder 3GH hubs to provide similar high-bandwidth access to several of the centralized servers on the company's 22-building campus.

In addition, according to Dave Leinweber of Microsoft's Information Technology Group, some of their engineering workstations that download 70MB-plus files of software code on a daily basis have been given dedicated 10Mbps Ethernet segments. Those engineers have the bandwidth available to get their work done efficiently, and their activities don't impact other network users.

COLLAPSED BACKBONE

Another major application for Ethernet switches is collapsing an extended backbone into the network hub. Don Benson, vice president of compute operations at Young & Rubicam, a large advertising firm in New York City, uses switches within a multi-function network hub to link client systems throughout the company's headquarters to centralized file servers. The Ethernet switch modules in the hub support multiple segments with 30 clients on each. Also in the hub is an FDDI switch that connects three file servers, each on its own FDDI ring.

Young & Rubicam was able to stop what was becoming an uncontrollable proliferation of servers and even reduce the total number of them in the network by implementing a switch, while providing everyone with high-speed access to data. In addition, by using a switching hub, Young & Rubicam has effectively collapsed its corporate backbone into a single hub, giving it more management control over the network elements.

FUNCTIONAL VARIATIONS

All the products currently on the market can be used to increase available bandwidth simply and cost-effectively by microsegmenting networks. But identifiable differences between these products are worth discussing because they directly affect which applications are best.

One category of product simply "switches" ports, usually using different Ethernet or FDDI backplane networks inside of a hub. Gartner Group's McClimans and Yankee Group's (Boston) Vice President of Data Communications Todd Dagres both term this type of device a *port switch.* On these products, all traffic from one port can be assigned via a software switch to one of the (usually three) separate backplane networks integral to the hub. To set up a connection between two ports the user can connect them both to one internal backplane network using the "switching" functionality.

Port switches can be used to segment a large network and provide permanent (until changed with the switch) connections between two or more segments. For example,

a segment with multiple workstations can be connected to one port and a single server to another, then those two ports can both be connected to the same internal network.

However, if a user on a different segment needs to access that server and his port isn't connected to the same internal network, his segment will have to be switched over using a software command. Port switches primarily allow for segmentation of the network and make adds, moves, and changes in the network easier to manage.

A functionally different type of product is one that switches individual packets between any two segments attached to the switch. McClimans calls these products *segment switches,* while Dagres terms them *network switches.* Whatever the name, these products provide flexible switching functionality between segments. Any node can exchange packets with any other node connected to the switch (unless security filters are set up to block traffic) because packets, not connections, are switched.

TECHNICAL DIFFERENCES

How these devices provide switching varies and has important ramifications for cost, application, and, to a lesser extent, performance.

First, bear in mind that the switch only handles packets that need to be transmitted between ports (from one segment to another). Intrasegment traffic is filtered at the port and never enters the switch itself.

The switching fabric is almost always some form of shared memory. In its most basic operation, an incoming packet is received into the shared memory space, its destination port is determined from an address table via some algorithm usually run by a RISC processor, and it is shipped out to that port. This process involves a number of other critical steps, and every vendor has a slightly different way of performing them. In all cases, however, the goal is to provide high throughput through the switch with a low or fixed delay (latency).

Probably the two most important differences in switch architecture are whether the device uses cut-through or buffered switching and whether it switches, bridges, or routes traffic. These differences can impact the cost, performance, and functionality.

Kalpana's EtherSwitch products use a cut-through cross-point switch. *Cut-through* refers to the fact that a packet arriving at one port in the switch is transmitted to

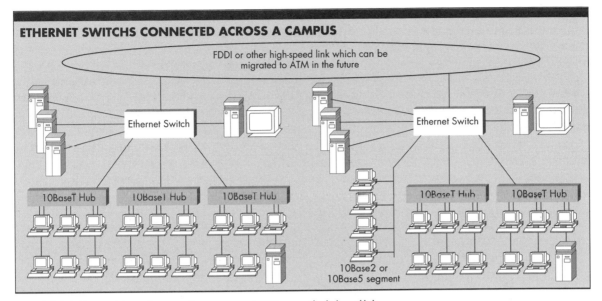

ETHERNET SWITCHS CONNECTED ACROSS A CAMPUS

FDDI or other high-speed link which can be migrated to ATM in the future

Ethernet Switch

Ethernet Switch

10BaseT Hub   10BaseT Hub   10BaseT Hub

10BaseT Hub   10BaseT Hub

10Base2 or 10Base5 segment

Figure 2: Multiple Ethernet switches can be connected across a campus via FDDI or some other high-speed link.

its destination port as soon as its destination address is read. The benefit of cut-through switching is that it introduces the least amount of latency in transmission between ports. The downside is that it can propagate collisions and bad packets to the destination segment.

This type of product is well suited to enhancing local workgroup throughput via microsegmentation at the workgroup level. As at Applied Materials, multiple segments can be created that comprise both client workstations and their servers. Or, servers and high-performance workstations can be placed on their own dedicated 10Mbps segments while lower-performance client stations can be grouped on other segments. The low latency will yield significant performance benefits in environments where a transmit-acknowledge protocol is used, such as pre-4.0 versions of Novell NetWare.

Other vendors' products use a store-and-forward scheme that *buffers* incoming packets in memory until they are fully received and checked to make sure there are no cyclic redundancy check (CRC) errors. Most of these products also employ bridging algorithms to determine where to send incoming packets. These products are, in effect, multiport 802.1d learning bridges. They typically incorporate the Spanning Tree Protocol (STP) as well, so that multiple redundant paths can exist.

One of the advantages of bridging is that it allows packets to be moved between media running at different speeds. For example, in a hub, when a packet is coming into a switching module from one of the 10Mbps Ethernet segments, it must be bridged to the hub's high-speed internal backplane for delivery to another module or to an external FDDI backbone.

Another advantage of bridging is that it allows for the use of address blocking to provide a level of network security. In other words, certain nodes can be prohibited from sending or receiving packets from other defined nodes. This capability is not implemented by every vendor that offers bridging, however.

Some vendors use routing protocols to move packets between segments. Most of these products offer routing as a configurable option to bridging. When so configured, the switches become multiport routers, which can route supported protocols (IP, IPX, DECnet, among others). The disadvantage of switching based on routing is that users are limited to the supported routing protocols.

PERFORMANCE AND COST

By far the most important benefit of LAN switches on the market today is that they offer better price-per-port and price/performance ratios than bridge and router products. Ethernet switches are no faster than many bridges and routers, according to Scott Bradner, director of the Harvard Network Device Test Lab (Cambridge, MA). Bradner's lab tests bridge and router performance of most of the Ethernet switches available. The big cost and performance advantages with Ethernet switching devices are that they provide the same high throughput across many more ports.

Port-to-port throughput in a switch should occur at Ethernet wire speed; that is, 14,880 packets per second using 64-byte packets. All the switches on the market today can achieve this rate between two ports when no others are active. The important number is the aggregate throughput for the switch across all ports, which indicates the switch's capability under load conditions.

Whether a product supports simple switching, bridging, or routing also impacts performance and cost. More complex functionality such as routing can slow down a switch. This shortcoming can be compensated for, but the components will cost more.

STANDALONE VS. HUBBING

Another important difference between switch products is whether they come in the form of a standalone device, a module for a switching hub, or a module for a multifunction network hub. Standalone products suit certain applications, while switching hubs are suited to others.

Standalone products come with a fixed number of ports. These switches are designed primarily to provide workgroup switching solutions. They are generally compact and offer a relatively low price per port.

Individual switches can also be linked, but the methods for doing so vary considerably among vendors. For example, Kalpana and Hewlett-Packard (Roseville, CA) use full-duplex Ethernet to provide interswitch connectivity, while Alantec (San Jose, CA) uses FDDI to link its PowerHubs, and Artel's standalone StarBridge Turbo switches are connected using 10Mbps or 20Mbps Ethernet.

At the other end of the spectrum are the multifunction hub vendors who offer switching modules to go inside their products. Companies such as 3Com, SynOptics (Santa Clara, CA), and Ungermann-Bass (Santa Clara, CA) have come out with network switching modules. Chipcom (Southboro, MA) and Bytex (Westboro, MA) offer port-

switching modules for their hubs. (Chipcom also offers a network switching product.)

These products are designed to be integral elements of the enterprise network. Users on segments connected to switch modules can access other nodes attached to the switch as well as any other module in the hub, including 10BaseT, 10Base2, or 10Base5; Token Ring; and FDDI concentrator modules. The connection between modules is made across the hub's backplane. Here the use of bridging or routing is important as opposed to straight switching, which cannot accommodate the speed differential between the Ethernet ports on the switch and the higher-speed backplane.

Some vendors offer and expandable switching hub that falls somewhere between the standalone device and the multifunction hub module. *Switching hubs* are simply hubs that only support switching modules. They allow a user to purchase a hub chassis and expand the number of switch ports. The modules plug into a high speed backplane for interswitch communications.

Like the standalone devices, switching hubs such as Artel's Glactica SuperSwitch, Synernetics' (Billerica, MA) LANplex hubs, of SMC's Elite SwitchingHub can be linked. Alantec's high-end PowerHub 5000 also fits in this category.

Introduced last year by Calios (Simi Valley, CA), the SwitchStak stackable switch product line uses another approach. Like the standalone products, each switch is a self-contained four-or eight-port unit. However, up to six switches can be stacked or placed adjacent to each other in a rack and connected via 300Mbps fiber links. When configured this way, they appear as a single unit to the network's Simple Network Management Protocol (SNMP) management system. Users can invest in only the number of ports they need and not pay for a large chassis up front, without sacrificing the capability to expand the system as needed.

DEDICATED ETHERNET

The term "dedicated Ethernet" has been coined to describe using a single port on a switch to dedicate a full 10Mbps Ethernet segment to a single network device, such as a server of high-performance workstation. All switches on the market today provide this function, but on most, this configuration is an option.

Some switches, however, only allow one MAC address per port, which forces this configuration. This configuration most resembles a pure ATM switch, which also has a dedicated path to each device, with much higher bandwidth than 10Mbps Ethernet. Chipcom's ONline Ethernet Interconnect Module and Grand Junction's (Fremont, CA) FastSwitch products allow only one MAC address per switch port, effectively requiring dedicated Ethernet configurations.

Switches that support only dedicated Ethernet are designed for the high-performance workgroup that doesn't require ATM speeds but does require a full, uncontended 10Mbps.

SWITCHED FUTURES

Ethernet switches have been around for almost four years but have only begun to catch fire the last year and a half. They have been very recently joined by Token Ring and FDDI switches. By the end of this year, Ethernet switching products should be available from all the major hub vendors, many of whom have been buying or merging with switch manufacturers. More vendors will introduce Token Ring switches, as well.

Switching these types of shared media technologies can prolong their useful life in many environments. But, perhaps more importantly, it will help users begin to understand how they can design networks to get the most out of ATM.

Some say Ethernet, Token Ring, and FDDI switching, combined with 100BaseX/100VG-AnyLAN, will eliminate the need for ATM on LANs except as a niche technology. But most vendors are investing in and planning for a different scenario in which switched Ethernet helps lead a smooth transition to ATM.

First the backbone link between hubs, which is predominantly FDDI today, will be replaced by ATM. Then the hub's internal backplane itself will become an ATM switch. All these changes can take place while users continue to make use of their existing LAN switches, adapter cards, and wiring.

The virtual LAN functionality incorporated in today's LAN switches will be standardized and melded with ATM's virtual LAN features and extended over the WAN to allow users to plug into their corporate networks anywhere in the world and be connected to their workgroups.

Ethernet switches are the first step most users will take toward evolving their networks to ATM and will play an important role in networks of all sizes and configurations over the next few years.

A POWERFUL SWITCHING FEATURE
Virtual LANs

Virtual LAN configuration is a powerful functionality associate with LAN switching products. Only a few of the Ethernet switch vendors offer what can truly be described as virtual LAN capability, and each of their implementations is somewhat different.

In effect, *virtual LAN configuration* is a method of creating virtual segments or subnetworks within the overall network. Workgroups can be established by defining all the members of the group as being on one virtual LAN. For example, the 20 members of a company's telemarketing department, located on the fourth floor, and their server connected to the network in the computer room on the second floor can comprise a virtual LAN.

In dynamic environments where workgroups are formed around short-lived projects, virtual LAN capability is a very powerful tool. When a network user moves from one project to another, the network manager can easily delete her MAC address from the first group and add it to the second using management software without physically changing any wiring.

In Ungermann-Bass' Virtual Network Architecture (VNA), two or more individual ports on the same or different switches in the network can be grouped together to form a virtual LAN. All users on segments connected to those ports would be able to access all other nodes within the group but not nodes outside of it.

U-B's VNA can also be used to create virtual networks based on MAC addresses. In this case, the network recognizes the addresses of the devices and gives the users access to their workgroups no matter where the users are located, even if they move within the network.

Alantec also supports virtual networking. In fact, that company was doing it well before Ungermann-Bass came out with its product. Initially, Alantec called its virtual networking capability "port subnet mapping," which didn't have quite the same pizzazz as VNA, according to Marketing Vice President Paul Schaller.

He is also quick to point out a fundamental difference

between U-B's VNA and Alantec's virtual networking. Alantec bases its virtual LAN functionality on IP network numbers, which are used to create virtual subnets within the network. Users can define these virtual LAN workgroups in much the same way as with VNA, except that an individual node can be a member of more than one virtual subnetwork at the same time.

This functionality allows the possibility for some resources, a mail server, for example, to be shared among several virtual LAN workgroups. The capability to share resources across workgroups can be a big advantage in networks where otherwise different workgroups need to share resources.

However, since Alantec's virtual LAN capability is based on higher-layer protocol processing, the PowerHub must be used in routing mode to make use of it. So, nodes that do not use one of the four routing protocols supported by Alantec (IP, IPX, DECnet, and AppleTalk) cannot participate in virtual LANs.

The SwitchStak product from Calios also incorporates a virtual networking capability similar to that of U-B. Virtual LANs can be defined using any combination of whole switches, ports, and MAC addresses. Both Calios and U-B have tried to stay independent of higher-layer protocols with their virtual LAN functionality so that they can trans-

parently support any type of node; their virtual networks cannot have common members.

Network managers can work around this limitation, however, by using multiport servers (for example, servers with multiple adapter cards) and connecting different ports to different virtual LANs or by using a router to link the different virtual networks.

Some of the other switch vendors' products can do some form of virtual LAN configuration via bridging with multiple user-selectable filters. By setting filters to allow or disallow packets to be transmitted between certain nodes, a network manager can create virtual LANs. But the filter-setting method is a far cry from the powerful, easy-to-use management interfaces provided by the Alantec, Calios, and U-B products.

Virtual LAN configuration is a big step toward ATM. ATM networks that integrate Ethernet and other "legacy" technologies will require some type of virtual LAN functionality to deal with their broadcast protocols.

In fact, perhaps the best implementation of virtual LAN today can be found in N.E.T.'s (Redwood City, CA) V-LAN feature that is part of its ATM switching product line. It developed V-LAN as part of the LAN-emulation capability it needed to build into its product, and it shows how much can be done with virtual LAN.

Section 5
Wide Area Networks

Networks are no longer confined to computers situated in a single location. Almost every LAN has some sort of attachment to a wide area link, whether that be to the building across the street or to a subsidiary halfway across the world. And establishing wide area connectivity involves gathering information from multiple competitive providers. You have to determine which transport services are available between points and then compare the overall speed and relative cost of those services.

Networks can be linked over the wide area using any number of technologies, including frame relay, Switched Multimegabit Data Service (SMDS), or Integrated Services Digital Network (ISDN), to name a few. The stories in this section focus on these topics and reveal the current state of development and deployment as well as the future capabilities of individual services. Each technology offers different capabilities at varying costs; some are tuned for data, while others can transfer voice and video as well. Knowing what your wide area connectivity needs are will be vital in determining which one is the right fit for the WAN.

A New Model for Frame Relay

LOOKING FOR NETWORK REDUNDANCY AND FLEXIBILITY IN
BANDWIDTH, ONE COMPANY FOUND ITS SOLUTION IN SPRINT'S NEW
MODEL FOR IMPLEMENTING FRAME RELAY.

BY SUSAN FITZGERALD AND LARRY KRAFT

Traditional frame relay network designs advocate a single access port for each LAN connecting to the frame relay cloud–regardless of the number of sites. When this idea is extended to networks of significant size this "single port" model can get stretched to the breaking point. Using a case study and a model presented by Sprint, we will demonstrate a method of addressing this design issue in large networks. The enhanced design also illustrates how to build additional fault tolerance into the frame relay network to take advantage of its scalability.

For the subject of our case study, a company we'll call Acme, Inc., we had to evaluate WAN services to provide transparent connectivity among an installed base of NetWare and AppleTalk LANs. The company has approximately 100 offices spanning six regions throughout the United States. Each region consists of a regional headquarters peppered with multiple smaller sites. As with many corporations, the timely receipt of information is of utmost importance. As a result, Acme has begun to develop truly distributed client-server applications and workgroup computing methods. Once these applications are completed, users will have to be able to communicate with any other user on the network and traffic will increase significantly.

At the time of our work with Acme, the exact impact of this development was difficult to judge, but clearly Acme needed a solution flexible enough to increase capacity as traffic increases without necessitating a complete network redesign. Acme's future could also include SMDS or ATM, so the infrastructure needed to be easily migrated to either environment. Redundancy in the network was also a major concern. None of the sites could be without communications.

We knew that frame relay offers a high degree of redundancy and alternate rerouting in the backbone of the network. But our objective in designing Acme's infrastructure was to achieve similar redundancy down to the site-level as cost-effectively as possible. The budget for the project was based on a meshed private-line solution using a combination of T-1 and fractional T-1 lines. Subject to the design, that this technology would put us at the high-end on the cost spectrum, but Acme was prepared to make the investment.

Acme's network can be clearly segmented along business lines. Each region includes a primary site. Together, these primary sites create a backbone for the entire network. The available information indicated a heavy amount of relatively uniform traffic between backbones, meaning that no site particularly dominated the traffic flow. We considered four options for connecting the backbone, three involving Clearline (Sprint's private-line product) and one using frame relay. Figure 1 shows the four options.

INITIAL COMPARISONS

Frame relay turned out to be the least costly option on a monthly basis. The star topology was 20 percent to 25 percent higher per month, the partial mesh topology was more than double, and the full mesh topology was five to six times higher than the cost of frame relay on a monthly basis. These cost ratios will change with geographic locations, so these figures should not be interpreted as general guidelines.

In a scenario in which traffic flow is centered at one site, depending on site locations and their distances from one another, a star private-line design could be cost com-

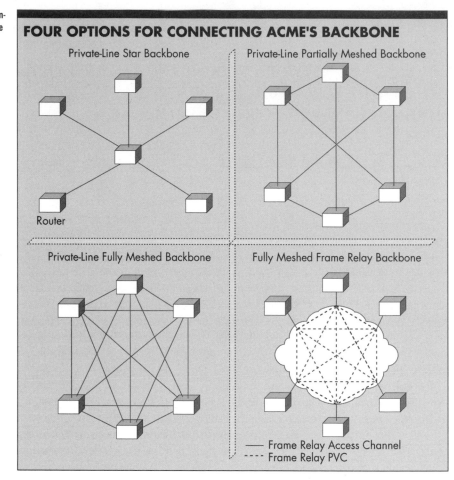

FOUR OPTIONS FOR CONNECTING ACME'S BACKBONE

Private-Line Star Backbone

Router

Private-Line Partially Meshed Backbone

Private-Line Fully Meshed Backbone

Fully Meshed Frame Relay Backbone

—— Frame Relay Access Channel
---- Frame Relay PVC

petitive with frame relay. But, with uniform traffic flow, as with that of Acme, the star design does not make sense because most traffic has to traverse two links, and the failure of one site would cripple the whole network.

In addition to being less expensive, the fully meshed frame relay option inherently provides site failure resiliency. Only the partially meshed or fully meshed private-line solutions approach the same level of resiliency. *Resiliency* describes a network's ability to automatically re-route data when a connection fails. Network designers should aim for complete site failure resiliency, meaning that the failure of any one site or any of that site's network links will not isolate any other site.

Achieving complete site failure resiliency with a private-line design is significantly more expensive. In the case of Acme, the cost of backbone options more than doubled.

THE SPRINT MODEL

Because WAN options can be mixed and matched, we evaluated the backbone and regional office designs independently. Frame relay's cost advantages and built-in resiliency made it the best transport solution for the backbone. At this point we applied Sprint's model for building a resilient network.

The basis of the model is exceedingly simple: Use more than one frame relay port at locations around the network. With strategic placement of additional ports and careful structuring of PVCs, you can design extremely resilient, flexible, and cost-effective networks. Key to this concept is

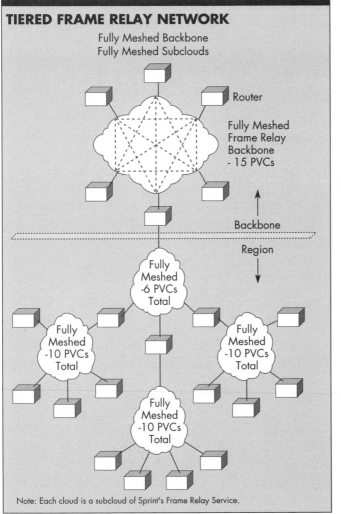

TIERED FRAME RELAY NETWORK

Fully Meshed Backbone
Fully Meshed Subclouds

Router

Fully Meshed
Frame Relay
Backbone
- 15 PVCs

Backbone

Region

Fully
Meshed
-6 PVCs
Total

Fully
Meshed
-10 PVCs
Total

Fully
Meshed
-10 PVCs
Total

Fully
Meshed
-10 PVCs
Total

Note: Each cloud is a subcloud of Sprint's Frame Relay Service.

FIGURE 2: In this tiered frame relay mesh de-sign, each small cloud is really a full mesh of PVCs between the attached sites, meaning that each site on the cloud has a PVC to every other site connected to the same cloud.

the famous 80-20 rule; typically, 20 percent of the sites in a corporation conduct 80 percent of the business. Generally, this rule of thumb translates into 20 percent of the sites creating 80 percent of the network traffic.

The best network designs take the 80-20 rule into account, along with the organizational structure and business relationships within a corporation, and the traffic flow.

The second key concept in the Sprint model is that the design should function using only today's standard capabilities, while providing a clear migration path to the future. Enabling easy migration is especially important be-

cause of the way in which routers deal with certain LAN protocols over frame relay. A design, especially for a large network, should not require static routing or other ad-hoc workarounds. Based on Sprint's model, the design begins to make sense with a minimum of 10 sites to 15 sites.

REGIONAL CONSIDERATIONS

In addressing the design for Acme's regional offices, we examined all available WAN options before deciding on frame relay. First, we looked at a potential private-line solution. The most cost-effective private-line design would mean that no site would be more than two router hops

FIGURE 3: To apply resilience to the entire region, we added one additional frame relay access port per site on each bottom-tier sub-cloud.

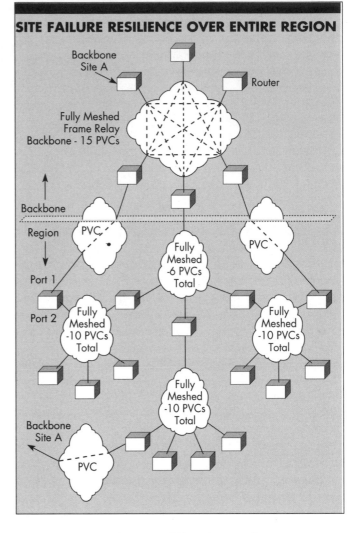

from the backbone. The "two-hop" limit ensures that no site in the network is more than five router hops from any other site (two to the backbone, one across the backbone, and at most two from the backbone to another site).

When planning your network design, keep hop counts to a reasonably low number because of the hop-count limitations of some routing protocols (for example, IPX RIP is limited to 15 hops). A lower hop count will also help provide relatively uniform service to all sites.

But, in Acme's case, the private-line design offered very little resiliency. The failure of a single router could result in the isolation of many other routers. Although possible,

adding resilience would have been costly–increasing costs by 50 percent.

Figure 2 shows a regional frame relay solution that preserves the maximum two hops to the backbone. This tiered frame relay mesh design is the crux of the new model. Each small cloud pictured is really a full mesh of PVCs between the attached sites, meaning that each site on the cloud has a PVC to every other site connected to the same cloud.

In actuality, each smaller cloud (called a subcloud) is part of the same overall frame relay network cloud. For simplicity's sake, consider each subcloud as its own logical frame relay network. Dividing the network this way reduces the number of PVCs required. Each link from a router into a subcloud is actually a distinct physical frame relay access port. So site A actually has two frame relay access ports using two synchronous router ports. Relative to the private-line design, this frame relay design costs Acme 20 percent less per month.

But the cost savings becomes even more clear in terms of network resilience. Making the sites within the private-line solution completely failure resilient costed only about 10 percent to 15 percent more per month.

Figure 3 shows the design when resilience is applied to the entire region. Basically, we added one additional frame relay access port per site on each bottom-tier subcloud. We also added separate frame relay ports to several backbone routers (creating a total of three frame relay access ports at these key backbone sites). A single frame relay PVC was defined from a router on each subtier to the backbone, creating extreme resilience. The failure of any one site in the network, regardless of the location of that site, will not isolate any other site.

Perhaps the most important benefit to the frame relay design is that sites can be cost-effectively grouped on subclouds based on business relationships, not only geographic proximity. This grouping truly allows the network to be matched to business objectives. And with today's rapidly changing business environment, the logical nature of frame relay means the network structure can be easily modified to reflect new requirements.

Sites can be added to subclouds, or shifted from subcloud to subcloud quickly and simply without affecting other sections of the network. Sites can also be grouped on clouds based on bandwidth requirements. Sites with lower bandwidth requirements can be grouped together with one site providing a link to another cloud with higher bandwidth. Although this subcloud design makes sense for Acme, other companies may want to implement a private-line subcloud on the backbone or at a different network tier.

In this scenario, with some strategic use of additional frame relay PVCs, the frame relay network could be used to back up the private-line subcloud links. A private-line scenario for a subcloud would make the most sense where sites are not widely geographically dispersed and where one or two sites dominate traffic flow.

PVC OPTIMIZATION

So, far we've been touting the benefits of a fully-meshed frame relay PVC architecture. However, a word of warning is in order: Try to limit the number of PVCs per port, otherwise as the number of sites increases the number of PVCs required on one physical interface increases exponentially and these PVCs slow router processing.

For example, a medium-size company with a 100-site network, would require 99 PVCs per interface for a meshed design. That number equates to a total of 4,950 PVCs. With this many PVCs per interface, a routing protocol update or any broadcast packet would likely consume the router's processing power, which would busily have to make copies of the packet. Internal router buffer issues might also make this setup unwise.

The maximum recommended number of PVCs per port is a difficult number to determine. The maximum will depend on the LAN protocol, traffic flow characteristics, applications, access-channel speed, router vendor, and processing power of the individual router used. Generally the "chattier" a protocol, the more the number of PVCs should be restricted.

Broadcast-intensive protocols, including bridging, argue for keeping the number of PVCs per interface relatively low. A rule of thumb is that more than 10 to 15 PVCs per router port should start worrying you. Of course, in some cases, you may want to exceed this number and, for other applications, an even lower number might make more sense, but when at this range of PVCs, you should carefully monitor performance.

Finally, consider that a fully-meshed frame relay network is in many respects similar to a LAN. Just as limiting the number of workstations on a LAN can improve performance, so does limiting the number of routers on a fully-meshed frame relay network. LAN applications are exploding and exactly how they will affect WAN requirements is open to speculation. But as applications evolve and create new demands on the WAN, frame relay's logical structure allows for comparatively simple network reconfigurations.

Outfit Your WAN with Frame Relay

FRAME RELAY'S RELIANCE ON UPPER-LAYER PROTOCOLS DICTATES THAT MANAGERS LEARN ABOUT THEIR NETWORK'S TRAFFIC PATTERNS AND THROUGHPUT REQUIREMENTS.

BY SUSAN FITZGERALD

If you're tired of trying to fit your square data requirements into the proverbial round WAN service hole, then frame relay may be the answer. It's cost-effective–at times saving more than 50 percent on network cost–but the real strength of a frame relay network is that it can be tailored to your communications needs.

But as the saying goes, nothing in life is free, and gaining such flexibility from a data communications service does not come without a cost. The first network managers to install frame relay can certainly attest to the difficulty of the network-design process. More significant than the steep learning curve required by any new protocol is the subtle, yet fundamental, shift in responsibility for network design that frame relay requires. Frame relay's reliance on upper-layer application protocols dictates that network managers possess a greater understanding of their network traffic patterns and data-throughput requirements. Conversely, it requires the telecommunications companies understand their customer's local protocol environment.

Education is paramount. Becoming fluent in frame relay is essential to a good network design. Too often, network managers begin by trying to decipher the services available and become discouraged as they realize service offerings vary widely among telecommunications companies. To minimize the frustration (for you and the carrier) of comparing components, start your design process by defining as many connectivity attributes for your network as possible.

TRAFFIC ANALYSIS

Although frame relay is often viewed as an alternative to private lines or slower X.25 services, surprisingly, the majority of frame relay customers are users with new applications, not those migrating from other services. New applications present a special challenge because of the lack of historical data on which to base traffic estimates. In addition, the underlying LAN protocols (particularly IPX and AppleTalk) are often "WAN-naive;" work has only recently begun to optimize these protocols for use over frame relay.

Depending on the size of your organization, the planning process can involve assessing user applications, coordinating requirements across multiple departments, and evaluating all of the organization's requirements. Don't beat yourself up to get every detail correct the first time. This assessment process is not a one-time assignment. Just as rushing water eventually carves a pattern through rock, your data patterns will become apparent. Fortunately, instead of taking years, the optimal design should become obvious in a matter of months. Expect to refine your service every two months to three months for the first two quarters following installation.

Begin your traffic assessment by identifying key applications and/or organizations that will account for 80 percent of the traffic. Ask your users a number of questions. Do their applications tend to be interactive or batch-like? Is usage heavier during certain times, or is the traffic pattern relatively constant?

Prior to evaluating frame relay, many companies installed asynchronous communications servers to transport corporatewide e-mail applications. The logs provided by the e-mail packages can offer a wealth of information because these logs provide communications patterns, and, since e-mail packages are frequently used to move files,

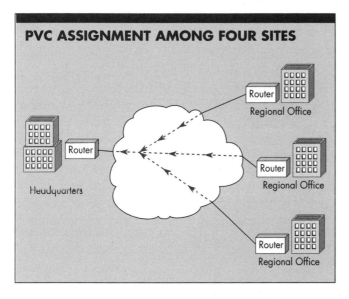

PVC ASSIGNMENT AMONG FOUR SITES

Figure 1. In this example, a minimum of three PVCs is needed for regional sites to communicate with headquarters.

the logs are a good source for making an initial assessment of traffic volume.

Next, ask the carriers and router vendors a series of "protocol behavior" questions. Collectively, they are the most likely to know how a particular protocol will behave over a WAN. Does the LAN protocol limit the number of device hops? Many protocols do. For example, IPX is limited to 15 hops, and NetBIOS is limited to seven hops. How are broadcasts handled? What types of filters are provided, and what information can reasonably be filtered without impacting the routing information on the network?

Finally, try to design the service to mirror the way you do business. One of the strong selling points of frame relay is that it provides meshed connectivity from a single access point.

With *meshed connectivity*, every site has a link to every other site; anyone on the network, regardless of location, can communicate with any other office. Although many companies look for this capability in a service, few have distributed applications in place to take advantage of meshed connectivity.

According to one carrier, "most companies ask for fully meshed connectivity to meet future requirements; the applications being used today tend to be hierarchical in nature." An advantage of using frame relay is that when the business requirements change, migrating from a hierarchical environment to a distributed environment is a very

simple process and can be accomplished with 30 days notice to the carrier.

DESIGN OPTIONS

Although telecommunications companies may disagree, only two types of services are available: private lines and virtual private networks (VPNs). Private lines provide dedicated connectivity between two locations.

VPN services take many forms, from being circuit switched, such as the public telephone network, to packet or frame based, such as frame relay. A VPN service is distinguished by the sharing of backbone resources among many customers.

Frame relay is a VPN service often said to be like a private-line service in that it provides a predetermined source and destination, referred to as a Permanent Virtual Circuit (PVC). To the user, it appears as a "nailed-up" or private circuit.

PVCs establish the logical connectivity of your network and are defined at the time of service subscription. A PVC is assigned between two sites requiring connectivity. For example, as shown in Figure 1, Company X has four sites: a headquarters site and three regional offices. For each regional site to communicate with headquarters, a minimum of three PVCs is needed. If, on the other hand, each site required the ability to communicate with every other office,

12 PVCs would be needed to provide a fully meshed network.

Some carriers use a simplex method of assigning PVCs, while others use a duplex method. Using the *simplex* PVC, traffic flows in one direction, in the same way that a car would travel on a one-way street. So, for example, as Figure 2 shows, information originating from the regional offices traverses a PVC and is transmitted to the headquarters. With a *duplex* PVC, traffic can run in two directions over two "one-way streets."

Understanding the method of assigning PVCs is beneficial when speaking with different carriers about the logical connectivity of your network. Contrary to what might be assumed, simplex and duplex PVC assignment are equally flexible. PVC assignment can quickly become overwhelming in a completely meshed network. With our simple example of four sites, we used 12 PVCs to provide complete connectivity between locations. As the number of PVCs increases so does the complexity of network management. Based on the number of sites you have and on the connectivity requirements, you should assign the minimum number of PVCs that will enable you to meet your needs.

COMMITTED INFORMATION RATE

The frame relay standards specify characteristics, typically referred to by carriers as "service parameters," which are assigned to each PVC. The Committed Information Rate (CIR) is the service parameter that will most affect your network-design effort.

The CIR is the data throughput in terms of bits per second that a network provider "guarantees" to support under normal network conditions. In actuality, carriers do not guarantee a *fixed* amount of bandwidth but rather an average amount of bandwidth calculated by measuring the *average* amount of traffic submitted to the network over a specified time interval. The interval measured is routinely very small, ranging from 0.25 seconds to 1.5 seconds.

Just as PVCs are assigned using a simplex or duplex method, CIRs can be assigned symmetrically or asymmetrically. *Symmetrical* CIRs commit the same amount of bandwidth for traffic flowing from source to destination as for traffic from destination to source. *Asymmetrical* CIRs, however, allow the network to become a true reflection of your bandwidth requirements; for example, asymmetrical

CIRs can accommodate more bandwidth from source to destination than from destination to source, if needed.

In my example, Company X is using a distributed database application to maintain inventory records at headquarters and in the field. Each evening a summary of the day's sales is transmitted to headquarters by each of the regional offices. After headquarters reconciles the inventory, a copy of the available inventory is downloaded to each regional office. Assume that the bandwidth required for downloading the inventory is three times as great as that required to upload the daily sales summary. The CIRs assigned from the regional sites to headquarters could be 128Kbps, while that rate for headquarters to the regional sites could be 384Kbps. Here frame relay offers substantial flexibility and economical gains over private lines.

In the preceding example, if private lines were substituted, you would have to drastically overbuild the network to get the same bandwidth capacity. Even if it were cost-effective to use a fractional T-1 line of 384Kbps, when headquarters downloaded the data, all other conversations would be precluded. And for the site that truly requires only 128Kbps, assigning 384Kbps would be like buying a baseball bat to kill a fly. Not only is it more power than is needed, but also the baseball bat is significantly more expensive than the better-suited fly swatter.

Establishing the correct CIR serves two functions. First, it will allow you to sleep at night knowing the data throughput agreed to at the time of service subscription is guaranteed. Even if the CIR selected is too low and the data submitted to the network exceeds your committed bandwidth, you don't have to lose sleep. Carriers attempt to deliver the data above the CIR on a best-effort basis. In the worst case, where the frame relay network experiences congestion and the data cannot be delivered, the upper-layer protocols used by your application will retransmit the information. Second, carriers charge, in part, based on CIR. The higher the CIR, the more money you pay. Establishing a CIR to reflect only your baseline connectivity requirements will save you money.

ASSIGNING CIRS

How do you assign CIRs? If your company is risk adverse or if the application is mission critical, set the CIR higher than you think is necessary. This CIR assignment theoretically represents the maximum amount of traffic

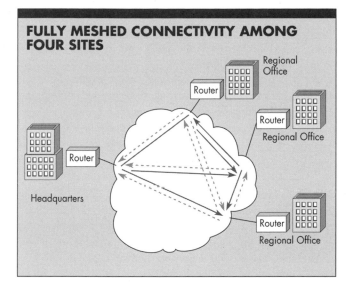

FULLY MESHED CONNECTIVITY AMONG FOUR SITES

Regional Office

Router

Router

Regional Office

Router

Headquarters

Router

Regional Office

Figure 2. Information originating from the regional offices traverse a PVC and is transmitted to the headquarters.

transmitted during periods of peak utilization. If, on the other hand, the frame relay network installation is viewed as a test–little information is known about the amount of traffic produced by each site and no mission-critical applications are in use–set the CIR very low. You can always increase the CIR later, and, in the meantime, this approach is more cost-effective.

At least two service providers offer a service in which the CIR can be set to zero. This setting alleviates much of the up-front traffic analysis because you are not asked to establish a CIR. The tradeoff is that none of the data is guaranteed. All data is delivered on a best-effort basis. At the end of the monthly reporting cycle, you can examine the amount of data submitted to the network for delivery and reassign the CIR accordingly.

To take advantage of the various CIR increments available, at least three months after installation you should establish CIRs (if you start out using a zero CIR) or refine them. The traffic statistics provided by the carrier should help make the decision to increase or decrease incremental bandwidth an easy one.

When data is transmitted above the CIR, the transmission is termed a burst. The standards define two types of burst: committed burst and excess burst. *Committed burst*, noted by the letters B_c ("B sub c") is the maximum amount of data that the network agrees to transfer under normal conditions during a specified time interval. In most situa-

tions, B_c is the same as CIR, but B_c is measured in bits while CIR is measured in bits per second.

Most users are familiar with *excess burst* (B_e, or "B sub e"). The excess burst is the maximum amount of uncommitted data that will be delivered through the network under normal network conditions in the specified time interval.

Some carriers support what is currently referred to as *extended burst* capability. This capability allows bursts to be sustained for long periods. This measure is subjective; however, for all practical purposes, a long burst is considered to last at least one second.

Other carriers do not offer an extended-burst capability; rather they handle excess data by buffering data in the frame relay switch's memory. With or without extended burst, carriers will deliver any data sent above the CIR on a best-effort basis.

Carriers not offering traditional burst capability use a credit-manager approach to burst allocation. By definition, bursty data is subject to peaks and valleys. During the valleys or periods of low usage, credits are accumulated which are then applied when high bandwidth is required. Although the approach is sound, it has been criticized for the small size of credits, equivalent to the length of one Ethernet frame. Carriers using a credit approach are expected to augment this implementation with an extended-burst capability next quarter.

After defining your logical connectivity through PVCs and your bandwidth requirement through CIRs, you must decide on port speeds for each site. Once again, this aspect of frame relay service differs significantly among carriers. The port speed selected is important, as it represents the size of the doorway between the local-access loop and the frame relay carrier's service. With a private-line service, port-speed selection is easy. If a 56Kbps line is used, a 56Kbps port is used.

With frame relay, the decision is a little more complex. The selected port speed can be less than, equal to, or greater than the sum of the CIRs. Given that the entire basis for frame relay is statistical multiplexing, the probability of all users hitting their keyboard to send information at the same nanosecond is remote. Therefore, some carriers permit the sum of the CIRs originating from one port to be greater than the port speed itself, a situation referred to as *oversubscription*. Other carriers take a more conservative approach and do not allow the sum of the CIRs to exceed the port speed.

If your organization has a steady flow of data from each location and is relatively risk adverse, you should pursue a port speed in which the sum of the CIRs represents 70-percent utilization. This percentage allows a safe margin for bursts even under peak traffic conditions. If your organization sporadically sends large chunks of data, then port-speed oversubscription could prove useful.

THE SUM TOTAL

How, you might ask, can the sum of my guaranteed bandwidth coming from one port be greater than the port speed itself? For carriers supporting this option the key word is "sum." Individual CIRs per PVC cannot exceed 100 percent of the port speed; however, the aggregate of the CIRs originating from one port can exceed the port speed by 200 percent or more. Such an implementation relies heavily on statistical multiplexing and buffers within the switches for safe data transmission.

In Company X's network, the sum of the CIRs originating from headquarters is 1,152Kbps. The port speed at the headquarters location must, at a minimum, be equal to 100 percent of the CIR, or 384Kbps. Using this port speed implies an oversubscription of 300 percent. Although possible, this level of oversubscription is recommended only under very stringent conditions where the traffic patterns

are precisely known. Most likely a port speed of 512Kbps would be used to bring the oversubscription to less than 200 percent. The port speed at the regional office sites would be 128Kbps.

All carriers allow port speeds to be mixed and matched within a frame relay network. In theory, sending information from a high-speed port to one with a lower-speed port would eventually flood the latter. But because of buffering throughout the network and the bursty nature of the traffic, carriers claim no noticeable effect. However, carriers recommend that when different port speeds are used, data being sent over the PVC connecting the two ports have the CIR of the lower-speed port.

Frame relay relies on the upper-layer protocol, such as Novell's SPX or TCP to provide error correction and retransmission. But the congestion-management techniques used by these protocols have raised undue concern on the part of network managers.

CONGESTION MANAGEMENT

Two types of congestion notification are specified in the CCITT standards: implicit and explicit. *Implicit notification* is the dropping of data when the network becomes overloaded. Although this type of congestion management typically makes network managers very nervous, it is actually commonly accepted for congestion management in bridge and router devices. If the buffers become full, subsequent data will be discarded.

If, after testing a frame relay service, you find an unacceptable amount of data is retransmitted, you may want to raise the CIR or add another PVC. You probably will not find yourself in this situation any time soon since the carriers have too few customers on their frame relay networks to stress these networks to the point of discarding data.

If you feel compelled, as one frame relay customer did, to test the congestion management of the network, you can do so by generating sufficient traffic sustained at the maximum excess burst rate for an extended period. After five days of sustained burst, this customer found data loss to be less than one bit per million.

Explicit notification is the setting of bits within the protocol to notify the end point to cut back the amount of data being submitted to the network. To date, the problem with explicit notification is the lack of industry support.

Until recently, router vendors have been reluctant to support this type of notification because it is the applications, rather than the routers, that in reality have to stop sending data. Look for explicit-notification support in the near future.

PRICING

Over the past 12 months, frame relay prices have dropped dramatically, making frame relay economically attractive for most networks. The difficulty lies not in finding an inexpensive service but in understanding how the prices are derived and which pricing approach is best for you. The most common pricing elements are local access, port speed, and CIR. Using some or a combination of these elements, carriers offer at least a flat-rate monthly service.

Carriers offering a zero CIR charge a per-packet fee. This approach has been used for many years by X.25 providers. It allows the user to pay "by the drink." The concept is similar to long-distance voice service, where you pay only for the minutes used. Some carriers offer a capped price, so that you will not be charged beyond a certain amount, even if your usage exceeds that amount.

A new distance-sensitive pricing strategy has recently been introduced. This per-mile charge is conceptually identical to private-line pricing. Under this pricing scenario, large regional connectivity using frame relay becomes economically attractive.

NETWORK DESIGN

Now that you have all the elements associated with defining your frame relay service, the only thing left to do is the design itself. Each design will be different based on your requirements, number of locations, and geographical dispersion.

Design a network that makes sense for you organizationally. The network should mirror your business and be designed around your business lines.

Ironically, one of the most important points to keep in mind is that frame relay is only one of the numerous services offered by each carrier. Even though you are designing a frame relay network, don't limit yourself to this technology. A good network design may be a hybrid of frame relay, private lines, switched services, and X.25.

Frame relay supports a maximum of 1,024 PVCs per port, approximately 20 percent of which are used for management purposes or reserved. Even with a theoretical maximum number of PVCs over 900, you will want to limit the PVCs per port to a manageable level. For most networks this number is probably no higher than 20.

Port-subscription strategies vary from carrier to carrier. To use the oversubscription aspect of a carrier's service, you must thoroughly understand your traffic patterns. Although oversubscription is a commonly touted feature, you are the only one who stands to lose if you guess wrong. The more risk adverse your company is, the higher you should set the CIR.

Frame relay does not currently offer dial-in services, so smaller sites must develop a piggyback strategy. These sites can dial in to locations with dedicated access.

CARRIERS: A SECOND GENERATION

With approximately 150 frame relay customers installed in 1992 and an estimated monthly growth rate of 20 percent, carriers are busy enhancing their service to stand out in what is becoming a crowded field. Initial service offerings included little, if any, network-management capabilities, PVC support, and utilization reports. Frame relay is becoming a second-generation service offering.

In addition to the aforementioned capabilities, one of the most significant changes to take place is the progress in addressing the installed base of 50,000 SNA networks–certainly a force to be reckoned with. SNA opens a new world of support issues. For example, SNA environments are time sensitive. If a response is not received within 7 seconds, the call is cleared. So, to successfully support this platform, SNA traffic needs to have priority over other types of traffic. This prioritizing can be done at the router or within the frame relay service. Router vendors are beginning to support traffic prioritization by protocol. The carriers may soon provide the same capability.

Carriers continue to have strong philosophical differences for service implementation. Their respective heritages are evident in the subtle differences in their service offerings. For example, Sprint's experience with X.25 prompted it to offer capped-usage pricing. MCI, which has a strong private-line orientation, offers a unique mileage-sensitive pricing scheme.

SUMMARY

With the evolving frame relay options, network design

continues to be an art rather than a science. Its multitude of options make frame relay the most flexible technology for developing an infrastructure that mirrors the way you do business. The key is to understand the options presented and to make the best decisions based on a knowledge of your traffic patterns and on an understanding of the peculiarities of LAN protocols. You will continue to benefit from your investment of time since frame relay offers a great migration to other technologies, such as ATM. The same backbone used for frame relay can be easily replaced with ATM without affecting the design.

A Work in Progress

JUST WHEN IT LOOKED LIKE ATM ALONE WOULD SHAPE THE FACE OF LAN/WAN CONNECTIVITY, USERS SHOW RENEWED INTEREST IN FRAME RELAY

BY CHERYL KRIVDA

The complete picture of developing technologies often resembles an M.C. Escher lithograph that twists and turns depending on your perspective. While vendors crow about product announcements and analysts furiously grapple with projections, prospective users wind their way through a maze of claims, promises, and predictions.

So it is with frame relay. Not long ago the golden child of WAN communications, frame relay suffered under the burden of the delays required to implement the carrier connections. At recent trade shows, some even pronounced frame relay "dead."

But frame relay is neither the savior promised in its early announcements nor the has-been naysayers allege. Rather, frame relay is a technology akin to a work in progress–one that can be expected to develop and mature during the next few years.

PRODUCTS TO MARKET?

Like most technologies, the success of frame relay depends on companies' needs, applications, and futures, and, to a great extent, a technology's success depends on timing.

Frame relay hit the market in mid-1991 in a blizzard of press stressing its role as the technology of choice for interconnecting discrete LANs into WANs. Still, vendors and carriers are only beginning to deliver products and services that enable frame relay–despite the technology's benefits. Standardized by the American National Standards Institute (ANSI) and International Telegraph and Telephone Consultative Committee (CCITT), frame relay offers low overhead, capacity up to 2Mbps with low delay, and reliable data transfer over modern networks.

Most importantly for some sites, frame relay can provide hardware savings of as much as 30 percent to 40 percent. In an environment with a headquarters and multiple remote sites, routers are used at each end of the leased-line connection. In a point-to-point Token Ring network with 500 branches, 500 routers are needed at the remote sites, which talk to 500 router ports at the central site. The expense of such a solution means that many networks defer connecting some remotes.

Depending on the traffic, a frame relay network can cut those 500 headquarters routers to 20 or 30, since dedicated bridging and routing is no longer necessary. In addition, frame relay allows any-to-any connectivity, so remote sites can communicate with one another, as well as with the central site. For many network managers, frame relay allows connection of sites that otherwise would not be cost-effective.

Migrating from point-to-point to a mesh architecture using a technology such as frame relay can pay for itself through the cost savings generated, explains Peter Galvin, product marketing manager of LAN products for Andrew (Orland Park, IL). "If you can cut your hardware cost by 30 percent or 40 percent by using frame relay instead of point-to-point connections, and you can also cut your point-to-point costs because you're using a frame relay network, you're talking about some significant cost advantages. Depending on your configuration, your period of payback may be very short."

PRELIMINARY TESTING

In some of the earliest investigations of frame relay's potential, Pacific Bell (San Ramon, CA) hosted a six-month technology test for several customers interested in frame relay, as well as for vendors who wanted to test their access-equipment products. From December 1991 through June 1992, PacBell evaluated the performance of AT&T and Northern Telecom frame relay switching equipment.

Kimberly Neverett, frame relay project manager for PacBell, qualifies the tests as a success. "We had nothing but high praise" for the frame relay network and associated products, she says. Because the traffic levels–generated by only four users–were not representative of a production frame relay network, PacBell's results are considered preliminary at best. As a first step, however, PacBell considered the testing results positive enough to pursue development of its own frame relay product and service offerings. Neverett says PacBell hopes to have service by mid-1993, pending Public Utility Commission approval.

The second benefit recognized by users is the relative speed of frame relay. Because it eliminates the overhead of transmission error checking at each node, frame relay is faster than other comparable packet-switching technologies, such as X.25.

FRUSTRATED EXPECTATIONS

Unfortunately, after the initial frame relay announcements, the vendors' and carriers' speed in bringing the technology to market couldn't match user expectations. Vendors and carriers spent the latter part of 1991 and much of 1992 building the physical network links, developing the products, and planning the services. But about the time frame relay was really ready in late 1992, marketing blitzes on behalf of Asynchronous Transmission Mode (ATM) had begun.

Customer confusion and frustration hit a new high. In the warped kaleidoscope created by enthusiastic product announcements and perceived customer need, it suddenly seemed to the majority of the marketplace that frame relay had failed.

"When frame relay first came out, it was heralded by the press as the solution for every networking evil," says Kaye Hack, product manager for Wiltel, a Tulsa, OK, carrier. When the press and customers discovered it had more narrow applications and that there were finite limits to the problems it could solve, it went from being everything to being nothing.

"In fact," she says, "the truth is somewhere in between.

For certain customers and certain applications, it's a fantastic solution that provides savings. For other customers with different applications and solutions, it's not the answer."

By the summer of 1992, it seemed that frame relay was suitable for few sites and that its promise had been largely oversold.

Rosemary Cochran, principal at the consulting firm Vertical Systems Group (Dedham, MA), has been tracking the frame relay market since mid 1991. The results of her work appear in a report called "The Frame Relay Industry Analysis," which examines the industry's market drivers, technology, vendor implementations, and user experiences.

Based on her research, the frame relay market became rife with user frustration. Besides the delays, a lack of education about frame relay and its costs helped feed user dissatisfaction.

QUALMS WITH VENDORS

Adding to the problem, users realized that each vendor can implement frame relay in a different manner. Currently AT&T, Wiltel, CompuServe, and British Telecom offer a platform based on the StrataCom's FastPacket multiplexer platform. MCI and Sprint use other implementations. The net result of this disparity is that users trying to communicate using dissimilar equipment have experienced difficulties.

Few of the carriers publish their frame relay pricing, another obstacle for users who attempt to gauge the technology's relative costs. Vendors claim to be pricing the offerings to reflect a value-added service orientation, rather than a commodity-style product. But Cochran says for users who don't know whether frame relay makes any sense at all, the lack of readily available information impedes the process of understanding the frame relay market.

Additionally, vendor's announcement of their intentions to pursue ATM initially threw ice water on frame relay's momentum. Some network managers questioned the wisdom of investing in frame relay, given ATM's promise of even higher-speed bandwidth (to 1.2Gbps) for more intensive processing. But, conservative estimates project that the first ATM products might not arrive until 1995.

REGAINED MOMENTUM

Then a funny thing happened. As the initial ATM announcements began to shake out, a convergence of frame relay products and services arrived on the market, and frame relay's future seemed to brighten considerably.

Wiltel's Hack notes that her company is experiencing tremendous growth as a result of customer interest in frame relay technology. Monthly revenues for most of 1992 grew by an average 16 percent to 31 percent. Wiltel expects similar continued growth until 1995, when ATM may impact frame relay's fortunes.

Analyst projections support Wiltel's experience. According to Vertical Systems Group, frame relay's market futures are extremely encouraging. From a market of $14.7 million last year to a projected $591.7 million in 1996, frame relay seems to be poised for an incredible takeoff.

One satisfied user of frame relay technology is Coyne Gibson, manager of information technology for Convex Computers, a supercomputer manufacturer in Richardson, TX. The original beta user for Wiltel's product, Convex implemented a hybrid network of public and private frame relay links.

The private portion of the network uses StrataCom equipment; the public side includes 14 active public links to field locations. Gibson says the savings generated by switching to frame relay were enough to link sites that previously were too costly to connect.

"A fairly tremendous savings is involved if you compare a meshed or partial mesh network composed of private lines versus a frame relay network. Your capital equipment costs and recurring costs are much lower, and the frame relay access costs are cheap when compared with private lines," he says. Convex realized a 60 percent savings on capital equipment because of the reduction in the number of router interfaces. An additional 30 percent reduction for frame relay services over the cost of private lines capped the cost justification.

Gibson says Convex's plan to move to ATM eventually did not deter the company from making the most of existing frame relay services. "Frame relay is a fair stepping-stone toward ATM technology. If you're trying to get early experience with this kind of network technology, it's a good way to go," Gibson says.

SOME REASSURANCE

Analyst projections for the viability of the frame relay market are encouraging for both the vendors and users. Vertical Systems Group recently released projections for frame relay technologies that show the market growing through 1996. Cochran divided projections for the diverse frame relay market into the categories of access equipment, private network switches, and public central office switches.

Access equipment includes everything from routers that are upgraded for free to intelligent devices costing tens of thousands of dollars, she says. Even with the diversity of the measurement, the numbers clearly show that frame relay has a strong future in WAN connectivity.

As a first step in the migration toward frame relay, sites buy routers, bridges, and other equipment fitted with frame relay connectivity. A core group of major telecommunications carriers offers public and private frame relay network services and is developing a roster of new value-added services to help draw and keep clients.

WHO BENEFITS?

But frame relay is not for everyone. Certain sites benefit more than others.

Most of the current Wiltel frame relay customers have partially or fully meshed networks with five to 10 nodes, with about 80 percent of these connected to multiple points.

Christine Heckart, marketing manager for broadband services at Wiltel, says companies with multiple geographically dispersed remote sites gain the greatest benefit from frame relay. Because they typically use segregated networks, they achieve significant savings by consolidating applications onto one frame relay network.

Like every developing technology, frame relay needs some work. One problem is that many users do not have geographic access to every city that's needed. Dave King, marketing manager for LAN internetworking division of Racal-Datacom (Boxborough, MA), says some frustration initially resulted from the sparse population of carrier Points-Of-Presence (POPs).

Customers believed that carriers announcements' meant services would be available immediately. "I think they were really sold a bill of goods," King says.

But linking many geographic areas takes time, and unconnected areas can be linked using private lines to the nearest linked city. Carriers promise to continue implementing additional POPs across the country. In the next year, geographic access should cease to be an issue.

Another problem has been the issue of how frame relay handles congestion on the communications lines. Although a frame relay user contracts for a specific amount of bandwidth, frame relay "clouds" allow sites that have paid for a certain bandwidth to pay extra for additional bandwidth as available.

When one site uses "available" bandwidth, it does so hoping the owner of that bandwidth won't need it simultaneously. If, during a transmission, the available bandwidth is claimed by the owning user, the frame relay cloud recognizes congestion on the line and relinquishes the line to the rightful owner. The user whose transmission was aborted must determine which packets were sent and which need to be resent. With the difficulties in connecting the equipment of discrete vendors, users can become frustrated attempting to reconnect and resend the transmission.

SOME THINGS ARE PRIVATE

Another issue the carriers need to address is security. For users accustomed to private leased-line networks, carriers need to provide assurance that moving to frame relay does not mean a loss of network control. "For the most critical high-speed data applications, users are very hesitant to use a public network," explains Gigi Wang, vice president of communications research for International Data Corp. (IDC, Framingham, MA). "They feel they would lose control of the management of the network. And in using a switched access network, they would be concerned about the access portion and the reliability and availability of the network."

For those who really chafe at the idea of a "public" network, private frame relay services are available. Using leased lines and privately owned frame relay switches, users can gain from frame relay's economy of scale and create any-to-any networks, while maintaining their private status.

Carriers argue that software-defined logical connections make public frame relay as secure as any private

leased line. "It's a private data facility on a public platform allowing for public economies of scale," states Heckart.

Vendors apparently sense the user frustration and are responding with a host of value-added services. Wiltel, for example, plans to provide a family of service and support offerings to help users perform everything from initial installation to full system operation.

According to IDC's Wang, Wiltel and vendors pursuing similar strategies are on the right track. Only vendors who understand users' applications and network needs will succeed in the frame relay market, says Wang.

"Selling a network service such as frame relay is very different from what the carrier sales-and-support infrastructure is used to, which is selling private lines," says Cochran. "Most carriers are struggling with that aspect. Salespeople are more attuned to selling private lines or voice services, and this is a whole new world. When you sell a service, it becomes critical to understand the traffic characteristics, protocols, and configurations."

A PRICE DROP

With the increase in vendor service offerings has come a gradual decrease in carrier access charges. In recent months, access charges have dropped approximately 30 percent; a continuing migration to frame relay is likely to reduce prices further.

But vendors caution that they will not slash prices at the risk of turning the frame relay business into a commodity market. Lower prices that reduce margins too soon could dampen vendors' ability to reinvest in continued development efforts, they say. Instead, vendors are hoping to get prospective users to focus on value-added services.

"I think you'll see some adjustments in pricing, but more than anything, adjustments will be made on relative value," says Rob McKinney, product manager of internetworking services for CompuServe (Columbus, OH). "In all the business we've won, cost has been an issue," but service was more critical, he points out.

To expand service offerings, some vendors have entered into the education business. In addition to helping network users understand frame relay and how to implement it to their advantage, vendors and carriers find themselves explaining why migrating to frame relay is more cost-effective than waiting several years for the delivery of commercial ATM. Most networks, they argue, can benefit immediately from frame relay's hardware consolidation and speed. Even those sites that intend to pursue ATM can use frame relay as an important stepping stone toward advanced WAN communications technology.

Those wondering whether to forgo frame relay and wait for ATM or SMDS to materialize will be disappointed, analysts say. ATM services are as yet undefined, and the only ATM switch on the market appeared at a recent trade show with a $300,000 price tag.

SMDS functionality clearly overlaps frame relay and may be limited by the fact that it is expected to be primarily a localized service offered by the RBOCs. Initially, SMDS was to offer speeds matching T-3 lines, but expectations have been scaled down for SMDS to reach speeds of 1.5Mbps (T-1) and higher–well within the range of frame relay.

WHY WAIT?

For now, Hack says, only sites that have large, high-speed, database-to-database applications requiring more than a T-1's worth of capacity should think seriously about waiting for ATM. "Instituting a frame relay solution today gives users experience in working with cell-based and frame-based protocols and internetworking environments," she says.

Once ATM finds its market niche, frame relay may develop a new one: connecting public services to LAN backbones. "ATM will probably be used in a couple of ways but not necessarily [for] directly interfacing public services to private networks for some time. We believe that there's quite an opportunity for frame relay to be used to bridge those two environments for some time to come," Cochran states.

And undoubtedly the disappointment that initially plagued frame relay will follow ATM, which has had the same blizzard of promotion but will be unavailable for an even longer period. "ATM is at least three or four or even five years away. Many companies are announcing an ATM strategy, but ATM won't be available to the commercial market for at least two to three years, if not longer," Andrew's Galvin says.

Given the development of frame relay during the last six months as well as the projections for the future, several years of steady growth seem the likely outcome. Buyers can take solace in knowing that the major carriers, who have invested millions of dollars in establishing frame relay links, are not likely to walk away from frame relay– their work in progress– any time soon.

Lighten Up

SMDS OFFERS A FAST, CONVENIENT, CHEAPER METHOD FOR
TRANSPORTING GRAPHICS FILES.

BY RUSSELL SHARER

Using today's sophisticated desktop publishing tools, prepress organizations are creating ever more beautiful, more complex brochures, presentations, and catalogs. Printed materials that once took artists, typesetters, and image strippers days to produce can now be created electronically in just a few hours. However, until recently high-speed modern design tools have been slowed by traditional image transport. The electronic design was copied to magnetic media and physically carried to an imaging service bureau or printer for output to film.

The improvement in image transport has come about in the prepress industry with the introduction of Switched Multimegabit Data Service (SMDS). SMDS is a metropolitan area network standard supported by the Regional Bell Operating Companies (RBOCs) and other telephony service providers. SMDS offers an electronic delivery service for immediate delivery of large graphics files. It is transforming business models of prepress companies, from small imaging service bureaus to large commercial printers.

THE CHALLENGES OF COLOR

Apple invented the desktop publishing market in the 1980s with its Macintosh computers and affordable laser printers. For the first time, materials could look as if they had been typeset at prices below the cost of typesetting. Memos and newsletters started appearing with sophisticated graphics, and Aldus (Seattle) Pagemaker skills meant extra pay for administrative staff.

The last couple of years have seen color enter the world of desktop publishing. Image scanners, large-screen monitors, and high-resolution color printers simplify the enhancement of materials by adding four-color art.

But color comes with a price. High-resolution color images are large, requiring lots of disk space for storage and huge quantities of RAM. A single color image can often require 5MB to 8MB of disk space, and a one-page mailer or advertisement can take 16MB to 20MB of storage. Catalogs start at 30MB of disk space and can expand more than 10 times as the page and image quantity increase.

The sheer size of these graphics files disqualifies most usual file-transportation mechanisms. Floppy disks are futile, like trying to carry a lake in a tea cup. SyQuest magnetic tapes with 44MB or 88MB capacities are also too small. Newer optical media offer hope for the future but today are too expensive and suffer from a lack of standards. Even if the file can fit on the media, it must still be physically delivered. Typically the graphic designer puts the media in a pouch and transports it to the service bureau or printer via a courier or overnight delivery service.

Even more overwhelmed by large files is modem technology. At 14.4Kbps, the large files would literally take days to transfer. While better, the proposed V.Fast and V.32 Turbo standards are still at least an order of magnitude too small for frequent use with large files (see Figure 1 for a comparison of file-transfer speeds).

The problem of file transportation has yielded some creative solutions, including more efficient compression technology and file-division algorithms, which break a single file into multiple parts for transport. But these technologies are limited in their ability to handle really large files. Therefore, prepress has been searching for a better file-transfer method.

ENTER SMDS

Into this seemingly solutionless situation steps SMDS. SMDS offers four key benefits to prepress:

• First, it operates at high speeds, usually 1.17Mbps. Utilizing readily available DS-1 lines from telephone service providers, SMDS can transport large files between remote sites in a brief period of time.

• Simplicity is the second advantage of SMDS. Since the network is monitored and maintained by the service provider, users do not have to be technically sophisticated. If you can install and maintain an AppleTalk network, you can incorporate SMDS.

• Interenterprise communication is benefit No. three. A company can link its main office with remote offices, ad agencies, graphic design firms, service bureaus, and commercial printers for file exchange. Extending the electronic highway beyond your enterprise is easy and secure with SMDS.

• Finally, SMDS is priced at a reasonable fixed monthly fee that is not usage sensitive. Network managers know what the service will cost in advance and can experiment with new applications without cost concerns. In fact, companies like the ones I am about to profile are finding that the monthly cost of SMDS service is less than they had been paying for couriers or overnight delivery services that require more time (see Figure 2).

FALCON FLIES WITH SMDS

Falcon Microsystems (Landover, MD) is the leading supplier of Macintosh computers and peripherals to the federal government. To keep its customers aware of new products and special offers, Falcon makes extensive use of direct mail. Two to four times per year, it produces a 250-page full-color catalog on its complete product offerings and government services agency (GSA) contract terms. Six times a year, Falcon supplements the large catalogs with smaller, 24- to 32-page catalogs. Finally, a constant stream of advertisements and mailers can incorporate anywhere from 10 to 30 images.

Falcon's half-dozen graphic designers generate 60MB to 80MB of material a day for transport to their service bureau, Design Imaging of Washington, D.C. Last winter, Falcon decided to find a better, more cost-effective way to move images between its two facilities.

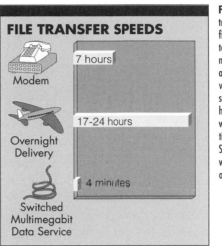

FILE TRANSFER SPEEDS

Modem — 7 hours

Overnight Delivery — 17-24 hours

Switched Multimegabit Data Service — 4 minutes

Figure 1. To transfer a 30MB file from Chicago to Philadelphia, modem technology and courier services require from seven hours to 24-hours compared with Switched Multimegabit Data Service (SMDS), which requires only munutes.

In Falcon's old system, a courier made an afternoon delivery run over the approximately 10 miles. Falcon saw two problems with this approach: The courier cost hundreds of dollars each month, and the firm's designers had to stop work at 3 p.m. daily to ensure the files got to Design Imaging before its 6 p.m. closing time. (Like many large cities, Washington suffers from horrible rush hour traffic, translating the 10-mile drive into an hour-and-a-half ordeal.) Since images would often take all night to process, if a file did not arrive on time and processing had to be delayed until the following morning, a full day could be lost in the production cycle. The worst scenario was to miss the delivery on a Friday, which would mean three days lost in the schedule.

Falcon worked with Bell Atlantic, its local telephone service provider, to investigate data-service options. It quickly settled on SMDS. Falcon ordered the service and acquired an SMDSTalk card from Multiaccess Computing (Santa Barbara, CA). The SMDSTalk card is a NuBus interface that provides the electrical interface to SMDS. When combined with the Apple Internet Router software, Falcon and Design Imaging created a single logical AppleTalk network.

The Falcon SMDS link came on-line in early Spring 1993. Will Foster, a systems analyst for Falcon, had previously installed a frame relay network between Falcon's remote offices across the United States. He found SMDS to be easier to bring up and more reliable and robust during operation than the packet-switching network. The only

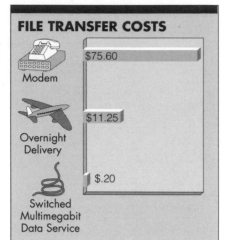

Figure 2. To transfer a 30MB file from Chicago to Philadelphia, Switched Multimegabit Data Service (SMDS), priced at a fixed monthly rate costs pennies. Courier services would cost $11 and modem technology $75 for the same file.

real issue was making sure the AppleTalk network zones were properly defined. Once zones were defined, the network worked well, and Falcon added its Crystal City, VA, office to the service (see Figure 3).

IMMEDIATE RETURNS

Falcon immediately profited from the service. Its designers could work a couple of additional hours each day and still meet Design Imaging's end-of-day deadline. This productivity improvement came with a hard-cost benefit. The monthly cost of SMDS is less than the amount Falcon had been paying for courier service.

Although Falcon actually would have paid less per month for Integrated Services Digital Network (ISDN), or T-1 service (approximately $1,450 plus usage fees for ISDN and $1,400 for T-1) than for SMDS (about $1,800), SMDS offers more potential growth. By using SMDS, Design Imaging can solicit other clients to deliver information digitally. Their SMDS port will accept traffic from any company on the SMDS network authorized by Design Imaging.

Design Imaging also liked the seamless look and feel of SMDS. The products available to attach its Macintosh networks to SMDS made access transparent. T-1 connections would have required the company's network manager to have greater knowledge of routing devices and protocols than SMDS does.

Over time, Falcon began to see additional benefits from the link. If a problem occurred during film processing, it

could be resolved jointly with the designer and service-bureau technician on-line. For example, anyone who has ever worked with prepress software knows the frustration of not having the correct font loaded or of missing an image link that aborts the film processing run. The next morning, rather than picking up film and delivering it to a commercial printer, the designer is loading files on magnetic media, updating links, and resubmitting the image for processing.

With SMDS, the Falcon designer and the Design Imaging technician have common access privileges for each file processed. If by some chance a font or image link is not found on the local disk, the design software can automatically find the item by looking across the SMDS link.

A GROWING RELATIONSHIP

The connection has expanded Falcon and Design Imaging's business relationship. For example, Design Imaging has a high-quality drum scanner that it offers clients for digitizing four-color photos and graphics. Rather than purchase its own expensive equipment, Falcon now has Design Imaging scan all necessary images and share them back across the SMDS link.

Design Imaging also invested in special image-management software to enable low-resolution versions of the images to be transferred to the Falcon designers for use in placement and proofs. The documents retain their links to the high-resolution images so when it's time to generate film for the printed piece, the high-resolution images are substituted for the low-resolution ones.

Improved communication between the two companies is another benefit. Falcon's Microsoft Mail system was extended to Design Imaging, allowing written communications to be easily exchanged. Design Imaging can even proofread draft versions of catalogs for Falcon, ensuring a higher-quality final result with minimal production schedule time for moving the file back and forth.

A MANAGEMENT REALITY

As the network connection approaches its one-year anniversary, both parties are pleased with the service. Zev Remba, vice president of Design Imaging, says the electronic link has deepened its business relationship with Falcon. SMDS has brought the concept of synergistic collaboration from the pages of management books to reality. The

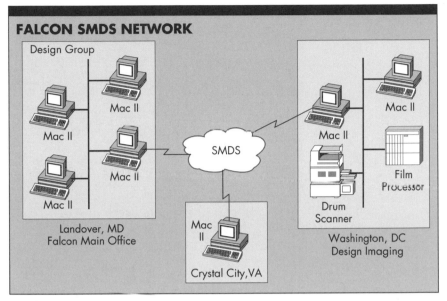

Figure 3. Falcon Microsystems used to send via courier the 60MB to 80MB of material its graphic designers generated each day to its service bureau, Design Imaging. Falcon decided to find a more cost effective way to move images and opted for SMDS.

firms are working together on network design and security issues, including the provisioning of storage on the network.

They are also developing a comprehensive image-management system that will enable Falcon to have on-line access to the more than 5GB of digitized images Design Imaging has scanned.

SMDS was a straightforward choice for Design Imaging. The company needed a data service that operated at a speed of at least 1Mbps and could link its geographically separate site to Falcon. When Remba reviewed what options were currently available, he found three: a leased T-1 line, primary rate ISDN, and SMDS.

The leased-line option was disqualified based on flexibility. Leased lines could not easily be expanded to link additional clients to the Design Imaging office. Primary rate ISDN lost because of its lack of complete and competitively priced hardware and software. Plus, its rate structure, based on usage, made the monthly cost difficult to budget. SMDS was priced right, was easy to expand, and offered multiple sources for interface equipment.

L.P. THEBAULT LINKS UP

SMDS is also impacting very large print operations. L.P. Thebault is a major commercial printer based in Parsippany, NJ. It specializes in high-quality corporate collat-

eral, such as brochures and annual reports in the financial services, pharmaceutical, and fashion markets. Two plants in New Jersey operate two half-Web presses, a full-Web press, and seven multicolor sheet presses around the clock.

For years, Thebault has linked its facilities with DS-1 lines. Recently, it added SMDS to broaden connectivity options. According to Clif Valentine, vice president of marketing for Thebault, its clients have been struggling to find a good way to transmit electronic images to Thebault's in-house film-processing center. Modems are too slow, and leased lines and Switched 56 services are too expensive. It should be no surprise that SyQuest tapes delivered via overnight courier is the transport vehicle of choice for Valentine's clients.

With his company's proximity to New York City, home of the country's largest advertising agencies, Valentine sees SMDS improving relationships between the agency, client, and printer by cutting time from the production schedule. Artists at an agency can design a new brochure, send it to the client for review and approval, and then immediately transfer it directly to Thebault for printing. This process, which can now take weeks, could be shortened to a handful of days (see Figure 4).

What's at stake is millions of dollars in company and printing business. Take a major company in the pharmaceuticals industry that is seeking to release a new mass

Figure 4. Clients of L.P. Thebault, a large commercial printer, have been clamoring for a good way to transmit electronic images to its in-house film-processing center. Recently, Thebault put SMDS into place.

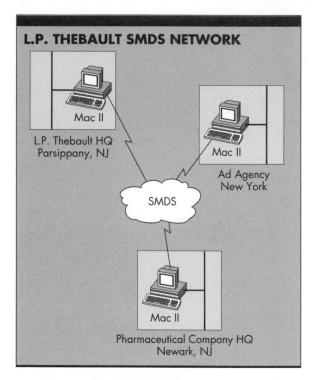

market pain reliever. A new product of this type can gather $1 million in sales revenue each day. If SMDS can save three days in the product launch by speeding up the materials-development process, it could theoretically increase that company's sales by millions of dollars. Commercial printers, such as Thebault, that support SMDS stand to profit from improved customer service and shorter production times.

SERVICE OF CHOICE

SMDS became the service of choice for Thebault based on its competitive monthly fee and the availability of interface equipment. Like Design Imaging, Thebault required at least 1Mbps of performance, the ability to span long distances, and availability of service. SMDS was the perfect fit.

SMDS is available in most of the metropolitan areas, and it is tariffed for use inside a single local access and transport area (LATA). Valentine says the only thing holding back SMDS in the prepress market is complete resolution of the intra-LATA traffic carrier.

The intra-LATA carriers are experimenting with a vari-

ety of approaches. MCI's SMDS service is in its infancy. Sprint is offering a routed service over frame relay. Ameritech, through an unregulated subsidiary, is routing SMDS over ISDN lines. When one of these, or another approach, is standardized, SMDS should become very common in prepress and printing applications. When Asynchronous Transfer Mode (ATM) is fully deployed in the latter half of this decade, it will also be able to carry SMDS traffic.

MEETING AT A TRADE SHOW

To introduce the prepress industry to SMDS, a group of vendors has been participating in industry trade shows. The Graphic Communications 3 event in Philadelphia is scheduled for March 24 through 26. Bell Atlantic and Ameritech lead the consortium of service providers, application software vendors, commercial printers, and network equipment suppliers that demonstrate SMDS under the banner of Instant Image Delivery. The group is taking a nontechnical approach to explaining the service, drawing the analogy that Instant Image Delivery offers the best of modems and overnight delivery services.

According to Mara Spaulder, manager of broadband product development at Bell Atlantic (Arlington, VA), response at previous meetings has been overwhelming. Long stymied by no electronic solution for image transfer, attendees are glad to see a service such as Instant Image Delivery.

Prepress people are already familiar with electronic design software and computers. Most use networks based on either AppleTalk or Novell NetWare. SMDS can plug in and immediately offer time and cost savings.

Because SMDS offers immediate payback for busy graphics designers and service bureaus, and because money is the best force for driving technology acceptance, more companies with needs like those of Falcon, Design Imaging, and L.P. Thebault will start using SMDS. If time and money are important to your print jobs, you should investigate the technology with your local telephone service provider.

WHAT IS SMDS?

SMDS is a connectionless, high-speed, public packet-switched data service. It was defined by Bellcore and is being implemented by the Regional Bell Operating Companies (RBOCs) and other public network local exchange carriers. SMDS is specified to operate at speeds from 1.544Mbps (DS-1) to more than 155Mbps (SONET's OC-3).It was designed for Intra-LATA service as a metropolitan area network. Initially implemented on a subset of the IEEE 802.6 MAC- and Physical-layer standards, SMDS will migrate to an ATM switching fabric as ATM is deployed. The service offers multicast and group addressing.

Changing Channels

AN ALTERNATIVE TO ATM AND FDDI, FIBRE CHANNEL COMBINES THE ELEGANCE OF PROTOCOL COMMUNICATIONS WITH THE SIMPLICITY OF CHANNEL ARCHITECTURE.

BY GARY KESSLER

If speed is what you want or need, you'll find no shortage of new alternatives. High-speed technologies and services, such as Fiber Distributed Data Interface (FDDI), Asynchronous Transfer Mode (ATM), and Switched Multimegabit Data Service (SMDS) have garnered a great deal of industry attention. But at least one channel-oriented approach is emerging for many of the same applications, or, perhaps more aptly, *reemerging:* Fibre Channel communications.

In many ways, Fibre Channel is a throwback to the internal channel-based communications of computer systems. Think of a computer's bus, which literally provides a physical link or channel for the transfer of information between parts of the system.

Because Fibre Channel architecture resembles this pipe-like functionality, it can provide high-speed data transfer between devices. It transfers data between a buffer at the source device and a buffer at the destination device, moving only the buffer contents from one device to another without regard to the format or meaning of the data. In this way, Fibre Channel avoids the overhead involved in handling different network communications protocols. It provides only control of the transfer and simple error detection.

In contrast, protocol-based networking technologies are, by nature, software intensive and, consequently, slower–albeit more flexible.

The Fibre Channel specification is an effort to combine the best of two technologies–the simplicity and speed of channel communications with the flexibility and interconnectivity that characterize protocol-based network communications.

INTO THE CHANNEL

Channels and networks have several fundamental differences.

Channels typically interconnect processors and high-performance peripherals at very high speeds over relatively short point-to-point links. Networks can interconnect processors at moderate to high speeds using some form of switching over relatively large distances.

Channels are, by definition, hardware intensive. Since their main task is to provide high-speed data transport between two devices with minimum delay and error, simple error correction or data retransmission (in the case of a busy condition) is handled by the hardware without requiring intervention by software. Networks, on the other hand, are software intensive and typically less efficient than channels because of high protocol overhead.

Channels provide a connection between a closed, usually small, set of devices, where the address of every device is predefined for the operating system. Networks must be able to provide connections between any pair of devices attached to the network, where addresses and routes are usually not predefined.

The American National Standards Institute (ANSI) X3T9.3 Task Group formed the Fibre Channel Working Group in 1988 to develop a high-performance serial link for data transfer between host mainframes, supercomputers, PCs, workstations, and peripheral devices.

Fibre Channel couples very high-bandwidth communications with a flexible switching topology to interconnect many devices. Traditional LANs, as well as circuit- and some packet-switched networks, were originally designed in the 1970s. At that time, bandwidth on the communica-

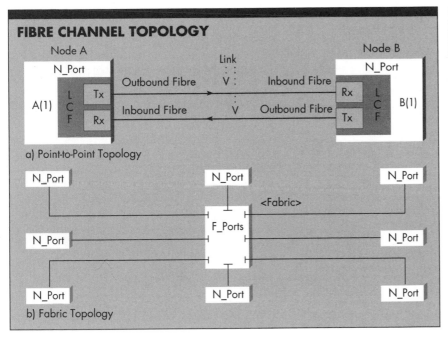

FIBRE CHANNEL TOPOLOGY

a) Point-to-Point Topology

b) Fabric Topology

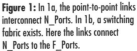

Figure 1: In 1a, the point-to-point links interconnect N_Ports. In 1b, a switching fabric exists. Here the links connect N_Ports to the F_Ports.

tions link was the network bottleneck; switches and the switching function, therefore, were distributed throughout the network.

Today, optical fiber has a theoretical maximum bandwidth 1,000 times greater than the electrical-optical conversion capabilities of the switch interfaces. The switches, then, are now the network bottleneck, and today's emerging broadband networks are being designed to minimize the number of switches (hence the attraction of photonic switching).

On a traditional channel, a central processor handles all but simple error handling. In LANs and other networks, every end node must be capable of detecting and correcting network errors. Neither of these solutions was considered appropriate for Fibre Channel; typical channels rely too heavily on the central processor and typical networks rely too heavily on end-user stations.

Fibre Channel moves the complexity of device interconnection and switching to a *fabric*, the networking structure that is protocol independent, largely distance insensitive, and may be based on any technology. An individual Fibre Channel end station is only responsible for managing a simple point-to-point connection between itself and the fabric; the fabric, in turn, is responsible for routing be-

tween end stations, error detection and correction, and flow control.

Regardless of any speed limitations of the physical links within the fabric itself, additional parallel paths may be added to a particular connection if additional bandwidth is required.

Fibre Channel provides a logically bidirectional point-to-point serial data channel for high-performance communications. It does so either through the interconnection of multiple user attachments, called *N_Ports*, or through the connection of an end-user station to a switching fabric (*F_Port*).

Figure 1a shows a simple topology in which point-to-point links interconnect N_Ports; note that the link media is referred to as *fibre*, meaning any media supported by the Fibre Channel specification. A link control facility (LCF) is hardware that attaches to each end of the link to control its operation.

Figure 1b shows a switching fabric in which case the links connect N_Ports to the F_Port. A *link* is the physical point-to-point connection between two N_Ports or between an N_Port and an F_Port, while a *path* is the sequence of links that interconnects two N_Ports (when a fabric is present).

FIBRE CHANNEL ARCHITECTURE

ULPs	IPI-3	SCSI	HIPPI	IP	Others
FC-4	IPI-3 Mapping	SCSI Mapping	HIPPI Mapping	IP Mapping	Other Mappings
FC-3	Common Services				
FC-2	Signalling Protocol				
FC-1	Transmission Protocol				
FC-0	Interface				
	Media				

FC-PH

The Fibre Channel specification describes a layered architecture as Figure 2 shows.

While I will discuss each layer in detail, generally speaking FC-0 describes the Fibre Channel link and encompasses a wide variety of media, speed, and distance combinations. FC-1 describes the Fibre Channel Transmission Protocol, defining the electrical signaling used on the link. FC-2 describes the Fibre Channel Signaling Protocol, defining how data is transferred between nodes.

These three layers comprise the Fibre Channel Physical and Signaling Interface, known as FC-PH. The FC-PH specification is in Revision 4.1 and, once formally adopted, will be published as ANSI X3.230. Adoption of the FC-PH standard is expected to occur in 1994.

FC-3 defines a common set of services that the FC-PH will provide to Upper Layer Protocols (ULPs), while FC-4 describes a series of ULP-specific mapping protocols that provide an interface between the FC-PH and the ULPs. Some of the upper layers that will be supported by Fibre Channel are the High-Performance Parallel Interface (HIPPI), SCSI, Intelligent Peripheral Interface (IPI-3), and Internet Protocol (IP). A Fibre Channel node contains the functions of FC-0 through FC-4; any resident ULPs are beyond the scope of the Fibre Channel specifications.

MEDIA, TRANSMISSION, AND SIGNALING

The lowest function layer of the Fibre Channel architecture, FC-0 describes the physical characteristics of the transmission media, connectors, transmitter, and receiver.

Fibre Channel supports a wide range of options for the physical links in terms of transmission speed, media type, transmitter type, and link length. The FC-0 option employed is identified according to the following nomenclature:

speed-media_transmitter-distance

Speed indicates the transmission rate on the media; possible values are 100, 50, 25, and 12, representing 100MBps, 50MBps, 25MBps, and 12.5MBps, respectively.

Media_type indicates the type of media; possible values are SM (single-mode fiber), M5 (50-Ω multimode fiber), M6 (62.5-Ω multimode fiber), TV (CATV video cable), MI (miniature coaxial cable), and TP (shielded twisted pair).

Transmitter_type indicates the type of transmitter; possible values are LL (long-wave, or 1,300-nanometer, laser), SL (short-wave, or 780-nm, laser), LE (long-wave light-emitting diode, or LED), and EL (emitter-coupled logic, or ECL).

Distance indicates the maximum length of a single point-to-point link; options include L, I, and S representing long (≤10 km), intermediate (≤2 km), and short (≤100 m) link lengths, respectively.

For example, the designation 100-SM-LL-L indicates a long link operating at 100 MBps over a single-mode fiber using a long wavelength laser transmitter. Table 1 contains a list of the supported FC-0 options. By understanding this nomenclature, the network builder can understand exactly what he or she needs.

TABLE 1: FC-0 CONFIGURATION OPTIONS (ORGANIZED BY MEDIA TYPE)

Designation	Data Rate	Transmitter	Distance
Single-mode fiber			
100-SM-LL-L	100 MBps	1300–nm laser	2 m - 10 km
100-SM-LL-I	100 MBps	1300–mn laser	2 m - 2 km
50-SM-LL-L	50 MBps	1300–nm laser	2 m - 10 km
25-SM-LL-L	25 MBps	1300–nm laser	2 m - 10 km
25-SM-LL-I	25 MBps	1300-nm laser	2 m - 2 km
Multimode fiber (62-5 µm)			
50-M6-SL-I	50 MBps	780-nm laser	2 350 m
25-M6-SL-I	25 MBps	780-nm laser	2-700 m
25-M6-LE-I	25 MBps	1300-nm LED	0-1 km
12-M6 LE I	12.5 MBps	1300-nm LED	0-1 km
Multimode fiber (50µm)			
50-M5-SL-I	50 MBps	780-nm laser	2 m - 1 km
25-M5-SL-I	25 MBps	780-nm laser	2 m - 1 km
25-M5-LE-1	25 MBps	1300-nm LED	(not specified)
12-M5-LE-I	12.5 MBps	1300-nm LED	(not specified)
Video coaxial cable (150 Ω)			
100-TV-EL-S	100-MBps	ECL	0-25 m
50-TV-EL-S	50 MBps	ECL	0-50 m
25-TV-EL-S	25 MBps	ECL	0-75 m
12-TV-EL-S	12.5 MBps	ECl	0-100 m
Miniature coaxial cable (75Ω)			
100-MI-EL-S	100 MBps	ECL	0-10 m
50-MI-EL-S	50 MBps	ECL	0-20 m
25-MI-EL-S	25 MBps	ECL	0-30 m
12-MI=EL-s	12.5 MBps	ECL	0-40 m
Shielded twisted pair			
25-TP-EL-S	25 MBps	ECL	0-50 m
12-TP-EL-S	12.5 MBps	ECL	0-100 m

FC-1 defines the specific signaling and coding scheme used across Fibre Channel links. FC-1 uses an 8B/10B block code, where every eight-bit entity (a byte) is actually coded using 10 bits. This coding scheme is the same as that used on IBM's Enterprise Systems Connection (ESCON) and is conceptually similar to FDDI's 4B/5B code.

Although 8B/10B appears to be wasteful because of the additional 25-percent transmission overhead, the additional bits ensure an adequate number of signal transitions to provide clocking information on the serial line. This approach places the clock-recovery burden on the hardware rather than requiring that users scramble their data or take other measures to ensure an appropriate number of clock signals. The 8B/10B encoding also allows for the definition of special control characters and delimiters, ensuring that user data is never mistaken for control information.

As a final aside, some additional bits are reserved for physical-layer framing and error detection, accounting for an additional 6.25 percent of overhead when maximum-size frames are used. Fibre Channel product capacities, then, may sometimes be quoted in terms of user data rate (in MBps) or raw transmission rate (in millions of signals per second, or megabaud). The 12.5, 25, 50, and 100MBps data rates correspond to transmission rates of 133, 266, 531, and 1,060 megabaud, respectively.

SIGNALING PROTOCOL SERVICES

The Fibre Channel Signaling Protocol, or FC-2, defines the rules for the exchange of higher-layer information between nodes. FC-2 specifies types of messages, procedures for their exchange, and formats. In this way, FC-2 is functionally similar to the data-link layer functions of LAN medium access control (MAC) protocols.

Like the IEEE 802.2 Logical Link Control (LLC) protocol, FC-2 defines several different classes of service. Fibre

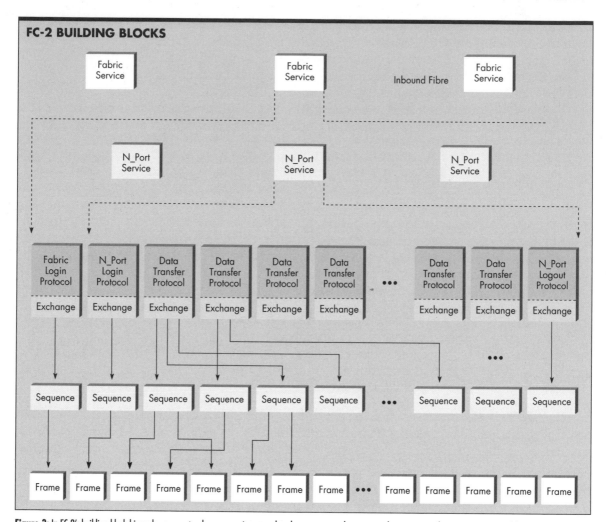

Figure 3: In FC-2's building-block hierarchy, one protocol may comprise several exchanges, one exchange several sequences, and one sequence several frames.

Channel service classes are categorized based on the way communication is established between two nodes and on the inherent integrity associated with the communications channel.

Class 1 service provides a *dedicated connection,* conceptually similar to a virtual circuit or other connection-oriented service (such as LLC Type 2). Connection-establishment and termination procedures are defined, and this type of service guarantees a maximum bandwidth between the two communicating nodes, as well as sequential ordering of frames.

Class 2 service is called *multiplex,* a type of connec-

tionless service. Neither frame delivery nor sequentiality is guaranteed in this type of service, although the fabric, if present, will notify the sender of frame delivery or nondelivery.

Class 3 service is called *datagram,* a connectionless service with no guarantee of delivery or sequentiality and no event notification; this service is similar to LLC Type 1. While frames are, of course, transmitted sequentially, they may be delivered out of order. *Resequencing,* or requesting retransmission of missing frames, is the responsibility of higher-layer protocols.

An *intermix* service has also been defined as an option

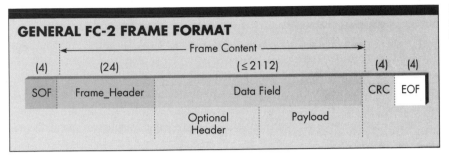

Figure 4: All of the FC-2 frames have the same general format, but specific fields exist within frames.

of Class 1, which allows interleaving Class 2 and Class 3 frames in an already established Class 1 connection between two N_Ports. While Class 1 service means a dedicated connection is established between a source and destination, the maximum bandwidth does not always have to be in use; this "excess" may be allocated to Class 2 and 3 traffic. In addition, a Class 4 service may be defined that combines several features of Classes 1 through 3.

In addition to basic service classes for the transport of data, Fibre Channel also defines a set of services required for the operation of the network, such as a name server, time server, and management server. Each of these services resides at a well-known address so that any node can access any services as needed (conceptually similar to well-known addresses in TCP/IP).

FC-2 BUILDING BLOCKS AND SERVICES

FC-2 defines a hierarchy of *transmission building blocks*, as Figure 3 shows. The Fibre channel fabric may offer a number of different services to users. The figure shows one fabric service comprising multiple N_Port services, which in turn comprise protocols, exchanges, sequences, and frames.

This building-block hierarchy appears to be unusually complicated when compared to most other network protocols but is actually rather straightforward: One protocol may comprise several exchanges, one exchange may comprise several sequences, and one sequence may comprise several frames. Consider the following example. Two devices (represented by N_Ports) communicate under the direction of some protocol; the protocol information transferred between the devices is represented by an exchange. An exchange is composed of messages going back and forth between the two entities; these messages are represented by sequences. Since a message may be too large for

a single transmission, messages may be fragmented into smaller transmission entities, called *frames*.

The frame is the basic unit of data exchange. Based on their function, frames are broadly categorized as being either Data frames of Link_Control frames. Data frames are used to transfer information between a source and destination N_Port. Data frames may be classified as:

• *Link_Data frames*, used to transfer link application information between N_Ports; these frames perform mandatory link-management applications such as the transmission of abort sequences, echo, and termination of Class 1 connections.

• *FC-4 Device_Data frames*, used to transfer higher-layer service data units from such protocols as Fibre Channel services, IEEE 802.2 LLC, IP, IPI-3 (master or slave), SCSI (initiator or target), HIPPI, or Futurebus.

• *Video_Data frames*, which allow an N_Port to transfer the frame contents directly to a video buffer without first directing them to an intermediate storage location.

If agreed on by both N_Ports, several Data frames may be outstanding at one time. Known as *pipelining*, this mechanism allows a single Link_Control frame to acknowledge multiple Data frames so that the source N_Port does not need to stop transmitting and wait to receive an explicit acknowledgement for one Data frame before sending the next. In that way, the source can send multiple messages at once.

Link_Control frames are used by the N_Port's LCF to manage frame exchange and to provide some control for FC-2 Class 1 and 2 services. In general, Link_Control frames are used to indicate successful or unsuccessful frame delivery, provide feedback for flow control and buffer management, indicate when a destination N_Port or the fabric is busy, and provide link credit information.

All FC-2 frames have the same general format, as Figure 4 shows. The fields within the frames and their functions are:

Start_of_Frame (SOF) delimiter. SOF is a four-byte sequence that precedes the frame content. Many types of SOF delimiters exist, indicating the establishment of a Class 1 connection or identifying the first or subsequent frames of a Class 1, 2, or 3 frame exchange.

Frame_Header. This field is a 24-byte sequence used by the LCF to control the link and device protocol data exchanges and to detect missing or out-of-sequence frames. Information contained in the Frame_Header includes: source and destination N_Port identifiers; originator and responder exchange identifiers; sequence identifier; frame type; and frame control information (such as the relative position of this frame in an exchange).

Data Field is a field containing optional higher-layer headers and data payload. This field, if present, may have up to 2,112 bytes.

Cyclic Redundancy Check (CRC) is a four-byte field used by the receiver to detect bit errors in the frame. Fibre Channel uses the same 32-bit CRC found in FDDI and most IEEE 802 MACs.

End_of_Frame (EOF) delimiter is a four-byte sequence used to indicate the end of the frame transmission. The EOF may be modified by an intervening fabric to indicate that the frame content is valid or invalid or that the frame content was corrupted and this transmission truncated.

FRAME BY FRAME

Fabric_Frames may be used within the fabric for communication between F_Ports. While Fabric_Frames may have the same general format as an FC-2 frame, the frame content is not defined by the Fibre Channel standard. Furthermore, N_Ports will ignore Fabric_Frames.

A set of one or more Data frames transmitted unidirectionally from one N_Port to another, along with any applicable corresponding Link_Control frame replies, forms a *sequence.* Sequences may comprise more than one frame should the amount of information in the sequence exceed the capacity of a single frame. Error recovery, controlled by a protocol layer above FC-2, will usually be performed at sequence boundaries. Thus, if a frame is received with an error, the receiver will notify the transmitter to terminate and restart the entire sequence.

An *exchange* is the mechanism used to transfer data between a pair of N_Ports. Exchanges may be unidirectional or bidirectional; they comprise one or more nonconcurrent sequences. Note that the restriction of nonconcurrent sequences means that data can flow in only one direction at a time between N_Ports.

Exchanges are closely tied to protocols related to the offered services. Protocols may be specific to higher-layer services (above Fibre Channel), although Fibre Channel provides its own set of protocols to manage its operating environment for data transfer. As Figure 3 shows, Fibre Channel-defined protocols include:

Fabric Login protocol, used by an N_Port to establish a specific class of service connection with the fabric, if present. Using this protocol, the N_Port is assigned an address and obtains the Fabric's working parameters.

N_Port Login protocol, used to exchange service parameters between two N_Ports prior to exchanging data. Service parameters define characteristics of the connection between two N_Ports and include such information as the Fibre Channel version number, amount of buffer space available for data transfer, total number of concurrent sequences that an N_Port can support as a recipient, supported service classes, an indication of whether sequential delivery is required, and an indication of support for pipelining Data frames.

Data transfer protocol, defining the transfer of ULP data between N_Ports.

N_Port Logout protocol, used by an N_Port to terminate a connection to another N_Port.

The Fabric and N_Port login procedures not only set up initial connections but also provide for flow control. Fibre Channel provides two types of flow control: *buffer-to-buffer flow control* across a link connecting an N_Port and the Fabric and *end-to-end flow control* across a path connecting two N_Ports. Both mechanisms are similar; a certain amount of buffer and end-to-end credit is assigned during the fabric and N_Port login procedures, respectively.

The amount of credit is decremented each time a frame is sent and incremented when an acknowledgement is received from the fabric or destination N_Port. The transmitting N_Port can transmit only as long as there is positive credit.

LAYERS ABOVE FC-PH

The current Fibre Channel specification only describes

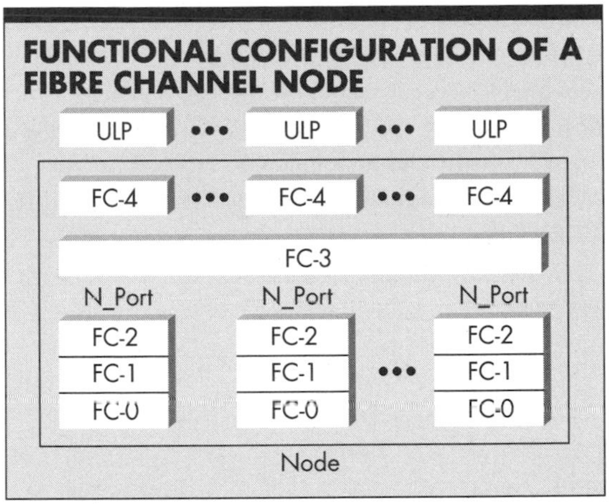

FUNCTIONAL CONFIGURATION OF A FIBRE CHANNEL NODE

| ULP | ••• | ULP | ••• | ULP |

| FC-4 | ••• | FC-4 | ••• | FC-4 |

FC-3

N_Port	N_Port	N_Port
FC-2	FC-2	FC-2
FC-1	FC-1 •••	FC-1
FC-0	FC-0	FC-0

Node

Figure 5: A Fibre Channel node contains one or more N_Ports, each comprising independent FC-PH functional entities.

the physical-layer aspects, or FC-PH, which comprises the FC-0, FC-1, and FC-2 functions (Figure 2). FC-3, FC-4, and the ULP functions are defined but not yet fully described.

A Fibre Channel *node* contains one or more N_Ports, each comprising independent FC-PH functional entities. FC-3 provides a set of services common across multiple N_Ports of a node. FC-3 services might include mechanisms for exchanging data, indicating service class or type of ULP, or multiplexing between an FC-4 and the FC-PH. The FC-PH and, optionally, the FC-3 provide a uniform service platform to higher-layer protocols.

The FC-4 provides a way to utilize existing protocols over Fibre Channel without modifying those protocols. As stated, FC-4 describes a series of ULP-specific mapping protocols that provide an interface between the FC-PH and the higher-layer services. Since the FC-PH/FC-3 services are as general as possible, they may not meet the specific needs of a given higher-layer protocol.

The FC-4, then, acts as a protocol-convergence layer, which ensures that the node appears to provide the exact lower-layer services the ULP requires. To do so, FC-4 may have to provide additional services such as buffering, synchronization, or prioritization of data.

FC-4 and ULP descriptions are beyond the scope of Fibre Channel standardization, although Fibre Channel is expected to accommodate a wide range of existing data communications protocols, including ATM, HIPPI, IBM's Block Multiplexer Channel Single Byte Command Code Set (SBCCS), IP, IPI-3, and SCSI; support for various internal buses, such as EISA, Futurebus, and VME, are also an-

ticipated. The standard will allow for the definition of up to 255 different FC-4 types.

HOW IT STACKS UP

Fibre Channel is quietly emerging as an efficient, cost-effective potential alternative to many standard technologies. Unlike most of the current LAN, MAN, and WAN strategies, Fibre Channel demonstrates:

• a wide variety of media and speed options;

• a nonconstrained physical topology; all N_Ports connect directly to each other or to the fabric, the internals of which are transparent to the end user;

• a nearly unlimited aggregate bandwidth, easily accomplishing gigabit speeds; by interconnecting nodes via a switching network (the fabric), full-link bandwidth is available to each node;

• a network size not constrained by the media access control scheme or by address size limitations; Fibre Channel's 24-bit addresses can accommodate a maximum of 16,777,216 N_Ports;

• multiple classes of service and support of a wide variety of higher-layer protocols;

• unlimited size of data units; although frames are limited in size to 2,112 bytes, any number of frames may be used to form a single-user data unit; and

• parallel transfer of data; if the network has x nodes, then x Data frames may be transferred at one time between pairs of N_Ports.

Fibre Channel, like many high-speed networking strategies, is designed to be used in a number of environments because applications are requiring ever-increasing bandwidth. Furthermore, Fibre Channel provides an attractive alternative to some of the options available today. ATM, for example, is not yet widely available and is still relatively expensive. Furthermore, ATM's underlying transmission infrastructure is the Synchronous Optical Network (SONET), which adds to ATM's cost.

Perhaps the best-known Fibre Channel test bed is a part of the High-Performance Switching System (HPSS) project at Lawrence Livermore National Laboratory in Livermore, CA. HPSS has, in fact, demonstrated transmission of 1,024-by-1,024 pixel-by-24 colorbits/pixel (2.5 MB) images at a rate of 30 images per second (75MBps). These Video_Data frames can be routed from the Fibre Channel adapter in a workstation directly to the video RAM.

Such capabilities lead some to believe that Fibre Channel will provide direct competition to ATM since both can support voice, video, and data services. Others believe that Fibre Channel is ideally suited to the local communications environment while ATM is best suited to wide-area networking.

INDUSTRY ACTIVITIES

While Fibre Channel is not yet widely implemented, several companies are actively working in this area and designing or building products. In early 1993, Hewlett-Packard (HP), IBM, and Sun Microsystems formed the Fibre Channel Systems Initiative (FCSI), to advance the Fibre Channel-standards process and to promote use of Fibre Channel for networking high-power workstations.

Another industry consortium, the Fibre Channel Association (FCA), was formed in January 1993 to encourage utilization of Fibre Channel and to complement the activities of the X3T9.3 Task Group.

The FCA maintains a discussion list on the Internet at fca@amcc.com (users can join this list by sending a request to fca-request@amcc.com).

Most Fibre Channel products that have been an-nounced are still in the prototype stage, although a few manufacturers have off-the-shelf products available. Some of the products that have been described include:
• AMCC (San Diego, CA): A number of chips, including a 32-by-32 crosspoint switch, and FC-0 and FC-1 devices.
• AMD (Advanced Micro Devices, Santa Clara, CA): 8B/10B coding chip (in development).
• AT&T Microelectronics (Allentown, PA): Transmitter/receiver chip.
• Ancor Communications (Minnetonka, MN): A number of products under development including MCA, NuBus, and VME host adapters and a Fibre Channel switch (fabric).
• Cypress Semiconductor (San Jose, CA): A number of Fibre Channel chips, including a transmitter/receiver and evaluation board.
• HP Canada Network Operations (North York, Ontario, Canada): Fibre Channel switch (under development).
• IBM Advanced Workstation Division (Austin, TX): An MCA Host Adapter for the RISC/System 6000, under development with Ancor.
• SGS-Thomson (Santa Ana, CA): 32-way Fibre Channel crossbar switch chip.
• Siemens Fibre Optic Components (Totowa, NJ): Longwave LED receiver and transmitter.
• Triquint Semiconductor (Santa Clara, CA): Interface card chips and optical modules.

The Internet Engineering Task Force (IETF) is also sponsoring several Fibre Channel-related activities. One work in progress describes the use of the IP and Address Resolution Protocol (ARP) over Fibre Channel. A second describes a Simple Network Management Protocol (SNMP) management information base (MIB) for Fibre Channel.

If you are looking for more information about Fibre Channel, you might want to consult another Internet mailing list at fiber-channel-ext@think.com. Users may join this list by sending a request to fiber-channel-ext-request@think.com.

A Happy Union

COMPATIBLE WITH ISDN AND FOCUSING ON UTP AS THE PRIMARY
DISTRIBUTION MEDIUM, THE 802.9 STANDARD PROMISES TO UNITE
VOICE, IMAGE, VIDEO, AND DATA.

BY GARY KESSLER

Concurrent with the growth in the use of PCs and LANs, new voice and data services became available from public network service providers. The middle to late 1980s saw the introduction of the Integrated Services Digital Network (ISDN). ISDNs provide a viable WAN alternative, connecting LANs, hosts, and PCs. ISDN and emerging broadband ISDN services that *physically* integrate voice, image, video, and data on a single network will result in applications that will *logically* integrate these different information streams.

In February 1986, the IEEE 802 Executive Committee formed an ad hoc study group on integrated voice/ data (IVD) LAN solutions. Within a year, the IEEE 802.9 Working Group was formed to provide an interface for the "marriage of LANs and ISDN." The working group began to define a standard IVDLAN interface that was compatible with the existing IEEE 802 LAN and International Telecommunication Union Telecommunications Standardization Sector (ITUT, formerly the CCITT) ISDN standards, architectures, and services.

The IEEE 802.9 working group has a charter to: develop an integrated voice/data service interface at the medium access control (MAC) and physical layers that is compatible with other IEEE 802 standards and ISDN standards; develop an interface that operates independently of the backbone network; and focus on the use of UTP as the primary distribution medium. This point is particularly important because of the near-pervasiveness of UTP and the excess bandwidth and capacity usually present when UTP is employed for applications such as voice.

To be successfully deployed, the 802.9 standard must also: be attractive to manufacturers and users from the perspectives of economy, installation, and network operation; support the quality of voice service available today and expected improvements; and allow for the implementation of a range of centralized applications.

By the end of 1990, the IVDLAN standard was almost completed but industry support had fallen off. As ISDN and multimedia applications became increasingly available, however, this work garnered new enthusiasm. Renamed the Integrated Services LAN (ISLAN), the IEEE 802.9 standard was approved in the fall of 1993, and the vendor involvement in this activity suggests that products will be available by 1995.

ISLAN OVERVIEW

The ISLAN standard defines an interface between integrated services terminal equipment (ISTE) and a backbone network. The standard provides a high-bandwidth interface to the desktop in support of packet data service and isochronous (time-sensitive) services. It is intended for operation over an unshielded twisted-pair medium.

As Figure 1 shows, ISTEs are connected to an access unit in a physical star topology. These ISTEs may take on many forms; a *voice TE*, for example, might be a telephone, while a *data TE* might be a PC. A digital bit stream is sent over each point-to-point link between an ISTE and the access unit, carrying packet data or isochronous data (such as voice, image, video, and facsimile). These different traffic flows are carried in separate channels on the line using time-division multiplexing (TDM). The 802.9 standard describes the interface between the ISTEs and the access unit.

From the perspective of the ISTE, 802.9 defines only

Figure 1. The Integrated Services LAN (ISLAN) standard defines an interface between integrated services terminal equipment (ISTE) and backbone network. ISTEs connect to an access unit in a physical star topology.

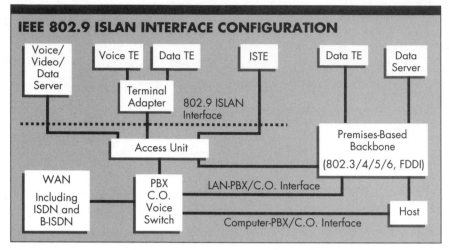

the interface to the access unit and the services provided by it. That definition implies that the 802.9 standard can apply to two general scenarios. In the first scenario, the ISTEs are connected to a standalone LAN, in which case the access unit actually does provide the integrated services. In the second scenario, the ISTEs access an integrated services backbone network, in which case the access unit is merely a gateway to the backbone.

This backbone network may be an existing IEEE 802 LAN, an ISDN (narrowband or broadband), a Fiber Distributed Data Interface (FDDI) metropolitan area network, or an ISLAN (such as 802.6 or FDDI-II). Figure 1 shows some of the possible interface configurations. The access unit-to-backbone connection is beyond the scope of the IEEE 802.9 standard and, in any case, is transparent to the ISTEs.

CHANNELS

One of the basic concepts common to ISDN and the 802.9 standard is that of multiple communications channels sharing the physical medium simultaneously. ISDN and 802.9 need to support multiple channels because each channel has a specific purpose or application. The easiest way to view the multiple channels is to compare them to a multiline telephone, where each line might serve a different user at any given time.

The multiple channels share the same physical medium by using TDM. A TDM system assigns every channel a fixed amount of time on the medium at speci-

fied intervals. The TDM bit stream between the access unit and ISTE comprises several different full-duplex digital channels, each defined for a different purpose.

The P-channel, or *packet data channel*, provides an IEEE 802 MAC service for packet-mode (bursty) data. The IEEE 802.9 MAC sublayer for the P-channel is described later.

The D-channel, or *signaling channel*, is a 16Kbps or 64Kbps channel that corresponds to the ISDN D-channel. In an ISDN, the D-channel is used primarily for the exchange of signaling information between the user and the network for the provision of user services (called *bearer services*).

The ITUT Q.930 protocol family is used for user-network signaling, including call control and the access to bearer services. The secondary function of the ISDN D-channel is to carry user packet-mode data. The 802.9 D-channel may be restricted for user-network signaling in some applications, but other applications may support packet data transfer over this channel.

The ISDN basic rate interface (BRI) specifies use of a 16Kbps D-channel, while the primary rate interface (PRI) uses a 64Kbps D-channel. The 802.9 standard will support both rates to facilitate interoperability with ISDN BRI terminals.

The B-channel, or *bearer services channel*, is a 64Kbps channel that is functionally identical to the ISDN B-channel. It provides ISDN circuit-mode bearer services, such as voice, video, and, optionally, packet-mode data services. A

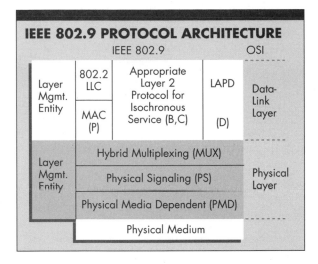

IEEE 802.9 PROTOCOL ARCHITECTURE

Figure 2. Like other IFEE LAN standards, the IFEE 802.9 protocol architecture corresponds to the Physical and Data-Link Layers (DLL) of the OSI reference model.

64Kbps rate is used on this channel because that corresponds to the rate of a single digital voice channel. The 802.9 standard requires two B-channels, corresponding to the two B-channels on the ISDN BRI.

The C-channel, or *circuit-switched channel*, is intended for circuit-switched services that require a bit rate greater than that available from a single B-channel. The C-channel operates in increments of 64Kbps; C_m indicates the size of the C-channel, where m is the number of 64Kbps multiples. C-channels are conceptually similar to ISDN H-channels, which are higher-rate channels equivalent to some defined number of B-channels. The 802.9 C-channels correspond to ISDN B- and H- channels as follows:

C_1 =B =64Kbps
C_6 =H_0 =384Kbps
C_{24} =H_{11} =1.536Mbps
C_{30} =H_{12} =1.920Mbps

802.9 PROTOCOL OVERVIEW

Figure 2 shows the IEEE 802.9 protocol architecture. Like other IEEE and ANSI LAN standards, these protocols correspond to the Physical and Data-Link Layers (DLL) of the OSI reference model.

The 802.9 interface must provide support for a number of different services depending on the user application and channel. For this reason, several different protocols are supported that correspond to the DLL:
• The P-channel is a packet data channel that will use a MAC scheme and frame format specific to the 802.9 standard. Like other IEEE 802 LANs (and ANSI's FDDI), the IEEE 802.2 Logical Link Control (LLC) protocol acts as the upper sublayer of the DLL on the P-channel.
• The 802.9 D-channel is essentially the same as the ISDN D-channel. Therefore, the 802.9 access unit will use the same data-link protocol as ISDN, namely the Link Access Procedures for the D-channel (LAPD), described in ITUT Recommendations Q.920 and Q.921.

Control of B- and C-channel services will be accomplished using basic ISDN call control procedures, described in the ITUT Q.930-series recommendations. The D-channel can also be used to support other ISDN services, such as frame relay and packet services, although this support has not yet been defined in the IEEE 802.9 standard.
• The B- and C-channels carry bit streams related to the requested bearer services. As in ISDN, no DLL is specified for bearer channels since any protocol may be used as long as it has been agreed to on both ends.

The B-channel was originally intended for any 64Kbps isochronous service, such as digital voice, but its scope has expanded to include other circuit-mode services, such as Switched 56 and 64Kbps digital data and Group 4 (digital) facsimile. Packet data transfers typically use either the ITUT Recommendation X.25 Link Access Procedures Balanced (LAPB) or LAPD protocol. The C-channels, like ISDN H-channels, are wideband isochronous channels for high-speed packet- and circuit-mode services, such as high-speed data transfers, video services, and image transfers.

Three sublayers in the 802.9 protocol model perform

Figure 3. The default time-division multiplexing (TDM) frame structure in 3a (top) includes a Synchronization (SYN) field, a TDM Maintenance (TDM MTN) field, a Hybrid Multiplexer Control (HMC) field, a Reserved (RES) field, a D field, B1 and B2 fields, and Access Control (AC) field, and a Payload field. A TDM frame for rates above 4.096Mbps, the AC field may need to be repeated periodically to minimize buffering, as 3b (bottom) shows.

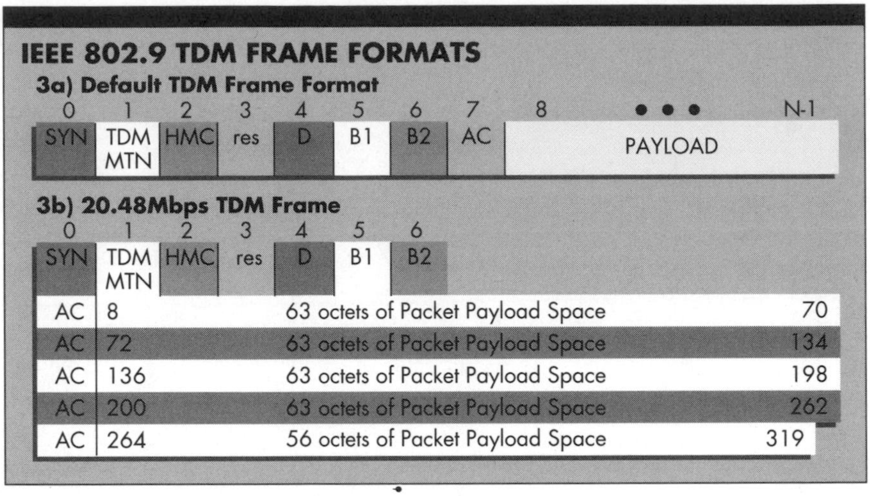

IEEE 802.9 TDM FRAME FORMATS

3a) Default TDM Frame Format

0	1	2	3	4	5	6	7	8	•••	N-1
SYN	TDM MTN	HMC	res	D	B1	B2	AC		PAYLOAD	

3b) 20.48Mbps TDM Frame

0	1	2	3	4	5	6
SYN	TDM MTN	HMC	res	D	B1	B2

AC	8	63 octets of Packet Payload Space	70
AC	72	63 octets of Packet Payload Space	134
AC	136	63 octets of Packet Payload Space	198
AC	200	63 octets of Packet Payload Space	262
AC	264	56 octets of Packet Payload Space	319

functions corresponding to those of the OSI Physical layer. The hybrid multiplexing (HMUX) sublayer multiplexes bits from the B-, C-, D-, and P-channels into a single bit stream between the ISTE and access unit. This sublayer provides the interface between the Physical layer and the user/control information.

The physical signaling (PS) sublayer provides an interface between the multiplexed bit stream and the actual physical bit stream on the line. The PS sublayer appends maintenance information to the frame, calculates parity and adds the appropriate parity bit, scrambles the bit stream, and appends framing information.

The physical media dependent (PMD) sublayer defines the electrical and mechanical characteristics of the specific medium used, in this case UTP. This sublayer defines the specific signaling scheme, cable and connector characteristics, and electrical properties of the transmitter and receiver.

Finally, the Layer Management Entities (LMEs) are part of the overall network management facilities of the interface. Each sublayer has a specific interface to its LME. The combination of all LMEs and the inter-LME communication define the network's Management (MT) entity. The network management features of the ISLAN standard will conform to OSI standards for system and layer management. Furthermore, management of the ISLAN interface will also conform to standards for managing the ISDN user-network interface.

PHYSICAL LAYER FEATURES

The 802.9 standard specifies that the ISTE and access unit be connected over unshielded telephone twisted pairs (UTTP), as defined in the EIA/TIA-568 premises wiring standard. Two different PMDs have been defined, which balance different speed and distance requirements.

The low-speed PMD operates at 4.096Mbps over a distance of up to 450 meters, using a Partial Response Class IV (PR4) encoding scheme. A high-speed PMD operates at 20.48Mbps over a distance of up to 135 meters and uses a 4-point carrierless AM/PM (4-CAP) encoding scheme. Both PR-4 and 4-CAP are used to achieve very high speeds over UTP in other standards, such as FDDI and ATM.

The physical connector for 802.9 ISTEs and access units is an eight-pin modular connector (specified in ISO standard 8877), commonly referred to as an RJ-45. This connector is the same one specified for the ISDN BRI and the IEEE 802.3 TYPE 10BaseT standard. Pin assignments for the connector are:

Pin	Function
1	STE Transmit
2	STE Transmit
3	STE Receive
4	Not used
5	Not used
6	STE Receive
7	Reserved
8	Reserved

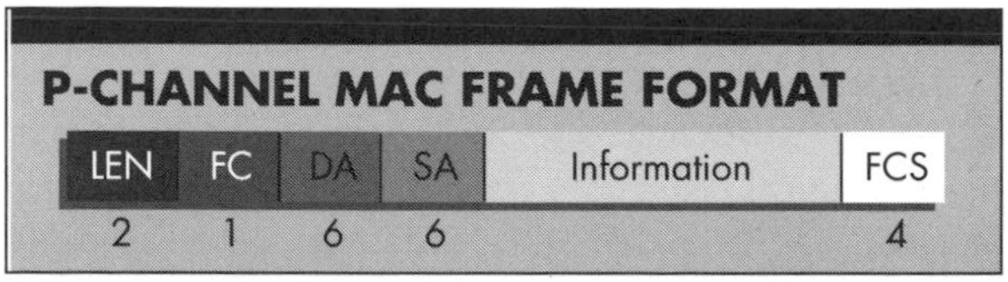

Figure 4. The fields in a P-channel medium-access control (MAC) from format include Length (LEN), Frame Control (FC), Destination Address (DA), Source Address (SA), Information, and Frame Check Sequence (FCS).

Pins 1 and 2 will be used for transmission in the ISTE-to-access unit direction, and pins 3 and 6 will be used for transmission in the access unit-to-ISTE direction. According to the standard, the access unit is not required to supply power to ISTE, but if it does it will use pins 7 and 8. Furthermore, the access unit may supply phantom power over pins 1 and 2 and 3 and 6, although the standard does not include specifications for this purpose. The standard does state, however, that any further 802.9 work with respect to powering should be as consistent as possible with the ISDN BRI Physical layer standard (ITUT Recommendation I.430).

The PS sublayer's major functions include frame synchronization and scrambling. Frame synchronization ensures that the transmissions between an ISTE and the access unit remain aligned and that the receiver correctly interpret the incoming transmission. Scrambling of the bit stream prior to transmission helps reduce the effects of electromagnetic interference (EMI) and aids in clock recovery.

The HMUX sublayer must take the bits from the incoming B-, C-, D-, and P-channels and place them into a single outgoing bit stream. The HMUX can operate in one of several modes:

• Mode 0–IEEE 802 Service Only. This mode is used by devices that have implemented only the 802.9 MAC, and the entire payload is dedicated to the P-channel. It does not support other bearer services.

• Mode 1–BRI ISDN Service Only. This mode is used by ISTEs that implement only the ISDN BRI and provides no support for IEEE 802 data services or the IEEE 802.9 MAC scheme.

• Mode 2–802 & BRI ISDN Service Only. This mode supports only the ISDN BRI and IEEE 802.9 data services. It does not support dynamic bandwidth management functions, meaning that the ISLAN C-channel is not used.

• Mode 3–Dynamic Bandwidth Management Service. This mode offers full support of ISLAN services, including the

dynamic use of C-channels and bandwidth negotiation over the D-channel.

Modes 4 through 7 are reserved for future definition.

TDM FRAME STRUCTURE

The bit stream exchanged between an ISTE and the access unit is called a TDM frame. A single TDM frame carries data from the B-, C-, D-, and P-channels as well as additional synchronization, control, and maintenance information. A *TDM frame* is generated 8,000 times per second, or once every 125 microseconds; this rate corresponds to the sampling rate necessary to digitize human voice. Each octet (eight bits) in the frame, then, represents a 64Kbps channel.

The 802.9 standard supports an ISDN BRI, which comprises two B-channels and a single D-channel (designated *2B+D*). Since each channel in an 802.9 TDM frame operates at 64Kbps while the ISDN BRI D-channel operates at only 16Kbps, the 802.9 D-channel will support both rates.

Figure 3a shows the default TDM frame structure, comprising the following fields:

• Synchronization (SYN)–used to establish TDM frame synchronization between the ISTE and access unit. The SYN field contains a seven-bit Frame Alignment Word that, when detected, indicates the first octet of the frame. (The eighth bit is reserved for future use.)

• TDM Maintenance (TDM-MTN)–used to transmit local Physical-layer status and control information to the device at the other end of the link. This octet is controlled by the layer management entities at the two ends. Functions include loopback testing and parity checking.

• Hybrid Multiplexer Control (HMC) –an 802.9 ISLAN interface that can support a variety of services that may require dynamic bandwidth allocation. ISDN-like call control mechanisms will be used on the D-channel for this purpose. The configuration of the bandwidth within the TDM frame, however, must use some procedure so that a given ISTE and access unit are always in agreement about their use of the TDM channels. This field indicates the speed of the D-channel (16Kbps or 64Kbps), the HMUX (0 to 3), and whether the exchange of this information is complete.

• Reserved (RES)–Reserved channel; use to be determined.

• D–The 16Kbps or 64Kbps D-channel. The D-channel may be restricted to conveying signaling information only. All information in this channel will be packetized according to the ISDN call control procedures defined in Recommendation Q.930.

• B1 and B2–one octet from each of the two ISDN B-channels. The B-channels may be used for any ISDN bearer service and may be non-switched, packet switched, or circuit switched.

• Access Control (AC)–contains information related to the 802.9 MAC scheme for the P-channel.

• Payload–has two parts. The first octet is called the Service Identifier (SID) and indicates the format of the data to follow. Current SID options support use of an 802.9-specific frame format or LAPD. The remaining octets are called the Payload Information field and carry P- and/or C-channel data. C-channels will carry isochronous information. Therefore, time slots within this field will usually be allocated for the C-channels, and extra time slots will be used to carry non-isochronous P-channel data.

The smallest supported TDM frame contains 64 octets; at 8,000 frames per second, the line rate is 4.096Mbps. At rates above 4.096Mbps, the AC field may need to be repeated periodically to minimize buffering, as in the 20.48Mbps TDM frame in Figure 3b.

MAC FRAME STRUCTURE

P-channel data will be carried in an 802.9 MAC frame which, in turn, is transported in the Payload field of a TDM frame. Figure 4 shows the MAC frame fields, described as follows:

• Length (LEN)–a two-octet field indicating the length of the MAC frame, excluding the Length and Frame Check Sequence (FCS) fields. The maximum MAC frame size is 5,119 octets.

• Frame Control (FC)–a one-octet field containing the priority of the frame. The priority is a three-bit value from 0 (lowest) to 7 (highest). The remaining bits are reserved and set to 0.

• Destination Address (DA) and Source Address (SA) fields–specifies the address of the destination station(s)

and the address of the sending station, respectively. The address fields are 48 bits in length and conform to other IEEE 802 48-bit addresses. The first address bit transmitted in the DA field is called the *individual/group* (I/G) *bit* and indicates if this address specifies an individual station or a group of stations. The transmitter sets the I/G-bit in the SA field to 0, and the receiver ignores this bit. The second bit transmitted is called the universal/local (U/L) bit and indicates whether the specified address is part of a locally administered addressing plan (0) or administered by a central authority, such as the IEEE (1). The remaining 46 bits contain the actual station address. The 46-bit field yields roughly 64 trillion possible station addresses.

• Information–contains up to 1,500 octets of user data.

• Frame Check Sequence (FCS)–a four-octet field containing the remainder from the CRC-32 calculation, used to detect bit errors in the SID and MAC frame.

MAC frames will, in all likelihood, be larger than a single Payload field, and, therefore, 802.9 MAC frames will have to be fragmented so they can be carried in multiple Payloads. A bit in the AC field indicates whether the following Payload contains the first fragment of a frame.

The 802.9 standard defines a point-to-point P-channel so an ISTE can access LAN services. The bandwidth of each P-channel will vary according to the services offered by the individual ISTE. Furthermore, the bandwidth available for the operation of a given P-channel will depend on how much of the payload fields reserved for P- and C-channels are dedicated to the isochronous C-channels.

A scheme called the Request/ Grant protocol controls access to the P-channel by the ISTE. The Request/ Grant protocol has the following general characteristics: It is associated only with the transmission of 802.9 MAC frames on the P-channel; the access unit controls the transmission of MAC frames from an ISTE to the access unit; and the intended ISTE receiver may govern the transmission of MAC frames from the access unit to the ISTE. If configured, the access unit may send MAC frames to an ISTE whenever it is ready without waiting for permission.

As Figure 5 shows, the Request/ Grant protocol works as follows: The AC field of the TDM frame contains one GRANT-bit and three request bits, called REQ3, REQ2, and REQ1. When an ISTE is ready to send a frame, it sets the appropriate REQ-bit corresponding to the MAC frame's priority (in the FC field). Although there is no direct rela-

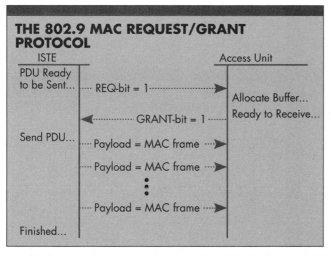

THE 802.9 MAC REQUEST/GRANT PROTOCOL

ISTE — Access Unit

PDU Ready to be Sent... REQ-bit = 1 → Allocate Buffer... Ready to Receive...

← GRANT-bit = 1

Send PDU... Payload = MAC frame →

Payload = MAC frame →

Payload = MAC frame →

Finished...

Figure 5. The Access Control field of the TDM frame contains one GRANT-bit and three request bits (REQ-bit). When an integrated services terminal equipment sends a frame, it sets the REQ-bit corresponding to the MAC frames's priority.

tionship between the request priority in the AC field of the TDM frame and the priority value in the FC field of the MAC frame, the standard recommends that frame priorities 6 and 7 map to REQ3 (high), 3 through 5 map to REQ2 (medium), and 0 through 2 map to REQ1 (low).

When the access unit sees an incoming REQ-bit, it must ensure that adequate buffer space is available to accommodate P-channel MAC frames. When it is ready to receive a MAC frame, the access unit sets the GRANT-bit to 1 in a TDM frame going back to the ISTE. If buffers in the access unit are available for each P-channel, all ISTEs could send 802.9 MAC frames simultaneously. Because of data traffic's bursty nature from the ISTEs, however, access units will probably be designed with fewer receive buffers than P-channels; in this case, some ISTEs may incur some delay before receiving permission to transmit.

When the ISTE sees the GRANT-bit set, it may send one complete MAC frame. Recall that a single MAC frame will probably be sent in multiple Payload fields of 802.9 TDM frames. This scenario would be reversed if the access unit's transmissions were controlled by the ISTE.

COMPATIBILITY WITH STANDARDS

Major additions to the current IEEE 802.9 specification are descriptions of how an ISLAN fits in with existing and emerging protocols.

ITUT Recommendation Q.931 describes basic ISDN call control for the establishment, maintenance, and termination of connections. IEEE 802.9 describes a subset of

Q.931, called *Q.93x*, that can be used for ISLAN control purposes for connections on the B- and C-channels. Q.93x is very similar to Recommendation Q.2931, describing B-ISDN extensions to Q.931.

Public ATM services started to become available in the United States in late 1993. The 802.9 specification also describes how the TDM frame can be mapped onto ATM cells.

Many addressing schemes are used in today's local and wide area networks, including IEEE 802 addresses, ITUT Recommendation E.164 international ISDN numbers, X.121 data network identifiers, F.69 telex addresses, and ISO data country codes. All these schemes are independent of each other, using a different address format, coding scheme, and length. IEEE 802.9 describes interworking between these different plans.

The IEEE 802.9 standard also provides a detailed specification of managed objects for the definition of network and layer management as well as security control for multimedia connections.

STATUS OF IEEE 802.9

Draft 20 (May 17, 1993) successfully passed the ballot stage and was established as an official IEEE standard in the fall of 1993.

Although very few ISLAN products or product announcements have yet appeared on the market, several companies actively participated in the standards process and have expressed interest in developing such products, including AT&T Paradyne (Largo, FL), Ericsson (Anaheim, CA), Hitachi America (Brisbane, CA), IBM (Boca Raton, FL), Luxcom (Fremont, CA), National Semiconductor (Santa Clara, CA), and NEC (Princeton, NJ). Stevens Institute of Technology (Hoboken, NJ) has announced that it will provide a beta test site for 802.9 equipment and applications. Its Advanced Telecommunications Institute (ATI) has also expressed an interest in developing a consortium to develop 802.9-based products.

Note that the 802.9 standard and ISLAN products cannot stand alone since they are conceptually associated with ISDN and B-ISDN. The development of these products, then, will succeed only if there is concurrent deployment of ATM in the local- and/or wide-area backbone.

ISDN Reemerges

ISDN HAS BEEN SLOW IN COMING, BUT NOW WITH BROAD AVAILABILITY OF ISDN SERVICES AND PRODUCTS, IT MIGHT BE WORTH A SERIOUS LOOK.

BY MICHAEL DURR

ISDN, that perennial example of technology-going-nowhere, has confounded conventional wisdom: Based on this voice-data hermaphrodite, a new family of business applications is ready to enable the downsized, distributed business model. If you're in a small or midsize business or are a strategic network planner in a large corporation, you should take a serious look at the technology that wouldn't die.

Integrated Services Digital Network (ISDN) is a carrier service offered by the telephone companies designed to combine voice and data traffic on the same network. Not surprisingly, given that in most U.S. companies voice and data are managed by separate fiefdoms, ISDN has been slow to take off.

These separate groups have correctly pointed out that, although voice and data are both communications technologies, their dissimilarities are myriad. Voice functions quite well on cheap, low-quality lines, while data is much more sensitive to interference and needs expensive, high-quality lines.

Voice traffic coasts along contentedly at relatively slow speeds, whereas the speed of a data line is continually pushed by insatiable new applications. The network design and support infrastructure for voice networks are so mature that the only issue remaining that's sure to ignite a fight is a good old tariff war. On the other hand, data network-design philosophies are continually evolving, forcing to the forefront the complex issue of how to build a stable infrastructure for a moving target.

All these factors seem to argue against voice-data integration. What does integrated service mean? High-quality voice lines–expensive, overly complex, and unnecessary–combined with inferior data lines?

Perhaps diverse voice-data requirements should be handled independently. If communications and business practices had remained static, that conclusion might still be true, but times have changed.

THIS YEAR'S MODEL

New business models rely on technology to increase the productivity of employees and resources. Companies no longer automatically design major remote locations that duplicate the home office. Instead, they set up lean remote offices that concentrate only on a specialized need, such as establishing a sales presence in a new territory. Businesses keep as many support functions as possible at the central location and reduce travel wherever possible to cut down on expenses and lost productivity. And they build in automated management to reduce administration costs and to enhance reliability.

You can't implement this model with traditional wide-area communications. Leased lines are too expensive to support an unconcentrated, distributed work force; the volume of point-to-point traffic seldom justifies a dedicated line in these environments. At the other end of the service spectrum, analog phone lines are slow, unreliable, and basically incapable of supporting high-bandwidth applications.

Bob Womack, director of computer services for Hale and Dorr, a Boston-based law firm, has recently become an active ISDN user. "We've been looking at the technology for the last couple of years but got actively involved about

Figure 1: One Integrated Services Digital Network (ISDN) line can serve multiple devices. For example, a single 2B+D Basic Rate Interface line installed for alternate voice and data can support multiple telephones, a fax machine, an X.25 packet network, and a LAN-to-LAN bridge.

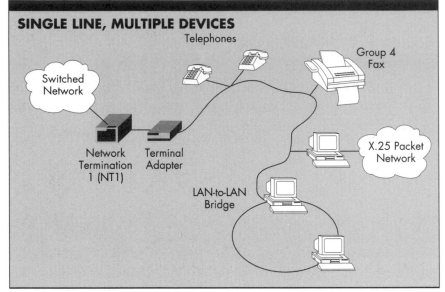

60 days ago. We ended up putting in an ISDN link to support a litigation matter. It worked so well that we put in ISDN circuits here in Boston and used ISDN to replace a leased line to an affiliated office in London."

The litigation support that Womack runs on ISDN is an image-based application developed by Just Law Computer Services (New York). The application is a large database application for retrieving and matching text and images.

Concerning the need for ISDN in these applications, Womack says, "We don't think it would have been feasible to do the image-based application without ISDN. The link to London is just doing the same things we did with the leased line but with equivalent or greater throughput at a cheaper price." Womack's applications use Gandalf (Cherry Hill, NJ) bridges, which plug into Wellfleet (Billerica, MA) routers to do LAN-to-LAN connections.

Bob Caveny, president of Telesynergy (San Jose, CA), has found similar advantages with ISDN as an applications enabler. Telesynergy is a service company that helps large corporations monitor their voice telephone networks, providing such services as call accounting.

"We first began using ISDN about a year and a half ago for two applications," says Caveny. "In one application, we gather data remotely and bring it to our facility for analysis. Our other ISDN application provides a remote login to Telesynergy's database. When the customer decides to log

in to our database, he or she turns on the communications software. The ISDN terminal adapter automatically makes the telephone call, and second later we have a login from their LAN to ours, and they're attached to our database."

Caveny's newest ISDN application uses the voice and data capabilities of ISDN. "We have a 2B+D Basic Rate Interface [BRI] line. As for customer premise equipment [CPE], we have a couple of telephones, a Group 4 fax machine, and a LAN bridge," Caveny says. "All these devices can make use of ISDN's two B channels. When a call comes in, the message packet signals the intended receiver. If a fax call comes in, it connects the call to the correct CPE (our fax machine). That's a pretty intelligent telephone system." (See Figure 1 for an illustration of how one ISDN line can handle multiple devices.)

Caveny says ISDN is opening a "great era" of new applications. "People aren't aware of a lot of what ISDN can do because they haven't explored it. Until you get knee deep into some technologies, you'll have no idea what that technology's capabilities are."

HOW IT WORKS

A digital carrier service, ISDN is typically purchased in the BRI 2B+D package. This package offers two Bearer (B) channels running at 64Kbps plus the Delta (D) channel operating at 16Kbps. All three channels are combined on a single pair of standard copper telephone wires. You can order the 64Kbps channels as voice only, data only, one channel voice and the other data, or data and voice on a call-by-call basis. Basically, any combination is available.

Industry discussion has focused on B-channel functionality, but the D channel is an important part of the package. If you're working on a BRI line, you also have a separate signaling channel, the D channel. This channel is where all the call initiation and termination information between the telephone or data device and the central office is sent. Because you have the separate signaling channel, both of the B channels are free of signaling overhead and provide a clear 64Kbps.

In addition to signaling information, the D channel can carry packet traffic. That capability provides a way of sending low-speed X.25 data, such as transaction-oriented data, over the signaling channel. Probably one of the most promising applications for a D-channel packet is for point-of-sale devices. A gas station or convenience store, for example, might have a BRI 2B+D line and assign the D channel to a point-of-sale application connecting to a central site. One B channel would be used for the station's direct telephone, and the other B channel would serve as the line to a pay phone.

For the home environment, a D-channel packet allows remote meter reading. It can provide a connection for security systems in building control systems. And it handles all of those functions without requiring the power of a voice channel and without adding overhead to the voice or data bearing channels.

In limited locations, ISDN also is available with Primary Rate Interface (PRI). The standard PRI service is 23B+D, which has 23 B channels running at 64Kbps and one 16Kbps or 64Kbps D channel.

CHOOSING AMONG OPTIONS

One of the options in setting up remote or wide-area communication links is a dedicated circuit. Dedicated circuits are used as backbone-type networks between remote facilities, and, when the volume of traffic is high, dedicated circuits are the standard choice.

A good breakpoint for choosing a dedicated connection is three hours to six hours of usage per day. Less than that and a dedicated line is difficult to cost justify. Large companies can negotiate very low tariffs and may be able to

justify a dedicated line with as little as three hours of usage a day. Smaller companies typically find dedicated lines more expensive and probably need six hours of usage a day to justify the expense.

The biggest issue in this era of distributed work forces, however, is that the dedicated line is a point-to-point service, not a multipoint service. Those three hours to six hours of connection time need to be between the same two facilities. If you communicate with multiple facilities, you must evaluate the cost-effectiveness of having a point-to-point line for each connection.

ISDN rates are based primarily on volume of usage rather than availability, which makes ISDN a good choice for businesses that sporadically need high bandwidth, such as for LAN-to-LAN communications, but don't need continuous connections.

Switched 56 is a data service that provides on 56Kbps digital channel per pair of phone wires. It does not support voice service. Switched 56 tends to be more expensive than ISDN but is also available in some remote locations where you may not be able to buy ISDN service. Currently, many offices support both ISDN and Switched 56 to provide coverage wherever necessary.

The other option for wide-area communications is analog service. One difference between digital ISDN and dial-up analog is speed. An ISDN connection, in the real world, runs four to eight times faster than an analog modem line. Dial-up analog can be pushed to a maximum of about 19.2Kbps, depending on the service and the type of data compression technique used.

In practice, the low quality of the analog line often reduces actual connection speed substantially as modems dynamically match speed to the range of acceptable error rates. But even at 19.2Kbps, the speed is inadequate for most applications other than simple text file transfers from PC to PC. LAN-to-LAN traffic and high-bandwidth applications, such as imaging or video, aren't practical.

LAN-to-LAN logon has been a desirable, if impractical, application for years. Because of slow analog connections, one way to enable remote connection to LANs is to connect remotely to a dedicated PC on the LAN and send keystrokes and screens of data back and forth.

A remote-control approach does not scale for most companies. It may be satisfactory for one or two casual users. But most companies balk at the idea of buying a PC at the remote site and a second one at the home office, both to allow the same user to work on the LAN. A high-speed LAN-to-LAN connection across ISDN enables remote PC users to attach directly to the LAN and use its resources.

ADDRESSING PROBLEMS

ISDN has had to overcome many problems–some more critical than others–to take its place as a practical technology for business. Some of these problems still aren't completely settled but are sufficiently resolved to open up ISDN to a broader class of user than technology pioneers.

Availability: By many counts, availability has been the biggest limiting factor. Today ISDN is available on close to 50 percent of the lines throughout the United States. Coverage in metropolitan areas is substantially higher.

Another major facet of availability is packaging. ISDN was released in most parts of the country as an option for Centrex customers. Centrex is a multiline service for larger business users. To be eligible for ISDN, you had to install two, four, or more lines (minimum requirements vary with regions). This requirement effectively excluded small offices or remote locations from using ISDN. Now, however, single line (non-Centrex) tariffs are blossoming throughout the country, and if you can't get them from your Regional Bell Operating Company (RBOC) right now, you will soon be able to.

Standardization: In late 1992, the National ISDN-1 standard was introduced. National ISDN-1 is a physical standard that makes all compliant lines look the same. The majority of RBOCs are moving to support National ISDN-1; you can verify support availability in your area.

A national standard that's not yet implemented nationally nonetheless has significant value. If you install an ISDN system that is based on National ISDN-1, you won't face any additional costs that might be required in moving from prestandard ISDN to the standard.

Some applications vendors have largely eliminated the standards-migration problem for their customers; these vendors have enabled their hardware to move to National ISDN-1 via a simple change in the configuration menu. If you're not in a National ISDN-1 area, you should find out about migration and perhaps select applications, in part, according to how easy standardization will be.

Enhancing ISDN Performance: ISDN BRI 2B+D provides a built-in capability for expanding available bandwidth. The two B channels can be used together in a process called *inverse multiplexing.* Multiplexing takes a large data pipe and divides it up to support multiple, low-speed terminals. With inverse multiplexing, the requirements are reversed. In the case of ISDN, you have a computer trying to send data over 64Kbps lines. The application, such as LAN-to-LAN communication or video conferencing, can easily need more than 64Kbps. An inverse multiplexer enables the data stream to use both 64Kbps bearer channels simultaneously so that the effective bandwidth is 128Kbps.

Another common technique for bandwidth enhancement is data compression. Many ISDN bridges and routers support data compression that increases throughput by four to eight times the basic rate of the connection.

Installation: ISDN users have plenty of horror stories, all of which seem to relate to installation rather than use. The phone companies have been addressing the problem. Almost all RBOCs and long distance carriers have set up a resource person for ISDN, who can be very helpful. Most applications vendors have also taken on the role of helping their customers get ISDN or at least pointing to specialists who can perform that service.

The telephone industry has a large group of third-party implementers, many of whom sell the services as well as install them. Within this third-party area a group is emerging called *data agents,* which provide ISDN expertise.

One such data agent is Telcom Service (Ann Arbor, MI), which serves vendors and their customers who want to install ISDN. As account manager for Telcom, Riley Trumbull's job is to figure out the most economical and practical way to get ISDN and then to work with the phone company to make it happen.

"I look at the local telephone supplier to see if they have what we need," she says. "If they don't have the right equipment, then I find out when they're going to have it and what can be done to go around the problem. I often end up trying to talk the RBOC into upgrading equipment or bringing equipment from someplace else, sometimes seeing if it's possible to defer costs. I negotiate that sort of thing on behalf of the customer," Trumbull says.

In many larger installations, Telcom works with data-system consultants, who handle the applications selection

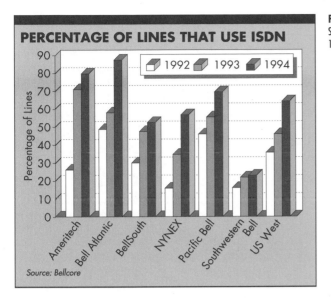

PERCENTAGE OF LINES THAT USE ISDN

Source: Bellcore

Figure 2: ISDN is finally available on about half the phone lines in the United States and according to predictions will be used on 80 to 90 percent of lines by 1994.

and implementation at the customer site. For example, Telcom Service worked with Technology Integration (Ann Arbor, MI) on a project for the National Center for Manufacturing Sciences (NCMS), a nonprofit teaching consortium, also located in Ann Arbor. Fred Champlain, vice president of technology for Technology Integration, provides outsource MIS services for NCMS. He says that NCMS is aggressively moving into ISDN.

"We consider ISDN to be a strategic technology for both small and midsize manufacturers," says Champlain. "One, it's affordable, and two, it greatly increases the numbers and types of applications compared to what's available using modems."

In describing the application, Champlain says, the first application is a centralized e-mail system, in which remote sites call up the central office and pick up their mail. NCMS uses a Network Express (Ann Arbor, MI) Interhub that supports multiple lines to provide ISDN connections to these remote sites. The remote sites have Combinet (Sunnyvale, CA) Interchange bridges, which support a single line each.

Today, these connections include sites in St. Louis; Huntington, WV; Toledo, OH; and Washington, D.C. According to Champlain, Network Express is looking at installing personalized video systems in each of these NCMS sites and has begun discussions with AT&T to provide this service.

ENTHUSIASM BREWING

Internationally, ISDN is a widely used, mature technology. Now, after a long and rugged introduction, ISDN is finally available on about half the phone lines in the United States. The major service suppliers, AT&T, MCI, and Sprint, have ISDN products and are promoting the service (see Figure 2). The RBOCs are rolling out service and expertise unevenly, but all have active ISDN programs.

Standards and tariffing are making ISDN feasible for business users. Many mature applications are available now, and, with several hundred vendors developing products either based on ISDN or supporting ISDN, the quantity and quality of ISDN applications is rapidly growing.

At the user level, the biggest problem with ISDN today is installation. ISDN installation is a challenging process, but vendors, data agents, and ISDN support people within the RBOCs are removing a lot of the pain. ISDN installation is a task for specialists; unless you're one of those folks who feel pain builds character, you should look for qualified support in designing and installing your ISDN system.

In researching this article and in conducting a previous survey of ISDN users, I found virtually unanimous enthusiasm for ISDN service after it's installed. Users like the cost structure and the line quality for their applications. They tend to be surprised and pleased with the performance of LAN-to-LAN connections.

Like any other technology, the appropriateness of ISDN will depend on your installation. ISDN is effectively here now and offers benefits to a broad group of users–benefits that are in many cases unmatched by competing technologies. In your data communications planning, ISDN is worth a long, hard look.

SUPPORT SERVICES AND INFORMATION

Dialing for ISDN

A good place to start looking for information on ISDN is the National ISDN HotLine at (800) 992-4736. The ISDN contacts for the Regional Bell Operating Companies are:

Company	Contact	Telephone
Ameritech	National ISDN HotLine	(800) 543-4376
Bell Atlantic	Bob Buehler	(201) 649-6167
BellSouth	National ISDN HotLine	(800) 428-4736
CBI	Al Castellani	(513) 397-6381
NYNEX	Roy Ray	(914) 644-5152
Pacific Bell	ISDN Information	(800) 622-0735
SNET	Donovan Dillon	(203) 553-2369
STENTOR	Steve Finlay	(604) 432-3527
Southwestern Bell	Fred Kemp	(314) 331-2865
US West	Louise Walsh	(303) 896-0793

Several informative publications also discuss ISDN. One of them covers ISDN applications: the *Catalog of National ISDN Solutions for Selected NIUF Applications*, available from National Technical Information Services, (800) 553-6847, reference number PB93-162881, at a cost of $44.50 (paper) or $17.50 (microfiche).

Another useful publication is the *Trip '92 Atlas*, subtitled "The Definitive Source Book on National ISDN-1." It is available from the Corporation for Open Systems, (800) 759-2674, at a cost of $74.

For ISDN planner, a third publication is *ISDN Deployment Data*, Issue 3, available through Bellcore, (800) 521-2673. This book provides ISDN deployment information across the United States. Its reference number is SR-NW2-002102, and it costs $110.

Never Say Die

PROPONENTS OF ISDN CONTINUE TO TOUT ITS LOW COST AND CURRENT AVAILABILITY, WHILE ADVOCATES OF OTHER TECHNOLOGIES SEE IT AS A HAS-BEEN.

BY CHERYL KRIVDA

Motivated by optimism or the hope of financial gain, most inventive souls face disappointment when a creation misses the mark. The inevitable what-if considerations buffer the bruising scrapes of reality until the creator finally moves on to the next idea.

And then there are the proponents of ISDN.

Long promoted as a future end-to-end technology for transmitting voice, data, and video over existing copper telephone lines, Integrated Services Digital Network eventually was dismissed by the technically and politically savvy as too little, too late, and certainly too bogged down by industry in-fighting. ISDN was DBA–dead before arrival.

Except ISDN's proponents never got the message. While analysts laughed off the technology as a has-been, several industry movers who wanted to see ISDN succeed plodded forward. In the United States, Bell Communications Research, known as Bellcore (Livingston, NJ), was the principal proponent of ISDN but had lost control of the standard.

Many of the regional Bell operating companies (RBOCs) developed protocols and tariffing structures to meet the equipment requirements of vendors with whom they agreed to partner. Over time, ISDN became less integrated and more unique to each RBOC; in industry circles, the joke was that the acronym stood for "I still don't know."

In February 1991, the interoperability stalemate ended. The Corporation for Open Systems (COS) and the North American ISDN Users' Forum (NIUF) announced a plan to establish National ISDN, a consistent interface providing interoperability among local exchange carriers, interexchange carriers, and customer-premises equipment to be connected across North America. The COS and the NIUF projected it would take approximately 18 months to complete the first stage of development, National ISDN-1.

GOING NATIONAL

In November 1992, Bellcore, the COS, and the NIUF introduced National ISDN-1 in a week-long public relations extravaganza, Transcontinental ISDN Project, or TRIP '92. To demonstrate unified commitment to the standardized ISDN, TRIP '92 participants hosted 150 open houses nationwide, demonstrated the launch of the national ISDN network, and organized a trade show in Reston, VA. The country's three largest interexchange carriers, AT&T, MCI, and Sprint, participated.

The results were pleasing to all involved. Zach Gilstein, executive director of data communications technology for Bellcore, says TRIP '92 "far exceeded expectations. Attendance at the ISDN trade show, where applications were demonstrated, was expected to hit 1,000. But the turnout was 4,000.

"The expectation wasn't for that many people," Gilstein notes, although those who understand ISDN's value "believe it deserves that level of attention for the significant upgrade it provides, using the current copper wiring infrastructure. While broadband certainly offers a lot more in terms of bandwidth, we don't have fiber to every house in the country like we do copper wires."

With such widespread copper access, Bellcore expects that 61.9 million telephone lines, more than 54 percent of the country's 115 million lines, will have ISDN services available by 1994.

In Europe, the ISDN implementation process may be

Figure 1. The NIUF indentifies five primary equipment configurations that can be used to enable National ISDN-1 applications.

ahead of that in the United States. ISDN is taken seriously in Europe, where many remote sites are connected to a smaller number of central sites. Speed is less critical to some users than is sheer connectivity.

NO UNITY IN STANDARDS

Not that uniformity is necessarily the net result. Mark Raymond, senior analyst for Datapro International (Maidenhead, Berkshire, England), says the European community may be working toward economic unification, but technology is another story. Currently each country has a separate telecom standard, which evolved before the introduction of ISDN. Each country also has formal standards defined by standards bodies.

As a result, the United Kingdom, France, and Germany–the main users of ISDN and other high-speed computer technology–all have different ISDN standards.

Standards bodies in the United Kingdom, France, and Germany plan to transition to the formal standards being defined by the International Telegraph and Telephone Consultive Committee (CCITT) and European Telecommunications Standards Institute (ETSI).

CCITT defines a Q series of protocols, the most important of which is Q.931, a network-level protocol addressing BRI (Basic Rate Interface) ISDN, and Q.921, which addresses the PRI (Primary Rate Interface) ISDN. In turn, the CCITT protocol forms the basis for the ETSI's standard, called Norm European Telecommunications, or NET. NET3 Part 1 and NET3 Part 2, the ETSI equivalent to Q.931, are the important standards.

Datapro's Raymond says the process of defining Q.931 was highly political and ran well over schedule when individual countries argued for country-specific codes and services. While the arguing continued, businesses became accustomed to using the country-specific protocols in the absence of the formal standards.

When standards are finally adopted, they will be more formal than standards in the United States, where industry standards are influenced more by vendors and changed often by users. Even now, telecom administrations are beginning to require hardware vendors to provide a migration path to Q.931.

Although Europe's protocol-development process is as complex as that in the United States, its progress toward ISDN market acceptance seems to be stronger.

"The path to ISDN today is clearer than it has been for several years. It is being promoted by telecom administrations increasingly in terms of availability and tariffing," Raymond notes.

CONTENDERS

On both continents, the hoped-for ubiquity of ISDN services is expected to benefit large and small sites that require low-cost, low-speed access. But some analysts wonder whether ISDN is too little, too late for heavy hitters. Many users eyeing the high-speed transmission of voice, data, and video are looking beyond ISDN's relatively slow speeds in favor of frame relay, Switched Multimegabit Data Service (SMDS), and Asynchronous Transfer Mode (ATM).

Frame relay offers packet-switched service from 56Kbps to 1.5Mbps, providing better utilization of LAN resources and customer equipment than ISDN. SMDS supports communication from 1.5Mbps to 155Mbps and offers both intraenterprise and interenterprise communication with better utilization of network resources and customer equipment. ATM, which promises speeds of 100Mbps to 2Gbps, is still in the planning stages but has been acknowledged by both the LAN and WAN markets as a key technology for the future.

Bellcore sees room for ISDN among the faster, more sophisticated technologies. ISDN's packet-switching capability, Bellcore argues, is attractive for applications requiring 16Kbps to 64Kbps of bandwidth. Multiple ISDN 64Kbps circuit-switched channels will provide up to 1.5Mbps of bandwidth. Bellcore expects some mapping of frame-relay services into ISDN transmission capabilities in the near future.

SMDS, others say, is still used in isolation, making connectivity between sites difficult. And although frame relay is packet-oriented and increasingly available, it is not applicable for voice and video applications, whereas ISDN is.

Despite Bellcore's optimism, others view ISDN less favorably. One recent study by Computer Intelligence (La Jolla, CA) cites lack of broad-based interest for what it sees as the inevitable failure of ISDN. The company, which surveys 130,000 establishments monthly about their computer equipment and services acquisitions, found that 110,000 ISDN lines are currently owned by fewer than 2,000 establishments.

A WAKE-UP CALL

The study, entitled "Field of Dreams" (for the movie about a farmer who followed the credo, "If you build it, they will come") suggests no evidence exists to support the idea that masses of customers are interested in ISDN technology. Approximately half of the existing ISDN lines are used by companies in the medical industry, in education, and in government. No other industry groups are forecast to migrate to ISDN in large numbers.

Stan Schatt, analyst for parent company InfoCorp (Santa Clara, CA), says most current ISDN installations are found in large establishments with 1,000 or more employees (about 82 percent). However, few large companies have ISDN installed (5 percent), and many of them (85 percent) have no plans to install ISDN. "In reality, it hasn't reached critical mass in terms of market segment to cause it to be propelled forward," he says. "You just don't see companies using ISDN for commercial purposes."

Moreover, Schatt adds, ISDN provides no singular application that sites cannot find elsewhere. "There are alternative solutions that make a lot more sense in speed in terms of price/performance," he says.

Yet some current users explain that attractive price/performance ratios drove them to ISDN in the first place. Compared to the cost of a leased line, ISDN's cost of $30 per month to $50 per month seems downright affordable.

AN URBAN SUCCESS

Dorothy Mulligan, director of academic computing and educational technology for Jersey City State College (Jersey City, NJ), says ISDN serves a current technical need while pleasing the college's business office.

The urban college, with a student population of 8,500, was interested in distance learning, video teleconferencing, and the creation of transparent networks for faculty members. Installing fiber in the 12 buildings on campus would have cost $100,000 per building, an impossible sum.

Mulligan thought ISDN held potential as a LAN interconnection method for video conferencing and distance education.

Using a series of grants from Apple Computer, Bell Atlantic, the state of New Jersey, and others, Mulligan's staff began designing the ISDN network. The staff created soft-

ware to help faculty dial in to office systems from Macintoshes at home as well as routing software to help them remotely access the campus network.

The college now uses a switch in the central New Jersey Bell office and a local server with five ISDN cards, providing links among five campus buildings through LocalTalk networks. A homegrown device driver called ISDNTalk tunnels the AppleTalk protocols through the ISDN line, solving the compatibility problem.

"I've got nailed-up connections [leased lines], and they cost me less than $50 a month," Mulligan says with a laugh, "which is really cost-effective. It's impressive when I talk to the people in the business office."

ISDN's lower cost may be a drawing card for remote users as well. Bellcore's Gilstein explains that home-based users can buy terminal adapters to gain access to two B channels for 128Kbps of bandwidth. While a large file transfer might take a few minutes using ISDN at $35 per month, instead of a few seconds with $500 per-month frame relay or SMDS, the technology is probably worthwhile, he says.

AN ISDN DELIVERANCE

Another ISDN user, Appalachian State University (Boone, NC), envisions similar connectivity. James Strom, vice chancellor for university advancement, explains that ISDN fits the technological needs of the applications required. "It's pervasive; it's ubiquitous. Telephone lines go everywhere," he says.

A rural, 11,500-student university, Appalachian State has an ongoing distance-learning program with two elementary schools and one high school. ISDN is used to link the four sites.

Appalachian State created a network backbone of 13 BRI ISDN lines provided out of Southern Bell's Boone central office. Three ISDN lines terminate in each of the three public schools, with four ISDN lines installed at Appalachian State. The system allows for interactive video, data, and voice transmission at 112Kbps.

The technology allows the public schools linked to the university to attain a quality of education matching schools in metropolitan areas, Strom says. Students communicate with college faculty using interactive video, voice, and data. Student teachers use the facilities to conference with faculty members and record teaching diaries.

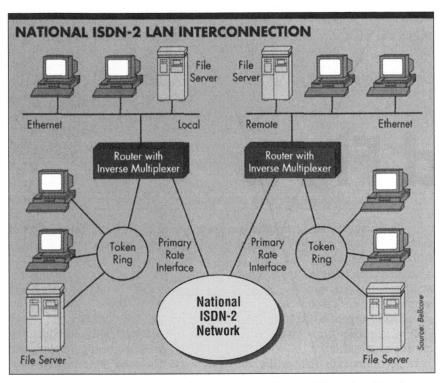

Figure 2. National ISDN-2 can be used to cost-effectively interconnect two large LANs with occasional need for high-speed communication.

Appalachian is currently the only university in the country using ISDN for distance learning, Strom says. While other institutions have implemented fiber optic for that purpose, he says ISDN was far more cost-effective for his university than other technologies could be.

But the costs for access and equipment to support ISDN may be more than anyone realizes, says Frank Dzubeck, president of analysis and consulting firm Communications Network Architects (Washington, D.C.).

The interexchange carriers that have created interfaces to the ISDN technology had it easy compared with the steps required of the local carriers. "They [local carriers] have to flush the existing central-office equipment," says Dzubeck. "It's going to inhibit the growth." As long as some carriers are less willing than others to proceed with ISDN, it will be impossible to achieve ubiquity of services and offerings on a national level.

And if the local carriers need to invest in expensive equipment to offer ISDN, their rate structures must change. Carriers will pass their costs on to consumers who may have trouble justifying ISDN under those conditions. "It's a much more complex economic model than is [typi-cally] analyzed by the communications press. Technology is not the issue," he says.

Which is not to say ISDN is too late for some piece of the market. Analysts agree that ISDN may have a prime place in the access market, particularly if frame relay or other low-speed services take off.

"There's no reason why you can't use ISDN for low-speed access even for ATM services," Dzubeck says. Some sites may want a system with switched access to a vari-able-bandwidth service where they can order services as needed, including ISDN. "A great many cost issues are in-volved, macro and micro economic issues that are actually stymieing the growth of [ISDN]," he says.

Yet the apparent success of National ISDN-1 via TRIP '92 has helped both vendors and users move closer to their goals of inexpensive connectivity. In Europe, Datapro's Raymond sees increasing ISDN interest in two areas: PRI ISDN, which, he says, is growing intrinsically as digitaliza-tion is introduced into the European infrastructure, and ISDN for leased-circuit and bandwidth-on-demand applica-tions.

The unification of the U.S. ISDN effort has helped promote the "whole concept of IDSN and stimulate vendors to create ISDN products," he notes. Rumors are circulating in Europe that an ISDN showcase may be held there later this year.

While some may fear that ISDN missed its chances by coming to market so slowly, others see the changes in the market since the introduction of ISDN as yet another market opportunity.

In Europe and the United States, the economies of scale for expensive technologies like ATM take time to achieve. In the interim, the relentlessly optimistic proponents of ISDN have yet another opportunity to bring their technology to the masses.

ISDN COMES IN TWO FLAVORS

A Taste of ISDN?

National ISDN-1 offers two services, Basic Rate Interface (BRI) and support of vendor-specific implementation of Primary Rate Interface (PRI). BRI includes two B channels that can transport 64Kbps of voice, data, image, or other information and one D channel of 16Kbps, which carries signaling information and, in some applications, packet data. BRI is sometimes designated "2B+D."

The B channels are called *bearer channels* since they carry the information transfer across the user-to-network interface. The D channel is a "delta" channel and carries signaling for specific types of call-control access to the ISDN bearer services. The D channel may also be used to carry packet-mode data.

BRI is typically used in one of two ways: to provide ISDN access between the customer and the ISDN central office or to provide ISDN access between user equipment and a PBX for off-site connections.

PRI includes 23 64Kbps B channels and one 64Kbps D channel and is sometimes designated "23B+D." It will be fully supported by National ISDN-2, which should be available late 1993 or early 1994.

One of the major features of National ISDN-2 is multirate Circuit Mode Data (CMD) service, also known as Switched DS1/ Switched Fractional DS1 (SWF-DS1). This service channels bandwidth at rates from 128Kbps to 1,536Kbps in 64Kbps increments over a PRI. Multirate CMD is well-suited for such applications as room-to-room video conferencing, bulk data transfer, customer network overflow, electronic imaging, and BRI applications that use inverse multiplexers.

A Free Ride for Data

WITH DATA/VOICE MULTIPLEXERS, YOU MAY BE ABLE TO PIGGYBACK DATA ON VOICE LINES, MAKING FOR AN EASIER COST JUSTIFICATION AND A MORE EFFICIENT NETWORK.

BY CHARLES FELTMAN

Glenn Leppla, technical support manager for the international law firm Davis Polk & Wardwell, is sketching a diagram of his company's worldwide data and voice network on a yellow legal pad. As he draws lines from the center box marked "NY" to boxes marked "London," "Paris," and "Frankfurt" on one side, and "Hong Kong" and "Tokyo" on the other, Leppla describes how subrate multiplexers allow his company to run voice and data over 56/64Kbps leased lines between the corporate offices in downtown Manhattan, Europe, and Asia for about what they once paid for toll voice calls alone.

It is just past noon in New York, which means it's a little after 7 p.m. at the Davis Polk & Wardwell offices in London, but at least one person is still there transferring a file, probably a legal brief that is stored on a server in Manhattan.

The Paris and Frankfurt offices have closed for the evening, and it is deep night at the Tokyo and Hong Kong branches, but the links are still being used to send time-delayed faxes back to corporate. Only the Washington, D.C., office is in full swing as Leppla talks about the various applications that are run over inexpensive 56Kbps and 64Kbps leased lines between the firm's remote branches.

Using Micom's (Simi Valley, CA) Marathon 5K data/voice muxes connected over 56Kbps and 64Kbps links between the remote sites in Europe, Asia, and its main office in Manhattan, the law firm supports remote networks, asynchronous terminal server applications using *telnet,* and synchronous AS/400 access, plus interoffice voice and fax calls. Only the Washington, D.C., office, with three T-1 lines (two to support a router and one for voice), is connected at speeds higher than 64Kbps.

"Each remote office has its own computing facility, and most of the data they need is local to that site," Leppla explains. "But there is some information available in New York that they don't have at the remote sites, so the wide area network is used to access it as needed.

"If we were using New York as the main computing facility we would probably run out of bandwidth at 64Kbps. But it works very well for what we do: e-mail, occasional file transfers from servers in New York, and terminal access via *telnet* to database servers.

"Our people also use the network for voice calls between the offices. In fact, the justification for the network came from the fact that we are paying just about the same for both data and voice as we would pay in voice toll calls. So I guess you could say our data rides for free."

The firm, which handles international corporate law, mergers and acquisitions, and tax law, has about 1,200 employees worldwide, with some 900 in the Manhattan office. Person-to-person voice calls are important to the company, but when it first installed the data/voice network, productivity increased because employees in remote offices could access data from New York electronically whenever it was needed.

"We couldn't cost justify a higher-speed WAN, and I doubt if we could have negotiated an SDN [switched data network] agreement with a long distance carrier that would have given us as much bandwidth for our money," Leppla concludes. "But we have benefited tremendously from the increased connectivity we get from this network."

ANATOMY OF A DATA/VOICE MUX

Typically a sub-T-1, or subrate, data/voice multiplexer

has some number of voice ports and some number of data ports to which users devices, such as PBXs, key systems, asynchronous terminals, remote controllers, packet assemblers/disassemblers (PADs), and bridges and routers, can be connected. These ports accept data at different speeds and support a variety of standard physical interfaces and data-link protocols. One or more of these ports can interface directly to a LAN.

The input to these ports is then multiplexed onto one or sometimes more wide-area *composite links* that are connected to leased wide-area lines such as those provided with a 56Kbps dataphone digital service (DDS). A CSU/DSU is sometimes integrated into the mux; otherwise an external CSU/DSU has to be included in the configuration. The composite links typically can be run at speeds between 1,200bps and 256Kbps, although the most common speeds used are 56Kbps in the United States and 64Kbps elsewhere.

Depending on the technology employed, the composite link may be divided into multiple channels for voice, asynchronous and synchronous data, and possibly network management. Channel-bandwidth allocation is user-selectable, so that the user can determine how much of the total bandwidth is to be allocated to the various types of inputs.

Subrate data/voice muxes with only one or two wide-area composite links are used to build point-to-point networks connecting several remote sites. Some vendors also offer systems with multiple composite ports that can be used as a central hub to link several remote sites.

Most vendors of subrate muxes target small to midsize companies that want to build wide area networks that run at sub-T-1 speeds throughout. Newbridge Networks is an exception to some extent, in that its 3606 and 3612 sub-T-1 data/voice muxes can be used as the only nodes in a network, or they can serve as feeder nodes into Newbridge's larger 3600 T-1 multiplexers. A few other subrate mux vendors also offer products that can be used as feeders into T-1 networks by providing fractional T-1 interfaces.

THE SQUEEZE ON VOICE

In the early 1980s companies such as Network Equipment Technologies (Redwood City, CA), Newbridge Networks, and Timeplex (Woodcliff Lake, NJ) introduced T-1 multiplexers capable of transmitting and switching both data and voice over leased T-1 lines. Large companies purchased these switches, leased T-1 lines from the carriers, and went about building large private telecommunications networks to serve their data and voice requirements.

This migration to private WANs was driven by the relatively high cost of voice toll calls and the justifiable concern at the time that the public telephone carriers couldn't be trusted with a company's data; the quality of service was too low.

But networks running at much less than T-1 speeds didn't supply enough bandwidth to carry both voice and data. So smaller companies that couldn't justify T-1 links between geographically remote sites were left with only one option: build private networks for their data and use public carrier services for voice calls.

Over the past five years, several developments have changed this situation, however. For one thing, the quality of digital links available from long distance carriers has improved considerably and dropped somewhat in cost at the low end, for 56/64Kbps, in particular.

More important at the low end, development of sophisticated voice-compression technologies has allowed users to get a great deal more out of a 56Kbps wide-area link than they used to. When voice circuits are run over digital lines, each analog voice channel is converted into a 64Kbps bit stream using Pulse Code Modulation (PCM). This technique used to mean that one entire 64Kbps link was needed for a single voice call, leaving no room for data. But various voice compression techniques have made it possible to squeeze voice signals to 4Kbps.

Clearly, the more bits per second used to represent voice-call information, the better the sound quality. However, today, even the lowest voice rates yield audible quality. Still, most compressed voice calls are made using either 16Kbps or 8Kbps digitization rates because they offer both good sound reproduction and leave quite a bit of bandwidth for data over a 56Kbps or 64Kbps circuit.

"You wouldn't want to play a high fidelity recording over a 16Kbps compressed voice call, but for just talking it works fine," says John Bennett, director of MIS for Crowley Foods of Binghamton, NY. Crowley Foods is a manufacturer and distributor of dairy food products that uses Newbridge's 3606 and 3612 data/voice muxes to link 11 sites scattered from New York state to the Mississippi.

Bennett's MIS group is currently using the muxes to

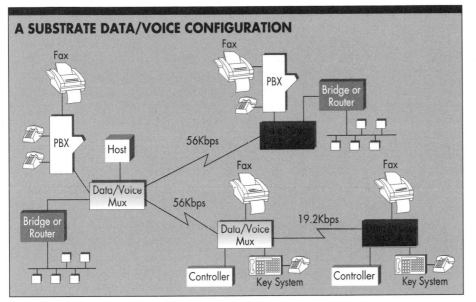

A SUBSTRATE DATA/VOICE CONFIGURATION

Fax

Fax

PBX

Bridge or Router

PBX

Host

56Kbps

Fax

Data/Voice Mux

56Kbps

Data/Voice Mux

19.2Kbps

Fax

Bridge or Router

Controller

Key System

Controller

Key System

Figure 1. A MUX CAN SAVE BUCKS: In this network, a central site is linked to three remote sites with a variety of data and voice equipment. If this company were to employ separate circuits for its data and voice links, it would probably pay a great deal more in telecommunications charges.

provide voice connections and 19.2Kbps data channels linking AS/400 systems at the different sites. However, within the next year it plans to put routers behind the muxes and add LAN traffic to run Lotus Notes and e-mail and to use the AS/400s as servers. The main reason Crowley Foods looked into building a WAN with subrate data/voice multiplexers was to support LAN internetworking. However, the company quickly realized the entire investment would yield a payback in less than one year.

Prior to putting in the data/voice mux network, Crowley had tie lines (a dedicated circuit linking two points, which does not require dialing the full phone number) to only seven sites, and these were often busy, forcing users to make "off-net" toll calls. Bennett estimates that the company will save as much as $73,000 in line costs with the new network, reach more of its locations, and support data as well as voice. As with Leppla's law firm, Bennett figures the data rides with the voice "for free."

CAN'T FORGET THE FAX

Compression is great for reducing bandwidth used by voice conversations, but it can wreak havoc on a fax transmission. Since fax machines are typically hooked to the same telephone lines used for voice calls, multiplexers with voice compression must be sensitive to the presence of a fax signal. Fax machines are designed to modulate a

9,600bps digital data stream into an analog signal for transmission over a voice line. If they are subjected to a speech-reduction technique, fax transmissions can be slowed, corrupted, or stopped altogether.

For this reason, most subrate data/voice multiplexers have some form of automatic fax-detection capability that identifies a fax signal. But simply identifying a fax signal and sending it along as an uncompressed analog transmission means it will take up an entire 64Kbps of bandwidth. Equally important, then, is demodulating the analog signal into a 9,600bps digital signal for transmission over the wide-area link to the far-end mux. At that end, the digital signal is again remodulated into an analog signal for presentation to the far-end fax machine.

TRANSMISSION CHOICES

Only six companies manufacture and sell the majority of subrate data/ voice multiplexers in use today, and the transmission technologies they employ vary. Most vendors rely on some type of time-division multiplexing (TDM) for their wide-area transmission but incorporate different ways of using the TDM bandwidth and compression technologies to maximize the amount of information carried over the network.

In a TDM transmission the total bandwidth of the link between two multiplexers is divided into multiple synchronized time slots. Each time slot corresponds to a unique channel in the link. Data for a specific channel can be placed into its designated time slot by the sending mux, and the receiver will know where to look for it in the bit stream at the other end.

TDM is a very good technique for voice transmission because it assures that a strong timing relationship is maintained between both ends of the connection to prevent the "satellite effect" of delayed sound. However, it does not always use network bandwidth efficiently.

For example, if a compressed voice call is given one 16Kbps channel, it will be allocated enough of the time slots to allow 16,000 bits per second to traverse the link. But about 60 percent of a typical a voice conversation is actually silence. And a typical link will only carry an average of one-and-a-half hours to three hours of voice calls per day; the rest of the time the voice channels are idle. In pure TDM transmission a lot of empty time slots would be sent across the link representing unused voice channels and the silent intervals in conversations.

Since bandwidth is a very limited commodity on a 56Kbps link, most subrate mux vendors that use TDM have at least devised ways to increase the speed of data channels when the voice channels are idle because the telephones are *on-hook* (not in use).

The most common way of allocating greater bandwidth to data when voice channels are idle is to increase the clock speed on the data port. When the voice channel goes *off-hook* (someone picks up the receiver to make a call or a call comes in from another site in the network) the clock or clocks on one or more data ports are slowed to the minimum speed set by the user. When the voice channel goes back on-hook, that bandwidth is given back to the data channels by increasing the clock speed for the data ports. This, of course, only works for devices that are not sensitive to varying clock speeds, such as bridges and routers, external PADs, or statistical multiplexers.

Micom, the market leader according to a 1993 study by International Data Corp. (IDC, Framingham, MA), has taken a different approach. It employs what it calls *cell relay/fast packet multiplexing,* conceptually similar to Asynchronous Transmission Mode (ATM). Data and voice/ fax input is packetized and multiplexed into cells for transmission over the WAN link. This packetization allows a Micom mux to allocate bandwidth to data and voice/fax

channels dynamically on the fly. Voice always takes precedence, but cells carrying data can be inserted into the transmission stream during silences within a voice call as well as when no voice calls are in progress. Bursts of data over a LAN-to-LAN connection can be accommodated without significant disruption of terminal-to-host traffic, as well.

Others are firmly in the TDM camp when it comes to subrate data/ voice multiplexers. Larry Starnes, president of Systems Express, a Charlotte, N.C., systems integrator specializing in LAN and WAN systems, and Noble Smith, one of his systems engineers, express a strong belief that users get the best voice quality using TDM transmission.

"TDM always assures clean, high-quality voice when it is compressed and still allows room for significant data transmission to take place," Smith says. "TDM's voice quality is especially important when a voice call is routed through more than one node in the network before reaching its final destination," he adds.

Dwight Buck, vice president of marketing for Pacific Communications Sciences, Inc. (PCSI, San Diego), says PCSI's philosophy is to let users make the decision about what is most important in their environments. "Ultimately, the user has to decide whether quality of voice conversations or a slightly higher aggregate data rate is the dominant criterion and choose their products accordingly."

THE LAN CONNECTION

Where do LANs fit into a subrate data/voice network? Originally, data/voice multiplexers were designed to carry one or two voice channels and some data, usually asynchronous or synchronous terminal-to-host communications, or a combination of the two, between a remote office and a central office or data center. The types of devices attached on the voice side were key systems and PBXs. On the data side, users connected asynchronous terminals, remote controllers, PADs, and sometimes statistical multiplexers.

As LANs have become ubiquitous at the larger corporate sites, users have begun looking for ways to connect terminals at their remote sites directly into the home-office LAN. Vendors such as Micom offer *telnet* and Local Area Transport (LAT) terminal server functionality within their muxes that allow remote terminals to connect to LAN-based hosts at a central site. A bridge or router can also be connected to a synchronous port on any data/voice mux. The issue is bandwidth. By now most users have realized that depending on the data flow between sites, as little as 19.2Kbps can suffice to link two LANs across a WAN, especially if the remote site is small. Many bridge and router products also provide their own compression, which helps.

As a general rule, if LAN-to-LAN traffic during the workday can be accommodated at between 14.4Kbps and 38.4Kbps and some level of voice traffic is also present, a subrate data/voice mux can be a cost-effective way to provide wide area networking. At night, when voice channels go unused, such products will automatically allocate more bandwidth to the LAN channel. With up to 56Kbps available, larger file transfers and server backups are feasible.

NOT A PANACEA

"You can't and shouldn't run any kind of 'real-time' LAN applications over the WAN with this kind of system," cautions Rocco Esposito emphatically. Esposito is manager of Microcomputer Services for Maidenform, the clothing manufacturer headquartered in Bayonne, NJ.

"We tried to run NetWare server applications in New Jersey from a remote site in Jacksonville, FL, and it just didn't work. There's not enough bandwidth," he concludes. "We have Micom Marathon 10Ks, and their forte as far as we are concerned is supporting background LAN file transfer, e-mail, and other terminal-emulation applications. If we want to do some kind of Novell server application we use Citrix [Coral Springs, FL]." Citrix's product, WinView for Networks, is a remote applications server for Windows, DOS, and OS/2.

A FUTURE FOR THE LOW END

IDC's July 1993 report on the data/ voice multiplexer market predicts that it will continue to grow at least through 1996.

But the environment is clearly changing. LANs are overtaking all other types of data communications and carriers are offering new, more cost-effective LAN interconnect services such as frame relay and SMDS. A variety of low-cost voice services are available. And ATM, with its ability to carry both data and voice is around the corner. Such services will undoubtedly have an effect on sub-T-1 networking.

Still, a large number of customers will continue to use low-speed lines for combined data and voice–those who simply can't justify SMDS or high-speed frame relay, for example. Whether they choose 64Kbps frame relay, DDS, or some other low-speed carrier service, such options will continue to be viable for smaller remote sites.

A SUBRATE DATA/VOICE NETWORK MAY BE FOR YOU

Can You Save Money?

Under the right conditions, integrating data and voice on a single sub-T-1 wide area network can save a company thousands of dollars a year in combined toll calls and leased-line charges.

To get some idea of the potential savings in telecommunication costs between two sites using subrate multiplexers, imagine a main office in Dallas and a smaller remote office in Atlanta. A typical set of communications requirements between these two sites might include a remote controller linked to the central site and a router connection for LAN internetworking, each using 19.2Kbps leased lines. According to AT&T long distance tariffs published in April 1993, these lines would cost $969. Assume that voice communication is handled using long distance toll service which averages $1,500 per month. The monthly bill for communications between these sites would be $3,438.

By multiplexing the data and voice together over a single 56Kbps dataphone digital service (DDS) line that costs $1,288 per month, this user could save approximately $2,150 per month. The annual savings would be $25,800. Depending on the multiplexer equipment purchased to build the network, the payback period could be anywhere from eight months to 12 months. In addition to the savings, the user would most likely realize an increase in the average speed of the router connection over the original 19.2Kbps link because of the ability of most multiplexers to give bandwidth to other channels when the voice channels are in use.

Here are a few questions that will help you to assess whether your company can save money by putting in a sub-T-1 data/voice network.

1. Do you have more than one-and-a-half hours per day of voice/fax calls between remote sites? Chances are, if you have less than this, you will not benefit economically with a leased line. (This rule of thumb can vary, however.

For example, if you only make one hour of voice calls per day but your total requirement can be met using a 14.4Kbps line, you may still be ahead of the game.)

2. What carrier services are you currently using? What are your monthly charges? If you completely understand what your monthly charges are and what you're paying for, it will be easy to determine the cost-benefit of installing a subrate data/voice WAN.

3. Do you have one or more low-speed leased or dial-up traditional data and/or LAN connections between those same sites? What are your total data requirements between sites? You may be able to cost justify greater bandwidth for a LAN link by combining it with voice.

4. Do you have sites in Europe, Asia, or Latin America that need regular voice and data communication with each other or with U.S. locations? Connecting data and voice over a 64Kbps link to overseas locations can be an enormous cost saver.

5. What are the prices of 56Kbps or 64Kbps DDS, fractional T-1, Switched 56Kbps, microwave, or frame relay services between the sites? Subrate mux products support a varying range of services, so your choice of product, as well as the overall cost justification, may depend on what services are available to you at what cost.

An Amazing Aqua LAN

ONE RESEARCH INSTITUTE'S UNDERWATER WAN IS MORE THAN MOST CAN FATHOM.

BY MELANIE MCMULLEN

Tom Tengdin manages what he says is the deepest node on the Internet. Suspended 1,000 meters below the icy waters of the Pacific Ocean, Tengdin's remote seaworthy node is a critical part of a wide area network operated by the Monterey Bay Aquarium Research Institute (MBARI) in Pacific Grove, CA. The oceanographic institute, with the help of Tengdin, an electronics technician in the operations division there, operates a WAN so sophisticated it blows existing network technology right out of the water.

Sure, Tengdin deals with the basic problems of most network managers, such as cabling, remote access, management, and fault tolerance. But he and other MBARI engineers are submerged, as the case may be, in other daily predicaments. Instead of worrying about whether a user spills coffee on a keyboard and shorts out the desktop, Tengdin has to deal with sharks, whales, and other inquisitive sea critters snooping around his waterlogged technology wonder. And at a time when many network managers are learning to run fiber to the desktop, MBARI engineers are in a different league, concerning themselves with the difficulties of running fiber down into Monterey Canyon, a 4,000-meter chasm located 10 miles off the Pacific coast in Monterey Bay.

STRANGE SCIENCE

To understand why Tengdin and MBARI researchers are interested in hanging around this canyon, a science lesson is in order. In 1977, scientists and oceanographers in the waters east of the Galapagos Islands in the Pacific found something very fishy. A colony of underwater animals was discovered living happily in pockets where, biologically, because of the depth and lack of plants, they

shouldn't have been able to survive. Most animal communities eat plants, which require sunlight for photosynthesis.

After extensive research, biologists determined that these worms, crabs, and snails were living via chemosynthesis, an energy-conversion process related to photosynthesis. The chemosynthesis in the Galapagos occurs in areas fed by hot, almost 70-degree underwater geysers. Spewing from rock chimneys, these geysers provide the right environmental conditions needed for chemosynthesis.

Working in the darkness of the ocean depths, the chemosynthetic bacteria use energy present in sulphur compounds to provide the basis of an intricate food chain. Some animals, such as the worms, have symbiotic bacteria to nourish them, while others, such as the crabs and the shrimp, gobble the bacteria directly as they float from the vents. This phenomenon converts a normally barren deep-sea desert into an underwater sanctum of feasting for rare species of fish, shrimp, clams, oysters, anemones, limpets, crabs, and worms, creating a biologist's living library of research.

But back to Monterey. Although Monterey Canyon has no known hot flumes or fiery gushes, it does have chemosynthesis-based cities that appear to operate with the same type of bacteria support. Located around the seeps of cold water at the bases of the rock faces of the canyon, these communities of clams and crabs were first discovered in the deeper parts of Monterey Canyon in 1988 by geologists who stumbled on them in a deep-diving submersible.

These geologists were not alone in knowing that Monterey Bay's cool underwater biospheres were a hotbed for biological and geological research. One year prior to the discovery of the first chemosynthesis colonies, David Packard founded MBARI, a private, nonprofit research spinoff of the Monterey Bay Aquarium in Monterey, CA. Packard, better known for his role as cofounder of Hewlett-Packard (HP, Palo Alto, CA), created an ongoing trust fund, the David and Lucille Packard Foundation, through which he and others contribute several million dollars each year to sustain MBARI operations.

OVER LAN, OVER SEA

At the inception of MBARI, Packard's goal for the Institute was simple: to advance human knowledge of the deep ocean via science and technology. More specifically, Packard charged the Institute's 100 employees with the task of developing the equipment, instrumentation, systems, and methods necessary for doing state-of-the-art scientific research in the ocean.

And Packard hasn't been disappointed. While the Institute is relatively young in research years, MBARI has already made its mark on the biology as well as the technology front, which includes network technology.

Using mostly HP computers and PCs, MBARI engineers designed, installed, and now operate a 100-node, wide-area TCP/IP network. This WAN uses a combination of wireless microwave, Ethernet, and fiber transmission to relay both data and video to and from multiple sites, including a node mounted on the remotely operated vehicle (ROV), named Ventana, that sits aboard–or dangles from–the Institute's 100-foot Pt. Lobos research vessel.

Ventana and Pt. Lobos were put to use from their first day out. Using the ROV, MBARI geologists in 1991 discovered several more cold seeps, and the accompanying chemosynthesis colonies, in the Canyon at depths somewhere around 900 meters.

New seeps are discovered almost daily by MBARI's ROV. The 5-year-old Ventana, the technology beast of the sea, has five separate still and live video cameras, a robotic manipulator arm, a collecting drawer, and a suction sampler. It has its own 40-horsepower propulsion engine, allowing it to move independently of the Pt. Lobos ship. A 286 PC is also on board the ROV. This computer serves as the remote brain of Ventana, allowing the handful of pilots and scientists situated in the vessel's command room to control settings of the cameras and other robotics.

The Ventana is connected to Pt. Lobos via a tether that costs approximately $50 per meter. This pricey link, built by Boston Insulated Wire, contains three layers of Kevlar for strength, a sturdy urethane jacket, five electrical conductors for the motors and electronics, and 10 optical fibers for data and video transmission. The Ventana currently uses only four of these fibers, but Tengdin can switch to alternate fibers if one fails. "This tether is a precious commodity," says Tengdin. "We can't go down and splice it in the middle if it fails."

MBARI chose fiber because of its electrical isolation and distance capabilities. The cameras, computers, and other navigational electronics share transmission time on their links into the abyss via six-wave division multiplexers, three on Pt. Lobos and three on Ventana.

While the Ventana is in work mode, the Pt. Lobos captain tries to keep his ship directly over the ROV, constantly watching the tether and checking its tension. While this task may sound easy enough, "The process can turn into an exercise of doing science from a yo-yo, if bad weather occurs or if strong ocean currents are running," explains Tengdin.

TAKE THE PRESSURE OFF

The cable and some of the other electronic devices aboard the Ventana are encased in a layer of oil which allows them to sustain an underwater pressure of more than 1,500 pounds per square inch. The oil is a lighter way of protecting the electronics than encasing them in a thick-walled box, which is how the fiber transceivers and all the computers aboard the ROV are protected. Even with all the effort to lighten the vehicle and miniaturize the electronics, the Ventana still weighs in at 4,000 pounds. "Making electronic devices light and pressure tolerant is not a walk in the park," says Tengdin. "Sea water and electronics just don't mix very well."

Tengdin, who has worked at MBARI since May 1992, first learned how to mix electronics and sea water from his time spent at Woods Hole Oceanographic Institution in Woods Hole, MA. There he served as a pilot of Alvin, the three-person, 25-foot deep-diving submersible best known for carrying the first researchers down to the remains of the Titanic.

But now Tengdin focuses on the tools needed to maneuver Ventana close enough to scoop up rocks and sedi-

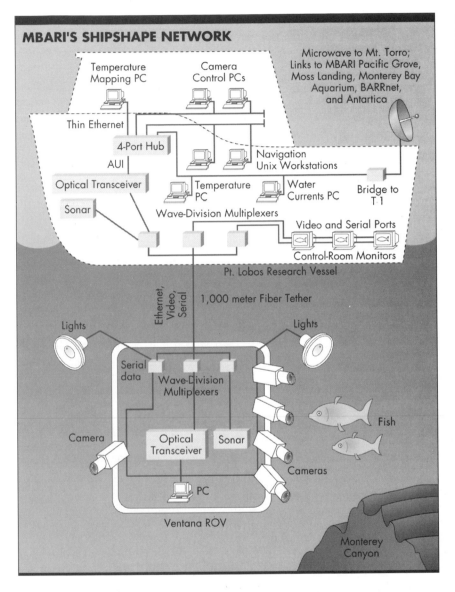

MBARI'S SHIPSHAPE NETWORK

Temperature Mapping PC

Camera Control PCs

Microwave to Mt. Torro; Links to MBARI Pacific Grove, Moss Landing, Monterey Bay Aquarium, BARRnet, and Antartica

Thin Ethernet

4-Port Hub

AUI

Navigation Unix Workstations

Optical Transceiver

Temperature PC

Water Currents PC

Bridge to T-1

Sonar

Wave-Division Multiplexers

Video and Serial Ports

Control-Room Monitors

Pt. Lobos Research Vessel

Ethernet, Video, Serial

1,000 meter Fiber Tether

Lights

Lights

Serial data

Wave-Division Multiplexers

Optical Transceiver

Sonar

Fish

Camera

Cameras

PC

Ventana ROV

Monterey Canyon

Far and Away: MBARI's wide area network uses a combination of wired and wireless transmission to connect a node in the depths of Monterey Canyon to places as far away as Antarctica.

ment, and most importantly, to capture a few canyon critters and bring them up to the ship secure and alive. Subsequently, these undersea urchins are transported back to MBARI headquarters for scientists to discover, among other things, how they are making a living in the cold canyon waters.

With daily excursions to the rim of the abyss, the scientific fishermen on Pt. Lobos, who reel out their remote rod Ventana, often have success in the hunt. And like most ichthyologists, they have a few tales of the ones that got away. "The pilot maneuvers the sampler around the squid, then he slams the lid on it," Tengdin explains. "But if our timing is off, they ink and run."

With stadium-power lights illuminating the view for Ventana's four forward cameras as well as the aft one, the roving ROV captures a detailed video feed of each fishing excursion. The Pt. Lobos crew broadcasts the ongoing underwater drama live to Institute headquarters and to the

Live Link Theater at the Monterey Bay Aquarium. The footage provides some exciting entertainment for aquarium visitors. "Even a little squid can look man-eating on a tight video," says Tengdin.

The link also includes a two-way audio circuit that allows the aquarium visitors and the Live Link interpreter to ask questions directly to the scientists on the boat about the images squirming across the screen.

FEED ME

The video feed is only one component of the Pt. Lobos and Ventana thin-Ethernet network that also transports sonar data, navigational and ocean current information, and temperature mapping statistics from Ventana to ship and also from ship to shore. The on-ship network is powered by 286, 386, and 486 DOS-based PCs as well as a couple of HP workstations running HP-UX. The copper-to-fiber conversion to and from Ventana is handled by two Optical Data Systems' (ODS, Dallas) fiber transceivers modified to boost transmission distances to the necessary 1,000 meters.

Tengdin uses FTP Software's (North Andover, MA) PC/TCP 2.05 for DOS as the network transport on the ship's PCs and on the nodes at MBARI headquarters. The crew of Pt. Lobos runs several custom software programs as well as Meridian Ocean Systems' Quils navigational program and GEM, software developed by Digital Research. The captain keeps the Pt. Lobos on course by doing real-time mapping of the vessel using the network along with Quils and Differential Global Positioning System (GPS) satellite navigation.

The Pt. Lobos network goes ashore using a wireless T-1 connection. A Network Application Technology (Campbell, CA) bridge connected to a T-1 modem from Graham-Patten Systems (Grass Valley, CA) work together to add the LAN signals to the video and audio transmissions carried across a 6.5GHz microwave link. The ship can transmit, from more than 50 miles offshore, to an antenna located atop Mt. Toro. The nearby peak is 19 miles inland from Moss Landing, a port city north of Monterey that also serves as the home port for the Pt. Lobos.

From Mt. Toro, the signal travels via 18GHz microwave to MBARI headquarters, where the video and audio is broadcast a few more miles to the aquarium, again using a microwave link. MBARI headquarters provides its re-searchers located anywhere on the WAN an Internet connection to the National Science Foundation Network (NSFnet) via a T-1 hook to its regional affiliate, the Bay Area Regional Research Network (BARRnet).

But the network doesn't end there. MBARI headquarters is connected to the Moss Landing marine operations office using a 56Kbps dedicated line. And Moss Landing has a T-1 link to NASA Ames Research Center in Moffett Field, CA, which in turn connects to another ROV cruising the seas near Antarctica.

TIP OF THE ICEBERG

In addition to managing MBARI's deep-sea node and wide-area connections, Tengdin and other MBARI engineers have been tinkering with technology that enters into other undiscovered realms. MBARI is currently experimenting with an acoustic LAN as well as building the Institute's next-generation research ship, the Western Flyer, and its accompanying ROV, Tiburon (which, incidentally, is Spanish for "shark").

Tengdin's pet project is the acoustic LAN, technology that, for ocean-based networking, sounds good both from a technical and practical perspective. While radio waves can travel only a few feet in sea water, sound waves can be heard for miles underwater, as any marine biologist who listens to dolphins chatting can verify. This long-distance propagation makes sound waves one of the most viable carriers of wireless data signals through the ocean.

MBARI and researchers from Woods Hole Oceanographic Institution are collaborating on the experimental acoustic LAN. The acoustic LAN has two 5Kbps data channels and two slow-speed command channels. Initial testing began at the end of 1993. The acoustic LAN uses separate request and acknowledgement channels to transfer data from underwater devices, such as tilt meters drilled into the canyon, to stationary buoys in Monterey Bay.

Using radio-based wireless network gear from Telesystems (Toronto), the buoys forward the information sent from below to MBARI collection stations on shore. The instrument-laden buoys, which should be able to bob unattended at sea for several years at a time, get their transmission power from solar-collection panels.

Although the transmission speed of the acoustic LAN is slow in comparison to wired or radio speeds, Tengdin says the first step in developing any cutting-edge technology is establishing the basic transmission path, leaving the performance as an aspect that can be bumped up later. "The jump from zero to any baud rate is the most important step you make. You have to establish the path first, then run it later at the speed of light," he says.

In addition to the acoustic LAN, MBARI is focusing on construction of its next research ship and ROV as well as a new $9.7 million research and administration facility in Moss Landing. The Western Flyer, one of the first small wetted-area twin-hull (SWATH) vessels to be used for research, will have berths and laboratories for up to 24 researchers and crew and will have a cruising range of more than 2,500 miles.

Scheduled for a 1995 deployment, Western Flyer will be the floating home for Tiburon, a lightweight electric ROV which, like Ventana, will have microprocessor-based ports of call to control its assortment of robotics and cameras. Tiburon, which will be able to sink to depths of 4,000 meters, will sport a hydraulic titanium arm for scooping up sediment and deep-sea denizens.

MBARI will continue to operate Pt. Lobos and Ventana as well as the Western Flyer/Tiburon mates. These floating technology marvels will double the amount of research the Institute can do in Monterey Bay. "Oceangoing scientists have long been hampered by a lack of technology. One of MBARI's missions is to develop new technology and make it available to the community," says Tengdin.

CHIPS AHOY

Although he uses the latest in sophisticated computing and network equipment, Tengdin still has to deal with the most basic of problems with those tools–equipment failures. "Once you go out to sea, the equipment is bound to fail," he says.

Tengdin also tosses in that he and the other operations personnel frequently have ocean-specific obstacles. "The network lives in a different, constantly moving environment. To fix components, you have to brace yourself against a wall before you can unscrew anything. And you have to hope that your tools don't slide away as a wave crashes against the boat."

And, of course, problems come in waves. He adds, "Try troubleshooting a network when you're seasick."

Section 6
Portable Computing

The average network user is no longer linked to the company LAN solely through the desktop machine. Laptops, subnotebooks, and Personal Digital Assistants (PDAs) have migrated from novelties owned only by top executives to basic tools of the trade for millions of roving workers.

The current choices in portable network devices allow mobile users to work in a variety of ways, sharing information locally within a building or accessing information via wide area links from the field. Corporate users can free-float within the office and take their laptops to the meeting room, building an ad hoc network that allows them to share information with each other as well as access corporate servers via wireless links.

A couple of innovative transmission methods, Cellular Digital Packet Data (CDPD) and Personal Communications Services (PCS), allow for both local and wide area portable-based networking. "Cellular Hero" and "Personal Space" explain the benefits and drawbacks of using each of these technologies. Other stories in this section look at the hardware and connectivity options available for those with a lust for mobile computing. Is a pocket-sized PDA right for you, or should you stick with a notebook? "Toys of the Trade" should help you decide.

Cellular Hero

CDPD WILL ALLOW YOUR APPLICATION TO SEND DATA OVER THE VOICE CELLULAR NETWORK, ENGENDERING A SLEW OF NEW APPLICATIONS FOR FIXED AND MOBILE USES.

BY PATRICIA SCHNAIDT

If you've ever tried to get a Coke from a vending machine and found that only orange soda is left, a new technology may be right for you. If you've ever tried to use your notebook computer to send a message from a hotel room but found that the telephone didn't have a modular jack, a new technology may be right for you. If you've ever waited for a taxi in the rain, a new technology may be right for you.

Oddly enough, the same technology is potentially viable for these applications and many more. Cellular Digital Packet Data (CDPD) is a nascent technology that will help keep vending machines stocked with comestibles people want, help people send messages from their notebook computers or personal digital assistants, and help them call for cabs more easily.

CDPD works in conjunction with the analog cellular system, allowing users to send data packets in between voice calls. CDPD can use the cell sites, transmission towers, and some radio-frequency (RF) equipment of the existing voice cellular networks. Many of the analog cellular carriers are in the midst of building and testing their CDPD networks, and service should begin to be available by the end of 1994.

COMPETING WITH RAM AND ARDIS

CDPD competes with other wireless packet networks, primarily RAM Mobile Network (New York) and Ardis (Schaumberg, IL), but CDPD has a couple of advantages. For one, CDPD has industry support. It was developed by eight major carriers in North America: Ameritech Cellular (Chicago), Bell Atlantic Mobile Systems (Bedminster, NJ), Contel Cellular (now part of GTE Mobilnet), GTE Mobilnet

(Atlanta), McCaw Cellular Communications (Kirkland, WA), Nynex Mobile Communications (Orangeburg, NY), Pacific Telesis Cellular (San Ramon, CA), and Southwestern Bell Mobile Systems (Dallas). From the start, these carriers have worked together to ensure that their individual CDPD networks will operate as one nationwide network.

Proponents contend that the CDPD network will provide greater bandwidth with lower latency, increased geographic coverage, and lower costs than other wireless packet networks.

CDPD provides a 19.2Kbps wireless link between the user's device and the CDPD base station, although multiple users share that link. RAM Mobile Data supports an 8,000bps data rate. Ardis supports 9,600bps and will be extended to support 19.2Kbps in 1995. Transmissions over Ardis and RAM can suffer from several-second delays, which makes them unsuitable for two-way interactive communications. In contrast, CDPD promises only subsecond delays, although the exact latency will be determined by the design and implementation of each CDPD carrier's network.

When fully built, the CDPD network stands to have the largest geographic coverage, since analog cellular provides nationwide coverage from approximately 10,000 cell sites, all of which could have CDPD equipment added. RAM has about 800 base stations serving about 100 metropolitan areas. Ardis has about 1,300 base stations serving approximately 400 metropolitan areas.

One important side effect of broader geographic coverage is increased power consumption. Transmitting within a small cell site requires less power than transmitting in a large one, since the receiver is closer. Power consumption is vital for battery-powered devices, as mobile devices will be. Ardis and RAM have larger cell sites than analog cellular, and each requires two-watt transmitters. CDPD will require 600 milliwatts, 1.2 watts, or 3.0 watts, depending on the device and application.

Although pricing has yet to be set for CDPD, it is expected to cost less than sending data over RAM, Ardis, or circuit-switched cellular networks.

WHERE CDPD WILL BE USEFUL

Although CDPD proponents engage in one-upmanship with RAM and Ardis over which network has the greatest bandwidth, the stark reality is that CDPD provides a 19.2Kbps wireless link that's shared among all users in a particular cell.

In an era when network users are crying out for more bandwidth on the LAN, an era when users routinely have 14.4Kbps wire-line modems and still complain about the slowness, 19.2Kbps isn't much bandwidth, especially since wireless is a much less-effective transmission medium than wire.

The upshot: CDPD is particularly suited to sending small messages and transactions. CDPD won't be appropriate for sending multimegabyte files; you'll need circuit-switched cellular, which is another burgeoning service, to send large files or faxes. However, if you wish to send short messages, CDPD may be a technology for you.

Although cellular phones quickly became a status symbol with corporate executives, CDPD is likely to be deployed as a top-down effort as companies try to make a key application more efficient. The mission-critical application may be for executives or salespeople on the road dialing in to the corporate network, but more commonly CDPD will be used for delivering packages, managing field service engineers, dispatching taxis, or monitoring the status of vending machines. CDPD is likely to be used first in these vertical-market applications rather than in horizontal applications (see Figure 1).

The early applications are going to be sales-force automation, field service, fleet management, and telemetry, says Charles Parrish, general manager of mobile data at GTE Personal Communications Services. "Over a longer term, you'll see the horizontal applications emerge. These are less structured, where you have the individual worker who wants access to corporate e-mail and databases. In the

long run, this application is going to be the biggest," says Parrish.

McCaw Cellular, the leader in CDPD, outlines four classes of applications that are suitable for CDPD:
• transaction applications,
• location services,
• broadcast applications, and
• multicast applications.

Transaction applications provide limited communication between two users. Transactions typically consist of one message to request an operation and another to acknowledge the success or failure of that operation, although in some cases, multiple messages must be exchanged. CDPD can be used for transaction-oriented applications, such as credit card verification; point-of-sale; taxi, truck, and job dispatch; package pickup, delivery, and tracking; inventory control; emergency dispatch services; message services; and notification of voice mail or e-mail.

CDPD can be used to locate people and devices, particularly if used in conjunction with a global positioning satellite. In this vein, CDPD can be used for location services such as managing fleets of vehicles or recovering stolen vehicles.

Fixed telemetry is an important application. CDPD can be used to deliver the status of vending machines, engines, or vehicles. It can also be used to deliver instrument measurements, such as for reading gas, electric, and water meters or the flow through pumps and valves.

Broadcast and multicast services, along with messaging services, are more likely to be deployed across a variety of industries. In a broadcast service, messages may be delivered to a single cell or group of cells. Since broadcasts are not acknowledged by the receiver, the messages may have to be sent several times to increase the probability of reception. General information, such as news, weather advisories, traffic advisories, movie guides, television guides, and restaurant guides, can be delivered to mobile users.

Both broadcast and multicast services are one-way, unacknowledged messages, except multicast messages are sent to a specific group. Multicasts are useful for information services and private corporate bulletins.

HOW CDPD WORKS

CDPD is deployed alongside the existing analog cellular system, which makes it less expensive for the cellular

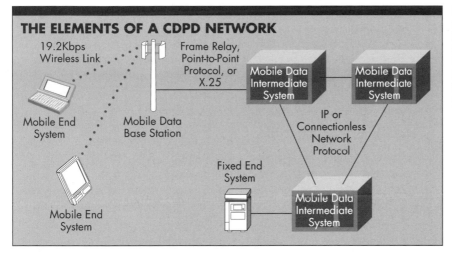

THE ELEMENTS OF A CDPD NETWORK

19.2Kbps Wireless Link

Frame Relay, Point-to-Point Protocol, or X.25

Mobile Data Intermediate System

Mobile Data Intermediate System

Mobile End System

Mobile Data Base Station

IP or Connectionless Network Protocol

Fixed End System

Mobile End System

Mobile Data Intermediate System

Figure 1. Corporations are likely to deploy Cellular Digital Packet Data (CDPD) as part of their business reengineering process. In the short term, CDPD is likely to be used in vertical-market applications, but over the long term, CDPD is likely to be a key compnent in horizontal applications.

carriers to build than a system that carries only data. How are data packets sent along with voice calls? It's all in the architecture.

CDPD runs in conjunction with any cellular system that's Analog MultiPoint Service (AMPS) or AMPS-compatible, which is the predominately installed analog cellular system in the United States. The analog cellular system has additional bandwidth which allows it to support data and voice calls.

In analog cellular, the channel must remain idle for a set period between each voice call. CDPD uses channel hopping to move data packets through these interstices across different frequencies. Voice calls take precedence over data, so cellular phone users shouldn't experience any delays. Since data is not a time-sensitive service as is voice, data can be packetized and reassembled at the receiving end.

The eight originators of the CDPD specification intended to create a system that could be deployed rapidly, economically, and with technology that was generally available in the marketplace. It had several other objectives, including:
- compatibility with existing data networks;
- support for multiple protocols;
- minimal impact on end systems, so existing applications operate without change;
- interoperability between service providers, without compromising the service provider's ability to differentiate its offering based on features and service;

- subscriber roaming between serving areas;
- protection against casual eavesdropping; and
- protection against fraudulent use of the CDPD network.

The CDPD Group released version 1.0 of its specification in July 1993. It included definitions for the necessary components and communications protocols to support its outlined objectives. Figure 2 shows the components of a CDPD network.

The *mobile-end system* (M-ES) is the subscriber's device. As the physical location of the user with an M-ES changes, the M-ES remains in continuous contact with the CDPD network. Because the CDPD Group's intent was to work with existing applications, CDPD does not require any changes to protocols above the OSI Network layer. IP and OSI's Connectionless Network Protocol (CLNP) are currently supported. Although OSI protocols are not popular in the United States, the CDPD system uses OSI messaging, directory service, and network management protocols for network management. Also, support for OSI is essential for building CDPD networks in Europe and the Pacific Rim.

The M-ESs communicate with the *mobile-data base system* (MDBS) over a 19.2Kbps wireless link. The MDBS provides the link between the cellular radio and the wired CDPD network. From the MDBS, data is transported over the CDPD carrier's wired network to the destination's MDBS, and then to a fixed-end system, such as a file server, a mobile-end system, or another user.

Mobile-data intermediate systems (MD-ISs), or routers,

are responsible for the transportation. Internally, the carriers use frame relay, T-1, or X.25 networks to carry the traffic.

All M-ESs in the same sector of a cell use the same channel. Access to this shared frequency is governed by a protocol called *Digital Sense Multiple Access* (DSMA). Unlike Collision Sense Multiple Access (CSMA), which allows Ethernet stations to act as peers to gain access to the cable, in DSMA the MDBS referees the M-ES's access to the bandwidth. Otherwise, DSMA's operation is similar to CSMA's.

How many users can share this 19.2Kbps wireless link? "It depends on how the application is architected and what traffic it sends or receives," says Rob Mechaley, senior vice president of McCaw Communications and general manager of the company's Wireless Data Division.

GTE's Parrish says, "Based on our analysis, a cell will support hundreds of users. In a market like San Francisco, you literally have hundreds of cells. The bottom line, even with single data stream per cell, is that we have the capacity to absorb the entire market in the early years."

As corporations buy and use CDPD service, if a 19.2Kbps wireless link becomes heavily loaded, the carrier can subdivide the cell, making additional transmission frequencies available and effectively doubling the number of users it can support.

ROAM AS FREE AS THE DATA

The users see and use the M-ESs; the MDBSs and MD-ISs are transparent to them. The three components play a critical role in allowing the user to roam from one cell to another even amid a data transmission.

Each M-ES has a permanent address that identifies its home router or MD-IS. When a user travels from cell to cell, the M-ES identifies itself to the new serving MD-IS. The serving MD-IS registers the user, authenticates the user's identity, and verifies the user's access rights and billing status. A subscriber device must register with the serving MD-IS every time it is powered on or it moves to a new serving MD-IS.

Data sent to an M-ES is always sent through the subscriber's home MD-IS, since the home MD-IS maintains a database of location information so it can always discover in real time where its M-ESs are located. Sending data through the home router ensures that data can reach a subscriber no matter where he or she is located, even if the subscriber is mobile.

Users can roam from one carrier's network to another while maintaining the connection. Much of the handoff is procedural. When moving from one carrier's region to another's area, the second carrier will ask the first carrier if the user has access rights. If so, the user is transferred. The user's identity, the type of service, and the rates are not visible to the second carrier, thereby creating a service that's beneficial for the user without the carrier having to expose competitive information.

Even the billing procedures were designed for intercarrier service. "We built the accounting functions into the stack so the accounting records are generated automatically and forwarded automatically to the right carrier," says Mechaley.

Anyone who's eavesdropped on a cellular phone knows security and privacy are major faults with analog cellular. The CDPD specification calls for stringent user-authentication procedures and encrypts data. For authentication, CDPD uses RSA Data Security's (Redwood City, CA) electronic-key exchange. For encryption, CDPD employs RSA's RC4 symmetric string cipher encoding. Both schemes are highly regarded for verifying users' identities and preventing casual eavesdropping.

LOOK, A CDPD APPLICATION

CDPD carriers contend that existing applications can run over the CDPD network with little or no modification. In November 1993, McCaw demonstrated its CDPD service in Las Vegas by running American Airlines' Sabre reservation system. "The American Airlines' reservations person said she thought it was just a little bit faster than the system she usually uses," says Mechaley.

While applications will probably run over CDPD with little or no modification to the Transport layer, the Application layer may need more changes. "Making an application wireless requires more than just hooking up an adapter and sending it out over the airwaves," says Glenn Kaufman, business development manager of Lotus Development's Mobile Computing Group (Cambridge, MA). Lotus has a version of cc:Mail for RAM and is working with McCaw to ready its mobile applications for CDPD service.

The wireless environment is different than wired. Applications may time out because of the network's low

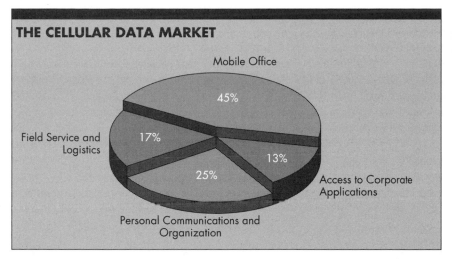

THE CELLULAR DATA MARKET

Mobile Office

45%

Field Service and Logistics

17%

13%

25%

Access to Corporate Applications

Personal Communications and Organization

Figure 2. From the 19.2kbps wireless link, a mobile-data base station receives the data transmission and forwards it to the Cellular Digital Packet Data (CDPD) carrier's wired network. Mobile-data intermediate systems then route the packets to their destinations, which could be other mobile-end systems or fixed-end systems.

bandwidth and high and variable latency, unless the protocol's timers are se carefully. The actual latency will depend on where the sending station is located in relation to the receiving station. If there are 10 routers between the two devices, the latency will be greater than if there are two.

"For the past couple of years, we've spent so much time talking about ATM and other high-speed networking technologies. Bandwidth is certainly not free when it comes to wireless," says John Reidy, director of new business development at Retix (Santa Monica, CA). Retix is providing its RX 7000 MD-IS routers to McCaw and PacTel Cellular for their CDPD networks.

Some applications can be changed with relatively little effort; some will require a greater undertaking. "There are existing applications that can be easily modified. 'Easily' means four or five people can work for a few months," says Andy Papademetriou, business manager for wireless data products at Motorola (Schaumberg, IL). "The excitement will be in '95 when many more people will see the light of what wireless can do. New applications will be invented."

Applications, whether modified or brand new, need to understand how to operate in a world of precious bandwidth. Existing applications, particularly messaging, will be optimized for wireless. Using filters to select what information users wish to receive on the road is an important first step. Agent software, such as General Magic's (Mountain View, CA) TeleScript, will enable software to act on the user's behalf.

"The goal is to reduce the amount of information over a narrow pipeline. We are facing these challenges right now," says Kaufman. How do those applications have to change? Kaufman won't say exactly, but he comments, "The Application-layer protocol has to be designed so that it's not chatty. Over a LAN, a protocol sends data, gets a response, sends data, gets a response. You can't do that over a wireless network."

Client-server applications will tend to be more suitable for CDPD. The more data that has to be transmitted between the client and server, the slower the response time.

"It's hard to express how useful wireless is until you're in the middle of a meeting," says Kaufman. "You can't pull out a cellular telephone because it's considered rude, so you open up your HP 100LX and compose the message, 'The meeting is running late. Meet me at the restaurant.'"

FOLLOWING PROTOCOL

The CDPD network currently supports IP and CLNP as transport protocols, although others can be added. Since CLNP is not widely supported in applications, IP is the key protocol for corporate applications. If you are not using an IP application, CDPD also supports the AT modem command set.

Novell's IPX is not supported. IPX's origin as a LAN protocol becomes obvious in a wired WAN; it's doubly clear in a wireless WAN. One twist that may help is Novell's IPX WAN, which reduces the broadcast burst. "IPX Wide Area would work and could be instantiated very easily on a CDPD network. The question is whether it's worth the effort," says McCaw's Mechaley. "It looks to me like Novell is moving toward supporting IP as the wide-area protocol as opposed to native IPX." If you have a Macintosh-based application, get familiar with MacIP. AppleTalk protocols are particularly unsuitable for wireless networks.

CLNP may play a large role in vertical-market applications. IP is running out of addressing space. "In parcel services or taxi dispatching, thousands of devices have to be accommodated. The kind of application that says 'I need six cases of Coke, two cases of Pepsi, and a case of a ginger ale' is machine-readable, and the machine doesn't have any embedded bigotry as to what the correct protocol should be," say Retix's Reidy.

CDPD FOR REAL

CDPD is in its earliest stages. In January 1994, aggressive carriers were building their networks in limited geographic areas. The number of CDPD users can be counted on one hand, and you'd be hard-pressed to find a paying customer. Interoperability testing among the different CDPD carriers hasn't begun–not enough carriers have built their networks to warrant testing until later this year. Pricing hasn't been set, and CDPD carriers mostly negotiate a custom contract.

"The third quarter to fourth quarter is more likely to be when CDPD starts forming a picture," says Jim Wilson, Southwestern Bell Mobile Systems' director of network development. "It's like when they take the prebirth pictures of babies. Everyone 'oohs' and 'aahs' over them, but all I ever see is a blur. I see the blur with CDPD, and I want to see it more crisply."

McCaw is the most aggressive CDPD carrier, and it deployed its AirData CDPD networks, or at least parts of them, in New York, Dallas, Miami, Seattle, San Francisco, and Las Vegas at the end of February, 1994.

Bell Atlantic Mobile Systems is also pushing CDPD. In January 1994, it tested 10 cell sites in Baltimore, and it expects to offer the service commercially in April, according to Russ Brankley, product manager. It was also installing nine cell sites in Pittsburgh in January. "By the end of the year, we'll have CDPD in all of our markets in 15 states, which range from Massachusetts to the Carolinas, although not contiguous, and in parts of Arizona, New Mexico, and in El Paso, Texas," says Brankley.

At the end of January 1994, PacTel Cellular was ready to go into beta testing with its San Francisco CDPD network, which it built with McCaw. A beta test for its own network in San Diego was scheduled on the heels of the San Francisco test. "We're committed to begin deployment immediately," says Susan Rotella, director of marketing. "From San Diego, we'll roll into other markets: Atlanta, Sacramento [CA], and Los Angeles."

GTE, too, was building its networks in San Francisco and in Houston in January. "We're still in the network test process. We're not in field trial applications yet. During the winter and into the spring, we'll move from the testing of technology to the testing of applications," says Parrish.

Nynex Mobile Communications conducted two CDPD trials. "We haven't committed to a commercial deployment. We're looking at mid-'94. We're looking to get CDPD out as early as we can," says Jim Dukay, director of wireless data.

Of the members of the CDPD consortium, Southwestern Bell is the most conservative. "We won't see a substantial volume of subscriber units or applications before the third quarter. We need to be in a position in early '95 to turn up our CDPD networks. That time frame will be behind the other guys, but it's hard to gauge what we lose or give up. It's not much," says Wilson.

Southwestern Bell ran trials of digital cellular service but decided not to be a CDPD front-runner. "We've decided to let the market drive our technology. Our customers will tell us when it's time [to enter the market]. Everyone says CDPD is neat, but I'm not getting my door knocked down by people saying I want it and here's how much I'm willing to spend," Wilson continues.

Pricing is foggy, and the carriers uniformly say their offerings will be "cost-effective." Although GTE hasn't announced pricing, Parrish says, "What we're doing and what I think you'll see throughout the industry is that we're looking at a packet-oriented pricing structure rather than a distance-sensitive or time-oriented structure. The price structures will be developed with basic monthly amounts that look like your application, and perhaps the meter only runs after a large amount of traffic."

The real test of CDPD is yet to come: Users, whether vending machines or executives on the road, will determine its merits. Whether CDPD becomes a cellular hero or a celluloid flash can only be divined in 1995.

POWER, EMISSIONS, SIZE, AND HEAT
CDPD in the Palm of Your Hand

Once the carriers offer commercial Cellular Digital Packet Data (CDPD) service, subscribers will need a way to access it. CDPD is designed to work with the AT command set used by Hayes-compatible modems, although using IP or Connectionless Network Protocol applications will be much more efficient.

Issues of the CDPD devices' power consumption, radio-frequency (RF) emissions, size, and heat dissipation will arise, although they will be more pointed in mobile applications than in fixed telemetry applications. A vending machine doesn't move and doesn't complain about the weight of a CDPD modem; executives, salespeople, field service personnel, and package-delivery people do.

"You can't put RF inside of a device that wasn't designed to understand how it works. Microprocessors generate a tremendous amount of RF noise, so the receiver section of your device will be overwhelmed by what it's hearing from the microprocessor. There may not be a way to effectively shield the receiver. So you have a conundrum, which generally says put stuff outside," says Rob Mechaley, general manager of McCaw Cellular's Wireless Data Division (Kirkland, WA). He also points out that the RF transmitters will interfere with the LCD screen.

Cincinnati Microwave designed the MC-Dart 100 CDPD modem for fixed and mobile telemetry. "It's rea-sonably small, at 6.3 inches by 3.4 inches by one inch," says Greg Blair, vice president of Cincinnati Microwave'sOEM Division. One three-watt, half-duplex radio costs $495. Cincinnati Microwave plans to bring out the MC-Dart 200 for mobile applications by year-end. This modem will be full-duplex, with a 600-milliwatt transmit power (which is the voltage cellular phones use) and will include circuswitched cellular for fax and large file transfers.

Blair says, "We don't get to the PCMCIA form factor until version 3, and that's Extended PCMCIA. There are some significant technical challenges to make a Type 2 or Extended Type 2. When you put the radio inside, it's a challenge."

Power consumption is another issue for the CDPD user on the go. CDPD modems can use 600-milliwatt to three-watt batteries. The denser the cells in a CDPD carrier's network, the less power is required to transmit. Look for CDPD modems that "go to sleep" when not transmitting. CDPD modems will require external batteries over the near term. Down the road, notebooks and PDAs will understand that they contain a CDPD modem, and the power-management functions will be integrated.

Heat dissipation out of the transmitter must be tackled. "The smaller the device, the greater the heat. When you try to transmit at 600 milliwatts, heat will be a problem," says Blair The notebook and PDA manufacturers will have to work with the makers of CDPD subscriber equipment to resolve these issues.

Personal Space

WITH STANDARDS ON THE HORIZON AND THE HOPE OF A NEW UNLICENSED PERSONAL COMMUNICATIONS SERVICES BAND, WIRELESS NETWORKS MAY FINALLY BE UNLEASHED.

BY MELANIE McMULLEN

Radio networks of all varieties suffer from an ongoing wave of problems. For example, anyone who has ever tuned in to late-night AM radio has experienced the frequent frustration of frequency fade-outs. Halfway through a commercial-free broadcast of Meat Loaf Live, in chimes some station operating in turbo-transmission mode from Omaha that overpowers the Loaf with some rappin' 2 Live Crew.

Unfortunately, this type of transmission crowding isn't confined to your AM/FM radio dial. The electromagnetic spectrum is currently the carrier of millions of disparate wireless services. And the radio portion of the spectrum, a scarce and finite resource, has a seemingly infinite number of users and potential users. This creates one basic problem–airwave overpopulation.

Some recent contributors to this ongoing frequency crowding include a slew of companies sprinkling the market with spread spectrum-based networking devices. While years ago the number of vendors in the market was negligible, the laundry list of wireless radio network companies now includes AT&T's Global Information Solutions (owners of NCR, Dayton, OH), Motorola's Wireless Data Group (Schaumburg, IL), Windata (Northboro, MA), Proxim (Mountain View, CA), Digital Equipment Corp. (DEC, Littleton, MA), Symbol Technologies (Bohemia, NY), Metricom (Los Gatos, CA), and Solectek (San Diego), to name a few.

The big guns of hardware, such as IBM, Apple Computer, and Compaq (Houston), are also tentatively slated to release radio-based products sometime in 1994. The newcomer list from last year alone contains several formidable forces of networking: Xircom (Calabasas, CA), National Semiconductor (Santa Clara, CA), Digital Ocean (Overland Park, KS), Aerocomm (Lenexa, KS), and Aironet Wireless Communications (Akron, OH), a merger of Telesystems, Telxon Radio Frequency Group, and Software Engineering.

While lack of new competition and technology is no longer an impediment to the wireless network market, growth has ushered in a new set of obstacles. Two problems currently cloud the future of wireless networking: an absence of frequency dedicated specifically to wireless data communications and a lack of any IEEE standards.

But don't give up on this market, not yet at least. Help is on the way in both areas, with airwave relief coming in the form of a new spectrum allotment for wireless Personal Communications Services (PCS) and standards help coming via the IEEE 802.11, which promises to offer up a preliminary draft of its first wireless standard by November 1994.

CROWDS AND CRIMPS

To understand why a dedicated frequency is needed for wireless data networks, take a look at the crimps in the shared areas of transmission. Debates are raging as to which currently available frequency band can provide optimum transmission for spread spectrum-based networking. Many of the first devices on the market were designed to work in the extremely crowded 902MHz to 928MHz unlicensed Industrial, Scientific, and Medical (ISM) band. In 1993, the trend shifted up, with many companies starting to eke out their space in the other two high-range ISM bands, the 2.400GHz to 2.4835GHz and the 5.850GHz to 5.725GHz bands (see figure).

Note that the ISM bands were originally earmarked in

1985 for use by factory radio devices, such as the machine that seals the plastic over a TV dinner. These bands are now used for cruise missile testing, baby monitors, cordless phones, and car tracking devices, as well as wireless networking. "ISM is the kitchen sink of the radio spectrum," says Bennett Kobb, a wireless communications consultant based in Arlington, VA. "And over a period of time, the bands have simply become too crowded."

And a crowd, whether sharing space in the bleachers at a soccer match or in the airwaves of a network spectrum, can wreak havoc. "An immense amount of redundancy and error correction is needed to operate in a crowded band," says Bob Rosenbaum, vice president of product marketing at Windata.

The two higher microwave ISM bands, which are a little less crowded than the 902MHz space, do offer network users less interference. But they come complete with other drawbacks. "The higher the frequency, the more the components cost. Making components for the 2.4GHz band is the upper limit of cost that the market can bear," Rosenbaum adds.

SOMEONE'S IN THE KITCHEN

The higher microwave bands also have inherent sharing problems; other devices in that air space are cooking up all sorts of trouble for wireless networks. Wireless networks operating in that frequency could likely suffer a performance burn if located near the kitchen, or more specifically, near a microwave oven. Essentially, the network packet has to share the air with the bursty energy needed to heat up a coworker's Lean Cuisine.

While nobody is sure of the amount of interference a microwave oven could cause to a wireless office network, the effects have been noted in early demonstrations. Jeff Alholm, the president of Digital Ocean, makers of the Macintosh-based Grouper, tells of such an incident at a recent IEEE 802.11 meeting. During a demonstration of a 2.4GHz product, he explains, "A funny thing happened around noon. The radio started working significantly worse." He says the best explanation anybody could come up with was that the building had several microwaves humming along in the kitchen.

In addition to oven-based interference, the microwave bands have other drawbacks–power and performance. Power requirements in these two areas are more stringent,

which can put a strain on portable devices. Throughput, as well as distance, in the 2.4GHz band is also questionable. "You have limited coverage in the 2.4 band," explains Cees Links, director of product marketing for NCR's Wireless Communications and Networking division in Utrecht, the Netherlands. "You get the coverage of a telephone booth in that band."

Despite these drawbacks, NCR is developing a version of its WaveLAN product that will operate in the 2.4GHz band. Why? Here's the upside to microwave LANs. The 2.4GHz band affords a worldwide opportunity. This frequency is about to become available internationally, specifically in most of Europe and in Japan. The European Telecommunication Standards Institute (ETSI) will vote in March to allocate a 2.4GHz band as well as a high-performance band in the 5.2GHz range. Radio products designed for that space can operate–and be sold into–an international market.

"Demand in the international market for wireless networks is as strong or stronger than in the United States," says Links. He adds that offices in countries such as India and China are not wired during construction as most U.S. buildings are, making wireless networks a viable and even affordable option.

SEND HELP

While the crowded ISM bands are currently the only unlicensed bands available for data networking, help is coming–maybe. The Federal Communications Commission (FCC) is the master of the spectrum domain, deciding through a lengthy petition process who can legally use which parts of the spectrum, including both the licensed and unlicensed portions. Several years ago, the FCC entered a proposal for rulemaking to reallocate spectrum in the 1.85GHz to 2.2GHz range for use by what the government dubbed "emerging technologies."

These technologies have now emerged under the popular name of PCS. The technologies and devices vying for spectrum space in the PCS area will run the gamut from pagers, phones, Personal Digital Assistants (PDAs), and a variety of pocket-size, low-power communications devices. Devices in the PCS area will operate at a more intelligent level than those in the ISM band, with the ability to sense each other's presence and share the frequency more efficiently.

In 1993, the FCC further divided the PCS bands into licensed and unlicensed areas, then had to determine how much to allot for each area. After intense lobbying from Apple and the Wireless Information Networks Forum (WINForum, Washington, D.C.), the Commission earmarked 40MHz for unlicensed use.

Concerning the licensed PCS portions, the FCC divvied up a 120MHz bank of frequencies into seven trading areas consisting of a variety of allotment sizes ranging from 10MHz to 30MHz. These areas will be up for grabs, or rather for sale, as early as June 1994. The government intends to raise $10 billion in revenue from the reallocation of these frequencies, according to Becky Diercks, program manager for wireless research services at Business Research Group (BRG, Newton, MA). While these frequencies can be used for both voice and data, the cellular providers will most likely provide the more profitable voice services first, Diercks adds.

PCS services in the licensed spectrums will operate over a network of base stations and operating areas, called microcells. PCS will function much like the cellular network, allowing users to roam from one cell to the next. However, PCS devices will operate with lower power, meaning the microcells in the network will be smaller and necessarily more numerous within a given area. PCS will use a digital voice transmission, unlike cellular, which uses analog. The strongest competitor to licensed PCS services will be the emerging Cellular Digital Packet Data, or CDPD, network.

THE FREE BAND

While the licensed portion of the PCS spectrum appears to be moving forward, the unlicensed area, which falls in the 1.890GHz to 1.930GHz range, is a hotbed of controversy. The area was originally targeted by companies interested in developing the market for wireless, roving, low-power computing devices, such as PDAs. Specifically, Apple was interested in obtaining the area as part of Sculley-vision–a world of spontaneous networks comprised of millions of nomadic users. While developing the vision was easy enough, the efforts needed to obtain the necessary spectrum were a little more difficult, as Apple quickly discovered.

The first step Apple took in its attempt to accrue spectrum began in 1991 when it organized a lobby group, WINForum, made up of those companies interested in garner-

ing an unlicensed PCS band. While thousands of lobbyists in Washington protect those who have, "Organizing a lobby group for people who don't have something is a formidable task," says Kobb, who was president of WINForum until 1994. "Pulling this group together was as hard as forming a group for people who don't have a driver's license."

As WINForum developed and grew closer to achieving its goals, more companies became interested in this free band, including the powerful–and very wealthy–telecommunications companies such as Northern Telecom (Ottawa, Canada) and AT&T (Basking Ridge, NJ). "The movement for more spectrum for unlicensed use started with the data companies, but then the phone companies got involved. The two factions had tremendous disagreements," explains Kobb. The politically savvy phone companies managed to do what they do best in Washington–exercise clout. "The FCC wasn't as interested in the computer companies with the telephone people breathing down its neck," says Kobb.

Over the past year, the voice forces also began to dominate WINForum itself, and Apple and a handful of other data companies dropped their membership and financial support of the organization. "A lot of cantankerous things have happened at WINForum," says Nancy Bukar, a Washington, D.C., attorney who is serving as project coordinator of the group. "Billions of dollars are at stake, so really everyone is upset."

THE BETTER HALF

All the squabbling between the voice and data factions eventually pushed the FCC into going halvsies with the band. In the fall of 1993, the Commission decided to split unlicensed PCS into two distinct areas: a 20MHz area from 1.900GHz to 1.920GHz dedicated to asynchronous communication, and two 10MHz bands, located at 1.890GHZ to 1.900GHz and 1.920GHz to 1.930GHz, earmarked for isochronous communication, or voice-based networking.

The split, while harmless at first glance, contains a costly loophole. The FCC requires that the manufacturers interested in using these frequencies pay to relocate the incumbents that currently operate in this area of the spectrum. And to make the relocation fair, or rather miserable, for both sides, the FCC split the 40MHz so that each group, voice and data, has one portion that is not heavily laden with incumbents and one portion that is.

"The FCC believes in inequality and unfairness for

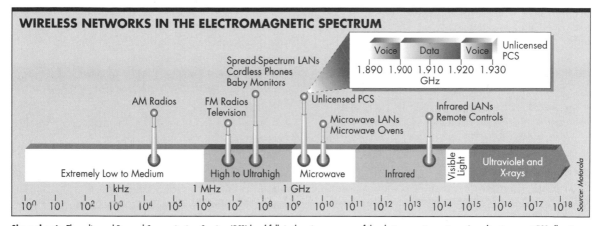

Share the air: The unlicensed Personal Communications Services (PCS) band falls in the microwave area of the electromagnetic spectrum. According to current FCC allocations, a 20MHz data portion of the PCS band will be encased by two 10MHz voice areas.

everybody," says Dave Murashige, director of product marketing and U.S. PCS marketing at Northern Telecom's Richardson, TX, branch.

Keep in mind that moving just one incumbent can be colossally expensive, costing as much as $250 million to move just one pair of transmission towers. And the total number of incumbents in the unlicensed band is somewhere around 100, according to Kobb. The cost of moving incumbents would eventually have to trickle down into the retail price of the products to be used in the PCS area, creating a mark-up that most wireless manufacturers cannot afford to tag on to their already expensive radio portables.

"When the voice guys and the incumbents in the unlicensed band reared their ugly heads, the promises of PCS got really bleak," says Greg Hopkins, chairman of Windata. "Most of the data companies have backed away from it."

Other wireless company leaders interested in the PCS band have also expressed disappointment. "With the cost of relocation borne by the makers of the new products, the notion of moving people out of the band is a big challenge that is too costly and complex," says David King, president and CEO of Proxim. "If a manufacturer has a million users and only sells a $50 product, then this action will kill the market before it starts."

LOBBY TILL YOU DROP

Even though the first promise of a clear, unlicensed PCS band looks dim, hope is not dead. The PCS band would al-low devices to operate at low power levels at a high data rate with little interference, an offer too good to refuse. In addition, the FCC intends to adopt a type of spectrum etiquette, parts of which were developed by WINForum, for this band which would regulate how products can communicate. This move would keep out any ham radio operators or other hobbyists that might produce interference and thereby hinder device throughput and performance.

Apple has already sent several petitions for reconsideration to the FCC. Other computer industry powers, including Compaq and Microsoft, have also sent detailed letters pleading for reconsideration. The Compaq letter dubbed the current allotment of unlicensed PCS "a black hole," saying it would be a complete flop for the computer industry. Microsoft offered the FCC a detailed list of the types of products that could operate in the band–if the frequency situation is remedied.

"The FCC is looking things over and will have to decide what to do," says Kobb. "Reconsiderations can take a year or longer. It will be a political dogfight over who is most persuasive." NCR's Link estimates that moving the incumbents and clearing the way for PCS products in the unlicensed area won't happen until at least 1996.

MOVERS AND SHAKERS

To get the moving process going, the FCC has sanctioned an Unlicensed Transition and Management (UTAM) committee to come up with two proposals: an acceptable financial plan of incumbent relocation and the relocation plan itself that specifies a new location for each incumbent.

The UTAM committee is comprised of officials from Northern Telecom, AT&T, Motorola, and Sony, among others. Northern Telecom's Murashige notes that conspicuously absent from the lineup are any data-only companies. He blames this absence on a lack of political organization among the data ranks. "There is less of a consensus among data people for working with the FCC," he says. "The voice people have been doing this for years."

Windata's Hopkins sums up the battle for bandwidth this way. "Unlicensed PCS, with its high data rates, was once wonderful and altruistic. Then the voice people got greedy, and the incumbents got greedy. Greed is what did us poor LAN guys in."

WIRELESS STANDARDS ALMOST A REALITY
The Real Missing Link

After three years of debating and politicking, the IEEE 802.11 wireless group finally has a focus. If all goes as planned, the committee may have a long-awaited draft of the first wireless network standard by November of 1994, with final approval coming in 1995.

While IEEE standards meetings traditionally are not fast-moving proceedings, 802.11, encumbered by more than 200 members, has been particularly slow to come to a consensus. "When the group first started, our original focus, or lack of focus, was to cover everything that had to do with wireless," says Bob Rosenbaum, vice president of product marketing at Windata (Northboro, MA). "Now we're focused on addressing the portable, mobile marketplace and making sure that laptops and handheld devices can all play together in the same area."

To make the devices play, the group adopted a Media Access Control (MAC) protocol, dubbed the foundation protocol, jointly developed by NCR (Dayton, OH), Symbol Technologies (Bohemia, NY), and Xircom (Calabasas, CA).

The basic access method of the protocol is distributed, based on Carrier Sense Multiple Access (CSMA) with collision avoidance. The protocol can support two types of peer-to-peer wireless LANs: ad hoc LANs and infrastructure LANs interconnected via access points to a wired network. The foundation protocol supports asynchronous data service and time-bounded services.

While the one-size-fits-all MAC foundation is close to being set, the physical layer (PHY) side of the standard will take more work. The 802.11 committee intends to develop PHY standards for three differ-ent methods of wireless transmission: direct sequence, frequency hopping, and infrared.

In direct sequence, signals are spread over a continuous band of frequencies. Each bit of information is replicated many times and transmitted as smaller pieces. The receiver, using a unique code, then reassembles the package into the original bit. Products such as NCR's WaveLAN use this method.

Frequency hopping does what its name implies–it switches signals from one frequency to another. Multiple bits are transmitted on a specific sequence of frequencies, where each frequency is used only for a short duration. Xircom's Netwave uses frequency hopping. Infrared uses infrared light to transfer signals. It is cheaper to implement than the other two radio-based wireless methods. Photonics (San Jose, CA) uses infrared in its Collaborative and Co-operative product lines.

The direct sequence and frequency hopping PHY groups are each looking into developing a dual-mode 1Mbps standard and a 2Mbps standard. The frequency of interest is the 2.4GHz ISM band. The speed issue has led to some heated debates, although most members seem to agree that two levels are necessary. "Having only a slow standard would be like standardizing only Arcnet," says David King, president and CEO of Proxim (Mountain View, CA).

As far as future progress is concerned, the committee members are optimistic. "We still have a few religious issues to get over," says Rick Heller, president and CEO of Aironet Wireless Communications (Akron, OH). "But with a lot of players, everyone eventually has to line up and support something."

Portable Apples: Young and Restless

AT THE BEACH, AT THE OFFICE, OR ON THE PLANE–POWERBOOKS AND PERSONAL DIGITAL ASSISTANTS CREATE A MOBILE LINK TO YOUR NETWORK INFORMATION.

BY MELANIE McMULLEN

He spotted her from across the plane. Sitting a mere two rows ahead, she was the ultimate woman of his dreams. She had flowing blond hair, gorgeous, well-tanned skin, a pearly white smile, and, most importantly, she had the quintessential travel essential–a Macintosh. With her PowerBook 180 perched on her tray-table, he watched in marvel as her mango-tinted fingernails floated gracefully across the keyboard, creating a masterful spreadsheet. She had treated herself with this high-end model of the Power-Book, he thought, splurging for more power, the high-res display, and the math coprocessor. He began to sweat.

Throughout the flight, he dreamed of them spending time together on The Island, fishing, swimming, dancing, spending the evenings talking only of LocalTalk (or did she prefer EtherTalk?) while sharing some fresh, grilled Mahi-Mahi on the beach as the orange Hawaiian sun set over the cresting waves of the horizon.

He couldn't stand it any longer. Only one hour until Honolulu. He really wanted to see her After Dark, and he didn't have much time. For once in his life, he was thankful for Bill Gates–Microsoft Mail could make his dreams come true. He spotted her infrared adapter, flickering like warm embers above her screen. He fired up his own infrared; eager anticipation now had to be transformed into some serious messaging. With his Chooser, he could choose her, and the rest would be history. Maybe.

Out goes the message, direct and to the point: *Hello, gorgeous 17D. This is 19A. Let's share some RAM over some rum. How about it?*

After anxious seconds that lasted for hours, back comes the response. *Drop dead.*

If only getting a date were as simple as impromptu PowerBook networking. Sharing files Mac to Mac is as easy as booting up, which explains why more than 65 percent of all Macs are networked, according to Pieter Hartsook, editor of the *Hartsook Letter*, a Macintosh market-research newsletter and service in Alameda, CA. And mobile Macs, high in functionality but low on storage and processing, are even more likely to want connectivity to the home LAN, dropping in and out of the network like planes at an airport.

While the PC world is quietly shifting from desktop to laptop machines, Apple Computer is forging the path of mobile computing with two separate extensions to the enterprise: the PowerBook and the Personal Digital Assistant (PDA). Both of these road warriors fulfill the vision of computing held by John Sculley, chairman and CEO of Apple, who says simply, "The obstacles of time and place must be overcome."

ANYWHERE, EVERYWHERE

First, the PowerBook. Not yet 3 years old, the Macintosh PowerBook has become one of the top sellers in portable computing. According to International Data Corp. (IDC, Framingham, MA), the worldwide PowerBook installed base topped 550,000 at the end of 1992. Figures from the first half of 1993 reveal a continued PowerBook buying frenzy, with Apple's second-quarter earnings statement showing a 70 percent increase in demand worldwide and a 100 percent increase in the United States.

Demand for the PowerBooks has been so high that parts shortages have restricted Apple's ability to keep up with shipments. "It's nice to know that you're loved," says Bruce Cooper, PowerBook product manager at Apple.

"We've been actively chasing the parts problem." Cooper says that Apple now has larger inventory balances and is currently running 24-hour shifts in manufacturing.

Modern economics dictates that high demand equals high sales. PowerBook sales have generated more than $1 billion in revenue for Apple, which couldn't have come at a better time. Recent price cuts and an industry price war forced Apple into some sacrificial margin cuts on its hardware, dropping the company's net income 18 percent in the second quarter of 1993. Apple is counting on the Newton and its workgroup servers announced in March to boost fourth-quarter sales. In the meantime, the Power-Book will be its cash cow.

"PowerBooks have gone from nowhere to capturing major market share," says analyst Hartsook. He estimates that Apple currently has a 25-percent to 30-percent share of the portable market. And note that the portable market isn't just a niche anymore. Dataquest (San Jose, CA) estimates that, at the end of 1992, more than 1.6 million notebooks were in use in the United States. Currently, 15 percent of all computers sold are portables, and Dataquest predicts that number will grow to 30 percent by 1995.

"Replacement machines will be mobile computers," says Jeff Leopold, director of integrated computing at the Yankee Group, a market-research firm based in Boston. "Unless desktop computers become dirt cheap, buyers will have no good reason to buy anything other than a portable."

But when comparing portables, why buy an Apple? Although buyers use a variety of criteria when purchasing portable computers, a few crucial elements can sway the decision. Leopold says the price of the PowerBook has entered into the attractive "buy me" zone. The low-end PowerBook 145, for example, sells for $2,149, much more attractive than Apple's first portables, which sold for $5,000 and, according to Leopold, were just too heavy. "The weight, the high-quality screen, and the price-performance ratio has brought Apple success in the mobile market," he adds.

Hartsook says the PowerBook lure is its sleek design and inherent networking capabilities. He attributes Apple's success to its understanding of the needs of the mobile user in all areas, ranging from such unrelated features as remote network access to trackball placement. "Apple offers intelligent human engineering better than anyone else around, " says Hartsook. "Other laptop makers just

don't get it. They're unclear on the concepts of mobile computing."

MOBILE MANIACS

To be clear on the concepts, a vendor must first understand the mobile workforce and the computing needs of the roving users. The actual numbers of the mobile mob are staggering. The Yankee Group estimates that 25 million Americans work outside their offices. Another 13 million workers have jobs that require them to travel at least 20 percent of the time. And the last group, a large mass whose numbers simply can't be counted, are those corridor crawlers who have office-wandering syndrome, going from meeting to meeting or floor to floor, and could greatly benefit from impromptu networks.

These workers don't want to choose between being connected or mobile–they simply want to be both, and subsequently they use a variety of methods to maintain contact. According to Forrester Research, a Cambridge, MA-based market-research firm, mobile users access the LAN on average four times a week. In the Apple sphere, long-distance connectivity methods currently available include PowerBook modems that use either regular analog phone lines or cellular links, which require you to have a cellular-phone account.

On the receiving end, these users can make contact either by remote control of a device on the LAN or by a client-server connection in which the mobile user dials in to a router or communications server and becomes a peer on the network.

And, of course, Apple assists you with the connection. It offers a PowerBook Express Modem for $319 that includes fax capabilities. The Apple modem can transfer data at 14.4Kbps (or 57.6Kbps with data compression). This modem, combined with AppleTalk Remote Access, creates a relatively painless way to phone home.

LOCAL MOTION

Local network-connectivity options for the PowerBook vary depending on the model. For the person who can't decide between a desktop and a laptop, Apple offers its dynamic duo, the Macintosh Duo Dock and Duo MiniDock models that can provide a desktop home for the PowerBook Duo. The dock portion provides a full-fledged desktop machine, with a full-size screen, keyboard, and two

NuBus slots. The pop-out PowerBook Duo sidekick measures a mere 1.5 inches thick and weighs in at 4 pounds.

The freestanding PowerBook models include two serial ports for LocalTalk networking and a speedier SCSI port that can facilitate multiple devices, including an Ethernet connection, which doesn't come standard on the Power-Book. While a serial connection offers a maximum data-transfer rate of 57.6Kbps, SCSI emulation can be much faster. Companies such as Farallon Computing (Alameda, CA), Compatible Systems (Boulder, CO), and Asanté Technologies (San Jose, CA) all recently announced products that connect PowerBooks via a SCSI port to an Ethernet network.

"Connecting PowerBooks to Ethernet has become a problem," explains Wilson Wong, president and CEO of Asantœe. "We wanted to come up with something the size of a pack of cigarettes that the user could carry around." Shipping in March, Asanté's Virginia Slim is the 6-ounce Mini EN/SC, which can link the PowerBook via the SCSI port to thin Ethernet and 10BaseT. It sells for $459. Wong says the PowerBook's built-in LocalTalk support is no longer enough. "The line between PCs and Apples is getting fuzzy. Mobile users just want the best possible machine, and then they have to integrate it with mixed networks on Ethernet," he says. "Having only LocalTalk would freeze you out."

In addition to SCSI connections, Farallon offers a more inexpensive, but slower, method of reaching Ethernet from a PowerBook. Using Farallon's PowerPath, the mobile computer is hooked up via LocalTalk to the host Ethernet Mac. Working much like a router, PowerPath uses Farallon's Forward Transfer Algorithm, making PowerBooks appear as a node on the primary LAN. PowerPath, which includes the necessary software, PhoneNet StarConnectors, and cable, costs $149.

In contrast to Asanté, Farallon is a LocalTalk believer. "LocalTalk is a simpler and much cheaper solution," says Larry Jones, product manager for networking at Farallon. "LocalTalk is easier to install, and it's not constrained by the distance requirements of 10BaseT."

He predicts that Apple's PDAs, which will have a LocalTalk connection, will be a boost for products such as PowerPath that can connect these devices to the network. "LocalTalk is dirt cheap for Apple to put into the Newton. It makes sense to go that route."

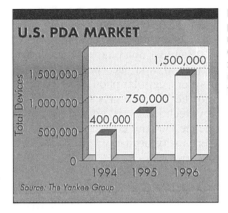

Figure 1. Analysts predict the PDA market will take off, going from zero to 1.5 million units in the next three years.

BABY SLOT

A final connectivity remedy, coming from the Power-Book's cohorts on the PC side, will be the Personal Computer Memory Card International Association (PCMCIA) slot. This tiny form factor will most likely first be seen in the Newton, with an eventual migration to the PowerBook.

"PCMCIA is a good multipurpose slot that addresses the customer issue of adding a modem, expansion, and a network link" to a PowerBook, says Apple's Cooper. Apple hasn't announced a specific time frame for development of PCMCIA slots.

According to other vendors, Apple was initially hesitant to jump on the PCMCIA bandwagon because of a few technical problems. "PCMCIA was designed around an Intel processor, leaving it with a few software problems for the Apple environment," explains Farallon's Jones. "PCMCIA is just a different beast for the Macintosh." Jones says that despite these problems, "PCMCIA is still an obvious solution."

Even though Apple hasn't publicly disclosed its PCMCIA path, Asanté is already developing PCMCIA cards for the Mac. "PCMCIA is where everyone is headed," says Wong. "Apple will have to support it. PCMCIA is becoming a significant bus standard, more important than the AT bus. PCMCIA is becoming almost universal." He points out that PCMCIA cards could fit into a desktop Mac, Power-Book, or Newton, making the cards the form factor of choice for the buyer.

DON'T FENCE ME IN

Note one important contradiction with all these cable-based network options: You just took a mobile device and hooked a wire to it. That's a mobility don't. Apple and others are not sitting on their hands in this area, either. Apple is interested in two very different forms of wireless transmission: spread-spectrum radio transmission and infrared. Each offers specific benefits to the user.

"Wireless networking is hot and exciting," says Apple's Cooper. "But integrating it into a PowerBook requires the cooperation of software, hardware, and communications companies. This is no slam dunk."

Apple has already begun passing the ball in the spread-spectrum game. In 1991, Apple petitioned the FCC to allocate a 40MHz frequency band to an area it dubbed Data Personal Communications Services (Data-PCS), targeting this area for unlicensed use by buyers of its PDAs and other wireless devices. Apple then helped form a lobby group, dubbed Wireless Information Networks Forum (WINForum), based in Washington, D.C., to help politick its wishes to fruition. In response to Apple's request, a nonenthusiastic FCC divvied out a small 20MHz slice of bandwidth, that is still currently in the petition stage, to an area it dubbed User-PCS.

WINForum is still pushing for more bandwidth. "In the world of mobile computing and portable devices, adequate bandwidth in the user premises is vital," says Benn Kobb, executive director of WINForum. He explains that Apple and others need the new band, with adequate bandwidth, to allow the devices to transmit at low power without having to "shout" over interference–such as baby monitors, cruise missiles, and antitheft devices–that currently transmit in the unlicensed band.

The new PDAs will be "highly intelligent devices that can detect each other's presence," says Kobb. WINForum is coming up with a set of rules, or spectrum etiquette, that would outline to vendors a method in which one device would not overpower another device sharing the spectrum. Essentially, the device would monitor the frequency before transmitting and not lock out other devices.

Users could also realize other benefits in this bandwidth. Apple's requested space, in the 1910MHz to 1930MHz range, is also adjacent to carrier-based frequencies, which would allow for synergy and interaction between licensed and unlicensed devices, facilitating long-distance messaging and other services.

And keep in mind that Apple and Motorola have multiple development agreements, so jumping from the unli-

censed user band with the PDA to a carrier-based messaging band could be more than a remote possibility.

The FCC could reach a bandwidth decision as early as this summer, according to Kobb. The Clinton/ Gore pro-technology administration has "pushed the accelerator even more," says Kobb. WINForum has to battle powerful government and railroad lobbies fighting to keep Apple and others from legally stealing their bandwidth.

But the wireless industry is optimistic about Apple's politicking power. "Apple will be successful in acquiring bandwidth," says David Frankland, vice president of Digital Ocean (Overland Park, KS). "Look who was sitting next to Hillary Clinton on inauguration day." (That would be John Sculley, for those who are television impaired). "The entire bandwidth will probably be redistributed."

IN THE SWIM

Digital Ocean does have a vested interest in this redistribution. It is one among a school of new wireless third-party products for the PowerBook .Among those are Photonics' (San Jose, CA) Collaborative Mac infrared adapters. Another is, Digital Ocean Grouper, a spread-spectrum product designed specifically for the PowerBook.

Photonics, owned 17 percent by Apple, will have a Collaborative Mac adapter that is a user-installed infrared device for Mac desktops and PowerBooks. It will allow users to create an instant network, in an office, classroom, or plane.

PowerBook users who feel fenced in by infrared's inability to penetrate walls might prefer to network with radio devices, such as the Grouper. Then they could network without having to look at one another, which is a coup in some office environments.

The Grouper, with a wedge-shaped design, can be attached to any PowerBook model or be used freestanding with desktop Macs. The Grouper provides wireless network access within a 250-foot radius in an average office. Groupers network by joining a group called–you guessed it–a "school," which includes up to 15 Groupers. Groupers also can connect directly to wired LocalTalk networks, with one centrally located Grouper in each school directly attached to the network and acting as a hub.

IT KEEPS GOING, AND GOING . . .

Now that the Grouper is shipping, Frankland says, Dig-

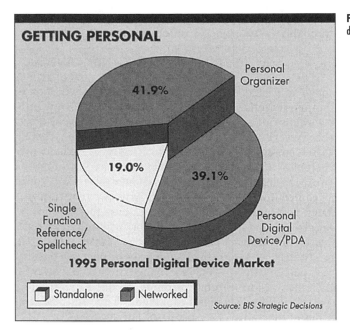

GETTING PERSONAL

Personal Organizer — 41.9%

19.0% — Single Function Reference/Spellcheck

39.1% — Personal Digital Device/PDA

1995 Personal Digital Device Market

☐ Standalone ▣ Networked

Source: BIS Strategic Decisions

Figure 2. Although designed strictly for mobility, most personal digital devices will have built-in network-connectivity options.

ital Ocean will look to Apple for possible technology integration. "Apple doesn't have the not-invented-here syndrome anymore," he says. Specifically, Frankland says the Grouper's low power consumption may be most interesting to Apple. The Grouper, with its patented power technology, lessens the power required to network using chatty AppleTalk, which can swiftly drain an already quick-to-die portable battery. "We use one-sixtieth the power of other wireless products out there," says Frankland. "This will be one of the secrets to our success."

Power is a critical problem among all laptops, and PowerBooks are no exception. Forrester Research estimates that if wireless connections drain the portable battery more than 25 percent, they won't be feasible.

"You just don't have a big enough battery if you incorporate wireless adapters, cellular phones, and pagers into the laptop," says Cooper. "Battery technology is now a rampant science, but the expectation from the user is way beyond what science can now provide."

PC MUTANTS

Science (and Apple) in 1993 provided a new device, though, that could exceed user expectations–PDAs. These small, hand-held devices, sitting somewhere in the computing food chain between calculators and laptops, are called everything from PC mutants by analysts to network appliances, organizers, personal information managers, and miniature mobile offices. They could provide messaging, sports scores, stock reports, weather, traffic, and even standard office functions, such as e-mail, faxing, and enterprise connectivity. As Jay Leno quipped, be careful when you put one in your pocket–the paper cutter could slice your finger when you try to get it out.

While PDAs fit into the bevy of products that no one knew they needed until they had one (for example, portable CD players), analysts already foresee a growing market (see Figure 1). BIS Strategic Decisions (Norwell, MA) says the personal digital-device market will hit $396.9 million by 1995, with 81 percent of them networked (see Figure 2).

Apple's first PDA, the Newton, is scheduled for shipment in the summer of 1993 and will be marketed toward individual business users, according to the company. Priced under $1,000, the Newton will run on its own operating-system software and use pen technology, both print and cursive, along with a keypad limited to symbols and icons. The Newton is based on a RISC processor from Advanced RISC Machines Ltd, a British firm.

Apple describes the Newton as the third layer of a network, sort of a detachable extension for the road. "On a client-server network, this is a client to your desktop client," says Larry Tesler, vice president of development in Apple's Personal Interactive Electronics (PIE) division.

He says the Newton will have built-in intelligence that "completes your thought." For example, if you note in the Newton that you have a lunch date with mom on Thursday, you won't have to exit your current program and enter your calendar; your Newton will do it for you.

Tesler says the Newton will initially use paging technology for wide-area communications. On the local front, it will have a few LAN-connect options. Apple confirms it will have network connectivity via AppleTalk on first shipment, but details have not been disclosed. "You can assume the Newton will have a serial port with a LocalTalk connection," says analyst Hartsook. He says the device will also have point-to-point infrared connectivity.

Apple will sprout a whole family of Newtons, with the second member destined for delivery in November of 1993. That device will be slate-size, have a faster processor, and most likely have a PCMCIA slot. Apple's future PDA plans include devices sophisticated enough to support multimedia.

ANYTHING, EVERYTHING

Portable devices must contain everything the user needs, according to John Sculley. "There is no space for add-on boards in a briefcase," he says. Vendors are speculating that the Newton will have built-in e-mail along with the messaging functions.

BIS Strategic Decisions found, in a survey of 200 prospective PDA buyers, that remote database access via an e-mail link was one of the most desired applications for PDAs. Another typical application was the ability to remotely update appointment schedules for staff in the field.

As with any new technology, the Newton will have its share of problems coming out of the barrel, the first one being cost. Rolling all these applications and functions into one small device dictates a high price tag. "Cost is a barrier. Would you pay $1,000 to be able to read your e-mail on the bus? Probably not," says Yankee Group's Leopold.

And like the PowerBook, another Newton problem could be battery based. These devices need to last at least a day without a recharge, according to the Yankee Group.

In addition, the Newton could have a literacy problem. Pen-based computing is still unproven, leaving most peo-

ple unconvinced of its accuracy. "Initially, the handwriting technology is just not there," says Hartsook. "You wouldn't want to take notes with the Newton." This shortcoming puts the Newton directly in the forms-based, vertical markets–used by UPS and Federal Express–that Grid and other companies are already aiming at.

But eventually the Newton will be able to read the handwriting on its wall, and, as Hartsook says, then "people will actually use these things." In the meantime, Apple will try to sell the Newton as the greatest thing for mobile communication since, well, the PowerBook. As Hartsook puts it, "There's always a group of people who just have to have the latest toy. They'll buy a Newton."

USING APPLETALK REMOTE ACCESS
Cruisin' with the PowerBook

The black Volvo comes cruising into the rounded driveway of the white Southern mansion, and the tuxedoed man and his shimmering mate flow out the door. Or should a red Volvo come careening to the beachfront, with the top of the surfboard jutting out of the sunroof? These are the kinds of crucial decisions that ad agency producers and executives at Messner, Vetere, Berger, McNamee, and Schmetterer have to make on a daily basis.

And needless to say, they don't have time to fly from commercial shoots in Los Angeles back to agency headquarters in New York to discuss the latest outtake. Instead, their scripting takes place using Apple Remote Access via their PowerBooks, which allows the ad execs to keep in touch with both the home base and, through an e-mail link, with Volvo, one of the agency's largest clients.

"AppleTalk Remote Access is amazing. It's as easy as plugging into a phone jack," says Tripp McCune, network manager for the firm. And although another one of the agency's largest clients is MCI, McCune boldly says, "It's the next best thing to being there."

Connectivity is fairly straightforward with AppleTalk Remote Access. You first establish the connection with the remote Mac running System 7, then log on to the services you want. If you call the same connection frequently, you can set up an alias. Clicking on that icon will then start a series of events: It activates AppleTalk Remote Access, dials the remote number, establishes a network connection, and mounts the remote disk of your choice on your laptop's desktop.

McCune's users access the network through Shiva (Cambridge, MA) LanRover/L, which connects to the LocalTalk workgroups.

To accommodate a flood of users, the company also has the multiport LanRover/E, which can handle simultaneous connections to the Ethernet mail and file servers. The agency's 260 users use CE Software (West Des Moines, IA) QuickMail.

"AppleTalk Remote Access is simple and very reliable," adds McCune. "People don't even realize that they're getting e-mails from someone in Hong Kong. It's that transparent."

Toys of the Trade

USING PCMCIA CARDS AND WIRELESS CONNECTIVITY, PDAS MAY
BECOME HANDY MOBILE CLIENTS THAT GIVE USERS ON THE RUN
UNLIMITED ACCESS TO THE NETWORK.

By Melanie McMullen

Vanna White, Al Gore, Ed McMahon, Igor, the Newton MessagePad. Each of these will be remembered in history for their starting roles as The Assistant. some will fare better in the books than others. Vanna, for instance, has one up on the Newton; she can easily recognize the letters of the alphabet. But the MessagePad, with its ballyhooed Newton Intelligence, probably ranks highest in the brains department among all assistants, especially inept Igor.

Despite their perceived shortcomings, each of these assistants has a certain value. Because no matter what type of activity and interaction a job requires, most people need some variety of lovely assistant to polish off the nagging, mostly mundane details of a job. Whether that assistant is vital to business or merely provides entertainment and diversion in those wasted moments waiting for trains or planes, everyone would agree that an assistant of some sort is great to have.

But in the world of mobile computing companions, or more specifically personal digital assistants (PDAs), the agreements end right there. The first point of dissension is who, besides the early technology gadgeteers, will really want, and subsequently buy, these expensive toys of the trade. This question is followed closely by *how* the aforementioned group will use these devices, specifically in terms of work vs. pleasure.

While buyers will most likely not pay $700 for a Game-Boy that can also store their addresses and appointments, they might shell out the bucks if the device can also serve as a mobile access point for communications, that is, if it offers network connectivity. If it doesn't, then PDAs may be doomed to failure as illiterate, Pretty Dumb Assistants that will forever be trapped in a small niche. "PDAs with-out network connectivity are good doorstops and book-ends," says Geoff Goodfellow, founder and chairman of RadioMail in San Mateo, CA).

But buried within the hype of PDAs is hope. While the application developers hash out the uses, PDA makers and other mobile mavens fortunately all agree that networking and PDAs should be one and the same. Tossing in a variety of connectivity options could move PDAs up exponential notches on potential buyers' "I want it" lists.

THE DETACHABLES

The first network assistants have mutated to market in all shapes and form factors, ranging from the basic palm-tops, such as the Hewlett-Packard (Palo Alto, CA) 95LX and 100LX, to the pen-based devices, such as EO's (Mountain View, CA) Personal Communicators and Apple's firstborn in the Newton family, the MessagePad. Sharp, which manufactures the Newton for Apple, in 1993 shipped its own version of the product, the ExpertPad.

Another PDA that came to market in 1993 is the Zoomer, a product codeveloped by Tandy (Ft. Worth, TX) and Japan-based Casio, who along with AST Research (Irvine, CA) market the product.

Two other mobile devices shipped in 1994, one low-end PDA, the Amstrad PLC PenPad, and one high-end device designed for vertical markets, the TelePad SL. The PenPad, manufactured by Amstrad, an Essex, England, consumer-electronics company, has already been a hit in Europe, with buyers scooping up more than 30,000 in its first months on the market. It sports a battery life of 40 hours, runs off three separate 8-bit chips, and costs $499. Scottsdale Technologies in Arizona distributes the PenPad in the United States.

The TelePad SL, made by TelePad Corporation (Reston, VA), is a true hybrid PC and PDA. Manufactured by IBM, the TelePad was originally only sold to government field work forces, such as the U.S. Air Force. The company decided to make it commercially available in 1993. The TelePad is equipped with an Intel 386 processor, and although it's pen based, it has a detachable keyboard and even a plug-in camera for multimedia applications. The TelePad is armed with Proxim's (Mountain View, CA) RangeLAN wireless technology. It costs $2,500 to $3,500.

In a relatively short period of time on the market, these first PDAs have already started to make a reputation for themselves as the detachable add-ons to the desktop, forging a new layer of networking: client client-server computing. Future PDAs will have a variety of options, ranging from sending and receiving e-mail and fax messages to actually running scaled-down versions of desktop applications. PDAs with third-party e-mail connections are already being successfully put to use.

"The most compelling aspect of PDAs is using them on the network, says Jeffrey Henning, senior industry analyst at BIS Strategic Decisions, a market research firm based in Norwell, MA. "People have to be able to easily access the network with these devices. That will sell the products."

But Henning points out that since network capabilities are limited in the early PDA renditions, potential buyers–and even Doonesbury–have been focusing on other aspects of the devices, which unfortunately for the makers is the less-than-perfect pen-computing capabilities. Predicted sales of PDAs over the next year will remain on the conservative side, with only 215,000 units in use in 1994, according to BIS forecasts (see figure).

But despite the poor pen performance of PDAs, analysts aren't totally writing them off. As connectivity options and availability increases, PDA sales will skyrocket, hitting annual sales of more than 4 million units in six years, according to BIS. This figure represents faster growth than any other advanced technology product, including cellular phones.

THE MISSING LINKS

As Apple seeds the market–it claims to have sold more than 50,000 Newtons in the first month after its September launch–PDA-to-network connectivity is becoming a hotbed of commotion among optimistic PDA makers and numerous third-party developers.

Connectivity from PDA to the desktop, PDA to PDA, or PDA to other services such as the Internet currently comes in a variety of forms, ranging from wired and wireless local connections to wide-area solutions that use phone lines or existing cellular links. The high-end devices such as the EO Communicator have the components necessary for communications built-in, while Apple offers connectivity for the MessagePad as add-ons.

And, of course, wherever the PDA hardware manufacturer leaves off, someone else is there to make the connection or add value. "PDAs will realize their full potential when they have integrated communications," explains Roberta Wiggins, research director for wireless mobile communications at The Yankee Group (Boston). Wiggins says the door is open for other companies to provide the missing links.

Whether the network link is integrated or provided by an add-on product, one concept is vital to understanding the basics of PDA connectivity: A mobile user with a handheld device will almost always be sending and receiving only small bits of information. The power and internal storage on a PDA, right now at least, is limited, and although automatic data compression is included in most of them, these mobile data appendages are targeted for information use, not information creation. "A Newton is not a computer at all," says Apple's Wirt. "If you want to create documents, a computer is the right thing. If you want a mobile personal device that can access information, the Newton is the right thing."

Other developers agree with this assessment. "The PDA user will mostly pull data from other sources," says David Larson, vice president of marketing at Notable Technologies (Foster City, CA), a firm that develops communications software for mobile computing devices. "Data is a huge asset that needs to be moved around and accessed on demand. The new mobile platform should allow you to leverage small pieces of existing information on host-based systems and networks." Notable announced its flagship product in August, dubbed Mobile Access Personal. This software links a PDA running Go's (Foster City, CA) PenPoint OS to public and private host-based systems, such as CompuServe.

OFF THE WIRE

Since PDAs will transfer data in small, byte-size pieces, all varieties of information transportation come into play. On the wireless side, spread-spectrum radio and infrared transmission are already available for PDAs, as well as paging and cellular services. Almost 70 percent of new PDAs sold in 1999 will have wired or wireless communications capability, according to analyst Henning. "With PDAs, wireless communication is the holy grail," he adds.

In addition, the Cellular Digital Packet Data (CDPD) group, spurred forward quickly by the AT&T takeover of McCaw Cellular Communications, has already released the 1.0 specification. This spec outlines details of the CDPD architecture, including airlink, external network interfaces, and network support and applications services.

CDPD technology, ideally suited for applications that require short bursts of data, could quickly become a boon for PDA connectivity. CDPD-enabled mobile devices can be constantly connected, allowing them to function much like a live, connected node, sending and receiving e-mail and faxes with no user intervention.

PADDING THE INFORMATION

Priced from $699 to $949, the Newton MessagePad offers faxing capabilities, wireless messaging, and alphanumeric paging via MobileComm's local, regional, or national services; e-mail via the NewtonMail service and a modem; infrared Newton-to-Newton beaming; and both local and network printing functions. Newton has an RS-442 serial port, one PCMCIA slot, and a 19.2Kbps infrared transceiver.

While all these features sound impressive, remember that Apple was anxious to get the Newton to market, shipping the device several months before the communications basics, such as faxing, paging, and desktop connection software, were ready. "Newton was squeezed out the door," says Larson of Notable Technologies.

Larson adds that his developers, who are working on a cross-platform product called Shared Whiteboard that will allow various PDAs to communicate graphically with one another, are finding Newton's operating system difficult to work with. Even Apple has struggled with the OS, shipping four revisions to it in the first month after its release.

Other companies interested in offering platform sup-

port for the Newton are in more of a wait-and-see mode. "Communication is one of the least-developed aspects of the Newton," says Dan Schwinn, president, CEO, and chairman of Shiva (Burlington, MA). He intends to offer support for PDAs as a dial-in client to all his remote access products by the end of next year. But he adds that right now, "the Newton is just unbelievably slick but not quite useful."

But Apple and Newton users are quick to come to its defense. Wirt says the Newton is exactly what its name implies–a personal device–and has to be customized to be appreciated. "If I took my shoes off and asked 12 people on the street to try them on, and I asked them, 'hey, are these comfortable?' they would probably say, 'no.' Newton is the same way. You learn it, you train it, and then it fits your needs," Wirt adds.

But Newton does indeed seem to be the shoe that fits, according to a sample of some of its first users on the street. "At least two-thirds of the people I know who use the Newton are happy with it," says Steve Costa, executive director of the Berkeley Macintosh User Group (BMUG) in Berkeley, CA. The group there and the Apple user group in Boston are both forming special interest groups (SIGs) for users of the PDA, appropriately dubbed SIG Newton.

MAKING THE CONNECTION

The SIG Newtons may soon have more to play with, as Apple intends to have two pieces of desktop connectivity software, Newton Connection kit for the Macintosh and Newton Connection kit for Windows, ready for distribution in the last quarter of 1993. Apple plans to sell the software kits for approximately $150 each.

On the Mac side, Newton Connection will use Apple Events to allow Macintosh applications to talk to Newton. Since the object-oriented Newton operating system is quite unlike that on the Macintosh, "Newton Connection will serve as the main gate to the Newton from a Mac," says Rick Kapur, product manager for Newton Connection.

The Mac desktop running Newton Connection will have an application set equivalent to the Newton, allowing users to plug the Newton into the desktop via a serial or LocalTalk port and automatically synchronize data. In addition to supporting Newton's built-in applications, Newton Connection will support data transfer with three or

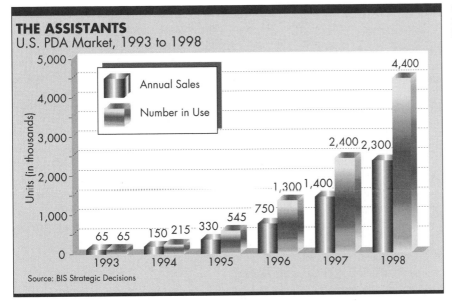

THE ASSISTANTS
U.S. PDA Market, 1993 to 1998

tCommuter Computers: PDA sales will rise slowly, hitting the $4 million mark by 1998..

Source: BIS Strategic Decisions

four applications in other categories, such as databases or spreadsheets, says Kapur.

Newton Connection for Windows is codeveloped by Traveling Software (Bothell, WA). The Newton has Traveling Software's universal communications object embedded in ROM. The first version of the Newton-to-Windows software will use Dynamic Data Exchange (DDE) to transfer data, while the next version will use Object Linking and Embedding (OLE), according to Mark Eppley, CEO of Traveling Software.

He says one of the key elements of linking PDAs with networks is keeping the applications on both the desktop and the portable Newton in synch, not an easy task when platforms differ. "This product is the first automatic synchronization software between different platforms," adds Eppley.

THE TRAVELING LAN

Keeping automatic data synchronization in mind, Traveling Software codeveloped with National Semiconductor (Santa Clara, CA) a wireless portable-to-desktop product. It's scheduled to be announced by the end of the quarter. The connection kit will contain two National Semiconductor Airshare spread-spectrum transceivers, the necessary antennas, and LapLink Remote Access and synchronization software for both the desktop and the portable.

By plugging a transceiver into the portable and the desktop, the product maintains a wireless, 1Mbps link between a DOS or Windows portable and the desktop machine, automatically updating data anytime the portable device comes within 30 feet of the desktop. The product will sell for less than $200. The next form factor for this product will be a PCMCIA version that will have drivers for PDAs and other portables, according to Eppley.

Eppley's product fits into the slot of choice for PDA connectivity, the PCMCIA slot. This I/O hole may become the one unifying element between desktops, laptops, and PDAs. "The market for PCMCIA cards will take off with PDAs," says Andy Prophet, president of AP Research (Cupertino, CA). Prophet predicts that the PCMCIA LAN card market will top 2.6 million by 1997.

Prophet says that since PDAs may have only one slot, makers of PCMCIA cards may start to bundle functions, such as fax/modem and LAN interfaces, on the same PCMCIA card, which will make them very functional but also more expensive. "PDAs fall under the razor-blade theory of hardware, where 40 percent to 50 percent of the revenue from the product comes from add-ons. In the case of PDAs, these will be PCMCIA cards," he says.

Apple is developing some PCMCIA cards of its own for the Newton, with the first one, a Type II modem card, due for shipment by the end of the year, according to Kapur.

OTHER TWISTS

Connecting the PDA directly to the network via a PCM-CIA card is the first order of business for New Media (Irvine, CA), a new start-up. The company is currently working on a Newton LAN card and some wireless LAN connectivity cards.

Once modem PCMCIA cards become available, Newton users can go on-line via Ex Machina's (New York) PocketCall, terminal emulation software that allows Newton users to view incoming information or queries from host systems. It costs $99. The company is also developing Notify! for PowerTalk, a wireless messaging add-in for Apple's Open Collaboration Environment. Notify! will cost $149.

If Newton users don't want to tie up the PCMCIA slot, they could physically connect the PDA to the network by the old-fashioned, cable-based LocalTalk port methods. Apple has combined serial port and LocalTalk port functions into one slot, calling it the Communication port. Existing LocalTalk connectors, such as Farallon Computing's (Alameda, CA) PhoneNet Connector and StarConnector products, work in this port.

In addition, Farallon has plans to release the EtherWave family of daisy-chain 10BaseT connectivity products by year's end. EtherWave allows users to chain up to eight connections in an Ethernet link, creating a desktop landing pad for the mobile Newton and other LocalTalk devices. The EtherWave Newton adapter sells for $379.

MOBILE COMPUTING: IS IT FOR THE BIRDS?

One in the Hand

Dragging a hand-held portable computer out into the wilderness may at first seem like a birdbrained idea. After all, the machine is one more thing that can fill up the already packed backpack, and it adds a few extra pounds to be hauled over that next hill. But to bird-buffs Chip Haven and Jane Becker-Haven, portable computing has engendered new possibilities in seeking the endangered.

The Havens, who reside in Palo Alto, CA, are avid bird-watchers and have been faithfully pursuing their hobby for 15 years. Since that time, their bird-watching expeditions have led them near and far in pursuit of possible sightings of rare birds, including a two-mile hike up a 2,000 ft. mountain in Big Bend, TX, to catch a glimpse of the Colima Warbler, a Mexican species that has been spotted in that one location.

To map out their searches for fine feathered friends, the Havens regularly swoop on-line to the Internet's Birdchat forum. Birdchat is a service hatched by the University of Arizona that now has more than 400 subscribers who electronically discuss sightings of rare birds all across the U.S. "Birdchat is a very active, ongoing way of letting others know when an unusual bird arrives in a certain vicinity," says Haven

ON THE FLY

This fall, Haven, a network consultant at Stanford University, heard from a coworker about RadioMail, a service based in San Mateo, CA, that allows mobile computer users to send wireless e-mail messages to and from the Internet. The company set him up with the necessary software and some portable gear, including a Hewlett-Packard 95LX palmtop and an Ericsson cellular modem, and he headed for the hills.

After his first outing with the gear, he quickly discovered that portable computing, with a wireless link to Birdchat, could be a birdwatcher's bonanza. "People fly miles and miles just to spot rare birds," says Haven. He explains that people on the Internet already give excellent directions as to where birds are, such as under this bush or that tree, but the information quickly becomes dated as birds dart hither and yon, never to be seen again.

Mobile computing could change the way bird-watchers watch, says Haven, allowing birders to report and update sightings on the spot. "Instant access is desirable in this kind of work," he adds.

Section 7
Network Operating Systems

The future of networking is very dependent on the future of the network operating system. The ability to share applications efficiently over a local or wide area network can be either limited or enhanced by the choice of network operating system.

Like operating system software, network operating systems are becoming very sophisticated, with complex directory services, security, and management capabilities being the norm. The distinctions between OS and NOS are no longer there; a merging, or at least a very tight integration, of the two components is a trend that will likely continue with each new generation of OS and NOS. The enterprise NOS is even inheriting some of the powerful elements of its early ancestors, the mainframe operating system, as "NOSs Mimic Mainframe" explains.

The latest Microsoft offerings, Windows NT and Windows NT Advanced Server, have emerged as 32-bit powerhouses that incorporate both NOS and OS. Since the first generation of any software always has its glitches, some performance tuning and add-on software enhancements may be necessary before NT should be unleashed on a large, mission-critical network. "NT on the WAN" and "Far and Wide with NT" offer some practical tips and insights into optimizing that software for the enterprise.

NT on the WAN

ALMOST ONE YEAR OLD, WINDOWS NT NEEDS SOME HELP TO BE
ENTERPRISE-READY. HERE ARE A FEW BYPASSES AND PRODUCTS TO FILL
NT'S CONNECTIVITY GAPS.

BY STEVEN BAKER

Windows NT is Microsoft's hearty entree on the menu of operating systems available for your enterprise. The first version of Windows NT is a complex and powerful operating system with many interesting attributes. But nearly a year after the "new technology" has emerged and the massive marketing has diminished, does the product really satisfy? What are its limitations? Here is a look at how NT integrates with existing "old technology" for networking and at some recent products that fill in some gaps in NT's connectivity fabric.

To understand where the future of NT on the network will be, look at the desktop evolution. The lowly IBM PC started with a mere 64KB of memory, a 160KB single-sided 5 1/4-inch floppy diskette drive, and a monochrome monitor. A dozen years later, siblings of the IBM PC commonly pack 16MB of memory and hard disks of more than a gigabyte. This power dwarfs mainframes and minicomputers sold less than a decade ago. Yet the same operating system, PC-DOS and MS DOS developed by IBM and Microsoft, successfully lives on.

Meanwhile, desktop PCs are ubiquitous from corporate America to home offices and bedrooms. Once standalone, most PCs have become networked into small enterprises. Even home users are finding that connectivity to machines at work and to resources on the Internet are becoming an important consideration. Windows NT is one of the handful of operating systems competing for this enhanced PC marketplace.

DESKTOP OF ENTERPRISE ELITE?

While more than adequate in the early 1980s, DOS now shows its age, displaying numerous shortcomings.

These liabilities include the 640KB memory limit (which has generated a variety of schemes for subverting it), the DOS File Allocation Table (FAT) file system constrained to 8.3 character uppercase file names, the 64KB segmented 16-bit architecture of the 80x86 scorned by programmers, and the single-tasking nature of the operating system. These restrictions have traditionally reduced other options, including the ability to run large programs, to execute several applications at once, and to feature enhanced networking capabilities for connectivity.

Both IBM and Microsoft have offered DOS replacements–OS/2 (originally termed advanced DOS), Windows, and Windows NT. While Windows is a DOS system enhancer, IBM OS/2 2.1 and Microsoft Windows NT 3.1 are complete operating systems.

Both products can run 16-bit Windows and DOS programs alongside new native 32-bit applications. But Windows NT offers more–scalability to other platforms such as MIPS and Digital Equipment Corp. (DEC) Alpha, symmetric multiprocessing (support for multiple CPUs), a New Technology File System (NFTS), and enhanced network connectivity. Taking full advantage of these features requires rewriting applications to use the appropriate Win32 APIs.

Originally, Windows NT was positioned as a high-end desktop replacement for DOS and Windows. But last February, Microsoft changed its marketing approach, positioning NT as two distinct flavors–a workstation (desktop client) and an enterprise server. A year earlier, Novell had chosen a similar strategy with its UnixWare x86 offering. In both cases, the client or desktop version is missing certain key network capabilities offered with the server edition. Other than that, the workstation and server products are basically the same.

Windows NT workstation and NT Advanced Server (NTAS) are based on the same architectural design. A microkernel hardware abstraction layer that is machine-dependent forms the foundation for a number of subsystems (see Figure 1). These subsystems or personality modules provide the capability to run applications originally written for other operating systems. Currently, Windows NT can run programs written for DOS, 16-bit Windows, 16-bit OS/2 1.x, Portable Operating System Interface for Computer Environments (POSIX), and native 32-bit Windows NT applications. Other subsystems, such as Unix and OS/2 2.x, could conceivably be added by Microsoft, but this support appears unlikely, since these systems directly compete with NT.

Microsoft combined the Windows NT base platform with a version of LAN Manager retargeted to run on Windows NT to create Windows NTAS. Microsoft has since decided to end further development of OS/2 LAN Manager. This decision was more a marketing than a technical one. LAN Manager ran on the 16-bit version of OS/2 1.3, an aging system at best. Microsoft's choice was either to port to IBM OS/2 2.1 and provide de facto support to its competitor or to move to its own Windows NT platform. The choice was obvious.

NETWORK SMOKE STACKS

In the DOS realm, running several network protocol stacks at the same time is definitely a challenge. It can be done but with some pain and suffering. Unfortunately, with the mix of computer systems currently found even in smaller companies, running one or more stacks is often a requirement for connectivity.

A number of network protocols might share an enterprise. My own state agency, for example, has PCs connected to NetWare file servers, Sun SPARCstations running Unix using Sun's Network File System (NFS), and Macintosh computers networked using AppleTalk (LocalTalk and EtherTalk). All of these share the same wiring fabric. Over a wide area network, my coworkers and I connect to IBM mainframes and VAX VMS hosts for accounting and database access. A myriad of other network systems are used at other agencies just one hop from our agency's router. We also have a connection to the Internet for easy communication with colleagues across the state and the globe.

Windows NT attempts to bridge this gap by bundling support for part of our network alphabet soup–TCP/IP, IPX/SPX, NetBEUI, and the Data Link Control (DLC) protocol (for mainframe access). NT Advanced Server adds AppleTalk (EtherTalk, TokenTalk, and LocalTalk) support to the menu (see Figure 2). Be forewarned that this support is somewhat uneven–the protocol stacks may be provided without the appropriate software applications to use all of them.

NODE WARRIOR

If your hot Windows NT workstation is used merely as a desktop machine, then various server functions may be unnecessary. The network protocols to be supported can also be limited to those in your specific environment. However, all protocols are not treated equally in Windows NT. Some network stacks have far better support than others in the current product.

NetBEUI was introduced in 1985 with the IBM PC LAN Program. NetBEUI assumed that LANs would be small, containing a modest number of workstations segmented into workgroups. NetBEUI remains the protocol of choice for Microsoft. It forms the basis for LAN Manager and is well-supported in NT. In fact, the default behavior for both NT and NTAS is to install only the NetBEUI protocol. Of the stacks shipped with NT, NetBEUI is supposedly the fastest for small LANs when delivering large packets. The Windows NT documentation often calls NetBEUI the NetBIOS Frame (NBF) format protocol.

NetBEUI's problem is that it is not routable, so its use is not suitable for a larger enterprise. NT and NTAS support NetBIOS over TCP/IP, encapsulating NetBIOS frames in TCP packets where routing is necessary. LAN Manager and LAN Server do so as well. The Department of Defense developed the NetBIOS over TCP protocol.

An inconvenience with NetBIOS over TCP in large enterprises is the necessity of setting up and maintaining static routing tables between domains. The NT and LAN Manager products omit support for protocols such as Routing Information Protocol (RIP) or Open Shortest Path First (OSPF), which are commonly used over TCP/IP to dynamically adjust packet routing based on congestion and router failures.

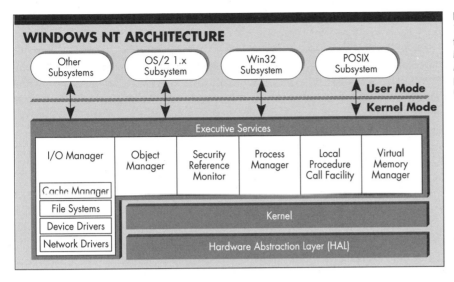

WINDOWS NT ARCHITECTURE

Other Subsystems | OS/2 1.x Subsystem | Win32 Subsystem | POSIX Subsystem

User Mode
Kernel Mode

Executive Services

I/O Manager | Object Manager | Security Reference Monitor | Process Manager | Local Procedure Call Facility | Virtual Memory Manager

Cache Manager
File Systems
Device Drivers
Network Drivers

Kernel

Hardware Abstraction Layer (HAL)

Figure 1: On Intel platforms, DOS and 16-bit Windows applications run within the Win32 subsystem in Virtual DOS Machines (VDMs). On MIPS and DEC Alpha processors, Win16 and DOS programs run in a 286 emulator and the OS/2 1.x subsystem is not available.

To support access to NetWarc, NT and NTAS provide an IPX/SPX stack. A Novell-compatible NetBIOS implementation over the IPX stack is also included. Until a NetWare client or requester for NT is available, this IPX/SPX stack has very limited value.

A similar set of protocol stacks is available with Windows for Workgroups 3.11. So between NT servers, NT workstations, and Windows for Workgroups nodes, any one of these three protocols can be used for supporting basic file- and print-sharing services. The upper-level networking is handled by the Server Message Block (SMB) protocol, which runs over some form of NetBIOS API. The primary difference between an NT workstation and NTAS is inclusion with the server of powerful management tools to set up, monitor, and maintain users and domains in a large enterprise. For example, NTAS includes a global name service provider using Microsoft's remote procedure call (RPC) mechanism.

By supplying TCP/IP and IPX/SPX stacks, NT comes with enabling technology for accessing NetWare servers and the world of TCP (Unix and the greater Internet). But the appropriate client applications, redirectors, or requesters aren't included in the package.

Both Microsoft and Novell are trying to remedy this NetWare-on-NT vacuum by developing separate Windows NT NetWare requesters. As a starting point for its technology, Microsoft purchased WebCorp, the developers of Web, a successful peer-to-peer networking system based on

IPX/SPX with Novell compatibility. While Microsoft clearly has an interest in enhancing NT's connectivity, Novell doesn't appear to be in any rush to help out its competitor. In March, beta software was available from both vendors. By summer, one of these products should be ready for commercial release.

In contrast with Unix systems that come loaded with powerful TCP/IP networking applications, Windows NT comes with only a few minimal network tools. The lack of TCP/IP tools is currently one of the larger holes in the NT networking fabric.

INTERNET WIMP

TCP/IP is the dominant protocol used by most Unix systems, and it must well-supported if Windows NT is to fulfill an enterprise role. The TCP/IP protocols also form the core of networking on the Internet. Because of the immense and growing wealth of resources available via the Internet (on-line databases and convenient e-mail access to 25 million users worldwide, for example) it's clearly where the action is for tomorrow's networking.

The Unix community is already fully equipped and remains the hotbed for experimentation with the latest network wonders (such as audiocasts and video broadcasts across continents). The PC desktop world of DOS lags far behind. The tools that currently ship with NT are barely adequate to let NT be considered a player in this arena.

TCP/IP is based on the client-sever model of networking. A server process on some host computer fields requests from a client node that may be located across the globe. The distinction in the Unix realm is that both client and server networking applications are commonly supplied with each Unix workstations, so Unix machines act more like a network of peers than subordinates. To play ball in the enterprise, Windows NT must offer comparable tools–server applications as well as clients.

PLUG IN TO SOCKETS

Windows NT is supposed to run 16-bit Windows programs seamlessly, but many TCP/IP applications pose difficulties. While software written to the Windows Socket specification is supposed to be portable to Windows NT, many programs are not.

Some require access to custom Windows device drivers of virtual device drivers (VXDs) that access the hardware directly and won't work under Windows NT. Many of the 16-bit Windows Socket applications that I tried from various vendors would not work under NT. None of the 16-bit products that provide an NFS client will function under Windows NT.

While testing 16-bit Windows networking applications on NT's Windows on Windows (WOW) subsystem, network throughput suffered dramatically. The Win16 API calls in a 16-bit program that must be translated (thunked, in programmer's jargon) by the system to the native Win32 API, requiring considerable overhead. The most important goal of the NT design team was application compatibility. So while some parts of Windows on Windows deliver reasonable performance, network thunking does not. This aspect could well be improved in a future upgrade.

Windows NT offers a potential replay of the DOS market, where several vendors have made a solid reputation by providing TCP/IP stacks and applications. So far, software developed for Windows NT, including networking products, has been slow to arrive. Porting is clearly more difficult than Microsoft had thought, and the market appears smaller than anticipated. Although limited compared with the range of tools available for DOS and 16-bit Windows, the first TCP/IP products are beginning to appear.

Windows NT and NTAS come bundled with a handful of TCP/IP tools from Microsoft, most of which are crude command-line utilities similar to ones that NT marketers

lambast in DOS and Unix. Remember, NT is supposed to be the next-generation operating system, where mouse clicks replace cryptic key strokes. In contrast, Frontier Technology (Mequon, WI) and NetManage (Cupertino, CA) supply attractive, easy-to-use 32-bit Windows applications modeled after their 16-bit Windows products. For the operation of some tools such as the *file transfer protocol (ftp)*, the Microsoft NT version and its competitor are miles apart in ease of use.

Of the TCP/IP tools available for NT, the most common are some basic client applications and X Window servers. Corresponding network server tools for NT are quite limited (see Table 3). NetManage's Chameleon32NFS is the only product shipping with an NFS client (the regular Chameleon32 product does not include NFS). The NetManage product also has an NFS server, but this server is built as a Win32 application and functions only when a user is logged in to a Windows NT machine to start it.

Requiring that a privileged user has to be logged in provides a potential security hole, unless the machine is locked in an office. In fact, all the TCP server tools currently shipping (except Microsoft's *ftp* server) are application-level programs rather than NT service providers. While application-level tools for NT are relatively easy to write using the Win32 API, true NT server processes are much more involved and require knowledge of the Windows NT device driver and kernel-mode interfaces.

SunSelect (Chelmsford, MA) has been developing a PC-NFS for Windows NT product for the OEM market, which will be similar to its popular DOS/16-bit Windows offering. The SunSelect software includes a full kernel-mode PC-NFS client, a Network Time Protocol (NTP) client for synchronizing the time with a NTP server, and a remote shell (*rshd*) server. This remote shell server is the only product I've used thus far that runs as an NT service (no desktop user is necessary) and allows executing commands on a remote NT machine over TCP/IP and the Internet.

The PC-NFS software package also provides a set of developer tools that could be used to port Unix network client-side applications to Windows NT. The tools consist of Dynamic-Link Libraries (DLLs) and supporting files offering transport-independent RPCs. Unfortunately, SunSelect has put off further development of an end-user product until 1995, when the NT market is expected to pick up.

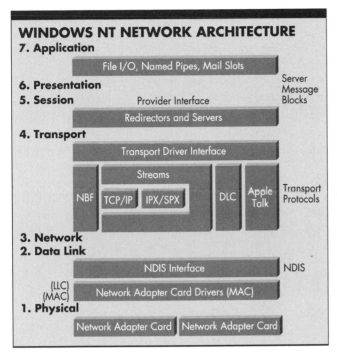

Figure 2: Windows NT is built on a seven-layer network cake. Transport support includes TCP/IP, IPC., NetBEUI, and DLC.

WINDOWS NT NETWORK ARCHITECTURE

7. Application
File I/O, Named Pipes, Mail Slots

6. Presentation
5. Session   Provider Interface   Server Message Blocks
Redirectors and Servers

4. Transport
Transport Driver Interface

Streams
NBF   TCP/IP   IPX/SPX   DLC   Apple Talk   Transport Protocols

3. Network
2. Data Link
NDIS Interface   NDIS
(LLC) (MAC)   Network Adapter Card Drivers (MAC)
1. Physical
Network Adapter Card   Network Adapter Card

GO X YOUNG MAN

Three vendors are now shipping X Window server software: AGE Logic (San Diego), Digital Equipment Corp. (DEC), and Hummingbird Communications (Markham, Ontario). The same companies offer similar products for 16-bit Windows. However, running the 16-bit Windows product on Windows NT (if it would run) would provide abysmal performance, since these applications are both network-and graphics-intensive. The thunking overhead going from 16-bit network and graphics code to the native Win32 API and kernel cripples performance.

All three products support X11 Release 5, making them suitable for use with most Unix systems. Hummingbird's eXceedNT comes with several standalone TCP/IP tools, including *telnet* and *ftp* clients for troubleshooting. Hummingbird and AGE Logic offer flexible scripting and debugging options to facilitate connecting to a networked host computer and starting up X client applications.

The AGE and the Hummingbird X servers both offer two operating modes. One scheme uses Windows NT as the window manager with X applications executed in separate Windows NT-style windows. The second mode uses a remote window manager (OpenLook or Motif, for exam-

ple) on the remote client to handle one large X root window. The user can choose the preferred configuration during installation or before starting up X clients. With the DEC product, the default behavior is to use NT as the window manager. To set up another behavior requires client configuration on the Unix system that is not described in the manuals.

The DEC product has some special features (keyboard maps for DEC keyboards and support for DECnet) to fit more easily into DEC networks. DEC's eXcursion setup program also offers a convenient feature when connecting to a DEC VMS, DEC Ultrix, or Sun OpenWindows host. If one of these system types is selected, Windows NT icons are created for starting the standard DEC Motif or Sun Open Look applications. So for a Sun host (one of my test systems), icons were conveniently created for Sun's Mail-Tool, File Manager, Calculator, Calendar, Clock, TextEdit, and CmdTool (VT100 terminal emulation) application. However, eXcursion lacks easy-to-use diagnostic and debugging tools for testing login scripts. This shortcoming makes debugging configuration problems with eXcursion much more difficult than with its competitors.

Both DEC and Hummingbird offer X software development kits (SDKs) that allow programmers to build local X client applications that run on the Windows NT machine instead of on some Unix host. Both SDKs include the OSF/Motif Toolkit supporting Motif 1.2. These SDKs have the potential to move powerful X and Unix applications to Windows NT. The price of the DEC SDK ($495) includes the eXcursion X server, while the Hummingbird SDK ($695) is a more expensive separate product.

None of the products was completely stable and ready for less-experienced users. Of the three products, eXceedNT has by far the best documentation. From a subjective point of view, the Hummingbird product felt slightly faster, but it also had problems mapping to proper fonts when connected to a Sun SPARCstation running Solaris 2.3. AGE's XoftWare/32 was still a beta version that performed quite well with only a few wrinkles. Until the startup scripts were fully working (debugged using the other products), DEC's eXcursion was quite buggy, generating execution exceptions. Overall, the user feel of all three products was similar. These products need stability before beginning a comparison on performance issues.

UNIX SEA SHELLS

To establish Windows NT as an enterprise player requires wooing Unix developers with powerful applications to the NT platform. The Unix environment comes with a rich set of command shells (like COMMAND.COM in DOS) and command-line utilities to ease development. Unix developers often write complex build scripts for software development based on these Unix tools. Fortunately, Unix-like shells and utilities are available for Windows NT from several vendors: Mortice Kern Systems (MKS, Waterloo, Ontario), Hamilton Laboratories (Wayland, MA), and Hippo Software (Salt Lake City).

The most familiar product is MKS Tools for NT. MKS has been offering similar products for DOS and OS/2 for many years. The Windows NT version is just the latest evolution. The MKS toolkit includes a *korn* shell for NT and a large collection of Unix-like utilities (more than 120 tools) that comply with the POSIX.2 standards. All of the tools are native Windows NT 32-bit utilities except for two Win16 applications: a visual *diff* utility and a *vi* editor. The MKS tools come with excellent printed documentation and on-line manual pages in the Unix tradition. Unfortunately, the NT version omits the useful *uucp* communica-

tion utility that is supplied on some of the other platforms. Raw devices (tape drives and floppy diskettes, for example) are supported by the *cpio, dd, pax,* and *tar* commands which should ease moving files via tape from Unix to NT. A powerful make tool and the latest version of *awk* are included.

The Hamilton C Shell has also been around for some time, since it was written originally for OS/2. It is a very powerful multithreaded C shell with a collection of Unix-like utilities (more than 40 tools). In a number of cases, the utilities provided with the Hamilton Labs product differ from the POSIX standards, a result of maintaining compliance with earlier versions. The C Shell utilities also include tools for manipulating tapes and reading and writing Unix-compatible *tar* files. A useful *cron* utility is included to run tasks at a later time. Printed documentation is solid and on-line help is provided within each tool using an '-h' help switch. The centerpiece of the Hamilton product is the C Shell.

Windows NT provides a POSIX subsystem for writing console-based applications necessary for compliance with many federal procurements. Unfortunately, the POSIX subsystem in Windows NT is minimal–just enough to meet a procurement officer's checkoff box–and is poorly documented for use by programmers. Hippix from Hippo Software tries to address this problem. The package consists of two parts: a large set of Unix-like utilities and a set of programming libraries to provide an environment similar to the full POSIX 1003.1 and 1003.2 standards under the Win32 subsystem. The utilities and the libraries may be purchased together or separately. The Hippix manual is overly brief, depending on on-line manual pages for reference. Since some of the utilities are based on code written under the GNU public license umbrella, source code for these GNU-based utilities is also supplied. The Hippix libraries provide a POSIX interface to the Win32 subsystem adding 230 functions designed to emulate the Unix environment. The libraries have been tested with the Microsoft Windows NT SDK C/C++ compiler and should work with other development tools.

SERVING UP NT

So far, many of the features discussed relate more to a Windows NT desktop client than to an enterprise server. Fortunately, some powerful enterprise-enabling products are becoming available for Windows NT. Although this software will run on either an NT workstation or NTAS, most users will likely opt for NTAS, since it provides some powerful user and domain management utilities.

Microsoft SNA Server for Windows NT offers a client-server model for connecting with IBM mainframes and other legacy systems. A server runs on the Windows NT machine that handles the connections to the mainframe using either the DLC or the TCP/IP protocols and several proprietary hardware products. Users who wish to access the mainframe may run client software on either the Windows NT machine or on PCs with network connections to the NT server. The base product provides a modest SNA client applet for DOS, OS/2 1.x, Windows, and Windows NT along with enabling technology for many other vendors offering SNA connectivity. Third-party products offer enhanced SNA client software compatible with SNA Server along with various hardware options for extending connection possibilities.

Microsoft recently enhanced SQL Server for Windows NT. The new version uses the multithreading features of Windows NT and multiple CPUs, if available on the hardware platform, to deliver significantly improved performance. Support is also incorporated for Microsoft's Messaging API (MAPI), allowing the corporate messaging and e-mail functions to be integrated into transaction-based applications. Microsoft added better support for different network protocols, including compatibility with Banyan VINES and TCP/IP clients. SQL Server now supports PC clients accessing the server over TCP/IP and the Windows Sockets API.

I briefly tested a 10-user Workgroup System on a dual-CPU Intel machine and found about double the performance from the earlier release. SQL Server supports Intel, MIPS, and DEC Alpha hardware, so its performance is scalable.

For developing custom applications, Microsoft offers a SQL Programmer's Toolkit that supports C and Visual BASIC. This toolkit can use the Open Database Connectivity (ODBC) APIs for SQL access. A similar toolkit is also available for COBOL programmers.

If your enterprise uses NetWare, Beame and Whiteside (Raleigh, NC) offers MultiConnect IPX, a software package that emulates a NetWare 3.11 file server on Windows NT. The product comes with both the NT server software and a few NetWare-like DOS client utilities designed to emulate the normal NetWare tools. This emulation allows an administrator to use this product in an environment without other NetWare servers.

I worked with a beta version of the software installed on an Intel NTAS machine. PC clients could access disk files and printers on the Windows NT machine using IPX/SPX just as easily as using a real NetWare server. The DOS client utilities provided were minimal, consisting of LOGIN, LOGOUT, ATTACH, SLIST, and MAP lookalikes. An IPX/SPX client stack is not provided for PC workstations (Novell's IPX and NETX TSRs), but this is not an issue in a mixed environment with NetWare file servers.

Windows NT comes with a Remote Access Server (RAS) and client software to connect over remote links. While the RAS software works adequately over a direct dial-up link (one NT machine to another), the RAS AsyncBEUI protocol is not yet supported by any of the router and terminal server vendors. This lack of support makes RAS virtually useless for remote access over the Internet. Microsoft has negotiated agreements with Cisco (Menlo Park, CA) and 3Com (Santa Clara, CA) for supporting RAS in future products. In contrast, the Serial Line Interface Protocol (SLIP) and Point-to-Point Protocol (PPP) are widely implemented in products now and can be used to connect remote computers directly to networks through routers and across the Internet.

For writing distributed applications, Windows NT includes support for the Distributed Computing Environment (DCE) developed by the Open Software Foundation (OSF). DCE provides an RPC mechanism different from the more common Sun RPC scheme. While NT supports the DCE protocols at the network packet level, the development tools and NT APIs available are not a direct port of the OSF code. Unfortunately, this fact makes moving a DCE application to NT more difficult than to other DCE systems. While DCE provides a rich environment for constructing distributed applications, DCE system software and development tools are just now coming to market on IBM, DEC, and other platforms. Currently, the dominant scheme for writing distributed applications is Sun's RPC protocol.

UNIX AND THE GREATER INTERNET

A weak link in the Windows NT networking fabric is

connectivity with Unix machines over TCP/IP and the Internet. One way to solve this problem is to use a Unix machine to provide connectivity. UniPress (Edison, NJ) has recently released a version of LAN Manager for Unix (LMU) 2.2 on the UnixWare x86 platform. I tested a current version of LMU on UnixWare 1.0 on a 486DX2/66MHz machine and later upgraded the operating system to UnixWare 1.1 without difficulty. I also worked with a similar beta test version for Sun SPARC machines running SunOS 4.1.3

The SPARC and UnixWare products provide a full implementation of the LAN Manager file and print services on Unix. DOS, Windows, and Windows NT client machines connect to the Unix boxes as if they were normal LAN Manager servers. Unix files can be easily shared among PC, Windows NT, and Unix users. A full NetBEUI protocol stack is added on the Unix machine, so either NetBEUI or TCP over NetBIOS connections can be used. In a mixed environment with Windows NTAS, the NTAS machine must be the primary domain controller. The familiar LAN Manager (now Windows NT) networking APIs are available on the Unix machine as linkable libraries for writing custom applications.

The low-level NetBEUI and NetBIOS over TCP/IP stacks used by UniPress are from Micro Computer Systems (MCS, Irving, TX). If you require only these protocol stacks and libraries for writing custom applications, MCS offers its NetBIOS/ix product on a wide range of Unix platforms (SCO, SunSoft Interactive, AT&T SVR4, UnixWare, AIX/RS600, SunOS, Solaris, and HP-UX). MCS also sells SMB/ix, an emulation of LAN Manager 1.1 for the same platform.

OLD TECHNOLOGY LIVES ON

Window NT offers many new features, but its network support for some older, well-established protocols is somewhat uneven. Products from other vendors can fill some of these holes but not all of them. TCP/IP and NetWare access are the most obvious problem areas.

The next version of Windows NT (code-named Daytona) should be available sometime this summer. It is supposed to have new TCP/IP and IPX/SPX stacks, a Microsoft NetWare requester, and better support for TCP/IP applications. Servers for the Domain Name System (DNS) and a version of the Bootstrap Protocol (BOOTP) are promised. The PPP protocol will be included to facilitate remote access. Unfortunately, some substantial changes in the Daytona kernel will possibly break some existing file server code.

While NT waits for greater Internet connectivity, the UniPress and MCS products can provide this access on a Unix workstation where it is ubiquitous. So users could be running the latest multimedia applications on Unix and connecting via NetBEUI or NetBIOS over TCP/IP from Windows NT and PC desktop machines.

Microsoft's new technology offers much to the desktop and the enterprise, but it also needs to have a solid smattering of old technology to be more useful.

Far and Wide with NT

WINDOWS NT MAY STILL BE STRUGGLING TO PROVE ITSELF, BUT ITS MODULAR DESIGN SHOULD EVENTUALLY WIN OVER MANAGERS OF MULTIVENDOR LANS AND WANS.

BY MICHAEL CHACON AND CLAUDE KING

We all saw the ads: "Nice Try," "Not There," "New Theology." But marketing skirmishes aside, now that Windows NT is finally shipping, Microsoft's real challenge is to demonstrate to a wary and cynical industry that New Technology is better and, more importantly, that this newness enhances current infrastructures–including WAN infrastructures.

Not only has NT faced criticism from competitors, but prospective users, many of whom have invested considerable amounts of money and effort in their networks, do not want to make serious changes without commensurate benefits. Managers of multivendor LANs and WANs, where the dollar investment is greatest, may be particularly reluctant to implement NT–at least unless they understand its modular architecture.

Network managers who come to understand NT's design should then grow to fully appreciate the elegance of a protocol-independent operating system. While many areas of Windows NT take advantage of its modular architecture, we will focus on the modularity that enables integration into heterogeneous WANs through protocol independence and well-defined APIs.

NT'S MODULAR APPROACH

NT Advanced Server has been designed as a modular system based on a Mach kernel architecture. In essence, this design means that the fundamental chores of the OS, such as scheduling and prioritizing of such key objects as processes and threads, are handled by an abstracted modular kernel. This abstraction, or subsystem architecture, permits the OS to run across multiple processors and allows significant new subsystems to be added to the system without changing the kernel. The modularity of subsystems is what makes the operating system so extensible.

For example, if yet another file system (such as Cairo) comes along or if a new protocol spurs interest, a network developer need only make sure the new component communicates through the well-defined interface. While the industry may not resolve the standards battle for some time, Windows NT is architecturally ready to accept all standards with significantly less heartache for developers and integrators.

In the WAN world, high- and low-level access interfaces provide the protocol independence for integration (see Figure 1). The low-level access interface is the Network Driver Interface Specification (NDIS 3.0), used by hardware manufacturers to write drivers for their networks boards. NDIS allows different protocols to be used on a network without the hardware manufacturers having to write separate drivers for each.

At the higher levels of the protocol stack, the Transport Driver Interface (TDI) is another kernel-mode, common-access interface. It is designed to allow multiple protected-mode transport protocols running on Windows NT Advanced Server to communicate concurrently with other operating systems. In addition, NT takes advantage of the TDI internally, abstracting, or separating, the redirector and services, such as file and print, from the protocol. So, because of TDI, you can establish a session using Net-BIOS, Windows Sockets, or any other method you choose.

Although more clients may actually be running IPX, a derivative of the routable XNS, the accepted standard for WAN connectivity is TCP/IP. IP is a standard supported across all major operating system platforms, and realistically TCP/IP is what you have to work with for heterogeneous WAN connectivity. And because NT can run any transport protocol supporting the NDIS 3.0 specification, the best way to implement Windows NT in a WAN is to utilize TCP/IP as the transport protocol.

VERY SUPPORTIVE

NT Advanced Server allows a client using TCP/IP to access information across an enterprise WAN at three fundamental levels.

Windows NT uses NetBIOS as the basic ISO session-layer connection interface. By using the B-node protocol (NT's implementation of NetBIOS over TCP/IP defined in the RFC 1001/1002), NT includes support for all basic networking features, including printer sharing, domain administration, file sharing, resource browsing, and peer-to-peer sharing of information. These functions establish ISO session-layer connection, which would include the use of virtual drives–standard LAN stuff and the first level of connectivity to the WAN.

Second, NT provides IP support by establishing terminal-type connections to host operating systems such as Unix, VMS, and SunOS. Once connected, a client can access the host applications using standard methods, such as Telnet, and, if their account privileges allow, can act as any other client on the host systems. Also, the clients can use standard TCP tools, such as the File Transfer Protocol (FTP), to transfer files from the host to other systems. In addition, various third-party TCP/IP products can provide Network File Services (NFS), X Window, and other TCP-based support.

In addition to these two traditional methods of IP support, users can bypass the use of NetBIOS altogether by using Microsoft's APIs: Windows Sockets, Remote Procedure Calls (RPCs), and named pipes support client-server development connectivity.

Windows Sockets is Microsoft's preferred method for developing enterprise applications, and the company is mounting a strong campaign for TCP/IP developer acceptance. This connectivity method is more popularly known as the Windows Open System Architecture (WOSA).

According to Microsoft, the big advantage of WOSA is that it would provide developers a common set of APIs independent of the underlying protocols or other network layers. Microsoft's strategy is to have a strong stable of developers bring a multitude of WOSA-compliant applications to the hungry Windows customer base.

For Unix developers, the big carrot in WOSA compliance is that a program can access a common API and access support for different protocol implementations right out of the box. WOSA addresses the biggest headache for the Unix developer and user–the multitude of source-code revisions necessary for widespread support across different platforms.

Of course Novell, Lotus, and Apple are battling for market acceptance of their own standards. For example, for e-mail transmission, Novell uses the Message Handling Services, Lotus uses Vendor-Independent Messaging, and Apple uses the Apple Open Collaborative Environment. Each of these standards will probably have a place in the WAN. The real question is what place and how large of a place will the various standards occupy? Be prepared to step up your efforts to integrate applications rather than simply enabling them to coexist on a LAN.

MESHING NT WITH TCP/IP

Implementing NT's TCP/IP requires the basic network configuration necessary for any TCP/IP network. You must establish all relevant IP addresses, any subnet maskings, and default gateways in your IP network. Then you must make fundamental decisions about how workstations are going to interact with the network: What level of connectivity do you want? Are you going to use applications on hosts through terminal emulation? Or will you mount NFS drives from Unix servers? Or will you do both–use terminal emulation and mount drives?

If you have a significant investment in legacy systems, you will probably go the terminal-emulation route, using emulation software to turn your workstations into terminals. The emulation solution is not the best utilization of the considerable resources necessary to run Windows NT. However, sites that cannot quite let go of their legacy host applications can still enhance terminal-emulation method functionality.

As with OS/2, the multithreaded kernel in the Windows NT client can sustain many terminal sessions with different hosts active in real time. These sessions can also forward and retrieve information between the host and LAN-based applications. In such instances, Windows NT can be the infrastructure that glues together the heteroge-

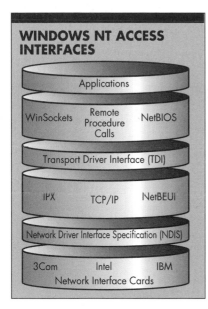

Figure 1. Hardware manufacturers use the low-level access interface Network Driver Interface Specification (NDIS 3.0) to write drivers for their network's boards, for example. At the higher levels of the protocol stack, the Transport Driver Interface (TDI) allows multiple protected-mode transport protocols running on Windows NT Advanced Server to communicate concurrently with other operating systems.

neous environment. The terminal-emulation method of integration is the easiest because you don't change the original model. You simply add a client to an existing applications set that appears to the hosts as just another terminal.

Once all the IP addressing information has been added, communication will traverse IP routers and WAN links as if they were local resources. When two Windows NT workstations or Advanced Servers on different networks try to establish a NetBIOS session across a router, an interesting problem occurs. NetBIOS is designed for local connectivity and not for routing–a problem not particular to NT but associated with any application that uses NetBIOS as an application interface, such as gateways, some imaging systems, and workflow applications, including the NetBIOS version of Lotus Notes.

BUT IT WORKS ON THE LAN

NetBIOS' unique characteristic of broadcast works great on LANs as the means by which clients communicate with servers, requesting access to drives, printers, and messaging applications. NetBIOS is limited to a 15-character unique name space and uses network broadcasts for name registration claims and releases on a network. When a client requests access to the network resources, it sends out a broadcast signal declaring its existence and attempts to claim a unique NetBIOS name. If another device on the

network is already using that name, that NetBIOS device will respond and report the error, and the second client on the network will not be permitted to participate.

Therefore, at the ISO session layer, in addition to their IP address, clients have a unique NetBIOS name, which is abstracted from the network protocol layers and the physical media such as Ethernet or Token Ring. The three layers of name/address abstraction are the MAC address (network card address), the network address (IP address), and WinSockets (Berkeley Unix 4.2 Sockets) and the NetBIOS name. By means of the session-layer naming convention services, such as domains and named pipes, users can dynamically locate resources through the Browser Service.

On LANs, the mapping of the NetBIOS name to the physical-layer MAC address is all that is needed for point-to-point communication. With the IP network portion of TCP/IP, a third and fourth address abstraction is possible. The Internet address, which identifies the network and the client along with Domain Name Service (DNS), abstracts the Internet number identifier into a somewhat-meaningful name, such as cking@jou.ufl.edu (for Claude King at the Journalism Department, University of Florida, Education Industry).

When all goes well, a request for a connection to a resource is answered with a response that includes the desired resource's IP address. This mapping allows applications to communicate using the NetBIOS names over the IP network. Wonderfully simple. However, on the WAN, there is still a slight problem. NetBIOS broadcasts and listens for its name across a network. Broadcasts, by their very nature, do not cross routers.

MICROSOFT'S SOLUTION

To resolve this problem, Microsoft uses the LMHOST file which resides at each Windows NT node on the LAN. The LMHOST file permits NetBIOS names to be manually mapped to other resources across IP routers. This solution was first offered in LAN Manager, which shares some of NT's NetBIOS session-layer connectivity characteristics. Fortunately, the LMHOST functionality in NT has been greatly enhanced in terms of both capacity and functionality.

LMHOSTis an ASCII file that contains a listing of resources that can exist outside the broadcast area of a network. These resources would typically include routers but could also include a filtering bridge, server, peer, or PC gateway device. Such resources would be listed by IP address, NetBIOS name, and a comment field.

When a workstation requests a resource, the workstation examines the cached portion of the LMHOST file. If the workstation does not find the address in cache, it searches for the resource with a broadcast following the standard B-node protocol. If that search fails, the LMHOST file is then read into memory.

Knowing the order of that search can be very useful in a fully bridged environment. Keeping the most-used addresses in cache will minimize broadcast traffic, enabling network bandwidth to be better utilized. The network administrator determines which resources are kept in cache. Up to 100 NetBIOS names can reside in cache without modification of the Windows NT Registry, where all Windows NT configurations are stored. The administrator determines which NetBIOS names and IP numbers are loaded in cache with the #PRE keyword as shown.

If that LMHOST file were loaded on the 128.003 network, then the order of resolution would be as follows: The Remote Server, Server_3, would be loaded in memory, so the workstation would know the address of Server_3. If a request for Server_3 were initiated, the request would be resolved immediately without the B-node broadcast.

If a request for Server_1 were initiated, a search of the LMHOST cache would fail, and the B-node broadcast protocol would then find the resource. If a request for Peer_3 were initiated, then the cache search would fail, and the B-node broadcast would fail. The workstation would then search the LMHOST file to find the address, and the connection would then be established through the IP router, eliminating the need for broadcast traffic.

The size of the LMHOST file is limited only by the time it takes to resolve the NetBIOS name and the IP address. The TDI will time out after 15 seconds of searching. This time is quite long for a resource request and provides for a file that can support thousands of entries.

The LMHOST file can also be used to permit domains in the Windows NT environment to span routers. Domains are important with Windows NT because they are used to maintain the access rights of the users and other network services. By including the #DOM keyword in aLMHOST file, a domain controller across a router can then help authenticate the user or provide other services.

JUST BROWSING?

Among the useful services provided by a domain controller is a convenient list of resources available with a Master Browser Service in each NT domain. This information is kept up to date by the various servers in a domain broadcasting changes in resources to the Master Browser Service. This master service is provided by the primary domain controller in a Windows NT Advanced Server network.

With the #DOM keyword in LMHOST files, the domain controllers in each of the respective broadcast areas can receive local and remote resource updates that keep them synchronized. In addition, with the proper #DOM keyword entries, even non-NT clients can browse resources outside the broadcast area.

The Master Browser in each broadcast area acts as a surrogate for your requests. It then uses the LMHOST file to find the Browser for the broadcast area you're interested in, contacts that Browser, and downloads the information you requested. Thus, to the individual client, the entire network looks and acts like the resources are all local.

Because the resources look local, networks can be configured logically and not by physical area or broadcast region. Logical configuration is an important concept in the maintenance and configuration of large multisite and multivendor networks. This configuration allows peer-to-peer, client-server, user, and resource domains to be configured according to your company's structure rather than the physical location of resources.

As with any technical solution, this one has its drawbacks. The main disadvantage of the LMHOST file is that it is essentially equivalent to a static routing table. The use of static routing requires your network to be well designed in terms of resource location. It also means the network administrator must keep tabs on the files to ensure users can make the appropriate connections.

DON'T WORRY, YOU'LL MANAGE

The next obvious question is, "How do I manage the LMHOST file?" Another feature of the LMHOST file is the ability to insert a #BEGIN_ALTERNATES keyword statement to permit the inclusion of a remote LMHOST file. Following the #BEGIN_ALTERNATE keyword is the #INCLUDE keyword that points to an LMHOST file on another server.

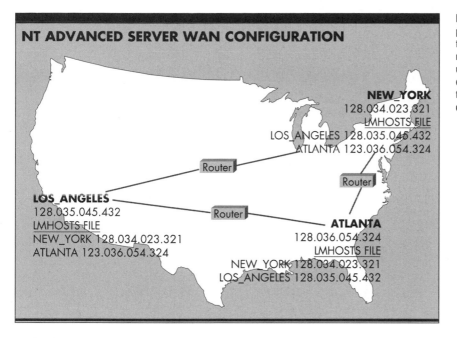

NT ADVANCED SERVER WAN CONFIGURATION

NEW_YORK
128.034.023.321
LMHOSTS FILE
LOS_ANGELES 128.035.045.432
ATLANTA 123.036.054.324

Router

Router

LOS_ANGELES
128.035.045.432
LMHOSTS FILE
NEW_YORK 128.034.023.321
ATLANTA 123.036.054.324

Router

ATLANTA
128.036.054.324
LMHOSTS FILE
NEW_YORK 128.034.023.321
LOS_ANGELES 128.035.045.432

Figure 2. This basic WAN configuration permits Windows NT Advanced Servers to update all their administration information, such as access rights, domain updates, and browsing. The workstations on each LAN can use the information in the LHMOST file to access resoources across the routers.

These global server-based LMHOST files can contain the entries for the main resources that exist across the routers. The administrator can maintain a master global file that can then be used by all the client's files pointing to this file. The master global LMHOST file also can be easily distributed to other servers through the Replicator Service. In addition to the central management aspect of this configuration, the #ALTERNATES keyword provides redundancy in case a single server fails.

How can you put all this information together? Consider the following configuration for a server in New York, Los Angeles, and Atlanta, with X number of workstations; the networks are distinct but routed with IP (see Figure 2).

The basic configuration in Figure 2 will permit Windows NT Advanced Servers to update all their administration information, such as access rights, domain updates, and browsing. In addition, if an SQL application were distributed across these servers, the local application client would be able to make a request to its local server. If the data requested were located on a remote server, the two servers would be able to communicate seamlessly using the IP routers. Clients can get access across the routers using the LMHOST file residing on their local server.

With the addition of an LMHOST file and the Master

Browser service, Windows NT Advanced Server can offer all the resources on the WAN in what appears to clients and end users as a seamless contiguous LAN. NT can be arranged in a flat, hierarchical, or distributed environment depending on an administrator's design philosophy directed by the company's organizational structure.

NT is another step in the movement toward the abstraction of all programs and data into objects, enabling the user to leave behind the baffling concepts of links, virtual drives, sessions, regions, and servers.

NOT THERE . . . YET

So what's wrong with this picture? Even if we can put Windows NT Advanced Servers all over the country, what would we do with them?

Windows NT Advanced Server needs applications that take advantage of its considerable power. Ultimately, NT's ability to run 16-bit Windows at lightening speeds compared to DOS or OS/2 becomes irrelevant. Running 16-bit applications in a 32-bit environment is somewhat foolish with NT, OS/2, or Unix. It's like trying to drive a Volkswagen as if it were a race car.

Third-party developers need to step forward and build the object-oriented applications around WOSA that can take real advantage of the preemptive multitasking and symmetrical processing Window NT Advanced Server provides. Microsoft needs to release associated products, such as Hermes and Chicago, so in-house enterprise developers can design, implement, and manage rightsized distributed applications. It also needs to get Object Linking and Embedding 2.0 accepted and implemented in more applications than Microsoft Office.

NOSs Mimic the Mainframe

NOS VENDORS RECREATE THE CENTRALIZED FUNCTIONS OF MINIS AND MAINFRAMES.

BY TED BUNKER

Evangelists of microcomputer networks have decried hierarchical, host-based computer systems forever, it seems. Yet as soon as desktop computer networks became ubiquitous in American offices, the high priests of networking took a turn toward the data center. Now, the major NOS makers seem all-too eager to provide the kinds of systems-management tools mainframe users take for granted and networkers have long ignored.

What's going on here?

Industry watchers say NOS vendors have recognized the value of providing operating systems that are as stable, as easy to manage, and as functional as host-based computer operating systems.

Some NOS vendors say they're reaching for that value because they realize the market for NOS is fragmenting, leading to greater competition and lower profit margins on their basic systems. To make acceptable returns on their investments, NOS vendors are reaching into higher layers of system software, sometimes called *middleware*, to provide added value to their basic systems. Executives of those companies openly discuss another motive: that growing the network market increasingly requires coaxing MIS managers to migrate core applications from host-based systems to networks.

As those applications move onto networks, industry watchers say, NOS vendors have come under increasing pressure to make their products easier to manage by MIS professionals more accustomed to running host-based systems.

STONES AT GLASS HOUSES

But to satisfy those concerns, NOS vendors are edging closer to recreating the centralized, restrictive functions of minis and mainframes–the very sorts of things that drove users to PCs and networks in the first place. That shift makes the irony hard to escape in this rush toward the glass house. For instance, Microsoft Founder and Chairman Bill Gates, speaking in New York in the summer of 1992 to a gathering populated with corporate chief information officers, described his company's computer system: a thousand workstations in racks inside a glass-enclosed, air-conditioned room with a raised floor.

And consider what one Novell official said about its key NetWare product: "1993 is a real turning point for Novell, because of this delivery of enterprisewide solutions with not only the platform NetWare 4.x . . . but also [with] associated products that support its function in the enterprise," said Peter Troop, director of corporate communications at Novell, in one of a series of meetings between Novell executives and investment managers earlier in 1993.

"We can now support networks and internetworks of departmental networks, so that the departmental network here in New York is connected to networks in Chicago and likewise to [networks in] San Jose, CA," he declared.

"That's something we couldn't do before because we never had a directory environment," Troop noted, referring to a key addition to NetWare. "Up through [NetWare] 3.11, servers are only aware of themselves. They don't realize that they're one of a population of servers. When you log in, you do just that, you log in to that one server.

"With NetWare 4.0, you log in to the network, and you have access to all of the servers and resources that are specified by MIS people who have packaged the network."

Does this scenario and the physical setup Gates described at Microsoft sound familiar? It should, if you've ever used a host-based computer system.

Typically run out of insular computer rooms by technicians, such systems and their rigid, restrictive hierarchies of access and control provided the impetus for the development of PCs and then networks of PCs a few generations ago. To the gurus of networking, centralized management and control formed the antithesis of what they preached.

That was all fine and good until so many desktops became wired together. By some estimates, more than 60 percent of all PCs in use by business today are linked together in some form of network, and the pace of growth shows no sign of slackening. But with that growth has come complexity. And managing that complexity extracts a considerable price from organizations.

In some documented cases, the price of supporting a networked user runs more than $3,000 a year. Until recently, support services–chiefly personnel, often including the savviest PC-meister in the workgroup rather than a technician–remained largely hidden. That scenario changed once MIS managers realized they were losing control of critical information to ad hoc networks springing up outside their operations through the efforts of end users.

RESPONSIVE TO MIS

As networks grew and became more unwieldy, users who had been driving that growth were overwhelmed and tossed the problem in the laps of systems professionals in MIS shops, says Jeff Leopold, director of integrated computing at The Yankee Group in Boston. "Now, MIS has inherited it," Leopold says, adding, "This caused the OS makers to become sensitive to MIS."

"MIS people came back in and standardized it for lower costs," says Jim Tolonen, Novell's chief financial officer. As MIS managers took control of networks running in their organizations, they began looking for the kinds of tools they customarily used to efficiently operate larger systems. What they found, in NetWare as well as other NOSs, was that these tools are clearly lacking.

Novell and other NOS vendors–Microsoft (Redmond, WA), Banyan Systems (Westboro, MA), and a host of Unix developers–took steps to supply what the MIS managers

wanted and began rolling out products with tools and utilities added, such as directory services in NetWare 4.0 and support for symmetric multiprocessing in Windows NT. But these and other systems have a long way to go.

"There's still a great gulf to be filled between these LAN and PC environments and the mini/mainframe," assays Neal Hill, senior analyst with Forrester Research in Cambridge, MA. Hill points out that network systems lack transaction-monitoring tools, network-management applications, and configuration utilities and controls available in minicomputer and mainframe operating systems, such as Digital Equipment's VMS or IBM's MVS/ESA.

"You look at what minicomputers offered–they offered two things. One was an integration thing. The other was specific work that someone could do by themselves," explains David Stone, once a key Digital software executive who is now president of AT&T's operations systems business unit, a part of the company's Network Systems group.

"The piece that was taken away [by microcomputers] was the specific work that people did by themselves. Integration has never been touched and still isn't being touched by the products they're offering," he says, referring to Microsoft, Novell, and other microcomputer NOS vendors. Stone adds that it will probably be several years at least before NOS vendors get to that point.

Apparently, the bigger NOS vendors recognize their faults and are making efforts to remedy them. For instance, Microsoft has been working on its Hermes package of network-management utilities for Windows NT for more than a year. And NT, at least on systems powered by Digital's Alpha chips, is expected to benefit from Accessworks, a package of systems-management and other utilities developed by Digital for use with its VMS operating system. Digital is said to be in the process of porting the tool set to NT.

With NetWare 4.0, Novell took a big step down the same path. "NetWare 4.0 is the culmination of four and a half years of work, to provide the systems software infrastructure to support our reaching out to the delivery of full enterprisewide networks," said Novell's Troop. He added that Novell sees such efforts as key to moving corporate data flows off the 50,000 SNA networks that still dominate the enterprise market.

In future releases, Troop added, Novell will offer products "that extend the capabilities of the core platform, the

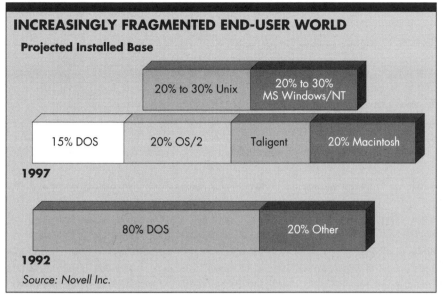

INCREASINGLY FRAGMENTED END-USER WORLD

Projected Installed Base

20% to 30% Unix	20% to 30% MS Windows/NT

15% DOS	20% OS/2	Taligent	20% Macintosh

1997

80% DOS	20% Other

1992

Source: Novell Inc.

Figure 1. As the battle for OS market share heats up, DOS will no longer enjoy its 80-percent lead.

server operating system, and deliver system software that's required for these networks to behave like host computers have always behaved."

For example, in October of 1993, Novell released App-Ware to developers, a developer's tool kit designed to shield applications from the underlying operating system–a form of middleware layering to help users cope with the fragmented world Novell expects to exist by 1995 or so. Troop said Novell expects to see Windows NT, Unix, and OS/2 all with roughly equal market shares by then–a far cry from the 80 percent dominance enjoyed by DOS today (see Figure 1). Novell madea general release of AppWare for May 1994.

YOURS, MINE, OURS

"They recognize they don't have it all, and they recognize that people are a little bit nervous about being controlled by them," Stone says, offering a different interpretation of what moves Novell. "They want to make it possible for people to still rely on them but somehow access everything else.

"By making it possible for you to access everybody's networks through mine, I make it more likely for you to buy mine," Stone explains, taking the position of an OS vendor. He says this reasoning applies to IBM, Novell, Microsoft, Banyan, and a host of other NOS vendors, includ-

ing Sun Microsystems and Apple Computer, that are all promoting their own microcomputer operating systems.

Stone's rationale puts remarks by industry executives in context, such as the following from Microsoft's Gates:

"The idea of the Windows family is to provide capabilities across the whole range of computing equipment," Gates told his New York audience.

Discussing Windows NT, which at that point still had not reached the market, Gates went on to recount some of the thinking that got Microsoft moving on the project some four years ago: "The idea was that heretofore people, in putting together an application, had to choose between PCs, with their low cost and wide variety of software, or a workstation, which had high power and reliability, or a minicomputer-type solution. Any one of these three approaches had benefits, but no one had really pulled all of those things together.

"We felt with advances in the hardware, things like Pentium, and the right kind of operating system, we could have the best of the minicomputer, the best of the workstation, and the best of the PC pulled together in one system definition.

"That's what we believe we have achieved with this product."

Gates went on to say that a key ingredient of NT is the ability to make it work with systems on desktops all the way up to mainframes. But he added that making it work across platforms meant providing system-level services in the OS, such as license administration, security, and directory services.

"Every one of these things has been homogenized," Gates said. "So that if you have a heterogeneous network with lots and lots of different types of systems, as long as you're writing most of your code in this approach, in a Windows environment, that variety won't be a factor slowing you down."

Network-applications developers, such as Lotus Development and Oracle, couldn't be happier about the trend to provide networked services that make NOSs more manageable. Officials from both those companies say those management services will relieve some of the burden from their applications to provide similar functions.

"There's a range of those things, some of which we've had to build into Notes and cc:Mail that don't really belong in those products and that we'd be happy to see in network operating systems," says Frank Ingari, marketing vice president at Lotus. "For example, name and address services, directory services, certain kinds of gateways, and message transport services."

So even though Lotus will have to modify some of its products to take advantage of new services in NOSs, Ingari says Lotus welcomes those additions.

"To me, that's just where NOSs have to go," Ingari says. "[Networked systems] management is abysmal, so they've got to make it better. That should be integral to how you run a network. To us that's fully complementary. I don't have anything but joy when I see better management tools for networks."

But analysts such as Forrester's Hill and others, including some NOS users, aren't convinced that recreating the hierarchical mainframe world in a NOS is the smartest thing for Gates and Novell Chairman Ray Noorda to do.

THINK GLOBALLY

Myles Trachtenberg, vice president and manager of distributed technology services at Chase Manhattan Bank, says virtually all the NOS vendors are developing systems-management tools for use in their operating systems. As an example, he says Novell is developing Simple Network Management Protocol (SNMP) agents for use with a NetWare systems-management console. But he finds this focus on providing a single point of network control misguided when it comes to helping Chase run its global operations.

"Too much emphasis is being placed on the single, omnigod console," Trachtenberg says. "There isn't enough breakup of roles. . . . Not any one area is going to be able to address all the needs." Trachtenberg points out that a systems administrator in New York isn't likely to be as much help to a client user in Hong Kong as he will be to a user down the hall. So he'd like to see more distributed systems-management tools as well as distributed applications.

Hierarchical, host-centric network management systems are a disappointment to Trachtenberg.

"That really gets away from the whole point of it all," he says. "I think we should treat people with some more respect. . . . Your feedback mechanism is the people out there," he says. "If the tools are placed in the hands of a few, then their phone mail is always filled up and they've always got their hands full."

But some analysts, along with applications vendors, praise the addition of systems-management utilities.

"What you really want from a network is a single view of what's out there," observes Paul Cubbage, a principal analyst with Dataquest in San Jose, CA.

Novell's addition of global directory services, in NetWare 4.0, is a step in that direction.

"It's going to help users a lot in terms of making networks more manageable," says Jamie Lewis, an analyst with the Burton Group in Salt Lake City.

But analysts and others say Novell still has a long way to go. For instance, NetWare still comes up short of providing the kind of bulletproof stability in a high-performance system typically associated with mainframes and minicomputers, analysts and industry executives say.

"I wouldn't bet my enterprise on NetWare now," says Ed Zander, president of Sun's SunSoft (Mountain View, CA) software unit. As a provider of NOSs (with its Unix-based Solaris 2.0 product) for departmental and enterprise networks, Zander says, "We think we have an advantage in that area."

For instance, Zander says a Solaris network with 150 users can be run by one systems administrator, while he claims a NetWare system with that many users would require at least two administrators. Zander says Sun can lower the ratio of administrators to clients to one to 400.

Notoriously difficult to manage in large configurations, NetWare's stability has also been a nettlesome issue for Novell, analysts say. Along with adding directory services to ease management, the latest NetWare version attempts to provide greater stability by providing a special shell in which new applications can be tested before the entire network is exposed to them.

But The Yankee Group analyst Leopold notes that NetWare 4.0 forces users to accept a severe performance penalty for the safety of running applications one step removed from the rest of the OS. To avoid the penalty, he says, users face the risk that came with earlier NetWare versions: The failure of a single application could bring down the whole network.

"If you're talking about a mission-critical application, how could you put it on NetWare?" Leopold asks.

In NetWare 4.0 and in discussions about future enhancements, Novell is trying to address these and other issues of concern to MIS managers. Executives such as Tolonen point to the company's $350 million acquisition of Unix Systems Laboratories from AT&T and what USL will bring to NetWare when they talk about Novell's future growth.

The USL deal provides Novell with ownership of the source code for Unix System V.4, a general-purpose OS that is as much at home on a mainframe as on a desktop. Novell expects that once it is integrated with NetWare, it will go a long way to easing the problems MIS managers face in migrating applications off larger systems and into a distributed computing environment.

JUST DO IT

"The relationship between applications being integrated with the network and growth of networks is inextricable," Novell's Troop said. "At one level, Novell doesn't care whether people use OS/2 or use NT in the future or use Taligent or use UnixWare to integrate applications to the network, as long as they do it."

As networks become friendlier to applications, Troop said, MIS managers will become more comfortable putting their most important applications onto networked platforms. And that move is expected to help the dominant provider of NOSs–Novell.

"These applications aren't Lotus 1-2-3 or WordPerfect. They're in-house, mission-critical apps that currently run on host computers. And they aren't going to be moved to OS/2 or NT–or, for that matter, our product–until there is a very real understanding that the move will work," Troop said. He added that Novell believes NT will eventually become a major NOS, but not until 1995 at the earliest.

"We think we have a head start with UnixWare, to really build in that capability and to bridge down from the installed base which is in the mid-range and higher systems, into these desktop lower-end systems with Unix technology," Troop said. By "tightly integrating" Unix V.4 with NetWare, Troop went on, Novell expects to have a competitive advantage over NT in providing enterprise NOSs.

But experiences in the field with UnixWare cast doubt on Novell's ability to carry out that strategy. Forrester's Hill says UnixWare appears to have been cobbled together in haste and suffers from conspicuous lapses as a result. He says he knows of one user who struggled for two weeks to get UnixWare to run in his corporate network. One big problem: It wouldn't run TCP/IP.

"It doesn't even support Novell's own adapter cards on the server," Hill asserts. "It has all the earmarks of a product that was just rushed out the door."

Moving users into a NetWare environment could take more than simply integrating Unix V.4 into the NOS, however. Mike Prince, director of information services at discount clothing retailer Burlington Coat Factory in Manchester, NH, says his company began moving to Unix several years ago. Burlington picked Sun Microsystems' implementation and runs a Sun SPARC-based LAN in each store, with 10 to 12 PC-based point-of-sale systems connected to the server using TCP/IP.

Prince, who describes NetWare 4.0 as "really nice" but a "specialized OS," says he found NetWare particularly deficient compared to the Sun OS in that he couldn't use NetWare as a general-purpose applications platform; he can with Sun's system. And he noted that the extra charges Novell sought for TCP/IP extensions of NetWare pushed the cost per user up to near $1,000.

Although NetWare can be made into an application server with its NLMs, Tom Kucharavy, president of Summit Technology in Boston, says he doubts it will be employed for much beyond basic file and print services. For more than that, he sees users turning to Unix systems or, when it ships, to Windows NT. "NetWare's primary advantage is that it is there," in so many of today's LANs, he notes.

To Prince, the future success of any OS hinges on its ability to emulate the Windows API. "They've got to run the Windows API as seamlessly as NT will," Prince says. "The guy who can do that the best is going to win this thing." Sun, he adds, is trying to do just that.

Zander, SunSoft's president, said that in the fall of 1993, Solaris will incorporate Windows Application Binary Interface (WABI) technology Sun acquired through a merger in 1992. WABI implements the Windows API by mapping it on X Window, providing execution of Windows applications on a 32-bit platform. Zander maintains that WABI-equipped workstations can run Windows programs faster than any 386-based system.

BETTER THAN WINDOWS

IBM takes that kind of assertion one step further. It claims its OS/2 2.1 runs Windows applications better than Windows itself. While independent software vendors (ISVs) would like to see OS/2 survive to counterbalance Microsoft's marketplace power, Kucharavy and other analysts say that it isn't enough to keep ISVs making versions of their applications that take advantage of OS/2's unique features. "I just think it's too late for OS/2," Kucharavy says.

IBM may have come to that conclusion as well, at least as far as the name of the OS. John Soyring, director of software development programs for IBM's microcomputer software unit, suggests that the technology will be renamed to strip away any association with IBM's PS/2 PCs. He points out that IBM's Workplace OS runs OS/2, as well as DOS and Windows, but adds that Workplace is merely a working name for a collection of systems and utilities based on the Mach III kernel developed at Carnegie Mellon University in Pittsburgh, PA.

Microsoft may figure it has the OS contest in the bag on the basis of its ability to run Windows applications. But analysts point to several deficiencies in Windows and Windows NT that are likely to keep the competition in business.

For one thing, there's the memory-hogging size of NT. Microsoft recommends users have available 70MB of fixed disk space and at least 12MB of system memory on each client for the $495 NT package. For the server version of NT, expected to list from $2,995, Microsoft recommends a minimum system memory of 16MB and 100MB of free disk space. In contrast, NetWare 4.0 demands 6MB of system memory and anywhere from 12MB to 60MB of free disk space.

"The client cost is significant, I think," says Yankee's Leopold. "That's something that's going to slow the adoption of 32-bit operating systems," he adds, whether it's NT or Unix.

Not everyone agrees with that analysis.

"I don't think cost is the issue. Users want these services, so they're going to be willing to pay for them," says Burton Group's Lewis. But, he adds, Microsoft has another problem that could keep competitors coming.

"Microsoft is clearly trying to tie everybody to Windows, and as long as that remains their strategy, they're guaranteeing success for other vendors in the NOS world," Lewis says.

Microsoft rivals–a group that seems to include almost everyone in the industry these days–regard Windows and NT as blatant attempts to seize control of the computer industry. Gates denies any such motive–in fact, he says that kind of control is impossible in today's fragmented, horizontally segmented industry. But when he talks about Microsoft's role in the industry, it starts at the NOS layer and rises through middleware, systems utilities, and applications development to database programs, word processors, and other end-user applications.

Ingari says Microsoft's strategy "is wholesale conversion, it really is. . . . They're going to make NT a very good system if you're all NT or if you're all NT and Chicago."

Chicago is Microsoft's yet-to-be-introduced effort to blend its 32-bit Windows NT OS with DOS, the standard OS that runs on some 100 million PCs in use today.

Referring to Gates and his strategy, AT&T's Stone observes: "His game is, if he can have everybody use that interface, his interface and everybody knows it's his interface, then he can lead you through that interface to his other added-value things.

"This is a little bit like your favorite spreadsheet doing word processing and graphics on the side," Stone says. "Once they've got you doing their spreadsheet, if they can get you to do everything else through their human interface, then somehow or other, they are adding a piece of value to what you do."

By trying to find new ways to add value to their products, OS vendors from Microsoft and Novell to IBM and Sun are struggling to cope with the same trend that has shaken up other parts of the computer industry: commodity pricing.

"They're looking at the price that you're willing to pay for things and the commoditization of the lower layers of added value," says Stone, a veteran software marketer. "At one point the OS itself, not the NOS, the OS, was a high-priced item. What with Unix wars and NT wars, the price of a PC-class or a server-class operating system is getting driven down to practically zero.

"And so now where do I get my added value? Well, you go up the chain to the middleware," Stone continues. "Middleware has been fairly expensive. But it is getting bundled in and will become a commodity next. I think what is happening [is that] people are moving their added value up this chain, hoping to create more margin, but recognizing that it, too, will get commoditized pretty quickly."

But before that happens, Stone says he sees Microsoft and others trying to carve out permanent places for themselves. Microsoft, with its enormously broad market reach, appears to be doing just that. Analysts concur, noting that many vendors are abandoning development of OS/2 native applications and focusing their resources on Windows and NT.

But NT test sites have demonstrated more than just the system's finer points. Gary Curtis, an executive with the Boston Consulting Group in Chicago, says he's seen two such sites where problems that have cropped up compound with the size of the network. And, he adds, users "need a high level of expertise to set it up and do it right."

In terms of effective NOS management utilities, Curtis says Computer Associates' (Islandia, NY) UniCenter for Unix provides "a great improvement over any other solution I've seen."

"I think Microsoft has a lot of really fundamental problems to solve before they worry about the finer points of that stuff," says Tim Negris, vice president for server product marketing at Oracle in Redwood Shores, CA. Negris points out that Microsoft lacks experience as a server-software maker.

"If you look at the NT server, it's kind of like the NT client only it's got a few extra things added on," Negris continues. "The notion that a server is just kind of a client that swings both ways–it's not reasonable," Negris concludes, particularly when compared to software designed from the ground up for servers. "Microsoft's immaturity is sort of showing in that regard."

Microsoft's attempts to be an all-encompassing software provider with Windows NT has another penalty, according to Jonathan Handler, senior consultant at Blue Cross, Blue Shield of Illinois.

"If portability [of NT] is the benefit, what is the cost? The cost is performance," Handler says, citing tests his organization has run. Handler says this performance penalty translates into dollars and cents in a particularly prominent way when you get into multiprocessor systems. For instance, he claims an OS/2 system with two processors will go just as fast as a three-processor machine with Windows NT. Couple that statistic with the cost of today's fastest processors and the higher disk and memory requirements of NT, and the penalties become significant for sizable organizations, Handler submits.

Handler's suggestion, if OS/2's portability issues run counter to your shop's open-systems goals, is to take a closer look at Unix systems to escape the performance penalties and overhead costs of NT. Multithreaded client OSs, such as Unix, NT, or OS/2, will be a must for distributed-computing setups in his and other Blue Cross, Blue Shield insurance systems, Handler says. He adds that these systems will be connected to servers typically running Unix and that those servers will be connected to mainframes.

Forward into the past, in other words. For those who want a more radical solution–one that eliminates host systems–analysts suggest they not lose sight of what got them to that frame of mind.

"You get things out of these distributed systems that you never got and never will get from centralized host systems," says Hill of Forrester Research. The core benefit of client-server systems, he adds, is "maximizing the individual, the end user. That's the key resource."

NOS and OS Cross

THE MATURE DESKTOP MAY SOON HAVE AN OPERATING SYSTEM WITH BUILT-IN NETWORKING. BUT WILL NO NOS MEAN CALM OR CHAOS IN CONNECTIVITY?

BY MELANIE McMULLEN

The Nose family had an inhouse toy-sharing problem. The clan consisted of your garden-variety set of parents and eight noisy, unruly children–Dave, Michelle, Christina, Joel', Ken, Patricia, Tova, and baby Laura. Father Nose had decided to put all the children's toys down in the basement, so the children could more freely locate and share playthings.

They would check with Father or Mother Nose who were responsible for equal distribution of the toys. But as the children began to drag and click toys all over the house, Mother Nose spent most of her days in a futile attempt to organize and relocate fire trucks, blocks, and Barbies, not to mention putting out kiddie wars over whose toy belonged to whom.

Eventually Father Nose decided to rely on the maturity of his offspring to solve the situation, and he let each individual Nose regulate his or her own toys. Each would have the responsibility of determining which sibling could play with a given toy and which one would be banned.

To evaluate how well this worked, let's look at what 3-year-old Christina did. She let Michelle, Tova, and Patricia play with any of her dolls; she knew they could be trusted not to destroy them. She banned Ken and Dave from her tea set; they were boys, after all, and liked to crush cans as an afternoon pastime. She didn't allow baby Laura any access to the Magnadoodle, since she might drool on it and cause the magnets to malfunction. And she put her favorite Winnie the Pooh book into a locked drawer, where nobody could touch it.

If you take her situation and compound its difficulties with the seven other children's requests for toy access and security, can it actually work? Mother and Father Nose can rest easier, since they are no longer responsible for the chaos. But does Father Nose know best?

Microsoft (Redmond, WA) seems to think that kind of sharing will work in networking, and even Novell is willing to give it a try. And if Windows and DOS dictator and NOS king think it can work, so it will be. Products such as Microsoft's Windows for Workgroups 3.1 and Apple's System 7 are already out of the chute. With upcoming DOS 6.0, Novell's DR DOS and NetWare Lite blend, and IBM's commitment to tagging peer-to-peer to OS/2, odds are your desktop will soon know how to network.

GOOD, BAD, OR UGLY

Since the merging of OS and NOS is still a relatively novel idea, the jury is just beginning to contemplate whether this blurring of power is a good idea or a really bad one. Even the vendors are squabbling over how many and what type of users can be trusted to pull it off. Issues such as good performance and ease of use come up on the positive side, while topics of security and management are issues of debate on the down side.

First, the evangelistic believers. "I fell in love with Windows for Workgroups. It's a nice blending of networking features into operating system features," says Cheryl Currid, president of Currid & Co., a market research firm based in Houston. "It made networking natural."

She cites the user's need for control as an underlying reward of network-intrinsic operating systems. She says network managers should accommodate that user desire by giving up control of basic file and print sharing, if the users are willing to take on the responsibility at the operating system level. "Mature users who go about their own way could set up networks of hundreds and even thousands of connections," Currid continues. "You could run big, big companies like this."

Other analysts tend to agree philosophically with the principle of merging NOS capabilities into the desktop but take a more conservative stand on the number–and type–of users who will make it successful. "It's a good idea, and eventually it will happen," says Michael Howard, president of Infonetics Research, a San Jose, CA-based research firm specializing in internetworking. "You could buy one operating system and get it all." He says the experience of the users is the crucial factor in the success of embedded networking. "Even if the users are mature, you'll have organized chaos at best." He recommends that a network of 10 to 20 users would need a file server with a NOS, for backup purposes alone.

"Peer-networking services are definitely going to be embedded into the desktop OS," says Janet Hyland, director of network strategy research at Forrester Research (Cambridge, MA). "It won't kill server-based networks. A hybrid of server and peer networking will occur." She predicts users will want to use peer-to-peer OS services for sharing files between desktops, but networks of even moderate proportion will require servers for backup, security, database support, and software distribution.

Like Howard, Hyland says peer networking via the OS could have its problems. "If a server-based network is a hierarchy in structure, a peer one is an anarchy. There is no rigid structure for where files really are," she says. "Networks need the security of servers along with the fluidity of people-centric peer-to-peer systems."

MICROSOFT GOES FIRST

Microsoft went for serverless fluidity. At the end of 1992, Microsoft took advantage of its Windows, operating system, and application clout and attempted to transfer it into the network market–an area it has struggled in with LAN Manager–by releasing Windows for Workgroups 3.1. The software, which Microsoft describes as "easy to buy, set up, and use," works essentially like Windows 3.1 but offers file and printer sharing, e-mail, group scheduling, and network Dynamic Data Exchange (DDE). DDE allows users to create live links or cut and paste between documents on different PCs.

The one-stop shopping network can be purchased as a starter kit bundle that includes Windows for Workgroup software, two 16-bit network cards, 25 feet of thin Ethernet cable and connectors, and an installation video. Microsoft even throws in a screwdriver, in case you don't have one handy on your desk.

Microsoft prides itself on the product's simplicity. "For peer-to-peer file sharing, we tried to keep it simple," says Rogers Weed, product manager for Windows for Workgroups at Microsoft. "Our feeling was to make a product straightforward enough for Joe Enduser to easily grasp."

Weed says Windows for Workgroup is Microsoft's first step in its three-tiered strategy to embed network functions into operating and application software. After extending the OS to include network services, Microsoft's second goal is to evolve existing applications to include workgroup features or make application software more shareable and network-aware.

The third tier involves a new class of Microsoft application software whose primary benefit to the user is to solve a group-oriented need. Weed cites Schedule+, software that allows users to set up group calendars and meetings, as an example of a product that fits into that category.

"Networking is coming down to the system level in software," says Weed. "If the PC is a group tool, the operating system has to have certain services, such as networking and messaging, built in systemwide."

UNDER SCRUTINY

While the NOS, OS, and application software merge sounds easy enough, Microsoft has had its share of headaches doing it, both technically and legally. Currently, it is the subject of a two-year inquiry by the Federal Trade Commission (FTC) concerning possible antitrust violations. While previously Microsoft maintained that it had a Wall of China between its OS and application groups, that may no longer be the case, especially when Microsoft is shipping OS software that doesn't just work with application software–it contains them, such as the e-mail in Windows for Workgroups.

The FTC investigators submitted a 250-page report in December of 1992 but took no punitive action against Microsoft, according to the Washington-based newsletter *FTC: Watch.* That report dealt with the topic of licensing DOS "in a manner calculated to prevent competing operating systems from being established," the newsletter stated.

Another problem facing Microsoft is Windows for Workgroups' incompatibilities with NetWare. Although positioned as a workgroup solution for up to 50 users, Windows for Workgroups clients are inevitably going to need access to existing NetWare servers. Windows for Workgroups clients access one another or a LAN Manager server by using NetBEUI. To access a NetWare server, the client runs IPX in parallel with NetBEUI. Although both companies admit this approach has problems, neither company is specific on the details. But they do agree that a solution is mandatory.

Concerning progress made toward finding a cure, Weed says, "I'm encouraged by the last couple of months. We just need to hammer it through." Novell chimes a similar tune. "We're working hard to support Windows for Workgroups," says William Donahoo, director of marketing for the desktop systems group at Novell. "But we would tell customers to be careful of that product."

Microsoft says the problems originated because it didn't consult Novell during software development. "We didn't involve them in beta, since Windows for Workgroups competes with their products," says Weed. "We wanted to involve the NetWare server people, but we didn't want the DR DOS and NetWare Lite people to get hold of the product. Novell was taken off guard, and that created a strain in our relationship."

Analysts say the technical problems between NetWare and Windows for Workgroups will have to be resolved. "Windows for Workgroups will simply have to work with NetWare," says Forrester's Hyland. "And Microsoft will have to come back with something positioned differently than where this product is, which is a low-end, serverless LAN with bundled applications."

CALLING DR NETWARE

With a multitude of illnesses plaguing Windows for Workgroups, Microsoft has left the door open for Novell, which is already talking about an operating system to be released in the first half of this year that will meld DR DOS and NetWare Lite. "The competition for the client side is becoming a war between Microsoft and Novell," says analyst Howard. And Novell is by no means sitting on its hands.

"There ought to be tighter integration with the desktop system," says Donahoo. "Novell will be a strong player at the desktop." He says Novell will create a combination NOS/OS, similar to the one found in the Mac environment with System 7, but it will support a mix of clients. Apple provides networking only to other Apples, he says, and Windows for Workgroups only connects Windows, which is a big negative.

"There has to be something beyond the homogeneous environment. Novell is aiming toward a heterogeneous OS solution to connect diverse environments," he says. "Networking has to be neutral enough to support all networks, without breaking the paradigm of the Apples and Windows."

Although touting the power of a desktop OS with networking hooks, Donahoo also admits that purely peer networking can have its share of dilemmas. "You don't want a 5GB database running on your desktop. And would you really want someone to actually work on the machine that the company depends on for its business?" He doesn't view serverless networks to be quite as simple as Microsoft sees them. "Connecting people is important, but having to map 15 drives to your desktop is absolutely too confusing for the user."

Additionally, Donahoo says an operating system with integrated networking should be supplemented with a server NOS at about 10 users, allowing companies scalability. "The desktop and the server have to play together," he says. "Microsoft is saying peer-to-peer is better, but that's shortsighted. It's a lie, and they know it. Only two years ago, they were saying client-server is important."

Although Novell has not announced details, analysts speculate that the OS will function as a universal client that includes a single set of APIs to access NetWare Lite networks or NetWare 2.x, 3.x, and 4.x servers or clients. The product will most likely be modular, allowing users to choose not to load the peer network functions as well as giving users the option to use MS-DOS instead of DR DOS. Donahoo says Novell also plans to release versions of the product for Windows and Macintosh computers. "It's a big challenge technically to mix clients," says Microsoft's Weed. "But Novell is in the best position of any of us to do that."

THREE'S A CROWD

The only other company in a position to make a networking OS work is IBM (Armonk, NY). With a network-aware operating system such as OS/2 already in place, IBM would have a fairly easy time embedding peer-to-peer functionality. While DOS requires an NOS as a bolt-on to kidnap files and redirect calls, OS/2 integrates well with networking. "In OS/2, you're not a growth on the side," says Donahoo. "You have a place to sit. With DOS, you had to find your way around."

At the end of 1992, IBM announced some general development plans that included peer services being added to OS/2, but specific products have not been disclosed.

"There's an attraction for building a peer platform, in terms of DDE over the LAN and clipboard over the LAN, that also includes file and print sharing," says Art Olbert, personal systems director of IBM's LAN systems division in Austin, TX. In November of 1992, IBM added peer-to-peer functionality to LAN Server 3.0.

IBM's offering will most likely be a modular one also. "The idea of putting a bundle together goes against our experience in the market," says Olbert. He related IBM's experience with OS/2 Extended Edition, which at first IBM released as one piece of tightly integrated software containing the base operating system, communications manager, database manager, and the LAN requester. "Then we spent the last year and a half taking them apart," says Olbert, explaining that customers repeatedly told the company that they wanted more choices.

IBM's networking OS/2 would also contain some connection to a server-based system, which is where the vast majority of the OS/2 installed base already resides. Forrester Research predicts IBM will have two versions of OS/2–one for the desktop and one for the server.

Olbert explains the user-based reason why servers would always play a role in IBM's strategy: "We've done significant research in this area, and we found that peer networks over eight systems don't exist. We literally find a breakdown at six or eight when people do a wonderful, logical thing and say, 'Wait a minute. Instead of dealing with eight other connections in my workgroup, let's buy something to put our shared information in.' "

For IBM to make any sort of dent with a networking OS/2 offering, it would have to reduce the software's hardware requirements and simplify installation, something that Forrester Research says IBM should do on the basic product to make it successful.

THE NOS/OS MARRIAGE

Since the inevitable marriage of the desktop operating system with the network operating system has already taken place, this year should be the experimental honeymoon for Windows for Workgroups and Novell's and IBM's releases along those lines. Following close behind will be the release of Microsoft's DOS 6.0. DOS 6.0 will have a TSR that starts the network and connects, disconnects, and browses the servers. It will also feature network client support for Windows for Workgroups, Windows NT, and LAN Manager.

Even with the popularity of Windows, don't toss DOS for dead. Analysts predict that a network-aware DOS 6.0 could be a best-seller. Forrester's interviews with 100 Fortune 1,000 companies revealed that DOS will maintain a 43 percent market share in 1994, followed by Windows at 33 percent.

With a deep-rooted market share, thousands of applications, and now embedded networking, DOS 6.0 could lead to more linking by the previously non-networked. "When you implement networking at the OS level, it's ubiquitous. It's not a kludge," says Pieter Harsook, editor of the Harsook Letter, a Macintosh market research newsletter and service in Alameda, CA. He suggests that the new DOS could lead to the high network numbers found in Mac environments using System 7. He estimates that 65 percent to 70 percent of all Macs are networked, double the current figures of the DOS world. He says simply, "If it's there, you tend to use it."

Section 8
Managment and Security

As networks grow in leaps and bounds, so does the amount of maintenance and tending required to keep them going. While a few years ago the network manager could slink by with a minimum amount of management and security software and savvy, that is no longer the case. The modern network, whether consisting of ten nodes or tens of thousands of nodes, needs ongoing management and stringent security.

The network management schemes of the future will be centered around alliances. Management capabilities for individual components will be consolidated onto a few platforms and built into every piece of hardware that sits on the network. "DMI: Desktop Detente" and "Management Framework" describe a couple of ways in which this could be achieved.

Security is also an issue that will become more vexing in the future. Hackers looking to destroy and tinker with information are rampant, yet data integrity has to be ensured and maintained. You have to know how to properly batten down the network hatches. "Stump the Cipher Punks" and "Make It Real" offer some fundamental methods of making sure that information that is broadcast across a network can be seen and deciphered only by those with the proper privileges and authorizations.

DMI: Desktop Détente

AS THE DMTF EMERGES, VENDORS JOIN FORCES TO BETTER COMMUNICATION AND COEXISTENCE WHILE THEY DESIGN A COMMON MANAGEMENT INTERFACE.

BY BONNY HINNERS

This decade is proving to be one of revolutionary peace with the end of the Cold War and the signing of the Middle East peace agreement. Even major players in the personal computer marketplace have been asking themselves if they might reach an accord that would leave the PC a tranquil place. Can multiple vendors not only coexist but also acquire meaningful information about one another?

Yes, they have said, it can be done, and they established the Desktop Management Task Force (DMTF) to fulfill the goal.

Originally, five companies were involved: Intel (Hillsboro, OR), Microsoft (Redmond, WA), Novell, SunConnect, (Mountain View, CA) and SynOptics (Santa Clara, CA). IBM, DEC, and Hewlett-Packard (HP) were quick to join the effort. As other companies sought to become members, the eight charter members chose to limit participation. They allow other companies to join only as participating members in the hopes that the DMTF can avoid becoming bogged down in bureaucracy if it stays small. In addition to interest from companies throughout the industry, the Personal Computing Asset Management Institute (PCAMI) contributed recommendations from the end-user perspective.

The DMTF set four primary goals:

• Design a programming interface to allow desktop systems to become more intelligent and easily manageable.

• Specify a method for adding manageability to desktop components.

• Specify a venue for management applications to gain information and control over desktop components.

• Simplify implementation of the technology.

In less than a year and a half, the DMTF released a beta version of the Desktop Management Interface (DMI) and made it available at conferences, on bulletin boards, and through charter members. The DMTF appears well on its way to achieving its goals, with the final specification expected this quarter.

ALL TOGETHER NOW

These goals extend to five categories of desktop products: platforms, add-ons, peripherals, management applications, and management consoles. *Platforms* are the actual desktop PC systems and network servers. *Add-ons* comprise the adapters and software that reside on the platform. *Peripherals* are those devices that attach to the platform. *Management applications* are those that access the desktop information, and *management consoles* are those based on industry standards.

As part of the DMTF effort, participating companies are grouping together to determine what information common products should make available. Working groups for printers, network adapters, modems, software applications, and storage were organized last. The purpose of these groups is to agree on the manageable aspects of a specific component. Working groups for consoles and operating systems were also formed to ensure the viability of DMI from their perspectives.

Chris Thomas, chairman of the DMTF and manager of technology and alliances for Intel's networking division, feels the working groups provide the DMTF with an opportunity for a coincidental contribution to the computer industry: the ability to unify standardization efforts. Ron Smith, manager of printer technology development at Texas Instruments (Temple, TX), agrees. Considering existing printer standardization efforts, he says that for the printer working group, "The first major step was to get all the major printer manufacturers to meet in one room and to agree to meet again." PostScript, HP, and the Network Printer Alliance are represented in the group, and it is starting to tackle problems of printer and print-job management.

With the scope of products considered by the DMTF, conceivably anything purchased for the desktop in the future will be DMI-compliant. For example, Acer Computers and MAG Technology (both in Taipei, Taiwan) monitors will implement DMI. Intel plans for all its networking products to be DMI-compliant, from fax boards and network adapters to the StorageExpress backup system and LANDesk management software. Management consoles from Microsoft, Trend Micro Devices (Torrance, CA), and Microcom (Norwood, MA) are also expected to be DMI-compliant.

With the open nature of the DMI, the sky is the limit when it comes to determining what products can benefit from the DMI. It has the potential to touch all aspects of desktop system management.

For hardware and software installation, products can retrieve information about the existing status of the system and its resources to better automate installation. No more selecting which printer drivers need to be installed, for example.

With DMI information, automatic software distribution across the network can be based on up-to-the-minute desktop characteristics. The latest IPX.COM and NEXTXCOM, for example, can be installed based on the current network adapter settings rather than on information in a sometimes-outdated database.

Troubleshooting becomes easier when diagnostics, which previously couldn't talk to anything else, can share information across the system. An off-line printer or paper jam, for example, can be reported to users rather than the vague "cannot print to . . ." message now offered.

COMPONENTS OF DMI

The DMI was designed for flexibility and extensibility. Spry (Seattle) President Dave Pool says these features are one of the DMI's primary advantages, "The PC market changes every nine months. Extensibility is required to hit a moving target like that."

The DMI consists of four major components. They are the management information file (MIF), component interface, management interface, and service layer (see figure).

The *MIF* describes the manageable aspects of a given component, whether it be the platform itself or any of its add-ons and peripherals. This ASCII file contains static information and is defined by the component manufacturer. It is the goal of DMTF working groups to develop a common MIF for similar products–a common printer MIF or network adapter MIF, for example.

The *component* and *management interfaces* are APIs defined for component manufacturers and management-application developers respectively. The primary commands for both APIs are GET and SET, allowing both management applications and desktop components to retrieve or specify information about the desktop when needed.

In addition, management applications can LIST information in the MIFs. This capability allows management applications to gain information with no previous knowledge of the system. Pool says that one of the main advantages of the DMI is that it enables management applications to "learn" about the desktop.

Another important command offered by the component interface is an EVENT. This command allows components to send notification of occurrences that might be of interest to management applications. It can be used for a variety of functions such as notifying management applications when an adapter card loses a connection with a specific server. "The event notification is key for printers," according to Smith. "Printers are dynamic devices. They run out of toner and paper and you never know when that's going to happen." With event notification, the printer initiates the message when it needs attention, eliminating the overhead of polling the device constantly for changes in its state. Smith says, "Now all the information the printer knows about itself and reports on its LCD can be reported on the desktop."

The *service layer* coordinates information exchanges between the component and management interfaces. This portion of the DMI is the actual code that resides on the PC platform to facilitate the DMI. Originally, the DMTF developed a TSR and DLL to act as the service layer for DOS and Windows, respectively, followed by code for OS/2 and Windows NT.

Eventually, the DMTF hopes to see the service layer built into operating systems rather than it being a separate

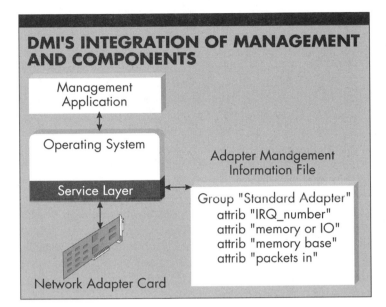

DMI'S INTEGRATION OF MANAGEMENT AND COMPONENTS

Management Application

Operating System

Service Layer

Network Adapter Card

Adapter Management Information File

Group "Standard Adapter"
attrib "IRQ_number"
attrib "memory or IO"
attrib "memory base"
attrib "packets in"

HOW WILL YOU MANAGE? The network adapter card registers with the service layer when it is installed. The Management Information File describes the adapter's manageable characteristics. Management applications communicate with the adapter card via the service layer.

program. A service layer built into the operating system will eliminate the need for TSRs on the desktop, such as those common to inventory and control programs. TSRs are particularly troublesome because users sometimes remove them and because they can conflict with other memory-resident programs. With the service layer built into the operating system, and the component interface built into the component, management applications can rely on the fact that a desktop is always prepared to offer information.

When a component is installed, it passes a MIF to the service layer. Management applications can request information through the service layer for installed components. Likewise, components can indicate unsolicited information through the service layer. Components also notify the service layer when they are removed.

The separation of management and component interfaces is another advantage of the DMI according to Smith: "Management-application development proceeds independently of component development." Component manufacturers don't have to busy themselves with every management aspect from the component through the application. And management-application developers don't have to worry about a lack of standards between components. Smith continues, "DMI should spur on applications because it's gotten rid of the bottleneck of 'I have to write to this device and that device. Which one do I do first?' "

The DMI was designed to be independent of the operating system, network, network protocol, and existing management protocols. This independence makes it possible to develop DMI-compliant code for any existing desktop system. It is, of course, necessary to develop service-layer code appropriate to the operating system if components and management applications expect to share data on any given platform. Once a service layer exists for an operating system, any DMI-compliant application written for the same platform should operate as it would on any other platform.

Dan Shelly, group product manager for Enterprise Systems at Microsoft, says operating system independence makes the DMI attractive to network administrators. "Probably the biggest advantage is that by providing cross-platform support, it really solves problems for customers who have heterogeneous environments," he says. "They have a variety [of operating systems] and they'd like it all to work together."

SOME SHORTCOMINGS

While initially the service-layer code was provided only for DOS, Windows, Windows NT, and OS/2, charter members, such as IBM, Novell, and SunConnect, can be instrumental in having the code ported to operating systems such as Unix and DR-DOS. Even so, the Macintosh may go unsupported. As of last year, Apple was not even a participating member nor part of the printer working group. A Macintosh service layer would certainly be useful to a lot of desktop users and network administrators who need to manage resources on those computers.

And because the DMTF is dedicated to resource management on the *desktop* (thus the name), the DMI does not specify how network applications and resources will function. This shortcoming is DMI's biggest, according to Jundar Huong, program manager for Trend Micro Devices. Management applications trying to retrieve data remotely and peripherals that attach directly to the network, such as some network printers, are not covered by the DMI. That's not to say they couldn't be. At the DMTF Developer's Conference last fall, Trend Micro Devices demonstrated an application under development that enables a management console to scan any desktop on the network for viruses.

Even so, the Simple Network Management Protocol (SNMP) and other existing standards for network management must still be used. Steve Dauber, product-line manager for network management at Novell, says NetWare servers will continue to be managed through SNMP and directory services. Presumably, activities such as inventory control on the server will take place as they have in the past, by downing the server and running a DOS application to retrieve information not otherwise attainable, such as port and memory configurations.

NetWare servers won't be readily manageable through DMI, but SNMP management consoles, such as Novell's NMS, will still be able to manage desktop systems thanks to the DMI. The DMTF designed MIFs to be easily mappable to SNMP management information blocks (MIBs) and has even written a sample translation utility to demonstrate how the MIF can be ported to other protocols. It is this mapping capability that enables products such as the current release of NMS to manage the desktop. However, the DMTF will probably not supply translations to work with the Common Management Information Protocol (CMIP) or with CMIP over Logical Link Control (CMOL).

Why not expand existing standards such as SNMP to better embrace the desktop rather than developing yet another management standard? Pool explains that not only is the DMI "very well layed out and logical," but also it has the commercial backing of companies such as Intel, IBM, Microsoft, and Novell. Standardization efforts such as

SNMP don't have similar backing, nor are they able to respond as quickly to the ever-changing market, he believes.

Thomas says, "We didn't want to be coupled with one specific [network protocol], but our goal was to be mappable to the popular ones."

Network administrators and desktop users alike will discover that the DMI offers them less advantage with existing components than with updated and future DMI-compliant components. Existing components that are not updated for DMI will continue to be maintained as they have been in the past in relatively static databases. Management applications will treat them as they have always been treated with little advantage from the DMI. If management and inventory-control applications translate existing databases to MIFs, data should be interoperable. That alone would be a benefit we haven't readily enjoyed without the DMI.

When the service layer is finally built into the operating system, another benefit will be the elimination of those irritating TSRs and DLLs that users sometimes delete. Even before the service layer is built into the operating system, the DMI eliminates the need for multiple, possibly conflicting TSRs as long as all your management applications are DMI compliant.

When exactly will the service layer be built into operating systems? Even though the service-layer code was developed last year, Microsoft, for example, has not announced plans to incorporate it into future operating system releases.

According to Shelly, Microsoft has not determined when it will add the service layer to its operating systems. "When [the specification] is finalized, then we'll have plans for how we're going to implement and support it. We're certainly not saying [it will be in] the next release of the operating systems." Shelly would not speculate on when the specification might be finalized even though Microsoft's management console, code named Hermes, promises to support DMI components.

Microsoft's "plug-and-play" Windows, which has some capabilities similar to those offered by DMI, is a proprietary technology not related to the DMI. According to Shelly, Microsoft has written a "translation layer that takes the plug-and-play information and puts it in a format accessible to DMI." All this work toward DMI compatibility seems to indicate Microsoft's commitment to the technology, even if its announced operating system plans don't yet include DMI.

MANAGEMENT FIRST

Thomas is optimistic about DMI's future. He expects the specification to be finalized this quarter and DMI-compliant products to begin shipping promptly. "We're doing what we should have done in the first place," he says, "embedding management into the products instead of tacking it on at the end."

Dauber believes the biggest disadvantage to the DMI is that the products that implement it on the desktop aren't available now. He says Novell is anxious to give network administrators access to desktop management, and DMI provides that opportunity.

The ability to manage desktop resources will be a boon to network administrators and will bring down the cost of computing. "Much of the cost is in management and support, not acquisition," says Dauber.

All aspects of managing the desktop could be affected by the DMI, but don't expect it to become an official standard. The DMTF does not plan to submit any part of the DMI to any standardizations organizations because it doesn't believe there is a suitable organization to consider it. The IEEE and ANSI are not particularly focused on the desktop system itself. Instead, the DMTF plans to continue working with companies and end users to assist with DMI implementation.

The DMTF expects to increase the number of working groups and support for their efforts. It also hopes to assist end users by considering an end-user group specific to DMTF in addition to the PCAMI. DMTF will provide other help for end users in the form of documentation, for example a deployment guide to help those hoping to develop their own DMI-compliant products and to explain the benefits of such products.

A Management Framework

A NEW VERSION OF SNMP ARRIVES–SNMPV2–TO MAKE UP FOR SOME OF THE PROTOCOL'S EARLIER SHORTCOMINGS, WHILE ENABLING COEXISTENCE WITH SNMPV1.

BY WILLIAM STALLINGS

In 1992, President Clinton (then candidate Clinton) popularized the word "infrastructure." While several years before, Bush had promised a kinder, gentler nation, and more recently Perot vowed to run the United States as if it were a larger version of one of his companies, Clinton capitalized on the idea of "rebuilding" the country–from the ground up. Goodbye to the hard times that came to characterize the preceding administration. Don't stop thinking about tomorrow, beginning with a newly installed management framework.

If any industry can, the networking industry can out-PR someone as high-profile as a presidential candidate. Years before Clinton's name achieved household-word status, the network industry was abuzz with talk of the need to re-lay the foundation of corporate management. Computers and networks had irrevocably changed the way business was conducted, but companies had changed neither their management habits nor their basic infrastructure to keep pace. The ideal would be an intersection of the two–a technology that would help lay the foundation for new network-aware forms of management, a protocol that simplified network management–a Simple Network Management Protocol (SNMP).

In August of 1988, SNMP was issued and rapidly became the dominant network-management standard. The speed with which SNMP was accepted caught even its most passionate supporters by surprise.

SOME SHORTCOMINGS

But as the protocol gained widespread use, its deficiencies became apparent. These deficiencies include functional shortfalls and the lack of a security facility. To deal with the lack of a security capability, an enhancement, known as Secure SNMP, was published in July 1992 as a proposed standard. A further enhancement, the Simple Management Protocol (SMP) incorporates, with minor changes, the security features in Secure SNMP and provides additional functionality to SNMP.

SMP became the starting point for an open process that would lead to the next generation of SNMP, to be named SNMP version 2 (SNMPv2). A draft set of SNMPv2 specifications was published early in 1993 as proposed Internet standards.

The SNMPv2 specifications are technically stable. Even though the process by which the specification becomes an official standard will take a few more months, vendors have already begun work on SNMPv2 products. Expect a flood of SNMPv2 product announcements.

GIVE ME STRUCTURE

Surprisingly, SNMPv2 does not provide network management at all. Instead, it provides a framework–or infrastructure–on which network-management applications can be built. Figure 1 shows the type of infrastructure that SNMPv2 can create.

The essence of SNMPv2 is a protocol that is used to exchange management information in the form of a message. Each "player" in the management system maintains a local database of information relevant to network management, known as the *Management Information Base* (MIB).

Essentially, the MIB is a collection of objects or data variables that represent one aspect of the managed agent. The MIB functions as a collection of access points at the agent for the *management station*.

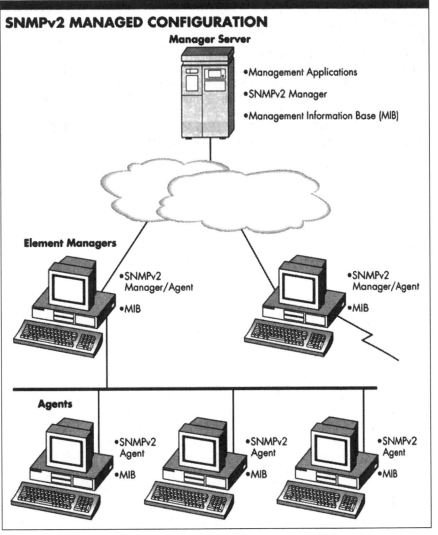

Figure 2. Within the SNMPv2 framework, manager and agent stations maintain a local database of information, called a MIB, which defines acceptable data structures.

At least one system in the network must act as the management station. Any network-management applications are housed at this station. More than one of these management stations may exist to provide redundancy or simply to split duties in a large network. Other systems can act as agents or, in some cases–as in distributed environments–they may act as both management stations and agents.

An agent collects information locally and stores it for later access by a manager. The information includes data about the system and may also include traffic information for the network or networks to which the agent attaches.

The MIB's *objects*, or access points, are standardized across systems of a particular class (for example, bridges all support the same management objects). The management station monitors the network by retrieving the value of MIB objects. A management station can cause an action to take place at an agent or can change the configuration settings of an agent by modifying the value of specific variables.

The SNMPv2 standard defines the structure of this information and the allowable data types; this definition is known as the *Structure of Management Information* (SMI).

LISTING 1—AN EXAMPLE OF AN SNMPv2 TABLE

```
grokTable     OBJECT-TYPE
  SYNTAX      SEQUENCE OF GrokEntry
  MAX-ACCESS       not-accessible
  STATUS           current
  DESCRIPTION
    "The (conceptual) grok table."
  ::= | adhocGroup 2 |

grokEntry     OBJECT-TYPE
  SYNTAX           GrokEntry
  MAX-ACCESS       not-accessible
  STATUS           current
  DESCRIPTION
    "An entry (conceptual row) in the grok table."
  INDEX                | grokIndex |
  ::= | grokTable 1 |

GrokEntry ::= SEQUENCE |
    grokIndex         INTEGER,
    grokIPAddress     IpAddress,
    grokValue         Counter32,
    grokStatus        RowStatus |

grokIndex     OBJECT-TYPE
  .SYNTAX          INTEGER
  MAX-ACCESS       not-accessible
  STATUS           current
  DESCRIPTION
    "The auxiliary variable used for identify instances of the
    columnar objects in the grok table."
  ::= | grokEntry 1 |
```

```
grokIPAddress    OBJECT-TYPE
  SYNTAX         IpAddress
  MAX-ACCESS     read-create
  STATUS         current
  DESCRIPTION
    "The Ip address to send grok packets to."
  ::= | grokEntry 2 |

grokCount     OBJECT-TYPE
  SYNTAX         Counter32
  MAX-ACCESS     read-only
  STATUS         current
  DESCRIPTION
    "The total number of grok packets sent so far."
  DEFVAL-| 0 |
  ::= | grokEntry 3 |

grokStatus    OBJECT-TYPE
  SYNTAX         RowStatus
  MAX-ACCESS     read-create
  STATUS         current
  DESCRIPTION
    "The status object used for creating, modifying, and
    deleting a conceptual row instance in the grok table."
  DEFVAL-| active |
  ::= | grokEntry 4 |
```

SMI is the language for defining management information: It defines the general framework within which a MIB can be constructed–which data types can be used and how resources are named. The standard also supplies a number of MIBs generally useful for network management. In addition, vendors and user groups can define new MIBs.

SMI encourages simplicity and extensibility within the MIB. Thus, the MIB can store only simple data types: scalar numbers and two-dimensional arrays of scalars, called *tables*. SMI does not support the creation or retrieval of complex data structures; this pared-down approach actually expands interoperability.

DUAL ROLES

SNMPv2 will support either a highly centralized network-management strategy or a distributed one. In the latter case, some systems operate as both manager and agent.

When acting as an agent, a system accepts commands from a superior management system. Some of those commands relate to the local MIB at the agent. Other commands require the agent to act as a proxy for remote devices. In this case, the proxy agent assumes the role of manager to access information at a remote agent, then assumes the role of an agent to pass that information to a superior manager.

All these exchanges take place using the SNMPv2 protocol, a simple request/response type of protocol. Typically, SNMPv2 is implemented on top of the User Datagram Protocol (UDP), which is part of the TCP/IP protocol suite.

The final concept you should understand to make sense of Figure 1 is that of *parties*. Any SNMP implementation includes one or more parties, which, in essence, are the roles taken by the protocol. Information is exchanged between the parties, and the parties assumed by the protocol

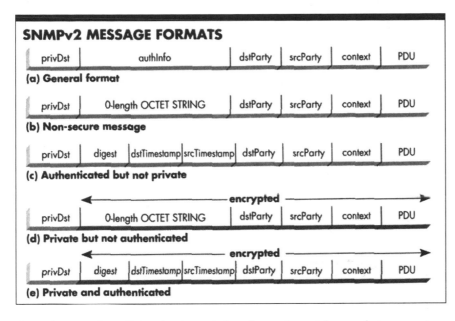

Figure 2. The SNMPv2 protocol contains an outer message wrapper and an inner Protocol Data Unit (PDU). Five fields within the message header define security-related information.

determine security policies. Access-control and security policies differ depending on the combination of manager, agent, and desired information. This loose definition gives the user considerable flexibility in setting up a network-management system and assigning levels of authorization.

WHEN SIMPLER IS BETTER

Because it does not support the creation or retrieval of complex data structures, SMI systems management differs from OSI systems management, which supports these structures and retrieval modes to provide greater functionality. Whereas the more complex model makes achieving interoperability more difficult, SMI's simplified approach enhances interoperability. But MIBs will inevitably contain vendor-created data types and, unless restrictions are placed on the definition of such data types, interoperability will suffer.

SMI contains three key elements. At the lowest level, SMI specifies the data types that may be stored. Then, SMI specifies a formal technique for defining objects and tables of objects. Finally, SMI provides a scheme for associating a unique identifier with each object in a system so data at an agent can be referenced by a manager.

SMI's set of allowable data types is fairly restricted. For example, real numbers are not supported. However, SMI is rich enough to support most network-management requirements.

The SNMPv2 specification includes a template, known as an *Abstract Syntax Notation One* (ASN.1) macro, which provides the formal model for defining objects. Listing 1, which defines a table I created, shows how this collection of templates can define objects and tables of objects. The first three definitions (grokTable, grokEntry, and GrokEntry) apply to a table (grokTable) stored at an agent.

As with all SNMPv2 tables, grokTable is organized as a sequence of rows, or entries, each of which has the same sequence of objects. The INDEX clause specifies that the object grokIndex serves as an index into the table; each row of the table will have a unique value for grokIndex.

The grokIPAddress is a read/create access type, which means that the object is read/write and that a management station may assign the object at the time that the manager creates the row containing this object.

Each row of the table maintains a counter for the number of grok packets sent to the grokIPAddress. The grokCount object is read-only; its value cannot be altered by a manager but is maintained by the agent within which this table resides. The manager uses the grokStatus object when creating and deleting rows. Both manager and agent use the RowStatus object to track the state of a row during creation and deletion.

Each object definition includes a *value*, which is a unique identifier. For example, the value for grokEntry is {grokTable 1}; the identifier for grokEntry is the concatenation of the identifier for grokTable and 1. The objects in a MIB are organized in a tree structure, and the identifier of an object is found by walking the tree from its root to the position of the object in that structure. For scalar objects, this scheme provides a unique identifier for any given object instance. For objects in tables, each object occurs once in each row of the table, so the object must be further qualified. A manager specifies an instance by concatenating the value of the INDEX object to the identifier of each object in the table.

PROTOCOL OPERATION

The heart of the SNMPv2 framework is the protocol itself. The protocol provides a straightforward, basic mechanism for the exchange of management information between manager and agent.

The basic unit of exchange is the message, which consists of an outer message wrapper and an inner Protocol Data Unit (PDU). The message header consists of security-related information contained within five fields, as Figure 2 illustrates.

The srcParty identifies the party at a manager or agent that is sending this message. The dstParty identifies the party at a manager of the agent to whom the message is sent. The context may indicate that this exchange relates to access to a MIB local to the agent; in this case, the context value serves to identify a portion of the agent's MIB, known as a *MIB view*. A MIB view is simply a subset of the MIB at the agent, which is the subject of this protocol exchange.

Otherwise, the context value indicates that this exchange involves access to a third system by means of a proxy relationship. In this case, the context value serves to identify the proxied device and the access-control privileges associated with accessing that proxied device. In either case, the combination of source party, destination party, and context value determine the access-control privileges for this exchange.

The authInfo field carries the information required by an authenticated exchange. If this pair of parties uses authentication, then a message digest is computed over the message using a secret key by the source party. The destination party computes the same digest; a match verifies that the message was indeed sent by the party indicated in the srcParty field. The authInfo field also includes two time stamps to maintain synchronization between party clocks at source and destination. These clocks assure the timeliness of the message.

In addition, SNMPv2 uses encryption to ensure that communication between two parties may be protected from eavesdropping. SNMPv1 does not include this capability. With SNMPv2, the entire message, with the exception of the privDst field, is encrypted. The privDst field repeats the dstParty field–a value that must remain clear to enable delivery to the intended party.

As Figure 2 indicates, the communication between two parties may be nonsecure, may provide either authentication or privacy, or may provide both.

MIND YOUR PDUS

An SNMP message may carry seven types of PDUs. Figure 3 illustrates the general formats. Several fields are common to a number of PDUs. The request-id field is an integer assigned in such a way that each outstanding request can be uniquely identified. This unique identification enables a manager to correlate incoming responses with outstanding requests. It also enables an agent to cope with duplicate PDUs generated by an unreliable transport service. The variable-bindings field contains a list of object identifiers; depending on the PDU, the list may also include a value for each object.

The GetRequest-PDU, issued by a manager, includes a list of one or more object names for which values are requested. If the "get" operation is successful, then the responding agent sends a Response-PDU. The variable-bindings list contains the identifier and value of all retrieved objects. For any variables that are not in the relevant MIB view, its identifier and an error code are returned in the variable-bindings list.

Thus, SNMPv2 permits partial responses to a GetRequest, a significant improvement over SNMPv1's handling of such occurrences. In SNMPv1, if an agent does not support one or more of the variables in a GetRequest, the agent returns an error message with a status of noSuchName. To cope with such an error, the SNMP manager must either return no values to the requesting application, or it must include an algorithm that responds to the error

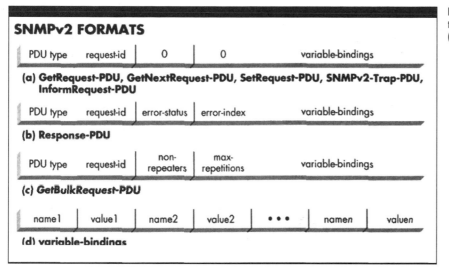

Figure 3. An SNMPv2 message carries these seven types of Protocol Data Units (PDUs).

by removing the missing variables, resending the request, then sending a partial result to the application.

The GetNextRequest-PDU also is issued by a manager and includes a list of one or more objects. For each object named in the variable-bindings field, a value is to be returned for the object that is next in *lexicographic order*, meaning next in the MIB's tree structure. As with the GetRequest-PDU, the agent will return values for as many variables as possible. One of the strengths of the GetNextRequest-PDU is that it enables a manager to discover dynamically the structure of a MIB view. This dynamic identification is useful if the manager does not know a priori the set of objects that is supported by an agent or that is contained in a particular MIB view.

WAIT, THERE'S MORE

One of the major enhancements SNMPv2 provides is the GetBulkRequest-PDU. This PDU minimizes the number of protocol exchanges required to retrieve a large amount of management information. The GetBulkRequest-PDU allows an SNMPv2 manager to request that the response be as large as possible given the constraints on message size.

The GetBulkRequest operation uses the same selection principle as the GetNextRequest operation; that is, selection is always of the next object instance in lexicographic order. The difference is that, with GetBulkRequest, multiple lexicographic successors can be selected.

In essence, the GetBulkRequest operation includes a list of (N + R) variable names in the variable-bindings list. For each of the first N names, retrieval is done in the same fashion as for GetNextRequest. That is, for each variable in the list, the next variable in lexicographic order plus its value is returned; if no lexicographic successor exists, then the named variable and a value of endOfMibView are returned. For each of the last R names, multiple lexicographic successors are returned.

The GetBulkRequest-PDU has two fields that other PDUs do not: nonrepeaters and max-repetitions. The nonrepeaters field specifies the number of variables in the variable-bindings list for which a single lexicographic successor is to be returned. The max-repetitions field specifies the number of lexicographic successors to be returned for the remaining variables in the variable-bindings list. To understand the algorithm, you must know the following variables and their definitions:

L = the number of variable names in the variable-bindings field of the GetBulkRequest-PDU

N = the number of variables, starting with the first variable in the variable-bindings field, for which a single lexicographic successor is requested

R = the number of variables, following the first N variables, for which multiple lexicographic successors are requested

M = the number of lexicographic successors requested for each of the last R variables

The following relationships hold:

$N =$

MAX [MIN (non-repeaters,L), 0]

$M = $ MAX [max-repetitions, 0]

$R = L - N$

If the value of either nonrepeaters or max-repetitions is less than zero, a value of 0 is substituted.

If N is greater than 0, then the first N variables are processed as for GetNextRequest. If R is greater than 0, and M is greater than 0, then for each of the last R variables in the variable-bindings list, the M lexicographic successors are retrieved.

That is, for each variable,

• obtain the value of the lexicographic successor of the named variable;

• obtain the value of the lexicographic successor to the object instance retrieved in the previous step;

• obtain the value of the lexicographic successor to the object instance retrieved in the previous step;

• and so forth, until M object instances have been retrieved.

If, at any point in this process, there is no lexicographic successor, then the endOfMibView value is returned, paired with the name of the last lexicographic successor or, if there were no successors, with the name of the variable in the request.

Using these rules, the total number of variable-binding pairs that can be produced is N + (M x R). The order in which the last (M x R) of these variable-binding pairs are placed in the Response-PDU can be expressed as follows:

for i : = 1 to M do

    for r : = 1 to R do

        retrieve i-th successor of

        (N+r)-th variable;

With this definition, the successors to the last R variables are retrieved row by row, rather than all successors being retrieved to the first variable, followed by all successors to the second variable, and so forth. This process matches the way in which conceptual tables are lexicographically ordered, so if the last R values in the Get-BulkRequest are columnar objects of the same table, the Response returns conceptual rows of the table.

BEYOND SNMPv1

The GetBulkRequest operation removes one of the major limitations of SNMP–its inability to efficiently retrieve large blocks of data. Moreover, use of this operator can help reduce the size of management applications the management protocol supports, creating further efficiencies. The management application does not need to concern itself with some of the details of packaging requests.

The management application need not perform a trial-and-error procedure to determine the optimal number of variable bindings to put in a Request-PDU. Also, if a request is too big, even for GetBulkRequest, the agent sends back as much data as it can, rather than simply sending a tooBig error message. Thus, the manager simply has to retransmit the request for the missing data; it does not have to figure out how to repackage the original request into a series of smaller requests.

The SetRequest-PDU is issued by a manager to request that the values of one or more objects be altered. The receiving SNMPv2 entity responds with a Response-PDU containing the same request-id. The SetRequest operation is atomic: Either all of the variables are updated or none is. If the responding entity is able to set values for all of the variables listed in the incoming variable-bindings list, then the Response-PDU includes the variable-bindings field, with a value supplied for each variable. If at least one of the variable values cannot be supplied, then no values are returned, and no values are updated. In the latter case, the error-status code indicates the reason for the failure, and the error-index field indicates the variable that caused the failure.

When an unusual event occurs, the SNMPv2-Trap-PDU is generated and transmitted by an SNMPv2 entity acting in an agent role. It provides the management station with asynchronous notification of a significant event. The variable-bindings list contains the information associated with the trap message. Unlike the GetRequest, GetNextRequest, GetBulkRequest, SetRequest, and InformRequest-PDUs, the SNMPv2-Trap-PDU does not elicit a response from the receiving entity; it is an unconfirmed message.

The InformRequest-PDU is sent by an SNMPv2 entity acting in a manager role, on behalf of an application, to another SNMPv2 entity acting in a manager role, to provide management information to an application using the latter entity. As with the SNMPv2-Trap-PDU, the variable-bindings field conveys the associated information. The manager receiving an InformRequest acknowledges receipt with a Response-PDU.

For both the SNMPv2-Trap and the InformRequest, the agent can define various conditions that indicate when the notification is generated, and the information to be sent is also specified.

The objects defined as part of SNMPv2 are organized into three MIBs: the *SNMPv2 MIB*, the *manager-to-manager MIB*, and the *party MIB*. In turn, each MIB is organized into a number of *groups*. A group is simply a related collection of objects. Typically, implementations are characterized in terms of which groups they include. An implementation includes a group if it supports all of the objects in that group.

The SNMPv2 MIB defines objects that describe the behavior of an SNMPv2 entity. This information enables a manager to monitor the amount of SNMPv2-related activity at an agent and the amount of dedicated SNMPv2-related resources at the agent. This MIB contains five groups: SNMPv2 statistics, SNMPv1 statistics, object resource, traps, and set.

The *SNMPv2 statistics* group provides some basic measurements of the SNMPv2 entity. It consists of counters used to record the number of incoming and outgoing SNMPv2 messages, broken down into successful messages and those that have suffered various error conditions. The *SNMPv1 statistics* group includes several objects useful if an SNMPv2 entity also implements SNMPv1. The *object resources* group enables an SNMPv2 entity acting as an agent to describe its dynamically configurable object resources; essentially, this group consists of a table with one entry for each resource and a text description of the resource. The *trap* group consists of objects that allow the SNMPv2 entity, when acting in an agent role, to be configured to generate SNMPv2-Trap-PDUs.

Finally, the *set* group consists of a single object, snmpSetSerialNo, that can be used to coordinate set operations. This object is integer-valued and obeys the following rules: When a manager wishes to set one or more object values in an agent, it first retrieves the value of snmpSet object. It then issues a SetRequest-PDU whose variable-bindings list includes the snmpSet object with its current value. If two or more managers issue SetRequests using the same value of snmpSet, the first to arrive at the agent succeeds (assuming no other problems exist), resulting in an increment of snmpSet; the remaining set operations fail because of an inconsistent snmpSet value.

The Manager-to-Manager (M2M) MIB supports the distributed management architecture. It enables a superior manager to define events that a subordinate manager can then use as triggers for sending alert-type messages to the superior manager. The M2M MIB allows an intermediate manager to function as a remote monitor of network media traffic. It may also be used to allow an intermediate manager to report on activities at the intermediate manager or at subordinate agents. This MIB consists of two groups: the alarm group and the event group. The *alarm* group helps define a set of threshold alarms. Each threshold alarm specifies some object in the local MIB that is to be monitored. When the value of that object crosses a threshold, an event is triggered. Typically, the triggered event is an InformRequest-PDU that is sent to a superior manager. Each alarm in the alarm group points to an entry in the event group, which, in turn, defines the information to be sent with that InformRequest-PDU.

The party MIB is concerned with the security-related aspects of SNMPv2.

COEXISTENCE WITH SNMPv1

The benefits of SNMPv2 are likely to make MIS managers desire it. Announcements of SNMPv2-based products will flood the market throughout the remainder of 1993. Customers and vendors will begin migration from the same point–the huge installed base of SNMPv1-based products. As usual, the problem of migrating a large installed base to a new generation is vexing. Fortunately, the developers of SNMPv2 have given this problem a great deal of thought.

In all cases, an existing SNMPv1 installation consists of one or a small number of SNMPv1 management stations and a larger number of SNMPv1 agents. The easiest way to accomplish migration on an existing network is to upgrade the manager systems to support SNMPv2 in a way that allows coexistence of SNMPv2 managers, SNMPv2 agents, and SNMPv1 agents.

That SMI's definition for SNMPv2 is nearly a proper superset of its definition for SNMPv1 eases the transition. Therefore, without much trouble at all, an SNMPv2 management station can understand the MIB at an SNMPv1 agent. The major technical problem is that the protocol itself is different.

But because SNMPv2 uses proxy agents, the protocols

can coexist. SNMPv2 proxy agents can reach existing SN-MPv1 agents, thereby enabling coexistence at the protocol level. An SNMPv2 entity acting in an SNMPv2 agent role can be implemented and configured to act as a proxy agent on behalf of SNMPv1 agents.

The proxy agent needs to perform two mappings. SN-MPv2 PDUs coming from an SNMPv2 manager are converted to SNMPv1 PDUs to be sent to an SNMPv1 agent according to the following rules: GetRequest-, GetNextRequest-, and SetRequest-PDUs are passed unchanged, and a GetBulkRequest-PDU is converted to a GetNextRequest-PDU with the same variable-bindings list. The effect of this mapping is that only the first "row" of the max-repetitions portion of the variable-bindings list is retrieved. SNMPv1 PDUs coming from an SNMPv1 agent are converted to SNMPv2 PDUs to be sent to an SNMPv2 agent according to the following rules: A Response-PDU is passed un-changed, and a Trap-PDU is converted into an SNMPv2-Trap-PDU; the latter conversion involves a small format change.

An alternative way to achieve coexistence is to use management stations that "speak" both SNMPv2 and SN-MPv1. When a management application needs to contact a protocol entity acting in an agent role, the entity acting in a manager role uses either SNMPv2 or SNMPv1 PDUs based on information in a local database that assigns each correspondent agent to one of the two protocols. This dual capability in the management station should only be visible at the SNMPv2/SNMPv1 level. Management applications can be written as if they were using only SNMPv2. For communication with SNMPv1 agents, the manager can map operations as if the manager were acting as a proxy agent.

Make It Real

DIGITAL SIGNATURES ADD A LEVEL OF SECURITY BEYOND DATA ENCRYPTION BY VERIFYING THE AUTHENTICITY OF MESSAGES TO PROTECT AGAINST ACTIVE ATTACK.

BY WILLIAM STALLINGS

When the term "network security" is used, most people think immediately of encryption and its use to ensure the secrecy of transmitted messages. Encryption protects against passive attack (eavesdropping). But network security must also protect against active attack (falsification of data and transactions). Protection against such attacks is known as *message authentication*.

A message, file, document, or other collection of data is said to be authentic when its contents have not been altered and when its source is verified. By verifying these two elements via a message-authentication procedure, communicating parties verify that received messages are authentic. The parties may also wish to verify a message's timeliness (that it has not been artificially delayed and replayed) and sequence relative to other messages flowing between two parties.

You can perform authentication simply by using conventional encryption. Assuming that only the sender and receiver share a key, then only the genuine sender would be able to successfully encrypt a message for the other participant. Furthermore, if the message includes an error-detection code and a sequence number, the receiver is assured that the message has not been altered and that sequencing is proper. If the message also includes a time stamp, the receiver is assured that the message has not been delayed beyond the time expected for network transit.

DIGITAL SIGNATURE

Authentication using conventional encryption protects two parties exchanging messages from any third party. However, it does not protect the two parties from each other. Several forms of dispute between the two are possible.

Suppose John sends an authenticated message to Mary, using conventional encryption. Consider the disputes that could arise. In one scenario, Mary could forge a different message and claim that it came from John. Mary would simply have to create a message and encrypt it using the key that John and Mary share. In a second scenario, John could deny sending the message. Since Mary could forge a message, there is no way to prove that John did, in fact, send the message.

Both these scenarios are of legitimate concern. In the first scenario, the transmission could, for example, be an electronic funds transfer in which the receiver increases the amount of funds transferred and claims the larger amount had arrived from the sender. Suppose that in the second scenario an electronic mail message contains instructions to a stockbroker for a transaction that subsequently turns out badly. The sender could pretend that the message was never sent.

If sender and receiver do not have a relationship based on complete trust, some security measure beyond authentication is needed. The most attractive solution to this problem is the digital signature. The digital signature is analogous to the handwritten signature. It must have the following properties:

• It must be able to verify the author and the date and time of the signature.

• It must be able to authenticate the contents at the time of the signature.

• The signature must be verifiable by third parties, to resolve disputes.

Thus the digital signature function includes the authentication function. A variety of approaches has been proposed for the digital signature function, among them public-key encryption for providing authentication and digital signature.

Figure 1a illustrates a simple digital-signature scheme using public-key encryption. This scheme exploits an important characteristic of all public-key encryption algorithms: The two keys can be used in either order. That is, one can encrypt with the public key and decrypt with the matching private key or encrypt with the private key and decrypt with the matching public key.

Figure 1a illustrates the latter application. A prepares a message to B and encrypts it using A's private key before transmitting it. B can decrypt the message using A's public key. Because the message was encrypted using A's private key, only A could have prepared the message. Therefore, the entire encrypted message serves as the signature. In addition, the message cannot be altered without access to A's private key, so the message is authenticated.

In the preceding scheme, the entire message is encrypted. While this encryption validates both author and contents, it would require a great deal of storage. Each document would have to be kept in plaintext to be used for practical purposes. A copy also would have to be kept in ciphertext so the origin and contents could be verified in case of a dispute. A more efficient way of achieving the same results is to encrypt only a portion of the document. A minimal portion would include the sender's name, the receiver's name, a sequence number, and a checksum. If this portion of the message is encrypted with the sender's private key, it serves as a signature that verifies origin, content, and sequencing.

This encryption process does not provide secrecy. That is, the message being sent is safe from alteration but not safe from eavesdropping. This exposure is obvious in the case of a signature based on a portion of the message, since the rest of the message is transmitted in the clear. Even in the case of complete encryption, as shown in Figure 1a, secrecy is not provided since any observer can decrypt the message using the sender's public key.

However, the double use of the public-key scheme provides both the digital signature function, which includes authentication and secrecy. Figure 1b illustrates this doubling of the public-key scheme.

As in the preceding example, begin by encrypting a message using the sender's private key. This step provides the

digital signature. Next, encrypt again, using the receiver's public key. The final ciphertext can only be decrypted by the intended receiver, who alone possesses the matching private key. Thus secrecy is maintained. The disadvantage of this approach is that the public-key algorithm, which is complex, must be exercised four times, rather than two, in each communication.

WITHOUT SECRECY

We have seen several schemes for message authentication that rely on encryption of the entire message, but several other approaches exist in which an authentication tag is generated and appended to each message for transmission. The message itself is not encrypted and can be read at the destination independent of the authentication function at the destination.

Because these approaches do not encrypt the message, they do not provide message secrecy. Since conventional encryption will provide authentication, and since it is widely used with readily available products, why not simply use that approach, which provides both secrecy and authentication? Message authentication without secrecy may actually be preferable in a number of instances.

First, in a number of applications the same message is broadcast to a number of destinations, for example, notification to users that the network is unavailable or an alarm signal in a control center. In these cases, it is cheaper and more reliable to have only one destination monitor authenticity. Thus, the message must be broadcast in plaintext with an associated message-authentication tag. One system is responsible for performing authentication. If a violation occurs, the other destination systems are alerted by a general alarm.

Another scenario in which authentication without secrecy is desirable is an exchange in which one side has a heavy load and cannot afford the time to decrypt all incoming messages. Authentication is carried out on a selective basis, with messages randomly checked.

Authentication of a computer program in plaintext is also attractive. The computer program can be executed without being decrypted every time, which would be wasteful of processor resources. However, if a message-authentication tag were attached to the program, the tag could be checked whenever assurance is required of the authenticity of the program.

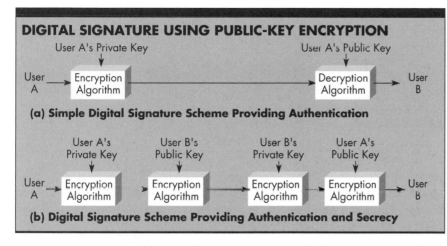

Figure 1. The top half of this diagram shows a simple digital signature scheme using public-key encryption. The two keys can be used in either order. In the bottom half of this diagram, the final ciphertext can only be decrypted by the intended receiver, who alone possesses the matching private key.

Thus both authentication and encryption have their place in meeting security requirements.

MESSAGE AUTHENTICATION CODE

One authentication technique involves the use of a secret key to generate a small block of data, known as a *message-authentication code*, that is appended to the message. This technique assumes that two communicating parties, say A and B, share a common secret key KAB. When A has a message to send to B, it calculates the message-authentication code as a function of the message and the key: MACM = F(KAB, M). The message and the code are transmitted to the intended recipient. The recipient performs the same calculation on the received message, using the same secret key, to generate a new message-authentication code. The received code is compared to the calculated code (see Figure 2). If we assume that only the receiver and the sender know the identity of the secret key, and if the received code matches the calculated code, then:
• The receiver is assured that the message has not been altered. If an attacker alters the message but does not alter the code, then the receiver's calculation of the code will differ from the received code. Since the attacker is assumed not to know the secret key, the attacker cannot alter the code to correspond to the alterations in the message.
• The receiver is assured that the message is from the alleged sender. Since no one else knows the secret key, no one else could prepare a message with a proper code.
• The receiver can be assured of the proper sequence if the message includes a sequence number (such as is used with

X.25, HDLC, TCP, and the ISO Transport Protocol), since an attacker cannot successfully alter the sequence number.

A number of algorithms could be used to generate the code. The National Bureau of Standards, in its publication *DES Modes of Operation*, recommends the use of the DES algorithm. The DES algorithm is used to generate an encrypted version of the message, and the last number of bits of ciphertext are used as the code. A 16- or 32-bit code is typical.

The process just described is similar to encryption. One difference is that the authentication algorithm need not be reversible, as it must be for decryption. Because of the mathematical properties of the authentication function, it is less vulnerable to being broken than encryption.

ONE-WAY HASH FUNCTION

A variation on the message-authentication code that has received a great deal of attention recently is the one-way hash function. As with the message-authentication code, a hash function accepts a variable-size message M as input and produces a fixed-size tag H(M), sometimes called a *message digest*, as output. However, no secret key is involved; the hash function is simply a mathematical function that produces a known output for a given input. In general, a hash function is easier to compute than a message-authentication code.

Since the hash function does not depend on a secret key, some means is required to protect the message and the hash function to ensure authenticity. Several approaches are possible. The message digest can be en-

Figure 2. A message-authentication code involves the use of a secret key to generate a small block of data that is appended to the message.

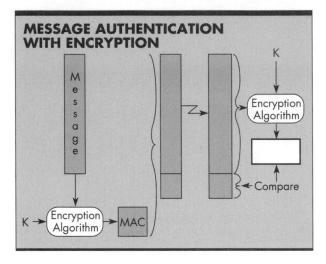

crypted using conventional encryption; assuming that only the sender and receiver share the encryption key, authenticity is assured. The message can also be encrypted using public-key encryption. The public-key approach has two advantages: It provides a digital signature as well as message authentication, and it does not require the distribution of keys to communicating parties.

These two approaches have an advantage over approaches that encrypt the entire message in that they require less computation. Nevertheless, interest has grown in developing a technique that avoids encryption altogether. Several reasons for this interest are:

• Both encryption and the hash function have to be performed for every message. Even though the amount of data to be encrypted per message is small, there may be a steady stream of messages into and out of a system.

• Encryption hardware is optimized for use on large blocks of data. For small blocks of data, typical in many networking applications, a high proportion of time is spent on initialization/invocation overhead.

• Encryption algorithms may be covered by patents. Some encryption algorithms, such as the Rivest-Shamir-Adelman (RSA) public-key algorithm, are patented and must be licensed, adding a cost.

• Some encryption algorithms, including DES, are subject to export control.

Figure 3 shows a technique that uses a hash function but no encryption for message authentication. This technique assumes that two communicating parties, say A and B,

share a common secret value SAB. When A has a message to send to B, it calculates the hash function over the concatenation of the secret value and the message: MDM = H(SABM).1 (note that indicates concatenations). It then sends [MMDM] to B. Since B possesses SAB, it can recompute H(SABM) and verify MDM. Since the secret value itself is not sent, an attacker cannot modify an intercepted message. As long as the secret value remains secret, it is also not possible for an attacker to generate a false message.

HASH FUNCTION REQUIREMENTS

The purpose of a hash function is to produce a "fingerprint" of a file, message, or other block of data. To be useful for message authentication, a hash function H must have the following properties:

1. H can be applied to a block of data of any size.

2. H produces a fixed-length output.

3. $H(x)$ is relatively easy to compute for any given x, making both hardware and software implementations practical.

4. For any given code m, it is computationally infeasible to find x such that $H(x) = m$.

5. For any given block x, it is computationally infeasible to find $y \cdot x$ with $H(y) = H(x)$.

The first three properties are requirements for the practical application of a hash function to message authentication. The fourth property is the "one-way" property: It is easy to generate a code given a message but virtually impossible to generate a message given a code. This property

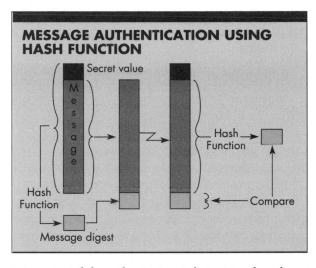

MESSAGE AUTHENTICATION USING HASH FUNCTION

Figure 3. This technique uses a hash function but no encryption for message authentication. It assumes that two communicating parties share a common secret value.

is important if the authentication technique involves the use of a secret value. The secret value itself is not sent; however, if the hash function is not one-way, an attacker can easily discover the secret value. If the attacker can observe or intercept a transmission, the attacker obtains the message M and the hash code MDM = H(SABM). The attacker then inverts the hash function to obtain SABM = H-1(MDM). Since the attacker now has both M and SABM, it is a trivial matter to recover SAB.

The fifth property guarantees that an alternative message hashing to the same value as a given message cannot be found. This aspect prevents forgery when an encrypted hash code is used. If this property were not true, an attacker could observe or intercept a message plus its encrypted hash code, generate an unencrypted hash code from the message, and generate an alternate message with the same hash code.

In addition to providing authentication, a message digest also provides data integrity. It performs the same function as a frame-check sequence: if any bits in the message are accidentally altered in transit, the message digest will be in error.

MD5 MESSAGE-DIGEST ALGORITHM

The MD5 message-digest algorithm was developed by Ron Rivest at M.I.T. (whose name is represented by the R in the RSA public-key encryption algorithm). The algorithm takes as input a message of arbitrary length and produces as output a 128-bit message digest. Looking at

two simple examples of a hash function will help explain why MD5 must be complex.

Simple Hash Function. All hash functions operate using the following general principles. The input (message or file, for example) is viewed as a sequence of n-bit blocks. The input is processed one block at a time in an iterative fashion to produce an n-bit hash function.

One of the simplest hash functions involves taking the bit-by-bit exclusive-or (XOR) of every block. This type of code produces a simple parity for each bit position and is known as a longitudinal redundancy check. It is reasonably effective for random data as a data integrity check. For random input, each 128-bit hash value is equally likely. Under such conditions, the probability that a random data error will occur such that the hash value of the message with the error equals the hash value without the error is 2^{-128}. In other words, the probability that a random error will not be detected by the hash value is 2^{-128}. With more predictably formatted data, the function is less effective. For example, in most normal text files, the high-order bit of each octet is always zero. Therefore 16 bits in the hash will always be zero, and in effect, a 112-bit hash value is left and the effectiveness is reduced to 2^{-112}.

A simple way to improve matters is to perform a one-bit circular shift, or rotation, on the input as each block is processed. This operation has the effect of "randomizing" the input more completely and overcoming any regularities that appear in the input.

Although the second program provides a good measure

TABLE 1. Truth table of logical funtions.

X	Y	Z	F	G	H	I
0	0	0	0	0	0	1
0	0	1	1	0	1	0
0	1	0	0	1	1	0
0	1	1	1	0	0	1
1	0	0	0	0	1	1
1	0	1	0	1	0	1
1	1	0	1	1	0	0
1	1	1	1	1	1	0

of data integrity, it is virtually useless for data security. Consider the following task of a potential attacker: Given a hash code, produce a message that yields that hash code. The attacker would simply need to prepare the desired message and then append a 128-bit block that forces the new message plus block to yield the desired hash code.

Thus we need a hash algorithm that is a much more complex function of the input bits.

MD5 Algorithm. The MD5 algorithm produces a 128-bit hash code, or message digest, of an input file. The algorithm was designed for speed, simplicity, and compactness on a 32-bit architecture. The algorithm processes the input in 512-bit blocks.

The algorithm consists of the following five steps:

Step 1: Append Padding Bits. The message is padded so that its length is congruent to 448 modulo 512. That is, the length of the padded message is 64 bits less than an integer multiple of 512 bits. Padding is always added, even if the message is already of the desired length. For example, if the message is 448 bits long, it is padded by 512 bits to a length of 960 bits. Thus, the number of padding bits is in the range of 1 to 512.

The padding consists of a single 1-bit followed by the necessary number of 0-bits.

Step 2: Append Length. A 64-bit representation of the length of the original message (before the padding) is appended to the result of Step 1. If the original length is greater than 2^{64}, then only the low-order 64 bits of the length are used. The inclusion of a length value at the end of the message makes a type of attack known as a padding attack more difficult.

The outcome of the first two steps yields a message that is an integer multiple of 512 bits in length. Equivalently, the result is a multiple of 16 32-bit words. Let M[0 . . . N-1] denote the words of the resulting message, with N an integer multiple of 16.

Step 3: Initialize MD Buffer. A 128-bit buffer is used to store intermediate and final results of the hash function. The buffer can be represented as four 32-bit registers (A, B, C, D). These registers are initialized to the following hexadecimal values (low-order octets first):

A = 01 23 45 67
B = 89 AB CD EF
C = FE DC BA 98
D = 76 54 32 10

Step 4: Process Message in 128-Bit (16-Word) Blocks. The heart of the algorithm makes use of four functions. Each function takes three 32-bit words as input and produces a 32-bit word output. Each function performs a set of bitwise logical operations; that is, the nth bit of the output is a function of the nth bit of the three inputs. The functions are:

F(X,Y,Z) = (X•Y) + (X'•Z)
G(X,Y,Z) = (X•Z) + (Y•Z)
H(X,Y,Z) = X Y Z
I(X,Y,Z,) = Y (X+')

where the logical operators (AND, OR, NOT, XOR) are represented by the symbols (, +, ', '). Function F is a conditional function: If X then Y else Z. Function H produces a parity bit. Table 1 is a truth table of the four functions.

The algorithm also makes use of a 64-element table T[1 . . . 64] constructed from the sine function. The ith element of T, denoted T[i] has the value equal to the integer part of 2^{32} 4 abs(sin(i)), where i is in radians. Since abs(sin(i)) is a number between 0 and 1, each element of T is an integer that can be represented in 32 bits. The table provides a "randomized" set of 32-bit patterns, which should eliminate any regularities in the input data.

Step 5: Output. The message digest is produced as output.

The MD5 algorithm has the property that every bit of the hash code is a function of every bit in the input. The complex repetition of the basic functions (F, G, H, I) produces results that are well mixed; that is, it is unlikely that two messages chosen at random, even if they exhibit similar regularities, will have the same hash code. The author of MD5 conjectures that the difficulty of generating two messages with the same MD5 digest is on the order of 2^{64} operations, and the difficulty of generating a message that produces a given digest is on the order of 2^{128} operations.

Stump the Cipher Punks

DATA ENCRYPTION HELPS ELIMINATE THE FEAR OF NETWORK ATTACK AND OBVIATES THE NEED TO STORE SENSITIVE APPLICATIONS ON A SEPARATE LAN.

BY GLENN HYATT

Suppose you had a user who could read any data flowing across your LAN, any file being accessed by any other user, any financial data, any payroll data, any personnel data, any product development data. Suppose that user could do so without any special hardware, with only some public-domain software. Suppose that user were someone your organization didn't designate but who designated himself or herself. In fact, suppose that any user with just a little motivation and curiosity could sit at a workstation and sift through every bit that flows across your network.

This scenario isn't hypothetical; it illustrates the status quo on most LANs. Data that flows across a LAN is broadcast, not "narrowcast." That is, when a user at a client opens a file on a server, the LAN sends one or more packets containing the data to all nodes. The packets are labeled with the address of the client node from which the user opened the file. That client node recognizes its own address on the packet's frame and accepts the data.

But many network interface cards can be placed into promiscuous mode using software alone. In this mode the network interface card (NIC) accepts all data flowing on the network. The user can then read the data, whether or not it was addressed to his or her workstation.

Some shops recognize this exposure, and they prohibit NICs that allow promiscuous mode. However, what's to prevent bringing in such a NIC on a portable PC and attaching it to the LAN?

NODES IN SPY MODE

As Martin Hellman, professor of electrical engineering at Stanford University and cryptology guru, points out, each network node is designed to spy on the network and pick off its own data. Well, it can just as easily be configured to spy on the network and pick off the CEO's data.

Management may be aware of these possible exposures or, at least, vaguely uneasy about the level of security afforded by LANs. If so, managers may avoid placing applications on LANs if the information is sensitive, or they may dedicate a separate LAN to a sensitive application. These constraints wouldn't be necessary if encryption were used.

Even LANs that don't carry confidential data or applications are exposed to this sort of illicit "spying." If a user signs on to other environments from the LAN, the user ID and password go out across the LAN unencrypted. For example, users may be signing on to mainframe applications from terminal emulators on their LAN workstations, such as DCA (Cincinnati) IrmaLAN or Attachmate (Bellevue, WA) Extra. In effect, these users broadcast their mainframe passwords each time they sign on.

ENCRYPTION BASICS

The fundamental aim of encrypting data is to make it difficult for unauthorized people to read the information, even if they get hold of the transmitted or stored value. This goal is accomplished by running the original data (the *cleartext* or *plaintext*) through an encryption algorithm in conjunction with a cryptographic *key*, a bit or character string or a numerical value that, when applied with the correct algorithm, encodes the message. In a well-designed method, the resulting scrambled data (*ciphertext*) is different for each possible key. Given enough possible keys, trying each key (a *brute-force* attack) becomes an impractically large task.

Encryption methods may be categorized as symmetric or asymmetric. *Symmetric methods* (such as the Data Encryption Standard, or DES) use the same key to encrypt and to decrypt data. *Asymmetric methods* (such as RSA, named after its authors Rivest, Shamir, and Adleman) use different keys to encrypt and decrypt.

One very useful type of asymmetric method is *public-key algorithms*, again, such as RSA, in which data must be encrypted under one key and decrypted under another. One key is public and may even be published; the other is private and is kept secret. This way, for example, anyone can send Alice a message encrypted under her public key, but only Alice has the private key to decrypt it.

READ MY LIPS

Often managers or auditors concerned with the security of their systems ask whether certain data are encrypted. If the answer is yes, they may ask to see the data to ensure that it is, actually, encrypted. Often they are satisfied if they can't read it by casual browsing.

In fact, this limitation may, at times, be adequate. Internet users have access to electronic bulletin boards where a weary soul can find a joke or two (for example, through rec.humor.funny). Some of these jokes are offensive. Rather than censor the joke or offend some users, the originator of the joke or the moderator of the bulletin board will encrypt the posting. The posting can't be read with a casual glance.

The method used is called *ROT-13*. Each letter in the message is replaced with the letter 13 positions away in the alphabet. For example, the fourth letter *d*, is replaced with the seventeenth letter, *q*. The twentieth letter of the alphabet, *t*, is replaced with the seventh letter, *g*. Software used to read bulletin boards typically provides a hot key to decrypt these messages. The goal is met because the message need only be obscure to the most casual browser.

Most often, however, encryption must be tough enough to frustrate a determined and skilled observer trying to extract the protected information. Then the questions become: How determined is a potential adversary? How skilled is he? How much frustration must we subject him to? The answers to these questions in turn depend partly on the value of the data.

It may seem, then, that rationality would call for a manager to quantify:

- the value of the data,
- the cost of implementing encryption,
- the effectiveness of the proposed encryption method, and
- the probability of a successful attempt to break the code.

After weighing these considerations, the manager can then make a shrewd business decision based on the potential cost of disclosure vs. the cost of applying encryption. A manager familiar with the data and its market can estimate the value of a given set of data. He or she can easily figure the cost of a given application of encryption by accounting for the cost of any hardware and software involved, plus the cost of increased capacity required. (Software encryption can place significant demands on a CPU.) Evaluating the effectiveness of an encryption method and figuring the likelihood of an attack can be touchy business, though.

WEIGHING EFFECTIVENESS

WordPerfect 4.2 provided a user the ability to supply a password to be used as a key to encrypt ("lock" in WordPerfect terminology) a file as it was saved. A locked file looked to the casual browser like random information, when, in fact, the encryption method was not trivial.

Documentation warned users that information couldn't be recovered without the password. However, an article appeared in the public press describing the encryption method and how the author went about attacking it. (The article, "An Analysis of the Encryption Algorithm Used in the WordPerfect Word Processing Program," by John Bennett, appeared in *Cryptologia*, vol. 11, no. 4, page 206.)

The author concluded by offering a copy of the decryption program if the reader sent a blank disk "with a note explaining your interest." (WordPerfect has since strengthened the encryption method.)

Another interesting article in the same journal analyzes the encryption components of five commercial PC security products available at that time (see "A Survey of Data Insecurity Packages," by Martin Kochanski, *Cryptologia*, vol. 11, no. 1, page 1). As promised in its introduction, the article "describes the algorithms we found and how to break them."

The vendors of these products no doubt worked hard on making these encryption algorithms difficult to break, but in the end they were thwarted. Simply put, judging an encryption method's resistance to attack is very difficult.

What motivates a potential code cracker? We tend to worry about someone who wants to get at our information. But the security of the packages discussed here was breached by people attacking *products,* not some particular encrypted *data.* The authors' motivation would, of course, be impossible to discern, but the former article was written by a software consultant, and the latter was written by the developer of a rival security package. Perhaps pursuit of bragging rights and potential financial gain played their parts, but who could guess all the reasons someone would put his or her hand into such a project? And if it's this difficult to predict who may break your code, it's impossible to guess how motivated that person may be or to predict the likelihood of attack.

EVALUATING THE METHODS

The best indication of a given encryption method's strength comes when the method has been subjected to plenty of scrutiny. If no one has demonstrated–not just boasted–an ability to crack it, the method is a relatively safe bet. The DES, for example, has been a standard for more than 15 years and has apparently withstood attempts to find shortcuts to decryption (see sidebars). DES may need replacing soon, but for now it seems a good choice unless you're protecting very valuable or sensitive data that must be protected for a long time.

The RSA public-key algorithm has been around nearly as long as the DES and has also proven resistant to *cryptanalysis* (cracking the encryption scheme). It's based on the difficulty of factoring the product of two very large prime numbers and so has suffered apparent setbacks with advances in factoring and primality testing. These advances, though, barely dent the algorithm's armor.

Rather than try to evaluate the strength of a given encryption method yourself, a safer bet would be to place your money on methods that have been published and proven resistant to cryptanalytic attacks. Assume that a potential attacker of an encryption scheme is much more capable than you are at cryptanalysis. If a vendor uses a proprietary, even idiosyncratic algorithm, it could conceivably prove strong in the face of attempts to crack it. However, as previously noted, such algorithms can fail under such a test. While standard methods are often more CPU-intensive than the proprietary methods, they are also more likely to hold up over the long haul.

In any case, though, key management is a potential weak link in the chain. The secrecy of the keys (except public keys) is the foundation on which the encryption structure rests. When you implement encryption, the way you handle the keys and the way the product handles the keys are critical.

To evaluate a product that provides the encryption capabilities then, ask what cryptographic method is used and how the keys are handled. If the method used is a standard, ask if the product has been certified by the National Institute of Standards and Technology (NIST). If it's the vendor's own nonstandard, proprietary method, be aware of the risks involved. Remember the articles previously cited in which the authors detail how to break commercially available encryption schemes.

A final word of warning: If you need to share encrypted information among sites in different countries, your task will be more complicated. Software and hardware that include cryptographic technology are subject to U.S. export restrictions, requiring licenses that can be a long time in the works, if granted at all.

Other countries also regulate the flow of encryption technology. France and Taiwan, for example, restrict the import of such products.

YOU'VE GOT INTEGRITY

The bottom line when trying to safeguard the confidentiality of encrypted data is to make it difficult for an unauthorized person to reverse the encryption process. However, encryption techniques that assure data confidentiality can also be applied to assure data integrity.

Suppose Alice wants to send a message to Bob, and they want to make sure that the message Bob gets is exactly the message Alice sent. If they are worried about a noisy communications link corrupting that message, they can use an error-detecting or error-correcting code, such as those used in modems.

But if Alice and Bob fear that the message might be corrupted by a third person of dubious intent, they have a different problem. Ordinary error-detecting and error-correcting codes are easily analyzed and understood by a competent eavesdropper. The dastard could unravel the code, reformulate the message, apply the code, and resend the altered message.

Designing a method to assure integrity and to resist

such attacks is similar to the task of designing a good algorithm to encipher data. One general approach is for Alice to subject the message to an algorithm that depends on a secret key, and which produces a *hash value*, a relatively short bit string whose value depends on the content of the message but which cannot be decrypted. She appends this value to the message.

When Bob receives the message, he performs the same function on the message he received, using the same key. If either the message or the key is different, the hash value will also be different. If they are the same, the hash value will be the same.

AUTHENTICATE YOUR SOURCE

Another use for cryptographic methods is to verify the source of data. The mere fact that Bob received a message encrypted with a symmetric algorithm under a key shared only by himself and Alice assures Bob that Alice sent the message.

Suppose, though, that the message is a contract of some sort, and Bob claims Alice sent it, but Alice denies it. How does Bob prove he didn't forge the message? After all, they both know the key.

Enter public-key systems. Alice encrypts the message (or, in practice, more likely a hash value of the message) under her private key. This method is known as a *digital signature*. Bob can decrypt it under her public key to verify that she sent it. Because only someone with the private key could have encrypted the message, Alice can't disavow the message's authenticity.

NETWARE'S CRYPTOGRAPHY

No current LAN system transmits or stores users' LAN passwords in cleartext. They store either an encrypted password or a hash value of the password. A common approach is to use one-way encryption. When a user enters a new password, it's encrypted and stored in such a way that it can't be decrypted. Then when the user attempts to sign on, the password entered is encrypted and compared with the encrypted password stored for that user. If they match, the user is allowed on.

On a NetWare LAN, a hash value of the password is stored on the server. The file containing these hash values cannot be accessed from client nodes. To get access to the file, one must have physical access to the server (or to the server's backups).

Originally, in NetWare 3.x, if a privileged user were signed on, any client workstation could masquerade as any other signed-on user. By monitoring network traffic, one could get the information needed to construct a packet that appeared to the server to come from the client node where a privileged user had signed on. Masquerading in this way would allow a nonprivileged user to do anything the privileged user is authorized to do. Novell created a fix based on cryptographic techniques to authenticate that each packet comes from the purported sender.

NetWare 4.0 uses the RSA algorithm to provide a different sort of authentication. When a user ID is created or an administrator changes a user's password, NetWare generates a public and a private key for the user. The user's private key is stored on the server encrypted under the user's password. When a user signs on, his or her private key is downloaded, in encrypted form of course, to the client node. If the user has access to two servers and is already signed on to one, he or she may access the second server without signing on again.

To vouch for the user's identity, NetWare creates a "certificate" on the user's workstation and uses the private key to generate a digital signature for this certificate. Rather than pass the digital signature over the LAN (which could be intercepted by another user), Novell has the second server initiate an exchange based on a *zero-knowledge proof*. With this technique, the client node proves to the server that it "knows" the contents of the digital signature without revealing anything about the contents of that signature.

In the future, Novell will furnish the option of encrypting the data within packets.

CRYPTOGRAPHIC LAN PRODUCTS

LAN managers can choose from among hardware- and software-based products available to provide cryptographic services for LANs. Generally speaking, hardware implementations are more expensive and faster. The keys used are typically encrypted in a hierarchy, ultimately based on a key protected by tamper-proof hardware.

Software implementations are generally slower because they use the CPU cycles of the servers and clients, but they are less expensive. The keys must be protected by software schemes.

Among the hardware solutions available are products from Digital Equipment Corp. (DEC, Maynard, MA), Semaphore (San Jose, CA), and Cylink (Sunnyvale, CA).

DEC has a DES product for Ethernet LANs called Digital Ethernet Secure Network Controller (DESNC) based on an encryption unit with four ports. The unit is installed between a part of the network and the Ethernet backbone. Only nodes on the same port as the originating node can pick up cleartext packets from the originating node. DESNC also can enforce access-control policies.

Semaphore's Work Group and Work Group Plus products allow you to divide a LAN into *subnets* that are encrypted. They use DES to encrypt data and RSA for key management protocols. Their equipment is protocol transparent and independent of the topology of any WAN to which the subnets are attached.

Cylink manufactures hardware to encrypt data flowing among LANs or between LANs and WANs, rather than within a LAN. Its products offer encryption under various algorithms, including DES and proprietary algorithms. The products' key exchanges take place via public-key methods, including RSA.

Among the software available, Fischer International (Naples, FL), with its Watchdog and Director security products, offers encryption. The user can choose DES or a proprietary method to encrypt selected directories. Files are passed around the network in encrypted form and are decrypted in workstation memory. Keys are stored on the workstations, encrypted under users' passwords. Fischer's MailSafe product applies the RSA technique to provide encryption and digital signatures for "any PC-based messaging system."

A relatively new type of product is the LAN-based forms tool that allows attaching digital signatures to electronic forms. WordPerfect (Orem, UT), Block (Coral Gables, FL), and Delrina (San Jose, CA) offer such packages that provide RSA digital signature capability.

THE TIME HAS ARRIVED

Unless you already encrypt data on your LAN, you're broadcasting it to anyone who can connect to the LAN. If this accessibility troubles you or if it has inhibited your organization from placing sensitive applications on LANs, carefully implemented encryption could be your answer.

RUMORS POINT TO NSA INVOLVEMENT
Through the DES Door

Rumors have persisted that the National Security Agency (NSA, Fort Mead, MD) influenced IBM's design of the DES. Suspicion has focused on a feature of the algorithm called the S-boxes. The rumor is that the NSA dictated at least part of the design of the S-boxes in order to build in an obscure weakness. Exploiting this "trap door," they could more easily decrypt intercepted messages. The problem with such a trap door, of course, would be that the NSA and anyone else who found it could subvert users' efforts to protect their data.

The authors of the DES emphatically deny that the NSA dictated any feature of the algorithm. It is certain, though, that IBM classified some of the notes on the design of the S-boxes. The authors say that the NSA requested to participate because some of the design criteria reflected secrets that the NSA was using in their own encryption algorithms. (See "Data Encryption Gurus: Tuchman and Meyer," by Paul Kinnucan, Paul, *Cryptologia*, vol. II, no. 4, page 371.)

Perhaps the best refutation of the theory, though, is that the DES, and the S-boxes in particular, have been subjected to years of scrutiny and have actually been found to be quite well-designed. The closest anyone has come to claiming bragging rights to breaking the DES was when two cryptologists, Biham and Shamir, developed an attack called differential cryptanalysis. (See "Differential Cryptanalysis of DES-Like Cryptosystems" by E. Biham and A. Shamir, *Journal of Cryptology*, vol. 4, no. 1, page 3.)

They demonstrated that if the attacker could choose the plaintext to be encrypted under the key to be discovered, then the attacker's analysis could reveal the key in 2^{47} to the 47th power iterations. A brute-force attack could accomplish this in 2^{56} to 56th power iterations. The analytical method itself, however, requires significantly more computation than a brute-force attack. Also, in the real world, it's very difficult for an attacker to create a situation in which he chooses the text to be encrypted.

Contributors

EDITOR

Melanie McMullen is the editor-in-chief of LAN Magazine and Interoperability. She has been involved in the computer industry for six years and has written hundreds of articles on LAN and WAN technology. She specializes in the areas of portable computing and wireless networking. Her work has been published in MacWorld and Cadence magazine as well as in the Computer Security Institute newsletter.

STAFF CONTRIBUTORS

Dave Brambert is editor-in-chief of Stacks magazine and executive editor of LAN Magazine.

Patricia Schnaidt has served as editor-in-chief of LAN Magazine.

OTHER CONTRIBUTORS

Steve Baker works for the Oregon Department of Energy coaxing energy conservation out of new state buildings. He is the networking columnist for Unix Review, former editor of Programmer's Journal, and a coauthor of Extending DOS.

Ted Bunker is a Washington, D.C.-based journalist who writes about regulation, technology policy, and other issues.

Michael Chacon is a network consultant for Inacom's national integration services. He is based in Garden Grove, CA.

Mike Durr is founder and chief analyst for Michael Durr and Associates, a market research company in Cape Coral, FL. He is a former director of strategic marketing for Novell and has written several books on networking and communications.

Charles Feltman is a marketing and management consultant with Insight Communications in Santa Barbara, CA.

Susan Fitzgerald is a principal with Dimensions Enterprises (Centreville, VA), a consultancy that focuses on LAN/WAN interconnection.

Ned Freed is chief development officer at Innosoft International in West Covina, CA. He is also one of the coauthors of the MIME standard.

Leslie Goff is a freelance writer based in New York.

Tom Henderson is vice president of engineering at Unitel and director of its subsidiary, Beach Labs, both located in Indianapolis.

Bonny Hinners, a freelancer based in San Francisco and Windsor, CT, specializes in networking and Windows programming.

Mike Hurwicz is a freelance writer and consultant based in Eastsound, WA. He specializes in LANs, e-mail, and imaging.

Glenn Hyatt, founder of HighGate Solutions, is a data security consultant based in Wilmington, DE.

Gary Kessler is a senior member of the technical staff of Hill Associates, a data communications, education, and consulting firm in Colchester, VT.

Cheryl Krivda is a Philadelphia-based technical journalist specializing in data communications.

Suketu Mehta is a technical writer based in Ridgewood, NJ, who writes about networking in Europe and the United States.

Jack Powers is the director of Graphics Research Lab, an international media technology research firm based in Brooklyn, NY.

Russ Sharer is a principal at imageMakers, a Santa Barbara, CA, firm that provides market analysis and consulting services.

Joel Snyder is a senior analyst with Opus One in Tucson, AZ, a company that specializes in networks and international aspects of information technology.

Peter Stephenson has been an independent consultant in the network industry for 10 years.

William Stallings is president of CompComm Consulting in Brewster, MA. A frequent lecturer on networking topics, he is the author of more than a dozen books on data communications and computer networking

LAN Magazine Glossary of Terms

Professionals ostensibly use jargon to aid communication among peers, but the plethora of obscure terms, invented words, and acronyms serve often serve to confuse not only the uninitiated, but after awhile, confuse the initiated as well. Here is a glossary of networking terms meant to dispel the mystery of network argot.

3+. 3+ was 3Com's network operating system that implemented Microsoft MS-Net file sharing and Xerox's XNS transport protocols. 3Com no longer sells 3+.

3+Open. 3+Open was 3Com's network operating system based on Microsoft's OS/2 LAN Manager. 3Com no longer sells 3+Open.

1Base5. 1Base5 is the implementation of 1Mbps Starlan, which is wired in a star topology.

10Base2. 10Base2 is the implementation of the IEEE 802.3 Ethernet standard on thin coaxial cable. Thin Ethernet or thinnet, as its commonly called, runs at 10Mbps. Stations are daisy-chained and the maximum segment length is 200 meters.

10Base5. 10Base5 is the implementation of the IEEE 802.3 Ethernet standard on thick coaxial cable. Thick, or standard Ethernet, as its commonly called, runs at 10Mbps. It uses a bus topology and the maximum segment length is 500 meters.

10BaseF, 10BaseFO. This is the draft specification for running IEEE 802.3 Ethernet over fiber-optic cable. It specifies a point-to-point link.

10BaseT. 10BaseT is the implementation of the IEEE 802.3 Ethernet standard on unshielded twisted-pair wiring. It uses a star topology, with stations directly connected to a multi-port hub. It runs at 10Mbps, and it has a maximum segment length of 100 meters.

802.1. This is the IEEE standard for hardware-level network management. It includes the spanning tree algorithm for Ethernet MAC-layer bridges and the Heterogeneous LAN Management (HLM) specification for managing Ethernet and Token Ring wiring hubs.

802.2. This IEEE standard specifies Logical Link Control (LLC), which defines services for the transmission of data between two stations at the data-link layer of the OSI model.

802.3 This IEEE standard governs the Carrier Sense Multiple Access/Collision Detection (CSMA/CD) networks, which are more commonly called Ethernet. 802.3 networks operate at varying speeds and over different cable types. See 1Base5, 10Base2, 10Base5, 10BaseF, and 10BaseT.

802.4. This IEEE standard defines the use of the token bus network access method. Token bus networks are sometimes used in manufacturing networks, but are rarely used in office-automation networks.

802.5. This IEEE specification standard defines a logical ring network that uses a token passing access method. It is commonly called Token Ring. It comes in 4Mbps and 16Mbps speeds. It is physically wired in a star topology, with multistation access units, or hubs, as the center, to which workstations, servers, and other network devices are attached. Token Ring runs over shielded twisted-pair, unshielded twisted-pair, and fiber-optic cabling.

802.6. This IEEE specification standard defines metropolitan area networks (MANs). The MAN standard implements a distributed queue, dual-bus access method over a fiber-optic cable plant. Switched Multimegabit Data Services, an emerging high-speed WAN service, can run over a MAN physical network.

802.7. Defined by the IEEE, the 802.7 standard defines broadband LANs. They can carry video, data, and voice traffic. Broadband LANs are constructed of cable television-like components and use RF to transmit information in separate channels in a single cable. They are built using a tree topology. Broadband LANs are rarely used anymore. Do not confuse with Broadband ISDN or wideband networking, which is a term used to denote a wide-area network service with substantial bandwidth, usually in the hundreds of megabits per second.

802.9 The IEEE 802.9 standard defines integrated digital and video networking.

802.11 When finalized by the IEEE, the 802.11 standard will define wireless networking. The standard will encompass many different methods of wireless transmission, including infrared and spread spectrum radio. Many data communications, computer, and telephone vendors are involved in the wireless LAN committee.

A

access method. An access method is the set of rules by which the network arbitrates access among the nodes. Collision Sense Multiple Access Collision Detection and token passing are two access methods used in LANs.

address. An address is a unique identification code that is assigned to a network device, so it may independently send and receive messages.

Address Resolution Protocol (ARP). Within TCP/IP, ARP is the protocol that determines whether a packet's source and destination addresses are in the Data-Link Control (DLC) or Internet Protocol (IP) format. ARP is necessary for proper packet routing on a TCP/IP network.

Advanced Program-to-Program Communications (APPC). APPC is the protocol suite within IBM's Systems Application Architecture that provides peer-to-peer access, enabling PCs and midrange hosts to communicate directly with mainframes. APPC is key for distributed computing within an IBM environment. APPC can be used over an SNA, Token Ring, Ethernet, or X.25 network.

Advanced Peer-to-Peer Networking (APPN). APPN is the network architecture within IBM's Systems Application Architecture that provides for peer-to-peer access among computers. Under APPN, a mainframe host is not required. It also implements concepts such as dynamic network directories and routing in SNA.

American National Standards Institute (ANSI). ANSI is the principal group in the United States for defining standards. ANSI represents the U.S. in ISO, the international standards-making body. Fiber Distributed Data Interface, a 100Mbps network, is one network standard developed by ANSI.

AppleShare. Apple Computer's network operating system designed to run primarily with Macintoshes, but also accommodates DOS and Windows PCs. AppleShare Pro runs under A/UX, Apple's version of Unix, and is a high-performance version of the network operating system.

AppleTalk. AppleTalk is the name of Apple Computer's networking specification. AppleTalk includes specifications for the physical layer as LocalTalk, EtherTalk, and TokenTalk; network and transport functions as Datagram Delivery Protocol and AppleTalk Session Protocol; addressing as Name Binding Protocol; file sharing as AppleShare; and remote access as AppleTalk Remote Access.

application programming interface (API). An API is set of programming functions, calls, and interfaces that provide access to a particular network layer.

application layer. The seventh and uppermost layer of the OSI model, the application layer allows users to transfer files, send mail, and perform other functions where they interact with the network components and services. It is the only layer that users can communicate directly with.

Arcnet. Datapoint designed this 2.5Mbps token-passing, star-wired network in the 1970s. Its low cost and high reliability can make it attractive to those companies on a tight network budget, although it is not endorsed by any IEEE committee. ArcnetPlus is a proprietary product of Datapoint that runs at 20Mbps.

Asynchronous Transfer Mode (ATM). ATM is a method of data transmission used by Broadband ISDN. It is specified as 53-octet fixed length packets that are transmitted over a cell-switched network. Speeds up to 2.2 gigabits per second are possible, and it is capable of carrying voice, video, and data. ATM has been embraced by the LAN and WAN industries, who have proclaimed it as the solution to integrating disparate networks across a large geographic distance. It is also called cell relay.

asynchronous communication server (ACS). An asynchronous communication server is some combination of a computer motherboard, asynchronous modems, and software that enable multiple people to dial out of a LAN. ACSs also provide dial-in service, where users not in the office can use modems to call up their network services in the office. ACSs are also called dial-in/dial-out servers or modem servers.

attenuation. Attenuation is amount of power that is lost as the signal moves over the cable from the transmitter to the receiver. It is a measured in decibels (dBs).

B

backbone. A backbone is the main "spine" or segment of a campus network. Departmental networks are attached as "ribs" to the central backbone.

bandwidth. Bandwidth is the amount of data that can be transmitted over a channel, measured in bits per second. For example, Ethernet has a 10Mbps bandwidth and FDDI has a 100Mbps bandwidth. Actual throughput may be different than the theoretical bandwidth.

bandwidth on demand. A concept in wide area networking in which the user can dial up additional WAN bandwidth as the application warrants. It enables users to pay only for bandwidth that they use, when they use it. Implementing bandwidth on demand requires switched services, such as ISDN or Switched 56 lines.

Basic Rate ISDN (BRI). BRI is an ISDN service that offers two "bearer" channels (B) with a 64Kbps bandwidth that can be used for bulk data transfer plus a "data link" (D) 16Kbps channel for control and signalling information.

blackout. A blackout or power outage is an interruption or total loss of commercial electrical power. Uninterruptible power supplies provide battery-backed up power that will supply electricity during a blackout (while their batteries last).

bridge. A bridge connects two networks of the same access

method, for example, Ethernet to Ethernet or Token Ring to Token Ring. A bridge works at the OSI's Media Access layer, and is transparent to upper-layer devices and protocols. Bridges operate by filtering packets according to their destination addresses. Most bridges automatically learn where these addresses are located, and thus are called learning bridges.

Broadband ISDN (B-ISDN). A class of emerging high speed data and voice services for the wide-area network. Switched Multimegabit Data Services and Asynchronous Transfer Mode are two emerging B-ISDN services that will provide megabits and gigabits of bandwidth across a wide-area network.

broadcast. A broadcast message is addressed to all stations on a network.

broadcast storm. In a broadcast storm, network congestion occurs because large numbers of frames are transmitted by many stations in response to a transmission by one station.

brownout. A brownout is an abnormally low voltage on commercial power distribution lines. Power utilities may intentionally produce a brownout when there is near overload demand for power, or natural conditions, such as storms, fires, or accidents, may cause a brownout.

brouter. A brouter is a device that can transparently bridge protocols as well as route them. It is a hybrid of a bridge and a router.

bus topology. A bus topology is a network architecture in which all of the nodes are connected to a single cable.

C

campus network. A campus network connects LANs from multiple departments within a single building or campus. Campus networks are local area networks, that is, they don't include wire-area network services, but they may span several miles.

campus wiring system. A campus wiring system is the part of a structured wiring system that connects multiple buildings to a centralized main distribution facility, local exchange carrier, or other point of demarcation. It is also referred to as a backbone.

Carrier Sense, Multiple Access with Collision Detection (CSMA/CD). Ethernet and 802.3 LANs use the CSMA/CD access method. In CSMA/CD, each network device waits for a time when the network is not busy before transmitting and it detects transmissions already on the wire that were put there by other stations.

cascaded star. A cascaded star topology is a network configuration in which multiple data centers or hubs are constructed for the purposes of redundancy. It is also called a tree topology.

Category 1. The Electronics Industry Association/Telecommunications Industry Association (EIA/TIA) specifies a five-level standard for commercial building telecommuncations wiring. Category 1 wiring is old-style unshielded twisted-pair telephone cable and it is not suitable for data transmission.

Category 2. The EIA/TIA 568 standard certifies Category 2 UTP for use up to 4Mbps. Category 2 UTP is similar to the IBM Cabling System Type 3 cable.

Category 3. The EIA/TIA 568 standard specifies Category 3 UTP for speeds up to 10Mbps, and it is the minimum cable required for 10BaseT. The wire pairs should have at least three twists per foot, but no two pairs should have the same twist pattern.

Category 4. The EIA/TIA 568 standard specifies Category 4 as the lowest grade UTP acceptable for 16Mbps Token Ring.

Category 5. The EIA/TIA 568 standard specifies Category 5 is certified for speeds up to 100Mbps but 155Mbps will be possible. It is suitable for FDDI and other high-speed networks.

cell. A fixed-length packet. For example, Asynchronous Transfer Mode (ATM) uses 53-octet cells.

cell relay. Cell relay is a form of packet transmission used by Broadband ISDN networks. Also called ATM, cell relay transmits 53-octet fixed-length packets over a packet-switched network. ATM is important because it makes it possible to use a single transmission scheme for voice, data, and video traffic on LANs and WANs.

client. A client is a computer that requests network or application services from a server. A client has only one user; a server is shared by many users.

coaxial cable. Coaxial cable has a inner conductor made of a solid wire that is surrounded by insulation and wrapped in metal screen. Its axis of curvature coincides with the inner conductors, hence the name coaxial. Ethernet and Arcnet can use coaxial cable. It is commonly called coax.

concentrator. A concentrator is a multiport repeater or hub that brings together the connections from multiple network nodes. Concentrators have moved past their origins as wire concentration centers, and often include bridging, routing, and management devices.

Connectionless Network Protocol (CLNP). Of the two OSI transport protocols–CLNP and Connection-Oriented Network Service (CONS)–CLNP is more efficient for LANs. Like TCP/IP, it uses datagrams to route network messages by including addressing information in each.

Connection-Oriented Network Service (CONS). Of the two OSI transport protocols–CLNP and CONS–CONS is more efficient for WANs. CONS allows the transport layer to bypass CLNP when a single logical X.25 network is used.

Consultative Committee for International Telegraphy and Telephony (CCITT). The CCITT defines international telecommunications and data communication standards. In March of 1993, the group changed its name to ITU-TS.

Controlled Access Unit (CAU). A CAU is a managed Multistation Access Unit (MAU), or a managed multiport wiring hub for Token Ring networks. Management features include turning ports on and off.

common carrier. A common carrier is a licensed, private utility company that provides data and voice communication services for a fee. For example, Sprint and MCI are common carriers.

Common Management Information Protocol (CMIP). CMIP is the OSI management information protocol for network management. It is not widely implemented.

compression. A technique to "squash" files, making them smaller as to optimize bandwidth utilization. Compression is important for WAN transmission and disk and tape storage.

D

Data Access Language (DAL). DAL is Apple's database query language that is based upon SQL, but it provides far greater functionality.

data dictionary. In a distributed database, a data dictionary keeps track of where the data is located and stores the necessary information for determining the best way to retrieve the data.

Data Encryption Standard (DES). DES is the United States government's standard for encryption, in which data is scrambled and security codes called keys are added, so data cannot be deciphered by unauthorized users.

data-link layer. The data-link layer is the second layer of the OSI model. It defines how data is packetized and transmitted to and from each network device. It is divided into two sublayers: medium access control and logical link control.

database server. A database server is a database application that follows the client-server model, dividing an application into a front end and a back end. The front end, running on the user's computer, displays the data and interacts with the user. The back end, running on a server, preserves data integrity and handles most of the processor-intensive work, such as data storage and manipulation.

DECnet. Digital Equipment Corporation's network system for networking personal computers and host computers. DECnet can use TCP/IP and OSI, as well as its proprietary protocols.

departmental LAN. A departmental LAN is a network that's used by a small group of people laboring toward a similar goal. Its primary goal is to share local resources, such as applications, data, and printers.

directory services. Directory services provide a white pages-like directory of the users and resources that are located on an enterprise network. Instead of having to know a device or user's specific network address, a directory service provides an English-like listing for a user. The OSI's X.500 and Banyan's StreetTalk are examples of directory services.

distributed computing. In a distributed computing architecture, portions of the applications and the data are broken up and distributed among the server and client computers. In the older model, all applications and data resided on the same computer.

distributed database. A database application where there are many clients as well as many servers. All databases at remote and local sites are treated as if they were one database. The data dictionary is crucial in mapping where all of the data resides.

Distributed Queue Dual Bus (DQDB). The medium access method of the IEEE 802.6 standard for metropolitan area networks.

downsizing. Downsizing or rightsizing is the process of porting mission-critical applications from a mainframe to a minicomputer or PC LAN or from a minicomputer to a PC LAN.

Dual-Attached Station (DAS). In FDDI, a DAS connects to both of the dual, counter-rotating rings. Concentrators, bridges, and routers often use DAS connections for fault tolerance. In contrast, a single-attached station is connected to only one ring.

dual homing. In FDDI, dual homing is a method of cabling concentrators and stations in a tree configuration that permits an alternate path to the FDDI network in case the primary connection fails.

Dynamic Data Exchange (DDE). DDE is Microsoft's specification for Windows that enables applications to communicate with each other without human intervention.

E

E-1. In Europe, E-1 is the basic telecommunications carrier, and it operates at 2.048Mbps. In the U.S., the basic carrier is T-1, which operates at 1.544Mbps.

electromagnetic interference/radio frequency interference (EMI/RFI). EMI and RFI are forms noise on data transmission lines that reduces data integrity. EMI is caused by motors, machines, and other generators of electromagnetic radiation. RFI is caused by radio waves.

Electronic Data Interchange (EDI). EDI is a method of electronically exchanging business documents, such as purchase orders, bills of lading, and invoices. Customers and their suppliers can set up EDI networks. EDI can be accomplished through OSI standards or through proprietary products.

electronic mail. E-mail is an application that enables users to send messages and files over their computer networks. E-mail can range from a simple text-based system to a messaging system that accommodates graphics, faxes, forms-processing, workflow, and more.

encapsulation. Encapsulation or tunnelling is the process of encasing one protocol into another protocol's format. For example, AppleTalk is often encapsulated into TCP/IP for transmission over a WAN because TCP/IP is more efficient over a WAN.

end system. In Internet terminology, an end system is a host computer.

End System To Intermediate System (ES-IS). ES-IS is an OSI routing protocol that provides the capabilities for hosts (or end systems) and routers (or intermediate systems) to find each other. ES-IS does not handle the router-to-router protocols; the Intermediate System to Intermediate System protocol does.

Enterprise Management Architecture (EMA). EMA is Digital

Equipment Corp.'s umbrella architecture for managing enterprise networks. EMA is a distributed approach.

enterprise network. An enterprise network is one that connects every computer in every location of a company, and runs the company's mission-critical applications.

Ethernet. Ethernet is a 10Mbps CSMA/CD network that runs over thick coax, thin coax, twisted-pair, and fiber-optic cable. A thick coax Ethernet uses a bus topology. A thin coax Ethernet uses a daisy chain topology. Twisted-pair Ethernet uses a star topology. A fiber Ethernet is point-to-point. DIX or Blue Book Ethernet is the name of the Digital Equipment Corp., Intel, and Xerox specification; 802.3 is the IEEE's specification; 8802/3 is the ISO's specification.

EtherTalk. EtherTalk is Apple Computer's implementation of Ethernet.

F

fault management. Fault management, one of the five categories of network management defined by ISO, is the detection, isolation, and correction of network faults.

fault tolerance. Fault tolerance is the ability of a system to continue operating in the event of a fault. You can implement fault tolerance in many places in a network, including in file servers with Novell's NetWare SFT III, in disks with RAID, and in bridges with the spanning-tree algorithm.

fast packet. Fast packet is a technique for asynchronously transferring data across the network.

fiber-optic cable. Fiber-optic cable can be used to transmit signals in the form of light. Glass fiber is composed of an outer protective sheath, cladding, and the optical fiber. It comes in single mode and multimode varieties. Single-mode fiber is more often used in the public-switched telephone network; multimode fiber is more often used in local and metropolitan area networks. Single-mode fiber uses lasers to transmit the light; multimode uses light-emitting diodes.

Fiber Distributed Data Interface (FDDI). FDDI is the ANSI X3T9.5 specification for a 100Mbps network that is logically implemented as dual, counter-rotating rings. A fiber FDDI network can support up to 500 stations over 2 kilometers. FDDI, originally specified to run over fiber, can also operate over shielded and unshielded twisted-pair, although the distances are greatly shortened.

File Transfer, Access, and Management (FTAM). FTAM is the OSI protocol for transferring and remotely accessing files on other hosts also running FTAM.

File Transfer Protocol (FTP). FTP is the TCP/IP protocol for file transfer.

filtering. Filtering is the process by which particular source and destination addresses are prevented from crossing a bridge or router onto another portion of the subnetwork.

firewall. A firewall is an impermeable barrier through which broadcast or other types of packets cannot pass. Routers, not bridges, are used to set up firewalls.

flow control. A router controls the progress of data through the network in a process called flow control. It ensures that other routers are not being congested by a heavy traffic flow, and it will route around congestion points.

forwarding. Forwarding is the process by which a bridge copies a packet from one side of the subnetwork to the other after it has been filtered.

fractional T-1. Many telephone companies and service providers offer fractional T-1 service. In fractional T-1, the 1.544Mbps T-1 bandwidth is divided into 64Kbps increments. Users can order as many channels as they need, but they are not required to purchase the entire 1.544Mbps from the service provider.

fragmentation. Fragmentation is the process in which larger frames from one network are broken up into smaller frames–and into the frame size that is compatible with the network to which they'll be forwarded.

frame relay. Frame relay is the CCITT standard for a low-overhead packet-switching protocol that provides dynamic bandwidth allocation at speeds up to 2Mbps. Frame relay is in its early stages of deployment in the United States. It is considered a second generation X.25 in that it is more efficient.

front-end application. Users present, manipulate, and display data via front-end applications, which are client applications. These applications work with back-end applications, such as a mail or database engine.

G

gateway. In OSI terminology, a gateway is a hardware and software device that connects two dissimilar systems, such as a LAN and a mainframe. It operates at the fourth through the seventh layers of the OSI model. In Internet terminology, a gateway is another name for a router.

global network. A global network spans all departments, campuses, branch offices, and subsidiaries of a corporation. Global networks are international, and bring with them the problems of dealing with multiple languages, cultures, standards, and telephone companies.

Government OSI Profile (GOSIP). GOSIP is the U.S. government's specification for OSI conformance. Some level of GOSIP support is required for all bids made on government projects.

H

heterogeneous network. A heterogeneous network is made up of a multitude of workstations, operating systems, and applications of different types from different vendors. For example, a heterogeneous network may contain 3Com Ethernet adapter cards, Dell 486 PCs, Compaq SystemPros, Novell NetWare, FTP TCP/IP, and an HP 9000 Unix host.

Heterogeneous LAN Management (HLM). HLM is an IEEE 802.1 specification for jointly managing mixed Ethernet and Token Ring networks with the same objects.

High-level Data Link Control (HDLC). HDLC is an ISO standard for a bit-oriented, link-layer protocol that specifies how data is encapsulated on synchronous networks.

High Level Language API (HLLAPI). HLLAPI is a set of tools developed by IBM to help developers write applications that conform to its Systems Application Architecture.

High-Speed Serial Interface (HSSI). HSSI is a standard for a serial link up to 52Mbps in speed over WAN links.

homogeneous network. A homogeneous network is comprised of similar components–one type of workstation, server, network operating system, and only a few applications.

horizontal wiring subsystem. This part of a structured wiring system connects the users' computers in the departments. It is attached to the vertical wiring system. The horizontal wiring system is often copper cable, such as twisted-pair or coax.

hub. A concentrator is a multiport repeater or hub that brings together the connections from multiple network nodes. Concentrators have moved past their origins as wire concentration centers, and often house bridges, routers, and network-management devices.

I

impedance. Impedance is the resistance equivalent for AC, and it affects a network's propagation delay and attenuation. Each protocol and topology has its own impedance standards. For example, 10BaseT has an impedance of 100 ohms to 105 ohms, while 10Base2 has an impedance of 50 ohms.

infrared. Infrared electromagnetic waves are above that of microwaves but below the visible spectrum. Infrared is used for wireless LANs.

intermediate system. In Internet terminology, an intermediate system is a router.

Institute of Electronics and Electrical Engineers (IEEE). The IEEE is a professional society of electrical engineers. One of its functions is to coordinate, develop, and publish data communications standards for use in the United States.

Integrated Services Digital Network (ISDN). ISDN is the CCITT standard for carrying voice and data to the same destination. ISDN specifies 23 "B" 64Kbps channels plus one "D" 16Kbps channel. Although ISDN is not popular in the United States, it is a common method of wide area networking in Europe (especially in the U.K., Germany, and France) and in Japan.

Intermediate System-to-Intermediate System (IS-IS). IS-IS is an OSI routing protocol that provides dynamic routing between routers or intermediate systems.

International Standards Organization (ISO). ISO is a multinational standards-setting organization that formulates computer and communication standards, among others. ISO defined the

OSI reference model, which divides computer communications into seven layers: physical, data-link, network, transport, session, presentation, and application.

Internet. The Internet is a collection of more than 2,000 packet-switched networks located principally in the United States, but also in other parts of the world, all linked using the TCP/IP protocol. It links many university, government, and research sites.

Internet Activities Board (IAB). The IAB is the coordinating committee for the design, engineering, and management of the Internet. The IAB has two main committees: the Internet Engineering Task Force (IETF) and the Internet Research Task Force (IRTF). The IETF specifies protocols and recommends Internet standards. The IRTF researches technologies and refers them to the IETF.

Internet Protocol (IP). IP is part of the TCP/IP suite. It is a session-layer protocol that governs packet forwarding.

internetwork. An internetwork is collection of several networks that are connected by bridges and routers, so all users and devices can communicate with each other, regardless of the network segment to which they are attached.

Internetwork Packet Exchange (IPX). IPX is the part of Novell's NetWare stack that governs packet forwarding. This transport protocol is based on Xerox Network System.

interoperability. Interoperability is the ability of one manufacturer's computer equipment to operate alongside, communicate with, and exchange information with another vendor's dissimilar computer equipment.

inverted backbone. An inverted backbone is a network architecture in which the wiring hub and routers become the center of the network, and all subnetworks connect to this hub. In a backbone network, the cable is the main venue of the network, to which many bridges and routers attach.

isochronous transmission. An isochronous service transmits asynchronous data over a synchronous data link. An isochronous service must be able to deliver bandwidth at specific, regular intervals. It is required when time-dependent data, such as video or voice, is to be transmitted. For example, Asynchronous Transfer Mode can provide isochronous service.

J

jitter. Jitter is a form of random signal distortion that interferes with the reception of signals.

L

LAN Manager. LAN Manager is Microsoft's network operating system based on OS/2. It uses NetBEUI or TCP/IP network protocols. LAN Manager supports DOS, Windows, OS/2, and Macintosh clients. Through LAN Manager for Unix, it offers connections to various Unix hosts.

LAN Server. LAN Server is IBM's network operating system that is based on the OS/2 operating system and the NetBIOS network protocol. LAN Server supports DOS, Windows, OS/2, and Macintosh clients.

LANtastic. LANtastic is Artisoft's peer-to-peer, NetBIOS-based network operating system. It supports DOS, Windows, Macintosh, and Unix clients.

leased line. A leased line is a transmission line reserved by a communications carrier for the private use of a customer. Examples of leased-line services are 56Kbps or T-1 lines.

line of sight. Laser, microwave, and infrared transmission systems require that no obstructions exist in the path between the transmitter and receiver. This direct path is called the line of sight.

local area network (LAN). A LAN is a group of computers, each equipped with the appropriate network adapter card and software and connected by cable, that share applications, data, and peripherals. All connections are made via cable or wireless media, but a LAN does not use telephone services. It typically spans a single building or campus.

Local Area Transport (LAT). LAT is Digital Equipment's protocol suite for connecting terminals to an Ethernet network. Because LAT lacks a network layer, it must be bridged in an enterprise network, not routed.

LocalTalk. LocalTalk is one of Apple's physical-layer standards. It transmits data at 230Kbps using Carrier Sense Multiple Action/Collision Detection (CSMA/CD) over unshielded twisted-pair wire.

Logical Link Control (LLC). OSI Layer 2, the data-link layer, is divided into the Logical Link Control and the Media Access Control sublayers. LLC, which is the upper portion, handles error control, flow control and framing of the transmission between two stations. The most widely implemented LLC protocol is the IEEE 802.2 standard.

Logical Unit (LU). IBM's LU suite of protocols govern session communication in an SNA network. LU1, LU2, and LU3 provide control of host sessions. LU4 supports host-to-device and peer-to-peer communication between peripheral nodes. LU6.2 is the peer-to-peer protocol of APPC. LU7 is similar to LU2.

M

mail-enabled applications. Mail-enabled applications are a class of software that incorporates e-mail's functionality, but provides additional services, such as workflow automation, intelligent mail handling, or contact management software.

main distribution facility. In a structured wiring system, the main distribution facility is the portion of the wiring that's located in the computer room. From the main distribution facility extends the campus wiring subsystem, which runs to each building.

management information base (MIB). A MIB is a repository or database of the characteristics and parameters that are managed in a device. Simple Network Management Protocol (SNMP) and Common Management Information Protocol (CMIP) use MIBs to contain the attributes of their managed systems.

Manufacturing Automation Protocol (MAP). MAP is an ISO protocol for communicating among different pieces of manufacturing equipment.

Media Access Control (MAC). The MAC is the lower sublayer of the data-link layer (Logical Link Control is the upper sublayer), and it governs access to the transmission media.

mesh topology. In a mesh network topology, any site can communicate directly with any other site.

Message Handling System (MHS). MHS is Novell's protocol for electronic mail management, storage, and exchange. MHS is the most widely installed e-mail protocol.

Message Handling Service (MHS). MHS is another name for ISO's X.400 protocols for store-and-forward messaging.

Message Transfer Agent (MTA). In ISO's X.400 electronic messaging protocols, the MTA is responsible for storing messages then forwarding them to their destinations. The MTA is commonly implemented as the mail server.

metropolitan area network (MAN). A MAN covers a limited geographic region, such as a city. The IEEE specifies a MAN standard, 802.6, which uses the Dual Queue, Dual Bus access method and transmits data at high speeds over distances up to 80 kilometers.

Microsoft API (MAPI). When using MAPI, application developers can add messaging to any Windows application and the program remains independent from the message storage, transport, and directory services.

mission-critical application. A mission-critical application is one that is crucial to a company's continued operation. As corporations downsize from mainframes, many mission-critical applications are moved to networks.

multicast. Multicast packets are single packets that are copied to a specific subset of network addresses. In contrast, broadcast packets are sent to all stations in a network.

multimedia. Multimedia is the incorporation of graphics, text, and sound into a single application.

multimode fiber. Multimode fiber-optic cable uses light-emitting diodes (LEDs) to generate the light to transmit signals. Multimode fiber is prevalent in data transmission.

multiplexing. Multiplexing is putting multiple signals on a single channel.

Multipurpose Internet Mail Extension (MIME). MIME is an Internet specification for sending multiple part and multimedia messages. With a MIME-enabled e-mail application, users can send PostScript images, binary files, audio messages, and digital video over the Internet.

multistation access unit (MAU). A MAU is a multiport wiring hub for Token Ring networks. IBM calls MAUs that can be managed remotely Controlled Access Units, or CAUs.

N

Narrowband ISDN. Narrowband ISDN is another name for

ISDN. Narrowband ISDN offers a smaller bandwidth than the Broadband ISDN services, such as Asynchronous Transfer Mode (ATM) and Switched Multimegabit Data Services (SMDS).

NetBIOS. NetBIOS is a protocol developed by IBM that governs data exchange and network access. Because NetBIOS lacks a network-layer, it cannot be routed in a network, which makes building large internetworks of NetBIOS-based networks difficult. Examples of NetBIOS-based NOSs include IBM LAN Server and Artisoft LANtastic.

NetBEUI. Microsoft's version of NetBIOS is called NetBEUI. It is a protocol that governs data exchange and network access. Because NetBEUI lacks a network-layer, it cannot be routed in a network, which makes building large internetworks of NetBEUI-based networks difficult.

NetWare. NetWare is Novell's network operating system. NetWare uses IPX/SPX, NetBIOS, or TCP/IP network protocols. It supports DOS, Windows, OS/2, Macintosh, and Unix clients. Through NetWare for Unix, users can gain access to various Unix hosts. NetWare versions 4.x and 3.x are 32-bit operating systems; NetWare 2.2 is a 16-bit operating system.

NetWare Loadable Module (NLM). An NLM is an application that resides in the NetWare server and coexists with the core NetWare operating system. NLMs provide better performance than applications that run outside the core.

network. A network is a system of computers, hardware, and software that is connected over which data, files, and messages can be transmitted and end users communicate. Networks may be local or wide area.

network layer. The third layer of the OSI model is the network layer, and it governs data routing. Examples of network-layer protocols are IP and IPX.

Network Driver Interface Specification (NDIS). NDIS is a specification for generic device drivers for adapter cards that is used by LAN Manager networks.

Network File System (NFS). NFS is Sun Microsystems' file-sharing protocol that works over TCP/IP.

network interface card (NIC). A network interface card is the adapter card that plugs into computers and includes the electronics and software so the station can communicate over the network.

network operating system (NOS). A network operating system is the software that runs on a file server that governs access to the files and resources of the network by multiple users. Examples of NOSs include Banyan's VINES, Novell's NetWare, and IBM's LAN Server.

network-aware application. A network-aware application knows that it is running on a network and has file- and record-locking features.

network-ignorant application. A network-ignorant application has no knowledge that it is running on a network. It lacks file

and record locking, and cannot guarantee data integrity in a multiuser environment.

network-intrinsic application. A network-intrinsic application knows it is running on a network and takes advantage of a network's distributed intelligence. For example, a client-server database is a LAN-intrinsic application.

noise. Noise is sporadic, irregular or multifrequency electrical signals that are superimposed on the desired signal.

O

Object Linking and Embedding (OLE). OLE is Microsoft's specification for application-to-application exchange and communication. It is more powerful and easier to use than Microsoft's Dynamic Data Exchange (DDE) API, but it is not as widely implemented by independent software vendors.

Open Data-Link Interface (ODI). ODI is Novell's specification for generic network interface card device drivers. ODI enables you to simultaneously load multiple protocol stacks, such as IPX and IP.

Open Shortest Path First (OSPF). The OSPF routing protocol for TCP/IP routers takes into account network loading and bandwidth when moving packets from their sources to their destinations. OSPF improves on the Routing Information Protocol (RIP), but it is not as widely implemented.

open systems. In open systems, no single manufacturer controls the specifications for the architecture. The specifications are in the public domain, and developers can legally write to them. Open systems is crucial for interoperability.

Open Systems Interconnection (OSI). The OSI model is the seven-layer, modular protocol stack defined by ISO for data communications between computers. Its layers are: Physical, Data Link, Network, Transport, Session, Presentation, and Application.

optical drives. Optical drives use lasers to read and write information from their surface. Because of their slow access times, optical drives are used for archiving and other activities that are not as time-sensitive. Several types of optical drives are available. CD-ROMs, or compact disk read-only memory, can be remastered. Information can be written to WORM, or write once, read many, disks only once; they cannot be erased. Data can be written to and removed from erasable optical disks.

OS/2. OS/2 is IBM's 32-bit multithreaded, multitasking, single-user operating system that can run applications created for it, DOS, and Windows.

outsourcing. Outsourcing is the process of subcontracting network operations and support to an organization outside your company.

P

packet. A packet is a collection of bits comprising data and control information, which is sent from one node to another.

packet switching. In packet switching, data is segmented into packets and sent across a circuit shared by multiple subscribers. As the packet travels over the network, switches read the address and route the packet to its proper destination. X.25 and frame relay are examples of packet-switching services.

peer-to-peer. In a peer-to-peer architecture, two or more nodes can directly initiate communication with each other; they do not need an intermediary. A device can be both the client and the server.

personal communications services (PCS). PCS is a category of applications that includes wireless local and personal area communications for portable and desktop computers, wireless notepad and messaging devices, and wireless office and home telephone systems. The FCC is in the process of allotting both licensed and unlicensed frequency ranges for PCS-based devices.

Physical Layer. The lowest layer of the OSI model is the Physical Layer, and it defines the signalling and interface used for transmission media.

point-to-point. A point-to-point link is a direct connection between two locations.

Point-to-Point Protocol (PPP). PPP provides router-to-router and host-to-network connections over asynchronous and synchronous connections. It is considered a second-generation Serial Line Internet Protocol (SLIP).

Presentation Layer. The sixth, or Presentation Layer, of the OSI model is responsible for data encoding and conversion.

Primary Rate ISDN (PRI). PRI ISDN is a T-1 service that supports 23 64Kbps B channels plus one 16Kbps D channel.

propagation delay. Propagation delay is the time it takes for one bit to travel across the network from its transmission point to its destination.

protocol. A protocol is a standardized set of rules that specify how a conversation is to take place, including the format, timing, sequencing and/or error checking.

proxy agent. A proxy agent is software that translates between an agent and a device that speaks a different management information protocol. The proxy agent communicates the data to the network manager.

public data network (PDN). A PDN is a network operated by a government or service provider that offers wide area services for a fee. Examples are networks from British Telecom and Infonet.

Q

query language. A query language enables users to retrieve information. Structured Query Language (SQL) is one example.

R

Redundant Array of Inexpensive Disks (RAID). RAID 1 is disk mirroring, in which all data is written to two drives. In RAID 2, bit-interleaved data is written across multiple disks; additional disks perform error detection. A RAID 3 disk drive has one par-

ity drive plus an even number of data drives. Data is transferred one byte at a time, and reads and writes are performed in parallel. Like RAID 3, RAID 4 has a dedicated parity drive, but the data is written to the disks one sector at a time. Also reads and writes occur independently. In RAID 5, the controllers write data a segment at a time and interleave parity among them. A segment is a selectable number of blocks. RAID 5 does not use a dedicated parity desk. It offers good read performance, but suffers a write penalty. RAID 1, 3, and 5 are appropriate for networks.

remote MIB (rmon). Rmon defines the standard network monitoring functions and interfaces for communicating between SNMP-based management consoles and remote monitors, which are often called probes.

Remote Operations Service Element (ROSE). ROSE, an OSI Application-Layer protocol, supports interactive applications in a distributed open systems environment.

Remote Procedure Call (RPC). An RPC is a set of conventions that governs how an application activates a process on another node on the network and retrieves the results.

repeater. A repeater is a Physical Layer device that regenerates, retimes, and amplifies electrical signals.

requirements analysis. A requirements analysis is the process through which you define and evaluate the business needs of your network system.

request for proposal (RFP). An end-user company issues an RFP document that asks systems integrators and manufacturers to bid on their network designs and specifications.

request for information (RFI). An end-user company issues an RFI document to ask systems integrators and manufacturers to propose and design a system that will fulfill the corporation's business requirements.

Request For Comment (RFC). An RFC is the Internet's notation for draft, experimental, and final standards.

return on investment (ROI). Calculating an ROI enables MIS shops to gauge the network's success from a business profit-and-loss standpoint. Calculate a ROI by subtracting the total cost of the network from the total benefit.

ring topology. In a ring topology, the network nodes are connected in a closed loop. Information is passed sequentially between active stations, and each one examines or copies the data and finally returns it to the originating station, which removes it from the network.

risk analysis. A risk analysis is the process by which a company analyzes the business and technology risks of installing a new system.

RJ-11. An RJ-11 is a four-wire modular connector that is used by the telephone system.

RJ-45. An RJ-45 is an eight-wire modular connector that is used by 10BaseT Ethernet and some telephone systems.

roll back. A database application's ability to abort a transaction before it has been committed is called a roll back.

roll forward. A database's ability to recover from disasters is called a roll forward. The database reads the transaction log and re-executes all of the readable and complete transactions.

router. A router is a network-layer device that connects networks using the same Network-Layer protocol, for example TCP/IP or IPX. A router uses a standardized protocol, such as RIP, to move packets efficiently to their destination over an internetwork. A router provides greater control over paths and greater security than a bridge; however, it is more difficult to set up and maintain.

Routing Information Protocol (RIP). RIP is the routing protocol used by most TCP/IP routers. It is a distance-vector routing protocol, and it measures the shortest distance between the source and destination addresses by the lowest "hop" count.

S

sag. A sag is a short-term drop (up to 30 seconds) in power-line voltage that typically is in the region of 70 percent to 90 percent of the nominal line voltage.

server. A server is a computer that provides shared resources to network users. A server typically has greater CPU power, number of CPUs, memory, cache, disk storage, and power supplies than a computer that is used as a single-user workstation.

Serial Line Internet Protocol (SLIP). SLIP is used to run IP over serial lines, such as telephone lines.

Sequential Packet Exchange (SPX). SPX is Novell's protocol for the transmission of data in sequence.

session. A session is a communications connection between two nodes.

session layer. The fifth OSI layer, the Session Layer, defines the protocols governing communication between applications.

shielded twisted-pair (STP). STP is a pair of foil-encased copper wires that are twisted around each other and wrapped in a flexible metallic sheath to improves the cable's resistance to electromagnetic interference.

Simple Mail Transfer Protocol (SMTP). SMTP is TCP/IP's protocol for exchanging electronic mail.

Simple Network Management Protocol (SNMP). SNMP is a request-response type protocol that gathers management information from network devices. SNMP is a de facto standard protocol for network management. Two versions exist: SNMP 1 and 2. It provides a means to monitor and set configuration parameters.

single-attachment station (SAS). In FDDI, a single-attachment station is one that is connected to only one of the dual counter-rotating rings. Workstations and other noncritical devices are normally connected using SAS, which are less expensive than dual-attached stations.

single-mode fiber. Single-mode fiber uses lasers, not light-emitting diodes, to transmit signals over the cable. Because single-mode fiber can transmit signals over great distances, it is primarily used in the telephone network, and not for LANs.

SNA mainframe gateways. An SNA mainframe gateway is a hardware and software device that connects a LAN to an SNA mainframe. It translates between the different systems, making the PC look like a 3270 terminal to the SNA host, so the PC user can access mainframe applications, files, and printers.

source-explicit forwarding. Source-explicit forwarding is a feature of MAC-layer bridges that enables them to forward packets from only those source addresses specified by the administrator.

source routing. Source routing is normally used with Token Ring LANs. In source routing, the sending and receiving devices help determine the route the packet should traverse through the internetwork. The route is discovered via broadcast packets sent between these two points.

source-routing transparent (SRT). Source-routing transparent addresses the coexistence of Ethernet, Token Ring, and FDDI. A SRT bridge passes both source routing and transparently bridged data. The bridge uses source-routing to pass packets with the appropriate embedded routing information, and transparently bridge those packets that lack this information.

spanning-tree algorithm. The spanning-tree algorithm is an IEEE 802.1D technique for configuring parallel MAC-layer Ethernet bridges to increase redundancy. The spanning-tree algorithm manages the illegal loop created by the redundancy of having dual bridges.

star topology. In a star topology network, the nodes are connected in a hub and spoke configuration to a central device or location. The "hub" is a central point of failure.

standby power supply (SPS). A standby power supply is a backup power device that is designed to provide battery power to a computer during a power failure. A SPS experiences small interrupts during switch-over to battery operation.

Station Management (SMT). SMT is part of the FDDI specification, and it defines how to manage nodes on the FDDI.

StreetTalk. StreetTalk is Banyan's distributed global naming and directory service for its network operating system, VINES.

Structured Query Language (SQL). SQL is an IBM and ANSI standard query language for extracting information from relational databases.

structured wiring. Structured wiring is a planned cabling system which systematically lays out the wiring necessary for enterprise communications, including voice and data. IBM's Cabling System and AT&T Premises Distribution System are two such structured wiring designs. A structured wiring system is made up of horizontal, vertical, and campus subsystems.

A horizontal subsystem is the system between the wiring closets and the users' systems. A vertical subsystem or backbone includes the wiring and equipment from the wiring closets to the central equipment room. The campus subsystem interconnects the buildings to a central distribution facility, local exchange carrier, or other point of demarcation.

superserver. A superserver is a computer that is designed specifically to serve as a network server. It typically has several CPUs, error-correcting memory, large amounts of cache, large amounts of redundant disk storage, and redundant power supplies. It is designed to provide high speed, high capacities, and fault tolerance.

surge. A surge is a short term (up to 30 seconds) rise in power-line voltage level.

Switched 56. A Switched 56 service is a dial-up connection that uses bandwidth in 56Kbps increments. A user can order a maximum of 24 channels from the telephone service provider, for a maximum bandwidth of 1.5Mbps.

Switched Multi-Megabit Data Service (SMDS). SMDS is a high-speed metropolitan area network service for use over for T-1 and T-3 lines. SMDS' deployment is being stalled by the enthusiasm for Asynchronous Transfer Mode, although SMDS can run in conjunction with ATM.

Synchronous Data Link Control (SDLC). SLDC is IBM's bit-synchronous link-layer protocol. It is similar to HDLC.

Synchronous Optical Network (SONET). SONET will establish a digital hierarchical network throughout the world that will enable you to send data anywhere and be guaranteed that the message will be carried over a consistent transport scheme. The existing telephone infrastructure is digital but is designed for copper lines; SONET is digital and has been designed to take advantage of fiber. SONET offers speeds up to 2.5Gbps.

synchronous transmission. A transmission wherein the events occur with a precise clocking.

Systems Application Architecture (SAA). SAA is IBM's set of rules for computer communications and application development. SAA was designed to help create programs that will run on a wide variety of IBM computing equipment.

Systems Network Architecture (SNA). IBM's protocols for governing terminal-to-mainframe communications. It is IBM's older architecture.

systems integrator. A systems integrator is a company who is paid to combine disparate pieces of technology into a unified, working system for an end-user company.

T

T-1. The CCITT specifies a four-level, time-division multiplexing hierarchy for the telephone system in North America. T-1 provides 24 channels of 64Kbps bandwidth, for a total bandwidth of 1.544Mbps. A T-1 circuit can transport voice, video, data, and fax. T-1 service sold in 64Kbps increments is called fractional T-1.

T-2. T-2 is the equivalent of four T-1s, and it offers 6.3Mbps of bandwidth. Each T-2 link can carry at least 96 64Kbps circuits. T-2 is not a commercially available service, but it is used within the telephone company's hierarchy.

T-3. A T-3 circuit carries in one multiplexed signal stream the equivalent of 28 T-1 circuits. It provides 44.736Mbps of bandwidth. T-3 is not widely used for LANs.

Technical Office Protocol (TOP). TOP is the OSI protocol stack for office automation; it is not widely implemented.

Telnet. Telnet is the TCP/IP protocol for terminal emulation.

terminal emulation. A terminal emulator makes a computer of a different type appear to a host as a node in the host environment.

time domain reflectometer (TDR). A TDR is a troubleshooting device that is capable of sending signals through a cable to check continuity, length, and other attributes.

token. A token is an electronic character sequence that mediates access on a Token Ring or Token Bus network.

token passing. Token passing is a network access method that requires nodes to possess the electronic token before transmitting their frames onto the shared network medium. Token Ring, Token Bus, and FDDI use token-passing schemes.

Token Ring. Token Ring is the IEEE 802.5 specification for a 4Mbps or 16Mbps network that uses a logical ring topology, a physical star topology, and a token-passing access method. It works with UTP, STP, and fiber optic cable. Each ring can have up to 256 stations.

transceiver. A transceiver is a device for transmitting and receiving packets between the computer and the wire. The transceiver is usually integrated directly onto the network adapter card.

Transmission Control Protocol/Internet Protocol (TCP/IP). TCP/IP is the protocol suite developed by the Advanced Research Projects Agency (ARPA), and is almost exclusively used on the Internet. It is also widely used in corporate internetworks, because of its superior design for WANs. TCP governs how packets are sequenced for transmission on the network. IP provides a connectionless datagram service. The term "TCP/IP" is often used to generically refer to the entire suite of related protocols.

transparent bridging. Transparent bridging connects similar LANs and is usually used with Ethernet. In transparent bridging, when the station transmits a frame, that frame does not know what path it will take. Instead, the bridges determine the best path at the time the frame is sent. In contrast, in source routing, the path is determined at the start of the transmission, rather than frame by frame.

transport layer. The transport layer is the fourth layer of the OSI model, and it provides reliable end-to-end data transport, including error detection between two end user devices. Examples of transport protocols are the Internet Protocol (IP), Sequenced Packet Exchange (SPX), and Transport Protocol Class 0 (TP0).

Transport Protocol Class 0, Class 4 (TP0, TP4). These protocols are OSI transport protocols. Transport Protocol Class 0 is a connectionless transport protocol for use over reliable networks. Transport Protocol Class 4 is a connection-based transport.

Trivial File Transfer Protocol (TFTP). TFTP is a simplified version of FTP, or the TCP/IP file transfer protocol.

tunneling. The process of encasing one protocol in another's format is called tunneling. For example, AppleTalk packets are often enveloped in TCP/IP packet formats for transmission on an enterprise network. Tunneling is also called encapsulation.

twisted-pair. Twisted pair is type of copper wiring in which two wires are twisted around one another to reduce the amount of noise absorbed. The Electronics Industry Association/Telecommunications Industry Association (EIA/TIA) specifies a five-level standard for commercial building telecommunications wiring. Category 1 wiring is old-style unshielded twisted-pair telephone cable and is not suitable for data transmission. Category 2 is for use up to 4Mbps; it resembles IBM Cabling System Type 3 cable. Category 3 UTP is specified for speeds up to 10Mbps, and it is the minimum cable required for 10BaseT Ethernet. Category 4 is the lowest grade UTP acceptable for 16Mbps Token Ring. Category 5 is certified for speeds up to 100Mbps, but it can handle speeds of up to 155Mbps. Category 5 cable is suitable for FDDI and other high-speed networks.

two-phase commit protocol. In a distributed database, a two-phase commit protocol ensures data integrity by asking the multiple database engines for permission before committing each transaction.

Type 1. The IBM Cabling System specifies different types of wire. Type 1 is a dual-pair, 22 American Wire Gauge (AWG) cable with solid conductors and a braided shield. It is a type of shielded twisted-pair.

Type 2. Type 2 is the IBM Cabling System's specification for a six-pair, shielded, 22 AWG wire used for voice transmission. It is the same wire as Type 1, but has an additional four-pair wire.

Type 3. Type 3 is the IBM Cabling System's specification for a single-pair, 22 or 24 AWG, unshielded twisted-pair wire. It is common telephone wire.

Type 5. Type 5 is 100/140 micron fiber; IBM now recommends 125 micron fiber.

Type 6. Type 6 wire is two-pair, stranded 26 AWG wire used for patch cables.

Type 8. Type 8 wire is a two-pair, 26 AWG, shielded cable without any twists; it is commonly used under carpet.

U

undervoltage. In an undervoltage condition, a lower-than-usual power-line voltage lasts from several seconds to several hours.

uninterruptible power supply (UPS). A UPS is a power conditioning and supply system that affords protection against short-term power outages. A UPS rectifies the incoming AC line voltage to DC, which is then applied to batteries. An inverter, driven by DC power, supplies AC voltage for equipment that requires conditioned power. During outages, the converter is driven by battery power.

Unix. Unix is a 32-bit multitasking, multiuser operating system. Versions of Unix are available for nearly every type of computer platform. Unix was initially popular in universities and research labs, but it is now the basis of many corporate applications. Since its purchase of Unix Systems Labs, Novell owns the license to Unix.

unshielded twisted-pair (UTP). UTP is a pair of foil-encased copper wires, twisted around each other. UTP is classified into several levels of wire quality suitable for different transmission speeds (see "Category").

user agent (UA). In X.400 mail systems, the user agent is the client component that provides the X.400 envelope, headers, and addressing. The user agent sends the messages to the X.400 mail server, or Message Transfer Agent, which then routes the messages to their destinations.

User Datagram Protocol (UDP). UDP is the connectionless transport protocol within the TCP/IP suite. Because it does not add overhead, as the connection-oriented TCP does, UDP is typically used with network-management applications and SNMP.

V

value-added reseller (VAR). Also called an integrator, a VAR is an independent company that resells manufacturers' products and adds value by installing or customizing the system.

VAX. Digital Equipment's brand name for its line of minicomputer and workstation hardware is VAX.

vertical wiring subsystem. The vertical wiring subsystem is the part of the structured wiring system that connects the campus wiring system to the departmental wiring system. It runs in a building's risers.

VINES. Banyan's NOS based on a Unix core and TCP/IP protocols. VINES supports DOS, Windows, Mac, and OS/2 clients and is especially popular in large enterprise networks. Its crowning feature is StreetTalk, its distributed directory service.

virtual circuit. A virtual circuit is a shared communications link that appears to the customer as a dedicated circuit. A virtual circuit passes packets sequentially between devices.

Virtual Terminal (VT). VT is the OSI terminal-emulation protocol. A terminal-emulation application makes one computer appear to a host as a directly attached terminal.

virus. A virus has the ability to reproduce by modifying other programs to include a copy of itself. Several types of viruses exist. Bacteria or rabbits do not explicitly damage files but do reproduce and eat up disk or processor space. A logic bomb lies dormant in a piece of code or program until a predefined condition is met, at which time some undesirable effect occurs. A password catcher mimics the actions of a normal log on but catches user IDs and passwords for later use. A Trojan horse is a program that appears to function but also includes an unadvertised and malicious feature. A worm scans a system for available disk space in which to run, thereby tying up all available space.

V.21. V.21 is the modem standard for the trunk interface between a network access device and a packet network. It defines signalling data rates greater than 19.2Kbps.

V.22, V.22 bis. V.22 is a 1200-bps duplex modem for use in the public-switched telephone network and on leased circuits. V.22bis is a 2400-bit modem that uses frequency division multiplexing for use on the public telephone network and on point-to-point leased lines. (The CCITT uses "bis" to denote the second in a series of related standards and "ter" to denote the third in a family.)

V.32, V.32 bis. V.32 are two-wire duplex modems operating at rates up to 9600bps (with fallback to 4800bps) for use in the public telephone network and on leased lines. V.32 bis offers speeds in increments of 4800bps, 7200bps, 9600bps, 12,000bps, and 14,400bps.

V.42 error correction, V.42 bis data compression. The V.42 error-correction standard for modems specifies the use of both MNP4 and LAP-M protocols. V.22, V.22 bis, V.26 ter, and V.32 bis may be used with V.42. With V.42 bis compression, data is compressed at ratio of about 3.5 to 1, which can yield file-transfer speeds of up to 9600bps on a 2400-bps modem. Manufacturers can provide an option that will allow a V.42 bis modem to monitor its compression performance and adjust the ratio accordingly.

V.35. Prior to 1988, V.35 was a modem specification that provided data transmission speeds up to 48Kbps. V.35 was then deleted from the V-Series Recommendations.

VMS. VMS is Digital Equipment's proprietary operating system for the VAX.

vulnerability analysis. A vulnerability analysis is a type of risk analysis in which you calculate the effects of a project's success or failure on your overall business.

W

wide area network (WAN). A WAN consists of multiple LANs that are tied together via telephone services and/or fiber optic cabling. WANs may span a city, state, a country, or even the world.

Windows. Microsoft's popular 16-bit GUI that runs on top of DOS. Windows 4.0, code-named Chicago, will be a 32-bit OS that integrates DOS and Windows. Windows for Workgroups is Microsoft's peer-to-peer network that uses a Windows interface and NetBIOS communications.

Windows NT. Microsoft's "New Technology" is the company's 32-bit, multitasking operating system that includes peer-to-peer file sharing. Windows NT Advanced Server provides high-end networking services. Cairo is Microsoft's code name for its next generation Windows NT.

wireless LANs. A wireless LAN does not use cable to transmit signals, but rather uses radio or infrared to transmit packets through the air. Radio frequency (RF) and infrared are the most commonly used types of wireless transmission.

Spread spectrum is used to access the low-frequency RF in the Industrial, Scientific, and Medical (ISM) bands. Most wireless LANs use spread spectrum transmission. It offers limited bandwidth, usually under 1Mbps, and users share the bandwidth with other devices in the spectrum; however, users can operate a spread spectrum device without licensing from the Federal Communications Commission (FCC). High-frequency RF offers greater throughput, but it is used less often because it requires an FCC license for the right to transmit.

Infrared may also be used as a wireless medium, and has greatest applicability for mobile applications due to its low cost. Infrared allows for higher throughput–measured in several megabits per second–than spread spectrum, but it offers more limited distances. Infrared beams cannot pass through walls.

wiring closet. A wiring closet is a room or closet that is centrally located and contains operating data-communications and voice equipment, such as network hubs, routers, cross connects, and PBXs.

workflow software. Workflow software is a class of applications that help the information worker manage and route his or her work. It is also called groupware or workgroup software.

X

X Window System (X). X Window System, developed by MIT, is a graphical user system most often implemented on Unix systems. The Open Software Foundation's implementation of X Window is Motif. Sun and HP use a version called OpenLook.

X.25. X.25 is the CCITT and OSI standard for packet-switching networks that provide channels up to 64Kbps. Public and private X.25 networks can be built. In the United States, common X.25 networks are British Telecom, AT&T, CompuServe, and Infonet.

X.400. X.400 is the OSI and CCITT standard for store-and-forward electronic messaging. It is used for large enterprise networks or for interconnecting heterogeneous e-mail systems. X.400 divides an electronic mail system into a client, called a User Agent, and a server, called a Message Transfer Agent. Message Stores provide a place to store messages, submit them, and retrieve them. Access Units provide communication with other device types, such as telex and fax. Distribution Lists are routing lists.

X.500. X.500 is the OSI and CCITT specification for directory services. For computer users, a directory service provides a function similar to the function the telephone company's white pages provides telephone users. Using a directory service, computer users can look up easily the location of resources and other users.

Xerox Network System (XNS). XNS is Xerox's data-communication protocol; it is the basis for the IPX/SPX network protocols used in NetWare.

Index